BI 3372143 2

D0420693

The Esse

Weber is increasingly being recognized as *the* theorist of modernity. Avoiding the mistakes of other classical thinkers, his sociological analysis has an increasing validity and relevance. Weber explained the work ethic, impersonal bureaucracy, the criteria for profit maximization, charismatic and legal rulership, the fate of salvation doctrines and the place of science. With the triumph of capitalistic modernity his writings on disenchantment, the force of community, the separation of law and justice, and the reduction of personality to instrumental expertise have a ring of prophecy.

The Essential Weber, selected by one of the world's leading Weber scholars, will introduce the work of this key thinker to a new generation of readers. Central themes highlighted in the collection are:

- the developmental logic of world religions
- the rise of modern capitalism
- the multi-dimensionality of power in societies
- the dilemmas of modernity
- the theory of social action
- ideal types and the objectivity of knowledge

The majority of the readings have been specially translated for this collection both to improve accuracy and to make Weber speak anew in the twenty-first century. Each part opens with a short introduction explaining the sequence of readings, the flow of ideas and their intellectual context, and concludes with a guide to further reading.

Sam Whimster is Reader in Sociology at London Metropolitan University and editor of *Max Weber Studies*.

BIRMINGHAM CITY
UNIVERSITY
DISCARDED

The Essential Weber

A reader

Edited by Sam Whimster

Routledge
Taylor & Francis Group

LONDON AND NEW YORK

UNIVERSITY OF
CENTRAL ENGLAND

Book no.   3 3 7 2 1 4 3 2

Subject no.   3 0 1   W e b

LIBRARY SERVICES

First published 2004
by Routledge
11 New Fetter Lane, London EC4P 4EE

Simultaneously published in the USA and Canada
by Routledge
29 West 35th Street, New York, NY 10001

Routledge is an imprint of the Taylor & Francis Group

Selection and editorial matter © 2004 Sam Whimster; Readings, as
detailed in the Acknowledgements

Typeset in Times by RefineCatch Limited, Bungay, Suffolk
Printed and bound in Great Britain by
The Cromwell Press, Trowbridge, Wiltshire

All rights reserved. No part of this book may be reprinted or
reproduced or utilized in any form or by any electronic, mechanical, or
other means, now known or hereafter invented, including photocopying
and recording, or in any information storage or retrieval system,
without permission in writing from the publishers.

British Library Cataloguing in Publication Data
A catalogue record for this book is available from the British Library

Library of Congress Cataloging in Publication Data
Weber, Max, 1864–1920.
   [Selections. English. 2003]
   The essential Weber: a reader/edited by Sam Whimster.
p. cm.
Almost all the selections in this reader are taken from Economy and
Society and the 'Collected Essays in the Sociology of Religion' – Introd.
Includes bibliographical references and index.
1. Sociology. 2. Economics. 3. Religion and sociology. I. Whimster,
Sam. II. Title.
HM585.W42 2003
301–dc21   2003011946

ISBN 0–415–24426–9 (hbk)
ISBN 0–415–24427–7 (pbk)

Contents

Acknowledgements   vii
Abbreviations   ix

Introduction to Max Weber   1

PART I
Comparing civilizations and the origins of modernity   11

  Introduction   13

1 Puritanism and the spirit of capitalism   25

2 Confucianism and Puritanism compared   35

3 Introduction to the Economic Ethics of the World Religions   55

4 The religions of civilization and their attitude to the world   81

5 Prefatory remarks to the Collected Essays in the
   Sociology of Religion   101

  Further reading   113

PART II
Structures of power and stratification   117

  Introduction   119

6 Politics and the state   131

7 The three pure types of legitimate rule   133

8 The nation   146

9 The belief in common ethnicity   150

10 The household community   156

11 Capitalism in Antiquity   161

12 The conditions of maximum formal rationality of
    capital accounting   171

13 Status groups and classes   176

14 The distribution of power in society: classes, status
    groups and parties   182

15 Parties   195

    Further reading   200

PART III
The dilemmas of modernity   203

    Introduction   205

16 Intermediate reflection on the Economic Ethics of the
    World Religions   215

17 Bureaucracy   245

18 Formal and substantive rationalization: theocratic and
    secular law   250

19 The vocation of politics   257

20 The vocation of science   270

    Further reading   288

PART IV
Methodology of the social sciences   293

    Introduction   295

21 Basic sociological concepts   311

22 The 'objectivity' of knowledge in social science and
    social policy   359

    Further reading   405

    Glossary   407
    Index   414

Acknowledgements

The idea of this book originated some time ago with Gordon Smith when he was the Sociology editor at the publishing house of George Allen & Unwin. Why, he inquired, could not the basic ideas of Weber be presented between the covers of one book, as had happened to many other giants of social theory? In principle this was a very sound question, in practice a somewhat harder accomplishment. What has made this, at last, possible is the immense amount of scholarship and progress achieved in the international community of Max Weber studies – not least the Max Weber *Gesamtausgabe* that has painstakingly revealed the full extent and reach of Weber's oeuvre and its work-history. In addition, in the English-speaking world, there has been a new wave of translations slowly replacing the old and heroic translations of Talcott Parsons and the German émigré translators, most notably Hans Gerth and Ephraim Fischoff, to whom the social sciences owe a huge debt.

I have to admit this was no easy project and my first debt of gratitude is to those who stuck me back together, knowingly or unknowingly, especially Sue Whimster. My father James Whimster died during the course of this book. He himself in his upbringing on the East coast of Scotland was touched by those geographically peripheral but influential Puritan sects – only in part I should add – and I would like to think this book can explain something to the educated layperson of the Puritan heritage that so affects our culture, even now.

In particular I would like to thank for their suggestions and support Ola Agevall, Martin Albrow, Karl-Ludwig Ay, Edward Brunsdon, David Chalcraft, Sven Eliaeson, Klaus Fischer (who sustained my belief in the syntax of the German sentence), John Gabriel, Nick Gane, Peter Ghosh, Michael Greven, Austin Harrington, Rainer Lepsius, Scott Lash, Edith Hanke, Mohammad Nafissi, Guenther Roth, Ralph Schroeder, Vic Seidler, and Stephen Turner. I am most obligated to Keith Tribe for his translations (Readings 21 and 22) and for his unfailing help and advice. My thanks also to Gerhard Boomgaarden at Routledge who brought the project to completion so effectively. The final cut is, of course, solely the editor's responsibility.

The editor wishes to thank Routledge for permission to use excerpts (Readings 1 and 5) from *The Protestant Ethic and the Spirit of Capitalism*, translated by Talcott Parsons, and an excerpt (Reading 20) from *Science as a Vocation*, edited by Peter Lassman and Irving Velody; Cambridge University Press for an excerpt (Reading 19) from *Weber. Political Writings*, edited by Peter Lassman and Ronald Speirs, and an excerpt (Reading 14) from *Weber: Selections in Translation*, edited by W.G. Runciman and translated by Eric Matthews; Verso for an excerpt (Reading 11) from *The Agrarian Sociology of Ancient Civilizations*, translated by R.I. Franks; University of California Press for excerpts (Readings 8, 9, 10, 12, 13, 15, 17, and 18) from *Economy and Society*, edited by Guenther Roth and Claus Wittich; and University of Liverpool Press for a quote (p. 14) from *The Protestant Ethic Debate*, edited by David Chalcraft and Austin Harrington.

Abbreviations

China   *The Religion of China*, translated and edited by Hans Gerth, New York, Free Press, 1951.

E&S   *Economy and Society. An Outline of Interpretive Sociology*, edited by Guenther Roth and Claus Wittich, New York, Bedminster Press, 1968.

FMW   *From Max Weber*, translated and edited by Hans Gerth and C.W. Mills, London, Routledge & Kegan Paul, 1947.

GARS   *Gesammelte Aufsätze zur Religionssoziologie*, 3 vols, Tübingen, J.C.B. Mohr (Paul Siebeck), 1920–21.

GEH   *General Economic History*, translated and edited by Frank H. Knight, London, Allen & Unwin, 1927.

India   *The Religion of India*, translated and edited by Hans Gerth and Don Martindale, New York, Free Press, 1958.

MSS   *Methodology of the Social Sciences*, translated and edited by Edward Shils and Henry Finch, New York, Free Press, 1949.

MWG   *Max Weber Gesamtausgabe*, edited by Horst Baier, M. Rainer Lepsius, Wolfgang J. Mommsen, Wolfgang Schluchter and Johannes Winckelmann, Tübingen, J.C.B. Mohr (Paul Siebeck), 1984–.

PESC   *The Protestant Ethic and the Spirit of Capitalism*, translated by Talcott Parsons, London, Allen & Unwin, 1930.

Rel   *The Sociology of Religion*, translated and edited by Ephraim Fischoff, London, Methuen, 1965.

WL   *Gesammelte Aufsätze zur Wissenschaftslehre*, 4th edn, edited by Johannes Winckelmann, Tübingen, J.C.B. Mohr (Paul Siebeck), 1973.

WuG   *Wirtschaft und Gesellschaft*, 5th edn, edited by Johannes Winckelmann, Tübingen, J.C.B. Mohr (Paul Siebeck), 1972.

Max Weber at Castle Lauenstein in the summer of 1917. The listener to his immediate right is the dramatist and political anarchist, Ernst Toller. (From Eduard Baumgarten, *Max Weber. Werk und Person.*)

Introduction to Max Weber

Let us state at the outset the reasons for Weber's importance, both as a pre-eminent social scientist and as commentator on the cultural condition of modernity. Weber provided many concepts that have proved central to the understanding of how societies develop and, with this, how modern citizens can reflect upon the significance of this development in the pursuit of their own lives. It is worth listing his major contributions. This will give an indication of the scope of his thinking and, just as importantly, the debates they have triggered.

- Weber gave us the concept of the work ethic, which he formulated as a religiously driven obsession that performed a crucial role in the formation of modern, rationalistic capitalism.
- He provided a set of specifications of what we mean when we term economic action, institutional performance, or social action as rational. It is from Weber that we derive the idea of capitalism as a rationally calculative enterprise, of bureaucracy – whether in a government, an army, a corporation, a church, or a voluntary organization – as ordered through a set of rational rules, and of legal systems operating according to rational principles. When individuals, groups, or governments adopt rational criteria as the basis for their action it gives them a basis of control over their future.
- Weber also pointed out that the consequence of a rational ordering of society was discipline, the potentiality for subordination and the loss of the individual's autonomy, an estrangement from simpler forms of communal association, a growing fragmentation of social existence and values, and a sense of disenchantment.
- Weber analysed the sociological dilemma that we use rationality to give control over our lives but that the structures of society and other people's actions mean that we never have complete control. It is in the nature of social reality that there will always be some element of irrationality of outcomes. He also analysed the ethical repercussions of this dilemma.
- Weber provided the basis of understanding power and rulership in terms of the legitimacy of why a command is obeyed. He formulated a

typology of legitimate rulerships: traditional, charismatic, and legal rational. History has been characterized by the interplay of traditional continuity and charismatic disruption. The modern era is one of legal rational legitimacy characterized by the interplay of bureaucratic routinization and strong political leadership.
- Weber took the theological ideas of salvation and theodicy (why good and evil co-exist in the world) and turned them into key components for explaining the directions of civilizational development.
- Weber took Marx's ideas on classes and made them a component of a general theory of power in the political, social and economic orders.
- Weber developed his own distinctive and highly influential methodology, partly for the pursuit of his own studies and partly as a critique of approaches he regarded as erroneous. His ideas here include:

  – The actions of people have to be placed within the social and cultural context of meaning which frames the motives and reasons for actions. It is the business of social science not only to understand these meanings but also to verify that the course of action in empirical reality is in line with its imputed cause.
  – Ideal types are used by social and cultural scientists to provide clarifying models of complex social action. Ideal types intensify and isolate cultural meanings. Causality and verification belong to the investigation of the empirical level of concrete reality.
  – Social science is invalidated by the importation of overall views of the world that are derived from religion, politics, or culture. The results and implications of science belong to the evaluation and decisions of citizens. This is the dual postulate of value-freedom: freedom *from* values in science and freedom *for* values by the citizen.

The issues and problems which Weber addressed are still with us today:

- The contemporary (and often excessive) work ethic may no longer be attributed to a Puritan mentality. But that was already noted by Weber: the original religious compulsion to rationally ordered work at the start of the twentieth century had already turned into an 'iron cage' or a strait-jacket imposed by the impersonal economic order.
- Bureaucratic rationality still remains indispensable for all medium and large organizations, whether public, private or voluntary, even though great ingenuity has been exercised to undermine or divert this condition.
- Religions, both old and new, are still with us and the tide of enlightenment secularism has reached only so far. In the twenty-first century, one of the major distinguishing factors of civilizational and societal particularity will be religion. Weber's comparison of the world religions has never been more relevant, even though contemporary comparisons will produce different conclusions to those drawn by Weber.

- Power, and the stratification of societies in terms of the degree to which power is distributed, was for Weber a constant feature of all human societies. Weber regarded socialist and anarchist utopias for the abolition of oppression as fantasy. In particular, he predicted that Bolshevik communism would discredit the egalitarian and reform policies of socialism – with which he was sympathetic – for decades. Our contemporary world produces new inequalities of power along the inter-related dimensions that were analysed by Weber – political, economic, and status inequalities.

Weber's methods have been taken up and used throughout the social sciences. It is almost impossible to envisage the social sciences without the use of ideal types, and of approaches that take as their starting point the inter-pretation of social and cultural meaning. To an extent Weber's ideas have proven to be too popular. They have been used to underpin some very diverse sociological approaches; for example, empirical sociology, phenomenology, system theory, and rational choice theory. This may of course be a tribute as much to his interpreters' inventiveness as to Weber's originality.[1]

This set of readings confines itself to the exposition of his writings, leaving to one side the very rich resource of commentary and critique. (This is however outlined in the Further reading sections.) Weber died in 1920 and since then he has proved to be the most influential social scientist of the 'classical' period, his reputation gaining as the twentieth century unfolded. Something needs to be said first about who Max Weber was – partly in the context of his own times, partly in a wider context of intellectual ideas. I will then give a brief explanation for my selection of his writings and how best to use this Reader.

Outline sketch of Weber's intellectual biography

Weber was born in Prussia on 21 April 1864. In 1871 Prussia's Chancellor Otto von Bismarck created the German Empire that quickly established itself as the dominant power in continental Europe. It was then a much bigger geographical entity than today's German Federal Republic. It stretched from Holland in the west to Königsberg on the Russian border in the east, over 550 miles. In the south-west it embraced the kingdom of Bavaria, and in the south-east it extended to Upper Silesia on the Austro-Hungarian border. Its capital Berlin was then over 200 miles from the eastern border whereas now it is only 60 miles, and in the south-east Silesia is now part of present-day Poland. Germany and Austro-Hungary were then the hegemonic powers in Eastern and Central Europe.

Weber was brought up in Berlin and so was at the heart of the German

---

1 See the recent study by Sven Eliaeson, *Max Weber's Methodologies*, Cambridge, Polity Press, 2002.

political, cultural and scientific elite. His father, who started his career as a journalist, was a politician and a supporter of Bismarck. He had significant responsibilities for the development of Berlin as well as sitting in the national parliament, the Reichstag. His mother, Helene, was brought up in Heidelberg, then, as now, a beautiful city on the banks of the River Neckar in the province of Baden. Her father, Georg Friedrich Fallenstein, was a German patriot who had fought against Napoleon's rulership over the German states. Patriotism and a belief in a German national culture did not exist then – around 1810 – and it was irrepressible and energetic characters like Fallenstein who worked to give Germans a sense of national and cultural identity. Weber's mother had inherited a considerable fortune from her parents who were one of the leading merchant families of Frankfurt. She, like many of her sisters, was intensely religious in an ethical rather than superstitious way. She tended towards Unitarianism, a church that placed very little emphasis on metaphysical ideas such as the after-life and the holy spirit. She devoted much of her time and wealth to Christian-inspired social reform and charity. Her gospel was a social gospel.

Max was the first-born and he had three brothers and four sisters, two of whom died in infancy. Both of his parents came from similarly large families, and Max Weber was brought up within the dense network of an extended family whose main locations were Berlin, Heidelberg, Strassburg (which was then occupied as part of the German Empire) and Frankfurt. Apart from the political, merchant, and religious prominence of members of this extended family it included many leading academics in history, theology, and geology.[2]

Weber's generation witnessed three major structural transformations. First, the rise of the organized factory system and the bureaucratic organization of clerical work. Second, the flight from the land and traditional village life into the only semi-planned expansion of the cities – urbanization. (Weber's father would return home completely exhausted from his responsibilities for the expansion of Berlin.) Third, the emergence of the constitutional nation state and the superseding of the semi-monarchical 'concert of powers' that had regulated European international relations in the nineteenth century. The transition to international diplomacy based on the co-existence of nation states was not a success and its first phase ended in the European catastrophe of the First World War. Weber died in June 1920, distraught at the loss of German power and territories and not fully comprehending his country's fall from international approval.

These transformations are obviously relevant to the conventional side of Weber's academic life as sociologist, social psychologist, economist, and

---

2 Guenther Roth has recently completed an extensive historical study of the family: *Max Webers deutsch-englische Familiengeschichte 1800–1950 mit Briefen und Dokumenten*, Tübingen, Mohr Siebeck, 2001. See the review essay, in English, by Wolfgang J. Mommsen, *Max Weber Studies*, 3, 1, 2002, pp. 99–109.

political commentator, all of which were subjects he embraced and concerning as they did modernization, social reform, social policy, and political analysis. In addition, he supported his wife Marianne who was a leading reformer in the area of rights for women, in particular property and matrimonial rights, and education. *The Essential Weber* includes almost none of Weber's extensive activity and writings in these fields.[3] This is an important part of Weber's biography, but perhaps no longer so relevant for our understanding of his significance. While Weber worked at the 'coal-face' of contemporary issues using the newest of social scientific discourse, he also had the capacity to stand back and place these modernizing processes in a wider historical and cultural perspective.

Today there is a tendency to take modernity for granted, and also to assume a global convergence of societies patterned on some version of western modernity. Weber is the great analyst of modernity, who had the ability to place and gauge the significance of what we, unwisely, take for granted. Because Weber lived through the major structural transformations mentioned above, he could so to speak stand on the watershed of world history and look forward in time – to what might become of modernity. But he could also look backward to the world of his childhood, his travels, family memories and traditions, and his reading and education; what Peter Laslett called 'the world we have lost'.[4]

Weber's intellectual formation needs to be examined if we want to share his sense of perspective; also if we want to understand the curious sense of distance that he manifests in his studies. Needless to say, Weber attended a typically high-standard gymnasium school in the Berlin suburb of Charlottenburg where he would have studied maths, science, and modern languages. But the core subjects were 'humanistic': history and in particular the languages and history of Antiquity. This was not so much a backward-looking education as one offering an alternative universe. Weber could read Cicero (whose Latin is intricate) at the age of 12, when he also wrote long precocious letters to his cousin Fritz Baumgarten on Roman politics. Many of the greatest minds of his day never entirely stepped out of this alternative universe, using the values of Greek politics, culture, and personality as a template for judging German society and history. Nietzsche, Theodor Mommsen, Wilamowitz, and Eduard Meyer belong in this galaxy of intellects.[5]

---

3 As a way into this enormous subject see Dirk Kaesler, *An Introduction to his Life and Work*, Cambridge, Polity Press, 1988; David Beetham, *Max Weber and the Theory of Modern Politics*, Cambridge, Polity Press, 1985; Wolfgang J. Mommsen, *Max Weber and German Politics. 1890–1920*, translated by Michael Steinberg, Chicago, Chicago University Press, 1984.

4 See Wolfgang J. Mommsen, 'Universal Historian and Social Scientist', in his *The Age of Bureaucracy. Perspectives on the Political Sociology of Max Weber*, Oxford, Blackwell, 1974, pp. 1–21; Peter Laslett, *The World We have Lost*, London, Methuen, 1965.

5 This classical worldview is discussed by M.S. Silk and J.P. Stern in their *Nietzsche on Tragedy*, Cambridge, Cambridge University Press, 1981.

Weber entered but then was able to step outside this incredibly rich world of scholarship. His second 'doctoral' dissertation, which German academics have to complete to obtain the right to lecture in a university, concerned the legal forms of property ownership in the late Roman Empire. He was publicly examined on his thesis by the great classicist Theodor Mommsen, who while not agreeing with all the points in Weber's thesis declared him worthy to step into his own shoes. Weber, however, declined the invitation. In 1894 at the age of 30 he turned his back on an assistant professorship in commercial and German law at the University of Berlin for a full professorship in economics at the University of Freiburg. Prior to the Freiburg appointment he had already moved into the field of what is now called 'evidence-based' social policy with an extensive survey of the contemporary crisis in farming and employment in the eastern regions of Prussia.

The intellectual style that emerges with Weber is someone who shuttles between contemporary social analysis and historical studies. He would bring modern economic and legal thinking to his historical studies and, conversely, use historical templates as a way of situating contemporary problems.[6] This makes him very hard to place in current disciplinary boundaries. As a historian, he was trained to use historical documents and, where at all feasible, he would base his historical and civilizational analysis on primary data. He also studied law and his mode of analysis is very often that of a lawyer. He appears to have been mainly self-taught in economics, which at that time was called *National-ökonomie* with a pronounced bias to historical analysis. Weber was not unsympathetic to historical economics, but he was one of the few German economists to embrace the new Austrian school of marginalism, which is the basis of current neo-classical economics. In his first doctoral dissertation on the history of medieval trading companies he was particularly quick to pick up the elements of the analysis of risk and return, which today is called decision making and is playing an increased role in mainstream economics.

In the 1890s his career was built on a formidable pile of publications in the area of policy analysis, culminating in membership of a government inquiry for the reform of the German bourses (stock and commodity exchanges) and a massive analysis of the legal and economic framework of financial trading that strongly recommended the continuance of options and futures trading. (This progressive recommendation was rejected as a result of lobbying by reactionary agrarian political interests.)[7] At this point in his career it would be reasonable to assume he would be called to Berlin at the heart of the Empire to occupy a chair in economics and policy science. But at this point, in 1898, his career begins to falter. He moved to Heidelberg, which, while

6 I discuss this in 'Max Weber. Text and Interpretation', in G. Ritzer and B. Smart (eds) *Handbook of Social Theory*, London, Sage, 2001, pp. 54–65.

7 See Knut Borchardt, 'Max Weber's Writings on the Bourse: Puzzling Out a Forgotten Corpus', *Max Weber Studies*, 2, 2, 2002, pp. 139–62.

intellectually illustrious and liberal, was no power centre like Berlin. In addition, long-suppressed personality and health problems rose to the surface and resulted in a clinical depression, which is an absolutely debilitating condition. The years 1899 and 1900 were desperate for both Weber and his wife Marianne, who was ever supportive but also tremendously ambitious for her husband.

It is at this low point in his life that the Protestant ethic study, on which his posthumous intellectual reputation rests, emerges from the shadows. In actuality, the study took shape amid the bright landscape of Italy, where Weber travelled and convalesced for months at a time. In Italy there was no pressure to 'get on' and to conform and Weber, while a non-believer himself, found the Catholic communal sense of religiosity a source of fascination. Italian conviviality contrasted to Prussian rigidity and Protestant individualism. It was in Italy that Weber set about thinking about the forces that lay behind the modern lifestyle and mode of conduct which in comparative terms he was to find so distinctive and peculiar. It is reasonable to suppose that there was a degree of self-analysis involved – what forces had driven Weber himself to such a catastrophic collapse.

His work, henceforward, placed a clear and insistent emphasis on investigating cultural meanings. The relentless work ethic and pleasure-averse behaviour of the Puritan sects could be explained only in terms of salvation hopes and fears. Dynamics of historical development could be grasped by isolating significantly important strata such as Norman rulers, papal officials, medieval burghers, Puritan sects, Renaissance 'man', and asking what were the cultural ideas that controlled the practical conduct of their lives. The Protestant ethic study was for Weber a brilliant vindication of this new method, and if one reads his 'Objectivity' essay (Reading 22) which was written at the same time, Weber is insistent that over and beyond the objective trends established by economics or demography, for instance, there remains an additional subject matter: the meanings people took as the guidelines for their behaviour. In his study Weber showed it was possible empathetically to re-experience the determining meanings, values and ideas by which people, or more precisely, social strata lived their lives. The forms of shared meanings of practical action had therefore to be factored into any account of historical and societal development.

The other outcome of his collapse, from which he never fully recovered, was a preoccupation with individual and social psychology. What factors had contributed to his own formation of self? Weber made it his business to be informed about the early forms of behavioural psychology, the physiological causes of mental illness, and the new discourse of Freudianism. Psychotropic drugs were then in their infancy, and through the use of opiates he was able to gain some control over his mood swings (even if this did mean whole summers given over to weaning himself off the ensuing addiction).

Weber thought that Freud's thesis of the sexual libido as the driving force of all behaviour did have some justification in the field of cultural studies, but he rejected its claim to be a science (on the grounds that its far too few case studies had yet to establish any law of behaviour).[8] He was extremely hostile to the idea of undergoing therapy, not least from the distrust of the therapists he had encountered. He did provide his clinical psychologist with a self-analysis of his condition (subsequently lost or destroyed). There is evidence of sexual incompatibility in his marriage, and any intimacy the marriage might have had was replaced by a pact between two workaholics. Over a long period of time, he harboured a distant love for the charismatic Else von Richthofen that stretched back to the convalescence in Italy. It was a love that was only realized in the last year of his life. Mrs Else Jaffé, as she became, was elder sister to Frieda von Richthofen, who married the English writer D.H. Lawrence. Both Else and Frieda had relationships with the libertarian psychoanalyst Dr Otto Gross, who triggered something of a covert sexual revolution in Heidelberg in 1907 that left Weber an interested onlooker. He later developed an affectionate and erotic relationship with a professional pianist Mina Tobler, but renounced continued intimacy with her for the cause of his own scientific work.[9]

Weber's biography did inevitably leave traces in his academic work, especially in the 'Intermediate reflection' (Reading 16) where the power of the erotic constitutes its own separate value-sphere. With the complete publication of Weber's letters we will be in a better position to estimate reliably the significance of the biography for the work. Besides, Weber's insistence on the objectivity of scientific work has to be respected, and for the majority of his writings collected in this anthology Weber maintained a clear demarcation between his own personal views of politics and values and his academic writings.

None the less, as a conclusion to this brief biographical sketch, I return to his curious sense of distance which he displayed from the actualities of his own life and his ability to couch contemporary events in historical terms. Overall, he placed the rise of modernity, of which the Puritan sects were but one (crucial) moment, in a very long time perspective. He outlined this in the 'Prefatory remarks' (Reading 5). Western rationalism, which advances up the shore of modernity where we stand like so many successive waves, developed in the Greek and Roman world, was carried forward in canon law, the citizenry of the towns, and the Renaissance. The next wave, the reformation of the Christian churches, was formative not only for a capitalistic mentality but for empirical science and the Enlightenment advance of human rights.

8 On Weber's views of Freud, see *Weber. Selections in Translation*, edited by W.G. Runciman and translated by Eric Matthews, Cambridge, Cambridge University Press, pp. 383–90.

9 The cultural historian Martin Green discusses the period and the personalities with great verve in his *The von Richthofen Sisters. The Triumphant and the Tragic Modes of Love*, Albuquerque, University of New Mexico Press, 1974. Also useful is S. Whimster (ed.), *Max Weber and the Culture of Anarchy*, Basingstoke, Macmillan, 1999. Rainer Lepsius' article on Weber's friendship with Tobler in *Max Weber Studies*, 4, 1, 2004 (forthcoming) provides valuable new information.

Today's secular rationalism, in both its socialist, liberal, and conservative guises, places the emphasis on the Enlightenment of the eighteenth century. That was not Weber's view. Puritan freedom of conscience and religious rationalism were the underpinnings of a subsequent secular rationality. While Weber was the founder of the new science of interpretative sociology, he did this, so to speak, with a very old head.

His other trait, which stems from the difficulties of his own personality and being a little 'out of joint' with his own world, is his extraordinary empathy with modes of conduct in civilizations quite other than his own. Eminent Weberian commentators have taken this empathy for a form of self-identification; however, their choice of strata differ. He has been variously selected as a heroic Puritan, a Chinese Mandarin, a Hindu Brahman, a Judaic prophet, and a chivalrous knight. Nobody has volunteered him for a Buddhist mystic, but here, like all the other cases, he does display remarkable powers of imaginative re-creation. It goes too far, though, to suggest that he displays a fundamental sympathy in his sociological typologies, which are invariably intellectually sharp and totally without sentiment. But as a universal historical sociologist, he was able to reach out and grasp the ultimate meanings and goals that drove and possessed humankind.

Using *The Essential Weber*

Almost all the selections in this Reader are taken from *Economy and Society* and the 'Collected Essays in the Sociology of Religion'. This means that most of the excerpts date from the last decade of his life or, as in the case of the Protestant ethic study, were revised in that period. *Economy and Society* was an enormous project that remained uncompleted in his lifetime. In Part I I have tried to include all the world religions discussed by Weber, but it should be appreciated that the German edition of his sociology of religion comprises three weighty volumes. Guidance for additional reading needs to be followed up in the Further reading section. Part II makes a selection from *Economy and Society*, which in its English version runs to over 1400 pages. The length is slightly misleading owing to the peculiar history of the work that overlaps and duplicates an older version with a revised newer version. Once again the advice on Further reading is important. Part III is drawn from a variety of sources, which have a common theme of problematizing modernity. Part IV is centred on the methodological introduction to *Economy and Society*, which provides the most coherent and mature summary of Weber's approach to social science. It is complemented by an earlier essay on 'Objectivity'.

This in itself is a fairly drastic curtailment of Weber's two main projects. In addition, a vast mass of Weber's other writings have been excluded. These include his voluminous writings on German politics, his numerous studies on contemporary socio-economic issues, and all his work prior to 1904.

The Essential Weber justifies itself by selecting his key themes and ideas. It has always been extremely difficult to contain Weber's different projects within one volume, and this has created a major problem in grasping the overall range and structure of his writings. As this anthology has taken shape, I have become far more aware of the dense network of cross-references many of which are made by Weber himself. Wherever possible I have given cross-references within the Reader. The four parts of the book are not self-contained but interrelate almost all the time. Thus the user of this Reader should take every opportunity to cross and re-cross from one part to another, making full use of the glossary and index. I have provided what I hope are plain explanations to the background to the Readings in each of the four parts.

I have also provided explanatory footnotes when Weber becomes a little too remote from us in his historical and cultural references. Unless indicated otherwise, all footnotes are mine. The Further reading sections are only indicative of current debates. Alan Sica's *Max Weber: A Comprehensive Bibliography* (New Brunswick, NJ, Transaction Publishers, 2004) lists almost 5,000 items.

Finally, a great deal of effort has been put into the English translations for this volume, two-thirds of which are new. New translations are something of a treat – they remove the old varnish from the text and reveal new contours in the original German. I have on occasion made minor changes to translations other than my own to achieve consistency of conceptual terminology (which has not been achieved before in English). The first Reading in Part IV contains the majority of his conceptual vocabulary, and in a sense is Weber's own conceptual dictionary. Where a concept first appears or its meaning is open to interpretation, I supply the original German. Despite reports to the contrary, Weber is mostly a very fluent writer – but it is a fluency of *argument* that the reader, like the translator, has to learn to swim with.

Part I

Comparing civilizations and the origins of modernity

Introduction

Reading 1 (Puritanism and the Spirit of Capitalism) counts as one of the most eloquent passages written in the social sciences. It summarizes one of the best-known arguments in economic history and sociology, which Weber had advanced in his book-length essay of 1904 to 1905, 'The Protestant ethic and the spirit of capitalism'. This thesis holds that the Puritan outlook defined an austere and pleasure-averse conduct of life which came to have a direct influence on the development of modern capitalism.

Puritans formed sects in the sixteenth and seventeenth centuries in Northwest Europe and North America that broke away from the established Christian Church. They fragmented the monopoly of religious mediation by priests and demanded instead direct access to holy scripture in the vernacular language rather than the learned language of the Church (Latin). Their way of life and conduct was marked by an intensity of belief. Puritans belonged to a sect of the morally pure as opposed to the broader church, as they saw it, of the morally suspect and morally indifferent. Puritans possessed a fundamental restlessness, which stemmed from an acute uncertainty whether they would be saved or damned. This salvation anxiety was displaced into a sober and systematic way of life – that through good conduct one could assure one's fate in the life hereafter. The Puritans became a key social stratum in the economy (as merchants and manufacturers), in science, knowledge, print, and in politics (but *not* in art and culture). It was the Puritan outlook and ethic which accelerated the pace of historical development in early modernity in the seventeenth century and effected the transition to modernity itself – modern capitalism, the modern state and organizations.

The terms in which Weber couched his argument have been greatly debated and much misunderstood, and it is as well to be clear what Weber is and is not saying. He is *not* saying that religion was solely responsible for the rise of capitalism – other factors such as economic geography, the balance of political power, the prior development of technology and capitalism in the medieval period, and legal forms are all also part of the complex combination of events that led to the decisive emergence in the seventeenth century of rational and methodical capitalist mentality in North-west Europe and North America. He is saying that the role of religion was crucial in this complex of factors as precipitating the emergence of modern capitalism. He does not make Protestantism the centre of his study, but argues instead that a subset of Protestantism, which he terms the Puritan sects (Baptists, Quakers, neo-Calvinists, Pietists, Methodists, and so on) generated a particular frame of mind conducive to rationally pursued economic activity. (Weber was less interested in the large Protestant churches, such as Lutheranism and Anglicanism.)

In reply to his critics Weber provided the following succinct statement of the train of his argument:

> I therefore proceeded by first
>
> 1 calling to mind examples of the remarkably strong congruence disputed as yet by no one between Protestantism and modern capitalism, and in particular capitalistic choice of occupation and capitalistic success. Then, by way of illustration, I
> 2 gave some examples of just those ethical life-maxims (Franklin) that I see as testifying indubitably to the 'capitalist spirit', posing the question of how they differ from other, particularly medieval, maxims. And then I
> 3 sought to *illustrate*, again through examples, how these spiritual attitudes relate *causally* to the modern capitalist economic system. This then
> 4 led me to the ideas of the 'calling', along with the unique and long-established elective affinity of Calvinism to capitalism (and also of Quakerism and similar sects), that Gothein in particular has noted. At the same time I
> 5 sought to demonstrate that our contemporary conception of vocation is in some way *religiously* based.[1]

This is a very useful guide to reading the whole study (*PESC*) and how to understand the way in which Weber steered his own particular route through the historical debates on the causes and consequences of the rise of modern capitalism. In the *PESC*, (1) can be termed the thing to be explained (*explanandum*) – the correspondence of two phenomena that Weber assumed most people took as a given. Weber will seek to provide an explanation for this correspondence. The spirit of capitalism (2) is exemplified in the maxims of Benjamin Franklin, such as 'remember that time is money', 'remember that credit is money'. Honesty, punctuality, industry, and frugality are all virtues, Puritan in their particular origin, that create the utilitarian outlook of Benjamin Franklin and other capitalist entrepreneurs. Franklin was a secular rationalist whose entrepreneurial outlook was shaped by his Calvinist

---

1 *The Protestant Ethic Debate*, edited by D.J. Chalcraft and A. Harrington and translated by Harrington and Mary Shields, Liverpool, Liverpool University Press, 2001, p. 107.

upbringing, argues Weber. (3) The *practice* or exercise of Franklin's everyday virtues is known by the technical term 'asceticism'. Weber pointed out that in the medieval world it was the monks who were the great proponents of asceticism, dividing the day rigidly into prayer, meals, silence, and work. Monks withdrew from the world into their self-contained monastic communities, hence their asceticism is 'otherworldly'. Weber's Puritans live and work in the world, and their behaviour is guided from within; it is an 'innerworldly' asceticism. 'Calling' (4) is the New Testament evangelical idea of being called to the faith, carrying out Christ's message and so achieving salvation and going to heaven. Following the Reformation, the idea of calling was associated with work; people spoke of their occupation, trade or profession as a vocation. Calvinists achieved their distinctive life conduct from the psychological impact of the belief in predestination: that one's salvation had already been decided *before* one's birth. This resulted in acute salvation anxiety that Calvinists displaced into ascetic conduct and, in particular, hard work and frugality. Behaviour and belief among the Puritans was focused and enforced through their membership of sects. Unlike the Catholic Church that was open to all who sought ecclesiastical grace whatever their conduct, the Puritan sect was a congregation open only to those whose conscience was pure. (5) makes the point that our contemporary work ethic is a compulsion rooted originally in a religiously determined psychological disposition, but whose religious motives are now largely discarded. 'Since asceticism undertook to remodel the world and to work out its ideals in the world, material goods have gained an increasing and finally an inexorable power over the lives of men as at no previous period in history. To-day the spirit of religious asceticism – whether finally, who knows? – has escaped from the [iron] cage' (see below, p. 33).

Reading 2 (Confucianism and Puritanism Compared) presents Weber's return to the subject several years later, when he widened the scope of his argument to examine why Confucianism in China, in contrast to Puritanism, failed to promote a rational capitalism as it had developed in the West. There was nothing to suggest that the Chinese would be less gifted in meeting the demands of modern capitalism, and a comparison of the material, political, and social structural factors showed that China was not in any significant degree more disadvantaged than pre-modern Europe. What was strikingly different, argued Weber, was the outlook of China's leading social stratum – the literary educated official – when compared to the Puritan stratum. A religion such as Puritanism has a propensity to move historical development forward, whereas a belief system such as Confucianism has a propensity to hold historical development in a stationary state.

China emerged from a period of feudal warfare into a loosely unified empire (around 300 BC) that remained in place until 1911. For over 2000 years this empire was administered by a bureaucratic social stratum, the mandarins, whose influence was decisive over all areas of life. Their lifestyle was dedicated to the Confucian ideals of self-perfection, material well-being, equanimity, and knowledge of literary texts and calligraphy. Confucianism, as a way of life, was underpinned by the belief in magic. China, in Weber's words, was a magic garden full of good and bad spirits. All decisions were influenced by the findings of magicians – geomancers, chronomancers, astrologers, feng shui experts – who would advise on how best to maintain the harmony of the spirit-infected world of material objects. Magic was a form of rationalism used to secure favourable outcomes, even though its assumptions were basically irrational.

The Confucian outlook was fearful of change and innovation, it endorsed tradition and respect for ancestors, and behaviour was governed by convention and good manners. The Puritan way of life was also determined by irrational beliefs, but whose content was entirely different. Instead of spirits inhabiting the material world of the Confucian, the Puritan believed in a hidden god who existed as a transcendental being beyond and outside this world. Puritanism was a reform religion, and it sought to purify the existing Christian Church by the removal of all sacraments and rituals, which for the Puritan were rooted in magic. For example, Jehovah's Witnesses – one of today's better-known sects – do not celebrate Christmas, seeing its festivities as pagan and magical in origin.

Ethical conduct within the Puritan sects is highly developed. An all-seeing and all-powerful god can look into the conscience of the Puritan. This divine surveillance forces Puritans to exercise the strongest possible control over their behaviour. Sin can be avoided by diligent and systematic hard work. The Confucian, by contrast, is immune to the idea of sin. The Puritan believes in the corruption of the flesh, the Confucian in the perfection of the self. Confucianism repressed all signs of religious prophecy, religious frenzy, and salvation beliefs as dangerous disturbances to the cultivation of the ordered self. The Confucian outlook strove to keep things as they are, whereas Puritans thought of themselves as the instruments of god, charged with changing the world. The Confucian would have regarded the Puritan as a dangerous revolutionary (and this was one of the reasons for the extreme resistance, initially, of the Chinese to Christian missionaries).

Reading 3 (Introduction to the Economic Ethics of the World Religions) is nothing less than a general theory of religion in its sociological aspect. It is one of Weber's key essays, crucial to the understanding of the many parts of his writings. It presents the reader with a complex of issues, which I will outline briefly below.

We have seen in Reading 2 that Weber had extended his study of Puritanism to a comparison with Confucianism. To this Weber added studies on Buddhism and the civilization of India, and Judaism in the ancient world. The 'Introduction' outlines how the economic effects of different religions can be assessed. The essay opens with a careful statement on how, from one direction, economic ethics are influenced by economic geography and historical factors and how, from the other direction, they are formed by religion acting through defined types of conduct of life. Confucianism is a type of conduct of life – *lifestyle* is another term for this – that is determined by magical beliefs; as an economic ethic, it is also determined by the history and economic geography of the Chinese Empire. From both directions of determination, argues Weber, Chinese economic ethics tended to be unadventurous and inward-looking.

Somewhat breaking the thread of his own argument, Weber at this point plunges into a critique of Marx and Nietzsche who, in his mind, offered too one-sided accounts of how religious ideas were determined by social class. The intellectual context needs to be explored briefly, if we are to appreciate the depth and rigour that Weber achieves in his 'Introduction'.

Marx is a constant presence in this anthology as well as in Weber's other numerous writings. He is the person whose arguments have to be debated and challenged, although, as we have noted above, Weber wants to assert his own thinking on the ideal (religion and magic) and material (economics and power) determination of history. Throughout the late nineteenth century and into the twentieth century Marxism exerted a massive influence on philosophy, intellectual and academic thinking, and politics. This current was running strongly during Weber's lifetime. Weber objected to a schema which held that the progress of history was determined by the dialectical conflict of social classes. As a philosophy of history, Marxism was arguing that it was scientifically demonstrable that capitalist social relations would collapse under the weight of their contradictions. The working-class movement would seize power and abolish all property ownership, and socialism would be created as the transitional form to communism, where all social classes, exploitation, and power would be abolished.

Marx's view of religion – he was one of history's more famous atheists – is caught by his remark that religion 'is the sigh of the oppressed creature, the heart of a heartless world, and the soul of soulless conditions. It is the opium of the people.'[2] Weber argued that religion could not be reduced to an ideology that cloaked the real nature of the interests of the ruling class, but there was some truth in Marx's assertion. Throughout history, oppressed social classes have held religious beliefs which have accommodated and explained away social injustice in the world. The Marxist explanation for this is that religion obscures the real basis of oppression – the Christian priest in the Middle Ages upheld the social order as the expression of divine will. And if religion is demystified, as happened prior to the French Revolution in 1789, then even monarchs can lose their legitimacy. Weber's comparative observation was that the lower social classes in urban societies have come to accept the social order as part of the design of the cosmos. Religions provide cosmological accounts for the way the world is, and these religions are mediated and propagated by urban intellectuals and priests. Hindus accept the caste system

2 Karl Marx, 'Contribution to the Critique of Hegel's Philosophy of Law', *Collected Works of Karl Marx and Friedrich Engels*, vol. 3, London, Lawrence & Wishart, p. 175.

as part of the process of reincarnation, Chinese ancestor cults revere tradition and authority, the urban Muslim accedes to the fatalism expressed in the Koran. One of the central tenets of Judaism is God's justice, which is experienced by the unworthy Jewish community as the injustice of the world, justice only appearing in the future in the form of the Messiah. The Christian believes that a person's suffering will be redeemed in an after-life.

Nietzsche asserted that Christianity was a slave morality believed in by the masses out of resentment for their subordination to political and economic masters. Christianity was plebeian not noble. It glorified suffering as a common condition, and through its doctrine of renunciation it denied to the individual person the realization and enjoyment of their true, instinctual nature. Only the superman has no religion, refuses to belong to the herd, and makes his own destiny. (Marx also shared this romantic Promethean conception of man and had hoped that a revolutionary class would act in this independent self-determining manner.)

Having criticized Marx, Weber also distances himself from Nietzsche's exclusive derivation of religion from oppression, but he does use Nietzsche against the contemporary Marxists of his day. Weber thought that the adherence of the German working class to a Marxist political party (the German Social Democratic Party) was a kind of substitute religion. Present injustice would be redeemed at some, unspecifiable, time in a future socialist utopia, and because the revolution was never called into existence, the working class was condemned to political quiescence and resentment.

This is, however, something of a detail in Weber's more general theory. Weber turned Nietzsche's ideas into a sociology of theodicy. This is the theological term for explaining why God, who is all powerful, allows the existence of evil alongside good in the world. Seen sociologically, a theodicy is a form of justification to explain why there is no moral meritocracy in the world. For the most part, those who act virtuously receive no reward in this life, while conversely those who are rich and enjoy the pleasures of the world have done little to deserve such happiness. Religions, in the context of large urban and stratified communities, are adapted to explain the gulf between virtue and social situation; 'just rewards' are rarely realized in the here and now. It is one of the constants in all forms of religion. Weber, then, was taking a psychological insight of Nietzsche's and providing it with a sociological validity. His sociological purpose is to show how sets of beliefs are moulded and mediated by the intellectuals and priests within the social context of interests and powers.

Weber also sociologized Nietzsche's theory of sublimation. This is now more usually understood in its Freudian form. As is well known, Freud argued that the elemental driving force of the personality was libido, an eternal demand for the fulfilment of sexual desire. Civilization was built on the taming and disciplining of this force. Unconstrained sexuality was brought under control through a series of encounters of the child with the patriarchal authority of the father. Freud termed the unformed libidinous core of personality 'the id'. Culture and civilization is the product of the psychological sublimation of the id and the work of the disciplined part of the personality, the superego.

Nietzsche had first formulated these arguments, using a different language and drawing different consequences. The primitive energy of human life is the Dionysian, named after the Greek god of wine, dance, and orgy. In his *The Birth of Tragedy* (1872) Nietzsche argued that this raw energy was culturally tamed and given artistic form. This was the relation of the culturally superior Apollo over Dionysius. Later in his life Nietzsche argued for a naturalistic psychology – that individuals should be true to their own instincts and find their own way to giving form and value to their life energies; this is sometimes termed 'vitalism'. Nietzsche added, ominously, that when individuals repressed their natural selves, the repressed would return to revenge itself on individuals and their culture. Freud made the same point, warning against overly repressive cultures. The idea of the return of the repressed is not entirely absent from Weber's thought, either (see pp. 74–5).

Weber and Freud stand for different appropriations of Nietzsche's insights. When Weber speaks of the sublimation of orgy and ecstasy in the direction of ritual and sacraments, this is a religio-sociological version of what Freud understood in terms of personality. Freud directly confronted the irrational with his new psychoanalytical theory, whereas Weber centred his thinking on the way people's conduct is given cultural form by the process of religious rationalization.

Religious rationalization would appear to be a contradiction. None of the main religions have a rational basis for their beliefs. Confucianism is based on magic. Islam, Christianity, and Judaism are based on revelation set down in sacred texts. Hinduism is based on the supernatural activities of a richly complex set of mythical gods and goddesses, and Buddhism on the idea of a self progressing through reincarnated lives towards enlightenment. Weber's 'Introduction' offers an explanation of how religions develop from the primal, Dionysian states in which people have always tried temporarily to escape from the mundane and the ordinary into well-worked cosmologies of the universe and the place of human beings in it. Religions, through the work of priests, who are the first intellectuals, are successful rationalizations of unformed primal experiences. Unformed experiences are induced through techniques – intoxicating drugs and rhythmic music that produce frenzy, ecstasy, and trance. But these occasions, like today's techno-clubs which use the same techniques, leave no lasting impression – the feeling of oneness with the world and humanity is strictly temporary. Religions as well as magic sublimate these vitalist experiences through the creation of sacred rites and ceremonies (and which are never far removed from their original profane rites and ceremonies) and, through intellectual rationalization, they create permanent understandings of extraordinary states of being.

In his 'Introduction' Weber shows just how difficult and sometimes an accidental accomplishment this is – for example, the chance survival of a prophet in an urban community who introduces the new idea of holiness in place of magic. Readers can judge for themselves whether Weber commits himself to saying there are universal 'religious' needs. Certainly he points to the continuously occurring need to explain social injustice (theodicy), to give cosmological explanations for what would otherwise be brute existence, and to indulge in religious-type experiences. At this point Weber is still a long way from home in explaining how religious or magical cosmologies exert their differential effects on economic ethics, which is the explicit purpose of his essay. His answers turn on the degree of religious rationalization and its contents, and here Weber shows himself to be a supreme intellectual in the way he compares and characterizes each of the world religions.

Magic, as we have seen in the case of China, is a complex form of rationalization of irrational beliefs. The rationalization proceeded to the level of overall theory (in this case the need for harmony in the face of the incompatible spirits of yin and yang), but the idea of the supernatural remains attached to the particularity of material objects such as rivers, trees, rocks. Puritanism represents the greatest contrast in its religious rationalization. Its supernatural concepts include a single transcendental god, salvation, and prophets. According to Weber this is a process of theoretical and practical rationalization. Prophets and priests have constructed *worldviews*, such as salvation beliefs concerning 'from what' one is saved and 'to what' will be given to the true believer. In literal terms a worldview is the picture of how we see the world, and each culture will have its own kind of lens through which the world is seen and understood. In Weber's hands worldviews are enormously influential as representations of the world. Prior to the rise of evidence-based science in modernity, peoples saw the world through the lens of religiously rationalized belief systems. The contents of these beliefs have the capacity to set the direction of whole civilizations. Islam, Christianity, and Zoroastrianism find salvation through behaviour that Weber terms an active asceticism in the world. Followers of these religions have the capacity to engage and change the world. This is not a sociological law, and it does not follow automatically that all such religions will be as consequential as Islam and Christianity. Zorastrianism, for instance, remained specific to Persia. Other religions, such as Buddhism, Taoism, neo-Pythagoreanism, Gnosticism, and Sufism, have an entirely different conception of their god, one that encourages a contemplative mysticism or apathetic ecstasy. Their worldview is one of otherworldly quietism that has little impact upon economic or social development.

Weber, as he explicity states, wants to allow an autonomy to the workings of religious ideas. This does not exclude the influence of material factors. To relate the material to the ideal factors, Weber produces two intermediating concepts: carriers or bearers (*Träger*) and elective affinity (*Wahlverwandtschaft*). Religious ideas do not drop out of the sky, but they are formulated by thinkers and priests who are part of a wider social stratum. Beliefs have their carriers, and the carriers need to be in a position of influence within a social order so as to have the capability to propagandize their ideas. Confucianism is carried by the mandarin stratum, Hinduism by Brahmans, Buddhism by mendicant monks, Islam by warriors, Judaism by petit-bourgeois intellectuals, and early Christianity by a wandering brotherhood of artisans. Each of these religions has achieved a high level of practical efficacy because there is a mutual attraction between idea and social status – what Weber referred to as an elective affinity. The nature and content of beliefs in some ways entirely suit the interests and outlook of its main carrier stratum. This has helped to propel all of the above religions, except Judaism which in terms of numbers is a smaller religion, to become world religions. A religion that goes against the grain of the social and economic structure of its host society will remain insignificant.

Likewise any religion that over-rationalizes its ideas into what Weber terms a 'virtuoso' accomplishment is in danger of losing its mass base. The masses in all civilizations are prone to relapses into magic and more primal states. A ready flow of charismatic miracle workers (magicians) and exemplary prophets revitalize salvation religions. At points in his 'Introduction' Weber thinks of successful religions as selling a good to a mass customer base. He speaks of salvation not as an ideal or higher experience, but as a 'salvation good' (*Heilsgut*) in the sense of a commodity. While Weber demonstrates a quite extraordinary empathy with all forms of religious experience, he is quite capable of treating them almost materialistically, or, as he says, in 'value-free' terms.

Weber's 'Introduction to the Economic Ethics of the World Religions' should be regarded as the most pivotal essay he wrote and it needs to be read carefully. His purpose was to provide a method of comparing religions in their effects on practical economic behaviour, and this involved him in elaborating a theory of the process of religious rationalization and the differential consequences of opposing worldviews. At the heart of the essay Weber offers the reader the following crucial formulation of his entire project:

> It is interests (material and ideal), and not ideas, which have directly governed the actions of human beings. But the 'worldviews' that have been created by ideas have very often, like switches, decided the lines on which the dynamic of interests has propelled behaviour.

In Reading 4 (The Religions of Civilization and their Attitude to the World) Weber sustains a running comparison of Puritanism, Talmudic Judaism, Catholicism, Islam, ancient Buddhism, Hinduism, and early Christianity. One of the commonalities of the pious in all these religions is that they adopted an ascetic way of life, but only in Puritanism did this asceticism lead directly to a modern economic mentality. In Buddhism and Hinduism, even though asceticism may be directed from within, the nature of the 'salvation goods' (dharma and reincarnation) led to a worldview that rejected the world. Religiosity taught that salvation was best achieved by devaluing the world. While these two religions produced remarkable ways of life, they were unable to produce an inner-directed asceticism that would change the world through methodical conduct.

Talmudic Judaism was a prescriptive code in which behaviour was exactly regulated according to taboos and rituals (which led, argued Weber, to the effective social segregation of the Jewish community). The point of the whole exercise in Talmudic Judaism was the correct observance of the Law (the oral and written code of the Talmud and its interpretation by rabbinic scholars). This was not quite the same as an inner-directed asceticism, which controlled the behaviour of the Puritan. For example, the Talmud retained a naturalistic attitude towards sex, indeed demanded it within marriage; whereas the Puritan renounced all conjugal pleasures except for the purposes of procreation. The one gap in Talmudic Law was in respect to the treatment of strangers (non-Jews). In economic transactions the Jew was not obliged to treat the stranger as he would a fellow Jew. The stranger was not subject to ethical norms. For the Puritan, conscience dictated that no one could be treated as ethically indifferent. While Sombart argued that the Jews were crucial in the formation of modern capitalism (and that the Puritans inherited those characteristics), Weber counters that their economic activity was peripheral to the decisive feature of modern capitalism, namely rationally organized industrial concerns. Jews suffered from what Weber termed their 'pariah' status. Though they are a people chosen by their god, Yahweh, they are continuously rejected by their god as unworthy of redemption. In addition, they suffer from the hostility of other religions. Because of their 'outsider' status, they could never enter the profit-making activities of productive capitalism. The Puritan through his sober systematic conduct was ideally suited to pursue such economic activities.

Islam has a lesser degree of asceticism and it turns towards the world, but its economic ethic is determined essentially by its warrior origins. This favours a feudalistic style of life that exhibits a degree of ostentation. Its religious prescriptions are explicit and, while they have to be adhered to, they are not as morally taxing as the Puritan's sense of conscience and sin. Islam has a worldview that is adjusted to the world.

At the end of Reading 4 Weber presents a brief outline of early Christianity. Its origins lay in the poor artisans of the towns and countryside of Palestine. These were the people who could not afford to follow all the commandments of Jewish Law, as could the urban strata of Pharisees and Hellenized nobility. Jesus responded to the needs of the lower strata by emphasizing not the observance of the Law but the inner attitude towards ethical behaviour. He took rural customs such as helping a neighbour and turned this into an ethical attitude approved by God. His ability to alter Jewish religion was based on the charisma of his preaching, the identification of the community with him, and his magical gifts. The historical significance of Christianity lay in its everyday ethical attitude that was religiously open to all peoples, and in particular could offer Jews the possibility of breaking out from their social segregation. In the next generation St Paul argued that Jesus was the Jewish Messiah whom God had allowed to be crucified.[3] This act released the Jews from their pariah status. This was a series of almost accidental events that lifted Christians from being just another Jewish splinter cult, like the Essenes, into a line of world historical development.[4]

In his study on *Ancient Judaism*, Weber summarizes the historic role of Jewish religion not only on Christianity but more generally:

> Judaism has been, moreover, a great stimulus and a partial model for the teachings of Mohammed. Quite apart from the significance of the Jewish pariah people for the economy of the European middle ages and modernity, when we consider the factors in the development of Judaism, especially on the basis of its universal-historical effects, we find ourselves at a turning point of the whole cultural development of the Occident and the near-eastern Orient. Only the following are of equal historical significance to it: the development of hellenistic intellectual culture, and, in western Europe, Roman law, and founded on the Roman concept of office, the Church of Rome; in addition, the medieval society of the estates; and finally in the field of religion Protestantism, which shatters the old order but has a progressive influence on its institutions.[5]

In the above quote Weber is outlining key moments of the historical development of the West, which is taken up in the next Reading as well. Before leaving his comparative sociology of religion, however, let us summarize the developmental potential of the different world religions. Islam, Judaism, and Christianity all have the potential to 'switch' the path of development towards change; their worldviews 'turn towards the world' and they all inculcate in their believers varying degrees of asceticism. But the realization of this potential for change very much depends on historical circumstances. Hinduism and Buddhism, while carrying high-level salvation messages, in their emphasis on mysticism and contemplation their believers 'turn away from the world', so producing a negative developmental potential. Lastly, Confucianism through its magical practices remains embedded in the world and sends out no high-level message to its believers to change the world.

Reading 5 (Prefatory Remarks to the Collected Essays on the Sociology of Religion) was written in the last year of Weber's life and provides a summation of his comparative sociology. In it he posed the grand question of

---

3 These arguments are handled more systematically by Ernst Troeltsch in his *Social Teachings of the Christian Churches*, London, Allen & Unwin, 1931, pp. 39–89.
4 Unfortunately this is only a glimpse of Weber's thinking on early Christianity as well as Islam. Early as well as medieval Christianity, Islam considered over a longer time period, and later phases of Judaism were to receive more extensive treatments as part of the 'Economic Ethics' project, but Weber never achieved his plan.
5 *GARS*, vol. 3, p. 7.

historical sociology: why did modern rational capitalism originate in the West? Conversely, why did it not originate in other civilizations that were equally or more gifted in matters of technology, scholarship, law, music, architecture, art, political structures and, moreover, already pursued various forms of capitalism? His essays on the Protestant ethic and the Protestant sects are his contribution to the first question, and his essays on the religions of China, India, and Ancient Judaism provide answers to the second question. Weber characterizes his own project as a search to identify 'the special and distinctive rationalism of Occidental culture'.

Rationalism, just to remind ourselves, is a form of pure reasoning that seeks to arrive at substantial knowledge about the nature of the world. It is the product of thinking rather than experience. Western rationalism seeks to control the world through the intellectual imposition of ideas. What distinguishes western history is that its law, its art and architecture, its press and printing, its universities, science and training, and its capitalism all developed rational methods: systematization in Roman law, rationalized interval scales in music, perspective in art, the Gothic arch in architecture, mass communication in printing, experiment and science in the universities, and calculation and budgets in capitalism. This occurred at a level and with a consistency that has no rival in other civilizations. This vastly deepens the question that is left hanging in the opening paragraph: to what chain (*Verkettung*) of circumstances is this to be attributed? 'For in all the above cases it is a question of the specific and distinctively formed rationalism of Western culture.'

The nature of religious rationalization in conjunction with unique conditions of social structure found only in North-west Europe (townspeople with citizenship rights) meant that a specific rationalism informed all spheres of life and culture in the West, so enabling the development of a specific form of dynamically expanding rational capitalism.

Weber has no problem with the idea that in the twentieth century other civilizations will be able to develop, through imitation and importation, modern rational capitalism. He observes in his China study that this was already happening in Shanghai (around 1910). But modern capitalism, as it achieves greater universality in our globalized world, will always retain the taint of its Puritan origins – the remorseless search for profits as a way of honouring a hidden god.

1 Puritanism and the spirit of capitalism[1]

Let us now try to clarify the points in which the Puritan idea of the calling and the requirement it placed upon the ascetic conduct of life was bound to have a direct influence on the development of a capitalistic way of life. As we have seen, asceticism turns with all its force against one thing: the *spontaneous enjoyment* of life and the pleasure existence has to offer. This is perhaps most characteristically brought out in the struggle over the *Book of Sports* which James I and Charles I made into law expressly as a means of counteracting Puritanism, and which the latter ordered to be read from all the pulpits. The fanatical opposition of the Puritans to the ordinances of the King, permitting certain popular amusements on Sunday outside of Church hours by law, was not only explained by the disturbance of the Sabbath rest, but also by resentment against the intentional diversion from the ordered life of the saint, which it caused. And, on his side, the King's threats of severe punishment for every attack on the legality of those sports were motivated by his purpose of breaking the *anti-authoritarian ascetic* tendency of Puritanism, which was so dangerous to the State. The feudal and monarchical forces protected the pleasure seekers against the emergent middle-class morality and the anti-authoritarian ascetic conventicles, just as to-day capitalistic society tends to protect those willing to work against the class morality of the proletariat and the anti-authoritarian trade union.

As against this the Puritans upheld their most decisive characteristic, the principle of the ascetic conduct of life. Apart from this, though, the Puritan aversion to sport, even for the Quakers, was by no means simply one of principle. Sport was accepted if it served a rational purpose, that of recreation necessary for physical efficiency. But as a means for the spontaneous expression of undisciplined impulses, it was under suspicion; and in so far as it became purely a means of enjoyment, or awakened competitive ambition, raw instincts or the irrational gambling instinct, it was of course strictly condemned. Impulsive enjoyment of life, which leads away both from work in a calling and from religious devotion, was as such the enemy of rational asceticism, whether in the form of 'seigneurial' sports, or the enjoyment of the dance-hall or the public-house of the common man.

Its attitude was thus suspicious and often hostile to the aspects of culture

---

1 Taken from *PESC*, pp. 166–83.

without any immediate religious value. It is not, however, true that the ideals of Puritanism implied a solemn, narrow-minded contempt of culture. Quite the contrary is the case at least for science, with the exception of the hatred of Scholasticism. Moreover, the great men of the Puritan movement were thoroughly steeped in the culture of the Renaissance. The sermons of the Presbyterian wing of the movement abound with classical allusions, and even the Radicals, although they objected to it, were not ashamed to display that kind of learning in theological polemics. Perhaps no country was ever so full of graduates as New England in the first generation of its existence. The satire of their opponents, such as, for instance, Butler's *Hudibras*, attacks directly the pedantry and highly trained dialectics of the Puritans. This is partially due to the religious valuation of knowledge which followed from their attitude to the Catholic confusion of faith (*fides implicita*).

But the situation is quite different when one looks at non-scientific literature, and especially the arts that appeal to the senses. Here asceticism descended like a frost on the life of 'Merrie old England.' And not only worldly merriment felt its effect. The Puritan's ferocious hatred of everything which smacked of superstition, of all survivals of magical or ritualistic means of grace, applied to the Christmas festivities and the May Pole and the uninhibited use of art in churches. That there was room in Holland for a great, often uncouthly realistic art proves only how far from completely the authoritarian moral discipline of that country was able to counteract the influence of the court and the regents (a class of *rentiers*). It also shows the joy in life of the parvenu bourgeoisie after the short supremacy of the Calvinistic theocracy had been transformed into a moderate national Church, and with it Calvinism had perceptibly lost in its power of ascetic influence.

The theatre was obnoxious to the Puritans, and with the strict exclusion of the erotic and of nudity from the realm of toleration, a radical view of either literature or art could not exist. The conceptions of idle talk, of superfluities, and of vain ostentation, all designations of an irrational attitude without objective purpose, thus not ascetic, and especially not serving the glory of God, but of man, were always at hand to serve in deciding in favour of sober utility as against any artistic tendencies. This was especially true in the case of decoration of the person, for instance clothing. That powerful tendency toward uniformity of style of life, which to-day so immensely aids the capitalistic interest in the standardization of production, had its ideal foundations in the repudiation of all 'idolatry of the flesh'.

Of course we must not forget that Puritanism included a world of contradictions, and that the instinctive sense of eternal greatness in art was certainly stronger among its leaders than in the atmosphere of the Cavaliers. Moreover, a unique genius like Rembrandt, however little his conduct may have been acceptable to God in the eyes of the Puritans, was very strongly influenced in the character of his work by his religious environment. But that does not alter the picture as a whole. In so far as the development of the Puritan tradition could, and in part did, lead to a powerful spiritualization

(*Verinnerlichung*) of personality, it was a decided benefit to literature. But for the most part that benefit only accrued to later generations.

Although we cannot here enter upon a discussion of the influence of Puritanism in all these directions, we should call attention to the fact that the toleration of pleasure in cultural goods, which contributed to purely æsthetic or athletic enjoyment, certainly always ran up against one characteristic limitation: *they must not cost anything.* Man is only a trustee of the goods which have come to him through God's grace. He must, like the servant in the parable, give an account of every penny entrusted to him, and it is at least hazardous to spend any of it for a purpose which does not serve the glory of God but only one's own enjoyment. What person, who keeps his eyes open, has not met representatives of this view-point even in the present? The idea of a man's *duty* to his possessions, to which he subordinates himself as an obedient steward, or even as an acquisitive machine, bears with chilling weight on his life. The greater the possessions the heavier, if the ascetic attitude toward life stands the test, the feeling of responsibility for them, for holding them undiminished for the glory of God and increasing them by restless effort. The origin of this style of life also extends in certain roots, like so many aspects of the spirit of capitalism, back into the Middle Ages. But it was in the ethic of ascetic Protestantism that it first found a consistent ethical foundation. Its significance for the development of capitalism is obvious.

This worldly Protestant asceticism, as we may recapitulate up to this point, acted powerfully against the spontaneous *enjoyment* of possessions; it restricted *consumption*, especially of luxuries. On the other hand, it had the psychological effect of *freeing* the acquisition of goods from the inhibitions of traditionalistic ethics. It broke the bonds of the search for gain in that it not only legalized it, but (in the sense discussed) looked upon it as directly willed by God. The campaign against the temptations of the flesh, and the dependence on external things, was, as besides the Puritans the great Quaker apologist Barclay expressly says, not a struggle against the rational *acquisition*, but against the irrational use of wealth.

But this irrational use was exemplified in the outward forms of luxury which their code condemned as 'idolatry of the flesh', however natural they had appeared to the feudal mind. On the other hand, they approved the rational and utilitarian uses of wealth which were willed by God for the needs of the individual and the community. They did not wish to impose *mortification* on the man of wealth, but the use of his means for necessary and *practical* things. The idea of comfort characteristically limits the extent of ethically permissible expenditures. It is naturally no accident that the development of a manner of living (*Lebensstil*) consistent with that idea may be observed earliest and most clearly among the most consistent representatives of this whole attitude toward life: the Quakers. Over against the glitter and ostentation of feudal magnificence which, resting on an unsound economic basis, prefers a sordid elegance to a sober simplicity, they set the clean and solid comfort of the middle-class home as an ideal.

On the side of the *production* of private wealth, asceticism condemned both dishonesty and impulsive avarice. What was condemned as covetousness, Mammonism, etc., was the pursuit of riches for their own sake. For wealth in itself was a temptation. But here asceticism was the power 'which ever seeks the good but ever creates evil'; what was evil in its sense was possession and its temptations. For, in conformity with the Old Testament and in analogy to the ethical valuation of 'good works', asceticism looked upon the pursuit of wealth as an *end* in itself as highly reprehensible; but the attainment of it as a *fruit* of labour in a calling (*Berufsarbeit*) was a sign of God's blessing. And even more important: the religious valuation of restless, continuous, systematic work in a worldly calling, as the highest means to asceticism, and at the same time the surest and most evident proof of rebirth and genuine faith, must have been the most powerful conceivable lever for the expansion of that attitude toward life which we have here called the 'spirit' of capitalism.

When the limitation of consumption is combined with this release of acquisitive activity, the inevitable practical result is obvious: *accumulation of capital* through *ascetic compulsion to save*. The restraints which were imposed upon the consumption of wealth naturally served to increase it by making possible the productive *investment* of capital. How strong this influence was is not, unfortunately, susceptible to exact statistical demonstration. In New England the connection is so evident that it did not escape the eye of so discerning a historian as Doyle. But also in Holland, which was really only dominated by strict Calvinism for seven years, the greater simplicity of life in the more seriously religious circles, in combination with great wealth, led to an excessive propensity to capital accumulation.

It is further evident that the tendency which has existed everywhere and at all times, and is quite strong in Germany to-day, for middle-class fortunes to be absorbed into the nobility was necessarily checked by the Puritan antipathy to the feudal way of life. English Mercantilist writers of the seventeenth century attributed the superiority of Dutch capital to English to the circumstance that newly acquired wealth there did not regularly seek investment in land. Also, since it is not simply a question of the purchase of land, the Dutch did not seek to acquire feudal habits of life, and thereby to forgo the possibility of capitalistic investment. The high esteem for *agriculture* as a particularly important branch of activity, which the Puritans held and one also consistent with piety, applied (for instance in Baxter) not to the traditional landlord (*Junker*) but to the yeoman and farmer; and in the eighteenth century not to the squire, but the 'rational' cultivator. Through the whole of English society in the time since the seventeenth century goes the conflict between the squirearchy, the representatives of 'merrie old England', and the Puritan circles of widely varying social influence. Both elements, that of an unspoiled naïve joy of life, and of a strictly regulated, reserved self-control, and conventional ethical conduct are even to-day combined to form the English 'national character'. Similarly, the early history of the North

American Colonies is dominated by the sharp contrast of the adventurers, who wanted to set up plantations with the labour of indentured servants, and live as feudal lords, and the specifically middle-class outlook of the Puritans.

As far as the influence of the Puritan outlook extended, under all circumstances – and this is, of course, much more important than the mere encouragement of capital accumulation – it favoured the development of a bourgeois, economically *rational* way of life; it was the most important, and above all the only consistent support for the development of that life. It stood at the cradle of the modern economic man.

To be sure, these Puritanical ideals tended to give way under excessive pressure from the temptations of wealth, as the Puritans themselves knew very well. With great regularity we find the most genuine adherents of Puritanism among the classes which were rising from a lowly status, the small bourgeois and farmers, while the *beati possidentes*, even among Quakers, are often found tending to repudiate the old ideals. It was the same fate which again and again befell the predecessor of innerworldly asceticism, the monastic asceticism of the Middle Ages. In the latter case, when rational economic activity had worked out its full effects by strict regulation of conduct and limitation of consumption, the wealth accumulated either succumbed directly to the nobility, as in the time before the Reformation, or monastic discipline threatened to break down, and one of the numerous reformations became necessary.

In fact the whole history of monasticism is in a certain sense the history of a continual struggle with the problem of the secularizing influence of wealth. The same is true on a grand scale of the innerworldly asceticism of Puritanism. The great revival of Methodism, which preceded the expansion of English industry toward the end of the eighteenth century, may well be compared with such a monastic reform. We may hence quote here a passage from John Wesley himself which might well serve as a motto for everything which has been said above. For it shows that the leaders of these ascetic movements understood the seemingly paradoxical relationships which we have here analysed perfectly well, and in the same sense that we have given them. He wrote:

I fear, wherever riches have increased, the essence of religion has decreased in the same proportion. Therefore I do not see how it is possible, in the nature of things, for any revival of true religion to continue long. For religion *must necessarily* produce both industry and frugality, and these cannot but produce riches. But as riches increase, so will pride, anger, and love of the world in all its branches. How then is it possible that Methodism, that is, a religion of the heart, though it flourishes now as a green bay tree, should continue in this state? For the Methodists in every place grow diligent and frugal; consequently they increase in goods. Hence they proportionately increase in pride, in anger, in the desire of the flesh, the desire of the eyes, and the pride of life. So, although the form of religion remains, the spirit is swiftly vanishing away. Is there no way to prevent this – this continual decay of pure religion? We ought not to prevent people from being diligent and frugal; *we must exhort all Christians to gain all they can, and to save all they can; that is, in effect, to grow rich.*[2]

There follows the advice that those who gain all they can and save all they can should also give all they can, so that they will grow in grace and lay up a treasure in heaven. It is clear that Wesley here expresses, even in detail, just what we have been trying to point out.

As Wesley says, the full economic effect of those great religious movements, whose significance for economic development lay above all in their ascetic *educative* influence, generally came only after the peak of the purely religious enthusiasm was past. Then the intensity of the search for the Kingdom of God commenced gradually to pass over into sober vocational virtue; the religious roots died out slowly, giving way to utilitarian worldliness. Then, as Dowden puts it, the place occupied in the popular imagination by Bunyan's pilgrim, hurrying through 'Vanity Fair' in a lonely spiritual search for the Kingdom of Heaven, was taken by 'Robinson Crusoe' – the *isolated economic man* who carries on missionary activities on the side.

When later the principle 'to make the most of both worlds' became dominant in the end, as Dowden has remarked, a good conscience simply became one of the means of enjoying a comfortable bourgeois life, as is well expressed in the German proverb about the 'soft pillow'. What the great religious epoch of the seventeenth century bequeathed to its utilitarian successor was, however, above all an amazingly good, we may even say a pharisaically good, conscience in the acquisition of money, so long as it took place legally. Every trace of the *Deo placere vix potest* [it is scarcely pleasing to God] has disappeared.

A specifically *bourgeois vocational ethic* had grown up. With the consciousness of standing in the fullness of God's grace and being visibly blessed by Him, the bourgeois business man, as long as he remained within the bounds of formal correctness, as long as his moral conduct was spotless and the use to which he put his wealth was not objectionable, could follow his pecuniary interests as he would, and feel that he was fulfilling a duty in doing so. In addition, the power of religious asceticism placed at his disposal sober, conscientious, and unusually industrious workmen, who clung to their work as to a life purpose willed by God.

Finally, it gave him the comforting assurance that the unequal distribution of the goods of this world was a special dispensation of Divine Providence, which in these differences, as in particular grace, pursued secret ends

2 Quoted in Robert Southey, *Life of Wesley*, 2nd edn, vol. 2, New York, Harper & Brothers, 1847, ch. 29.

unknown to men. Calvin himself had made the much-quoted statement that only when the people, i.e. the mass of labourers and craftsmen, were poor did they remain obedient to God. In the Netherlands (Pieter de la Court and others), that had been 'secularized' to the effect that the mass of men only *labour* when necessity forces them to do so. This formulation of a leading idea of capitalistic economy later entered into the current theories of the 'productivity' of low wages. Here also, with the dying out of the religious root, the utilitarian interpretation crept in unnoticed, in the line of development which we have again and again observed.

Mediæval ethics not only tolerated begging but actually glorified it in the mendicant orders. Even secular beggars, since they gave the person of means opportunity for good works through giving alms, were sometimes considered an 'estate' and treated as such. Even the Anglican social ethic of the Stuarts was very close to this attitude. It remained for Puritan asceticism to take part in the severe English Poor Relief Legislation which fundamentally changed the situation. And it could do that, because the Protestant sects and the strict Puritan communities actually *did not know* any begging in their own midst.

On the other hand, seen from the side of the workers, the Zinzendorf branch of Pietism, for instance, glorified the loyal worker who did not seek acquisition, but lived according to the apostolic model, and was thus endowed with the charisma of the disciples. Similar ideas had originally been prevalent among the Baptists in an even more radical form.

Now naturally the whole ascetic literature of almost *all* denominations is saturated with the idea that faithful labour, even at low wages, on the part of those whom life offers no other opportunities, is highly pleasing to God. In *this* respect Protestant asceticism added in itself nothing new. But it not only deepened this idea most powerfully, it also created the force which was alone decisive for its effectiveness: the psychological sanction (*Antrieb*) of it through the conception of this labour as a *calling*, as the best, often in the last analysis the only means of attaining certainty of grace. And on the other hand it legalized the exploitation of this specific willingness to work, in that it also interpreted the employer's business activity as a 'calling'. It is obvious how powerfully the *exclusive* search for the Kingdom of God only through the fulfilment of duty in the calling, and the strict asceticism which Church discipline naturally imposed, especially on the propertyless classes, was bound to affect the productivity of labour in the capitalistic sense of the word. The treatment of labour as a 'calling' became as characteristic of the modern worker as the corresponding attitude toward acquisition of the business man. It was a perception of this situation, new at his time, which caused so able an observer as Sir William Petty to attribute the economic power of Holland in the seventeenth century to the fact that the very numerous dissenters in that country (Calvinists and Baptists) 'are for the most part thinking, sober men, and such as believe that Labour and Industry is their duty towards God'.

Calvinism opposed 'organic' social organization in the fiscal-monopolistic form which it assumed in Anglicanism under the Stuarts, especially in the conceptions of Laud, this alliance of Church and State with the monopolists on the basis of a Christian-social ethical foundation. The Puritan leaders were universally among the most passionate opponents of this type of politically privileged commercial, putting-out, and colonial capitalism. Over against it they placed the individualistic motives of rational legal acquisition by virtue of one's own ability and initiative. And, while the politically privileged monopoly industries in England all disappeared in short order, this attitude played a large and decisive part in the development of the industries which grew up in spite of and against the authority of the State. The Puritans (Prynne, Parker) repudiated all connection with the large-scale capitalistic 'courtiers and projectors' as an ethically suspicious class. On the other hand, they took pride in their own superior middle-class business morality, which formed the true reason for the persecutions to which they were subjected on the part of those circles. Defoe proposed to win the battle against dissent by boycotting bank credit and withdrawing deposits. The difference of the two types of capitalistic attitude went to a very large extent hand in hand with religious differences. The opponents of the Nonconformists, even in the eighteenth century, again and again ridiculed them for personifying the spirit of shopkeepers, and for having ruined the ideals of old England. Here also lay the difference of the Puritan economic ethic from the Jewish; and contemporaries (Prynne) knew well that the former and not the latter was the *bourgeois* capitalistic ethic.

One of the fundamental elements of the spirit of modern capitalism, and not only of that but of all modern culture: rational conduct on the basis of the idea of the calling, was born – that is what this discussion has sought to demonstrate – from the spirit of *Christian asceticism*. One has only to re-read the passage from Franklin, quoted at the beginning of this essay,[3] in order to see that the essential elements of the attitude which was there called the 'spirit of capitalism' are the same as what we have just shown to be the content of the Puritan worldly asceticism, only without the religious basis, which even by Franklin's time had died away. The idea that modern labour has an *ascetic* character is of course not new. Limitation to specialized work, with a renunciation of the Faustian universality of man which it involves, is a condition of any valuable work in the modern world; hence deeds and renunciation inevitably condition each other today. This fundamentally ascetic trait of middle-class life, if it attempts to be a style of life at all, and not simply the absence of any, was what Goethe wanted to teach, at the height of his wisdom, in the *Wanderjahren*, and in the end which he gave to the life of his *Faust*. For him the realization meant a renunciation, a departure from an age of full and beautiful humanity, which can no more be repeated in the course of our cultural development than can the flower of the Athenian culture of Antiquity.

3 See *PESC*, pp. 47–58.

The Puritan *wanted* to work in a calling; we are *forced* to do so. For when asceticism was carried out of monastic cells into everyday life, and began to dominate innerworldly morality, it did its part in building the tremendous cosmos of the modern economic order. This order is now bound to the technical and economic conditions of machine production which to-day determine the style of life of all the individuals who are born into this mechanism, not only those directly concerned with economic acquisition, with irresistible force. Perhaps it will so determine them until the last ton of fossilized coal is burnt. In Baxter's view the concern for external goods should only lie on the shoulders of the 'saint like a light cloak, which can be thrown aside at any moment'. But fate decreed that the cloak should become an iron cage.[4]

Since asceticism undertook to remodel the world and to work out its ideals in the world, material goods have gained an increasing and finally an inexorable power over the lives of men as at no previous period in history. To-day the spirit of religious asceticism – whether finally, who knows? – has escaped from the cage. But victorious capitalism, since it rests on mechanical foundations, needs its support no longer. The rosy blush of its laughing heir, the Enlightenment seems also to be irretrievably fading, and the idea of 'duty in one's calling' prowls about in our lives like the ghost of dead religious beliefs. Where the fulfilment of the calling cannot directly be related to the highest spiritual and cultural values, or when, on the other hand, it need not be felt simply as economic compulsion, the individual generally abandons the attempt to justify it at all. In the field of its highest development, in the United States, the pursuit of wealth, stripped of its religious and ethical meaning, tends to become associated with purely competitive passions, which often actually give it the character of sport.

No one knows who will live in this cage in the future, or whether at the end of this tremendous development entirely new prophets will arise, or there will be a great rebirth of old ideas and ideals, or, if neither, mechanized petrification, embellished with a sort of convulsive self-importance. For of the 'last men' of this cultural development, it might well be truly said: 'Specialists without spirit, sensualists without heart; this nullity imagines that it has attained a level of civilization (*Menschentum*) never before achieved.'

But this brings us to the world of judgments of value and of faith, with which this purely historical discussion need not be burdened. The next task would be rather to show the significance of ascetic rationalism, which has only been touched in the foregoing sketch, for the content of socio-political ethics, thus for the types of organization and the functions of social groups from the conventicle to the State. Then ascetic rationalism's relations to

---

4 Talcott Parsons' translation – the iron cage – has now become iconic as an image of the inflexibility of the modern economic order. The original German is slightly different – a casing as hard as steel (*stahlhartes Gehäuse*).

humanistic rationalism and its ideals of life and cultural influence; further to the development of philosophical and scientific empiricism, to technical development and to spiritual ideals of culture would have to be analysed. Then its past development from the mediæval beginnings of innerworldly asceticism to its dissolution into pure utilitarianism would have to be traced out historically through all the areas of ascetic religion. Only then could the extent of the cultural significance of ascetic Protestantism in its relation to the other plastic elements of modern culture be estimated.

Here we have only attempted to trace the fact and the nature of the effect of ascetic Protestantism back to the motives of that influence in one, though a very important point. But it would also further be necessary to investigate how Protestant asceticism was in turn influenced in its development and its character by the totality of social conditions, especially *economic*. The modern man is in general, even with the best will, unable to give religious ideas a significance for conduct of life, culture and national character which they deserve. But it is, of course, not my aim to substitute for a one-sided 'materialistic' an equally one-sided spiritualistic causal interpretation of culture and of history. *Each is equally possible,*[5] but each, if it does not serve as the preparation, but as the conclusion of an investigation, accomplishes equally little in the interest of historical truth.

---

5 [Weber] For the above sketch has deliberately taken up only the relations in which an influence of religious ideas on the material culture is beyond doubt. It would have been easy to proceed beyond that to a regular construction which logically deduced everything characteristic of modern culture from Protestant rationalism, but that sort of thing may be left to the type of dilettante who believes in the 'unity' of the 'group mind' and its reducibility to a single formula. Let it be remarked only that the period of capitalistic development lying before that which we have studied was everywhere co-determined (*mitbedingt*) by religious influences, both hindering and helping. Of what sorts these were belong in a later chapter.

2 Confucianism and Puritanism compared[1]

Perhaps it will be most useful to place what has been said in the context of our approach, by clarifying the relationship of Confucian rationalism – for this is the term that best describes it – to the rationalism that is geographically and historically nearest to us, namely, the rationalism of Protestantism. For the assessment of the stage of rationalization represented in a religion, there are two measures that stand out and are internally connected to each other in various ways. First, the degree to which a religion has ridden itself of *magic*. Second, the degree of systematic unity that a religion has brought about in the relation of God and the world, and so a religion's particular ethical relationship to the world.

In regard to magic, ascetic Protestantism in all its different expressions represents a final stage. In most of its characteristic expressions it has terminated magic completely. Even in its sublimated form of sacraments and symbols, magic was eliminated as a matter of principle, so much so that the strict Puritan would have the bodies of his loved ones buried without ceremony in order to cut off the sources of any 'superstition', which in this case meant any trust in the manipulation of magical signs. It was only here that the complete *disenchantment of the world* was carried through with complete consistency. This did not mean freedom from what we today would tend to regard as 'superstition'. Witch trials flourished even in New England. But while in Confucianism magic was of unimpeachably *positive* significance for salvation, in Puritanism everything magical came to be considered as *diabolical*. What remained as religiously valued was rationally ethical behaviour, and this meant action that obeyed God's commands and flowed from the conviction in God's holiness. It has become perfectly clear in the course of the above presentation that in the magic garden, particularly in heterodox doctrines like Taoism, a rational economy and technology of the occidental type was quite simply ruled out. The magic garden remained in the power of chronomancers, geomancers, water diviners, and weather diviners.[2] It had crude and

---

1 The concluding chapter of Weber's study of Confucianism and Taoism, *GARS*, vol. 1, pp. 512–36. Translation by S. Whimster.
2 Magicians were used for a large number of decisions in China. Chronomancers advised on what day and time would be propitious for actions, and geomancers reported on the presence of the spirits and demons in the landscape. See *China*, pp. 196–202.

abstruse 'universistic' (*universistisch*) ideas of the coherence of the world.[3] It lacked any *natural scientific* understanding of the world and this was part cause, part consequence, of those primitive forces. And lastly, the prebendal holding of offices had an interest in charging fees for magical services and so was supportive of the magical tradition. The *preservation* of the magic garden belonged to the most intimate tendencies of the Confucian ethic. In addition to this there were also *internal* reasons that hindered any breaking of Confucian power.

While Confucianism adopted an open and unconstrained attitude (*unbefangene Stellungnahme*) towards the things and objects of the world, in the strongest possible contrast the Puritan ethic shifted this connection to one of a tremendous and pathetic tension in relation to the 'world'. Any religion which confronts the world with rational (ethical) demands becomes at some point involved in a relationship of tension with the irrationalities of the world, as we will shortly see in detail. These tensions appear in the individual religions at very different points and so both the manner as well as the strength of the tension vary accordingly. It depends to a large extent on the type of metaphysical promises that the individual religions have offered as the way to redemption. Above all, the degree of religious devaluation of the world is not thereby identical with the extent of its *practical* rejection of the world.

Confucianism, as we have seen, was (in intention) the rational ethic that reduced to an absolute minimum the tension towards the world, the religious devaluation of the world, and the practical rejection of the world. The world was the best of all possible worlds.[4] Human nature was disposed to the ethically good and while human beings might vary in this, as in all things, they were in principle similar and at any rate they were fully capable of perfection and capable of fulfilling the moral law. A philosophical and literary education in the ancient classics was the universal means to self-perfection. An insufficient education was the only reason for all failings and its most common cause was economic insufficiency. But these failings, and in particular those of the government, were the main reason for all disasters, since these failings disturbed the spirits, which were thought of in purely magical terms. The correct way to salvation was to adjust to the eternal,

---

3 Weber uses the term 'universistic' rather than 'universal'. One of his sources expounds on the animism that underlay the whole of Chinese religion as a form of universalism 'based on an implicit belief in the animation of the universe, and of every being or thing which exists in it'. The abstruse principles refers to 'the two souls or breaths, called *Yang* and *Yin*'. 'The *Yang* is subdivided into an indefinite number of good souls or spirits, called *shen*, the *Yin* into particles or evil spirits, called *kwei*, specters; it is these *shen* and *kwei* which animate every being and every thing' (J.J.M. de Groot, *The Religion of the Chinese*, New York, Macmillan, 1910, pp. 12–13).

4 Weber uses Voltaire's aphorism from *Candide* who satirized Leibniz's view that everything in the world had a purpose which was to increase happiness.

supra-divine (*übergöttlich*) orders of the world – the Tao, and thereby conform to the social demands of collective life that flowed from cosmic harmony. This meant above all a humble compliance with the fixed order of the earthly powers. The corresponding ideal for the individual was the development of the self as a harmoniously balanced personality in all respects and in this sense a microcosm.[5]

The 'grace and dignity' of the Confucian ideal of the person – the gentleman – was expressed through the fulfilment of traditional duties. Ceremonial and ritual propriety in all fields of life was, as a central virtue, the aim of self-perfection. A watchful self-control and the suppression of all the irrational passions that disturb the sense of balance was the appropriate means to attaining self-perfection. But 'salvation' of any sort, except that from the barbarism of lack of education, had no attraction at all for the Confucian. What he expected as a reward for virtue in this world were long life, health, and wealth and, after death, the preservation of his good name. What was lacking, and this was exactly the same for the genuine Greek of the ancient world, was any transcendental anchoring of ethics, any tension between the commands of a supra-worldly god and those of a creaturely world, any orientation to a goal in the world Beyond, and any conception of radical evil. The commandments were tailored to the average capability of human beings, and he who observed them was free from sin. The Christian missionaries tried in vain to awaken a sense of sin where these presuppositions were taken for granted. An educated Chinese would emphatically reject the idea that he was continuously burdened with 'sin', just as every superior intellectual stratum would have regarded the idea as embarrassing and lacking in dignity. Instead the concept of sin tended to be represented by conventional or feudal or aesthetically formulated variants, such as 'not proper' or 'lacking in taste'. Certainly there were sins, but in ethical terms they were offences against the traditional authorities – against parents, ancestors, superiors in the hierarchy of office – thus against traditional powers. From the standpoint of magic they were also serious infringements of inherited customs, the traditional ceremonial and, ultimately, the rigid conventions of society. All these offences were on the same level as one another. 'I have sinned' corresponded to our 'I beg your pardon' when we infringe against convention.

Asceticism and contemplation, mortification and flight from the world, were not only unknown in Confucianism but held in contempt as a dangerous parasitism. All forms of communal and salvation religiosity were in part directly driven out and eliminated, and in part treated in the same way superior Greeks in classical antiquity treated the orphic clerics – as a private matter of no great significance. The inner assumption of this ethic of unconditional affirmation of, and adjustment to, the world was the unbroken

---

5 The individual person was seen as correspondent to a wider macrocosmic harmony. See *Rel*, p. 200.

and continued existence of a purely magical religiosity. This started with the emperor who on account of his personal qualifications was responsible for the good behaviour of the spirits, the arrival of rain, and good weather for harvests. It extended to the cult of ancestral spirits which was absolutely fundamental to official and popular religiosity, to the unofficial (Taoist) magical therapy, and to the other earlier existing forms of animistic control of spirits – the belief in functional gods in the shape of humans and hero worship.[6]

The educated Confucian, like the educated Greek, combined in equal measure scepticism with the occasional succumbing to the fear of super-natural spirits, while the Chinese masses in a way of life influenced by Confucianism remained completely under the spell of magical ideas. The Confucian could say of the Beyond, as did the old Faust, 'Fool, who turns his eyes blinking in that direction', but like Faust was forced to add the qualification: 'If I could only remove magic from my path.'[7] Likewise in the ancient Chinese sense, the very educated high official seldom hesitated in his reverence for any old stupid miracle. A tension with the world never ever originated, since as far back as can be remembered the ethical prophecy of a supra-mundane god making ethical *demands* was completely unknown. The 'spirits' might provide prophecy and above all they required contractual faith, but this was no substitute for ethical prophecy. The protection of the spirits involved an *individual* duty, an oath or whatever, but this never amounted to the inner formation of the personality *as such* and the conduct of life. The leading intellectual stratum – officials and candidates for office – consistently supported the maintenance of magical tradition, in particular the animistic piety for the ancestors, as an absolute requirement for the undisturbed upholding of the bureaucratic authorities; they also suppressed all upheavals caused by salvation religiosity. Next to Taoist divination and sacramental grace, the only salvation religion permitted was Buddhist monasticism, since it was pacifist and therefore not a danger. In China it enriched practically the soul's range through the emphases it placed on the sense of inwardness, as we will see;[8] otherwise it worked simply as a further source of the magical sacraments of grace and as a traditional strengthening of ceremonies.

As has already been said, there are limits to the significance of this sort of intellectuals' ethic for the broad mass of the people. Local and above all social differences in education were enormous. Even until recent times subsistence needs were met by a traditionalistic and very naturalistic economy.

---

6 In the older popular religion spirits such as thunder and wind were personalized. See *China*, pp. 173–4. Taoist magical therapy refers to practices such as macrobiotics and breathing exercises as a way of improving health and longevity. See *Rel*, pp. 191–2.

7 A reference to Goethe's play *Faust* – Pt II, Act 5, midnight.

8 Weber followed this up in *India*, pp. 292–3. Buddhist monasticism gave an enlarged role to asceticism and meditation.

For the poor people, subsistence was maintained by an unbelievable virtuosity in thrift (in terms of consumption), rivalled nowhere else in the world, and this was only made possible by a standard of life that excluded any inner contact to the gentleman ideal of Confucianism. It was only the gestures and forms of the ruling stratum's external behaviour that became, as everywhere, a matter of general assimilation. The decisive influence of the educated stratum on the way of life of the *masses* in all probability only operated in negative ways: on the one side, obstructing completely the establishment of a prophetic religiosity and, on the other, the overall elimination of every orgiastic component from animistic religiosity. It could be possible that at least a part of those characteristics is co-determined by what one might occasionally term the racial qualities of Chinese. It is also today clear that experts have little definitive to say, here as elsewhere, about the extent of the influence of biological 'inheritance'. But for us an important observation can be easily made, and has been confirmed by reputable sinologists, that the further back in history one goes, the more *similar* the Chinese and their civilization (in what are the essential points for us) appear to be to our own. The ancient beliefs of the people, the old anchorites, the oldest songs of the *Schi king*,[9] the old warrior kings, the arguments of philosophical schools, feudalism, as well as the first signs of capitalistic development in the period of the Warring States[10] appear to us to be far more closely related to occidental phenomena than do the traits which are held to be characteristic of Confucian 'Chineseness'. What many like to see as its innate characteristics may therefore be considered as products of purely historically conditioned cultural influences.

The sociologist is dependent on the missionary literature that relates characteristics of this sort. This literature is certainly of very variable quality but ultimately is relatively the most reliable knowledge. Some observations are constantly stressed: the striking absence of 'nerves' in the specific sense of the word as it is attached to the modern European; the unlimited patience and the controlled politeness; the tenacity with which customs are adhered to; the complete tolerance of monotony and continuous ability to work; the slowness of reaction to unusual stimuli, especially in the intellectual sphere. These observations appear to present a coherent and comprehensible unity. But against this, there are some glaring contrasts apparent: the extraordinary horror, exceeding all normal levels and amounting to an inextinguishable mistrust, that is displayed above all to the unknown; the turning away from or the insufficient curiosity in everything that is not directly to hand and useful, and this contrasts with the apparently good-natured and easy belief in every

---

9 This was an ancient book of songs and poetry dating back to the sixth century BC.
10 A feudal period of Chinese history dating from the ninth to the third century BC when China was split up into competing states with no strong imperial centre of power. It was the period in which Confucius lived (551–479 BC).

fantastical and magical swindle. Then, it seems, there is very frequently a lack of warm sympathy for those persons personally closest to one that stands in apparent contradiction to the strong coherence of social groups. The (allegedly typical) lack of love and lack of respect for authority in small children, if really existing, seem difficult to reconcile with the absolute obedience and ceremonial piety of grown children towards their parents. Likewise, it appears difficult to reconcile an insincerity – as is continuously asserted – that has no equal in the world (for example, even to one's own lawyer) with the obviously very remarkable reliability of merchants in large commercial businesses; a reliability that is relative when compared to the countries with a feudal past such as Japan. (There seems to be little known about this in the small retail trade, and 'fixed' prices even among local Chinese seem to be mostly fictitious.) The typical *mistrust* of the Chinese to *one another* is confirmed by every observer and contrasts strongly with the trust in the honesty of the faith-brethren in the Puritan sects,[11] a trust that extended to those *outside* the congregation. Lastly, the general unity and unshakeability of the psycho-physical *habitus* contrasts with the often reported instability of all those characteristics of the Chinese way of life which are not regulated externally by fixed norms – though to be sure most characteristics are. Put more precisely, the absence of any core stance of attitudes that operates from within and looks outwards and generally regulates the integrity of the Chinese way of life stands in fundamental contrast with the subjugation achieved through innumerable conventions. How is all this to be explained?

The absence of a hystericizing asceticism and its proximate forms of religiosity and the elimination of all ecstatic cults[12] (if not completely, then a widespread elimination) could not occur without influencing the psychological and mental constitution of a human group.[13] In respect to the use of intoxicating substances the Chinese were a relatively 'sober' people from the end of the Warring States (in contrast to the importance of drinking in the ancient men's houses and in the princely courts). Frenzy and orgiastic 'possession' were stripped of any charismatically sacred evaluation and were seen merely as symptoms of demonic control. Confucianism condemned the use of alcoholic spirits except as a rudiment in sacrifices. The fact that alcoholic frenzy occurred quite often in China, especially among the lower strata, does not alter the *relative* importance of this distinction. But it was opium that was the intoxicating substance specific to China. It was imported only in the modern period and its admissibility into the country was strongly resisted by

---

11 Weber's source for these observations is Arthur H. Smith, *Chinese Characteristics*, New York, Fleming H. Revell, 1894. Successive chapters are titled 'The Absence of Nerves', 'The Absence of Sympathy', 'The Absence of Sincerity', and 'Mutual Suspicion'. See *MWG* I/19, pp. 455–7.

12 *Rauschkulte* – cults that achieve frenzy through intoxicating means such as alcohol or other drugs. See below, p. 67.

13 '*Die nervöse und seelische Konstitution einer Menschengruppe.*'

the ruling strata and was externally imposed through a war, as is well known.[14] Moreover its effects operate in the direction of apathetic ecstasy and thus in the direct line of '*wu-wei*'.[15] It did not operate in the line of heroic frenzy, nor in the unchaining of active passions. The Hellenic state of possession (*sophrosyne*) did not hinder Plato, for in the *Phaidros* everything magnificent was seen as being born from a wonderful madness. Like the Chinese educated stratum, the situation was completely different for Roman rationalism as well as the aristocracy of office who translated '*ekstasis*' as '*superstitio*'.[16]

The sense of being untouched by the gods,[17] as well as what is felt as indolence, goes together perhaps to a certain extent with the complete absence of Dionysian elements in Chinese religiosity that was a consequence of the deliberate decision by the bureaucracy to render the cults sober. For the bureaucrat there was nothing and should be nothing that could have disturbed the equilibrium of the soul. Any over-strong passion, especially rage – *ch'i* – produced evil charms, and with every pain it was first asked to what *ch'i* it should be ascribed.[18] Animistic magic was upheld as the only form of popular religion, and though condemned by the educated, it was supported because of the character of the official cults. It determined the traditionalist fear of anything new, which could produce evil spells and disturb the spirits. It explained the very great susceptibility to belief. The effects of upholding this belief in magic – that illness and unhappiness are symptoms of a self-incriminating anger of the gods – had to lead to the restricting of the warm sympathy that tends to flow from sense of community in salvation religions in the face of pain. In India this sympathy has always predominated in the popular ethic. The specifically cool temperament of the Chinese sense of friendship towards people that was tied to ceremonious correctness, even extending to relationships within the family, and a selfish fear of the spirits, were the result of the belief in magic. . . .

Genuine prophecy creates a systematic orienting of the conduct of life to *one* internal scale of values, and the 'world' is seen as raw material to be ethically fashioned according to norms. Confucianism is the reverse of this, being an adjustment from without, an adjustment to the conditions of the 'world'. A human being who is optimally adjusted to the world – one who has rationalized his conduct only to the degree that conformity demands – is not a systematic unity but a combination of useful individual qualities. The continuation of animist ideas in Chinese popular religion, that the individual

---

14 A reference to the Opium Wars (1839–42) when British traders bombarded the southern Chinese ports to gain access for trading in opium.

15 '*Wu-wei*' – 'an active inactivity that allows the way of Tao to be expressed', *Concise Dictionary of World Religions*, Oxford, Oxford University Press, 2000.

16 '*Superstitio*' meant an excessive fear of the gods.

17 '*Ungebrochenheit*' which Weber places in quotes.

18 *Ch'i* in Chinese religion is a vital energy.

possessed a plurality of souls, could almost be taken as a symbol of this fact. Where any stretching out beyond the world is absent, then the person's own stature in relation to the world is diminished. This then allowed the domestication of the masses and the good bearing of the gentleman. But the style which it bestowed on the conduct of life was perforce to remain characterized by negative traits. Any striving for a unity from within and facing outwards to the world, with which we associate the idea of 'personality', could not take root. Life remained a series of occurrences that lacked any methodical organization in the light of a transcendental goal.

The contrast of the Chinese social ethical position to the world with all occidental religious ethics was insurmountable. From the outside it is possible to demonstrate some apparent similarities between Confucianism and some of the patriarchal aspects of the Thomist and Lutheran ethic.[19] But this appearance is only superficial. The Christian ethic is implicated in such a close compromise with the orders of the world that it could not remove from the ground up the pessimistic tension between the world and the supra-mundane determination of the individual with its unavoidable consequences. The Confucian system of radical world-optimism could eliminate this tension like no other ethic.

The Confucian ethic was devoid of any tension between nature and the divine, ethical demands and human inadequacy, the consciousness of sin and the need for salvation, this-worldly acts and other-worldly recompense, and religious duty and politico-social realities. It therefore lacked any chance of influencing the conduct of life through internal forces other than those tied to tradition and convention. The power that exerted by far the strongest influence on the conduct of life was family piety, which was based on the belief in spirits. It was the power of family piety that, as we saw,[20] enabled and controlled the ever strong cohesion of the clan associations and the manner of the socialization of the friendly associations,[21] which could operate as extended family businesses with a division of labour – as mentioned earlier.[22] This strong cohesion was in its manner wholly religiously motivated, and the strength of the authentic Chinese economic organization extended just about as far as the personal ties were regulated through familial piety.

In strong contrast to the objectification of creaturely burdens that occurred within the orbit of the Puritan ethic, the Chinese ethic unfolded its strongest motives within the circle of people who formed associations on the basis of natural ties (or those associations affiliated and modelled upon them). In Puritanism, with its religious obligation to a supra-mundane, other-worldly god, all relationships with one's fellow human beings, including those close to

19 Thomas Aquinas and Martin Luther both stressed the role of the father in ethical conduct.
20 See *China*, pp. 86–95.
21 *'Vergesellschaftung in Genossenschaften.'*
22 See *China*, pp. 16–20.

one and standing within a natural order of life, are valued only as a means and expression of a conviction that extends beyond the organic social basis of life. And, conversely, the religious obligation of the pious Chinese is something that only realizes itself *within* an organic framework of personal relationships. Mencius rejected the universal 'love of mankind' with the remark that thereby piety and justice would be extinguished; not to have a father or a brother is a form akin to the beasts. The content of the duties of the Confucian Chinese was always and everywhere a piety towards concrete human beings, living or dead, who were close to him in the given orders of the world; and never to a supra-mundane god and *therefore* never to sacred 'causes' or 'ideas'. The 'Tao' was neither of these but simply the incorporation of binding *traditionalistic ritual*, and its decree was not 'action' but the 'void' (*Leere*).

The personalistic restrictions to impersonal objectification were without doubt of considerable importance for the economic mentality by acting as a constraint on an objectifying rationalization. These limits tended to bind the individual in his inmost feelings ever anew inwardly to his clan and the clan-related associates; that is, to people instead of objective tasks ('enterprises' – *Betriebe*). As the presentation has shown, the limits on objectification had the most intimate connection with the manner of Chinese religiosity and with the obstacles to the rationalization of the religious ethic. It was in the interests of the controlling educated stratum to maintain these obstacles as a way of upholding their own position. It is of very great economic significance if everything to do with *trust* – the foundation of all business relations – is always based within the family or family-type personal relationships, as was very much the case in China.

The great achievement of ethical religions, above all the ethical and ascetic sects of Protestantism, was the *shattering* of the fetters of the family clans and the establishment of the superiority of a communal way of life centred on belief and *ethics* rather than on *blood*, and to do this in large measure in the face of the family.[23] Seen economically, the founding of *trust in business matters on the ethical qualities* of particular individuals; qualities that were affirmed in impersonal *vocational* work. The consequences of a general mistrust of all against all, which was a result of the official pre-eminence of conventional insincerity and the general significance of the saving of face in Confucianism, probably have to be reckoned economically as quite high – although there are no reliable measures here.

Confucianism and the Confucian mentality that idealizes wealth could favour relevant economic-*political* measures (as did the Renaissance that was so open to worldly influences (*weltoffen*), as we have seen). But it is precisely here that one can see the limited significance of economic *policy* in respect to the economic *mentality*. In no other civilized country has material well-being

---

23 Weber's language here mimics Marx's *Communist Manifesto* which spoke of capitalism shattering the old feudal relationships.

ever been so emphatically represented as an ultimate goal as it has been in China.[24] The views of Confucius on economic policy corresponded roughly to those of our cameralists. The Confucian Ssu-ma Ch'ien emphasized the usefulness of wealth as well as the wealth created through trade. He even wrote a tract on the 'balance of trade' – one of the oldest documents of Chinese economics.[25] Economic policy was an alternation of fiscal and *laissez-faire* measures, but was not directed against the pursuit of money (*antichrematisch*). The merchant class (*Kaufleute*) were disdained in China, just as they were in our Middle Ages and are even now in literary circles. But economic *policy* did not create a capitalistic economic *mentality*. The income of the merchants in the time of the Warring States was the political profits derived from being state suppliers. The large mining concerns using servile labour (*Bergwerksfronden*) were used to search for gold. But no one adhering to the Confucian ethic, which was an ethic as strongly anchored as that of Christianity, crossed over to a *bourgeois* and *methodical* way of life. And this is what is crucial for us. Puritanism has created this methodical way of life – but always against its intentions. The paradox of the effect in relation to what was intended: this is a curious reversal of what seems 'natural', but only at the first and very superficial glance. It teaches us about the human being and fate, where fate is the *outcome* of actions when compared with the actions *intended* by the person.[26]

Puritanism presents a type radically opposed to the Confucian rational treatment of the world that, as we have seen above, is not a wholly unambiguous idea. '*Ecclesia pura*' [the church of the pure] signified in practical terms in its most proper sense the Christian community, cleansed of the morally rejected (*verworfen*), coming together for the glory of God in Holy Communion. The community might be placed on Calvinist or Baptist foundations and become according to the organization of the church either more synodal or more congregationalist. But in a broader sense one can see in this the ethically rigorous Christian-ascetic lay communities in general, those that include from their pneumatic and mystical beginnings the Baptists, Mennonites, Quakers, the ascetic Pietists, and the Methodists. What distinguished the Puritan type from the Confucian was this: it was the opposite of world flight. And this means the rationalization of the world, despite, or rather exactly because of, its form as the ascetic rejection of the world. Human beings in themselves are all equally reprehensible (*verworfen*) and in ethical terms totally inadequate, since in their creatural corruptness (*kreatürlichen*

---

24 [Weber] Compare what de Groot has to say on this in *The Religion of the Chinese*, New York, 1910, p. 130. [On Confucian religion de Groot wrote, 'Promotion of the material happiness of the world is its aim and end.']

25 [Weber] Printed in the edition of E. Chavannes, *Les mémoires historiques de Se-ma Ts'ien*, vol. 3, ch. XXX, Paris, Ernst Leroux, 1895–1905.

26 What would now be termed 'the unintended consequences of action'.

Verderbtheit) in relation to God there can be no distinction between them, and the world is a receptacle of sin. Conforming to the world and its vain customs would be a sign of rejection (*Verwerfung*) and the Confucian idea of perfecting the self would be a blasphemous, creature-idolizing ideal. Wealth and the surrender to its enjoyment would be a specific temptation, the insistence on human philosophy and literary education would be a sinful and creatural pride, and any trust in the power of magical spirits and gods would be not only an abominated superstition but an impudent blasphemy. Anything that recalled magic, every residue of ritualism and the magical power of priests, was rooted out. According to Quaker principles there could be no appointed preacher, and the majority of the ascetic sects did without a professional and paid preacher. Every last sign of religious emblems was absent in the small, light meeting places of the Quakers.

Although all human beings were by their nature equally sinful, their religious chances were not only unequal but highly unequal, and this was a definitive and not a temporary state of affairs. This operated either according to arbitrary (*grundloser*) predestination (in the Calvinists, the Baptists who believed in the particularism of grace, the Whitfield Methodists and the reformed Pietists), or according to how qualified individuals were in their spiritualistic gifts (*pneumatischen Geistesgaben*); or finally according to how intense their striving was and so the resultant varying success. For the old Pietists such striving could achieve a decisive act of conversion – the 'battle for repentance' ('*Bußkampf*') and the 'break-through' ('*Durchbruch*') – or however else the experience of being reborn was called. But what predominated in all these varieties was providence (*Versehung*) and the arbitrary, unmerited, and 'free' grace of a transcendental god. The belief in predestination therefore was indeed only one factor – but the most consequential one – in the dogmatic shaping of this virtuoso religiosity. Of the masses condemned to perdition, only a few were called to attain salvation. It did not matter whether it was defined for them by virtue of predestination from the beginnings of time onwards, or whether salvation was offered to all (even, for example, to non-Christians according to the Quakers), for only the small bunch who were able to grasp it would succeed. According to some Pietist doctrine salvation was offered only once in a lifetime, and according to others (the so-called Terminists) it was offered once and for all; whatever the case, the human being had to show that he or she was capable of acquiring it. Everything therefore turned on the free grace of god and on one's destiny in the Beyond, and life in this world was either a vale of tears or a mere transitional passage.

There was therefore a huge emphasis placed upon this tiny span of life and what occurred in it, in the sense perhaps of Carlyle's saying: 'Millennia will have passed before you come to life, and other millennia wait silently for what you will do with this your life.' And this was not because it would be possible to attain eternal salvation purely through one's own endeavours. That was impossible. Rather it was because the individual's own call to redemption could be received and, above all, only be perceived through the awareness of the central and unified relationship between his own short life and the transcendental god and his will, and the sacred observance of this. This observance could in its turn only be affirmed, like all active asceticism, in activity ordained by God and thus in ethical behaviour based on God's blessing, so giving the individual the certainty of salvation that was secured by being an instrument of God. This placed the strongest imaginable inner premiums on a rationally and ethically methodical way of life. Only a life that was regulated by fixed principles derived from a unified centre could be valued as ordained by God. If the unconstrained surrender to the world led in all certainty away from salvation, so nevertheless did this creatural world and creatural human beings remain God's creation. It was on his creatures that he placed definite demands and he created them according to the Calvinist conception 'for his glory' (*'zu seinem Ruhm'*). However depraved (*verderbt*) humans were as creatural beings, God wished to see his glory realized in them by subjecting sin, and where possible suffering, to the ethical discipline of rational order. 'While daylight lasts we must carry on the work of him who sent me'[27] then became a duty, and the work so given had a rational-ethical and not a ritualistic character.

The contrast with Confucianism is clear. Both ethics had an irrational anchoring: Confucianism in magic, and Puritanism in the ultimately unknowable mystery of a transcendental god. But magic, on account of its tried and tested magical means and a way of life that was ultimately rooted in custom, had the unalterable consequence that tradition could not be broken. In contrast, Puritanism in its relationship with a transcendental god and a creaturely, wicked, and ethically irrational world resulted in the complete lack of sanctity towards tradition and the never ending burden of ever renewed labour in the ethical mastering and control of the given world in a rational way: 'progress' was a rational matter of fact. In contrast to the accommodation towards the world stood the task of its rational transformation. Confucianism demanded a continuously vigilant self-control in the interests of maintaining the dignity of the all-round perfection of the man of the world, while Puritanism demanded this in the interests of the methodical unity of man attuned to the will of God. The Confucian ethic quite intentionally left people in either the natural relationships in which they had grown up or in the social relationships of the hierarchical order. It idealized these, and only these relationships, as ethical, and ultimately it recognized no other social obligations than those personal relationships created through a human sense of sympathetic obligation (*Pietätspflichten*), such as, of man to man, of prince to servant, of higher to lower official, of father and brother to son and brother, of teacher to pupil, and friend to friend. Although the Puritan ethic tolerated purely personal relationships as something natural so long as these

27 The New Testament, John, 9, 4.

were ethically regulated and not against the will of God, it nevertheless regarded them with suspicion since their worth was based in the creaturely. The relationship to God took precedence under all circumstances, and all intense human relationships as such, which idolized the creaturely, were to be unconditionally avoided. The trust that human beings placed on those things that had natually grown up closest to them would have endangered the soul. As we have seen, the Calvinist Duchess Renata d'Este would have cursed her own closest relatives if she became aware they were rejected by God (on account of the arbitrariness of predestination).[28]

Even though we will refer to these two ethics in terms of their practical application as 'rationalistic' and as 'utilitarian' in their consequences, very important practical differences flow from each. In China this was not just a matter of the social-ethical attitude taken towards the world but also of the autonomous working of the political structure of rulership. The maintenance of the kinship groupings had essential links with the political structure whose political and organizational forms were closely tied to the nature of personal relationships. These forms avoided in relatively quite striking ways the rational objectification and the abstract transpersonal character of purposeful associations, and led in the beginning to the absence of real 'communal organizations' (*Gemeinde*) especially in the cities and in course of time to the absence of associational and entrepreneurial forms created for purely instrumental reasons. These forms have never really originated on Chinese soil.[29] All communal activity remained encompassed and determined by personal and above all by kin relationships and, alongside these, by occupational fraternities. Against this, Puritanism objectivated everything, turning it into rational 'enterprises' and purely 'businesslike' relationships, and established rational law and rational association in place of tradition, local custom, and the specific personal favour of the official that in China was, in principle, all powerful.

There is another even more important difference. In China, the world-affirming utilitarianism and the conviction in the ethical value of wealth as a universal means to an all-round moral perfection, under conditions of very high population density, have intensified to an unheard-of degree of 'calculability' and self-sufficiency (*Genügsamkeit*). Every penny was haggled over and reckoned and the shopkeeper avidly counted his cash box each day. Reliable travellers report that money and money affairs appeared to be the main topic of conversation among locals to a degree seldom seen elsewhere. But what is most striking, in the field of economic activity at least, is that the

---

28 'But . . . as the famous letter of the Duchess Renata d'Este (Leonore's mother) to Calvin, in which she speaks of the hatred which she would feel toward her father and husband if she became convinced they belonged to the damned. . .', *PESC*, p. 237, n. 91. Renata d'Este was the daughter of the French king Louis XII and she married Ercole d'Este (1508–59).
29 [Weber] On the first signs of 'credit associations', see *China*, pp. 292–4, n. 40.

great conceptions of thinking about business in a *methodical* and a rational way, as is presupposed by modern capitalism, had not developed out of the infinitely intensive business activity and the crass 'materialism' that was so much complained about. This sort of thinking has remained foreign to all of China, except where past foreign influence (as, for example, among the Cantonese) or the now unstoppable impact of occidental capitalism has taught it to the Chinese. Forms of politically oriented capitalism have developed autonomously (especially, so it seems, as long as political divisions existed). Office usury and emergency credit, profits from wholesale trade and in the field of industrial production, the unfree workshops (*ergasteria*) (and also the larger workshops), occurred as they did in later Antiquity, in Egypt, and in Islam; and recently, the usual reliance of a system of domestic production on the distributor (*Verleger*) and buyer but without the strict organization of our Middle Ages.[30] Yet in spite of the quite intensive system of internal trade (and a reasonable foreign trade even if it was not permanent), there was no bourgeois capitalism, not even its late medieval form. There were none of the rational forms of the late medieval and the scientistic, European and capitalistic industrial 'enterprise' (*Betrieb*). There was no 'capital' formation in a European way (Chinese capital, which participated in modern risk, was predominantly accumulated by mandarins, and thus from office usury), nor was there any real rational organization of the commercial news services, no rational monetary system – not even a money economy as it was developing in Ptolemaic Egypt at that time. There were only the first traces of legal institutions as they appear in our business and company law, and in our legal regulation of credit, bonds, and shares (these beginings were characteristic, but only in terms of their lack of technical perfection). The use of numerous technical discoveries for purely economic purposes was highly limited,[31] and finally there was no really technically perfected system for writing, calculation and book-keeping for trading.

Thus, on account of the complete absence of slaves – a consequence of the pacification of the empire – China was very similar to the conditions of Mediterranean Antiquity, but in some respects those conditions were even further away from the 'spirit' of modern capitalism and its institutions. There existed extensive religious tolerance – despite the trials of heretics – (but this at least was not comparable to the intolerance of calvinistic Puritanism), extensive freedoms for the trading of commodities, peace, freedom of movement,

30 What in the European Middle Ages was referred to as a putting-out or cottaging system. These remarks link to Weber's comparative observations below, pp. 107, 162.

31 [Weber] It is abundantly clear that it was not the defectiveness of the Chinese gift for technology and invention that was responsible for the backwardness of mining (and the reason for currency crises), the failure to use coal in the production of iron (despite the alleged knowledge of the coking process), and the increasing restriction of shipping to traditional inland forms and waterways. Instead feng-shui, divination of all sorts (*Mantik*), and administration fees – that is, the products of magic and the form of the state – were decisive.

freedom of occupational choice and production methods, the acceptance of a shopkeeper mentality, yet all these factors in no way allowed the emergence of modern capitalism in China. The country that is most typified as one of acquisitiveness teaches us quite simply that the 'acquisitive drive', the enormous, indeed exclusive prizing of wealth, and utilitarian 'rationalism' have in and for themselves nothing to do with modern capitalism. The small and middle-ranking businessman in China (and also the large-scale businessman in the old traditions) ascribed his success, or lack of it, to divine powers, just as the Puritan did. The Chinese looked, however, to his (Taoistic) god of wealth. The divine powers were not for him symptoms of a state of grace but rather the effects of meaningful magical or ceremonial performance, or violation, that one could seek to balance out by further 'good works'. The Chinese businessman did not possess a core, and rationally methodical, way of life that was religiously determined and came from within, as was the case for the classic Puritan for whom economic success was not an ultimate goal and an end in itself, but instead a means of being affirmed. Unlike the Puritan, he was not consciously sealed off from the influences and impressions of the 'world'. The Puritan through a defined and rational will oriented in one direction strove to master the world just as he did himself. He simply subjugated the petty acquisitive greed, which so marked the Chinese shopkeeper mentality and which was destructive of any rational method of enterprise. The distinctive narrowing and repression of natural drives,[32] which accompanies the strict and volitional ethical rationalization that the Puritan acquired through upbringing, was foreign to the Confucian. The curtailing of the free expression of primitive drives bore a different character for him. The vigilant mastery of self of the Confucian stemmed from the dignity of outward gestures and manners in order to maintain 'face'. Self-control had an aesthetic and thereby an essentially negative character; 'bearing' ('*Haltung*') in itself, and devoid of definite substance, was prized and striven for. The equally vigilant self-control of the Puritan was directed towards something positive – a defined and designated behaviour that came from somewhere within him. It was the systematic mastering of one's own inner nature, which was regarded as corrupted by sin. The consistent Pietist established an inventory of sin in the manner of book-keeping, as it was undertaken on a daily basis by Benjamin Franklin, who was a descendant of Puritans. The transcendental and omniscient god looked into the core of one's inner *habitus*, whereas in contrast the world to which the Confucian conformed was a matter only of elegant gestures.

The Confucian gentleman, concerned only with his outward 'countenance',[33] had a general mistrust of other people and assumed they did not trust

---

32 [Weber] See the fine observations on this in the writings of Ludwig Klages. [The *MWG* I/19 editor refers the reader to Klages' article 'Zur Menschenkunde', *Graphologisches Monatshefte*, 3, 1899, pp. 8–42.]
33 Weber uses the English words 'gentleman' and 'countenance'.

him, and this was corrosive of all credit and business transactions. Whereas the Puritan had an unconditional and unshakeable trust in his fellow believer, especially in the field of economic activity, because the legality of this trust was religiously determined. This trust was just sufficient to allow the indispensable credit for capitalist trade in the face of the Puritan's deeply realistic and completely irreverent pessimism in relation to the creaturely corruption of the world and human beings, especially the high-ranking. It allowed him to make a sober and objective assessment of the (external and inner) competence of the other party, knowing the constancy of the essential motives – according to the principle that 'honesty is the best policy' – for the pursuit of business. The word of the Confucian was a nice and refined gesture, a thing in itself. The word of the Puritan was matter of fact, sparse, and an absolutely reliable business communication: 'Yes, yes, no, no, and anything more than that comes from evil.'[34] The frugality of the Confucian, at least with the gentleman, was tightly limited by what was becoming to his status. Where frugality became exaggerated, as through the mystically influenced humility of Lao-tzu and some Taoists, it was combated by the [orthodox] school. Frugality among the Chinese *petite bourgeoisie* was a common form of hoarding, just like the peasant squirrelling his money away in his stockings. Saving was undertaken to secure funeral rites and the good name of the family, and in addition the glory and delight in possessions as such; this natural attitude had not yet been mediated by an ascetic stance towards wealth.

For the Puritan, possessions as such were just as much a temptation as they were, say, for a monk. His acquiring wealth, just like the monastery, was a by-product and symptom of the success of his asceticism. John Wesley explicitly referred to the apparent paradox of rejection of the world and acquisitive virtuosity, which had been spotted early on by the Puritan denominations, when he said (as we have seen[35]) that we have no choice other than to advise: be pious, 'that is, in effect' – as an inevitable consequence – 'to grow rich', even though riches clearly placed the pious individual in jeopardy, just as it did the monasteries.

As was expressly taught by the founder of Confucianism, wealth was the most important means for living *virtuously*, that is, with dignity. It allowed the individual to devote himself to self-perfection. 'Enrich them' was given as the answer to the question of what was the best way to improve human beings, since only then could a person live according to his rank and status. Acquisitions were an unwanted consequence for the Puritan, yet a most important symptom of his own virtue, and the excessive spending of wealth

34 The quote comes from the New Testament, where Jesus is instructing on keeping one's word: 'But let your communication be, Yea, yea, nay, nay: for whatsoever is more than these cometh from evil' (Matthew, 5, 37).
35 *PESC*, p. 175.

for one's own consumption was an all too easy surrender to the world by a self-idolizing creature. The acquiring of wealth was not something to be spurned for Confucius, but it did bring with it uncertainties and so lead to the disturbance of the refined equilibrium of the soul, and all truly professional economic activity was a wretched form of ignoble specialism (*banausisches Fachmenschentum*). For the Confucian, the *specialist* could not attain a truly positive dignity despite his social-utilitarian value. What was really decisive was that the 'refined person' (the gentleman) was not an 'instrument'; that is, he was not a means to a substantive goal of any sort, but rather in his world-conforming self-perfection he was his own ultimate end. At the centre of the Confucian ethic was a rejection of specialization, the modern specialist bureaucracy and professional training and, most of all, economic training for acquisition. In direct contrast to the creature-idolizing maxim of the Confucian, the Puritan set himself the task of affirming himself through specialist and substantive worldly goals, and through a life of work as a vocation (*Berufsleben*).

The Confucian was a person of literary education, or more precisely, a bookish education, a man of the *script* and moulded by it. The Hellenic elevation and prevalence of speech and conversation, as well as the energy that went into making war and rational economic action, were equally alien to the Confucian. The majority of the Puritan denominations in relation to the absolute necessity of a thorough grounding in the Bible rejected philosophic-literary education (even if not all equally strongly) and the extreme ornateness of the Confucian as a temporal vanity and as religiously dangerous. (For the Puritan, the Bible was a kind of middle-class law book and doctrine of enterprise.) Scholasticism and dialectics, Aristotle and his tradition, was something both dangerous and horrendous. For example, Spener preferred Cartesian philosophy with its basis in rational mathematics. Real knowledge that can be used – especially knowledge with an empirically scientific and geographical orientation – the plain clarity of realist thinking, and specialist disciplines have been deliberately fostered as the purpose of education first of all in Puritan circles and, in Germany, especially by Pietists. On the one side, it was the only way of knowing God's glory and divine providence as expressed in the creation; on the other, it was a means in one's occupational vocation to master the world and to be able to do one's duty in honouring god. Confucianism and Puritanism were both positioned equally distant, but each in its own way, from Hellenism and the essence (*Wesen*) of the high Renaissance.

The indispensable 'ethical' qualities of the specifically modern capitalist entrepreneur included: the radical concentration on goals ordained by God; the ruthless practical rationalism of the ascetic ethic; the methodical conception of the matter-of-fact pursuit of enterprise; the abhorrence of the illegal political and colonial booty capitalism and monopolies, which were dependent on the favour of princes and men, as opposed to sober and strict legality and the controlled rational energy of ordinary business; the rationalistic appraisal of the technically optimal means; and practical solidity and effectiveness in place of the old craftsmen's traditionalistic enjoyment of the skills passed down and the beauty of the product. In addition to all of these was the specific willingness of the pious worker to labour. This ruthless, religiously systematized utilitarianism, whose distinctive rationalized asceticism meant living 'in' the world rather than being 'of' the world, has helped to create that superior rational disposition and so that 'spirit' of an occupationally vocational mankind (*Berufsmenschentums*). The Confucian and his conformity to the world – and this meant a conduct of life that was rationally determined from without, unlike Puritanism where rational conduct was determined from within towards the outside world – remained in the last analysis excluded from that spirit.

The contrast demonstrates that even simple sobriety and frugality in combination with an 'acquisitive drive' and the appreciation of wealth were far from the 'capitalist spirit' in the sense of the specifically modern, economically vocational mankind, and that they were unable to release that spirit. The typical Confucian spent his and his family's savings on a literary education and training for the examinations, thereby laying the foundation for a superior existence appropriate to his status. The typical Puritan earned much, consumed little, and put the income that resulted from his ascetic compulsion to save into further productive use as capital in a rational capitalistic enterprise. 'Rationalism' is the second thing that is demonstrated and it is common to both ethics. But it is only the transcendentally (*überweltlich*) oriented rational ethic of Puritanism that carried through the consequences of *inner*worldly economic rationalism. This occurred simply *because* nothing existed other than this ethic, and *because* innerworldly work was the only expression of the striving for a transcendental goal. The world fell to the Puritan ethic, as was promised, because it had set its 'mind on God's kingdom and his justice before everything else'.[36] It is here that is found the basic difference between the two types of 'rationalism'. Confucian rationalism meant a rational conformity to the world. Puritan rationalism meant the rational *mastery* of the world. The Puritan like the Confucian was 'sober'. But the rational 'sobriety' of the Puritan was based on an undercurrent of tremendous pathos that was entirely missing in the case of the Confucian, and this same pathos pervaded occidental monasticism. World-rejecting asceticism in the Occident was inextricably linked to its opposite: the desire to master the world, and this was decreed in the name of a transcendental god to the monk and adapted in an ameliorated form to the world.

The ideal of superiority in Confucianism resisted more than anything

---

36 The New Testament, Matthew, 6, 13: 'Set your mind on God's kingdom and his justice before everything else, and all the rest will come to you as well.'

else the idea of 'vocation'. The 'princely' man was an aesthetic value and therefore could not possibly be an 'instrument' of God. The genuine Christian, outwardly and inwardly the complete ascetic, wished for nothing other than to be just that. It was only in this way that he could seek his worthiness. And because this was what he wanted to be, he was a usable instrument for the rational revolutionizing (*umzuwälzen*) and mastery of the world.

The Chinese would in all probability be as capable as the Japanese, if anything more capable, in *adopting* the capitalism that technologically and economically has been fully realized in the modern era of civilization (*im neuzeitlichen Kulturgebiet*). There is nothing to suggest that the Chinese would not be naturally 'gifted' in meeting the demands of modern capitalism. But in spite of the very different external conditions that favoured the emergence of capitalism in comparison to the Occident, it was no more created in China than in occidental and oriental Antiquity, or in India and the Islamic sphere. And in all of these areas other, no less favouring conditions for the emergence of capitalism appear to have been present. Of the conditions that could or must have blocked its emergence in China, many of these were also operative in the Occident – and were so, indeed, right up to the period of the formation of modern capitalism; for instance, the patrimonial features of rulership and bureaucracy or the patchiness and lack of development of the money economy which was far more widely established in Ptolemaic Egypt than it was in the fifteenth and sixteenth centuries in Europe.

Feudal and seigneurial restrictions (and also in part the restrictions of the guilds), which we tend to regard as obstructing capitalist development in Europe, had been missing in China for thousands of years, as were apparently, to a large extent, the restrictive monopolies in the trade of goods that were typical in the Occident. The political circumstances, which since ancient Babylon and Antiquity have led to a politically determined capitalism *common* to both the whole of the past and to modernity, have originated from war and the preparation of war among competing states. China's past is far from being an exception in this regard. One might have thought that the subsequent disappearance in China of this essentially politically oriented accumulation of property and use of capital would have favoured the chances of specifically modern capitalism oriented to free exchange. This would be rather like the contemporary situation in North America, where the almost complete absence of the organization for war has offered the greatest latitude to the development of high capitalism. The pacification of the Chinese Empire at least provides a direct explanation of the absence of the *political* capitalism common to occidental Antiquity (until the Empire), the Orient, and to the European Middle Ages. What it does not explain is the absence of a purely economically oriented capitalism in China. It cannot of course be denied that political and economic fortunes have played their part in development of the basic characteristics (*Eigentumlichkeiten*) of the Chinese 'mentality' (*Gesinnung*) – in this case the practical attitude to the world. But notwithstanding that, the effects attributable to the autonomous workings (*Eigengesetzlichkeiten*) of this mentality have been deeply implicated in obstructing capitalist development.

3 Introduction to the Economic Ethics of the World Religions[1]

Under the heading of 'world religions' will be understood – in a completely value-free way – the five religions, or religiously determined systems for the regulation of life, which have known how to gather about them very large *numbers* of confessional followers, namely: the religious ethics of Confucianism, Hinduism, Buddhism, Christianity and Islam. To these needs to be added a sixth religion, that of Judaism, which contained the decisive historical pre-conditions for any understanding of the last two religions named above. As has been alleged, and is in part true, Judaism is also of uniquely historic significance for the unfolding of the modern economic ethic of the Occident, which is a subject that has been much debated recently.[2] Other

---

1 Weber subtitled his economic ethics of the world religions project, 'Comparative Essays in the Sociology of Religion'. He first published his 'Introduction' to them in the *Archiv für Sozialwissenschaft und Sozialpolitik* in 1915, and the version which is translated here by S. Whimster was published in 1920 for his *Collected Essays in the Sociology of Religion*. He prefaced the essays with the following footnote:

> Appeared in Jaffé's *Archiv für Sozialwissenschaft*, volumes 41–46 (1915–19) in instalments; the first parts unchanged from when they were written down and read out to friends two years before. Entry into military service made it impossible to include the scientific 'apparatus' as intended; in its place were supplied short notes on the literature at the beginning of each section. This also explained the differences in how thoroughly the particular subjects were treated. If the essays in spite of this were published at the time, it was because it seemed then that it would be impossible after the war had ended, which for everyone meant an epoch in their lives, to go back and pick up the threads of the ideas from the earlier period. It was, moreover, also intended that the essays should appear at the same time with the sociology of religion section of the treatise on 'Economy and Society' which was part of the 'Outline of Social-economics'. The essays would have interpreted and enlarged the sociology of religion section (and to be sure would have been interpreted in many points by that section). The essays seem to be publishable in the state that they were in at that time. What detracts from the essays' value, as a result of their inevitably somewhat outline character and the varying amount of detail presented, will surely be more improved in the future by the work of others than would have been possible by me. In order for the essays to be in any sense conclusive, they would have to rely less on the translated sources as were available to the author for the current presentation. Nevertheless the essays in their present form could be useful in some points for enlarging the terms of argument in the sociology of religion as well as here and there the sociology of economic life. I have sought to improve the essays, collected together for this edition, insofar as this is feasible for the non-specialist using the materials available to him. Some small oversights have been removed, the very much incomplete presentation, in particular of Chinese society, has been improved, and the references cited have been somewhat improved.

2 A reference to the debate caused by Sombart's books: *The Jews and Modern Capitalism*, translated by M. Epstein, New York, Collier Books, 1962 [German edn 1911].

religions will only be mentioned to the extent that they are unavoidably part of the complete historical picture. On Christianity, reference will initially be made to the earlier essays that have appeared in this collection, and knowledge of which will be presumed.[3]

It is hoped that what is meant by the 'economic ethic' of a religion will become increasingly clearer in the course of the exposition. Emphasis will be placed on the *practical impulses for action* that are grounded in the psychological and pragmatic contexts of religions, and the ethical theories of theological compendia will be used only as a means to knowledge (but are, under the circumstances, of not negligible importance). Although what follows is sketched only in broad outline, it will however allow it to be shown just how complicated a model a concrete economic ethic is and how multi-sided its determination tends to be. In addition it will be shown how organizational forms of the economy that on the outside appear similar are in fact linked to very different economic ethics, and that the particularity of an ethic is realized over time with very different historical consequences. An economic ethic is not a straightforward 'function' of the organizational forms of the economy, just as, conversely, an economic form cannot be unambiguously derived from a religious ethic.

No economic ethic has ever been determined solely by religion. It is evident that economic ethics possess to a high degree a lawlike autonomy (*Eigengesetzlichkeit*) closely determined by economic geography and historical conditions in contrast to the attitudes of human beings to the world as determined by religious or other 'inner' factors of a similar nature to religion. But it is true to say that among the determinants of an economic ethic – and these determinants, it should be noted, are *multiple* – belongs the religious definition of conduct of life (*Lebensführung*). The latter, in its turn, is naturally deeply influenced, within given geographical, political, social and national parameters (*Grenzen*), by economic and political factors. It would be a never-ending task if one wanted to chart these dependencies in all their details. What is presented here is merely an attempt to bring to light only those social strata which, in giving direction to the conduct of life, have most strongly influenced the practical ethic of the relevant religion and have imprinted on to the religion its characteristic features; by this is meant those features that distinguish it from other religious ethics *and* at the same time are important for the respective economic ethic.

This has never been the task of one social stratum alone, for in the course

3 Weber is referring to his 'The Protestant Ethic and the Spirit of Capitalism', and 'Protestant Sects and the Spirit of Capitalism', which are the first two Parts of his 'Collected Essays in the Sociology of Religion' and published as *Gesammelte Aufsätze zur Religionssoziologie* in three volumes (Tübingen, Mohr Siebeck, 1920–21). 'The Economic Ethics of the World Religions' forms the third and largest Part of that collection. What is translated here is the first two-thirds of his 'Introduction'. *The Essential Weber* presents his argument on Christianity in Readings 1, 3, 4 and 16.

of history the influential strata, which have this directive function, can change. And it is never the case that an individual social stratum has an exclusive influence. Despite this, it is possible in most cases to indicate the social strata whose conduct of life has been particularly decisive for each of the given religions.

To give some examples in advance:

- Confucianism was the status ethic of a humanistically educated and worldly-rationalistic group who lived off prebends.[4] Anyone, who did not belong to this *educated* stratum, simply did not count. The religious status ethic (or, if one will, irreligious status ethic) of this stratum has defined the Chinese way of life and extended far beyond its own group.
- The older Hinduism, in contrast, was carried by a hereditary caste of the literary educated who were remote from any official position. They operated a kind of ritualistic cure of the soul for individuals and communities, and, as the fixed centre point around which status divisions were organized, they shaped the social order. Only those Brahmans educated in the Vedas,[5] who were the carriers of the tradition, counted fully as the religious status group. It was only later that a non-Brahman caste of ascetics moved in as competition to the Brahmans, and still later in the Indian Middle Ages, that there appeared on the scene in Hinduism the fervent, sacramental religiosity, based on a saviour, which with the plebeian mystagogues[6] was found in the lower strata.
- Buddhism was propagated by homeless, wandering, and deeply contemplative monks, who, dependent on begging, rejected the world. They were the only group who belonged fully to the religious community. All the other groups were religiously inferior lay people – objects not subjects of religiosity.
- Islam in its first phase was a religion of world-conquering warriors – a knightly order of disciplined warriors of the faith, but without the sexual asceticism of their Christian counterparts in the Crusades. In the Islamic Middle Ages, however, contemplative-mystic Sufism came to the fore, and from it developed the sense of brotherhood of the small townspeople. They were not unlike the Christian Tertiaries[7] but were far more universally developed, and they gained at least an equal role among the leadership of the plebeian experts of the orgy.
- Since the Exile, Judaism was the religion of a town dwelling (*bürgerlich*) 'pariah-people' – and we will come to understand the meaning of this

---

4 A prebend, in its western sense, was an endowment in land or a pension in money used to support a priest in the early Christian Church.
5 'Veda' is the Sanskrit for 'knowledge'. They are the oldest books of Indian religion.
6 See n. 14 below.
7 These were a lay order of Franciscans, the 'third' order after the monks and the nuns.

pithy expression.[8] In the Middle Ages the religion fell under the leader-ship of an intellectual stratum, which had a literary and ritualistic train-ing, peculiar to Judaism, and which came to represent an increasingly semi-proletarian, rationalistic, and *petit-bourgeois* intelligence.

- Lastly, Christianity began its progress as the teaching of a wandering brotherhood of artisans. It was, and it remained, a specifically urban, and above all, civic (*bürgerlich*) religion during all the periods of its outward and inner upswing, whether in Antiquity, the Middle Ages, or Puritanism. The city of the Occident, unique in relation to all other cities, along with the middle classes (*Bürgertum*) in the sense in which they originated only in the Occident, was the main setting in which Christian-ity appeared. This was so for the spiritualistic religious communities (*pneumatische Gemeindefrömmigkeit*)[9] of Antiquity, for the mendicant orders of the high Middle Ages, and the sects of the reformation period through to Pietism and Methodism.

Now it needs to be made very clear what is being advanced in the following exposition. It is not being argued that a specific religiosity is a simple function of the social position of the stratum, which appears to be its characteristic carrier, as if it were the 'ideology' or a 'reflection' of the material and ideal interest situation of that stratum. It would be difficult to conceive of such a complete misunderstanding of what is being discussed here. The primary imprint of a religious ethic is received from religious sources – foremost being the content of its promises and message. It does not come from the politically and economically determined social influences acting in each case on a religious ethic, however far-reaching these factors may be. And on the fre-quent occasions when the message and promises of a religious ethic are reinterpreted by the next generation in order to meet the requirements of the community, this always occurs most of all for *religious* needs. The influence of other spheres of interest, while often quite emphatic and occasionally decisive, can only be of secondary importance. It will be convincingly shown that for every religion a change in its socially decisive stratum does indeed

8 The pariahs were the Indian untouchables, who existed outside the caste system. Weber uses the term to describe a people rejected by their god (but who promises to restore them their kingdom) as well as their ritualistic exclusion from local communities as a migrant people (*Gastvolk*). See Weber, *Ancient Judaism*, New York, Free Press, 1952, p. 3 and *Rel*, pp. 108–9. See below, Reading 4, pp. 84–5.

9 A reference probably to the Gnostic communities of early Christianity in the second century AD. Peter Brown writes, 'For Valentinus [a Gnostic Christian], the human soul was peopled by a host of unruly spirits, of *pneumata*. These were incomplete, needy creatures, who used the person to seek their own fulfilment, in the manner of a permanent, half-conscious state of possession' (*The Body and Society*, London, Faber, 1989, pp. 116–17). At the time of writing his Introduction, Weber had every intention of completing a full-length study of early Christian communities, but alas this was never done.

tend to be of far-reaching significance; but, on the other hand, once a religion has received its typical imprint, this influence tends to be quite extensive, even exerting control over the conduct of life of very heterogeneous strata.

Various efforts have been made to interpret the interrelationship between a religious ethic and the interest position of its carriers, so that the former appears only as a 'function' of the latter. This has occurred not just in so-called historical materialism[10] – and this cannot be debated here – but also in terms of pure psychology.

The linking of class to religious ethics in a very general and certainly very abstract way has been known about since Friedrich Nietzsche's brilliant essay on '*ressentiment*', an idea subsequently taken up with enthusiasm in the theories of psychologists.[11] The idea holds that the ethical transfiguration of compassion and brotherhood was an ethical 'slave revolt' of the disadvantaged, whether disadvantaged in terms of natural aptitudes or being condemned by fate to restricted life-chances. Thus, the ethic of 'duty' was a product of the 'repressed', who were the wretched artisans (*Banausen*) cursed by poverty of income and their work, but impotent in their feelings of revenge against the way of life of the ruling class, which lived free of all such obligations. Obviously, this idea would provide a very neat solution to the most important problems in the typology of religious ethics. While the discovery of the psychological meaning of *ressentiment* has in itself been welcome and fruitful, great care needs to be taken in estimating its social and ethical implications.[12]

More will be said later about the motives that defined the different kinds of 'rationalization' of the conduct of life purely as such. This has for the most part nothing whatsoever to do with *ressentiment*.

Within the religious ethic, the valuing of *suffering* has undoubtedly been subjected to a typical transition, and, properly understood, this indicates a certain correctness to the theory first advanced by Nietzsche. The original, natural attitude (*urwüchsige Stellungnahme*) towards the suffering of those who were ill or had befallen other sorts of persistent misfortune expressed itself most visibly in the religious celebrations of the community. The person who was permanently suffering, bereaved, ill or otherwise unfortunate was

10 I.e. Marxism.
11 This is a reference to a more generalist and philosophical psychology associated with Ludwig Klages, *Prinzipien der Charakterologie*, Leipzig, Barth, 1912, and Max Scheler, *Über Ressentiment und moralisches Werturteil*, Leipzig, Engelmann, 1912. See *Die Wirtschaftsethik der Weltreligionen. Konfuzianismus und Taoismus*, *MWG*, I/19, p. 88.
12 In this paragraph Weber summarizes Nietzsche's arguments and terminology from Section 10 of 'On the Genealogy of Morals'. See W. Kaufman (ed.), *The Nietzsche Reader*, New York, Modern Library, 1968, pp. 472–5. Nietzsche used the phrase 'the slave revolt in *morality*'. Like Nietzsche, Weber uses the French word '*ressentiment*'. This translates into English as 'resentment' but for Nietzsche the concept signified (a) the stimulus of a hostile external world, and (b) the vengefulness of the impotent.

reckoned, according to the manner of their suffering, to be either possessed by demons or burdened with the anger of a god whom the person had insulted. To tolerate this person in their midst could involve the cultic community in deleterious consequences. Such persons certainly could not take part in the meals and sacrifices of the cult. The sight of them was not pleasing to the gods and could arouse their wrath. The sacrificial meals were occasions for the joyful – even during the time when Jerusalem was under siege.

When religion treated suffering as a symptom of the hatred of the gods and a person's secret guilt, in psychological terms it encountered a very general need. The fortunate person was rarely content with the mere fact of his own good fortune. He needed more than that, he wanted to have the *right* to it. He has to convince himself that he 'deserves' his good fortune, and, above all, that he deserves it in comparison to others. And he also needs to believe that the person who is not the recipient of similar good fortune is getting what is only befitting. Good fortune has to be 'legitimate'. If one understands by the general expression 'fortune' all the benefits of honour, power, possessions, and pleasure, then this is the most general rubric under which religion had to perform its service of legitimation: the theodicy of good fortune. Religion legitimates both the outward and internal interests of the rulers, the rich, the victorious, the healthy, in short, all those who enjoy good fortune. Theodicy, as religious legitimation, is firmly rooted in the deep (and 'pharisaic'[13]) needs of men and women, and in this sense it is easy to understand, even though it is often insufficiently considered in its effect.

When the issue is looked at from the other way around – the religious transfiguration of suffering instead of good fortune – the lines of development are more intertwined. The primary experience here was the charisma of the ecstatic, visionary, hysterical and all those extraordinary states, which have been esteemed as 'holy' and whose invocation led to the making of magical asceticism into an object in its own right. These states of experience were created or at least favoured by the countless forms of mortification of the flesh and the abstinence from normal sustenance and sleep as well as sexual intercourse. The prestige of such mortification was the product of the idea that certain forms of suffering, and the abnormal conditions provoked by mortification, were ways to the attainment of superhuman, magical powers. Likewise the old taboo prescriptions and abstinence in the interests of cultic purity, which were the consequences of the belief in demons, worked in the same direction. But then, alongside these practices, there occurred, independently and innovatively, the development of 'salvation' cults that took up a principally new position in relation to the suffering of the individual.

The original community cults, especially the cults of political associations, had no interest in the suffering of the individual. Their gods belonged to the

---

13 Biblical term here meaning a self-righteousness that has formal justification.

tribe, the locality, the city, and the empire, and they concerned themselves only with the interests that related to the totality: rain and sun, the bag from hunting, and victory over the enemy. It was to these gods that the group as a whole turned in the form of the cultic community. For the rejection or elimination of evils, especially disease, that afflicted the individual, it was the magician to whom the individual turned and not to the cultic community; the magician was the oldest provider of cure of the soul to the individual person. The prestige of particular magicians, and those spirits or gods in whose name they performed their miracles, created a demand for them irrespective of any membership of the tribe. Under favourable circumstances, this led to independent community building separate from any ethnic body. Many, but not all, 'mysteries' went down this road.[14]

The mysteries promised to save the individual, as an individual person, from illness, poverty and all sorts of privation and danger. The magician changed into the mystagogue, who became the basis for hereditary dynasties or, rather, an organization of trained personnel with a head chosen according to particular rules. The head could be regarded either, in his person, as the incarnation of a superhuman being or as the messenger and executor of his god, that is, as a prophet. This then allowed the creation of a religious, communal organization for individual 'suffering' and for 'redemption' from that state. The next step, naturally enough, was for that message and promise to be turned towards those of the masses who were in need of redemption. The masses and their interests moved to the centre of the semi-professional enterprise of 'caring for the soul' which really only came into being at this point. The typical work of magicians and priests was now the ascertainment of what was responsible for suffering, and this was done by the confession of 'sins' – foremost being the infringement of ritual commands, and the advising of what behaviour would eliminate the suffering. The material and ideal interests of the priests, therefore, move increasingly towards specifically *plebeian* forces. A further step down this road is signified when a religiosity based on a 'saviour' develops under the pressure of typical and ever-recurring privation. This presumes the myth of the redeemer and so a (at least relatively) *rational* contemplation of the world, and whose most important object of attention has again been suffering.

The primitive mythology of nature very often offers the starting point for the process. The spirits, which control the coming and going of vegetation and the movement of the important heavenly bodies in the passage of the seasons, become the favoured bearers of the myths of a suffering, dying, and resurrected god who will guarantee to the people in their misery the return of

---

14 A mystery was a form of worship and rite in which some secret was revealed to the cult members, who had to be initiated into the cult. Mysteries were an essential element in the religiosity of Ancient Greece. The person who officiated the revealing of the mystery was a 'mystagogue'.

good fortune in this life or its certainty in the life beyond. Or, a figure, which has become popular from the heroic sagas, like Krishna in India, decked out with myths of childhood, love, and battles, has become the object of an ardent cult of the saviour. In the case of a politically repressed people, like the Israelites, the name of the saviour (Moshuach[15]), as the story was handed down in the heroic sagas, attached to those like Gideon and Jephthah, who have saved them from political immiserization, and so determined from this point onwards the people's 'messianic' promises. Because of the very particular circumstances of the Israelite people, this had the unique result that it was the suffering of the people as a *community*, rather than the individual's suffering, that became the object of the hopes of religious salvation. As a rule, though, the saviour bore a character that was both individual and universal, and salvation was guaranteed for the *individual* and available for *every* individual who would turn to the saviour. The figure of the saviour can assume different forms. In late Zoroastrian religion, with its countless abstractions, a purely constructed figure in the salvation-economy (*Heilsökonomie*)[16] assumed the role of a mediator and saviour. Or the situation was just the reverse: a historical person ascended to the role of saviour, legitimated through miracles and visionary reappearances. Purely historical events have been decisive in the realization of the various different possibilities.

But almost always some kind of theodicy of suffering has originated from the hopes of salvation.

The promises of salvation religions remained tied, certainly at first, not to ethical but to ritual pre-conditions. Ritual purity and the listening to the Eleusian mass conferred advantages, which were both worldly and other-worldly, on the participants of the Eleusian mysteries.[17] Special divinities, in whose care was placed the legal process, came to play a growing role in the increasing significance of law, so much so that they acquired the task of protecting the traditional order by punishing injustice and rewarding the just. And where prophecy exercised a determining influence on religious development, it is in the nature of things that 'sins' no longer appeared as infringements of magic but above all as a lack of faith in prophets and their commands, and so the basis for every type of misfortune.

In no ways should the prophet himself be regarded as the constant offshoot or representative of a repressed class. We will see that the opposite more often than not forms the rule. Also the content of the teaching in no way originated

---

15 Hebrew for Messiah. Jephthah and Gideon assumed the title of judge, even though they were seen as saviours to Israelite tribes. See the Old Testament, Judges, 6–12.

16 One of Weber's made-up terms that echoes the concepts of political-economy and national-economy.

17 Eleusis, outside Athens, was the most famous place where the mysteries were celebrated in Ancient Greece.

predominantly from the prophet's own social circle. But it was regularly the case that it was the oppressed, or at least those threatened by privation, who were in need of a redeemer and prophets, whereas the fortunate, the property-owners, and the rulers were in no such need. A religiosity of a saviour that was *prophetically* announced tended in the great majority of cases to be permanently located in the less favoured social strata, for whom it either completely replaced magic or instead rationally enlarged it. And when the promises of the prophet or the saviour himself did not adequately accommodate the needs of the less favoured, there developed with great regularity a secondary religiosity of salvation of the masses beneath the official teaching. The saviour myth contained the germ of a rational consideration of the world but as a rule it was thereby given the task of creating a rational theodicy of misfortune. And at the same time it frequently invested in suffering itself a positive evaluation, even though this would have been quite foreign to its original stance.

Mortification of the flesh, as a self-inflicted form of suffering, took on a new significance with the development of ethical divinities that punished and rewarded. The original control of magical spirits by the formula of prayers was intensified by self-mortification as a source of charismatic states. This mortification-with-prayer and the cultic prescriptions for abstinence were preserved even after the prayer formula for the control of magical spirits had become a plea to be heard by a divinity. To this was then added penitential mortification, as a means of appeasing the anger of the gods through repentance and of diverting the punishment incurred by punishing oneself. Also the very many abstinences, which initially were attached to the mourning of the dead (one can see this clearly in China) and whose purpose was to deflect the jealousy and anger of the dead, were then easily transposed on to the relationship with the relevant divinity. Self-mortification and finally even the occurrence of unintended abstinence purely as such seemed to be more pleasing to the divinity than the unrestrained pleasure in the good things of this world; and those who enjoyed those pleasures remained more inaccessible to the influence of the prophet or the priest.

These individual moments and events gained a far greater impetus in circumstances where, with the increasingly rational consideration of the world, there was an increasing need for an ethical 'meaning' for the distribution of the benefits of fortune between people. But with the increasing rationalization of the religious-ethical conception and the elimination of primitive magical ideas, theodicy came up against mounting difficulties. All too often it was the individual who ended up with 'undeserved' suffering, and this was not confined to a 'slave morality' alone. Even measured by the standards of the ruling stratum, it was only too often the case that it was the 'worst' rather than the best individuals who benefited most in life. The sins of the individual person in a previous life (transmigration of souls), or the guilt of ancestors that is avenged down to the third and fourth generation, or – in principle the clearest situation – the corruption of all things creaturely,[18] could serve the following functions: They could explain suffering and injustice, and as a form of compensation they could provide hope for a better future existence either within this world for the individual (the transmigration of souls), or for descendants (the messianic realm), or in the life beyond (paradise).

The metaphysical idea of god and the world, which was invoked by the inexhaustible need for theodicy, likewise enabled only a small number of systems of ideas to be produced – three in total, as we will see. The Indian doctrine of karma, Zoroastrian dualism, and the predestination decree of a *Deus absconditus*[19] gave rationally satisfactory answers to the question why there existed a lack of congruence between fate and merit. These solutions, which had rational closure, only appeared very exceptionally in their pure form.

The rational need for a theodicy of suffering – and of death – has had extraordinarily powerful effects. It has moulded important features of religions like Hinduism, Zoroastrianism, Judaism, and to a certain extent Pauline and later Christianity. In 1906, of a not inconsiderable number of proletarian workers answering a question about lack of belief, only a minority gave the repercussions of modern scientific theories as the reason for not believing in God. The majority referred instead to the injustice of this world and its social order, even though this was probably because they held to an innerworldly belief in equalization through revolution.[20]

The rational need for a theodicy of suffering can be coloured by *ressentiment*. But the need for compensation for the inadequacy of one's fate in this world has not always, and certainly not invariably, allowed the colouring of *ressentiment* to determine its essential characteristics. The belief that the unjust person only does well in this world because he is doomed to hell, whereas salvation is reserved for the pious, and also that the sins occasionally committed even by the pious must be atoned for in this life, certainly comes very close to the need for revenge. It is not however hard to show that even though this manner of thinking sometimes appears, it was by no means always determined by *ressentiment* and, above all, it was in no ways always the product of a socially downtrodden stratum. We will see that very little religiosity – and there is only one fully developed example – has been influenced in its *essential* features by *ressentiment*. It is only correct to say that *ressentiment could* certainly gain a significance everywhere, and often has done so, as one element (next to others) in the religiously determined

18 Human beings, as fleshly creatures, are continuously subverted by their own sins and weaknesses. All flesh decays, hence is 'corrupt'.
19 A 'hidden god' whose thoughts are inaccessible to human beings.
20 Weber is making a snide reference to Marxism as a belief system. Adolf Levenstein carried out the first questionnaire survey of the attitudes of German workers, publishing his findings in 1912 (*Die Arbeiterfrage*, Munich, Ernst Reinhardt).

rationalism of the socially less favoured strata. But the degree of significance achieved is highly variable and often evanescent, and this is anyway dependent on the nature of the promises of the particular religion. It would be completely mistaken at any rate to derive 'asceticism' in general from these sources.

In every genuine salvation religion as a rule there was a level of mistrust of wealth and power that had its natural basis in the experience of redeemers, prophets and priests. The strata, which were privileged and pampered in this world, had in general only a small need for salvation of whatever sort and were therefore less 'pious' in the sense of those religions. Likewise the development of a rational religious *ethic*, simply on the basis of socially less valued strata, found initial encouragement in the inner situation of those strata. By contrast, the strata that have secure possession of social honour and power tend to construct the legend of their status from a particular quality which is inherent within them, such as, most often, the quality of their blood; their *being (Sein)* (real or alleged) is what gives sustenance to their sense of self-esteem.

Strata that are socially repressed or are valued negatively (or, at least, not positively) feed their sense of dignity most easily from the belief in a particular 'mission' entrusted to them. Their sense of '*ought*' (*Sollen*) or their (functional) *performance* guarantees or constitutes for them its own value.[21] This moves them into a Beyond all of its own, into a 'task' imposed on them by god. The facts alone are sufficient to explain the ideal power of *ethical* prophecy that finds its first location in the socially less privileged and they do not require the extra leverage of *ressentiment*. The rational interest in material and ideal compensation in itself was a perfectly sufficient reason. It cannot be doubted that, alongside this, the propaganda of prophets and the priests has pressed the *ressentiment* of the masses into their service, whether intentionally or not, but this is a long way from being universally applicable. So far as it is known, this essentially negative power has nowhere been the source of those core metaphysical conceptions, which have given to each of the salvation religions its unique character. And most importantly, the type of religious promise was – speaking generally – in no ways necessarily, or even predominantly, simply a mouthpiece of class interests, whether they be of an external or internal sort. We will see that the masses of their own accord have everywhere remained stuck fast in a primitive sea of magic, unless a *prophecy*, with specific promises, was able to drag them into a religious movement of an ethical character. In short, the distinctiveness of the great religious and ethical systems was determined far more by particular social conditions than by the mere opposition of the ruling and the subordinated strata.

---

21 Weber contrasts *Sein* to *Sollen*. The rich justify their status in terms of their being, the poor in their feeling of carrying out a moral imperative.

In order to avoid repetitions about these issues, some observations will be made in advance. Religions promise and offer different salvation goods (*Heilsgüter*),[22] but empirical researchers do not study them only, or even mainly, as 'otherworldly'; leaving aside the fact, that by no means all religions, and also not all of the world religions, had an idea anyway of the Beyond as a site of definite promises. With the only partial exception of Christianity and a few other specifically ascetic faiths, the salvation benefits of all the religions, whether primitive or cultivated, prophetic or non-prophetic, belonged very much to this world. Health, long life, and wealth were promised by Chinese, Vedic, Zoroastrian, ancient Judaic, Islamic in exactly the same way as Phoenician, Egyptian, Babylonian, and old Germanic religions, as did Hinduism and Buddhism for pious lay persons. Only the religious virtuosi – the ascetic, the monk, the sufi, the dervish – strove for 'extra-worldly' (*außerweltlich*) salvation goods in contrast to those belonging most solidly to this world. The extra-worldly salvation goods however were by no means solely *otherworldly* (*jenseitig*), not even when they were understood by the believers to be so. For those who were seeking after salvation, it was instead to the present, *this-worldly* (*diesseitig*) *habitus*[23] that they primarily turned, if one looks at this psychologically. The Puritan's certainty of salvation – the permanent state of grace that belongs to the feeling of 'affirmation' – could only be grasped psychologically through the salvation goods of this ascetic religiosity.[24] The acosmic feeling of love that accompanied the assured Buddhist monk on entering into Nirvana,[25] the bhakti (the ardent love of divinity within)[26] or the apathetic[27] ecstasy of the pious Hindu, the orgiastic ecstasies of the Chlysts in the radjani[28] and of the whirling Dervish,[29] those possessed by god or seeking to possess god, the

---

22 *Heilsgüter* – this means literally salvation goods and is another of Weber's invented words. Sometimes I have translated it as salvation benefits.

23 *Habitus* is the Latin word for frame of mind, bearing, or psychological disposition. The Latin is retained, since it has subsequently preserved its importance as a concept in sociology.

24 The Puritan's sense of affirmation, while nominally holding to a belief in the world beyond, is psychologically made real by everyday ascetic practices. Then in the list that follows occur similar psychological states that are desired in the first instance solely for the positive feelings that they produce.

25 See n. 34 below.

26 A practice among Hindus where a deity, such as Krishna or Rama, becomes the object of deep reverence and contemplation. It is one of three paths to religious enlightenment.

27 Weber does not use 'apathetic' solely in its modern sense of 'disinterest'. The word here signifies a condition of 'a-pathos' or 'without suffering', and as such could also be read as pleasure.

28 A Christian sect founded in Russia in the seventeenth century. They had their own specific form of worship – the radjani – that involved ecstatic dancing.

29 An order of Islamic ascetics who sought through abstinence, singing, and dancing unification with the soul of the world.

'courtly' love of Mary and the saviour,[30] the Jesuitical cult of the heart of Jesus,[31] quietistic reverence, pietistic tenderness for the infant Jesus and the blood of the wounded Christ, the sexual and half-sexual orgies in the love of Krishna, the refined cultic dinners of the Vallabhacharyas,[32] the masturbatory practices of the Gnostic cults,[33] and the different forms of mystic union and the contemplative surrender to the All-oneness[34] – all of these states (*Zustände*) have clearly been sought in the first instance for what *they in themselves directly* contributed to the believer's positive feelings.

As positively valued states of feelings, these examples are very much the equivalents of the religious intoxication of alcohol produced in Dionysiac and soma cults, totemistic meat orgies, cannibalistic feasts, the use of hashish, opium, and nicotine which used to have a religious function, and in general all kinds of magical frenzy. There is almost an air of the consecrated and the divine about these psychically extraordinary states, which in their particular circumstances come to have their own *autonomous* value. And when, at the start, the rationalized religions managed in a specifically religious way to smuggle in a metaphysical sense of meaning alongside their direct appropriation of salvation benefits, and thereby sublimated the orgy to the 'sacrament', a sense of meaning was by no means completely absent from the existing primitive orgy.[35] But the orgy was purely magical and animistic and it did not have the capacity for, or even suggestion of, being included in a universal, cosmic pragmatics of salvation (*Heilspragmatik*) that is a feature of all religious rationalism. Actually, even after the transition from orgy to sacrament, the acquisition of the benefits of salvation by the pious still retained, naturally enough, a sense of belonging to the immediate *present* when seen psychologically. That is, in the *habitus* of feeling (*Gefühlshabitus*) of the pious there existed a condition that was directly called forth by a specific religious (or magical) act, or by methodical asceticism, or through contemplation.

---

30 Weber's German here is very idiosyncratic. He refers to 'Marien- und Heilandsminne' whose literal meaning is the courtly love of Mary (the virgin mother of Jesus) and the saviour. Maryology is a form of 'courtly love'. The 'courts of love' were made up of medieval feudal knights who wooed the ladies of the court with songs, verse, and a seemingly complete devotion. Love of the saviour could refer to the Lutheran Zinzerdorf's sentimental popularization of the love of Jesus (cf. *GARS*, vol. 2, p. 198).

31 The bleeding heart of Jesus became a devotional object in the Catholic Church.

32 An Indian sect that worshipped the deity Vishnu.

33 The early Christian bishops condemned Gnostics as heretics and ascribed to them irreligious sexual practices.

34 Although Weber does not specify its forms, all-oneness was and is a prevalent feature in many religions and philosophies. It is the idea that humanity is not separate from the cosmic and material world but is part of it and can merge into it. Nirvana is 'acosmic' because it is a state of pure spiritual enlightenment that has completely escaped the material and cosmic world.

35 Sublimation is a chemical process of refinement of materials. Weber's usage should not be directly equated with Freud's theory of sublimation. See above, pp. 18–19.

Because of its purely outward nature, this condition could not sustain an extraordinary *habitus* beyond being a simply temporary affair, and originally this was, of course, the case everywhere. There is no way of distinguishing the 'religious' from the 'profane' condition, except by the *extra*ordinariness of the first. But a condition attained by religious means could be made more permanent in its effects when what was striven for was to grasp the 'condition of salvation' of the whole person and his destiny. The transition was fluid. In religiously sublimated salvation doctrine the two highest conceptions are 'rebirth' and 'salvation', and it was rebirth that was in its age-old origins a magical good. It meant the acquisition of a new soul through an orgiastic act or through systematic asceticism. Its acquisition was temporary in ecstasy, but it could also be sought as a permanent *habitus* and be attained by means of magical asceticism. A youth required a new soul if he was about to enter into the warrior community as a hero, or wished as a member of a cultic community to take part in its magical dances or orgies, or wanted to commune with the deities at the cult dinner. The asceticism of the hero and the magician, the initiation of the youth, and the sacramental customs of rebirth at significant points of private and communal life were therefore an age-old phenomenon. Aside from the means employed, what was different was the goals of these actions, above all, the answer to the question 'for what' one should be reborn.

The differing and valued states (*Zuständlichkeiten*), allowed by religion (and magic), that gave a religion its psychological complexion, can be systematized from very different viewpoints. Such an attempt cannot be undertaken at this point. All that will be done here is to give some very general indications in relation to what has been said above. The kinds of experiential states of being saved or rebirth (in this world), which are striven for as the highest good of a religion, obviously must vary according to the character of the stratum that was the most important carrier of the respective religiosity. A class of chivalrous warriors, peasants, those who pursue trade, and literary trained intellectuals contained within themselves very different tendencies. As will become clear, these tendencies had the capacity to have a very long-lasting influence on the psychological character of a religion, even though this, on its own, was far from being an unambiguous determination. The contrast between the first two strata (knights and peasants) and the second (tradespeople and intellectuals) was everywhere especially significant.

In the second group, the intellectuals were always the carriers of a more theoretical rationalism, while those who pursued trade (merchants and artisans) were the possible carriers of a more practical rationalism. Rationalism took very different forms but always tended to exercise a significant effect on religious stance. The characteristics of the *intellectuals* as a stratum were in this respect of the greatest consequence. The distinctiveness of the intellectual classes has everywhere been important for religions in the past. For contemporary religious development, it is a matter of overall indifference whether our modern intellectuals perceive the need, alongside other sensations, to consume 'religious' states as an 'experience' rather as though they were fitting out their inner furnishings with stylish, genuinely authentic, old pieces. No religious renewal has ever grown from such a source.[36]

The task of the intellectuals has predominantly been to take the possession of religious salvation (*Heilsbesitz*) and to refine it into the belief in 'redemption'. If one thinks of the liberation from privation, hunger, thirst, disease and, finally, suffering and death, then the conception of the idea of salvation in itself was age-old. But redemption only achieved a specific meaning when it became the expression of a systematically rationalized 'worldview' ('*Weltbild*') and the stance taken to the world. What redemption could and wished to signify in terms of its meaning and its psychological quality has depended on that worldview and stance. It is interests (material and ideal), and not ideas, which have directly governed the actions of human beings. But the 'worldviews' that have been created by ideas have very often, like switches, decided the lines on which the dynamic of interests has propelled behaviour.[37]

It is the worldview that has directed 'from what' and 'for what' one would be 'saved' and, let us not forget, could be saved: whether from a political and social slavery to a messianic realm in this world; or from the defilement of ritual uncleanliness or from the impurity of being imprisoned within the body to the purity of body, soul, and beauty and a purely spiritual existence; or from the eternal and senseless play of human passions and desires to the calm peace of the pure sight of the divine; or from radical evil and the servitude of sin to the eternally free goodness in the arms of a fatherly god; or from the submission to the astrologically conceived determination of the constellation of the stars to the dignity of freedom and the partaking in the substance of a hidden divinity; or from mortality expressed in the constraints of suffering, privation and death and the threat of punishment in hell to an eternal bliss in an earthly or future existence in paradise; or from the cycle of rebirth and its pitiless revenge of living out time to an eternal peace; or from the senselessness of worry and contingency to a dreamless sleep. There are still plenty more possibilities. What stands hidden behind all of these examples is a stance taken towards something that was perceived as specifically 'meaningless' in the real world. This resulted in the demand that the fabric of the world in its totality be in some wise a meaningful 'cosmos', or rather, that it could or should be. This longing, which is the nucleus of *religious rationalism*, has invariably been carried by the intellectual strata. The directions and the results of this metaphysical need, and also the extent

36 Weber is taking a vigorous side-swipe against some of his contemporaries – poets such as Stefan George who assembled a pseudo-religion.
37 The original German says 'like switchmen', a word rapidly becoming obsolete.

of its efficacy, have varied greatly. Some general comments can nevertheless be made about this.

The modern form of rationalization, which is theoretical and practical as well as intellectual and purposeful, has had the following general consequences in its thorough rationalization of worldviews and the conduct of life. Seen from the standpoint of an intellectual construction of the worldview, the more this particular form of rationalization proceeded, the more religion was pushed into the irrational. This occurred for several reasons. On the one hand, the calculation of a consistent rationalism did not work out easily and smoothly. One example from music is the Pythagorean comma where the attempt to rationalize notes according to a perfect scale of tonal physics resisted a solution.[38] This meant that each of the great musical systems from all ages and peoples differentiated themselves above all through the manner and way they covered up or went around this inescapable irrationality, or conversely, knew how to put it to work in the service of the richness of tonalities. This seems to have happened far more so for the theoretical worldview and, above all, for the practical rationalization of life. Also each of the main types of the rational and methodical regulation of life have been characterized by those irrational presuppositions – that are simply accepted as given – that each type of regulation had incorporated into itself.

What these presuppositions were has been a matter, to no small degree, of the historical and social determination by the particular *interest situation* of the strata; this means the external and social, and the internal and psychological, factors operating on the strata who were the carriers of the relevant methodical way of life at the time when their influence was decisive.

The irrational elements (*Einschläge*) in the rationalization of reality were also the places to which the heavily suppressed need of intellectualism for supra-real values saw itself compelled to retreat, especially so the more the world appeared to be divested of values. The unity of the primitive worldview, in which everything material was a concrete manifestation of magic, then showed a tendency to split; on the one side, a rational understanding and a rational subordination of nature and, on the other, 'mystical' experiences whose inexpressible content was the only possible Beyond left remaining in the face of the godless mechanism of the world. In truth, the Beyond could not be understood, it was a hidden realm of god-dwelling, individual possession of salvation. Where the consequences of this split are taken to its limits, then the individual can only seek his salvation as an individual. This

---

38 In a musical scale the notes are not the same distance apart (the interval) throughout the scale when measured by acoustic physics. The residual irrationality inherent in scales is called 'the Pythagorean comma'. Modern 'tempered' scales are designed in part to aurally overcome this difficulty. A five-note scale, as used on the bagpipes, makes little or no attempt to achieve equidistance of intervals between notes, and so exploits the inherent irrationality of tonal scales to musical effect. Weber is using a seemingly esoteric example to make a very profound observation. See also below, p. 102.

phenomenon, with an increasingly intellectualistic rationalism, inserted itself in whatever form that appeared when men undertook the rationalization of the worldview as an image of the cosmos ruled by impersonal forces. This occurred at its strongest, naturally enough, in those religions and religious ethics that were especially influenced by the refined intellectual strata whose refinement came from their dedication to *thinking* about the world and its meaning. This occurred in Asiatic and, above all, in Indian world religions. Contemplation for all of them was the entering into the deep and blessed peace and stillness of the All-oneness, which offered them the highest and ultimate religious good that was accessible to man. All other kinds of religious states were, however, an extremely relative but valuable surrogate. This had far-reaching consequences, as we will see, for the relationship of religion to life, including the economy. These consequences stemmed from the general character of mystical experiences in this contemplative sense and from the psychological pre-conditions of striving for those experiences.

The situation is entirely different where the decisive stratum in the development of a religion has stood in a practical relationship to life, or belonged to the classes of the knightly warrior heroes, political officials or the economically productive, or lastly, where the religion was governed by an organized hierocracy.

The growing rationalism of *hierocracy*[39] stemmed from the specialist concern in cults and myths, or, at a higher level, with care of the soul and the confession of sins and guidance. In general terms hierocracy sought to monopolize for itself the provision of the benefits of salvation. It alone would confer 'sacramental grace' or 'institutional grace' and moderate that state of grace accordingly. This would be attainable not by individuals but only through ritual administered by the hierocracy. The individual search for salvation by individuals or by free communities using the means of contemplation, orgy, or asceticism was considered, naturally enough, highly suspicious from the standpoint of the power interests of the hierocracy; the search for salvation had to be regulated through ritual and, above all, be controlled by the hierocracy.

- On the other hand every *political* officialdom mistrusted all forms of the individual search for salvation and the free formation of communities as sources of emancipation from domestication by the institutions of the state. Political officialdom also mistrusted competition from priests in their institutional administration of grace, but most of all it despised in the final analysis the striving after the non-practical benefits of the Beyond in place of utilitarian innerworldly goals. For every officialdom, religious obligations were at base simply the official or social duties of citizens and status groups. Ritual was the equivalent of regulation, and

---

39 Hierocracy is the rulership of priests.

so every form of religiosity has taken on a ritualistic character where it
has been determined by bureaucracy.

- A *knightly* warrior stratum has tended in its interests to be quite this-
  worldly in orientation and to be distant to all 'mysticism'. What the
  knightly stratum lacked, as did heroism in general, was any rationalistic
  grip on reality; it lacked this as a rule, by inclination and by capability.
  Instead the irrationality of 'fate', and possibly the idea of a vague,
  deterministically conceived 'disaster' (of the Homeric 'moira'[40]), stood
  behind and above the gods and demons, who were thought of as passionate and mighty heroes bestowing succour and enmity, glory and booty, or
  death to earthly heroes.

- Magic appealed to the *peasants*, who were tied to nature and dependent
  on the power of the elements, as was their whole economic livelihood.
  Magic was used against the controlling spirits within and above the
  forces of nature, or simply to purchase divine goodwill. Magic stood
  so close to the peasant that only enormous transformations in the
  orientation of life could drag them free from this primitive and pervasive form of religiosity. This was accomplished by other strata or
  by mighty prophets who legitimated themselves as magicians and
  through the power of miracles. For the peasants, orgiastic and ecstatic
  states of 'possession' produced by intoxicated frenzy or by dance took
  the place of what 'mysticism' was for the intellectuals. To the knightly
  stratum's sense of esteem, the state of 'possession' was alien and lacked
  dignity.

- Finally, there were the *bourgeois* strata (*bürgerliche Schichten*) in their
  western European sense and what corresponded to them elsewhere: – the
  artisan, the merchant, the household-based entrepreneur, and their other
  derivatives found only within the modern Occident. In the number of
  possibilities in the position they adopted in their religion, they seem to be
  the most ambiguous of all the strata – and this is particularly important
  for us. Various forms of religiosity originated directly from the bourgeois
  strata, very much more so than in the other strata, and these forms
  included: the sacramental institutional grace of the Roman Church in the
  medieval cities – that was the foundation of the popes; the sacramental
  grace of the mystagogues in the cities of Antiquity and India; the orgiastic and contemplative religiosity of the Sufis and the Dervishes of the
  Middle East; Taoist magic; Buddhist contemplation and the ritualistic
  acquisition of grace through the direction of the soul by the mystagogues
  in Asia; all forms of love of the saviour throughout the world and the
  belief in the redeemer from Krishna to the cult of Christ; in Jewry,
  rational ritualism according to the Law and a synagogue service that has

40 Greek goddesses who controlled the fate of heroes.

discarded all magic; the pneumatic sects of Antiquity[41] and the ascetic sects of the Middle Ages; and the belief in predestination and ethical regeneration of the Puritans and Methodists; and all kinds of individual search for salvation.

The religiosity of the other three strata was certainly very different from the above forms. Religiosity was not straightforwardly dependent on the stratum's character, as presented above, with which it had a particular affinity. In this respect, however, the 'bourgeois stratum' appears at first sight to be definable overall in far more varied ways. Yet, in the case of the bourgeois stratum, elective affinities with certain types of religiosity do stand out.[42] It commonly displayed a tendency towards a conduct of life defined by *practical rationalism*, since its way of life had been released from a direct economic dependency on nature. The bourgeois stratum's whole existence was based on the technical and economic calculation and control, of however small a means, over nature and people. The sort of technique for living that the bourgeois stratum inherited could harden into traditionalism – something that overall has always happened everywhere. But in the case of the bourgeois stratum, and this happens to very differing degrees, there always existed in the tendency to technical and economic rationalism the *possibility* of an *ethically* rational regulation of life to arise. It was not able to carry this through everywhere against tradition that was mostly magically stereotyped. But where a religious basis was created through prophecy, then it could belong to one of two basic types: 'exemplary' prophecy and 'missionary'[43] prophecy, and these will be frequently referred to below.

An exemplary prophecy *sets an example* of a life directed towards salvation, usually a contemplative and an apathetic-ecstatic life. A missionary prophecy makes *demands* of the world in the name of a god; these demands naturally are ethical and often of an actively ascetic character. Missionary prophecy in its call to active behaviour in the world was more likely to find favourable grounds, understandably enough, the more so where the bourgeois stratum as such has prevailed socially and has been torn free from the bonds of taboos and the division into kinship groups and castes. Not divine possession nor abandonment to contemplation of the god within, which have

---

41 See n. 9 above.
42 'Elective affinity' (*Wahlverwandtschaft*) is a term taken from a novel of that name by Goethe. Its central idea was that individuals elect who their friends are, or rather, there is a mutual attraction between individuals according to compatible qualities of character – they bond together like chemical compounds. In his use of terms and phraseology, Weber is being very careful about the nature of the determination he is allowing. He never states the determination in an unqualified way – that a social stratum could choose its own type of religiosity.
43 'Missionary prophecy' (*'Sendungs'-Prophetie*) signifies that the prophet is an emissary of god – literally that he brings a message from god.

appeared as the highest good in those religions influenced by genteel intellectual classes, but active asceticism – *action* willed by god with the sense of being the 'instrument' of god – has tended to be the preferred religious *habitus* in the Occident. It was the *habitus* of active asceticism that more and more gained the upper hand over contemplative mysticism and orgiastic and apathetic ecstasy that was also known in the Occident. Not that this *habitus* would have been limited to these bourgeois strata. One cannot speak here of an unambiguous social determination. One can find this same active character in the Zoroastrian prophecy that was directed to the aristocracy and the peasantry and in the Islamic prophecy directed to the warriors, just as likewise one can find it in the Israelite and the early Christian prophecy and preaching. This stands in contrast to the Buddhist, Taoist, neo-Pythagorean,[44] Gnostic, and Sufi propaganda. But certain consequences of the missionary prophecy in the field of the bourgeois have nevertheless been drawn, as we will see.

Missionary prophecy, in which the religious see themselves as an instrument of god and not as a vessel of the divine, had a deep-seated elective affinity to a defined conception of the deity. Missionary prophecy had a transcendental, personal, angry, forgiving, loving, punishing creator-god in contrast to the supreme being of exemplary prophecy. As a rule, although not without exceptions, the latter was an impersonal deity whose being was only approachable through the state of contemplation. The first conception of the deity prevailed in the religions of Iran and the Middle East and the western religions derived from them; the second conception in the religions of India and China.

There is nothing primitive about these distinctions. Quite the opposite, for they have only come about through a far-reaching sublimation of representations of primitive animistic spirits and heroic gods – a process that was very similar everywhere. And this has proceeded strongly assisted by the inter-relationships mentioned above, whereby the salvation benefit relates to the desired and valued religious state of affairs. The direction in which the various conceptions of god were interpreted was dependent on the religious state of affairs: according to whether the highest sacred state was a contemplative and mystical experience, apathetic ecstasy, orgiastic possession of the divine, or visionary inspirations and 'commissions' (*Aufzüge*). Seen from the standpoint that today is widespread and obviously widely justified, it is the emotional contents that alone are primary and ideas are merely their secondary manifestations. This leads to the causal relationship of the primacy of the 'psychological' over 'rational' constructions as being exclusively important; the latter should be seen as *merely* an interpretation of the former. This would however go far beyond the evidence of the facts. The highly consequential

---

44 The neo-Pythagorean treated the mathematical philosophy of Pythagoras as a secret mystery. They wandered through the Greek world, forming sects, a century before Christ.

development of a transcendental or an immanent conception of god was influenced by a whole series of purely historical forces that, in their turn, have had a very long-lasting effect on the nature of formation of the salvation experience; above all, as we will repeatedly see, on the transcendental god. If on occasions Meister Eckhart expressly placed 'Martha' over 'Mary', this was ultimately because for him the mystic's own pantheistic experience of God could not be fully realized without abandoning the central tenets of the western belief in creation and God.[45]

The rational elements of a religion, its 'teaching', also have their own lawlike autonomy, as is in the Indian doctrine of karma, the Calvinist belief in predestination, the Lutheran justification by faith, and the Catholic doctrine of the sacraments. And the rational religious pragmatics of salvation that stem from the manner of the representation of God and of the 'worldview' has, depending on circumstance, achieved far-reaching effects for the framing of the practical conduct of life.

If, as it has been assumed in the observations up to this point, the nature of the salvation goods striven for was strongly influenced by the type of external interest situation of the ruling stratum and the way of life adequate to it, and thus by social stratification itself, so the converse also holds: The direction of an entire way of life, where it has been rationalized in an ordered way, has been defined most profoundly by the final values towards which the rationalization process has oriented itself. Although this was not invariably and far from exclusively the case, where the rationalization process was *ethical* and where its influence was sufficient, the values and stances taken were as a rule, and often decisively so, *religiously* determined.

There is one very important factor that needs to be taken into account in the reciprocal connections of the external and internal interest position. The 'highest' salvation benefits promised by a religion – those that have been discussed so far – are not the most universal. Entry into nirvana, the contemplative union with the divine, and the possession of the divine achieved through orgy or asceticism were by no means available to everyone. Religious frenzy or dream-states could be transposed in a weaker form into an object of a universal cult of the people, but even then they did not become constituents of everyday life as such.

Right at the beginning of the whole history of religion stands, for us, the important experiential fact that the religious *qualifications* of human beings are *unequal*. This receives its starkest rationalistic conception in

45 A reference to an incident related in the New Testament, Luke, 10, 38–42. Mary sat at Jesus' feet, listening to him, while her sister Martha got on with the housework. Jesus reproached Martha for complaining about this to Mary. Meister Eckhardt was a medieval Christian mystic, who, as Weber indicates, held back from a complete pantheistic embrace of the divine that dispensed with Christian doctrine. The reference comes from one of Eckhart's sermons, probably given to nuns.

the doctrine of Calvinist predestination, as a form of the 'particularism of grace'.[46] The most highly valued of religious salvation benefits – the ecstatic and visionary abilities of all kinds of shaman, magician, ascetic, and pneumatic spiritualist – were not attainable by everyone. The possession of this ability was a 'charisma' that could be invoked by some, but not by all.[47] From this follows the tendency in all intensive religiosity to make a kind of *status* division according to the differences in charismatic qualification. A religiosity of 'heroics' or 'virtuosi' stood in opposition to the religiosity of the masses.[48] What is meant by mass religiosity, it has to be said, is not those at the bottom of the secular social order but the *religiously* 'unmusical'. Under the heading of status carriers of religious virtuosity are to be counted the alliances of magicians and sacred dancers, the religious status group of the Indian sramana,[49] the 'ascetics' in early Christianity who were seen as a separate 'status group' in the community, the Pauline and the even more so Gnostic 'pneumatics', the pietistic 'little churches',[50] all proper 'sects' – defined sociologically as groups which only accept into themselves the religiously *qualified*, and lastly, all monastic communities throughout the world.

All virtuoso religiosity, following its own autonomous unfolding, comes into fundamental conflict with every hierocratic and official power of a 'church', defined as an institution-like community with officials for the organized administering of grace. A church, as the carrier of institutional grace, strives to organize the mass religiosity and to put its own officially monopolized and mediated salvation goods in place of the religious virtuosi who have their own religious qualification and status. A church, by its nature – that is the interest position of its office-holders – has to be 'democratic' in the sense of making salvation benefits generally available. It is a supporter of universal grace and of the ethical adequacy of all those who place themselves under the church's institutional power. This forms sociologically a perfect parallel to the political arena where a struggle is carried on by the bureaucracy against the autonomous political rights of the aristocratic estate. The church is a hierocracy and like every fully developed political bureaucracy it is necessarily 'democratic' in the sense of levelling and fighting against the estatist privileges that compete for power with it. Many and varied compromises arose as a result of the not always official but always latent struggle between

---

46 'Particularism of grace' (*Gnadepartikularismus*) under Calvinism restricts salvation to a predetermined few. See below, p. 223.

47 Charisma is a major concept in Weber's analysis of rulership; see below, pp. 138–45. Here he is using it in its religious sense of a 'divinely conferred power or talent' (*OED*).

48 [Weber] In using the concept 'virtuosity' in this context, any trace of contemporary evaluation must be removed. I would have preferred the expression of 'heroic'.

49 Mendicant monks.

50 Weber uses the Latinate *'ecclesiola'*.

the religiosity of the masses and that of the virtuosi: (the ulama[51] against the religiosity of the dervishes; the early Christian bishops against the pneumatics and the heroics of the sect members, and against ascetic charisma that was a key force; the Lutheran office of preaching (*Predigeramt*) and the priests of the Anglican church against asceticism in general; the Russian state church against the sects; the official provision of cults by Confucians against Buddhist, Taoist, and all kinds of sectarian search for salvation).

In order for the virtuosi to acquire and hold on to a mass customer base, both ideally and materially, they were forced to adjust their standards as a way of making concessions to the possibilities of everyday religiosity. *This*, in the first analysis, was naturally decisive for the manner in which religion influenced everyday life. If religion left the masses stranded in a magical tradition, as happened in almost all oriental religions, then its influence would be infinitely smaller than if it – even with many relaxations from its ideal requirements – still was able to change and universally to pursue an ethical rationalization of the everyday that included the masses, or indeed was directed solely at the masses. Alongside the relationship between virtuoso and mass religiosity, which finally becomes established as a result of this struggle, even the character of the concrete virtuoso religiosity itself was therefore of decisive significance for the development of the conduct of life of the 'masses', and so also for the economic ethic of the relevant religion. A religion has not only a genuinely 'exemplary' and practical effect, but through the conduct of life that it prescribed for the virtuosi it created in general a rational everyday ethic, whose possibilities varied greatly.

The relationship of virtuosi religiosity to *everyday life*, and to the locale of the economy, varied especially according to the character of the *salvation good* that it strove after.

Where the salvation goods and means of redemption of virtuoso religiosity bore a contemplative or orgiastic-ecstatic character, there could be no bridge linking it to the practical everyday action in the world. This rendered the economy, as indeed all activity in the world, as something religiously inferior. And indirectly it did not permit any psychological motives to be derived from a *habitus* prized as the highest good. Instead the contemplative and the ecstatic religiosity in its most inner being was hostile to the economic. The mystic, orgiastic, ecstatic experience belongs most definitely to the specifically extraordinary, and leads away from the everyday and from rational instrumental action, and so is regarded as 'holy'. In these religious orientations, therefore, a deep chasm separated the way of life of the 'laity' from that of the virtuosi community. The power of the virtuosi estate within the religious community moved easily therefore in the direction of a magical worship of the human person (*Anthropolatrie*). The virtuoso was worshipped directly as a saint or for his blessing and his magical powers were purchased by the laity

---

51 Someone who is learned in law and theology in Islam.

as a means to support worldly or religious salvation. The Buddhist and Jainist bhiksu[52] treated the layman rather like the landed lord treated the peasant – ultimately, indeed solely, as a source of tribute. This enabled the bhiksu to live solely for salvation without his having to undertake worldly work that would always jeopardize that salvation. The way of life of the laity could also thereby undergo a certain degree of ethical regulation, since the virtuoso was the factual carer of the soul – father confessor and *directeur de l'âme* to the layperson, and so frequently of great influence. But this influence was exercised over the 'unmusical' layperson wholly outside the virtuoso's own religious way of life, or at least only in its ceremonial, ritual, and conventional details. Any actions taken in the world were in principle religiously insignificant and in relation to the striving after the religious goal they lay in the opposite direction. The charisma of the pure 'mystic' was directed entirely to himself alone, not like the genuine magician who served others.

The situation was completely different where the religiously qualified virtuosi came together to form an ascetic *sect* that strove to form the life *in* the world according to the will of a god. For this to happen in the truest sense, two conditions have to be met. First, the highest salvation good could not be of a contemplative nature; it could not be a unification, in opposition to the world, with an eternally valid, transcendental being; nor could it be a mystical union achieved by orgy or apathetic ecstasy. These states lay on the margins of the workings of everyday reality and beyond the real world; they led away from the world. Secondly, the religion has to divest itself as much as possible of the purely magical or sacramental character of its *means* of grace. These features continually devalue action in the world in terms of religious significance as highly relative, and they tie the decision whether someone is to be saved to the success of procedures that are non-rational in an everyday sense.

Where an ascetic sect was fully successful, then it led to the disenchantment of the world and the transference of the path to salvation from contemplative 'world-flight' to actively ascetic 'working-in-the-world'. Disregarding some small rationalistic sects, which crop up all over the world, this was only achieved in the great formations of churches and sects of ascetic Protestantism in the Occident. This has occurred because of the coming together of the distinctive and purely historically determined destinies of occidental religiosity: partly in its social environment and, above all else, the principal stratum in its development; but partly in its real character as a religion which is equally important. Its religious character was given by a transcendental (*überweltlich*) god and the exceptionality of its means and path to salvation, which were historically defined at their inception by Israelite prophecy and

---

52 A wandering monk dependent on begging for his livelihood.

the teachings of the Torah. This has been expounded in part in the preceding essays, and will be looked at more closely later.[53]

The religious virtuoso was placed in the world as an 'instrument' of God with the demand that he 'prove' himself through the ethical qualities of his action in the orders of the world. As an instrument of God he was detached from all magical means of salvation, thereby only called before God to salvation, and this meant in the nature of the exercise proving his ethical qualities to himself. But since the world could from a religious viewpoint be devalued and rejected as creaturely and as a receptacle of sin, psychologically there was even more reason that it be affirmed through 'vocation' (*Beruf*)[54] where the world became the setting (*Schauplatz*) of a purposeful god. This innerworldly asceticism was very much a rejection of the world. It despised and outlawed the benefits (*Güter*) of dignity and beauty, of wonderful ecstasy and trance, and of purely worldly power and the pride of heroes as competitors to the realm of God. Yet it did not follow that it wished to flee the world as in the case of contemplation. Instead it desired to ethically rationalize the world according to God's decree and so it remained in a specifically more insistent way turned towards the world than the naïve 'affirmation of the world' of unbroken humanity (*ungebrochenen Menschentums*) as in Antiquity and among the Catholic laity. The grace and the sense of being chosen of the religiously qualified were proven in normal everyday life. Obviously this did not mean that the everyday was simply mundane, but rather how everyday action became methodically *rationalized* in the service of God. Everyday action, which had been rationally intensified through vocation, became the proof of salvation. In the Occident, the sects of religious virtuosi formed the leaven for the methodical rationalization of the way of life, including economic activity. But unlike the religious virtuosi in the communities of the contemplative, orgiastic, or apathetic ecstatics in Asia, they did not produce outlets for the yearning to escape from the meaningless of innerworldly work.

Within this extreme polarity there operated the most various transitions and combinations. Religions, just as human beings, are not perfect contrivances. They were historical constructions and not logical or even psychological constructions free of contradictions. They very often carried within them series of forces, which if each had been logically followed through would have produced a blocking of paths or head-on collisions. 'Consistency' in a religion is an exception and not the rule. The psychological regularities in the paths to salvation and the benefits of salvation were also not unambiguous.

---

53 The earlier reference is to *The Protestant Ethic and the Spirit of Capitalism* and 'The Protestant Sects and the Spirit of Capitalism' essays. On the Torah see *Ancient Judaism*, edited and translated by Hans Gerth and Don Martindale, New York, Free Press, 1952, pp. 284–5, 294–6.

54 *Beruf* has the meanings of profession, trade and occupation. Its religious origins are indicated by the older term, vocation or calling. See above, pp. 31–3.

The monk in early Christianity or the Quaker had a very strong contemplative element in their search for God. But the total content of their religiosity – above all a transcendental god of creation and the manner of guaranteeing the certainty of grace – always placed them back on the path of action. The reverse also holds. The Buddhist monk was active, but this action was completely removed from any consistent *inner*worldly rationalization because the ultimate orienting of the striving for salvation was to flee from the 'wheel' of rebirth. The sectarians and the other brotherhoods of the occidental Middle Ages, as carriers of the religious penetration of everyday life, found their counterpart in the brotherhoods of Islam that were even more universally developed. And both brotherhoods came from the same social stratum – the lower-middle classes and especially the artisanal stratum. But the spirit of each brotherhood was very different. Numerous Hinduistic religious communities appeared from the outside to be sects, just as much as those in the Occident, but the salvation benefit and the manner of attaining salvation lay in radically opposed directions.

Further examples need not be accumulated since we wish to consider individually the most important of the major religions. These religions in their relationship to one another are not to be divided up, in this or any other viewpoint, into a series of types by which each signifies in opposition to the others a new 'stage'. Rather they are complete historical entities of the most complex sort and make up, taken all together, only a fraction of the possible combinations which could be conceivably constructed from the numerous individual factors that come into consideration.

What follows therefore does not present any *systematic* 'typology' of religions. On the other hand, to be sure, it is not a purely historical work. But the following presentation is 'typological' in the sense that it considers what is important in the connection between the historical realities of the religious ethics and the major differences in the *economic* mentalities; and it is typological in what it omits.[55]

---

55 For reasons of space the translation stops here. In the next section Weber briefly discusses the concept of rationalism, and then concludes the essay with an outline of key sociological concepts, which he takes from *Economy and Society*. See *FMW*, pp. 292–301.

4   The religions of civilization and their attitude to the world[1]

How Judaism turns to face the world

Judaism in its post-exilic and above all Talmudic form[2] (whose sociological foundations we have already presented[3]) is the third[4] of the religions which to an extent is 'adjusted to' (*'angepaßte'*) or at least faces the world, even though it does reject society's hierarchical order. Its promises, as normally meant, obtain in this world, and a contemplative or an ascetic flight from the world is as exceptional an occurrence as it is for Chinese religion and for Protestantism. In broad terms Judaism distinguishes itself from Puritanism by its *relative* lack of systematic asceticism in general. The 'ascetic' elements of early Christianity do not derive from Judaism but from the Pagan-Christian communities of the Pauline mission.[5] Observance of Jewish 'Law',[6] like any ritual or taboo, has very little to do with 'asceticism'. The relationship of Jewish religiosity to wealth on the one side, and to sexuality on the other, is not in the least ascetic but instead highly naturalistic. Wealth is a gift from God, and the satisfaction of sexual drive, as long as it is legal, is obligatory, so much so that to remain unmarried beyond a certain age is morally suspect in the Talmud.[7] The view of marriage defined simply as an economic arrangement for the procreation and rearing of children is universal and is not specifically Jewish. Non-legal sexual intercourse is very much frowned upon (and most effectively so in pious circles), and Judaism shares this with Islam and all prophetic religions. In addition, the regulations on abstinence and purity in Hinduism along with the majority of all ritualistic religions should not be thought of in the *specific* sense of sexual asceticism. The regulations cited by Sombart do not meet the standards of

---

1 The last chapter of Weber's 'Sociology of Religion', *WuG*, pp. 367–81. Translation by S. Whimster.
2 The leading strata of the Judaic people were expelled by the Babylonians and were only allowed to return to Judah and Israel seventy years later in 538 BC. The Talmud is an oral and written commentary on the Hebrew or Old Testament Bible.
3 *Rel*, pp. 80–94.
4 A reference to Confucianism and certain forms of Islam.
5 St Paul had more success propagating the message of Christian asceticism outside the Jewish communities and within the Roman Empire.
6 'Law' throughout this section means the Jewish religious Law of the Talmud.
7 See Order III of the Mishnah, part of the Talmud.

Catholic casuistry of the seventeenth century and one can find many analogies in other taboo systems.[8]

The unrestrained enjoyment of life, even luxury, is in itself nowhere forbidden just so long as the actual prohibitions and taboos of the 'Law' are adhered to. . . . Since Judaism lacks the idea of predestination or equivalent ideas with the same effect, continuous work and success in business cannot be valued as a sign of 'proof', as was the case at its strongest in calvinistic Puritanism and to a degree in the whole of ascetic Protestantism (as, for example, John Wesley's remarks show).[9] The idea that success in business is a sign of God's gracious disposing can, of course, be found in the Jewish religion, just as it can be found in Chinese, lay-Buddhist, and all religions that do not turn away from the world. This has to be the case in the Judaic religion, since its transcendental god makes very specific promises in conjunction with explicit signs of his anger with a people chosen by himself. It is obvious that the significance of success in business, while adhering to God's commands, could and must have been taken as a symptom of God's personal benevolence. This in fact happened again and again. But the situation for the working (pious) Jew was actually fundamentally different to that of the Puritan, and this difference is not without practical consequences for the economic history of Judaism. But first, what is the economic significance of this?

In the polemic against Sombart's intellectually excellent book[10] one fact should not have been seriously disputed: Judaism has played a very important part in the unfolding of the capitalist economic system in the modern era. Sombart's thesis in my opinion requires further clarification. What are the *specific* economic contributions of Judaism in the Middle Ages and in the modern era? The lending of money, from pawn-broking to the financing of large states; particular types of trading in goods with an emphasis on small retail, peddling and specifically rural goods; part of the wholesale trade and trade in financial securities, especially trading on stock exchanges, money-changing, and the associated business of money transfers; government loans, the financing of war, and a preponderant role in the financing of colonial settlements; tax-farming (but not the farming of taxes that would be frowned upon such as the tax on Romans); credit and banking business and the floating of all types of bond issues. It is from this activity that certain charac-

---

8 In *The Jews and Economic Life* Sombart had argued that Jewish sexual life had been highly regulated in the direction of abstinence. Weber says that, compared to other doctrines, it was not.

9 John Wesley pointed to the association of 'proof' and wealth: 'we must exhort all Christians to gain all they can, and to save all they can; that is, in effect, to grow *rich*.' Quoted by Weber in *PESC*, p. 175.

10 Werner Sombart, *The Jews and Economic Life* [1911, translated 1913]. In the following passage Weber mounts a vigorous refutation of Sombart's view that the Jews were central to the rise of modern capitalism. In particular Sombart had argued, against Weber's Protestant ethic thesis, that Puritan doctrines were borrowings from Judaism.

teristic economic and legal business *forms* (of not negligible importance) have emerged in *modern* western capitalism (in contrast to the capitalisms of Antiquity, the Middle Ages, and the Asiatic past); on the legal side, for example, the creation of stock companies and capitalistic companies. While these forms do not have a specifically Jewish provenance, they have been introduced into the West (*Okzident*) by the Jews, even though they probably had a common oriental (Babylonian) origin. Hellenistic and Byzantine origins have been mediated by the Jews – at any rate by Jews and Arabs together.

On the other hand these business forms are medieval western innovations with in part a specifically German imprint, but the detailed evidence for this takes us too far afield. But to give some economic examples, the stock exchange as a 'market of tradespeople' was created by Christian traders and not by Jews. And the particular way in which medieval legal forms were adapted for rational business purposes – for example, the Kommanditen, Maonen,[11] all types of privileged companies, and then the joint stock company – all of these were created independently of Jewish influence, even though later the Jews were very much involved in setting up businesses. And a final example: the specifically modern principles of financing public and private debt originated and were first developed in the medieval cities, and then these medieval, and wholly un-Jewish, legal forms were adapted, economically, to the requirements of the modern state and other borrowers. But there is one omission above all else in the long list of Jewish economic activity. It may not be completely absent but in relative terms it is nevertheless most striking and it relates to what is characteristic of modern capitalism, namely: the organization of production in households, manufacturing, and factories. In view of the fact that at a time of a large proletariat in the ghettos and the establishment of every sort of industry, when royal patents and privileges were on offer (for appropriate pecuniary payments), and also guild-free zones were made widely available for the establishment of new industrial enterprises, how can it be explained in the light of the above that no pious Jew with the availability of a workforce of pious Jews from the ghetto did not think of creating an industry as was the case with so many pious Puritan entrepreneurs using pious Puritan workers and artisans?[12] And right up to the threshold of recent times there has been no specifically modern, and this means *industrial*, Jewish bourgeoisie of any importance that has originated from household production, despite the existence of a broad band of Jewish artisans suffering from deprivation.

For thousands of years and across almost the entire world supplying the

11 These were medieval Italian business associations created to finance marine expeditions. See *GEH*, p. 206 and below, p. 104.
12 Weber is being sarcastic at the expense of Sombart whose economic explanation he opposed.

state, tax farming, the financing of war, the financing of colonies and especially slave plantations, brokerage, and money-lending have been the ways of capitalistically increasing wealth. The Jews have participated in these activities throughout history and in all countries, and especially so in Antiquity, and now also in modern legal and business forms that were created in the Middle Ages – but not by the Jews. The Jews are almost completely absent from what is specifically unique to modern capitalism – the rational organization of work and above all production in the industrial 'enterprise'. They are especially marked by the economic attitude which was typical of the first traders and trade in the Ancient, the Middle East, the Indian and medieval worlds, and in small business and large-scale money-lending, namely: the will and the wit to go after every possibility of profit regardless of the risk – 'to go through Hell for the sake of a profit even if it singes the sails'.[13] But this attitude is a long way away from what is peculiarly specific to *modern* capitalism in comparison to *other* capitalist eras – quite the reverse, for there is nothing specifically Jewish about either the modern economic *system* or modern economic *mentality* (*Wirtschaftsgesinnung*).

The main reasons for this relate to the particular 'pariah' character[14] of the Jewish people and its religion. First, there were simple external difficulties to taking part in the organization of industrial labour. The position of the Jews was legally as well as factually precarious and this supported trade and especially money-trading but not rationally organized production on a per-manent basis with fixed capital. Then there was the inner ethical situation. The Jews as a pariah people maintained a double standard in morality that in economic exchange is basic to every community. What is abhorred between brothers is permitted in relation to strangers. The Jewish ethic is undoubtedly traditionalistic in the obligation to sustain fellow Jews and, as correctly shown by Sombart, the rabbis made concessions for this that included business conduct between Jews. Those who availed themselves of these con-cessions to laxity fell short of the highest demands of the Jewish business ethic, and they certainly did not thereby 'prove' themselves.[15]

Behaviour towards strangers in business belongs to the sphere of the ethic-ally indifferent and includes things that between Jews would be frowned upon. This is the original business ethic across the world for all peoples and that it persisted for Jews is perfectly understandable, since already in Antiquity they regarded the stranger (*die Fremde*) almost everywhere as an

---

13 Weber is quoting the anecdote of a Dutch sea captain; see *PESC*, p. 57.
14 The pariahs were the Indian untouchables, who existed outside the caste system. The reference is not direct but is used as an analogy. Weber's usage includes endogamy – the prohibition against marrying outside Jewish ethnicity, lack of independent political power, social discrimination, and a distinctive economic role. See *Rel*, pp. 108–9.
15 Weber refers back, briefly, to his Puritan argument. Puritan grace was affirmed by business success. Jewish business success on the contrary could be achieved by benefiting from the right to sustenance from fellow Jews.

'enemy'. All the well-known admonishments of the rabbis to trust and faith, and which were applicable to strangers, did not make any impression on the real situation where the [religious] Law forbade charging interest for Jews but permitted it for strangers. As Sombart has correctly stressed, there was less legal prohibition (for example, benefiting from the mistakes of other people) in relation to the stranger, who was seen as an enemy. And it requires no proof to show (and its opposite would be simply unbelievable) that a people, placed in a pariah situation through the promises of Jahwe and the resulting contempt of outsiders, could only react by operating a business ethic that was consistently different for trade with strangers than with fellow Jews.

Differing position of Catholics, Jews, and Puritans to economic life

Summarizing the contrasting situation of Catholics, Jews, and Puritans in relation to economic activity: The devout Catholic in the pursuit of his business life found himself continuously infringing or reaching the limits of papal authority. His behaviour was in part ignored in the confessional on the grounds that that is the way the world is (*rebus sic stantibus*) and it was permitted because of a lax (probabilistic) morality;[16] his behaviour was seen in part as dubious and in part, at the very least, as not pleasing to God. The pious Jew found himself unavoidably doing things that were directly against the Law, or were dubious, or permitted through very lax interpretation. His behaviour was allowed only with respect to strangers and was never endowed with a positive ethical evaluation; ethically, as an average form of wrongdoing, his behaviour was formally not against the Law, it was permitted by God, and regarded as ethically indifferent. This touches upon what have been taken to be the lower standards of legality of Jewish economic behaviour. That God crowned this with success could be taken for a sign only that the Jewish businessman had not done anything directly forbidden and that he had followed God's commandments in other areas. What he could not do was to ethically affirm himself through modern business activity.

This was exactly what the pious Puritan could do. He was not subject to a relaxed interpretation or a double standard in morality, nor through his ethical indifference did he do something dubious in an area that had proper ethical standards. The situation was exactly the reverse. With a perfectly clear conscience and to the extent that he could legally and unemotionally objectify the rational approach of his whole way of life in 'work' ('*Betrieb*'), the Puritan legitimated his behaviour in his own eyes and in the circle of his community; and because this legitimation was absolute and not relative his

---

16 The Catholic businessman, for example, by charging rates of interest, which were forbidden in the Bible as usury, *might* be committing a sin. Weber is saying there were no clear and fixed rules as to what was morally permissible in business.

behaviour stood beyond any reproach. No really pious Puritan – and this is the point – could have obtained a profit pleasing in the sight of God from lending at high interest rates, taking advantage of the other party's mistakes (which was permissible for Jews), dealing and haggling, and through earning money from political and colonial robbery (*Raubverdienst*). The Quakers and the Baptists have attributed their reliability to others through their fixed price and unconditionally legal business conduct untainted by any greed, so much so that the godless bought from them rather than their own and likewise entrusted their money for safekeeping and investment with them. This made the Quakers and Baptists rich and these same qualities have affirmed them before their God.

The Puritan reacted with disgust to the petty-minded grasping business mentality of the Jew that was allowed by the Law, despite many reservations in regard to the stranger, and that in practice was the law of the pariah. Yet this same mentality in the pious Jew was fully compatible with strict legality, complete observance of the Law, the inner sense of God in his religiosity, and the most selfless love of those who were bound to him by family and through community as well as pity and gentleness towards all of God's creatures. What was permitted towards strangers in business was never held to be equivalent to the practical life of Jewish religiousness, in which the genuineness of obedience to God's commands was confirmed. The pious Jew has never measured the internal standard of his ethic against what he held permissible in business. But just like the Confucian gentleman who developed himself ceremonially and aesthetically and who for his whole life had studied the literary classics, so the Jew, informed by the casuistry of Law and knowledge of the texts, has found his real ideal in the 'intellectual' – always researching the holy texts and commentaries and at the expense of his business, which he very often entrusts to his wife.

It was exactly this intellectualist and scholarly textualism of the genuine late Judaism against which Jesus rebelled. It is not Jesus' 'proletarian' instincts, which have been read into him, but the manner of his faith and the degree of observance of the Law appropriate to the small townsman and peasant artisan that stands in contrast to the virtuosi who know the Law and have grown up in the city environment (*polis*)[17] of Jerusalem. It is the latter class who like every inhabitant of the great cities of Antiquity pose the question, 'What possible good can come from Nazareth?'[18] Jesus' observance and knowledge of the Law accords with the average for a practical working person, who even on the Sabbath cannot leave a sheep lying in a well. The knowledge of Jewish Law demanded for the truly religious, and already present in the education of youth, far outstripped, both quantitatively and

---

17 Weber uses the Greek word for city, indicating Jerusalem's political community.
18 Nazareth was the small country town where Jesus was brought up. The quote comes from the New Testament, John, 1, 46.

qualitatively, that of the Puritan's knowledge of the Bible. Jewish knowledge can only be compared with the Indians' and Persians' knowledge of the ritual laws, and even then it has a far greater reach covering not only norms attached to rituals and taboos but ethical commands as well ...

Self-control and religion in Judaism and Puritanism

The workings of the Law and the effects of intellectual education in the Law result in the Jewish 'methodical' approach to life and its 'rationalism'. 'A person should never change a practice' is a fundamental tenet of the Talmud. The sole gap in this tradition was the (relatively) ethically irrelevant area of economic trade with strangers, but nothing else. In this tradition and its casuistry everything is relevant before God. There is no rational, self-oriented instrumental action derivable without any presupposition from 'natural law'. The 'rationalizing' effect of fear of the Law is ubiquitous and penetrating but indirect in its effect.

'Watchfulness', accompanied by continual self-control and equability, is also an attribute of the Confucian, the Puritan, the Buddhist and every sort of monk, the Arabic sheik and the Roman senator. But the basis and sense of self-control for each is different. The watchful self-control of the Puritan results from the necessity of subjugating his animal impulses under rational order and method in the interests of certainty of salvation. The Confucian's self-control is the product of a classical education resulting in manners and dignity and a contempt for uncouth irrationality. That of the religious Jew from the Ancient period stems from brooding over the Law, in which his intellect is trained, and the continuous preoccupation with its exact observance. This in its turn was coloured and affected by the consciousness of the religious Jew that only he and his people possess this Law and for this reason he was persecuted and insulted by everyone. Yet at the same time the Law was obligatory and a day would come – overnight, nobody knew when, and nothing could be done to hasten it – when the hierarchical order of the world would be turned upside down and a messianic realm created for those who have kept faith in all things with the Law. The pious Jew knew that innumerable generations have waited, and still wait, defiant of all mockery. He does so with an over-watchfulness, which is a product of the necessity that the longer he is forced to wait probably in vain, the more he feeds his own self-esteem through a meticulous observance of the Law for its own sake. Finally, and not least, he has to be on his guard and never give free rein to his passions even against superior and merciless enemies. This was combined with effects of *ressentiment*[19] whose unavoidable impact stemmed from the promises of Yahweh and the unparalleled fate of a people who had sinned against him.

19 See above, p. 59.

The 'rationalism' of Judaism in its essentials was founded on these circumstances, but 'asceticism' was not. There are 'ascetic' sides to Judaism but they are not central to it; rather, they are partly a by-product of the Law, and partly they stem from the peculiar complex of Jewish piety. Asceticism is secondary to Judaism just as is everything connected with mysticism. Jewish mysticism, whether in its cabalistic, chasidic[20] or other forms, has provided no typical motive for the practical behaviour of Jewish economic activity, even though these forms held a symptomatic importance for Jews. For this reason the subject of Jewish mysticism will not be discussed.

The 'ascetic' turning away from the artistic was in lesser part due to the second commandment,[21] which summarily prevented the well-developed angelology[22] of the time from attaining artistic expression, and had more to do with the doctrines and commandments of the typical divine service in the synagogue (during the Diaspora long before the destruction of the Temple cult[23]). Hebrew prophecy had already removed the plastic[24] element of the cults and had effectively eradicated the orgiastic and the musical and dance elements. Religion in both Rome and Puritanism also went down this path, although for very different reasons. So, sculpture, painting, and drama never made the normal points of contact with religion. That (secular) lyricism and, in particular, the erotic sublimation of the sexual were in strong retreat in contrast to the strongly sensuous highpoint found in the Song of Songs,[25] was because of the naturalism of ethical behaviour in the sphere of sexuality in the Jewish religion.

The overall situation then is made up of two factors. On the one side there is the mute, faithful and questioning expectation of deliverance from the hellish existence of being, in spite of everything, chosen by God to be his elected people. This situation results in the continual emphasizing of the Law and the ancient promises. On the other side, the totally uninhibited surrender to the artistic and poetic transfiguration of the world must have appeared as highly vain and a deviation from the ways and purposes of the Lord (the relevant rabbinical sayings have not been preserved), and the purposes of creation had already on occasions become problematic from the

20 The cabala was a received set of Judaic doctrines that could only be spiritually divined within the sacred texts. It held that God was the space of the universe but the universe was not his space. Chasidic Jews were especially pious and worked against Syrian hellenization of the Jewish faith in the second century BC.
21 This prohibited the carving of images or likenesses of anything in heaven or on earth (Exodus, 20, 4).
22 The doctrine of angels.
23 The exile, or dispersion of the Jews, occurred around 600 BC. Jewish rulership and religion (in a reformed version that expelled pagan cults from the Temple) was restored in 445 BC.
24 For example, moulded figures of deities such as the calf.
25 Book of the Old Testament containing eight love songs.

later Maccabean period.[26] The defining characteristic of 'innerworldly asceticism' is quite simply missing; that is, a unified relationship to 'the world' from the vantage point of the certainty of salvation that feeds everything else. Instead it is the pariah character of Jewish religiosity and the promises of Yahwe that are ultimately decisive. Treating the world from the Calvinist standpoint of innerworldly asceticism was obviously the very last thing that would have come into the mind of a traditionally pious Jew. For him, the world was fundamentally wrong because of the sins of Israel, and no human action could compel or hasten what only a miraculous act of God could rectify; nor could the world and all of its sins, as a 'project' and a 'showcase' of his religious 'vocation', be forced to follow the rational norms of a revealed divine will for the glory of God and as a sign of his own election.

Jews and Puritans compared

Compared to the Puritan who through his 'election' was certain of his salvation in the life Beyond (*Jenseits*), the religious Jew had a far more difficult inner destiny to overcome. He had to resign himself to the existing state of the world as one not amenable to promises, so long as God so decided. If he were to follow the injunctions of the rabbis, he had to be satisfied, when God sent him grace and success in dealing with the enemies of his people, in treating them neutrally, with legality and even-handedness, and without love and without hate. . . .

Compared to Catholicism, the institutional provision of grace was far less developed after the decline of the ancient Palestinian confession (*theschuba*), and this independence and lack of mediation gave to the Jewish conduct of life something essentially more methodically individualistic and systematic than that of the average Catholic. The absence of the specifically Puritan ascetic motive and the, in principle, unbroken traditionalism of Jewish internal morality set a limit on being methodical. While there are numerous single motives for acting like an ascetic, what is lacking is the unifying framework of religion for the primary ascetic motive. The highest form of Jewish religiosity tends towards the side of 'mood' and not active behaviour. So, just why should the Jew feel himself to be the executor of God's will, installing a new rational order in a world that is fundamentally wrong, unresponsive to human action (as he has known since the time of Hadrian[27]), and alien to him? The Jewish freethinker can think like that but not the pious Jew.

26 Maccabean rule in the second and first century BC emphasized the independence of the Jewish nation from Syrian influence and the restoration of rabbinic Law. It had less to say about eschatology and the life hereafter.

27 A Roman Emperor who in AD 132 forbade Jews from entering Jerusalem. Hadrian marked a period of the complete hopelessness of Jewish revolt and the total subjection of Judea to Roman power.

Puritanism has always felt an inner affinity (*Verwandtschaft*) with Judaism; but also its limits. Despite fundamental differences, the affinity is principally the same as it had been for the Christian followers of Paul. For the Puritans as well as the early Christians, the Jews were always the people God had originally chosen. The actions of Paul were uniquely consequential for early Christianity. On the one hand, he made the Jewish sacred book into one of the sacred books – and at the time, the only book – of the Christians, and this erected a stout defence against the inroads of Hellenic (Gnostic) intellectualism (as Wernle in particular has pointed out[28]). On the other hand, with the aid of the dialectic that only a rabbi could possess, Paul here and there broke away from what was specific to Judaism and specific to the workings of Jewish 'Law', namely the taboo norms and the messianic promises. Paul triumphantly advanced the most impressive proof that the early patriarchs of Israel lived in accordance with God's will long before the enactment of those norms and by virtue of a strong faith, which was the surety of their being chosen by God, that they had been blessed.[29] Paul gave an enormous lift to those Jews escaping their pariah status through the awareness that they could be Greeks among Greeks even as they were Jews among Jews, and this could be achieved not through an enlightenment hostile to faith but within the paradox of faith itself. This passionate feeling of liberation is the driving force of the incomparable work of the Pauline mission. The Jew had been freed from the promises of God by a saviour who felt himself to be abandoned on the cross by the selfsame God.

There were a number of accompanying reactions to the breaking of the chains that bound the Jews to their pariah status: the Jews of the Diaspora bore a terrible hatred against this one man, Paul; the early Christian community exhibited indecisiveness and uncertainty; the attempt of James and the 'pillar apostles'[30] to construct a legal 'ethical minimum' that was universally binding in line with Jesus' own lay understanding of the Law; finally, there existed the open hostility of the Christian Jews to Judaism. In every line that Paul wrote we feel the overwhelming joy, which had been bought with the blood of the Messiah, for the emancipation from the hopeless 'law of slavery'.[31] In a similar way the Puritans rejected the Talmudic and the specifically Jewish ritual laws of the Old Testament, but they did accept other parts of it as the expression of the will of God. Although the extent of what they accepted varied, it was nevertheless binding, and individual parts were often combined with New Testament norms.

It is not so much the pious Orthodox Jews who have been accepted by the

---

28 P. Wernle, *The Origins of our Religion* (1901, trans. 1904).
29 This was the argument deployed by Paul in his letter to the Romans, 4, 9–13.
30 Five apostles of the community who agreed to spread the Christian faith. See Paul's letter to the Galatians, 2, 9.
31 The slavery of sin.

Puritan countries, especially America, but rather the Reformed Jews who have escaped from orthodoxy – to give a recent example, the pupils of the Educational Alliance and the baptised Jew have been completely accepted. This absorption occurred earlier without any fuss and despite everything is still relatively easy, so that now there is no trace of distinctiveness. In Germany, by contrast, the Jews even after many generations remain 'assimilated Jews'.[32] What this demonstrates is the real affinity of Puritanism with Judaism. But it is precisely what is not Jewish in Puritanism that has equipped the Puritan for his part in the development of economic attitudes, and also allowed the absorption of Jewish converts. This has not been achieved in countries which have a different religious orientation.

How Islam is 'adjusted' to the world

Islam is a late-comer to Near-Eastern monotheism. It is 'adjusted' to the world in a quite different sense and it has been strongly conditioned by Old Testament and Judaic-Christian motives. In its first period in Mecca, the eschatological religion of Mohammed was an urban-based conventicle that was Pietistic and turned its face away from the world. Next, in Medina, and then in the development of the early Islamic community, it was transformed into a national-Arabic and above all a status-group-oriented warrior religion. Those who converted to Islam were overwhelmingly drawn from the most powerful families and they were decisive for the success of the prophet. The injunction to fight a holy war did not have conversion as its primary aim; rather its aim was to elevate the social prestige of Islam to pre-eminence in this world by forcing other religions into a tribute role – 'until they (followers of alien religions of the book) humbly pay the tribute' (*jisyah*). The exaction of tribute in conjunction with the significance that war booty held in the ordinances, promises and particularly the expectations of Islam, even from its earliest period, marked Islam as a master religion (*Herrenreligion*), and, ultimately, its economic ethic was simply feudal. Already among the first generation the most pious were the wealthiest, or more exactly, they became richer than other members of the faith through the spoils of war.

Property, obtained from booty and political enrichment, and wealth in general play a role in Islam that is entirely contrary to the standpoint of Puritanism. The Islamic tradition depicts with delight rich clothes, perfume, and the meticulous coiffure of the beard. This is the complete opposite of the whole of the Puritan economic-ethic and corresponds to feudal conceptions of status. When some wealthy people appeared before Mohammed in ragged clothing, according to tradition, he said that if God had blessed a person with

32 The Educational Alliance was an organization whose aim was the Americanization of the European Jew.

property he would like to see 'its signs made visible to him'; or, as we would now say, a rich person is obliged 'to live up to his status'.

Mohammed's forceful rejection of asceticism and all monasticism (*rahbanija*) in the Koran may, insofar as it involved chastity, have had similar personal grounds to that of Luther whose well-known sayings expressed an earthy sensuous nature;[33] likewise in the Talmud is found the conviction that whoever is not married after a certain age must be a sinner. This rejection did not extend to each and every form of asceticism since Mohammed showed his respect for fasting, beggars, and penitents. But when a saying of the prophet called into question the character of those who abstain from meat for forty days, and when a recognized pillar of early Islam, celebrated by some as a Mahdi, in response to the question why he, in contrast to his father Ali, used hair lotion is alleged to have answered: 'in order to succeed with the ladies', then these cases stand uniquely in the hagiology of an ethical 'salvation religion'.[34]

But then Islam was never a salvation religion. The concept of 'salvation' in the ethical sense of the word is directly alien to it. Its god is unlimitedly powerful yet merciful, and the fulfilment of his commandments is within the capabilities of human beings. The rules of Islam are essentially political. They include the elimination of private feuds and concentrating forces to attack external foes, the regulation of legitimate sexual intercourse along the lines of strict patriarchalism and the disapproval of all forms of non-legitimate sex (although the rich were in fact sexually privileged through their keeping of slave concubines and the ease of divorce), the disapproval of usury, the payment of military taxes, and the obligation to support the poor. Alongside these rules are the essential duties which make Islam distinctive as a religion: the straightforward declaration of belief in one god and his prophet as the unique requirement of dogma, the pilgrimage to Mecca once in a lifetime, fasting in daylight hours during the month for fasting, weekly attendance at religious service and daily prayers. To these are added the rules for everyday life: the type of clothing (this prescription had economic con-sequences for newly converted savage tribes), and the avoidance of certain unclean foods, wine, and games of chance. (This last rule was important for the attitude towards speculative businesses.)

The individual search for salvation and mysticism was alien to early Islam, and wealth, power, and honour were promised in this life (*Diesseits*). These are warrior promises and the life hereafter (*Jenseits*) is a sensual soldier's paradise. Islam's original and genuine concept of sin has an orientation similar to feudalism. The prophet was subject to strong sensual passions and

---

33 See below, p. 237.
34 A reference to Muhammed b. al-Hanafiya (637–701) whose father was taken by some to be a Mahdi – an Islamic saviour figure. Weber's source here is Ignaz Goldziher, *Vorlesungen über den Islam*, Heidelberg, Carl Winter, 1910.

outbreaks of unprovoked anger, and his 'sinlessness' is a later theological construction that was foreign to him and not part of the Koran. Even after his move to Medina[35] he lacked any sense of 'the tragic' that comes from the feeling of sin. This last characteristic has persisted in Orthodox Islam, where sin is in part ritual impurity, in part religious sacrilege – i.e. polytheism (*shirk*),[36] in part disobedience of the explicit commands of the prophet, and in part the loss of status dignity through infractions of custom and propriety. Among the many characteristics of Islam's specifically feudal spirit are the acceptance of slavery and serfdom as natural, polygamy and the contempt and domestication of women, and a religion which is predominantly ritualistic, very simple in its demands, and even more modest in its ethical requirements.

Islam derived its enormous range, on the one hand, from its origins in theological-juristic casuistry and the schools of philosophy, some of which were enlightened, some Pietistic; on the other hand, from the infiltration of Persian sufism which had come from India and the formation of Dervish orders, which also had Indian influences and are still strong today.[37] These factors have stopped Islam moving any closer in key matters to Judaism and Christianity. The last two religions had a very specific urban and civic character, while the city had only a political importance for Islam. The type of official cult in Islam as well as its sexual and ritualistic demands could produce a degree of sobriety in the conduct of life. The *petite bourgeoisie* is to a large extent the carrier of Dervish religiosity that has been spread almost universally and with its continuously increasing power it has outstripped the official church religion. And this partly orgiastic, partly mystical and always extraordinary and irrational religiosity together with its official and thoroughly traditionalistic everyday ethic, which has been propagandistically so effective because of its great simplicity, has placed the conduct of life on lines that in effect run in an entirely different direction to that of Puritanism. Conduct in Puritanism and every other form of innerworldly asceticism is governed by the methodical control of life.

Islam in contrast to Judaism does not demand a comprehensive knowledge of the Law and it lacks the casuistic training of the mind that contributed to Judaic 'rationalism'. The warrior and not the man of letters is the Islamic ideal of religiosity. The patriarchal character of Jewish religiosity and everything else that has flowed from this was founded on the Messianic promises of a kingdom on earth and the meticulous fidelity to the Law in conjunction

---

35 Mohammed's legendary escape (the *hijra*) from Mecca to Medina occurred in AD 622.
36 *Shirk* is any lessening of the complete belief in Allah as the one true god.
37 Dervish orders were monastic brotherhoods of believers that proliferated after 1100. What the Indian influence would be is unclear, unless Weber is drawing a direct connection to the Indian fakir.

with the priestly teaching on history, election, sin, and the exile of Israel; this was absent in Islam.

But there were ascetic sects. Broad sections of the early Islamic warriors were characterized by a simplicity that from the start placed them in opposition to the Umayyad rulership. The Umayyad's cheerful enjoyment of the world was seen as a fall from the strict discipline of the fortified encampments, in which Umar had concentrated his Islamic forces in the conquered territories, and it was from here that the feudal aristocracy originated.[38] This was, however, the asceticism of a military encampment or of an order of warlike knights. It was not monastic, it did not possess the genuine middle-class asceticism with a systematic way of leading's one life; instead it prevailed only periodically and it was always liable to turn towards fatalism. The quite different outcome, which is bound to unfold in a situation of belief in providence, has already been discussed.[39] The infiltration of cults that revere saints and so, eventually, of magic has led in a direction completely contrary to the genuine methodical conduct of life.

The rejection of the world by ancient Buddhism

Standing opposite to what are effectively economic-innerworldly religious ethics is the most extreme ethic of world rejection, that of the concentrated mystical illumination of ancient Buddhism – in its genuine form as opposed to the completely altered versions of it in Tibetan, Chinese, and Japanese popular religion. This is an ethic that is also 'rational' in the sense that it controls all natural drives with a constant watchfulness, but it does so for an entirely different goal to that of innerworldly asceticism. It seeks salvation not from suffering and sin alone but from the transitoriness of life itself, and it searches for the release of eternal peace in place of the 'wheel' of karma causality. This is, and can only be, the most special work of the individual person. Predestination and divine grace are both absent and there is neither praying nor a religious service. Under karma causality there is a mechanism of cosmic reward that automatically sets premiums and punishments, proportionately and for a limited time period, for every good and bad act. So long as the thirst for life is a motivating factor, the individual will always enjoy a new human existence as a consequence of his actions whatever his previous situation – whether it was animalistic, heavenly, or hellish; the individual necessarily creates for himself new possibilities in the future. The noblest enthusiasm and the most sordid sensuality both contribute equally in this chain of individuation. (It is erroneous to talk of a 'transmigration of

38 Umar-al-Khattab (634–44) was the second successor (Caliph) to Mohammed and vastly extended Muslim rule in the Middle East. The Umayyad was the dynasty (661–750) that took over power from the Caliphs.
39 A reference to Calvinism, see *PESC*, pp. 98–128.

souls', for Buddhist metaphysics does not recognize the soul.) This process continues so long as the 'thirst' for life in this world and beyond is not completely eradicated and the individual struggles, impotently, for his own existence with all its illusions – none more so than believing in an integral soul and a 'personality'.

All instrumentally rational action as such is always a deviation from salvation, except for the inner activity, focused on contemplation, that removes the desire for the world from the soul. Salvation is granted only to the few, even of those who have decided to live without property, chastely, without work (for work is a purposeful activity) and so have to live from begging, and who wander the world restlessly and unceasingly outside the rainy season, cut off from all personal ties to family and the world. In fulfilment of the requirements of following the right path (Dharma) they are striving for the goal of mystical illumination. When this point is reached, which is accompanied by a deep joy and a tender feeling of a love without object, this represents the highest blessing on earth short of the eternal and dreamless sleep of Nirvana, a state that uniquely is subject to no further change. Aside from the few, all others may improve their chances in that future life if they follow the requirements of the Rule and refrain from major sins. According to karma causality, that future existence is the unavoidable result of a new individuation that follows on from the unbalanced ethical account and a thirst for life that has not been, so to speak, worked through or 'abreacted'.[40] When their life expires, true, eternal salvation inevitably remains closed to them.

There is simply no way to get from what is uniquely a really consistent position of world flight to any form of economic or rational social-ethic. The universal in Buddhism that extends its compassion to all of creation is the rational consequence of the common solidarity, established by karma causality, of all living and so transitory being; and psychologically, it is the product of a mystical, euphoric, universal, and acosmistic[41] feeling of love. These characteristics render it incapable of sustaining rational action and indeed lead in directly the opposite direction.

Buddhism belongs to the wider circle of salvation doctrines which both pre-date it and post-date it in large numbers. These doctrines were created by the intellectualism of high-class (*vornehm*) sections of the educated laity in India, and Buddhism is simply its most consistently developed version. The calm and proud emancipation of the individual, who frees himself from being in the world as such (*Dasein als solches*), meant that Buddhism could never become a salvation faith for the masses. Its effect beyond educated circles was tied to the tremendous prestige which the '*sramana*' (the ascetic) had always

---

40 The release of emotion. See below, p. 330.
41 An awkward but important term. Cosmic love would be divinely guided, for example, the love of God. *A*cosmic love has no such determination and is a diffuse love for all things, and is probably best regarded as a form of mysticism. See above, p. 67.

enjoyed and which was characterized by magic and human worship. As soon as it became a missionary 'people's religion', it accordingly transformed itself into a saviour religion based on karmic rewards in relation to hopes in the hereafter. These hopes were guaranteed by devotional techniques, cultic and sacramental grace, and acts of mercy, and as a popular religion it naturally inclined to purely magical ideas.

In India itself among the upper strata Buddhism succumbed to the existing salvation philosophy that underwent a renaissance under Vedic influences. Among the masses the competition came from Hinduistic saviour religions in the various forms of Visnuism,[42] tantristic magic and the orgiastic religion of the mysteries, and most of all the piousness of bhakti (the love of God). In the form of Lamaism,[43] Buddhism became a purely monastic religion whose religious power over the theocratically ruled laity was thoroughly magical in character. As Buddhism spread into East Asia, its essential character was very greatly changed, competing – and in many cases combining – with Chinese Taoism. In pointing beyond this-worldly life and the ancestor cults and by offering grace and salvation, it became the region's popular religion. But none of these forms of piety – whether Buddhist, Taoist, or Hindu – contained any impulse for the rational and methodical control of life. As already indicated,[44] Hinduism in line with its assumptions is the strongest traditionalistic power that can occur anywhere. This is because it provides the most consistent religious foundation for the 'organic' conception of society and the unconditional justification of the given state of affairs; the distribution of power and happiness follows a fixed mechanism of proportional compensation according to the guilt and merit of a person in a previous life.

Capitalism and the religions of civilization

All these Asiatic popular religions gave room to the 'acquisitive drive' of the shopkeeper as well as the sustenance needs of the artisan and the traditionalism of the peasant, alongside which they allowed philosophical speculation and the conventional status-oriented way of life of the privileged strata to go their own way. This was feudal in Japan, patrimonial-bureaucratic in China and so strongly utilitarian, and India retained a mixture of knightly, patrimonial, and intellectual characteristics. None of these religions could provide any motive or instruction for the *rational* and ethical forming of a creaturely 'world' according to divine commandments. Instead the world was taken as fixed and given, as the best of all possible worlds. For the most pious type, the only choice of ways was either to adapt oneself to the 'Tao' as the expression

---

42 Visnu is a major Hindu deity.
43 A Lama is a Tibetan spiritual teacher. Lamaism has been discontinued as a term for Tibetan monasticism.
44 See *Rel*, pp. 41–3.

of the impersonal order of the world and as the uniquely divine, or, directly conversely, to save oneself from the remorseless chain of causality through one's own act of passing into the one and only eternal, the dreamless sleep of Nirvana.

'*Capitalism*' has always existed in the lands of these religions, just as it did in occidental Antiquity and in the western Middle Ages. But there was no development *nor any sign* of it that was equivalent to *modern* capitalism; above all there was no 'capitalist spirit' in the sense that it was found in ascetic Protestantism. It would fly in the face of facts, if one wished to ascribe a lesser 'acquisitive drive' to the Indian, Chinese, or Islamic shopkeeper, artisan, or coolie than to the Protestant. Rather, the situation is the other way around: what is specific to Puritanism is the rational and ethical taming of the 'desire for profit'. Likewise there is no proof that the Asiatic people were less naturally gifted in technical and economic 'rationalism', and it is here that the distinction lies. All these people today import rationalism as a 'commodity' and take it to be the most important product of the West. What acts as a constraint upon them, just as it did with us in the Middle Ages, is not capability or will but rather fixed traditions. The reasons for this difference lie predominantly in religiosity, insofar as purely political conditions do not come into play (the internal structural forms of 'rulership').

It was only ascetic Protestantism that really put an end to magic, the quest for salvation through the supernatural, and in its highest form intellectualistic contemplative illumination. Ascetic Protestantism, in its concern with inner-worldly 'vocation' and in contrast to the strongly traditionalistic conception of occupation in Hinduism, created the religious motives to seek salvation through the methodical and *rationalized* fulfilment of occupational vocation. In Asiatic popular religiosity of all kinds, by contrast, the world remained a giant magic garden. The way to salvation was through revering or driving off the 'spirit', or through ritual, idolatry, and sacraments, by which means one oriented oneself practically and secured salvation in this world and the world hereafter. Just as there was no way through to a rational and methodical control of life in the adjustment to the world under Confucianism, the rejection of the world under Buddhism, the domination of the world under Islam, and the pariah hopes and pariah economic law of Judaism, this was also the case for the magical religiosity of the non-intellectual strata in Asia.

Early Christianity's complete indifference to the world

Magic and the belief in demons accompanied the birth of the second great religion, early *Christianity*, that in the specific sense was world-rejecting. Its saviour above all else was a magician, and magical charisma was an ever current support to his particular self-esteem. But Christianity's uniqueness is at once conditioned by the promises of Judaism, which are in comparison to other religions most distinctive, and the arrival of Jesus that occurred during a period of extreme messianic hopes. In addition, Christianity is influenced by the intellectualist and scripturalist learning of Jewish piousness of the highest order. The Christian gospel, in contrast, originated as a proclamation by a *non*-intellectual to non-intellectuals, to the 'spiritually poor'. Jesus interpreted and understood the 'Law', from which he did not want to remove a single letter, in the manner of the uneducated common people – the religious in the countryside and the small towns who adapted the Law to the demands of their occupations. The interpretation stood in contrast to that of the Hellenized nobility and the rich and to that of the casuistic virtuosity of the scholars and Pharisees. Jesus was mostly more relaxed about ritualistic prescriptions, especially the observance of the Sabbath, and in some regards, for example, the principles of divorce, he was stricter. And it appears that the Pauline view is anticipated, when the requirements of the Mosaic Law are indicated because of the sinfulness of the supposedly pious. In any case Jesus on occasions pointedly counter-posed his own commandments to those of the old tradition.

It is not Jesus' alleged 'proletarian instincts' that give him his special self-esteem – the knowledge that he is at one with the divine patriarch and that through him and through him alone lies the path to God.[45] Instead it is because he, who is untutored in scholarship, possesses the charisma of the power over demons and a tremendous ability to preach, whereas the scriptural scholars and the Pharisees do not have this gift. The ability to control demons operates only where the people believe in him. This belief, which gives him a miraculous and magical power, is lacking among the heathen in his home town, in his family, among the noble and the rich of the land, and among the scholars and the virtuosi of the Law. But among the poor, the oppressed, the tax-collectors, the sinners, and even among Roman soldiers are the people who believe in his powers and who, it should never be forgotten, are the decisive components of his messianic self-esteem. So his 'lament' is to be heard around the towns of Galilee,[46] just as is his angry curse of the stubborn fig-tree,[47] and so likewise the election of Israel as God's chosen people becomes for him ever more problematic, the significance of the Temple ever more doubtful, and the reproving of the Pharisees and the scriptural scholars more assured.

Jesus recognized two absolute 'mortal sins'. One was 'to sin against the spirit'. The scriptural scholars committed this and they were also contemptuous of charisma and its bearers. The other was to call one's brother a fool, for this was the unbrotherly disdain of the intellectual against the spiritually poor. This anti-intellectualism, seen in the reproof of Hellenic and rabbinical wisdom, is the only very specific element of social rank in his preaching. His

---

45 This final section starts as a critique of the view that Jesus was some kind of 'class warrior', as had been suggested by the Marxist Karl Kautsky. But then Weber turns to the new religious sensibility represented by Jesus' evangelism.

46 In Matthew, 11, 20–4, Jesus denounced the towns of Chorazin, Bethsaida, and Capernaum, where most of his miracles had been performed, for not believing in him.

47 In Mark, 11, Jesus curses a fig-tree that is not in fruit and it withers and dies.

message to Everyman and the weak should not be taken to be socially directed. It may be that their burden is light, but that is only possible for those who can be like children again. In truth his message involves formidable salvation challenges and in this sense it is aristocratic. Nothing lies further from Jesus' thinking than the universalism of divine grace. Jesus' message argues the opposite: *few* are selected to enter the narrow gates of heaven – only those who do penance and believe in him. It is God himself who hardens the hearts of the rest and makes them stubborn, and naturally it is the proud and the rich who undergo this fate.

In relation to other prophecies this was nothing new. In the light of the elevation of the great from this earth, ancient Judaic prophecy eventually saw the arrival of the Messiah as a king who enters Jerusalem on the beast of burden of the poor. There was no social prestige in this. Jesus ate with well-to-do people, who for the virtuosi of the Law are an abomination. Also the rich young man should only give away his wealth if he wished to be 'perfect', that is, to become a disciple. This assumed breaking all ties to the world, from family as well as from property, as was the case with Buddha and other similar prophets. But obviously the attachment to 'mammon' remains one of the most difficult obstacles to being able to enter the kingdom of God, although with God anything is possible. Wealth deflects from the attainment of religious salvation, on which everything depends.

Although this is not explicit, it is assumed that wealth leads to a lack of brotherliness. Jesus' message contains within it the original ethical obligation to help in emergencies that was part of the neighbourly ties of association of poor people. This unquestioned ethical belief is systematized into the religious attitude of brotherly love and becomes a 'universalistic' command that applies to everyone who is simply one's 'neighbour'.[48] The acosmistic paradox is intensified by way of the proposition that God alone can and will visit retribution. Unconditional forgiveness, giving without limit, unconditional love extending even to enemies, unreserved acceptance of injustice, and not to oppose evil with force – these demands on religious heroism could be the product of a mystically conditioned and non-cosmic love.[49] But it should not be overlooked, as it often is, that Jesus' ethic of

48 Weber places neighbour in inverted commas – '*Nächste*'. The conceptual move Weber is drawing out is between neighbourliness, which was originally a pre-religious ethic, and brotherly love. In the German language these two ideas are conjoined, for brotherly love translates as '*Nächsteliebe*'. Weber's original German here contains a number of his important ideas: 'Aber freilich ist alles "gesinnungsethisch" zur brüderlichen Liebesgesinnung systematisiert, dies Gebot "universalistisch" auf jeden, der jeweils gerade der "Nächste" ist, bezogen' (*WuG*, p. 380).

49 Brotherly love would seem to have three possible forms: (1) the original obligation to a neighbour in need, (2) the religious maxim that one should love one's neighbour like a brother, (3) undifferentiated love for the other is a component of mysticism. Mystic love is not divinely determined – it is *acosmic*. Jesus' teaching is paradoxical because he invokes mystical love and then salvation turns out to be dependent upon the judgement of a god.

brotherliness is placed alongside the Jewish idea of retribution; at some point God will reward or punish. This is not of man's doing and nor should a person publicize his own good deeds; otherwise he will forgo his own reward. In order to amass treasures in heaven, it is necessary to lend to those from whom one will perhaps get no return payment, otherwise there is no virtue in the action. The just equalization of fate is a theme that runs strongly through the story of Lazarus and in other passages; therefore, riches are a dangerous gift.[50]

In short, absolute indifference to the world and its affairs is crucial for salvation. The kingdom of heaven is a realm of joy on earth, without sin and suffering, that is close at hand, and the present generation will not pass on without seeing it. It will come like a thief in the night and its day is already dawning in the midst of mankind. One must be like a friend to the injustice of Mammon instead of clinging on to wealth. One renders unto Caesar what is due, for why should one care about such things? One prays to God for one's daily bread and takes no thought for the following day. No human action can advance the coming of the kingdom of heaven, but one does prepare oneself for its arrival.[51] While the above does not mean the formal abolition of the Law, it does show how everything now turns on the manner of one's beliefs. The entire contents of the Law and the prophets are now identified with love of God and brotherly love, and to this is added the far-ranging proposition that the authentic conviction is to be recognized through its fruits and so in its affirmation.

A number of consequences followed on from the visions of resurrection, which to be sure were already under the influence of widely spread salvation myths. There was a tremendous outpouring of charismatic spiritualism and the building of communities, at the head of which was Jesus' own, at first unbelieving, family. Paul's conversion was extremely significant since it smashed the pariah religiosity while maintaining continuity with the old prophecy. Finally there were the Christian missions among the heathen. What remained important for the position of the Christian communities in the missionary lands in their attitude to the world was, first, the expectation of the Second Coming, and second, the overwhelming significance of charismatic gifts of the 'spirit'. The world remains as it is until the coming of the Lord. The individual remains in his position and in his occupational 'calling' (*klesis*),[52] subordinated to authority, unless it commands him to commit a sin.

50 Lazarus was a poor man who attained heaven and he is contrasted to a rich man who is condemned to hell for his selfishness. See Luke, 16, 19–31.
51 These are all sayings of Jesus as reported in the New Testament.
52 St Paul's Christian message was not status-group-specific but open to all. So, in his letter to the Corinthians (7, 20) 'Everyone should remain in the condition in which he was called'.

5 Prefatory remarks to the Collected Essays in the Sociology of Religion[1]

A product of modern European civilization (*Kulturwelt*), studying any problem of universal history, is bound to ask himself to what combination of circumstances the fact should be attributed that in Western civilization, and in Western civilization only, cultural phenomena have appeared which (as we like to think) lie in a line of development having *universal* significance and validity.

Only in the West (*Okzident*) does *science* exist at a stage of development which we recognize to-day as valid. Empirical knowledge, reflection on problems of the world and of life, philosophical and theological wisdom of the most profound sort, are not confined to it, though in the case of the last the full development of a systematic theology must be credited to Christianity under the influence of Hellenism, since there were only fragments in Islam and in a few Indian sects. In short, knowledge and observation of great refinement (*Sublimierung*) have existed elsewhere, above all in India, China, Babylonia, Egypt. But in Babylonia and elsewhere astronomy lacked – which makes its development all the more astounding – the mathematical foundation which it first received from the Greeks. The Indian geometry had no rational proof; that was another product of the Greek intellect, also the creator of mechanics and physics. The Indian natural sciences, though well developed in observation, lacked the method of experiment, which was, apart from beginnings in antiquity, essentially a product of the Renaissance, as was the modern laboratory. Hence medicine, especially in India, though highly developed in empirical technique, lacked a biological and particularly a biochemical foundation. A rational chemistry has been absent from all areas of culture except the West.

The highly developed historical scholarship of China did not have the method of Thucydides. Machiavelli, it is true, had predecessors in India; but all Asiatic political thought was lacking in a systematic method comparable to that of Aristotle, and, indeed, in the possession of rational concepts. Not all the anticipations in India (School of Mimamsa), nor the extensive codification especially in the Near East, nor all the Indian and other books of law, had the strictly systematic forms of thought, so essential to a rational

---

1 Taken from *PESC*, pp. 13–31.

jurisprudence, of the Roman law and of the Western law under its influence. A structure like the canon law is known only to the West.

A similar statement is true of art. The musical ear of other peoples has probably been even more sensitively developed than our own, certainly not less so. Polyphonic music of various kinds has been widely distributed over the earth. The co-operation of a number of instruments and also the singing of parts (*Diskantieren*) have existed elsewhere. All our rational tone intervals have also been known and calculated elsewhere. But rational harmonious music, both counterpoint and harmony, formation of the tone material on the basis of three triads with the harmonic third; our chromatics and enharmonics, not interpreted in terms of distance, but, since the Renaissance, of harmony; our orchestra, with its string quartet as a nucleus, and the organization of ensembles of wind instruments; our bass accompaniment; our system of notation, which has made possible the composition and production of modern musical works, and thus their very survival; our sonatas, symphonies, operas; and finally, as means to all these, our fundamental instruments, the organ, piano, violin, etc.; all these things are known only in the Occident, although programme music, tone poetry, alteration of tones and chromatics, have existed in various musical traditions as means of expression.

In architecture, pointed arches have been used elsewhere as a means of decoration, in antiquity and in Asia; presumably the combination of pointed arch and cross-arched vault was not unknown in the Orient. But the rational use of the Gothic vault as a means of distributing pressure and of roofing spaces of all forms, and above all as the constructive principle of great monumental buildings and the foundation of a *style* extending to sculpture and painting, such as that created by our Middle Ages, does not occur elsewhere. The technical basis of our architecture came from the Orient. But the Orient lacked that solution of the problem of the dome and that type of classic rationalization of all art – in painting by the rational utilization of lines and spatial perspective – which the Renaissance created for us. There was printing in China. But a printed literature, designed *only* for print and only possible through it, and, above all, the Press and periodicals, have appeared only in the Occident. Institutions of higher education of all possible types, even some superficially similar to our universities, or at least academies, have existed (China, Islam). But a rational, systematic, and specialized pursuit of science, with trained and specialized personnel (*Fachmenschentum*), has only existed in the West in a sense at all approaching its present dominant place in our culture. Above all is this true of the trained official, the pillar of both the modern State and of the economic life of the West. He forms a type of which there have heretofore only been suggestions, which have never remotely approached its present importance for the social order. Of course the 'official', even the specialized official, is a very old constituent of the most various societies. But no country and no age has ever experienced, in the same sense as the modern Occident, the absolute and complete dependence of its whole existence, of the political, technical, and economic conditions of its life, on a specially trained *organization* of officials. The most important functions of the everyday life of society have come to be in the hands of technically, commercially, and above all legally trained government officials.

Organization of political and social groups in feudal classes has been common. But even the feudal state (Ständestaat) of *rex et regnum* in the Western sense has only been known to our culture. Even more are parliaments of periodically elected representatives, with government by demagogues and party leaders as ministers responsible to the parliaments, peculiar to us, although there have, of course, been parties, in the sense of organizations for exerting influence and gaining control of political power, all over the world. In fact, the State itself, in the sense of a political institution (*Anstalt*) with a rational, written constitution, rationally ordained law, and an administration bound to rational rules or laws, administered by *trained* officials, is known, in this combination of characteristics, only in the Occident, despite all other approaches to it.

And the same is true of the most fateful force in our modern life, *capitalism*. The impulse to acquisition, pursuit of gain, of money, of the greatest possible amount of money, has in itself nothing to do with capitalism. This impulse exists and has existed among waiters, physicians, coachmen, artists, prostitutes, dishonest officials, soldiers, brigands, crusaders, gamblers, and beggars. One may say that it has been common to all sorts and conditions of men at all times and in all countries of the earth, wherever the objective possibility of it is or has been given. It should be taught in the kindergarten of cultural history that this naïve idea of capitalism must be given up once and for all. Unlimited greed for gain is not in the least identical with capitalism, and is still less its spirit. Capitalism *may* even be identical with the restraint, or at least a rational tempering, of this irrational impulse. But capitalism is identical with the pursuit of profit, and forever *renewed* profit, by means of continuous, rational, capitalistic enterprise. For it must be so: in a wholly capitalistic order of society, an individual capitalistic enterprise which did not take advantage of its opportunities for profit-making would be doomed to extinction.

Let us now define our terms somewhat more carefully than is generally done. We will define a capitalistic economic action as one which rests on the expectation of profit by the utilization of opportunities for *exchange*, that is on (formally) *peaceful* chances of profit. Acquisition by force (formally and actually) follows its own particular laws, and it is not expedient, however little one can forbid this, to place it in the same category with action which is, in the last analysis, oriented to profits from exchange.[2]

2 [Weber] Here, as on some other points, I differ from our honoured master, Lujo Brentano (in his work to be cited later). Chiefly in regard to terminology, but also on questions of fact. It does not seem to me expedient to bring such different things as acquisition of booty and

Where capitalistic acquisition is rationally pursued, the corresponding action is adjusted to calculations in terms of capital. This means that the action is adapted to a systematic utilization of goods or personal services as means of acquisition in such a way that, at the close of a business period, the balance of the enterprise in money assets (or, in the case of a continuous enterprise, the periodically estimated money value of assets) exceeds the capital, i.e. the estimated value of the material means of production used for acquisition in exchange. It makes no difference whether it involves a quantity of goods entrusted *in natura* [in kind] to a travelling merchant, the proceeds of which may consist in other goods *in natura* acquired by trade, or whether it involves a manufacturing enterprise, the assets of which consist of buildings, machinery, cash, raw materials, partly and wholly manufactured goods, which are balanced against liabilities. The important fact is always that a *calculation* of capital in terms of money is made, whether by modern book-keeping methods or in any other way, however primitive and crude. Everything is done in terms of balances: at the beginning of the enterprise an initial balance, before every individual decision a calculation to ascertain its probable profitableness, and at the end a final balance to ascertain how much profit has been made. For instance, the initial balance of a *commenda*[3] transaction would determine an agreed money value of the assets put into it (so far as they were not in money form already), and a final balance would form the estimate on which to base the distribution of profit and loss at the end. So far as the transactions are rational, calculation underlies every single action of the partners. That a really accurate calculation or estimate may not exist, that the procedure is pure guess-work, or simply traditional and conventional, happens even to-day in every form of capitalistic enterprise where the

---

acquisition by management of a factory together under the same category; still less to designate every tendency to the acquisition of money as the spirit of capitalism as against other types of acquisition. The second sacrifices all precision of concepts, and the first the possibility of clarifying the specific difference between Occidental capitalism and other forms. Also in Simmel's *Philosophie des Geldes* money economy and capitalism are too closely identified, to the detriment of his concrete analysis. In the writings of Werner Sombart, above all in the second edition of his most important work, *Der moderne Kapitalismus*, the *differentia specifica* of Occidental capitalism – at least from the view-point of my problem – the rational organization of labour, is strongly overshadowed by developmental factors which have been operative everywhere in the world.

3 [Parsons] *Commenda* was a form of mediæval trading association, entered into *ad hoc* for carrying out one sea voyage. A producer or exporter of goods turned them over to another who took them abroad (on a ship provided sometimes by one party, sometimes by the other) and sold them, receiving a share in the profits. The expenses of the voyage were divided between the two in agreed proportion, while the original shipper bore the risk. See Weber, 'Handelsgesellschaften im Mittelalter', *Gesammelte Aufsätze zur Sozial- und Wirtschaftsgeschichte*, pp. 323–8.

circumstances do not demand strict accuracy. But these are points affecting only the degree of *rationality* of capitalistic acquisition.

For the purpose of this conception all that matters is that an actual adaptation (*Orientierung*) of economic action to a comparison of money income with money expenses takes place, no matter how primitive the form. Now in this sense capitalism and capitalistic enterprises, even with a considerable rationalization of capitalistic calculation, have existed in all civilized countries of the earth, so far as economic documents permit us to judge. In China, India, Babylon, Egypt, Mediterranean antiquity, and the Middle Ages, as well as in modern times. These were not merely isolated ventures, but economic enterprises which were entirely dependent on the continual renewal of capitalistic undertakings, and even continuous operations. However, trade especially was for a long time not continuous like our own, but consisted essentially in a series of individual undertakings. Only gradually did the activities of even the large merchants acquire an inner cohesion (with branch organizations, etc.). In any case, the capitalistic enterprise and the capitalistic entrepreneur, not only as occasional but as regular entrepreneurs, are very old and were very widespread.

Now, however, the Occident has developed capitalism both to a quantitative extent, and (carrying this quantitative development) in types, forms, and directions which have never existed elsewhere. All over the world there have been merchants, wholesale and retail, local and engaged in foreign trade. Loans of all kinds have been made, and there have been banks with the most various functions, at least comparable to ours of, say, the sixteenth century. Sea loans,[4] *commenda*, and transactions and associations similar to the *Kommanditgesellschaft*,[5] have all been widespread, even as continuous businesses. Whenever money finances of public bodies have existed, money-lenders have appeared, as in Babylon, Hellas, India, China, Rome. They have financed wars and piracy, contracts and building operations of all sorts. In overseas policy they have functioned as colonial entrepreneurs, as planters with slaves, or directly or indirectly forced labour, and have farmed domains, offices, and, above all, taxes. They have financed party leaders in elections and *condottieri* in civil wars. And, finally, they have been speculators in chances for pecuniary gain of all kinds. This kind of entrepreneur, the capitalistic *adventurer*, has existed everywhere. With the exception of trade and credit and banking

4 [Parsons] The sea loan, used in maritime commerce in the Middle Ages, was 'a method of insuring against the risks of the sea without violating the prohibitions against usury. . . . When certain risky maritime ventures were to be undertaken, a certain sum . . . was obtained for the cargo belonging to such and such a person or capitalist. If the ship was lost, no repayment was exacted by the lender; if it reached port safely, the borrower paid a considerable premium, sometimes 50 per cent' (Henri Sée, *Modern Capitalism*, p. 189).
5 [Parsons] A form of company between the partnership and the limited liability corporation. At least one of the participants is made liable without limit, while the others enjoy limitation of liability to the amount of their investment.

transactions, their activities were predominantly of an irrational and speculative character, or directed to acquisition by force, above all the acquisition of booty, whether directly in war or in the form of continuous fiscal booty by exploitation of subjects.

The capitalism of promoters, large-scale speculators, concession hunters, and much modern financial capitalism even in peace time, but, above all, the capitalism especially concerned with exploiting wars, bears this stamp even in modern Western countries, and some, but only some, parts of large-scale international trade are closely related to it, to-day as always.

But in modern times the Occident has developed, in addition to this, a very different form of capitalism which has appeared nowhere else: the rational capitalistic organization of (formally) *free labour*. Only suggestions of it are found elsewhere. Even the organization of *unfree* labour reached a considerable degree of rationality only on plantations and to a very limited extent in the *ergasteria* of antiquity. In the manors, manorial workshops, and domestic industries on estates with serf labour it was probably somewhat less developed. Even real domestic industries with free labour have definitely been proved to have existed in only a few isolated cases outside the Occident. The frequent use of day labourers led in a very few cases – especially State monopolies, which are, however, very different from modern industrial organization – to manufacturing organizations, but never to a rational organization of apprenticeship in the handicrafts like that of our Middle Ages.

Rational industrial organization, attuned to a regular market, and neither to political use of force nor irrationally speculative opportunities for profit, is not, however, the only peculiarity of Western capitalism. The modern rational organization of the capitalistic enterprise would not have been possible without two other important factors in its development: the separation of business from the household, which completely dominates modern economic life, and closely connected with it, rational book-keeping. A spatial separation of places of work from those of residence exists elsewhere, as in the Oriental bazaar and in the *ergasteria* of other cultures. The development of capitalistic associations with their own accounts is also found in the Far East, the Near East, and in antiquity. But compared to the modern independence of business enterprises, those are only small beginnings. The reason for this was particularly that the indispensable requisites for this independence, our rational business book-keeping and our legal separation of corporate from personal property, were entirely lacking, or had only begun to develop.[6]

---

6 [Weber] Naturally the difference cannot be conceived in absolute terms. The politically oriented capitalism (above all tax-farming) of Mediterranean and Oriental antiquity, and even of China and India, gave rise to rational, continuous enterprises whose book-keeping – though known to us only in pitiful fragments – probably had a rational character. Furthermore, the politically oriented adventurers' capitalism has been closely associated with rational bourgeois capitalism in the development of modern banks, which, including the Bank of England, have for the most part originated in transactions of a political nature, often

The tendency everywhere else was for acquisitive enterprises to arise as parts of a royal or manorial *household* (of the *oikos*), which is, as Rodbertus has perceived, with all its superficial similarity, a fundamentally different, even opposite, development.

However, all these peculiarities of Western capitalism have derived their significance in the last analysis only from their association with the capitalistic organization of labour. Even what is generally called commercialization, the development of negotiable securities and the rationalization of speculation, the exchanges, etc., is connected with it. For without the rational capitalistic organization of labour, all this, so far as it was possible at all, would have nothing like the same significance, above all for the social structure and all the specific problems of the modern Occident connected with it. Exact calculation – the basis of everything else – is only possible on a basis of free labour.

And just as, or rather because, the world has known no rational organization of labour outside the modern Occident, it has known no rational socialism. Of course, there has been an urban economy, food-supply policies within cities, mercantilism and welfare policies of princes, rationing, regulation of economic life, protectionism, and *laissez-faire* theories (as in China). The world has also known socialistic and communistic experiments of various sorts: family, religious, or military communism, State socialism (in Egypt), monopolistic cartels, and consumers' organizations. But although there have everywhere been urban market privileges, companies, guilds, and all sorts of legal differences between town and country, the concept of the 'citizen' has not existed outside the Occident, and that of the 'bourgeoisie' outside the modern Occident. Similarly, the 'proletariat' as a class could not exist, because there was no rational organization of *free labour as a business*. 'Class struggles' between creditor and debtor classes; landowners and the landless, serfs, or tenants; trading interests and consumers or landlords, have existed everywhere in various combinations. But even the Western mediæval struggles between putters-out and their workers exist elsewhere only in beginnings. The modern conflict of the large-scale industrial entrepreneur and free-wage labourers was entirely lacking. And thus there could be no such problems as those of socialism.

Hence in a universal history of culture the central problem for us is not, in

connected with war. The difference between the characters of Paterson, for instance – a typical promoter – and of the members of the directorate of the Bank who gave the keynote to its permanent policy, and very soon came to be known as the 'Puritan usurers of Grocers' Hall', is characteristic of it. Similarly, we have the aberration of the policy of this most solid bank at the time of the South Sea Bubble. Thus the two naturally shade off into each other. But the difference is there. The great promoters and financiers have no more created the rational organization of labour than – again in general and with individual exceptions – those other typical representatives of financial and political capitalism, the Jews. That was done, typically, by quite a different set of people.

the last analysis, even from a purely economic view-point, the development of capitalistic activity as such, differing in different cultures only in form: the adventurer type, or capitalism in trade, war, politics, or administration as sources of gain. It is rather the origin of this *bourgeois business* capitalism with its rational organization of *free labour*. Or in terms of cultural history, the problem is that of the origin of the Western bourgeois class and of its distinctiveness, a problem which is certainly closely connected with that of the origin of the capitalistic organization of labour, but is not quite the same thing. For the bourgeois (*Bürger*) in the sense of a status group existed prior to the development of the specifically modern form of capitalism, though, it is true, only in the Western hemisphere.

Now the specifically modern Western form of capitalism has been, at first sight, strongly influenced by the development of *technical* possibilities. Its rationality is to-day essentially dependent on the *calculability* of the most important technical factors. But this means fundamentally that it is dependent on the distinctiveness of modern science, especially the natural sciences based on mathematics and exact and rational experiment. On the other hand, the development of these sciences and of the technique resting upon them now receives important stimulation from these capitalistic interests in its practical economic application. It is true that the origin of Western science cannot be attributed to such interests. Calculation, even with decimals, and algebra have been carried on in India, where the decimal system was invented. But it was only made use of by developing capitalism in the West, while in India it led to no modern arithmetic or book-keeping. Neither was the origin of mathematics and mechanics determined by capitalistic interests. But the *technical* utilization of scientific knowledge, so important for the living conditions of the mass of people, was certainly encouraged by economic considerations, which were extremely favourable to it in the Occident. But this encouragement was derived from the distinctive character of the social structure (*Ordnung*) of the Occident. We must hence ask, from *what* parts of that structure was it derived, since not all of them have been of equal importance?

Among those of undoubted importance are the rational structures of law and of administration. For modern rational business capitalism (*Betriebskapitalismus*) has need, not only of the technical means of production, but of a calculable legal system and of administration in terms of formal rules. Without it adventurous and speculative trading capitalism and all sorts of politically determined capitalisms are possible, but no rational enterprise under individual initiative, with fixed capital and certainty of calculations. Such a legal system and such administration have been available for economic activity in a comparative state of legal and formalistic perfection *only* in the Occident. We must hence inquire where that law came from. Among other circumstances, capitalistic interests have in turn undoubtedly also helped, but by no means alone nor even principally, to prepare the way for the predominance in law and administration of a class of jurists specially trained in rational law. But these interests did not themselves create that law. Quite different forces were at work in this development. And why did not the capitalistic interests do the same in China or India? Why did not the scientific, the artistic, the political, or the economic development there enter upon that path of rationalization which is peculiar to the Occident?

For in all the above cases it is a question of the specific and distinctively formed rationalism of Western culture. Now by this term very different things may be understood, as the following discussion will repeatedly show. There is, for example, 'rationalization' of mystical contemplation, that is of an attitude which, viewed from other departments of life, is specifically 'irrational', just as much as there are rationalizations of economic life, of education, of warfare, of scientific research, of the provision of justice, and its administration. Furthermore, each one of these fields may be 'rationalized' in terms of very different ultimate values and ends, and what is 'rational' from one point of view may well be 'irrational' from another. Hence rationalizations of the most varied character have existed in various departments of life and in all areas of culture. To characterize their differences from the view-point of cultural history it is necessary to know what spheres of life are rationalized, and in what direction. It is hence our first concern to work out and to explain through its origins the special character of Occidental rationalism, and within this field that of the modern Occidental form. Every such attempt at explanation must, recognizing the fundamental importance of the economic factor, above all take account of the economic conditions. But at the same time the opposite causal relation must not be left out of consideration. For though the development of economic rationalism is partly dependent on rational technique and law, it is at the same time determined by the ability and disposition of men to adopt certain types of practical rational conduct (*Lebensführung*). When these types have been obstructed by spiritual obstacles, the development of rational economic conduct has also met serious inner resistance. The magical and religious forces, and the ethical ideas of duty based upon them, have in the past always been among the most important formative influences on the conduct of life. In the studies collected here we shall be concerned with these forces.[7]

Two older essays have been placed at the beginning which attempt, at one important point, to approach the side of the problem which is generally most difficult to grasp: the influence of certain religious beliefs on the development of an economic mentality, or the *ethos* of an economic system.[8] In this case we are dealing with the connection of the modern economic ethos with the rational ethics of ascetic Protestantism. Thus we treat here only *one* side of

---

7 Weber is referring to his comparative studies on the economic ethics of world religions. See above, Reading 3.
8 *The Protestant Ethic and the Spirit of Capitalism*, London, Routledge, 1992, and 'The Protestant Sects and the Spirit of Capitalism', *FMW*, pp. 302–22.

the causal relationship. The later studies on the Economic Ethics of the World Religions attempt, in the form of a survey of the relations of the most important religions to economic life and to the social stratification of their environment, to follow out *both* causal relationships, so far as it is necessary in order to find points of comparison with the Occidental development. For only in this way is it possible to attempt a causal *attribution* of those elements of the economic ethics of the Western religions which differentiate them from others, with a hope of attaining even a tolerable degree of approximation. Hence these studies do not claim to be complete analyses of cultures, however brief. On the contrary, in every culture they quite deliberately emphasize the elements in which it differs from Western civilization. They are, hence, definitely oriented to the problems which seem important for the understanding of Western culture from *this* view-point. With our object in view, any other procedure did not seem possible. But to avoid misunderstanding we must here lay special emphasis on the limitation of our purpose.

In another respect the uninitiated at least must be warned against exaggerating the importance of these investigations. The Sinologist, the Indologist, the Semitist, or the Egyptologist, will of course find no facts unknown to him. We only hope that he will find nothing definitely wrong in points that are essential. How far it has been possible to come as near this ideal as a non-specialist is able to do, the author cannot know. It is quite evident that anyone who is forced to rely on translations, and furthermore on the use and evaluation of monumental, documentary, or literary sources, has to rely himself on a specialist literature which is often highly controversial, and the merits of which he is unable to judge accurately. Such a writer must make modest claims for the value of his work. All the more so since the number of available translations of real sources (that is, inscriptions and documents) is, especially for China, still very small in comparison with what exists and is important. From all this follows the definitely *provisional* character of these studies, and especially of the parts dealing with Asia.[9] Only the specialist is entitled to a final judgment. And, naturally, it is only because expert studies with this special purpose and from this particular view-point have not hitherto been made, that the present ones have been written at all. They are destined to be superseded in a much more important sense than this can be said, as it can be, of all scientific work. But however objectionable it may be, such trespassing on other special fields cannot be avoided in comparative work. But one must take the consequences by resigning oneself to considerable doubts regarding the degree of one's success.

Fashion and the zeal of the *literati* would have us think that the specialist can to-day be spared, or degraded to a position subordinate to that of the seer. Almost all sciences owe something to dilettantes, often very valuable view-points. But dilettantism as a leading principle would be the end of

9 [Weber] The remains of my knowledge of Hebrew are also quite inadequate.

science. He who yearns for seeing should go to the cinema, though it will be offered to him copiously to-day in literary form in the present field of investigation also.[10] Nothing is farther from the intent of these thoroughly serious studies than such an attitude. And, I might add, whoever wants a sermon should go to a conventicle. The question of the relative value of the cultures which are compared here will not receive a single word. It is true that the path of human destiny cannot but appall him who surveys a section of it. But he will do well to keep his small personal commentaries to himself, as one does at the sight of the sea or of majestic mountains, unless he knows himself to be called and gifted to give them expression in artistic or prophetic form. In most other cases the voluminous talk about intuition does nothing but conceal a lack of perspective toward the object, which merits the same judgment as a similar lack of perspective toward men.

Some justification is needed for the fact that ethnographical material has not been utilized to anything like the extent which the value of its contributions naturally demands in any really thorough investigation, especially of Asiatic religions. This limitation has not only been imposed because human powers of work are restricted. This omission has also seemed to be permissible because we are here necessarily dealing with the religious ethics of the classes (*Schichten*) which were the culture-bearers of their respective countries. We are concerned with the influence which *their* conduct of life has had. Now it is quite true that this can only be completely known in all its details when the facts from ethnography and folk-lore have been compared with it. Hence we must expressly admit and emphasize that this is a gap to which the ethnographer will legitimately object. I hope to contribute something to the closing of this gap in a systematic study of the Sociology of Religion.[11] But such an undertaking would have transcended the limits of this investigation with its closely circumscribed purpose. It has been necessary to be content with bringing out the points of *comparison* with our Occidental religions as well as possible.

Finally, we may make a reference to the *anthropological* side of the problem. When we find again and again that, even in departments of life conduct apparently mutually independent, certain types of rationalization have developed in the Occident, and only there, it would be natural to suspect that the most important reason lay in differences of heredity. The author admits that he is inclined to think the importance of biological heredity very great. But in spite of the notable achievements of anthropological research, I see up

---

10 [Weber] I need hardly point out that this does not apply to attempts like that of Karl Jasper's (in his book *Psychologie der Weltanschauungen*, 1919), nor to Klages' *Charakterologie*, and similar studies which differ from our own in their point of departure. There is no space here for a criticism of them.

11 [Parsons] The only thing of this kind which Weber ever wrote is the section on 'Religionssoziologie' in his large work *Wirtschaft und Gesellschaft*. It was left unfinished by him and does not really close the gap satisfactorily. [See also above, p. 55 n. 1.]

to the present no way of exactly or even approximately measuring either the extent or, above all, the form of its influence on the development investigated here. It must be one of the tasks of sociological and historical investigation first to analyse all the influences and causal relationships which can satis-factorily be explained in terms of reactions to environmental conditions. Only then, and when comparative racial neurology and psychology shall have progressed beyond their present and in many ways very promising begin-nings, can we hope for even the probability of a satisfactory answer to that problem.[12] In the mean-time that condition seems to me not to exist, and an appeal to heredity would therefore involve a premature renunciation of the possibility of knowledge attainable now, and would shift the problem to factors (at present) still unknown.

12 [Weber] Some years ago an eminent psychiatrist expressed the same opinion to me.

Further reading

Since its first appearance in 1904–5 the Protestant ethic thesis has over successive scholarly generations accumulated an enormous literature. This was summarized in 1959 by Robert W. Green in *Protestantism and Capitalism. The Weber Thesis and Its Critics*, Lexington, MA, D.C. Heath, 1959. An updated reassessment was undertaken by Hartmut Lehmann and Guenther Roth in their *Weber's Protestant Ethic: Origins, Evidence, Contexts*, Cambridge, Cambridge University Press, 1993.

It is only very recently that Weber's own replies to his critics were translated into English, so providing a clearer definition of the thesis. See *The Protestant Ethic Debate*, edited by D.J. Chalcraft and A. Harrington, translated by A. Harrington and Mary Shields, Liverpool, Liverpool University Press, 2001.

It is, of course, vital for students to read *The Protestant Ethic and the Spirit of Capitalism* in its entirety. It is undoubtedly one of the classic books of the twentieth century and any reader quickly discovers that its contents and scholarship defy any easy summary. The short section provided in this reader is only a 'taster' and also has had to omit Weber's detailed historical footnotes. The book, which Weber referred to as an essay – meaning an exploratory investigation – can now be had in three English translations with a fourth and historical edition to be published by Oxford University Press and edited by Peter Ghosh. See also his 'Max Weber's Idea of "Puritanism": A Case Study in the Empirical Construction of the Protestant Ethic', *History of European Ideas*, 29, 2003, pp. 183–221. The first translation (1930) was done by Talcott Parsons and this still retains its authoritative status even though it is marred by inexactitudes (which have been amended for use in *The Essential Weber*); its original foreword by R.H. Tawney is still well worth reading. The book has appeared as a Penguin Classic in its 1905 version (Weber extensively re-edited it for its appearance in 1920 in *GARS*). The Penguin version, edited and translated by Peter Baehr and Gordon Wells, also carries Weber's replies to his critics, and is accompanied by an informative introduction and explanatory footnotes. The 1920 version has also received the same treatment in a new translation by Stephen Kalberg (Los Angeles, Roxbury, 2000). Both of these new translations also carry Weber's accompanying essay, 'The Protestant Sects and the Spirit of Capitalism' which is an application of the thesis to American conditions. It also develops Weber's crucial distinction between church and sect.

A useful short account of the Protestant ethic thesis is provided by Frank Parkin in Chapter 2 of his *Max Weber*, London, Routledge, 2002; likewise the presentation by Gianfranco Poggi, *Calvinism and the Capitalist Spirit: Max Weber's 'Protestant Ethic'*, London, Macmillan, 1983. A sociologically as well as historically attuned investigation of the thesis is provided by Gordon Marshall in *In Search of the Spirit of Capitalism. An Essay on Max Weber's Protestant Ethic Thesis*, London, Hutchinson, 1982.

Many studies have been inspired by Weber's work to undertake something similar, combining the analysis of structures, belief, action, and change. Among the many are Robert K. Merton, *Science, Technology and Society in Seventeenth Century England*, New York, Fertig, 2001 [1938]; also his 'Puritanism, Pietism and Science' in his *Social Theory and Social Structure*, Glencoe, IL, Free Press, 1957; Gordon Marshall, *Presbyteries and Profits. Calvinism and the Development of Capitalism in Scotland, 1560–1707*, Oxford, Clarendon Press, 1980; Robert N. Bellah, *Tokugawa Religion: The Cultural Roots of Modern Japan*, New York, Free Press, 1985 [1957]; Randall Collins, *Weberian Sociological Theory*, Cambridge, Cambridge University Press, 1986.

Weber himself indicates at several points that his approach and his ethnography will be vulnerable to the charge of what has come to be known as 'Europocentrism'. The challenge of the twenty-first century will be to see what Chinese, Japanese, Indian, and Islamic scholars will write about cultural and historical development and their perception of 'western rationalism'. This process is already underway, indicated by Mohammed Nafissi, 'Reframing Orientalism: Weber and Islam', in R. Schroeder (ed.), *Max Weber, Democracy and Modernization*, Basingstoke, Macmillan, 1998; also in the same volume, Wolfgang Schwentker has reported on the debates from Japan, 'Western Impact and Asian Values in Japan's Modernization: A Weberian Critique', pp. 166–81.

Weber's own writings in the field of historical and comparative sociology are numerous and they have all been translated into English. Unfortunately, there is no English entity equivalent to Weber's *Gesammelte Aufsätze zur Religionssoziologie* (Tübingen, Mohr Siebeck, 1920–1) but instead individual book-length studies of his essays on the world religions. Working through *GARS*, we have *The Protestant Ethic and the Spirit of Capitalism* and 'The Protestant Sects and the Spirit of Capitalism', already referenced above. These were followed by a section which Weber entitled 'The Economic Ethics of World Religions' and comprise, in order: *The Religion of China*, translated by Hans Gerth, New York, Free Press, 1951; *The Religion of India*, translated and edited by Hans Gerth and Don Martindale, New York, Free Press, 1958; and *Ancient Judaism*, translated and edited by Hans Gerth and Don Martindale, New York, Free Press, 1952. The whole collection was given an opening Foreword by Weber: 'Prefatory Remarks' which is included above as Reading 5 and appears in all translations of *PESC*.

Weber's first major comparative work on historical development in the Mediterranean basin is translated as *The Agrarian Sociology of Ancient Civilisations*, London, New Left Books, 1976. And Weber's doctoral dissertation on medieval trading companies in which he developed his thinking on risk and return and legal forms has recently been translated by Lutz Kaelber, *The History of Medieval Partnerships in the Middle Ages*, Lanham, MD, Rowman and Littlefield, 2003. Weber gave a course at the University of Munich in the winter semester 1919 to 1920 entitled 'Outline of Universal Social and Economic History'. A plausible manuscript was reconstructed using students' lecture notes, and this was translated by Frank H. Knight and published as *General Economic History*, London, Allen & Unwin, 1927.

Finally, there is Weber's *magnum opus*, *Economy and Society*, edited by Guenther Roth and Claus Wittich, New York, Bedminster Press, 1968. This work was not completed by Weber in his lifetime and its editorial history is a matter of significant dispute, affecting as it does our whole conception of Weber's project. Guenther Roth's 'Introduction' to the English edition should be read; also Hiroshi Orihara, 'From "a Torso with a Wrong Head" to "Five Disjointed Body-Parts without a Head". A Critique of the Editorial Policy for Max Weber Gesamtausgabe I/22', translated by Yoshiro Yano, *Max Weber Studies*, 3, 2, 2003, pp. 131–64.

Weber's 'Sociology of Music' has been translated, but much of the text is unreliable, and we will have to await the publication of the definitive German version, edited by Christoph Braun. Braun has outlined Weber's studies on music, 'The "Science of Reality" of Music History: On the Historical Background to Max Weber's Study of Music' translated by Mary Shields, in S. Whimster (ed.), *Max Weber and the Culture of Anarchy*, Basingstoke, Macmillan, 1999.

The wider field of Weber's comparative historical sociology is harder to chart, since many authors have been influenced by rather than followed Weber's line, and often this influence has provoked scholars to develop alternative approaches (most notably in the area of neo-evolutionary approaches). On the wider field of Weber's own historical studies, see the exposition by Reinhard Bendix, *Max Weber. An Intellectual Portrait*, New York, Doubleday, 1960. Ralph Schroeder's *Max Weber and the Sociology of Culture*, London, Sage, 1992, is a valuable introduction to the field and develops the concept of status groups as carriers of religious messages. The historian Wolfgang J. Mommsen has several lucid essays on Weber's historical and comparative method in his *The Political and Social Theory of Max Weber*, Cambridge, Polity Press, 1989. The author who has done most to analyse Weber's religious studies and historical method is Wolfgang Schluchter in his collection of essays, *Rationalism, Religion, and Domination. A Weberian Perspective*, translated by Neil Solomon, Berkeley, University of California Press, 1989. Bryan Turner has reconstructed Weber's scattered

writings on Islam and evaluated them in the light of contemporary under-
standings of Islam; see his *Weber and Islam. A Critical Study*, London,
Routledge, 1974. See also Turner's *For Weber. Essays on the Sociology of
Fate*, London, Routledge, 1981, which addresses a range of Weberian
topics. Also valuable is Toby E. Huff and Wolfgang Schluchter (eds), *Max
Weber and Islam*, New Brunswick, NJ, Transaction Publishers, 1999.

A number of aspects of Weber's interpretation of Judaism have been disputed, in particular his concept of a 'pariah' people. See Wolfgang Schluchter
(ed.), *Max Webers Studie über das antike Judentum*, Frankfurt, Suhrkamp,
1981. For a recent view on the historical differentiation of Judaism and early
Christianity, see Daniel Boyarin, *Dying for God. Martyrdom and the Making
of Christianity and Judaism*, Stanford, CA, Stanford University Press, 1999.

Rationalism and rationalization, while pervasive in Weber's writings, are
quite hard to pin down with conceptual rigour. The seminal article on rationality, rationalization and the role of religion in this process is Friedrich H.
Tenbruck, 'The Problem of Thematic Unity in the Works of Max Weber',
translated by S. Whimster, in *British Journal of Sociology*, 31, 3, 1980,
pp. 313–51. Also vital to this discussion is Wolfgang Schluchter's *The Rise of
Western Rationalism. Max Weber's Developmental History*, translated with
an introduction by Guenther Roth, Berkeley, University of California Press,
1981; also Guenther Roth, 'Rationalization in Max Weber's Developmental
History' in *Max Weber, Rationality and Modernity*, edited by Sam Whimster
and Scott Lash, London, Allen & Unwin, 1987. This book of readings has a
series of articles on the theme of rationalization: Wolfgang J. Mommsen
('Personal Conduct and Societal Change'), Wolfgang Schluchter ('Weber's
Sociology of Rationalism and Typology of Religious Rejections of the
World'), Pierre Bourdieu ('Legitimation and Structured Interests in Weber's
Sociology of Religion'), Johannes Weiss ('On the Irreversibility of Western
Rationalization and Max Weber's Alleged Fatalism'), Martin Albrow ('The
Applications of the Weberian Concept of Rationalization to Contemporary
Conditions'), and Jeffrey Alexander ('The Dialectic of Individuation and
Domination: Weber's Rationalization Theory and Beyond'). Stephen
Kalberg's *Max Weber's Historical Sociology*, Cambridge, Polity Press, 1994,
develops an account of historical sociology that remains faithful to Weber's
theory of social action (which is outlined in Part IV, below).

Finally, if it is accepted that Weber's overall project was to crystallize the
singularity of Western development, then other developmental trajectories to
modernity should be investigated. This is a new research agenda known as
'multiple modernities' and is associated with Bjorn Wittrock, S.N. Eisenstadt,
and Peter Wagner. See B. Wittrock, 'Modernity: One, None, or Many?
European Origins and Modernity as a Global Condition', *Daedalus*, 129, 1,
2000, pp. 31–60 and 'Social Theory and Global History: The Three Cultural
Crystallizations', *Thesis Eleven*, 65, 2001, pp. 27–50.

Part II

Structures of power and stratification

Introduction

Part II introduces the reader to some of the most well-known definitions in sociology which have become indispensable to our understanding of politics and society. In the first Reading Weber points out that his definitions of politics and power are in line with how we normally use these terms. Politics and the pursuit of a policy is a matter of controlling and directing a situation so that a desired aim is achieved. Power and domination, says Weber, 'is the possibility of imposing one's will upon the behaviour of other persons'. What is meant by the successful application of power is the ability to enforce it against the resistance of another person or group of people. Weber regarded the dimension of power as present in all social situations and relationships – whether in the state, the church, a social gathering, in a lecture room, or even in a personal (and erotic) relationship. Michel Foucault is the social theorist who has taken the universality of power furthest in his analysis. Weber accepts the pervasiveness of power and domination, but his main purpose is to analyse the distribution of power within societies.

His approach is often referred to as 'realist' and this means that he is not primarily interested in the constitutional forms of government or how societies may best be governed. (It should be noted, however, that outside his academic sociology he was very much involved in debates on the best form of national and democratic constitution.) Reading 6 (Politics and the State) contains his definition of the state: ultimately it is the supreme and legitimate controller of physical force within territorial boundaries. The state, says Weber, has a monopoly on the legitimate exercise of violence. Civil war or the unpoliced activity of criminal gangs represent situations where this monopoly has been broken. The long history of the modern state is the story of the acquisition of this monopoly against competitors.

Reading 7 (The Three Pure Types of Legitimate Rule) is an analysis of the main structures of power throughout history. While power, ultimately, can be backed up by the sanction of force and violence, stable forms of rulership rest upon the assent of those who are ruled. They believe, says Weber, in the legitimacy of the ruler. In broad comparative terms, this legitimacy rests on three grounds: (1) rulership is seen to rest on legal authority. As citizens of constitutional governments we assent to authority because its powers are based on procedures and institutions which have been legally enacted. (2) Rulership is based on traditional power and this involves subjects accepting rule because the king or chief has always exercised power. (3) Rulership is based on the belief in the charismatic powers of an individual person. For this to happen charisma has to be successfully demonstrated by magic, religious prophecy, or extraordinary military achievements or heroism.

Reading 7 contains an obvious but vital argument. Any exercise of power requires an administrating organization and staff. Weber uses the same term for this in the three types of rulership: a *Herrschaftsverband*, which means the group body that is formed or banded together to exercise rulership. Concretely, this could include a modern bureaucracy, an imperial court, or a warrior band. Whatever the organizational form of the exercise of power over the ruled, it is subject to a set of constraints and dynamics. The modern state and government could not possibly operate without a rationally organized bureaucracy, where the occupants of posts fit into a defined hierarchy, are professionally trained, their sphere of power is strictly defined, and administration is based on permanent office files. In traditional rulership a medieval king or Chinese emperor also requires some form of organization to enforce his power, but in these cases the type of legitimacy – here traditional – influences the organization or power structure. 'Officials' in China, the mandarins, as we have already seen in Part I, operate on principles of fixed custom and magic. The organization of rulership in early medieval Europe involved sharing power with feudal lords, a tradition based on personal allegiance and grants of land. By preference, traditional rulers use unfree servants who are totally dependent on them, and the extreme case of this is what Weber terms 'sultanism'. In charismatic rulership the structuring and organization of power is inherently problematic, because everything is dependent on the specific nature of the ruler's charisma. Charisma is the most irrational basis for the organization of rulership and the most unstable. Traditional legitimacy acquires stability through habituation, but is low on rationality because people are not prepared to think of new ways of exercising power and executing policies.

The exercise and holding on to power was an endless source of fascination to Max Weber. Reading 7 is one of six other versions on the same theme (see Further reading at the end of Part II). Like Machiavelli, he lived through a period of both the instability and the consolidation of power. In *The Prince*, Machiavelli advised his master on how best to outwit and outmanoeuvre his enemies. Both Weber and Machiavelli are concerned with the realities of power – just as much as a ruler wants to build up his power, so equally there are competitors in this process, and people and groups who will resist the claim to power. Legitimacy is a resource on which a ruler draws but which also determines the limits and organization of rulership. Legal, traditional, and charismatic legitimacies represent a typology for all rulerships. They are 'pure' because Weber has abstracted the underlying logical principles from a mass of historical material. The reader should be aware that while Reading 7 does have quite an abstract feel to it, it draws on Weber's extensive knowledge of comparative history.

The other issue, which is very much open to discussion, is the balance between universal history on the one side and historical development on the other. Weber, in this relatively short Reading, is discussing the modern state, the traditional state – whether in China, the Near East, or elsewhere, and charismatic rulership. He places them alongside each other for the purposes of comparison. For instance, charismatic rulership is mentioned in the context of both traditional rule and modern legal rule. According to Weber, a democracy can produce a charismatic ruler who is elected by the people as a whole (through a plebiscite); likewise rulers of empires display, or alternatively are seen to inherit, charismatic gifts. As a universal historian Weber is asking sociological questions about what is common to how power is secured against competition, exercised, undermined, and legitimated. Modern democratic government is not exempted from these dynamics, and it is worth noting that Weber is quite prepared to discuss democracy in America or Europe on the same terms as Periclean Athens (some 450 years BC), where democratic advance is linked intrinsically to demagoguery and the interests of different social classes.

Democratic regimes, just to be clear about this, do not have a category of legitimacy all of their own. Weber does not say that legal rulership is empowered by universal suffrage and a constitution based on human rights but that, compared to traditional and charismatic rule, many different sorts of rulership have in common the idea of enacted laws and rules (as opposed to charismatic pronouncement or the reverence before tradition). These differing sorts of regimes could therefore include absolutist rule, democratic constitutions, and – a possibility unknown to Weber – one-party communist or fascist regimes. The legality is procedural – it has been enacted, and this does not imply that its law is based on an underlying legitimacy derived from, say, moral universalism. In addition, it will be noted that Weber places enacted rule as a form of legitimacy common to organizations in both politics *and* business.

Reading 7 is the most uncompromising of Weber's formulation in respect of democratic rule. In *E&S* (pp. 215–23), his formulation adds in the concept of rationality, where enactment proceeds on rational grounds and so elicits acceptance and obedience. But this rationality describes procedure of enactment and the organization of rule, and has no implication of a deliberative reason. At the end of Reading 7 Weber does mention democratic legitimacy. Charismatic legitimacy which is almost always authoritarian can, says Weber, reverse this inequality of power. The 'voters' – those who assent or acclaim a leader – can make their recognition the basis of a democratic legitimacy.

Weber here is not in line with most accounts of the historical emergence of democratic constitutions. The legal legitimacy of rulership, therefore, should not in any sense be seen as exclusively directed at democratic rule. In the Further reading section to Part II, what may be termed the 'democratic deficit' in Weber's writings is discussed. What concerns Weber, however, is that aside from legitimacies rooted in the values of socialism, liberalism, or human rights, there always exists a rulership structure whose dynamics of power has to be addressed sociologically.

Against his 'neglect' of democratic legitimacy needs to be set his historical sociology of citizenship, which he regarded as fundamental to the emergence of the conditions of liberty in the West. His observations are widespread and difficult to excerpt, but taken together they point to the Greek polis and the political state made up of citizens, the medieval town commune as both an economic and political unit, and the rights of freedom of conscience established by Puritans as the basis of modern human rights. This issue is taken up in Further reading.

As a developmental historian, on the other hand, Weber makes a clear distinction between legal rulership and the other two types. The modern state originates in Europe for a range of specific reasons and over a very long period of time – and Weber's periodization of developments will be of great interest to historians. Under the ideal type of traditional rulership, Weber notes its running can be carried out by servants obedient to a patrimonial ruler, or rulership can operate through the feudal 'officials' who are nobles in their own right. The nobility constituted an 'estate' of the realm, along with the Church and the councils of town burghers. Western European history was especially marked by estatist rulership, which acted as a crucial counterweight to arbitrary rulership by a monarch. Another factor in European history was the employment of non-feudal and literate staff in certain, successful rulerships. For example, under the papacy of Innocent III or the Emperor Frederick II, a class of officials 'modernized' the medieval structures of power. The development of administrating apparatuses is sensitive to the type of official and this gives a developmental direction to a rulership: Brahmans, plebeian clerics, mandarins will all have a determinative effect, and in Europe, says Weber, it pushed rulership towards a more rational administration. Weber's reasoning here is directly analogous to his argument about the social carriers of religions (in Reading 3). There is also the link, established in Part I (see especially Reading 5), between the type of attitude a religion holds towards the world and the development of a rational attitude. In the West this rational attitude has a formative effect on the development of rational bureaucracy, which becomes the distinctive characteristic of the modern state, the modern business enterprise, and all complex organizations with purposive goals.

The reader will begin to notice that in the Readings in Part II Weber is committed to a different type of academic project than in Part I. There he was concerned with drawing out the main developmental drives of the different world religions, and in doing this he had to acknowledge that other factors such as history, geography and politics are all also going to exert different effects on a society's capacity to progress, regress, or remain stationary. Part II charts his enormous effort to analyse the effects of political and social structures on development *and* their interaction with the factors of religion.

There is also a further point to note. Most of the Readings in Part II are taken from his book *Economy and Society*. The overall purpose of this very large, almost encyclopedic work was to relate all the main forms of society – its law, its religion, its household structure, its political structures, its stratification – to the economy. In one obvious sense it may be thought of as a major challenge to Marx's attempt to derive and relate all social forms – what Marx called the superstructure of society – to its economic base. Marx sought to establish a predominantly one-way line of determination from the economic and class basis of all societies, so making their politics, religion, and law projections that derived ultimately from the material base of society. Weber, in reply, established comprehensively that there was always a two-way or reciprocal determination between the major forms of society and their economic provision and underpinning. Thus, throughout his analysis of political structures of rulership, there is another sub-argument concerned with how rulers support economically the various organizations that exercise power. Weber instances the interdependence of economy and rulership as follows:

> Even though the full development of a money economy is thus not an indispensable precondition for bureaucratization, bureaucracy as a *permanent* structure is tied to the presupposition of the availability of *continuous* revenues to maintain it. Where such income cannot be derived from private profits, as it is in the bureaucratic organization of modern enterprises, or from land rents, as in the manor, a stable system of *taxation* is the precondition for the permanent existence of bureaucratic administration. For well-known general reasons only a fully developed money economy offers a secure basis for such a taxation system. Hence the degree of administrative bureaucratization has in urban communities with fully developed money economies not infrequently been relatively greater than in the contemporaneous and much larger territorial states. As soon, however, as these states have been able to develop orderly systems of taxation, bureaucracy has there developed far more comprehensively than in the city states, where, whenever their size remained confined to moderate limits, the tendency for a plutocratic and collegial administration by notables has corresponded most adequately to the requirements.
>
> (*E&S*, pp. 968–9)

In Reading 8 (The Nation) and Reading 9 (The Belief in Common Ethnicity) we arrive at strong political and social ideas, but in sociological terms 'nation' and 'ethnicity' are quite weak concepts. Weber puts his finger on the problem when he says that the 'idea of the nation' (Weber uses inverted commas for the term) is a completely ambiguous concept when it comes to its sociological specification. A nation is not composed of one anthropological type of person, nor is it to be identified with just one language or one culture. When he wrote the passage on 'the nation' a few years before the outbreak of the First World War, Weber was able to draw upon the many examples of multicultural and multilingual political units, such as the Austro-Hungarian Empire. Nation is a derivative concept upon the state about which, as we know, he was much more categorical. Groups within a state, usually intellectuals, construct the idea of the special culture of the nation as a way of enhancing the prestige of the state. Reading 8 opens with a discussion of the way in which leading strata in imperial power structures seek to enhance their power with prestige. During the twentieth century the nation state has come to be regarded as the normal political unit in the world, but for Weber it is a compound of two separate dynamics: nation is based on an urge towards community whereas state is an associational process. The modern state is a matter of growing rationality and monopolization of power within a territory, but that territory is never the basis of a pre-given cultural homogeneity that would allow one to link the two concepts – nation and state.

Likewise in Reading 9, ethnicity is seen by Weber as not having any objective basis in society. 'Ethnic groups' (Weber's inverted commas), he says, 'entertain a subjective belief in the common descent', and these feelings of commonality are fostered by a common experience such as colonization or migration. Weber reverses the presumed sequence of ethnic identity as leading to a political association. Instead artificial distinctions, politically imposed, lead to the myth of a common ethnic descent; Weber gives the example, here, of the twelve tribes of Israel that was originally a politically imposed division on heterogeneous kinship relations. Shared identity rests on an underlying assumption of some kind of original consanguinity (related through blood). This is not objectively the case, but the myth is created for political, religious, status, and lifestyle reasons. The presumption of shared ethnic identity does, however, have clear sociological consequences in terms of political conflict between groups as well as antagonism between social groups.

In this connection Weber's position on race should be mentioned, and this predictably is in line with his position on the nation and ethnicity.

A much more problematic source of social action [than kinship] . . . is 'race identity': common inherited and inheritable traits that actually derive from common descent. Of course, race creates a 'group' only when it is subjectively perceived as a common trait: this happens only when a neighbourhood or the mere proximity of racially different persons is the basis of joint (mostly political) action, or conversely, when some common experiences of members of the same race are linked to some antagonism against members of an *obviously* different group. The resulting social action is usually merely negative: those who are obviously different are avoided and despised or, conversely, viewed with superstitious awe.

(*E&S*, p. 385)

Weber was writing during a period when there was an extensive 'scientific' programme in Northern European and American societies to maintain and improve what was called 'racial hygiene'. Weber strenuously protested against the use of the concept of race in sociology. 'With race theories you can prove and disprove anything you want', and therefore in social scientific terms it is a worthless concept. Weber made this point when race-based theories of society came up for discussion at the German Sociological Association in 1910. (For Weber's complete critique of 'race', see *E&S*, pp. 385–7.) For biological influences to be determinative on the formation of human groups, different 'races', argued Weber, would have to have some built-in repulsion against marrying into another 'racial' group. This would be very difficult to prove. Intermarriage does of course occur throughout history, and when it is forbidden, it is for reasons of social status and class and not ' "natural" racial antipathy'. Today, Weber's point could be formulated the other way round: inter 'racial' marriages occur not because of some socio-biological urge to diversify genetic inheritance but for cultural reasons of exoticism and fashionability. Whichever way round, this is a somewhat convoluted way of arguing against racial and biological theories. It is perhaps simpler to note that any choice of partner can be positively or negatively influenced by issues of status, culture, and social class.

Reading 10 (The Household Community) comes closest to outlining Weber's sociology of the household, but it will be noted that he quickly introduces a disclaimer saying that he is not writing a general sociology but only describing the connection between certain social groups (here the household) in their relation to the economy. Weber shows little interest in the nuclear family. Instead his comparative history leads him to explore every variety of relationship of parents to each other and their children and the types of household organization. The line between the smaller unit of the family is fluid between the larger kinship group of the clan and the sib. Referring back to Part I (Reading 2), the wider kinship group of the sib is one of the building blocks for his analysis of the dynamics of Chinese society. Weber's sociology is always searching out the linkages between institutions. So, in his history of the European household, the separating out of production from consumption within the household is of formative importance for the development of the modern business enterprise.

Reading 11 (Capitalism in Antiquity) demonstrates Weber's impressive grasp of comparative history which he combines with a clear line of reasoning. Weber discusses whether different forms of economic production belong exclusively to different types of society. Does the householding economy belong to the medieval city and the guilds? Does the factory belong to modern capitalism, and the *oikos* (a large household production and consumption unit) to the ancient world? This was a debate triggered by the economic historian Rodbertus, who operated with these fairly rigid types of distinctions. The classical historian, Eduard Meyer, argued on the contrary that the ancient world did in fact know forms of capitalism. Weber's conclusion is that where 'property is an object of trade and is utilized by individuals for profit-making enterprise in a market economy, there we have capitalism'. Capitalism, therefore, is not exclusive to the factory production of the modern era. There are, rather, different forms of capitalism throughout history.

However, as Part I has shown, Weber in his sociology of religion was trying to explain the emergence of *modern* capitalism. Its specification is spelt out in detail in Reading 5 (pp. 107–8): rational capitalism involves the calculation that the return on factors of production exceeds the capital outlay and that this process necessitates rational book-keeping. This is accompanied by the phenomena of continuous trade in markets, the use of (formally) free labour, and the separation of the household from the business enterprise. Reading 11 is an earlier formulation that reveals more of his thinking on the subject: different capitalist mentalities and the ways in which capitalisms are embedded in society.

Reading 12 (The Conditions of Maximum Formal Rationality of Capital Accounting) provides an even more detailed specification of the definition and the pre-conditions of the specifically modern, capitalistic enterprise – market freedom, autonomy of owners to select managers, labour contracted in a free market, non-interference by outside bodies in prices, the complete calculability of both technology and the behaviour of legal government, separation of the business enterprise from private and household budgetary units, and a formal monetary system. This is very much an ideal type. Contemporary capitalism now demonstrates a variety of forms which have moved a considerable distance away from the criteria that Weber specifies as rational. For example, the manipulation of book-keeping (accounts) and the adjustment of profitability in the interests of managers rather than major shareholders are empirical phenomena that fall very far short of the ideal type of the rational business enterprise. No doubt this loosening of rationality criteria would have greatly surprised him and goes against the thesis of the progressive rationalization of the world.

Reading 13 (Status Groups and Classes) and Reading 14 (The Distribution of Power in Society: Classes, Status Groups and Parties) are generally regarded as fundamental texts for the analysis of social stratification in societies. It is usually argued that while Marx based his analysis of inequality on class conflict, Weber modified this picture considerably by adding the sociological dimension of status groups and lifestyle. For this reason many introductions to Weber speak of his separating 'class, status, and power' into independent variables. In fact, Weber's theory of power is as radical as that of Marx. Where Marx speaks in comparative terms of modes of production, Weber offers in its place an equally universal account of the modalities of power. Readings 13 and 14 need to be placed within the wider framework of Weber's analysis of power. So far in Part II we have already noted that power is a pervasive phenomenon in all societies and social relationships. This position is restated in the opening sentences of Reading 14.

The structure of every legal order (not only the 'state') has a direct influence on the distribution of power, whether economic or of any other kind, within the community concerned. By 'power' we mean very generally the chances which a man or a group of men have to realize their will in a communal activity, even against the opposition of others taking part in it.

(p. 182 below)

We can think of this as follows. Within the legal (i.e. modern political) order, the economic order, and the social order there is a distribution of power which is almost always unequal. Within the political order we have already outlined the three types of rulership. Within the economic order there is a distribution of power along class lines. Within the social order there is a distribution of power in terms of status groups. In addition, there is the complex matter of how, in the overall distribution of power, the economic, the political, and the social orders interact with each other. One of the difficulties in comprehending Readings 13 and 14 is that Weber is extremely keen to explore and exemplify the *interactions* between the orders, and the fundamental organization of his thinking on the distribution of power in the various orders of society is not immediately apparent. But it is the latter that needs to be grasped by the reader, even if it means that the passages have to be read more than once. At the end of Reading 14, Weber clarifies his analysis.

'Classes' are properly at home in the economic order, 'status groups' in the social order, that is, in the sphere of distribution of status; starting from this point, both reciprocally influence each other and influence the legal order and are in turn influenced by it.

(p. 193 below)

Analytically, then, let us first treat class and the economic order, and then move on to status groups and the social order. Class, says Weber, is all the people in the same class situation in respect of two factors: (1) they either own property or they are propertyless, (2) they either have commercial skills to sell on the market or they have a lack of skills (i.e. differences in market opportunities). From (1) we can derive the class distinction between slave owners and slaves, or the distinction between manorial or feudal lords and unfree peasants. These are property classes – one side owns property, the other has no property. Typical of (2) are entrepreneurs who have the capability as merchants, shipowners, industrialists, bankers, or professionals to control the market for their services and to benefit from that control. The groups of people, or class, who do not benefit from the market for services and goods are the skilled, the semi-skilled, and unskilled workers. Thus Weber's analysis turns strictly on the positive or negative possession of economic capacities.

'*Social* classes' are defined by Weber by the forms of social interaction within the economically defined classes. Landowners form a social class if they accept one another socially and intermarry. Typical social classes (i.e. they move among themselves rather than between classes) are the working class, and the lower-middle class in modern capitalism. These social classes will, respectively, tend to live in the same areas, have the same social interests, and marry among themselves.

Social classes may be able to develop into class-conscious organizations, but only if four pre-conditions are met (see p. 179). The passage is an implicit criticism of the Marxist writer György Lukács, to whom Weber refers as a 'talented author' (Reading 14). Lukács was for a few years a research student in Heidelberg and befriended by Weber, but – to Weber's annoyance – took on a revolutionary role in Hungary in 1917. Lukács argued that by virtue of class interest alone (in Marxist terminology, the relation to the means of production, and in Weber's term, positively or negatively privileged in relation to property), a social class such as the proletariat will inevitably develop a class-consciousness. (Lukács' essays on the subject were later published in 1923 as *History and Class Consciousness*.)

Status groups concern the distribution of power in terms of positive or negative social values within the social order. A status group is marked out by a distinctive style of life that separates it from other social strata in a society. Feudal knights in medieval times would be an example of a status group because they are marked out by law – they have rights to land, by convention – a strict military code, and by culture. In Part I, we have already come across a list of status groups – Brahmans, mandarins, Christian clerics, the Jews as a pariah group. These groups have some special capacity in education, knowledge, ritual, that place them above, below, or outside other social groups, thereby conferring on them differing amounts of power within the social order. When a status group becomes a completely closed social group – one is born, married and dies within the same status group – the group is then termed a caste. The Indian caste society is the best example of this, namely one that is hierarchically segregated with functional roles given to each caste that are reinforced by ritual differences.

The categories of class and status group are analytical. In empirical reality a large degree of overlap is common between the two categories, and Weber pursues these interrelationships in Reading 14. Certainly in contemporary societies there is a move towards the increasing correlation of status and class, to an extent that Weber would have found quite surprising. The professional middle class in the nineteenth century was a semi-exclusive status group. It used its knowledge as a way of monopolizing market services – hence it was also a positively privileged class in terms of commerce. Today, what is called the 'underclass' may be termed a status group with virtually no status – in education, lifestyle, residence as well as reduced contact with other parts of society. In class or economic terms it is similarly negatively privileged.

The main reason Weber makes this analytic distinction is to argue that one may possess high status independent of class position. An artist or musician may attract high social esteem, while in economic terms having low economic income. Conversely, a property developer may well have extensive wealth, but low social esteem. But equally, superior economic class position is able to buy and acquire status and lifestyle. Weber argued that this was not a rapid process – old wealth, which is a status group, distrusts newly acquired wealth – and is known by a variety of disparaging terms: the newcomer, *parvenu*, *arriviste*, etc. In England during the 1980s, which was an era of new money, it was suggested semi-seriously that the status test between old and new money was whether one had inherited or bought one's antique furniture. In terms of the distribution of power as defined by status group, the question that needs to be asked is whether the relative positions of old and new money, as status group designations, have been reversed. Had new money achieved higher status than old money? Many commentators think this did occur and that it is not a trivial matter (despite the furniture test!). Weber's argument would be that in times of rapid economic change new class differences produce new status distinctions. Higher social status gives better access to the dimensions of power in the political and economic orders; hence it is closely related to the overall distribution of power in society. Empirical social groups, like Brahmans in India or bankers in the City of London, accrete power on all three dimensions: status group, economic class, and political power.

Reading 15 (Parties) takes us to the role of the political party in history (and this Reading overlaps with the last page of Reading 14). In the overall distribution of power in society it is open to any association of individuals to pursue power within the political order. There may well be class and status group determinants of the formation of political parties. However, in principle, it is open to any association of people to organize themselves as a political association with agreed and defined goals. Ecology parties in modern nation states have followings whose membership cuts across class and status group distinctions, and in this way are said to transcend old left- and right-wing distinctions which belonged to the old politics of social class. Ecology parties also illustrate another of Weber's points. Certain political groupings search for power by going beyond territorial borders. This was a feature of the international women's movement in Weber's own time.

This links back to Reading 7. Parties need to be organized if they are to achieve their goals. In traditional rulership factions often exist to exploit differences of political direction. In charismatic followers there are arguments and schisms over just which person can rightfully claim to be the bearer of charisma. In legal rulership political parties are formed in order to solicit the support of voters. In ideal typical terms the organization of the party will be determined by the type of legitimacy. A party, however, is not the same as the organization of rulership. A party is a subset of the *Herrschaftsverband*, there to exploit and promote differences within the rulership group body. Weber also notes that parties can be formed to promote a split or a heresy within a religion, and it will operate in a way similar to a charismatic party. At the end of the excerpt Weber takes up the question of the influence of money and funding on the political party, pointing out that in America the party machine is open to being 'bought' and therefore the candidates in a party become dependent upon the machine. Weber clearly believed he was raising a number of important and crucial points about the operation and tendencies of parties, and he indicates that he wanted to pursue them more fully in a sociology of the state. Unfortunately he never wrote this, and we are therefore reliant on this compressed piece of writing.

6   Politics and the state[1]

What do we understand by politics (*Politik*)? The idea is extremely broad and comprises every sort of independent *directive* activity. So, one speaks of the foreign exchange policy of a bank, of the interest rate policy of the central bank, and of the politics of a trade union in a strike. One can speak of the educational policy of local government in a town or village, of the directive policies of the committee of a voluntary association, and even, finally, of the politics of a clever wife who seeks to guide her husband. This wider idea of politics and policy has to remain beyond our consideration tonight. Instead we will understand it as the leadership, or the influencing of the leadership, of a *political* group body (*Verband*), or of what we now call the *state*.

What, from the sociological viewpoint, is a 'political' group body, and what is a 'state'? A sociological definition cannot be derived from the contents of its activities. There is almost no task that one can say that a political group body has not been concerned with at some time or another; equally, there is simply no one *exclusive* task that is specific to those bodies which today we refer to politically as states, or which were historical predecessors of the modern state. Instead, the modern state can only finally be defined sociologically in terms of the particular *means* that is specific to it and every political association: namely, those of physical force (*Gewaltsamkeit*). As Trotsky said at Brest-Litovsk, 'Every state is founded on violence.'[2] That is in fact correct. If there were structures in which violence as a means was unknown, *then* the idea of the state would have disappeared and 'anarchy' in its literal sense would appear. Obviously, it should be understood that violence is not the normal or sole means of the state, but it is what is specific to the state. Today the relationship of the state to violence is particularly close. In the past the most different bodies, starting with kinship groups, have known physical force as a wholly normal means. Now, in contrast, we have to say that the state is that human community which within a defined territory successfully claims for itself the *monopoly of legitimate physical force*; and 'territory' it should be noted is a characteristic of the state. This is what is

---

1 Taken from the opening section of a lecture '*Politik als Beruf*' that Weber was invited to give to students in Munich in January 1919. Translation by S. Whimster.
2 Trotsky was the Bolshevik leader who led the Russian peace delegation at Brest-Litovsk in 1917. When the German negotiator, General Hoffmann, accused the Bolshevik regime of having seized power through force, Trotsky replied that in the whole of history government was always based on power and violence.

specific in the present situation: the right to physical force is ascribed to all other group bodies and individual persons only to the extent that the *state* itself permits it. The state is the sole source for the 'right' to exercise violence. So, 'politics' for us is the striving for a share of power, or the attempt to influence the distribution of power, whether this is between states or between human groups within a state.

In essentials this does correspond to normal usage. When one says that something is a 'political' question, or that a minister or a civil servant is a 'political' official, or that a decision is 'politically' determined, what is invariably meant by this is that the distribution and the holding of power as well as the intervention of power interests are important for the answering of these questions; or that they influence the decision or define the sphere of activity of the relevant official. Whoever pursues politics, strives for power: power as either a means in the service of other goals (whether ideal or egoistical), or power 'for its own sake' (in order to enjoy the feeling of prestige it gives).

The state, like its preceding political group bodies, is an instrument of legitimate violence (or rather, is seen as legitimate) supporting the relationship of *domination* (*Herrschaft*) of human being over human being. For the state to exist, it has to force those who are ruled to comply with the claimed authority of those actually ruling. When and why do people obey? On what internal grounds of justification and by what external means is this domination based?

7 The three pure types of legitimate rule[1]

Domination, and this means the probability of obeying a definite command, can be based on different motives for compliance (*Fügsamkeit*): It can be determined by the pure interest situation – the instrumentally rational assessment of advantages and disadvantages by the person commanded. Or, on the other hand, it could be mere 'custom' – the blind habituation of internalized behaviour. Or it can be based on affectual reasons – on the purely personal inclination of the person commanded. Domination that was based only on such footings would, however, be relatively unstable. Instead it is usual for rulers and ruled to ground domination in rights (*Rechtsgründe*), for the 'legitimacy' of those rights to be supported for internal reasons, and for the destruction of this belief in legitimacy to have far-reaching consequences.

Seen in their pure form, there are only three grounds for the legitimacy of domination, and each of these, as a pure type, is accompanied by a fundamentally different sociological structure of administrative staff (*Verwaltungsstab*) and means of administration (*Verwaltungsmittel*).

I. Legal rule on the basis of enactment. The purest type is bureaucratic rule. Its fundamental idea is that any law (*Recht*) can be created and any existing law can be changed by enactment that is decided by formally correct procedure. The group body that rules (*Herrschaftsverband*) is either elected or appointed, and it and all its parts are working concerns (*Betriebe*). A heteronomous and heterocephalic concern,[2] or part of one, should be termed an administrative authority (*Behörde*). The administrative staff are officials appointed by the ruler (*Herr*), and the persons who obey are members of the group body (either citizens (*Bürger*), or members (*Genossen*)).

It is not the person who is obeyed by virtue of his own right but the enacted rule, which is therefore decisive for who obeys the rule and to what extent. Also the person who commands has himself to obey the rule – the 'law' or the 'regulation' of a formally abstract norm – insofar as this was enacted. The type of person who gives orders is the 'superior' whose right to command is legitimated by enacted rules, and is based on a defined 'jurisdiction'

---

1 'Die Drei Reinen Typen der Legitimen Herrschaft', *WL*, pp. 475–88. Translation by S. Whimster. It was written sometime between 1917 and 1920 and was published after Weber's death in the *Preußische Jahrbücher* in 1922. I have tended to translate 'Herrschaft' as rule and rulership but have also employed, depending on context, 'domination', 'power', and 'authority'.

2 Heteronomous means an organization subject to external control; heterocephalic means an organization with more than one head or ruler.

('*Kompetenz*') that is limited by specialization according to effectiveness and according to the specialist requirements for the performance of the official. The type of person who is the official is the trained, professional official, whose terms of service are based on contract with fixed salary and pension rights, which are graded according to the rank of the office and not the amount of work and according to fixed rules of advancement. His administration is a *professional* activity (*Berufsarbeit*) on the basis of a defined obligation to the office. The administrative ideal is impartiality ('*sine ira et studio*') without any motives of personal or emotional influence, free from arbitrariness and unpredictability, and in particular, strongly formalistic according to rational rules without regard to respect of person; and where these are lacking the ideal operates according to an objective outlook defined by effectiveness. The duty of obeying is graded in a hierarchy of office super- and sub-ordination and a regulated procedure for complaint. The basis of technical functioning is the *discipline of the organization* (*Betriebsdisziplin*).

1. Obviously, the modern structure of the state and local government falls within the type of 'legal' rule, but so also does the organization of authority (*Herrschaftsverhältnis*) in the private capitalist enterprise, and in the purposive organization (*Zweckverband*) or the voluntary association (*Verein*) – of whatever sort – that dispose over an extensive, hierarchically layered administrative staff. Modern political bodies (*Verbände*) are only the most outstanding representative of the type. Authority in the private, capitalist enterprise is indeed partially heteronomous – the order is in part stipulated by the state; and in relation to the staff who enforce legal rule, authority is completely heterocephalous – the state's legal and police apparatus (normally) discharges these functions. But the capitalist enterprise is autocephalic in its increasingly bureaucratic administrative organization. Even though the entry into a ruling body (*Herrschaftsverband*) is formally freely chosen and dismissal is also formally 'free', subjecting the person who is commanded to the norms of the enterprise and so the conditions of the labour market, it does not alter its character of authority (*Herrschaftscharakter*). The sociological affinity of the capitalist enterprise with the rule of the modern state will be explained later on, so making the economic foundations of power (*Herrschaft*) even more clear. The capitalist enterprise is based on validity of 'contract' and this marks it out as an outstanding type of the 'legal' organization of the relations of authority (*Herrschaftsbeziehung*).

2. Bureaucracy is technically the purest type of legal rule. But no rule is purely bureaucratic, i.e. rule by only contractually engaged and appointed officials. That is just not possible. The highest posts of the political organization are either 'monarchs' (see below on the inherited charisma of rulers), or 'presidents' elected by the people (and so are plebiscitary charismatic rulers, see below) or they are elected by the parliamentary body. In this last case members of parliament or rather the leaders (whether party notables or charismatic – see below) of the predominating parties are the actual rulers. Likewise, the administrative apparatus is effectively almost never

purely bureaucratic, but tends to embrace all manner of forms, including notables and representatives of interests (and, at the most extreme, the so-called self-government).[3] But what is decisive, however, is that the continuous work rests predominantly and increasingly on bureaucratic strengths. The whole history of the development of the modern state is identical with the history of modern bureaucracy and the bureaucratic enterprise (see below),[4] just as the whole development of modern high capitalism is identical with the increasing bureaucratization of the economic enterprise. The share of the bureaucratic form of authority increases overall.

3. Bureaucracy is not the only type of legal rule. Officialdom through rotation, lots and election, parliamentary and cabinet government, and all kinds of collegial rule and governing bodies fall under this heading if the sphere of their authority (*Kompetenz*) is based on enacted rules and the exercise of the right to rule corresponds to the type of legal administration. Collegial corporate bodies (*Körperschaften*) made an essential contribution to the development of the legal form of rulership in the period at the beginning of the modern state; in particular, the idea of 'the authorities' ('*Behörde*') owes its emergence to them. On the other side, the elected officialdom played a very important role in the prehistory of the modern administration by officials (as well as today in the democracies).

II. Traditional rule is based on the belief in the sanctity of orders and powers of rule (*Herrengewalten*) which have existed since time immemorial. The purest type is patriarchal rule. The rulership body (*Herrschaftsverband*) is a communal form of social relationship (*Vergemeinschaftung*), the type of person who commands is the lord ('*Herr*'), the administrative staff are servants ('*Diener*'), and those who obey are subservient subjects ('*Untertanen*'). The lord is obeyed on account of the particular worthiness of his person that is sanctified through tradition; he is obeyed out of piety. The content of the command is fixed by tradition, and if the lord recklessly disregards this, then he would endanger his own power which is based on the sanctity of that tradition. In principle, it is not permissible to create new law in relation to the norms of tradition. In fact new enactments are established as verdicts based on 'knowledge' known 'since time immemorial'. On the other hand, outside the norms of tradition the power of the lord is only limited by the degree of approval that the particular case meets with, and there is far greater flexibility here. His power therefore divides into an area that is closely circumscribed by tradition, and an area of favour (*Gnade*) and arbitrariness (*Willkür*) in which he switches between favouritism, affection, dislike, and purely personal views, and he is influenced by favours done for him. So far as there are principles underlying governing and the arbitration of disputes, they consist

---

3 A reference to the Soviets as in Bolshevik Russia.
4 The cross-reference is not obvious and probably relates to a planned but unwritten chapter on the development of the modern state.

of ethico-pragmatic equity (*materiale ethische Billigkeit*), justness (*Gerechtigkeit*) or practical effectiveness (*utilitaristischen Zweckmäßigkeit*) rather than principles of a formal kind as in legal rule.

This is also the case for the lord's administrative staff. This is made up of personal dependants (members of the household or household officials) or from relatives or personal friends (favourites) or from those bound personally to him by oaths of loyalty (*Treuband*) (vassals, tributary princes). The bureaucratic idea of competence as objectively demarcated spheres of responsibility is absent. The extent of the individual servant's 'legitimate' power to command depends on the particular whim of the lord. Servants in the exercise of powers are also completely entrusted by the lord to perform roles more important and higher than their rank. In fact the power can be quite extensive – whatever is permitted to the servant by the compliance of the subject. In place of official duty or office discipline, the personal loyalty of the servant prevails within the relational organization of the administrative staff.

In the nature of traditional rule there are two forms different in character to consider:

1 The purely patriarchal structure of administration (*Verwaltung*): Servants are in complete personal dependence to the lord and are either recruited in a patrimonial way as slaves, bondsmen (*Hörige*), and eunuchs, or they are recruited extra-patrimonially from strata that are not totally without rights – favourites, and plebeians. Administration is completely heteronomous and heterocephalic; the administrators have no right of their own in office and there is no selection in terms of specialization and no status group (*ständische*) honour of the official; the practical means of administration (*sachlichen Verwaltungsmittel*) belong to the lord's household and are under his own direction. There is no guarantee at all against the arbitrariness of the lord, which is at its greatest extent in this situation, because of the complete dependence of the administrative staff on the lord. The purest type of domination here is *sultanism*. All true despotisms had this character, whereby power is treated as a customary property right.

2 The structure of estates (*ständische Struktur*): Servants of the lord are independent on account of having their own position as socially prominent people. They are invested in office because of their own privilege or because of concessions granted by the lord (whether actual or a legitimizing fiction). Alternatively, servants acquire the office in their own right through a business exchange (purchase, pledge, or lease) and it is not easy for the lord to reappropriate it from them. Their administration is accordingly autocephalic and autonomous, even if this is limited, and the substantive means of administration fall under their direction and not that of the lord. Rulership exercised through the estates means: the competition of the office-holders over

the extent of the power of their office (and its income) determines the reciprocal limitation on the sphere of their substantive administration, and this takes the place of the limits of authority. The hierarchical stratification by privilege very often restricted the monarch's right to be a court of appeal (*de non evocando, non appellando*).[5] The category of discipline is absent. Tradition, privilege, feudal or patrimonial loyalty, status group honour and 'goodwill' prevail over the whole situation. The power of the lord is therefore shared between himself and the staff who appropriate the administration and acquire privileges, and this estatist division of power is highly stereotypical for the manner of administration.

Patriarchal rule (by the head of the family, the head of the clan, and the father of the realm (*Landesvater*)) is only the purest type of traditional rule. Every sort of authoritarian rule ('*Obrigkeit*') that successfully claims legitimate authority simply on the basis of acquired custom belongs to the same category, although it may not be so clearly exhibited. The piety acquired through upbringing and custom by the children in relation to the head of the family stands in the clearest contrast, on the one side, to the contractually appointed worker in an enterprise and, on the other side, to the emotional bonds of belief of a member of a community to a prophet. In fact the household unit is a kernel of traditional rulership. The typical 'official' of the patrimonial and feudal state are household officials with tasks that belong primarily to the household (the carver, the chamberlain, the marshal, the cupbearer, the seneschal, the major-domo).

The juxtaposition of action strictly defined by tradition and a free sphere of action is common to all forms of traditional rule. Within the free sphere, the action of the lord or his administrative staff has to be bought or be earned through personal relationship. (This is the historical origin of fees [*Gebühren*].) The absence of formal law is decisive and, instead of this, rulership according to material principles and the arbitration of conflict is likewise common to all traditional forms of rule and has far-reaching consequences for its relation to the economy. The patriarch, just like the patrimonial lord, rules and decides according to the principles of 'khadi justice': on the one side strongly fixed by tradition, so much so that this permits freedom of what from the legal point of view is the making of judgements for individual cases on the basis of informal and irrational fairness and justness, and indeed with regard to the person. All codifications and laws of the patrimonial ruler breathe the spirit of the so-called 'welfare state': a mixture of the social-ethical and

5 *De non evocando de non appellando* was a principle of the Holy Roman Empire, when the electoral princes had the right to stop appeals going further up the hierarchy to the imperial court.

social-utilitarian principles predominates and breaks any formal strictness in the law.

The separation of the patriarchal from the estatist structure of traditional rule is fundamental for the entire sociology of the state of the pre-bureaucratic era. (At its full extent the contrast is comprehensible only in connection with its later equivalent on the economic side: the separation of the administrative staff from the substantive means of administration in contrast to the appropriation of the substantive means of administration by the administrative staff.)[6] The whole question of whether and which estate was the carrier of ideal cultural goods (*Kulturgüter*) is first and foremost co-determined by history.[7] The administration by patrimonial dependants (slaves, bondsmen) as it occurred in the Near East and in Egypt until the time of the Mamelukes is the most extreme and apparently the most consistent (not always in reality though) type of pure patriarchal rulership devoid of the division of rule by the estates. Administration by free plebeians stands quite close to rational officialdom. Administration by literati can have very different characteristics, depending on the character of the literati; the typical contrast is between Brahmans, on the one side, and mandarins, on the other, and both in relation to Buddhist and Christian clerics. Administration by literati is always close to the estate type of rule. This is represented at its clearest by administration by nobility, and in its purest form by feudalism; the whole relationship of personal allegiance and the appeal to the estatist honour of the enfeoffed knight who has been bestowed with office takes the place of objective, rational official duty.

All kinds of estatist rule, whether based on more or less fixed appropriation of administrative power, stand closer to legal rule than does patriarchalism in this respect. Estatist rule, on account of the guarantees which surround the jurisdictions of those who possess privileges, has provided a characteristic basis for rights ('*Rechtsgrund*') (and is an effect of the estatist division of powers); this is absent in patriarchal structures with their entrusting of administration to the complete arbitrariness of the lord. On the other hand, the strict discipline and the absence of their own rights among the administrative staff places patriarchalism technically closer to the office discipline in legal rulership than the estatist model, which because of appropriation has a stereotypically fragmented administration. Also the employment of plebeians (lawyers) in the service of lords in Europe has been a direct forerunner of the modern state.

III. Charismatic rule on the basis of affectual surrender (*Hingabe*) to the person of the lord and his gifts of grace, in particular magical capabilities,

---

6 I.e. the managers of a firm administer it solely on behalf of the owners, or alternatively they take over the control of the firm.

7 See above, pp. 71–3.

prophecies or heroism, spiritual power and oratorical powers. The search for what is continuously new, that which is beyond the mundane, for novelty, and the emotional suggestibility (*Hingenommenheit*) of the exceptional are the sources of personal devotion (*Hingebung*). The purest types are the power of prophets, or of military heroes, and of great demagogues. The rulership body (*Herrschaftsverband*) is based on a communal form of relationship in the locality (*Vergemeinschaftung*) or among the followers.

The type of person who commands is the leader. The type of person who obeys is the 'disciple'. The leader is obeyed exclusively for his purely personal, non-everyday qualities and not for his legal position or traditional honour. This continues as long as these qualities are ascribed to him, and his charisma confirms itself through proof. If he is 'abandoned' by his god, or he is robbed of his heroic strength or he loses the masses' belief in his leadership qualities, his rule collapses.

The administrative staff is selected according to charisma and personal devotion and not according to the specialist qualifications (of the civil servant), nor on account of status honour (as in estatist rulership), nor household and other personal dependency (so standing in contrast to the patriarchal administrative staff). The rational idea of competence is absent just as is estatist privilege. The mission (*Sendung*) of the lord and his personal charismatic qualifications are decisive for the reach of the legitimation of the followers or disciples who are engaged. In the administration, insofar as this term is adequate, there is a lack of any orientation to rules whether they are enacted or traditional. When measured against the standards of an enacted order, the actual revelation or creation, deeds and examples, or decisions on a case-to-case basis are all characterized by irrationality. Charisma is not tied to tradition: 'it is written, but I say unto you' is valid for the prophet; the military hero undermines the legitimate order through a new creation by virtue of the power of the sword, and for the demagogue by his pronouncement and suggestion of revolutionary 'natural law'. The genuine form of charismatic legal finding (*Rechtsweisung*) and conflict settlement is the pronouncement of a judgement by the lord or wise man ('*Weisen*'). The warriors or community of believers are obliged to recognize a pronouncement, lest it is challenged by an opposing finding by another person also claiming charismatic validity. In this case the challenge to the trust of the community can only be finally decided by a contest between the leaders, and only one person will be shown to be right while the other will be guilty of a wrong that has to be atoned (*sühnenpflichtiges Unrecht*).

(a) Charismatic rule was first brilliantly developed by R. Sohm in his book on the canon law of the early Christian community, and not without the knowledge that he was dealing with a type. The expression has since been used several times but without a realization of its implications.[8]

In early history next to the glimmerings of 'enacted' rule, which was never completely absent, the totality of rulership was divided up between tradition and charisma. Next to the [North American] Indian chief in charge of economic matters (*Sachem*),[9] who was one of the most important traditional figures, stood the charismatic military prince (equivalent to our 'duke') and his retinue. Hunting and martial qualities, both of which require the leader to be equipped personally with extraordinary abilities, are the secular side of charismatic rule, and magic is its 'spiritual' side. Ever since, charismatic power over people has accompanied prophets and military princes over the centuries. The charismatic politician – the 'demagogue' – is the product of the western city states. In the city state of Jerusalem he appeared in religious garb as the prophet; the Athenian constitution after the innovations of Pericles and Ephialtes was tailored to the existence of the charismatic politician, without whom the state machine would have no prospect of functioning.[10]

(b) Charismatic authority is based on the belief in the prophet and the acknowledgement (*Anerkennung*) which the charismatic warrior hero, the hero of the streets[11] or the demagogue obtains, but it also collapses together with that belief. Nevertheless charisma does not derive its authority from the acknowledgement of the ruled. Rather the reverse is true: belief and acknowledgement are to be counted as an obligation whose fulfilment is demanded by the person who is charismatically legitimated and he punishes any endangering of this recognition. Charismatic authority is indeed one of the great revolutionary powers of history, but in its pure form it has a thoroughly authoritarian and dominating character.

(c) It should be understood that the expression 'charisma' is used here in a wholly value-free sense. The manic fit of rage of the Norse 'beserker', the

---

8 Rudolf Sohm, *Outlines of Church History*, translated by M. Sinclair, Beacon Hill, Beacon Press, 1958 [German edn 1883]. Sohm enquired into the source of authority in canon (church) law. His answer was that the Church has authority by virtue of individuals who are graced with gifts (charismata) such as preaching, or miracle-making. This forms the basis of their leadership, which is acknowledged by the congregation. Weber's comment about the unrealized implications of Sohm's work means that charisma is not just an extraordinary gift but a structure of authority with its own form of self-validation. By contrast, the argument of the Roman Church was that the charisma of the apostles was institutionalized into the Church.

9 *Sachem* was an Iroquois name – responsibility did not extend to military affairs.

10 In 462 BC Pericles and Ephialtes managed to place the oligarchic power of ancient Athens on a wider decision making basis.

11 A reference to the revolutionary insurgence in Germany in 1918 to 1919, and to charismatic politicians such as Kurt Eisner who established a socialist government in Bavaria.

miracles and revelations of any hole-in-the-corner prophecy, the demagogic gifts of Cleon are in sociological terms just as good 'charisma' as
the qualities of a Napoleon, Jesus or Pericles. The decisive factor for us is
whether the charisma is effective and works – that it is acknowledged. Its
fundamental assumption, therefore, is being able to prove itself. The charismatic lord has to prove himself through miracles, successes, the good
fortune (*Wohlergehen*) of the retinue or the subjects, and that these are
the result of being graced by god. His charisma is valid for only so long
as he can demonstrate it. If success is denied to him, then his authority
totters. The charismatic concept of 'divine right' ('*Gottesgnadentum*')
had decisive consequences in those instances where it existed. The position of the Chinese monarch was threatened when drought, floods, failure in the field of battle and other misadventures appeared to place in
doubt whether he still received the grace of heaven. Public self-
accusation and penances threatened him, and with persistent disaster,
dethronement, and possible sacrifice. Accreditation by miracles is
demanded of every prophet (even of Luther by the Zwickauers[12]).

The existence of the most widely spread form of legal rulership is
based, insofar as its stability depends on the belief in legitimacy, on
mixed principles. Settled tradition and prestige (charisma) come together
with the belief in the significance of formal legality, which finally comes
to be based on habituation. A shock to one of them – unusual demands
on the ruled that run counter to tradition, exceptional misadventure that
eliminates prestige, or damage to the usual formally legal correctness –
shakes the belief in legitimacy in equal measure. But in all organizations
of power, however, it is above all the administrative staff itself and its
continuing direction of action towards the enforcement of order and the
(direct or indirect) adherence of the subordinated to authority that is
decisive for the continuing existence of the actual compliance of the
ruled. This is what is meant by the term 'organization' ('*Organisation*'):
the securing of those actions that realize domination (*Herrschaft*). The
loyalty of the administrative staff itself to the lord is, accordingly, of
overriding importance, and here its solidarity of interest – ideal as well as
material – with the lord is the decisive factor. For the relationship of the
lord to his administrative staff the following proposition is generally
valid: as a rule the lord is the stronger party in relation to any opposing
individual of his staff because of the individualization of each person
and the loyalty (*Sölidarität*) of every member to him. But the lord
becomes the weaker party if all of the members of the staff form an
opposition to him, as numerous categories of staff have occasionally

---

12 A reference to the Anabaptists from Zwickau (Thomas Münzer, Nicolas Storch, and Mark
Stübner) who in 1521 challenged Luther's authority as being too based in scripture and not in
revelation.

done in the past and the present. But this requires rational planning on the part of the members of the staff if they are to unify and oppose or undermine the control of the organization by the lord and so paralyse his power. And equally it is necessary to create one's own administrative staff.

(d) Charismatic rule is a specifically *extraordinary* and purely personal social relationship. Most recently, with the disappearance of personal carriers of charisma, the organization of power in this sense has, if not died out, continued in another way. Hence, the authority of the lord is transferred to his successor, and this is the tendency to *routinization* (*veralltäglichen*). This occurs through:

1   the process of making the structure of powers traditional. In place of the continuous creation or law and administrative command that is ever-new and charismatic by the carrier of charisma or the charismatically qualified administrative staff, steps the authority of judgements (*Präjudizien*) and precedents which they created or were ascribed to them;

2   the transition of the charismatic administrative staff, where the disciples or retinue turn themselves into a legal or estatist staff by taking over the internally created rights to power or by appropriating those rights created as privileges (fiefs and prebends);[13]

3   through the transformation of the meaning of the charisma itself. What is important in this case is the way in which the burning question of the successor is solved and this involves ideal as well as (indeed above all) material factors.

The successor problem can be solved in various ways: by simply waiting passively for the appearance of a new charismatically attested or qualified lord. This tends to be replaced by a more active approach to acquiring a successor, when the waiting is accompanied by strong interests of whatever kind in the continued existence of the ruling organization. This happens:

(a) By searching for the characteristics of charismatic qualification. A fairly pure type is the search for a new Dalai Lama.[14] The strong personality and extraordinary character of the charisma changes into a quality that can be established according to rules.

(b) By oracle, lot, or other techniques of designation. The belief in the person with charismatic qualifications changes itself thereby into a belief in the relevant technique.

---

13 Fiefs are tenancies of land granted to a person; prebends are rents that are granted.
14 The child candidates are searched for characteristics that would indicate reincarnation of the Buddha.

(c) By the designation of the charismatically qualified:

1   By the bearer of charisma himself. Naming one's successor is a very common form, both by warrior princes and by prophets. The belief in the unique legitimacy of charisma changes therefore into the belief in the legitimate acquisition of power on account of legal and divine designation.

2   The charismatically qualified disciples or retinue decide with the acknowledgement of the respective religious or warrior community. The constitution of the 'vote' or the 'nomination' for this procedure is a secondary consideration. It is entirely different to the modern concept of election. The original idea is not concerned with a 'ballot' for election candidates, between whom a free selection occurs, but the establishing and acknowledgement of the 'rightfully' charismatically qualified successor who is called to be the lord. A 'false' election was therefore a wrong that had to be expiated. The original idea was that it must be possible to reach unanimity, and failure to do this was a form of wrongdoing and weakness.

    In each case the belief no longer resides in the person as such, but in the process of designation of the ruler as 'right' and 'valid' (and possibly leading to his coronation) or else the person is installed in power as if a piece of property was being acquired.

3   The charismatic qualification resides in the blood and the idea that charisma is inherited.

    A closely related idea is first of all the inherited right to rulership. This idea has only prevailed in the medieval Occident. Very often charisma attaches to the kinship group and it only remains for the actual bearer to be established according to the rules and methods mentioned above (a–c). Where there are fixed rules that apply to the person, these are not unified. It is only in the medieval Occident and in Japan that the right of inheritance to the throne by primogeniture has been unambiguously established, having a definite stabilizing effect on rulership there in comparison to all other forms which give rise to internal conflicts.

    Belief then depends no longer on the person purely as such, but on the 'legitimate' inheritance of the dynasty. The actual and extraordinary character of charisma is then very strongly traditionalized and also the idea of possessing the 'grace of god' has a completely different sense of divine right (the ruler is lord in his own right and not through the acknowledgement of the rule of his personal charisma). The claim to rulership is completely independent of personal qualities.

4   There occurs an objectification (*Versachlichung*) of charisma through ritual: the belief that magical qualities are transferable or

can be generated through a definite sort of hierurgy[15] – anointing, the laying on of hands, and other sacramental acts.

The belief no longer attaches to the bearer of charisma as a person, from whose qualities the claim to rule has become completely detached (rather as the Catholic Church has established the principle of the indelible character of the priest), but to the efficacy of the relevant sacramental acts.

5   The principle of charismatic legitimacy that in its primary sense is authoritarian can be changed to an anti-authoritarian principle. The validity of the charismatic rule is in fact based on the acknowledgement of the actual person as charismatically qualified and affirmed by the ruled. In a genuine charismatic situation this acknowledgement of the pretenders to rule who are qualified is an obligation. This relationship can however become easily reinterpreted, so that the free acknowledgement from the side of the ruled is the premise and foundation of legitimacy (democratic legitimacy). Then the acknowledgement becomes 'election' and the lord who had charisma in his own right becomes the power-holder on the basis of the favour (*Gnade*) of the ruled and of mandate. Just as the designation of the ruler by the retinue by acclamation (in warrior or religious communities), so the plebiscite has often historically taken on the character of an election by the ballot. Thereby, the charismatic claims appropriate to a chosen ruler (*gekorener Herr*) is made into the elected official of the ruled according to their will.

It is the same process with the charismatic legal principle. A charismatic judgement on law is proclaimed to the community (of warriors or the religious) and this has to be recognized by the community. This presents the possibility of different and opposing rulings (*Weisungen*), and the decision is hit upon first by charismatic means, then by the declaration of the community's belief in the right judgement. From this the legal idea can easily develop that the ruled vote freely to declare their will over what law should be valid (*das geltensollende Recht*) and that the number of votes is therefore the legitimate means (the majority principle).

The distinction between an elected leader and an elected official turns on the sense of the meaning which the elected person gives to his own behaviour and, according to his personal qualities, what he is able to offer to his staff and to the ruled. The official is simply the holder of the mandate of his ruler, which here is the voter; whereas the leader holds himself as exclusively responsible for his own behaviour. So long as the leader enlists the trust of the

15 A generic word for a variety of sacred performances and in its Greek sense it means literally the work of sacrifice.

voters by his success, he acts throughout according to his own discretion (this is leadership democracy – *Führer-Demokratie*). The official, by contrast, acts according to the expressed or surmised will of the voters (according to an 'imperative' mandate).

8   The nation[1]

In addition to the direct and material imperialist interests, discussed above, there are the indirectly material as well as the ideal interests of strata that are in various ways privileged within a power structure and, indeed, privileged by its very existence. They comprise especially all those who think of themselves as being the specific 'partners' of a specific 'culture' diffused among the members of the power structure. Under the influence of these circles, the naked prestige of 'power' is unavoidably transformed into other special forms of prestige and especially into the idea of the 'nation'.

If the concept of 'nation' can in any way be defined unambiguously, it certainly cannot be stated in terms of empirical qualities common to those who count as members of the nation. In the sense of those using the term at a given time, the concept undoubtedly means, above all, that *it is proper* to expect from certain groups a specific sentiment of solidarity in the face of other groups. Thus, the concept belongs in the sphere of values. Yet, there is no agreement on how these groups should be delimited or about what community-oriented action should result from such solidarity.

In ordinary language, 'nation' is, first of all, not identical with the 'people of a state', that is, with the membership of a given polity (*politische Gemein-schaft*). Numerous polities comprise groups who emphatically assert the independence of their 'nation' in the face of other groups; or they comprise merely *parts* of a group whose members declare themselves to be one homogenous 'nation' (Austria is an example for both). Furthermore, a 'nation' is not identical with a community speaking the same language; that this by no means always suffices is indicated by the Serbs and Croats, the North Americans, the Irish, and the English. On the contrary, a common language does not seem to be absolutely necessary to a 'nation'. In official documents, besides 'Swiss People' one also finds the phrase 'Swiss Nation'. And some language groups do not think of themselves as a separate 'nation', for example, at least until recently, the White Russians. As a rule, however, the pretension to be considered a special 'nation' is associated with a common language as a culture value of the masses; this is predominantly the case in the classic country of language conflicts, Austria, and equally so in Russia and in eastern Prussia. But this linkage of the common language and 'nation'

---

1 Taken from *E&S*, pp. 922–6.

is of varying intensity; for instance, it is very low in the United States as well as in Canada.

'National' solidarity among men speaking the same language may be just as well rejected as accepted. Solidarity, instead, may be linked with differences in the other great culture value of the masses, namely, a religious creed, as is the case with the Serbs and Croats. National solidarity may be connected with differing social structure and mores and hence with 'ethnic' elements, as is the case with the German Swiss and the Alsatians in the face of the Germans of the Reich, or with the Irish facing the British. Yet above all, national solidarity may be linked to memories of a common political destiny with other nations, among the Alsatians with the French since the Revolutionary War which represents their common heroic age, just as among the Baltic Barons with the Russians whose political destiny they helped to steer.

It goes without saying that 'national' affiliation need not be based upon common blood. Indeed, especially radical 'nationalists' are often of foreign descent. Furthermore, although a specific common anthropological type is not irrelevant to nationality, it is neither sufficient nor prerequisite to nation founding. Nevertheless, the idea of the 'nation' is apt to include the notions of common descent and of an essential, though frequently indefinite, homogeneity. The 'nation' has these notions in common with the sentiment of solidarity of ethnic communities, which is also nourished from various sources, as we have seen before [*E&S*, ch. V:4]. But the sentiment of ethnic solidarity does not by itself make a 'nation'. Undoubtedly, even the White Russians in the face of the Great Russians have always had a sentiment of ethnic solidarity, yet even at the present time they would hardly claim to qualify as a separate 'nation'. The Poles of Upper Silesia, until recently, had hardly any feeling of solidarity with the 'Polish Nation'. They felt themselves to be a separate ethnic group in the face of the Germans, but for the rest they were Prussian subjects and nothing else.

Whether the Jews may be called a 'nation' is an old problem. Most of the time, the answer will be negative. At any rate, the answers of the Russian Jews, of the assimilating West-European and American Jews, and of the Zionists would vary in nature and extent. In particular, the question would be answered very differently by the peoples of their environment, for example, by the Russians on the one side and the Americans on the other – or at least by those Americans who at the present time still maintain American and Jewish nature to be essentially similar, as an American President [T.R.] has asserted in an official document.

Those German-speaking Alsatians who refuse to belong to the German 'nation' and who cultivate the memory of political union with France do not thereby consider themselves simply as members of the French 'nation'. The Negroes of the United States, at least at present, consider themselves members of the American 'nation', but they will hardly ever be so considered by the Southern Whites.

Only fifteen years ago, men knowing the Far East still denied that the

Chinese qualified as a 'nation'; they held them to be only a 'race'. Yet today, not only the Chinese political leaders but also the very same observers would judge differently. Thus it seems that a group of people under certain conditions may attain the quality of a nation through specific behaviour, or they may claim this quality as an 'attainment' – and within short spans of time at that.

There are, on the other hand, social groups that profess indifference to, and even directly relinquish, any evaluational adherence to a single nation. At the present time, certain leading strata of the class movement of the modern proletariat consider such indifference and relinquishment to be an accomplishment. Their argument meets with varying success, depending upon political and linguistic affiliations and also upon different strata of the proletariat; on the whole, their success is rather diminishing at the present time.

An unbroken scale of quite varied and highly changeable attitudes toward the idea of the 'nation' is to be found among social strata within single groups to whom language usage ascribes the quality of 'nations'. The scale extends from emphatic affirmation to emphatic negation and finally complete indifference, as may be characteristic of the citizens of Luxembourg and of nationally 'unawakened' peoples. Feudal strata, strata of officials, bourgeois strata of various occupational categories, strata of 'intellectuals' do not have homogeneous or historically constant attitudes toward the idea.

The reasons for the belief that one represents a nation vary greatly, just as does the empirical conduct that actually results from affiliation or lack of it with a nation. The 'national sentiments' of the German, the Englishman, the North American, the Spaniard, the Frenchman, or the Russian do not function in an identical manner – to take only the simplest illustration – in relation to the polity, with the geographical boundaries of which the 'idea' of the nation may come into conflict. This antagonism may lead to quite different results. Certainly the Italians in the Austrian state would fight Italian troops only if coerced into doing so. Large portions of the German Austrians would today fight against Germany only with the greatest reluctance; they could not be relied upon. The German-Americans, however, even those valuing their [former] 'nationality' most highly, would fight against Germany, not gladly, yet, given the occasion, unconditionally. The Poles in the German State would fight readily against a Russian Polish army but hardly against an autonomous Polish army. The Austrian Serbs would fight against Serbia with very mixed feelings and only in the hope of attaining common autonomy. The Russian Poles would fight more reliably against a German than against an Austrian army.

It is a well-known historical fact that within the same nation the intensity of solidarity felt toward the outside is changeable and varies greatly in strength. On the whole, this sentiment has grown even where internal conflicts of interest have not diminished. Only sixty years ago the [Prussian conservative] *Kreuzzeitung* still appealed for the intervention of the emperor of Russia in internal German affairs; today, in spite of increased class antagonism, this would be difficult to imagine.

In any case, the differences in national sentiment are both significant and fluid and, as is the case in all other fields, fundamentally different answers are given to the question: What conclusions are a group of people willing to draw from the 'national sentiment' found among them? No matter how emphatic and subjectively sincere a pathos may be formed among them, what sort of specific joint action are they ready to develop? The extent to which in the diaspora a custom, more correctly, a convention is adhered to as a 'national' trait varies just as much as does the importance of common conventions for the belief in the existence of a separate 'nation'. In the face of this value concept of the 'idea of the nation', which empirically is entirely ambiguous, a sociological typology would have to analyse all the individual kinds of sentiments of group membership and solidarity in their genetic conditions and in their consequences for the social action of the participants. This cannot be attempted here.

Instead, we shall have to look a little closer into the fact that the idea of the nation for its advocates stands in very intimate relation to 'prestige' interests. The earliest and most energetic manifestations of the idea, in some form, even though it may have been veiled, have contained the legend of a providential 'mission'. Those to whom the representatives of the idea zealously turned were expected to shoulder this mission. Another element of the early idea was the notion that this mission was facilitated solely through the very cultivation of the peculiarity of the group set off as a nation. Therewith, in so far as its self-justification is sought in the value of its content, this mission can consistently be thought of only as a specific 'culture' mission. The significance of the 'nation' is usually anchored in the superiority, or at least the irreplaceability, of the culture values that are to be preserved and developed only through the cultivation of the peculiarity of the group. It therefore goes without saying that, just as those who wield power in the polity invoke the idea of the *state*, the intellectuals, as we shall tentatively call those who usurp leadership in a *Kulturgemeinschaft* (that is, within a group of people who by virtue of their peculiarity have access to certain products that are considered 'culture goods'), are specifically predestined to propagate the '*national*' idea.

9 The belief in common ethnicity[1]

The belief in group affinity, regardless of whether it has any objective foundation, can have important consequences especially for the formation of a political community. We shall call 'ethnic groups' those human groups that entertain a subjective belief in their common descent because of similarities of physical type or of customs or both, or because of memories of colonization and migration; this belief must be important for the propagation of group formation; conversely, it does not matter whether or not an objective blood relationship exists. Ethnic membership (*Gemeinsamkeit*) differs from the kinship group precisely by being a presumed identity, not a group with concrete social action, like the latter. In our sense, ethnic membership does not constitute a group; it only facilitates group formation of any kind, particularly in the political sphere. On the other hand, it is primarily the political community, no matter how artificially organized, that inspires the belief in common ethnicity. This belief tends to persist even after the disintegration of the political community, unless drastic differences in the custom, physical type, or, above all, language exist among its members.

This artificial origin of the belief in common ethnicity follows the previously described pattern (cf. *E&S*, p. 346) of rational association turning into personal relationships. If rationally regulated action is not widespread, almost any association, even the most rational one, creates an overarching communal consciousness; this takes the form of a brotherhood on the basis of the belief in common ethnicity. As late as the Greek city state, even the most arbitrary division of the polis became for the member an association with at least a common cult and often a common fictitious ancestor. The twelve tribes of Israel were subdivisions of a political community, and they alternated in performing certain functions on a monthly basis. The same holds for the Greek tribes (*phylai*) and their subdivisions; the latter, too, were regarded as units of common ethnic descent. It is true that the original division may have been induced by political or actual ethnic differences, but the effect was the same when such a division was made quite rationally and schematically, after the break-up of old groups and relinquishment of local cohesion, as it was done by Cleisthenes. It does not follow, therefore, that the Greek polis was actually or originally a tribal or lineage state, but that ethnic

---

1 Taken from *E&S*, pp. 389–95.

fictions were a sign of the rather low degree of rationalization of Greek political life. Conversely, it is a symptom of the greater rationalization of Rome that its old schematic subdivisions (*curiae*) took on religious importance, with a pretense to ethnic origin, to only a small degree.

The belief in common ethnicity often delimits 'social circles', which in turn are not always identical with endogamous connubial groups, for greatly varying numbers of persons may be encompassed by both. Their similarity rests on the belief in a specific 'honor' of their members, not shared by the outsiders, that is, the sense of 'ethnic honor' (a phenomenon closely related to status honor, which will be discussed later). These few remarks must suffice at this point. A specialized sociological study of ethnicity would have to make a finer distinction between these concepts than we have done for our limited purposes.

Groups, in turn, can engender sentiments of likeness which will persist even after their demise and will have an 'ethnic' connotation. The political community in particular can produce such an effect. But most directly, such an effect is created by the *language group*, which is the bearer of a specific 'cultural possession of the masses' (*Massenkulturgut*) and makes mutual understanding (*Verstehen*) possible or easier.

Wherever the memory of the origin of a community by peaceful secession or emigration ('colony', *ver sacrum*, and the like) from a mother community remains for some reason alive, there undoubtedly exists a very specific and often extremely powerful sense of ethnic identity, which is determined by several factors: shared political memories or, even more importantly in early times, persistent ties with the old cult, or the strengthening of kinship and other groups, both in the old and the new community, or other persistent relationships. Where these ties are lacking, or once they cease to exist, the sense of ethnic group membership is absent, regardless of how close the kinship may be.

Apart from the community of language, which may or may not coincide with objective, or subjectively believed, consanguinity, and apart from common religious belief, which is also independent of consanguinity, the ethnic differences that remain are, on the one hand, esthetically conspicuous differences of the physical appearance (as mentioned before) and, on the other hand and of equal weight, the perceptible differences in the *conduct of everyday life*. Of special importance are precisely those items which may otherwise seem to be of small social relevance, since when ethnic differentiation is concerned it is always the conspicuous differences that come into play.

Common language and the ritual regulation of life, as determined by shared religious beliefs, everywhere are conducive to feelings of ethnic affinity, especially since the intelligibility of the behavior of others is the most fundamental presupposition of group formation. But since we shall not consider these two elements in the present context, we ask: what is it that remains? It must be admitted that palpable differences in dialect and differences of religion in themselves do not exclude sentiments of common ethnicity. Next to pronounced differences in the economic way of life, the belief in ethnic affinity has at all times been affected by outward differences in clothes, in the style of housing, food and eating habits, the division of labor between the sexes and between the free and the unfree. That is to say, these things concern one's conception of what is correct and proper and, above all, of what affects the individual's sense of honor and dignity. All those things we shall find later on as objects of specific differences between status groups. The conviction of the excellence of one's own customs and the inferiority of alien ones, a conviction which sustains the sense of ethnic honor, is actually quite analogous to the sense of honor of distinctive status groups.

The sense of ethnic honor is a specific honor of the masses (*Massenehre*), for it is accessible to anybody who belongs to the subjectively believed community of descent. The 'poor white trash', i.e., the propertyless and, in the absence of job opportunities, very often destitute white inhabitants of the southern states of the United States of America in the period of slavery, were the actual bearers of racial antipathy, which was quite foreign to the planters. This was so because the social honor of the 'poor whites' was dependent upon the social *déclassement* of the Negroes.

And behind all ethnic diversities there is somehow naturally the notion of the 'chosen people', which is merely a counterpart of status differentiation translated into the plane of horizontal co-existence. The idea of a chosen people derives its popularity from the fact that it can be claimed to an equal degree by any and every member of the mutually despising groups, in contrast to status differentiation which always rests on subordination. Consequently, ethnic repulsion may take hold of all conceivable differences among the notions of propriety and transform them into 'ethnic conventions'.

Besides the previously mentioned elements, which were still more or less closely related to the economic order, conventionalization (a term expounded elsewhere) may take hold of such things as a hairdo or style of beard and the like. The differences thereof have an 'ethnically' repulsive effect, because they are thought of as symbols of ethnic membership. Of course, the repulsion is not always based merely on the 'symbolic' character of the distinguishing traits. The fact that the Scythian women oiled their hair with butter, which then gave off a rancid odor, while Greek women used perfumed oil to achieve the same purpose, thwarted – according to an ancient report – all attempts at social intercourse between the aristocratic ladies of these two groups. The smell of butter certainly had a more compelling effect than even the most prominent racial differences, or – as far as I could see – the 'Negro odor', of which so many fables are told. In general, racial qualities are effective only as limiting factors with regard to the belief in common ethnicity, such as in case of an excessively heterogeneous and esthetically unaccepted physical type; they are not positively group-forming.

Pronounced differences of custom, which play a role equal to that of inherited physical type in the creation of feelings of common ethnicity and notions of kinship, are usually caused, in addition to linguistic and religious differences, by the diverse economic and political conditions of various social groups. If we ignore cases of clear-cut linguistic boundaries and sharply demarcated political or religious communities as a basis of differences of custom – and these in fact are lacking in wide areas of the African and South American continents – then there are only gradual transitions of custom and no immutable ethnic frontiers, except those due to gross geographical differences. The sharp demarcations of areas wherein ethnically relevant customs predominate, which were not conditioned either by political or economic or religious factors, usually came into existence by way of migration or expansion, when groups of people that had previously lived in complete or partial isolation from each other and became accommodated to heterogeneous conditions of existence came to live side by side. As a result, the obvious contrast usually evokes, on both sides, the idea of blood disaffinity (*Blutsfremdheit*), regardless of the objective state of affairs.

It is understandably difficult to determine in general – and even in a concrete individual case – what influence specific ethnic factors (i.e., the belief in a blood relationship, or its opposite, which rests on similarities, or differences, of a person's physical appearance and style of life) have on the formation of a group.

There is no difference between the ethnically relevant customs and customs in general, as far as their effect is concerned. The belief in common descent, in combination with a similarity of customs, is likely to promote the spread of the activities of one part of an ethnic group among the rest, since the awareness of ethnic identity furthers imitation. This is especially true of the propaganda of religious groups.

It is not feasible to go beyond these vague generalizations. The content of joint activities that are possible on an ethnic basis remains indefinite. There is a corresponding ambiguity of concepts denoting ethnically determined action, that means, determined by the belief in blood relationship. Such concepts are *Völkerschaft*, *Stamm* (tribe), *Volk* (people), each of which is ordinarily used in the sense of an ethnic subdivision of the following one (although the first two may be used in reversed order). Using such terms, one usually implies either the existence of a contemporary political community, no matter how loosely organized, or memories of an extinct political community, such as they are preserved in epic tales and legends; or the existence of a linguistic or dialect group; or, finally, of a religious group. In the past, cults in particular were the typical concomitant of a tribal or *Volk* consciousness. But in the absence of the political community, contemporary or past, the external delimitation of the group was usually indistinct. The cult communities of Germanic tribes, as late as the Burgundian period (sixth century AD), were probably rudiments of political communities and therefore pretty well defined. By contrast, the Delphian oracle, the undoubted cultic symbol of Hellenism, also revealed information to the barbarians and accepted their veneration, and it was an organized cult only among some Greek segments, excluding the most powerful cities. The cult as an exponent of ethnic identity is thus generally either a remnant of a largely political community which once existed but was destroyed by disunion and colonization, or it is – as in the case of the Delphian Apollo – a product of a *Kulturgemeinschaft* brought about by other than purely ethnic conditions, but which in turn gives rise to the belief in blood relationship. All history shows how easily political action can give rise to the belief in blood relationship, unless gross differences of anthropological type impede it.

Tribe and political community: the disutility of the notion of 'ethnic group'

The tribe is clearly delimited when it is a subdivision of a polity, which, in fact, often establishes it. In this case, the artificial origin is revealed by the round numbers in which tribes usually appear, for example, the previously mentioned division of the people of Israel into twelve tribes, the three Doric *phylai* and the various *phylai* of the other Hellenes. When a political community was newly established or reorganized, the population was newly divided. Hence the tribe is here a political artifact, even though it soon adopts the whole symbolism of blood-relationship and particularly a tribal cult. Even today it is not rare that political artifacts develop a sense of affinity akin to that of blood relationship. Very schematic constructs such as those states of the United States that were made into squares according to their latitude have a strong sense of identity; it is also not rare that families travel from New York to Richmond to make an expected child a 'Virginian'.

Such artificiality does not preclude the possibility that the Hellenic *phylai*, for example, were at one time independent and that the polis used them schematically when they were merged into a political association. However, tribes that existed before the polis were either identical with the corresponding political groups which were subsequently associated into a polis, and in this case they were called *ethnos*, not *phyle*; or, as it probably happened many times, the politically unorganized tribe, as a presumed 'blood community', lived from the memory that it once engaged in joint political action, typically a single conquest or defense, and then such political memories constituted the tribe. Thus, the fact that tribal consciousness was primarily formed by common political experiences and not by common descent appears to have been a frequent source of the belief in common ethnicity.

Of course, this was not the only source: Common customs may have diverse origins. Ultimately, they derive largely from adaptation to natural conditions and the imitation of neighbors. In practice, however, tribal consciousness usually has a political meaning: in case of military danger or opportunity, it easily provides the basis for joint political action on the part of tribal members or *Volksgenossen* who consider one another as blood relatives. The eruption of a drive to political action is thus one of the major potentialities inherent in the rather ambiguous notions of tribe and people. Such intermittent political action may easily develop into the moral duty of all members of tribe or people (*Volk*) to support one another in case of a military attack, even if there is no corresponding political association; violators of this solidarity may suffer the fate of the (Germanic, pro-Roman) sibs of Segestes and Inguiomer – expulsion from the tribal territory – even if the tribe has no organized government. If the tribe has reached this stage, it has indeed become a continuous political community, no matter how inactive in peacetime, and hence unstable, it may be. However, even under favorable conditions the transition from the habitual to the customary and therefore obligatory is very fluid. All in all, the notion of 'ethnically' determined social action subsumes phenomena that a rigorous sociological analysis – as we do not attempt it here – would have to distinguish carefully: the actual subjective effect of those customs conditioned by heredity and those determined by tradition; the differential impact of the varying content of custom; the influence of common language, religion and political action, past and present, upon the formation of customs; the extent to which such factors create attraction and repulsion, and especially the belief in affinity or disaffinity of blood; the consequences of this belief for social action in general, and specifically for action on the basis of shared custom or blood relationship, for diverse sexual relations, etc. – all of this would have to be studied in detail. It is certain that in this process the collective term 'ethnic' would be abandoned, for it is unsuitable for a really rigorous analysis. However, we do not pursue sociology for its own sake and therefore limit ourselves to showing briefly the diverse factors that are hidden behind this seemingly uniform phenomenon.

10 The household community[1]

An examination of the specific, often highly complex effects of the ways in which social groups satisfy their economic wants does not belong into this general review, and concrete individual instances will be considered merely as examples.

While abandoning any attempt to systematically classify the various kinds of groups according to the structure, content and means of social action – a task which belongs to general sociology – we turn to a brief elucidation of those types of groups which are of the greatest importance for our exposition. Only the relationship of the economy to 'society' – in our case, the general structures of human groups – will be discussed here and not the relationship between the economic sphere and specific areas of culture – literature, art, science, etc. Contents and directions of social action are discussed only insofar as they give rise to specific forms that are also economically relevant. The resulting boundary is no doubt quite fluid. At any rate, we shall be concerned only with certain universal types of groups. What follows is only a general characterization. Concrete historical forms of these groups will be discussed in greater detail in connection with 'authority' (*E&S*, pp. 1006–70).

The relationships between father, mother and children, established by a stable sexual union, appear to us today as particularly 'natural' relationships. However, separated from the household as a unit of economic maintenance, the sexually based relationship between husband and wife, and the physiologically determined relationship between father and children are wholly unstable and tenuous. The father relationship cannot exist without a stable economic household unit of father and mother; even where there is such a unit the father relationship may not always be of great import. Of all the relationships arising from sexual intercourse, only the mother–child relationship is 'natural', because it is a biologically based household unit that lasts until the child is able to search for means of subsistence on his own.

Next comes the sibling group, which the Greeks called *homogalaktes* (literally: persons suckled with the same milk). Here, too, the decisive point is not the fact of the common mother but that of common maintenance. Manifold group relationships emerge, in addition to sexual and physiological

1 Taken from *E&S*, pp. 356–60.

relationships, as soon as the family emerges as a specific social institution. Historically, the concept of the family had several meanings, and it is useful only if its particular meaning is always clearly defined. More will be said later on about this.

Although the grouping of mother and children must be regarded as (in the present sense) the most primitive sort of family, it does not mean – indeed, it is unimaginable – that there ever were societies with maternal groupings only. As far as it is known, wherever the maternal grouping prevails as a family type, group relationships, economic and military, exist among men as well, and so do those of men with women (both sexual and economic). The pure maternal grouping as a normal, but obviously secondary, form is often found precisely where men's everyday life is confined to the stable community of a 'men's house', at first for military purposes, later on for other reasons. Men's houses (*Männerhäuser*) can be found in various countries as a specific concomitant and a resultant of militaristic development.

One cannot think of marriage as a mere combination of sexual union and socialization agency involving father, mother, and children. The concept of marriage can be defined only with reference to other groups and relationships besides these. Marriage as a social institution comes into existence everywhere only as an antithesis to sexual relationships which are *not* regarded as marriage. The existence of a marriage means that (1) a relationship formed against the will of the wife's or the husband's kin will not be tolerated and may even be avenged by an organization, such as in olden times the kinsmen of the husband or of the wife or both. (2) It means especially that only children born of stable sexual relationships within a more inclusive economic, political, religious, or other community to which one or both parents belong will be treated, by virtue of their descent, as equal members of an organization – house, village, kin, political group, status group, religious group; while descendants who are a product of other sexual relationships will not be treated in such a manner. This and nothing else is the meaning of the distinction between birth in wedlock and out of wedlock. The prerequisites of a legitimate marriage, the classes of persons not allowed to enter into stable relationships with each other, the kinds of permission and kinds of kinship or other connections required for their validity, the usages which must be observed – all these matters are regulated by the 'sacred' traditions and the laws of those groups. Thus, it is the regulations of groups other than mere sexual groupings and sibling communities of experience which endow the marriage with its specific quality. We do not intend to expound here the anthropologically very significant development of these regulations, since it is only their most important economic aspects which concern us.

Sexual relationships and the relationships between children based on the fact of their common parent or parents can engender social action only by becoming the normal, though not the only, bases of a specific economic organization: the household.

The household cannot be regarded as simply a primitive institution. Its prerequisite is not a 'household' in the present-day sense of the word, but rather a certain degree of organized cultivation of soil.

The household does not seem to have existed in a primitive economy of hunters and nomads. However, even under the conditions of a technically well-advanced agriculture, the household is often secondary with respect to a preceding state which accorded more power to the inclusive kinship and neighborhood group on the one hand, and more freedom to the individual *vis-à-vis* the parents, children, grandchildren, and siblings on the other hand. The almost complete separation of the husband's and wife's means and belongings, which was very frequent especially where social differentiation was low, seems to point in this direction, as does the occasional custom according to which man and wife were seated back to back during their meals or even took their meals separately, and the fact that within the political group there existed independent organizations of women with female chieftains alongside the men's organizations. However, one should not infer from such facts the existence of an individualistic primitive condition. Rather, conditions that are due to a certain type of military organization, such as the man's absence from the house for his military service, lead to a 'manless' household management by the wives and mothers. Such conditions were residually preserved in the family structure of the Spartans, which was based on the man's absence from the home and separation of belongings.

The size and inclusiveness of the household varies. But it is the most widespread economic group and involves continuous and intensive social action. It is the fundamental basis of loyalty and authority, which in turn is the basis of many other groups. This 'authority' is of two kinds: (1) the authority derived from superior strength; and (2) the authority derived from practical knowledge and experience. It is, thus, the authority of men as against women and children; of the able-bodied as against those of lesser capability; of the adult as against the child; of the old as against the young. The 'loyalty' is one of subjects toward the holders of authority and toward one another. As reverence for ancestors, it finds its way into religion; as a loyalty of the patrimonial official, retainer, or vassal, it becomes a part of the relationships originally having a domestic character.

In terms of economic and personal relationships, the household in its 'pure', though not necessarily primitive, form implies solidarity in dealing with the outside and communism of property and consumption of everyday goods within (household communism). The principle of solidarity in facing the outside world was still found in its pure form in the periodically contractually regulated households as entrepreneurial units in the medieval cities of northern and central Italy, especially those most advanced in capitalist economy. All members of the household, including at times even the clerks and apprentices who were members by contract, were jointly responsible to the creditors. This is the historic source of the joint liability of the owners of a private company for the debts incurred by the firm. This concept of joint liability was of great importance in the subsequent development of the legal forms of modern capitalism.

There was nothing corresponding to our law of inheritance in the old household communism. In its place there was, rather, the simple idea that the household is 'immortal'. If one of its members dies, or is expelled (after committing an inexpiable ill deed), or is permitted to join another household (by adoption), or is dismissed (*emancipatio*), or leaves out of his own accord (where this is permitted), he cannot possibly lay claim to his 'share'. By leaving the household he has relinquished his share. If a member of the household dies, the joint economy of the survivors simply goes on. The Swiss *Gemeinderschaften* operate in such a way to the present day.

The principle of household communism, according to which everybody contributes what he can and takes what he needs (as far as the supply of goods suffices), constitutes even today the essential feature of our family household, but is limited in the main to household consumption.

Common residence is an essential attribute of the pure type of household. Increase in size brings about a division and creation of separate households. In order to keep the property and the labor force intact, a compromise based on local decentralization without partition can be adopted. Granting some special privileges to the individual household is an inevitable consequence of such a solution. Such a partition can be carried to a complete legal separation and independence in the control of the business, yet at the same time a surprisingly large measure of household communism can still be preserved. It happens in Europe, particularly in the Alpine countries (cf. Swiss hotel-keepers' families), and also in the large family firms of international trade that, while the household and household authority have outwardly completely disappeared, a communism of risk and profit, i.e., sharing of profit and loss of otherwise altogether independent business managements, continues to exist.

I have been told about conditions in international houses with earnings amounting to millions, whose capital belongs for the most part, but not exclusively, to relatives of varying degree and whose management is predominantly, but not solely, in the hands of the members of the family. The individual establishments operate in very diverse lines of business; they possess highly variable amounts of capital and labor force; and they achieve widely variable profits. In spite of this, after the deduction of the usual interest on capital, the annual returns of all the branches are simply thrown into one hopper, divided into equal portions, and allotted according to an amazingly simple formula (often by the number of heads). The household communism on this level is being preserved for the sake of mutual economic support, which guarantees a balancing of capital requirements and capital surplus between the business establishments and spares them from having to solicit credit from outsiders. The 'calculative spirit' thus does not extend to the distribution of balance-sheet results, but it dominates all the more within the individual enterprise: even a close relative without capital and working as an employee will not be paid more than any other employee, because calculated costs of operation cannot be arbitrarily altered in favor of one individual without creating dissatisfaction in others. Beyond the balance sheet, those lucky enough to participate enter the 'realm of equality and brotherhood'.

11 Capitalism in Antiquity[1]

Nevertheless it is still necessary to face the problem whether or not the economic organization of Antiquity had characteristics which rule out the use of the concepts used to analyse the economic history of medieval and modern Europe. This question has been debated with vigour, and sometimes with passion, during the last century. The starting point of this controversy was the theory of Rodbertus,[2] according to whom all Antiquity was dominated by what he called an '*oikos* economy', one in which production centred around the household and the household was extended to include unfree workers. He argued that division of labour in Antiquity was essentially only specialization within the great slave households, and that commerce was only an occasional and secondary phenomenon, serving merely to dispose of the excess production of the great households. Hence Rodbertus argued for 'the autarky of the *oikos*'; he regarded the great households of Antiquity as in principle economically self-sufficient.

Karl Bücher accepted Rodbertus' account of the *oikos*, but with a difference.[3] His views may, I think, be interpreted – on the basis of his own statements – in this manner: he considered the *oikos* as an 'ideal type', denoting a kind of economic system which appeared in Antiquity with its basic features and characteristic consequences in a closer approximation to its 'pure concept' than anywhere else, without this *oikos* economy becoming universally dominant in Antiquity, either in time or space. One may add with confidence that even in those periods when the *oikos* was dominant this meant no more than a limitation on commerce and its role in meeting consumer needs. This limitation was, to be sure, strong and effective, and caused a corresponding economic and social degradation of those classes which would have otherwise carried on a more extensive trade.

Despite these reservations Bücher's use of Antiquity as an exemplification of the concept '*oikos* economy' caused him to emphasize certain paradigmatic aspects of ancient economic history to such an extent that a mistaken impression resulted. Historians concluded that Bücher regarded an

1 Taken from *The Agrarian Sociology of Ancient Civilisations*, translated by R.I. Franks, London, New Left Books, 1976, pp. 42–54.
2 Karl Rodbertus outlined his theory in vols 4 and 5 (1865) of the *Jahrbücher für Nationalökonomie und Statistik*.
3 Karl Bücher, *Industrial Evolution*, New York, Franklin, 1901 [German edn 1893].

'*oikos* economy' as characteristic of all Antiquity, at the same time ascribing a 'city economy' (in the ideal-typical sense) to the cities, a formulation of his views which Bücher himself called inaccurate. It was against this formulation that Eduard Meyer argued, going so far as to reject entirely the use of special economic concepts in studying Antiquity.[4] Meyer then made the attempt to operate entirely with modern economic concepts, at least in his analysis of Periclean Athens, and so used such terms as 'factory' and 'factory worker'.[5] He aimed to show that otherwise we cannot understand how 'modern' the economy then was, even with respect to the importance of commerce and banking.

Now in the first place there is no evidence for the existence in Antiquity even of 'cottage industry', such as appeared in Europe as early as the thirteenth century, based on letting out production on contract. This system represents an advance on the simple exploitation of the producer by an experienced merchant, a phenomenon of course known even in Antiquity. (In short: the stage which preceded development of the factory system in modern times has no parallel in Antiquity.)

There is moreover no evidence whatever for the existence in Antiquity of factories even in the purely technical or operational sense of the term, such as would encompass phenomena like Russia's factories manned by serfs rendering corvée labour or state factories producing for state needs. Nor do our sources ever indicate the widespread existence of industrial factories – that is, centres of production deserving the name 'factory' because of their size, continuity of operation, and technological sophistication (involving concentration of production in workshops, division and organization of labour, and use of fixed capital).

For example: the factory was not the normal form of production even in the industries of the Pharaohs, nor in the monopolies of the Ptolemies and of the later Roman Empire – periods where one would most expect to find it (see below). The Hellenistic *ergastērion* was simply the servants' quarters of a wealthy man, usually a merchant – often an importer of costly raw materials such as ivory. There he kept his skilled slaves – they could be of any number, and would have been either purchased or else held as collateral on loans – who worked under the direction of an overseer (*hegemōn tou ergastēriou*) on that part of his raw material which he did not sell to free artisans (Demosthenes XXVII: 823.19; see below on Athens).[6] One could divide this *ergastērion* at will by selling a part of the slaves, just as one would divide

---

4 Eduard Meyer, 'Die Wirtschaftliche Entwicklung des Altertums', in his *Kleine Schriften*, I, Halle, Max Niemeyer, 1924, pp. 79–168 [first published 1895].

5 [Weber] The remarkable thing about these ancient 'factories' is that they could be confiscated' (*aphobos*) or lost through dissipation (*timerokos*) to such a degree that they disappeared without leaving any physical trace. No modern factory could do that!

6 An *ergastērion* was a workshop whose legal ownership and workforce took a number of forms. See *E&S*, pp. 134–6.

an ingot of lead; this indicates clearly that we are dealing here with an undifferentiated group of slave labourers, not a differentiated organization of labour.

Here and there 'subsidiary industries' existed to aid the market operations of large agricultural organizations, and there were workshops attached to the monopoly administrations in the Near East and under the Roman Empire. There were also textile enterprises owned by great noblewomen which undoubtedly sometimes grew to large dimensions as in medieval times. But all of these concerns were dependent on plantations or tax administrations or an *oikos*; they were not genuine 'factories'. If one does find evidence of first steps towards something like a genuine factory organization – and this of course could occur in Antiquity as it did in Russia during serfdom – it soon becomes apparent that these phenomena, like the Russian factories and for the same reasons (see below), only serve as 'exceptions that prove the rule', for they were never a regular feature of the private sector.

Such an exception is the banking industry, which is supposed to have surpassed in size and character that of the thirteenth century, quantitatively if not qualitatively. In fact, this ancient banking seems to have been in the hands of the tax farmers of a very few centres of political power, Rome in particular as well as Athens and a few others. Furthermore different kinds of business – bottomry loans, merchant partnerships (characteristic of the discontinuity of 'early capitalism'), bank payments and transfers – were transacted with legal instruments essentially similar to those of the early Middle Ages. Thus the bill of exchange, already known in early medieval times, existed in a rudimentary form; similarly the rates, terms and legal regulation of interest were all generally comparable to early medieval equivalents. There was however an absence of all forms of state debt, something which was already developed in the Middle Ages, and which would have provided a regular source of return for capital. Instead there were typically substitutes for a national debt, such as the colossal hoards of oriental and Persian kings and Greek temples, and their characteristic use. All these phenomena indicate how little the existing stocks of precious metals were used as 'capital'.

Nothing could be more misleading, therefore, than to describe the economic institutions of Antiquity in modern terms. Whoever does this underrates – as often happens – the basic changes effected during the Middle Ages in the legal institutions governing capital, though the medieval economy was itself none the less different from ours. As for state and semi-state financial institutions, such as the Ptolemaic bank with its enormous reserves and the companies of Roman tax farmers, even these have striking parallels in corresponding developments in medieval city-states (e.g. Genoa). They were moreover surpassed by the commercial techniques of the thirteenth century.

Furthermore one must also emphasize that the *oikos* as defined by Rodbertus did in fact play a very important role in the economy of Antiquity. On the one hand it developed – as I have described elsewhere[7] – in the last stage of Graeco-Roman antiquity (the Empire) as a link to the feudal economy and society of early medieval Europe. But the *oikos* also appears in the Near East and also to some extent in Greece at the earliest stage of Antiquity known to us, as the households of kings, princes and priests – sometimes parallel to the modest economy of the masses, sometimes – through corvées – dominant over it.

It is not true, however, that the *oikos* developed out of the autarkic house communities of the masses, as Rodbertus believed. Rather it was partly 'state socialist' in origin, as in Egypt where it arose perhaps mainly as a result of public regulation of the irrigation system. It was also partly shaped in the ancient Near East and in early Greece by the commercial profits reaped by the first promoters of regular trade relations, the chiefs and princes; they enjoyed an effective monopoly of trade through their exchanges of gifts, and also profited from their own ventures (including piracy), collecting treasure to support their prestige and extend their resources.

Naturally in these archaic '*oikos* economies' of the princes and the political ruling class, the bulk of necessities were provided by the natural economy. Requisitions, corvées, and slave raids gave the princes the resources to buy foreign products; but the precious metals of their treasuries did not serve the purpose of a continuous supply of necessities through a money economy, not even in Persia. Instead the treasuries were merely used for rewarding individuals and gaining particular political aims. Similarly at the end of Antiquity (from the third century AD), the natural economy increasingly dominated both the manors and the '*oikos* economy' of the state.

However, the same is not true for the great slave systems of the classical periods of Antiquity, certainly not to the degree which Rodbertus believed, nor even that which I myself was once inclined to assume. On this matter one must give credit to Eduard Meyer and several of his students (e.g. Gummerus). Likewise I think that it must be admitted that, though justified in themselves, the attempts made to define Antiquity's specific economic characteristics, one of which was undoubtedly slave labour, have usually led to an under-estimation of the quantitative importance of free labour. This error, of which I too have been guilty, has been corrected by the researches of Wilcken on Egypt, even though that country was somewhat atypical.

Antiquity knew not only the unfree and half-free but also the free peasant, as owner or tenant or share-cropper. Likewise there existed, side by side with cottage industry and slave labour shops, production by free artisans – some working on order, some for wages (this was much more common), and some as extra help (this was also common). There were family workshops, one-man shops (much the most frequent), and shops run by a master with one or more

7 See 'The Social Causes of the Decline of Ancient Civilization', in *The Agrarian Sociology of Ancient Civilizations*, op. cit., p. 403.

slaves and free or (generally) unfree apprentices. There also existed the joint cooperative of artisans (Greek: *synergoi*) similar to the Russian *artel*,[8] as well as the organized crew of skilled craftsmen brought together by a contractor (Greek: *ergolabōn*) for specific purposes, nearly always composed of state workers.

Nevertheless Antiquity had no word corresponding to our 'journeyman', a concept which arose out of the medieval struggle against the 'masters', another notion unknown to Antiquity. For throughout Antiquity, despite its wealth of civic associations, the crafts never reached that level of autonomous organization which was attained by the high Middle Ages, nor did they reach medieval levels of refined division and organization of labour. Consider the institution of the journeyman!

Where one finds a guild or something similar in Antiquity it is nearly always essentially a state organization for the forced imposition of public tasks. The social position of the artisan was very low, with ephemeral and partial exceptions in the Hellenic democracies, and these exceptions are apparent rather than real. But even the employers evidently never had sufficient political power to secure legal concentration of trade in the cities, such as was achieved in the Middle Ages. (See below on Athens for the causes of this.)

Finally, Antiquity knew the free, unskilled wage earner; this type developed gradually from people sold into temporary slavery by themselves or by others (children, debtors). Wage earners were hired for harvesting, and were used by the state in large numbers for excavation work, construction and other public projects. Otherwise their employment was generally scattered and irregular.

The question to be considered now, therefore, is this: did a capitalist economy exist in Antiquity, to a degree significant for cultural history? To begin with, there is this general factor: the economic surplus of the ancient city – and this applies to the Near East as well as to the archaic *polis* of the Mediterranean lands – always had its original basis in the rents which the landed princes and noble clans derived from their estates and from levies on their dependants. This was true to a degree unknown today except in the case of certain capitals centring on a royal court; a more appropriate comparison would be Moscow during the period of serfdom. The significance of this source of wealth, and with it the specific political conditions of the economic 'flowering' of the cities – and hence too their swift decline – remained very important throughout all Antiquity. The ancient cities were always much more centres of consumption than production, whereas the opposite is true of medieval cities.

Similarly the development of ancient cities, although producing numerous elements of 'an urban economy' (discussed below), never led to anything so closely resembling the 'ideal type' as appeared in a great many medieval cities. This was a consequence of the fact that ancient civilization was coastal in

---

8 See below, p. 350 n. 21.

character. Hence these characteristics of the ancient economy: (1) cities exported certain articles of high labour input and quality; (2) cities were constantly dependent on grain imports from distant lands; (3) slaves were purchased; (4) city policies were shaped by specific commercial interests. In the light of these factors, one must then ask: although there were periods of Antiquity marked by a dramatic rise and fall in wealth, were these developments really part of an economic structure which we can call 'capitalist'?

Our answer will depend on our definition of 'capitalist' – and that of course can take many forms. However, one element must be emphasized: capital always means wealth used to gain profit in commerce. Otherwise the term loses any classificatory use. Therefore we should expect a capitalist economy to be based on commerce. This means that goods are produced (in part at least) to become objects of trade, and also that the means of production are themselves objects of exchange. This excludes all manorial charges levied in rural areas on subject groups, like the various tributes – rents, dues and services – extracted from peasants in the early Middle Ages, who had to pay dues in kind and money on their possessions, inheritances, trade, and persons. For neither the land owned nor the people subjected can be regarded as 'capital'; title to both depended (in principle) not on purchase in the open market but on traditional ties. This was a form of manorialism and was known also in Antiquity.

There also existed in Antiquity the commercial practice of dividing estates into parcels and leasing them out, in which case the land is used as a source of rent and capitalist enterprise is absent. One also finds in the Ancient world the exploitation of subjects as labourers in lords' workshops, as cultivators on the land (Pharaonic Egypt, Roman imperial domains), as purchased slaves in large enterprises, and in combinations of the last two.

Analysis of domain agriculture (*Fronhofsbetrieb*) is difficult because one finds a great variety of gradations; they range from systems based on formally free transfer and lease of land to *coloni* on a market basis, to systems based on completely traditional social ties binding the lord and the cultivator owing him labour services to reciprocal obligations. Nevertheless the latter is by far the more common type wherever the land is worked by a colonate. In such cases the *coloni* are not themselves 'capital', for they are not part of an autonomous labour market, but their labour along with the land they work can become objects of trade, and in fact became such in the Near East and later Roman Empire. In these cases the system is intermediate in character: it is capitalist insofar as goods are produced for the market and the land is an object of trade; it is non-capitalist insofar as the labour force as a means of production cannot be bought or leased in the open market.

Generally the existence of domain agriculture is a transitional phenomenon, either from *oikos* to capitalism or from *oikos* to natural economy. It is always a symptom of relative lack of capital, especially risk capital. This shortage is reflected in the practice of forcing dependants to find their own working capital, and also in policies aimed at reducing capital expenditures on inventory and labour; thus instead of buying slaves or hiring labourers recourse is made to forced labour. Usually the reason for this lack of capital is a relatively low level of trading activity.

Slave agriculture, when the slaves are normal objects of exchange (it makes no difference whether particular labourers have been actually purchased or not), and the land worked is privately owned or leased, is of course capitalist in character from the economic point of view. That is because land and slaves are both acquired in the open market and are clearly 'capital'. The work force is bought, not hired as in enterprises conducted with free labour; or if labour is, exceptionally, hired, it is not from the slave but rather from his owner. Hence the capital needed for slave labour is significantly more than would be needed – other things being equal – for the same quantity of free labour. Similarly buying land demands commitment of more capital than would leasing it.

Finally there is the large-scale capitalist enterprise based on 'free' labour. It permits the maximum use of available capital at the same level of accumulation for the output of means of production. In general this form of enterprise was not a regular feature of private economic activity in Antiquity, either within agriculture or outside it. It is true that one finds 'country squires' in the Near East and in Greece, but precisely in those periods and areas governed by tradition – e.g. in inland regions in the Hellenic period, in references in the Talmud, and certain zones in the Hellenistic period – not in areas marked by advanced economic development. Large enterprises which were on a regular basis and used only hired (i.e. free) labour existed in certain state undertakings, but private enterprises of this sort did not play a significant role in the social or economic systems of the centres of classical culture. This does not apply entirely, however, to the later period of the Near East.

Today the concept of 'capitalist enterprise' is generally based on this last form, the large firm run with free wage-labour, because it is this form which is responsible for the characteristic social problems of modern capitalism. From this point of view it has been argued that capitalist economy did not play a dominant role in Antiquity, and did not in fact exist. However, to accept this premise is to limit needlessly the concept of capitalist economy to a single form of valorization of capital (*Kapitalverwertungsart*) – the exploitation of other people's labour on a contractual basis – and thus to introduce social factors. Instead we should take into account only economic factors. Where we find that property is an object of trade and is utilized by individuals for profit-making enterprise in a market economy, there we have capitalism. If this be accepted, then it becomes perfectly clear that capitalism shaped whole periods of Antiquity, and indeed precisely those periods we call 'golden ages'.

But we must avoid exaggeration. In particular, it is necessary to show the specific peculiarities of the various types of capital goods, and the manner of their valorization, which determined the course of ancient economic history. Among the types of capital goods we do not find, of course, are all those tools of production which were devised during the last two centuries of technological advance, and which today constitute what we call fixed capital. On the other hand Antiquity had a form of capital goods now in disuse: debt or chattel slaves. Similarly among the forms of capitalist enterprise a very small role was played by the workshop in Antiquity, and an even smaller one by the factory. On the other hand a form of economic activity now of little significance was of absolutely dominant importance in Antiquity: government contract.

The most important forms of capital investment in Antiquity were as follows: (1) government contracts for partial or total collection of taxes and public works; (2) mines; (3) sea trade, with ownership of ships or part ownership, especially through bottomry loans; (4) plantations; (5) banking and related activities; (6) mortgages; (7) overland trade. The last only sporadically became a regular, large-scale enterprise – in the West only during the first two centuries of the Roman Empire and only with respect to trade with the North and North-east; most overland trade was in goods sent on consignment by caravan. Also important were: (8) leasing out slaves (sometimes educated slaves) or establishing slaves as independent artisans or merchants in return for a percentage of income (or *obrok*, as the Russians would say); (9) finally, capitalist exploitation of slaves skilled in a craft, either owned or leased, sometimes in a workshop and sometimes not.

That slaves were frequently used in private economic enterprises cannot be doubted. Artisans were to be seen working alongside a few slaves of their own. Capitalistic exploitation in the type of enterprise called *ergastērion* has been mentioned above and will be discussed further below. Although there is no proof of its existence in the classical period proper, we can certainly presume that there existed the 'domestic system', in which the master provides raw materials and tools, and the slave produces the finished product in his own family household and then delivers it to him. Certainly this existed in the Near East, and it was dominant in ancient Egypt. We may, therefore, presume such a system in the Athenian pottery industry, even though many exports bear the same name (so far the largest group numbers about eighty). The name is of course that of an artist, not that of a 'manufacturer' or 'contractor'. The artist's name will have been that of a family of potters in which technical skill was passed on as an inheritance and as a secret, and the name would be kept as an eponym. In this connection we should note the existence of artisans' villages (*dēmoi*) in Attica, characteristic of the family-like organization of handicrafts.

The quantitative and also the qualitative importance of capitalist enterprise in Antiquity were determined by a number of independent variables which appeared in very different combinations at different times. These variables were as follows:

1   It is clear that the supply of precious metals had great importance for the tempo of capitalist development. However, there is a mistaken tendency now current to overestimate the importance of this factor for the structure of the whole economy itself. Thus Babylonia had no mines

and evidently very little precious metal supplies, as is indicated by the correspondence between Babylonia's kings and the Egyptian pharaohs, and also by the use of precious metals only as a measure of value; nevertheless from earliest times Babylonia's exchange system was as developed as that of any other Eastern land, and more developed than that of gold-rich Egypt. Similarly capitalism was not particularly important as a basic element of the economic structure of Ptolemaic Egypt, even though the Ptolemies had colossal hoards of precious metals (taking current estimates as at least approximately correct) and their economy was thoroughly monetarized. Indeed, capitalism developed to a greater extent in contemporary Rome.

There is also the strange theory that the rise of a natural economy in the later Roman Empire was the result of a fall in the productivity of the mines. This probably reverses the actual sequence of cause and effect; where a decline in mining productivity did occur, it was most likely caused by a shift from the classical period's mining system, based on a highly developed capitalist organization using slave labour, to a new system based on small contractors.

The foregoing, however, should not be taken as a denial of the significance of control over large supplies of precious metals and in particular the important effects for cultural history of the sudden appearance of such supplies. Some examples: (a) ancient customary kingship was supported by the 'royal treasure'; (b) without the mines of Laureion there would probably have been no Athenian fleet; (c) the transfer of many temple treasuries into the circulating money supply during the Hellenic period probably had much to do with price changes *c.* 500 BC; (d) the release of the Achaemenids' hoard furthered Hellenistic city-foundations; (e) the well-known effects on Rome caused by the colossal influx of precious metals won as war booty in the second century BC. However, the fact that this booty was used as it was and not otherwise – for example, it was not hoarded, as in the Near East – must have been due to prior existence of certain conditions. In other periods of Antiquity the presence of large stores of precious metals did in fact fail to have a 'creative' significance; that is, they did not lead to the development of qualitatively new forms of economic activity.

2   The economic specificity of the capitalist use of slave labour, as appears from comparison with free labour systems, is that a much greater amount of capital must be invested to assemble and maintain the work force. When low sales cause suspension of production not only does the capital invested in slaves bring no interest – as is true of capital invested in machines – but also the slaves literally 'eat up' additional amounts. The result is to slow down capital turnover and capital formation.

Furthermore there was a large risk in investing capital in slave labour. This was due first of all to the fact that slave mortality was very high and entirely unpredictable, causing capital loss to the owner. Then in addition any political upset could wipe out completely investments in slaves. This is particularly evident in the dramatic variations in slave prices; thus Lucullus sold prisoners into slavery at 4 drachmae apiece at a time when the regular market price, due to low supply, had risen to several hundred drachmae for an able-bodied labourer. The result of this was that capital invested in slaves could be drastically devalued at any time.

Moreover, there was no basis for reliable cost accounting, the necessary condition for large industrial enterprises based on division of labour. Along with this there was also the fact that patriarchal slavery, in the form prevalent in the Near East, either made the slave a member of the master's household or else conceded to him the right to have his own family household. In the latter case there could of course be no question of gaining maximum return on investments; the slave either paid dues, thus functioning as a source of rents rather than labour, or else performed work, possibly with his family, in which case he filled the role of labourer or unfree house worker with all the limitations on profit-making this implied.

Another limitation on the truly capitalist exploitation of slaves as a means of production was the fact that the slave market depended for supply on successful wars. For full capitalist exploitation of the work force was possible only if the slaves had no families, in fact as well as in law; in other words, if they were kept in barracks, which, however, made reproduction of slaves impossible. For the cost of maintaining women and rearing children would have been a dead ballast on working capital.

12 The conditions of maximum formal rationality of capital accounting[1]

The following are the principal conditions necessary for obtaining a maximum of formal rationality of capital accounting in production enterprises: (1) complete appropriation of all material means of production by owners and the complete absence of all formal appropriation of opportunities for profit in the market; that is, market freedom; (2) complete autonomy in the selection of management by the owners, thus complete absence of formal appropriation of rights to managerial functions; (3) complete absence of appropriation of jobs and of opportunities for earning by workers and, conversely, the absence of appropriation of workers by owners. This implies free labor, freedom of the labor market, and freedom in the selection of workers; (4) complete absence of substantive regulation of consumption, production, and prices, or of other forms of regulation which limit freedom of contract or specify conditions of exchange. This may be called substantive freedom of contract; (5) complete calculability of the technical conditions of the production process; that is, a mechanically rational technology; (6) complete calculability of the functioning of public administration and the legal order and a reliable purely formal guarantee of all contracts by the political authority. This is a formally rational administration and law; (7) the most complete separation possible of the enterprise and its conditions of success and failure from the household or private budgetary unit and its property interests. It is particularly important that the capital at the disposal of the enterprise should be clearly distinguished from the private wealth of the owners, and should not be subject to division or dispersion through inheritance. For large-scale enterprises, this condition tends to approach an optimum from a formal point of view: in the fields of transport, manufacture, and mining, if they are organized in corporate form with freely transferrable shares and limited liability, and in the field of agriculture, if there are relatively long-term leases for large-scale production units; (8) a monetary system with the highest possible degree of formal rationality.

Only a few points are in need of comment, though even these have already been touched on.

---

1 Taken from *E&S*, pp. 161–6.

1   With respect to the freedom of labor and of jobs from appropriation, it is true that certain types of unfree labor, particularly full-fledged slavery, have guaranteed what is formally a more complete power of disposal over the worker than is the case with employment for wages. But there are various reasons why this is less favorable to rationality and efficiency than the employment of free labor: (a) The amount of capital which it was necessary to invest in human resources through the purchase and maintenance of slaves has been much greater than that required by the employment of free labor; (b) the capital risk attendant on slave owner-ship has not only been greater but specifically irrational in that slave labor has been exposed to all manner of non-economic influences, par-ticularly to political influence in a very high degree; (c) the slave market and correspondingly the prices of slaves have been particularly subject to fluctuation, which has made a balancing of profit and loss on a rational basis exceedingly difficult; (d) for similar reasons, particularly involving the political situation, there has been a difficult problem of recruitment of slave labor forces; (e) when slaves have been permitted to enjoy family relationships, this has made the use of slave labor more expensive in that the owner has had to bear the cost of maintaining the women and of rearing children. Very often, he has had no way in which he could make rational economic use of these elements as part of his labor force; (f) hence the most complete exploitation of slave labor has been possible only when they were separated from family relationships and subjected to a ruthless discipline. Where this has happened it has greatly accentuated the difficulties of the problem of recruitment; (g) it has in general been impossible to use slave labor in the operation of tools and apparatus, the efficiency of which required a high level of responsibility and of involvement of the operator's self-interest; (h) perhaps most important of all has been the impossibility of selection, of employment only after trying out in the job, and of dismissal in accordance with fluctuations of the business situation or when personal efficiency declined.

Hence the employment of slave labor has only been possible in general under the following conditions: (a) Where it has been possible to main-tain slaves very cheaply; (b) where there has been an opportunity for regular recruitment through a well-supplied slave market; (c) in agri-cultural production on a large scale of the plantation type, or in very simple industrial processes. The most important examples of this type of relatively successful use of slaves are the Carthaginian and Roman plant-ations, those of colonial areas and of the Southern United States, and the Russian 'factories'. The drying up of the slave market, which resulted from the pacification of the Empire, led to the decay of the plantations of Antiquity. In North America, the same situation led to a continual search for cheap new land, since it was impossible to meet the costs of slaves and pay a land rent at the same time. In Russia, the serf 'factories' were barely able to meet the competition of the *kustar* type of household industry and were totally unable to compete with free factory labor. Even before the emancipation of the serfs, petitions for permission to dismiss workers were common, and the factories decayed with the introduction of shops using free labor.

When workers are employed for wages, the following advantages to industrial profitability and efficiency are conspicuous: (a) Capital risk and the necessary capital investment are smaller; (b) the costs of reproduction and of bringing up children fall entirely on the worker. His wife and children must seek employment on their own account; (c) largely for this reason, the risk of dismissal is an important incentive to the maximization of production; (d) it is possible to select the labor force according to ability and willingness to work.

2   The following comment may be made on the separation of enterprise and household. The separation in England of the producing farm *enterprise*, leasing the land and operating with capital accounting, from the entailed *ownership* of the land is by no means fortuitous, but is the outcome of an undisturbed development over centuries which was characterized by the absence of an effective protection of the status of peasants. This in turn was a consequence of the country's insular position. Every joining of the *ownership* of land with the *cultivation* of the land turns the land into a capital good for the economic unit, thus increasing the capital requirements and the capital risks of this unit. It impedes the separation of the household from the economic establishment; the settlements paid out at inheritance, for instance, burden the resources of the enterprise. It reduces the liquidity of the entrepreneur's capital and introduces a number of irrational factors into his capital accounting. Hence the separation of landownership from the organization of agricultural production is, from a formal point of view, a step which promotes the rationality of capital accounting. It goes without saying, however, that any substantive evaluation of this phenomenon is quite another matter, and its conclusions may be quite different depending on the values underlying the judgment.

The principal modes of capitalistic orientation of profit-making

The 'capitalistic' orientation of profit-making activity (in the case of rationality, this means: the orientation to capital accounting) can take a number of qualitatively different forms, each of which represents a definite type:

1   It may be orientation to the profit possibilities in continuous buying and selling on the market ('trade') with free exchange – that is, absence of formal and at least relative absence of substantive compulsion to effect any given exchange; or it may be orientation to the profit possibilities in continuous production of goods in enterprises with capital accounting.

2   It may be orientation to the profit possibilities in trade and speculation in different currencies, in the taking over of payment functions of all sorts and in the creation of means of payment; the same with respect to the professional extension of credit, either for consumption or for profit-making purposes.

3   It may be orientation to opportunities for predatory profit from political organizations or persons connected with politics. This includes the financing of wars or revolutions and the financing of party leaders by loans and supplies.

4   It may be orientation to the profit opportunities in continuous business activity which arise by virtue of domination by force or of a position of power guaranteed by the political authority. There are two main sub-types: colonial profits, either through the operation of plantations with compulsory deliveries or compulsory labor or through monopolistic and compulsory trade, and fiscal profits, through the farming of taxes and of offices, whether at home or in colonies.

5   It may be orientation to profit opportunities in unusual transactions with political bodies.

6   It may be orientation to profit opportunities of the following types: (a) in purely speculative transactions in standardized commodities or in the securities of enterprises; (b) in the execution of the continuous financial operations of political bodies; (c) in the promotional financing of new enterprises in the form of sale of securities to investors; (d) in the speculative financing of capitalistic enterprises and of various other types of economic organization with the purpose of a profitable regulation of market situations or of attaining power.

Types (1) and (6) (above) are to a large extent peculiar to the modern Western world. The other types have been common all over the world for thousands of years wherever the possibilities of exchange and money economy (for type 2) and money financing (for types 3–5) have been present. In the Western world they have not had such a dominant importance as modes of profit-making as they had in Antiquity, except in restricted areas and for relatively brief periods, particularly in times of war. Where large areas have been pacified for a long period, as in the Chinese and later Roman Empire, these types have tended to decline, leaving only trade, money changing, and lending as forms of capitalistic acquisition. For the capitalistic financing of political activities was everywhere the product of the competition of states with one another for power, and of the corresponding competition for capital which moved freely between them. All this ended only with the establishment of the unified empires.

It is only in the modern Western world that rational capitalistic enterprises with fixed capital, free labor, the rational specialization and combination of functions, and the allocation of productive functions on the basis of capitalistic enterprises, bound together in a market economy, are to be found. In other words, we find the capitalistic type of organization of labor, which in formal terms is purely voluntary, as the typical and dominant mode of providing for the wants of the masses of the population, with expropriation of the workers from the means of production and appropriation of the enterprises by security owners. It is also only here that we find public credit in the form of issues of government securities, the 'going public' of business enterprises, the floating of security issues and financing carried on as the specialized function of rational business enterprises, trade in commodities and securities on organized exchanges, money and capital markets, monopolistic organizations as a form of rational business organization of the entrepreneurial *production* of goods, and not only of the trade in them.

This difference calls for an explanation and the explanation cannot be given on economic grounds alone. Types (3) to (5) inclusive will be treated here together as 'politically oriented capitalism.' The whole of the later discussion will be devoted particularly to the problem of explaining the difference. In general terms, it is possible only to make the following statements:

1   It is clear from the very beginning that the politically oriented events and processes which open up these profit opportunities exploited by political capitalism are irrational from an economic point of view – that is, from the point of view of orientation to market advantages and thus to the consumption needs of budgetary units.
2   It is further clear that purely speculative profit opportunities and pure consumption credit are irrational from the point of view both of want satisfaction and of the production of goods, because they are determined by the fortuitous distribution of ownership and of market advantages. The same may also be true of opportunities for promotion and financing, under certain circumstances; but this is not necessarily always the case.

Apart from the rational capitalistic enterprise, the modern economic order is unique in its monetary system and in the commercialization of ownership shares in enterprises through the various forms of securities.

13 Status groups and classes[1]

Class situation and class types

'Class situation' means the typical probability of:

1   procuring goods
2   gaining a position in life and
3   finding inner satisfactions,

a probability which derives from the relative control over goods and skills and from their income-producing uses within a given economic order.

'Class' means all persons in the same class situation.

1   A *'property* class' is primarily determined by property differences,
2   A *'commercial* class' by the marketability of goods and services,
3   A *'social* class' makes up the totality of those class situations within which individual and generational mobility is easy and typical.

Associations of class members – class organizations – may arise on the basis of all three types of classes. However, this does not necessarily happen: 'Class situation' and 'class' refer only to the same (or similar) interests which an individual shares with others. In principle, the various controls over consumer goods, means of production, assets, resources and skills each constitute a *particular* class situation. A *uniform* class situation prevails only when completely unskilled and propertyless persons are dependent on irregular employment. Mobility among, and stability of, class positions differs greatly; hence, the unity of a social class is highly variable.

Property classes

The primary significance of a positively privileged property class lies in

1   its exclusive acquisition of high-priced consumers goods,
2   its sales monopoly and its ability to pursue systematic policies in this regard,

---

1 Taken from *E&S*, pp. 302–7.

3   its monopolization of wealth accumulation out of unconsumed surpluses,
4   its monopolization of capital formation out of savings, i.e., of the utilization of wealth in the form of loan capital, and its resulting control over executive positions in business,
5   its monopolization of costly (educational) status privileges.

Positively privileged property classes are typically *rentiers*, receiving income from:

(a) men (the case of slave-owners),
(b) land,
(c) mines,
(d) installations (factories and equipment),
(e) ships,
(f) creditors (of livestock, grain or money),
(g) securities.

Negatively privileged property classes are typically:

(a) the unfree (see under 'Status and status group'),
(b) the de-classed (the *proletarii* of Antiquity),
(c) the 'paupers.'

In between are the various 'middle classes' (*Mittelstandsklassen*), which make a living from their property or their acquired skills. Some of them may be 'commercial classes' (entrepreneurs with mainly positive privileges, proletarians with negative ones). However, not all of them fall into the latter category (witness peasants, craftsmen, officials).

The mere differentiation of property classes is not 'dynamic', that is, it need not result in class struggles and revolutions. The strongly privileged class of slave-owners may co-exist with the much less privileged peasants or even the de-classed, frequently without any class antagonism and sometimes in solidarity (against the unfree). However, the juxtaposition of property classes *may* lead to revolutionary conflict between:

1   landowners and the de-classed or
2   creditor and debtors (often urban patricians versus rural peasants or small urban craftsmen).

These struggles need not focus on a change of the economic system, but may aim primarily at a redistribution of wealth. In this case we can speak of 'property revolutions' (*Besitzklassenrevolutionen*).

A classic example of the lack of class conflict was the relationship of the 'poor white trash' to the plantation owners in the Southern States. The 'poor white trash' were far more anti-Negro than the plantation owners, who were often imbued with patriarchal sentiments. The major examples for the struggle of the de-classed against the propertied date back to Antiquity, as does the antagonism between creditors and debtors and land owners and the de-classed.

Commercial classes

The primary significance of a positively privileged commercial class lies in:

1   the monopolization of entrepreneurial management for the sake of its members and their business interests,
2   the safeguarding of those interests through influence on the economic policy of the political and other organizations.

Positively privileged commercial classes are typically *entrepreneurs*:

(a) merchants,
(b) shipowners,
(c) industrial and
(d) agricultural entrepreneurs,
(e) bankers and financiers, *sometimes* also
(f) professionals with sought-after expertize or privileged education (such as lawyers, physicians, artists), or
(g) workers with monopolistic qualifications and skills (natural, or acquired through drill or training).

Negatively privileged commercial classes are typically *laborers* with varying qualifications:

(a) skilled
(b) semi-skilled
(c) unskilled.

In between again are 'middle classes': the self-employed farmers and craftsmen and frequently:

(a) public and private officials,
(b) the last two groups mentioned in the first category (i.e., the 'liberal professions' and the labor groups with exceptional qualifications).

Social classes

Social classes are:

1   the working class as a whole – the more so, the more automated the work process becomes,
2   the *petite bourgeoisie*,
3   the propertyless intelligentsia and specialists (technicians, various kinds of white-collar employees, civil servants – possibly with considerable social differences depending on the cost of their training),
4   the classes privileged through property and education.

The unfinished last part of Karl Marx's *Capital* apparently was intended to deal with the issue of class unity in the face of skill differentials. Crucial for this differentiation is the increasing importance of semi-skilled workers, who can be trained on the job in a relatively short time, over the apprenticed and sometimes also the unskilled workers. Semi-skilled qualification too can often become monopolistic (weavers, for example, sometimes achieve their greatest efficiency after five years). It used to be that every worker aspired to be a self-employed small businessman. However, this is less and less feasible. In the generational sequence, the rise of groups (1) and (2) into (3) (technicians, white-collar workers) is relatively the easiest. Within class (4) money increasingly buys *everything*, at least in the sequence of generations. In banks and corporations, as well as in the higher ranks of the civil service, class (3) members have a chance to move up into class (4).

Class-conscious organization succeeds most easily:

1   against the immediate economic opponents (workers against entrepreneurs, but *not* against stockholders, who truly draw 'unearned' incomes, and also *not* in the case of peasants confronting manorial lords);
2   if large numbers of persons are in the same class situation,
3   if it is technically easy to organize them, especially if they are concentrated at their place of work (as in a 'workshop community'),
4   if they are led toward readily understood goals, which are imposed and interpreted by men outside their class (intelligentsia).

Status and status group (*Stand*)

'Status' (*ständische Lage*) shall mean an effective claim to social esteem in terms of positive or negative privileges; it is typically founded on:

1   style of life, hence
2   formal education, which may be

    (a) empirical training or

    (b) rational instruction, and the corresponding forms of behavior,

3   hereditary or occupational prestige.

       In practice, status expresses itself through:

    (a) connubium [marriage],

    (b) commensality [eating together], possibly

    (c) monopolistic appropriation of privileged modes of acquisition or the abhorrence of certain kinds of acquisition,

    (d) status conventions (traditions) of other kinds.

Status *may* rest on class position of a distinct or an ambiguous kind. However, it is not solely determined by it: Money and an entrepreneurial position are not in themselves status qualifications, although they may lead to them; and the lack of property is not in itself a status disqualification, although this may be a reason for it. Conversely, status may influence, if not completely determine, a class position without being identical with it. The class position of an officer, a civil servant or a student may vary greatly according to their wealth and yet not lead to a different status since upbringing and education create a common style of life.

A '*status group*' means a plurality of persons who, within a larger group, successfully claim

1   a special social esteem, and possibly also

2   status monopolies.

Status groups may come into being:

1   in the first instance, by virtue of their own style of life, particularly the type of vocation: 'self-styled' or occupational status groups,

2   in the second instance, through hereditary charisma, by virtue of successful claims to higher-ranking descent: hereditary status groups, or

3   through monopolistic appropriation of political or hierocratic powers: political or hierocratic status groups.

The development of hereditary status groups is generally a form of the (hereditary) appropriation of privileges by an organization or qualified individuals. Every definite appropriation of political powers and the corresponding economic opportunities tends to result in the rise of status groups, and vice versa.

Commercial classes arise in a market-oriented economy, but status groups arise within the framework of organizations which satisfy their wants through monopolistic liturgies, or in feudal or in *ständisch*-patrimonial fashion. Depending on the prevailing mode of stratification, we shall speak of a 'status society' or a 'class society'. The status group comes closest to the social class and is most unlike the commercial class. Status groups are often created by property classes.

Every status society lives by conventions, which regulate the style of life, and hence creates economically irrational consumption patterns and fetters the free market through monopolistic appropriations and by curbing the individual's earning power.

14 The distribution of power in society: classes, status groups and parties[1]

The structure of every legal order (not only the 'state') has a direct influence on the distribution of power, whether economic or of any other kind, within the community concerned. By 'power' we mean very generally the chances which a man or a group of men have to realize their will in a communal activity, even against the opposition of others taking part in it. 'Economically determined' power is not, of course, the same thing as 'power' in general. On the contrary, economic power may result from the possession of power which rests on other foundations. Conversely, men do not only aspire to power for the sake of economic enrichment. Power, even economic power, may be valued for its own sake, and it is very often the case that men seek power in part for the sake of the honorific social 'status' which it brings. Not all power, however, brings status with it. The typical American 'boss', like the typical large-scale financial speculator, consciously renounces such status; and generally speaking it is precisely 'pure' economic power, especially power based on 'naked' cash, which is not accepted in any way as a basis of social 'status'. On the other hand, power is not the only basis of social status. Quite the contrary: social status or prestige can be, and very often has been, the basis of power, even of economic power. The legal system may guarantee both power and status. But, in normal circumstances at least, it is not their primary source; it is merely an extra factor which increases the chances of possessing them but cannot always make it certain. The mode of distribution of social 'status' among typical groups of members of a community will be called the *social order*. Its relation to the 'legal order' is, of course, very similar to that of the economic order. It is not the same as the economic order, by which we mean only the mode of distribution and consumption of economic goods and services. But it is of course very much affected by the economic order and

---

1 Taken from *Weber: Selections in Translation*, edited by W.G. Runciman and translated by Eric Matthews, Cambridge, Cambridge University Press, pp. 43–56. The main title to Reading 14 is descriptive and not Weber's own. Throughout this excerpt Weber uses the term 'community' in a very broad sense and a few years later he substituted the term 'social action' for 'communal action'. See Hiroshi Orihara, 'From "A Torso with a Wrong Head" to "Five Disjointed Body-Parts without a Head". A Critique of the Editorial Policy for Max Weber Gesamtausgabe I/22', *Max Weber Studies*, 2, 3, 2003, pp. 131–64.

interacts with it. 'Classes', 'status groups' and 'parties' are phenomena of the distribution of power in a community.

Classes are not 'communities' in the sense we have adopted, but merely possible (and frequent) bases of communal action. The term 'class' will be used when (i) a large number of men have in common a specific causal factor influencing their chances in life, insofar as (ii) this factor has to do only with the possession of economic goods and the interests involved in earning a living, and furthermore (iii) in the conditions of the market in commodities or labour. This we shall call 'class situation'. It is an elementary fact of economic life that the manner in which the disposal of property in goods is distributed within a human group whose members encounter one another in the market for purposes of exchange and compete with one another is in itself sufficient to create specific chances in life. In accordance with the principle of marginal utility, it excludes the propertyless from taking part in the competition for highly valued goods in favour of the propertied and thus in practice gives the latter the exclusive opportunity to acquire such goods. It means that, other things being equal, those who, being already provided with goods, are not dependent on exchange, alone have the exclusive opportunity of profiting from exchange. Thus, in general at least, it increases their power in the price struggle against those who, having no property, have nothing to offer but their labour-power, either in its natural form or in the form of the products of their labour, and so are compelled to sell this labour and its products in order to keep body and soul together. It means that only those who own property have the possibility of shifting what they own from the sphere of benefit as 'wealth' to the sphere of employment as 'capital': hence they alone can become entrepreneurs and have the chance of directly or indirectly participating in capital profit. All this applies in the sphere of pure market conditions. 'Property' and 'propertylessness' are thus the basic categories underlying all class situations, whether in the form of struggles over prices or struggles between commercial competitors.

Within this general framework, however, class situations may be further differentiated in terms of the nature of the property which is a source of income, on the one hand, and in terms of the nature of the services offered on the market, on the other. The class situations of property-owners may be distinguished by the differences in the kind of property which they own: dwelling-houses, workshops, warehouses or shops, agricultural land (this last may be further subdivided in terms of the size of landholdings – a quantitative difference with possible qualitative consequences), mines, livestock, men (slaves), disposal of moveable means of production or industrial tools of all kinds, above all money or objects readily exchangeable for money at any time, products of one's own or other people's labour (this last depends on the stage of development of consumption), or commercially viable monopolies of any kind. Their class situation depends as much on these differences in kinds of property as on the 'meaning' which they can and do give to the use made of their property, especially their property with a money value; such factors

determine whether, for instance, they belong to the *rentier* or the entrepreneurial class. There is an equally marked distinction amongst those who
have no property but only their labour to offer, depending as much on the
nature of the services performed as on whether these services involve them in
a continuous or only a casual relationship to the consumer. The element
which is always present in all cases where the concept of 'class' is applied,
however, is that it is the nature of chances in the market which is the common
factor determining the fate of a number of individuals. In this sense, the 'class
situation' is ultimately a 'market situation'. It is only a first step towards the
formation of genuine 'classes' when in cattle-breeding societies the effect of
pure, naked ownership as such is to give over those without property into the
power of the cattle-owners as slaves or bondsmen. But it is certainly true that
such situations first reveal, in the practice of loaning cattle and the sheer
rigour of the law on debt in such communities, the way in which the mere
ownership of property as such can determine the fate of an individual: in this
there is a sharp contrast with agricultural communities based on labour. The
debtor–creditor relationship first formed the basis of 'class situations' in the
towns, where a credit market of a rather primitive kind developed, with interest rates which increased in proportion to the degree of distress and with
virtual monopolisation of lending by a plutocracy. With this, 'class struggles'
began. By contrast, when the fate of a group of men is not determined by
their chances of using goods or labour in the market (as in the case of slaves),
that group is not in the technical sense a 'class' but a 'status group'.

As we are using the term, then, 'classes' are clearly the product of economic interests, bound up with the existence of the 'market'. Moreover, the
concept of 'class interests' becomes ambiguous, indeed ceases to be in any
way a clearly empirical concept, as soon as it is taken to mean anything but
the actual direction taken by the interests of a specific cross-section of those
subject to a class situation, and following from the class situation with a
specific probability. In the same class situation, even when other things are
equal, the probable direction of the interests of an individual worker will vary
greatly according to whether, in terms of native ability, he is highly, averagely
or poorly qualified for the occupation in question. It will depend likewise on
whether or not there has developed out of the 'class situation' either communal action on the part of a larger or smaller section of those collectively
involved in it, or even some form of association, such as a trade union, from
which the individual can expect definite results. It is by no means always the
case that some form of association or even of communal action emerges from
the common class situation. Rather, its effects may be limited to generating an
essentially similar reaction: that is, to use the terminology we have adopted,
to generating a 'mass action'; and even this may not always result. Often,
moreover, such communal action as results is only of an amorphous kind. An
example of this is the 'grumbling' by workers which was recognized in ancient
Eastern ethical codes – the moral disapproval of their master's behaviour.
Presumably this had much the same practical significance as the phenomenon

which has once again become increasingly typical within precisely the most recently developed sectors of industry – the 'go-slow', or deliberate restriction of output by tacit agreement among the workers.

The extent to which there emerges from 'mass action' by the members of a class some form of 'communal action', or even possibly of 'association', depends on general cultural conditions, especially of an intellectual kind, and on the extent of the contrasts which have emerged on the basis, above all, of the visibility of the connexions between the causes and the consequences of the 'class situation'. Differences in chances in life, however marked, are certainly not sufficient in themselves, as experience shows, to create 'class action' in the sense of communal action by the members of a class. For that, it must be possible clearly to recognize that they depend on and result from the class situation. Only then can the contrast in chances in life be experienced as something which is not merely given and to be endured, but which results either (i) from the existing distribution of property or (ii) from the structure of the concrete economic order, and only then, therefore, can reactions to it take the form not of sporadic acts of irrational protest but of rational association. 'Class situations' of the first category existed in just such a characteristically blatant and visible form in the ancient world and in the Middle Ages in the towns, especially where great wealth had been accumulated by a virtual monopoly of trade in the local industrial products or food supplies; and they existed also in agricultural societies at various periods when commercial exploitation was on the increase. The most important historical example of the second category is the class situation of the modern 'proletariat'.

Every class may therefore give rise to some form of 'class action', of one of the numerous possible kinds; but it need not do so. In any case, a class itself is not a community, and it is misleading to treat classes as conceptually equivalent to communities. Finally, it is wrong to operate with such concepts as those of 'class' and 'class interest' in the kind of pseudo-scientific way which is all too common today, merely on the strength of the fact that men in the same class situation, faced with situations as emotionally charged as are those of economic life, regularly react by mass action in the direction which best approximates to their average interest – a fact which is as important for the understanding of historical events as it is basically simple. The most classical expression of this pseudo-scientific use of concepts is the contention of a gifted writer that the individual may well mistake his own interests, but the 'class' is 'infallible' about its interests.

If classes are not themselves communities, then, class situations arise only in the context of a community. The collective action which leads to the emergence of a class situation, however, is not in its essence an action undertaken by members of the same class but one involving relations between members of different classes. For example, the forms of communal action which directly determine the class situation of workers and entrepreneurs are the labour market, the commodity market and the capitalist enterprise. The existence of a capitalist enterprise in its turn, however, presupposes the existence of a form of collective action which is ordered in a very special way – one which protects the possession of goods purely as such, and in particular the power of the individual in principle to dispose freely of the means of production: that is, it presupposes the existence of a 'legal order' of a specific kind. Every sort of class situation, since it is primarily based on the power conferred by property as such, is realized in its purest form when all other factors which might determine the significance of the mutual relations between classes are excluded as far as possible, with the result that the use of the power of property on the market holds maximum sway. Amongst the impediments to a consistent realization of the naked market principle are 'status groups', which for the moment and in the present context are only of interest to us from this point of view. Before dealing briefly with them, we may simply point out that there is not much to be said in a general way about the more specific kinds of opposition between 'classes' (in the sense of that term which we have adopted). The radical change which has taken place between the past and the present may be connected, if a certain imprecision is admissible, with the fact that the struggle by which class situations are brought about has progressively shifted from the area of consumer credit, first to that of competition on the commodity market and then to that of price conflict on the labour market. The 'class struggles' of the ancient world – insofar as they were genuine 'class struggles' rather than conflicts between status groups – were primarily struggles between debtors threatened with debt-slavery (mainly peasants, but also including artisans) and their creditors who lived in the towns. For debt-slavery, both among cattle-breeders and in commercial towns, especially towns engaged in sea-borne trade, is the normal consequence of inequalities of wealth. The debt relationship as such gave rise to class action even as late as the time of Catiline. The next development, which resulted from the increasing tendency for the town's needs to be provided by foreign corn importers, was the struggle over the food supply, in the first instance the provision of bread and its price. This struggle lasted right through Antiquity and the whole of the Middle Ages; it grouped together all those without property in opposition to those who had a real or supposed vested interest in a high price for bread, and came more generally to cover all goods essential for the maintenance of life, including those required for artisan production. Conflicts over wages were not an issue in the ancient world or in the Middle Ages; even well into the modern era they existed only in embryonic form and were slow to develop. They took second place in every way not only to slave rebellions but also to struggles in the commodity market.

The objects of protest for those without property in the ancient world and the Middle Ages were such things as monopolies, pre-emptions, cornering of the market, or the holding back of goods from the market in order to raise their price. By contrast, today the central issue is the determination of wage levels. The transitional stage is represented by those struggles over access to the market and the determination of commodity prices which occurred between retailers and artisans working in cottage industry in the earliest days of the modern era. It is a general feature of those class conflicts which result from the market situation, and must therefore be mentioned here because of its generality, that the conflict is usually at its most bitter between those who actually and directly participate as opponents in the price struggle. It is not the *rentier*, the shareholder or the banker who suffers the resentment of the workers, even though it is his coffers which are filled by much more profit (for which he has done much less work) than are those of the manufacturer or the director of the enterprise. Rather it is the latter against whom resentment is directed, as the immediate opponents in the price struggle. This simple fact has often been decisive in determining the role of the class situation in the formation of political parties. It has, for instance, made possible the several varieties of patriarchal socialism and the attempts frequently made, at least in earlier times, to forge an alliance between threatened status strata and the proletariat against the 'bourgeoisie'.

Status groups, in contrast with classes, are normally communities, though often of an amorphous kind. In contrast with the 'class situation', which is determined by purely economic factors, we shall use the term 'status situation' to refer to all those typical components of people's destinies which are determined by a specific social evaluation of 'status', whether positive or negative, when that evaluation is based on some common characteristic shared by many people. This status may also be bound up with a certain class situation: class differences are connected in manifold ways with status differences, and, as remarked earlier, the ownership of property in itself comes to acquire a status value, not in every case, but with remarkable frequency in the long term. In the type of neighbourhood association to be found in subsistence economies in all parts of the world it is very often the case that the richest man as such becomes 'chief', which often means only a certain precedence in status. In modern 'democratic' society in what is called its 'pure' form, that is, in the form in which all explicitly regulated status privileges for individuals are done away with, it is the case, for instance, that only families belonging to broadly similar taxation groups dance with each other: this is reported, for example, of some of the smaller Swiss cities. But 'status' is not necessarily connected with a 'class situation': normally, it stands rather in glaring contradiction to the pretensions of naked property-ownership. Furthermore, those who own property and those who do not may belong to the same status group: this frequently happens and its consequences are very noticeable, so precarious may this 'equality' of social assessment become in the long run. The 'equality' of status of the American 'gentleman' finds expression, for instance, in the fact that, outside the context of the 'enterprise', where subordination is determined by purely realistic factors, it would be considered the height of bad taste – wherever the old tradition prevails – for even the richest 'chief' to treat his 'clerk' as in any way at all of unequal rank, even in the evening at the club, over billiards or at the card table. It would be unacceptable to treat him with that kind of condescending affability which marks a difference in position, and which the German chief can never avoid entirely – one of the most important reasons why German club-life has never managed to seem so attractive there as the American club.

In content, social status is normally expressed above all in the imputation of a specifically regulated style of life to everyone who wishes to belong to the circle. This goes together with a restriction of 'social' intercourse – that is, intercourse which does not serve any economic, commercial or other 'practical' purposes – including especially normal intermarriage, to the circle of status equals; this can extend to the point of totally exclusive endogamy. As soon as a communal action of this nature is in question – not a purely individual and socially irrelevant imitation of an alien style of life, but an action based on mutual consent – we say that 'status' development is under way. A typical development of articulated 'status' grouping of this kind on the basis of conventional lifestyles is taking place at present in the United States, where it is emerging out of a long-established democracy. One example of this is that only those who reside in a certain street ('The Street') are regarded as belonging to 'society' and as fit for social intercourse, and are accordingly visited and invited. The outstanding example, however, is the strict submission to the fashion prevailing for the moment in 'society', to an extent unknown in Germany, which is taken, even among men, as a sign that the person in question has pretensions to be regarded as a gentleman and so decides at least *prima facie* that he will also be treated as such. This is as important, for instance, for his chances of securing a position in a 'good' company, and above all of mixing socially and intermarrying with 'well-regarded' families, as being qualified to fight a duel is in Germany. For the rest, social 'status' is usurped by certain families who have resided in a certain area for a long time (and who are, naturally, correspondingly well-to-do), such as the 'FFV' or 'first families of Virginia', or the descendants, real or alleged, of the 'Indian princess' Pocahontas or the Pilgrim Fathers, or the Knickerbockers, or the members of some extremely exclusive sect, or all kinds of circles of associates who mark themselves off by some criterion or other. In this case it is a matter of a purely conventional social differentiation based essentially on usurpation (although this is admittedly the normal origin of almost all social 'status'). But it is a short step from this to the legal validation of privilege (and lack of privilege), and this step is usually easy to take as soon as a certain arrangement of the social order has become effectively 'settled' and has acquired stability as a result of the stabilisation of the distribution of economic power. Where the consequences are followed through to the limit, the status group develops into a closed *caste*. That is, distinction of status is guaranteed not only by convention and law, but also by ritual sanction to such an extent that all physical contact with a member of a caste regarded as 'inferior' is held to be ritually polluting for members of the 'superior' caste, a stain which must be religiously expiated. The individual castes, indeed, in part develop quite separate cults and gods.

Status differentiation, to be sure, only as a rule develops into these extreme forms when it is based on differences which are regarded as 'ethnic'. The 'caste' is actually the normal 'societal' form in which ethnic communities which believe in blood-relationship and forbid intermarriage and social intercourse with outsiders live alongside one another. This is true of the 'pariah' peoples which have emerged from time to time in all parts of the world – communities which have acquired specific occupational traditions of an artisan or other kind, which cultivate a belief in their common ethnic origin, and which now live in a 'diaspora', rigorously avoiding all personal intercourse other than what is unavoidable, in a legally precarious situation, but tolerated on the grounds of their economic indispensability and often even privileged, and interspersed among political communities. The Jews are the most striking historical example. A system of 'status' differences which has developed into a 'caste' system differs in structure from a system of purely 'ethnic' differences in that the former creates a vertical social hierarchy out of the horizontal relationships of the latter, in which different groups co-exist side by side in an unsystematic way. To put it more accurately: a more comprehensive consociation unifies the ethnically distinct communities to the point where they can engage in communal action of a specifically political kind. The difference in outcome is that the horizontal relationships of ethnic groups, which lead to mutual repulsion and contempt, permit each ethnic community to consider its own status as the highest, whereas a caste system brings with it a hierarchy of subordination and a recognition of the 'higher status' conferred on the privileged castes and status groups by virtue of the fact that the ethnic distinctions become differences of 'function' within the political sector of the total social system (warriors, priests, craftsmen whose work is of political importance for war, public building and so on). Even the most despised pariah people usually finds some way, moreover, of cultivating the belief in its own specific 'status', which is equally characteristic of both ethnic and status communities. This is true, for instance, of the Jews.

Only amongst underprivileged status groups does the 'sense of worth', the subjective precipitate of social status and of the conventional claims which the privileged status group makes on the lifestyle of its members, take a specifically deviant turn. Privileged status groups naturally base their sense of their own worth on their 'being', which does not transcend them – their 'beauty and excellence' (καλοκἀγαθία). Their kingdom is 'of this world': they live for the present and on the strength of their glorious past. The underprivileged strata, naturally, can only relate their sense of worth to the future, in this world or the next, but at all events at some point beyond the present: in other words, it must be nourished by a belief in a providential 'mission', in a specific status before God as a 'chosen people', and so by the conviction that there will either be a world beyond in which 'the last shall be first' or there will appear in this world a saviour who will bring out into the light the special status of the pariah people (such as the Jews) or pariah status group, which was hidden from the world which rejected them. It is this simple fact, whose significance is to be discussed in another connexion, and not the '*ressenti-ment*' which Nietzsche emphasizes so strongly in his much-admired account in the *Genealogy of Morals*, which is the source of the type of religion culti-vated by pariah status groups – a type of religion which, by the way, as we saw, is found only to a limited extent and, indeed, not at all in the case of one of Nietzsche's chief examples, Buddhism.[2] Moreover, it is by no means nor-mal for status systems to originate from ethnic differences. On the contrary, since it is by no means always the case that subjective feelings of 'ethnic' community are based on objective 'racial differences', it is right that all ques-tions about an ultimately racial foundation for status differentiation should be treated strictly on the merits of the individual case: very often a status group determines by effective exclusion the selection of personal qualities (as when knights select those who are physically and mentally fit for military service) and by so doing creates a pure-bred anthropological type. But selec-tion on the basis of personal qualities is far from being the only, or the predominant, way in which a status group is formed: political membership or class situation is the deciding factor at least as often, and nowadays the latter is by far the most important. After all, the possibility of maintaining the lifestyle of a status group is usually conditional on economics.

In practice, status differentiation goes together with monopolisation of cultural and material goods and opportunities in the manner we have already acknowledged to be typical. In addition to the specific honorific status, based always on distance and exclusiveness, and its associated privileges, such as the right to certain costumes or kinds of food forbidden by taboo to others, the right to bear arms (so important in its consequences), or the right to engage in certain non-utilitarian or dilettante forms of artistic activity (such as the use of certain musical instruments), there are also material monopolies of various kinds. These are seldom the only motive for the exclusiveness of a status group, but they are almost always to some extent the most effective one. Where intermarriage within a circle of status equals is concerned, the interest of families in monopolising control over their daughters as marriage partners is almost equally matched by their interest in having a monopoly of potential suitors within the circle in order to make provision for these same daughters. As status groups become increasingly exclusive, so the conventional priorities of opportunity for particular appointments develop into a legal monopoly over certain posts for certain groups defined in terms of status. Certain kinds of goods (characteristically, manorial estates), the ownership of bondsmen and serfs, and finally certain sectors of industry come to be the monopoly of particular status groups. This is true both in the positive sense that a particular status group alone has the right to own and exploit them, and in the negative sense that it may not own or exploit them because of the need to maintain its specific lifestyle. For it is a consequence of

2 See above, pp. 59–65.

the fact that it is lifestyle which determines social status that status groups are specifically responsible for all 'conventions': all 'stylisation' of ways of life, however expressed, either originates with a status group or is preserved by one.

Despite the enormous differences, there are certain typical features to be seen in the principles on which status conventions are based, especially amongst highly privileged strata. It is very common to find that privileged status groups are disqualified on the grounds of their status from engaging in the usual forms of physical labour: the first signs of this phenomenon can now be seen in America, although it runs counter to the diametrically opposed traditions which have long existed there. It is very often the case that all rational employment of a gainful kind, especially entrepreneurial activity, is regarded as disqualifying a person from high status; furthermore, artistic and literary work, if engaged in in order to earn a living, or if associated with hard physical exertion, is considered to be degrading. For instance, the sculptor, who works in overalls, like a stonemason, is thought to be of lower status than the painter, with his salon-like studio, or than certain kinds of musical performer who have an accepted status.

The extremely frequent disqualification of 'gainful employment' as such is, apart from the particular causes to be discussed later, a direct result of the ordering of society on 'status' principles, in contrast with the regulation of the distribution of power by purely market principles. The market and its economic processes are, as we saw, 'no respecter of persons': it is dominated by 'concrete' interests. It knows nothing of 'status'. The ordering of society in terms of status means precisely the opposite: differentiation in terms of 'social standing' and lifestyles peculiar to particular status groups. As such it is fundamentally threatened when purely economic gain and purely economic power, completely naked and clearly displaying the marks of its origin unconnected with status, can confer on everyone who has acquired it the same 'standing' which the interested status groups claim for themselves in virtue of their way of life – or even a consequentially higher standing, given that ownership of property adds an extra element, whether acknowledged or not, to the status of someone who is otherwise of equal standing. The interested parties in every status system therefore react with especial bitterness precisely against the claims of mere economic acquisition as such, and the more they feel threatened, the greater is their bitterness. The respectful way in which peasants are treated in the works of Calderon, in contrast with the open contempt shown by Shakespeare, writing at the same time, for the '*canaille*',[3] is an illustration of these differences in reaction. Calderon was writing within a clearly articulated status system, Shakespeare within one which was economically tottering. Their different reactions are an expression of a universally recurrent situation. Privileged status groups have for that

3 Rabble, the vulgar crowd.

reason never accepted the *'parvenu'* personally, and genuinely without reservations, however completely he has adopted their way of life; it is his descendants who are first accepted, since they have been brought up within the status conventions of their social stratum and have never defiled their standing as members of the status group by their own employment for gain.

In general, then, only one factor, though admittedly a very important one, can be cited as a consequence of status differentiation: the restraint imposed on the free development of the market. This applies, first, to those goods which status groups have directly withdrawn from free trade by either legal or conventional monopolisation: one example is inherited wealth in many Greek cities during the period when considerations of status were dominant and (as the old rule of trusteeship for spendthrifts shows) in the early days of Rome also; other examples are manorial estates, peasant landholdings, church property and above all the goodwill of a craft or trade held by a guild. The market is restricted, and the power of naked property as such, which places its stamp on 'class formation', is held back. The effects of this may be various: they do not necessarily, of course, have any tendency to weaken contrasts in economic situation – often the reverse. At all events, there is no question of genuine free market competition as we nowadays understand it when status differentiation permeates a community as completely as it did in all the political communities of the ancient world and the Middle Ages. But even more far-reaching than this direct exclusion of certain goods from the market is a consequence of the opposition mentioned earlier between the status order and the purely economic order. This is that, in most cases, the concept of honorific 'status' involves a general revulsion from precisely the most characteristic feature of the market, namely bargaining, both between close associates within the status group and occasionally between members of a status group in general. The result is that there are status groups in all societies, and often the most influential of them, which regard all forms of overt participation in trade as totally contaminating.

One might say, therefore (with a certain amount of oversimplification), that 'classes' are formed in accordance with relations of production and the acquisition of wealth, while 'status groups' are formed according to the principles governing their consumption of goods in the context of specific 'lifestyles'. An 'occupational status group', furthermore, is still a 'status group': normally, that is, it successfully lays claim to social 'status', by virtue first of all of its specific lifestyle, which in some cases is determined by the occupation which it pursues. Admittedly, it is often the case that the different types shade into each other, and it is precisely those communities which are most sharply separated in status – the Indian castes – which nowadays display (albeit within very strict and definite limits) a relatively high degree of indifference towards 'trade', which is pursued in the most varied forms, especially by the Brahmans.

In connexion with what has just been said, only one completely general point may be made about the general economic determinants which lead to the prevalence of status differentiation: a degree of relative stability in the bases on which goods are acquired and distributed favours it, whereas all technological and economic convulsions and upheavals pose a threat to it and thrust the 'class situation' into the foreground. Those ages and countries in which the naked class situation is of prevailing importance are generally periods of technological and economic upheaval; while every deceleration of the process of economic change immediately leads to the growth of 'status' structures and restores the significance of 'social standing'.

'Classes' are properly at home in the economic order, 'status groups' in the social order, that is, in the sphere of distribution of status; starting from this point, both reciprocally influence each other and influence the legal order and are in turn influenced by it. *Parties*, on the other hand, are primarily at home in the sphere of power. Their activity is concerned with social power, that is, with exerting influence on communal action, whatever its form: there can in principle be 'parties' in a social 'club' as much as in a 'state'. Communal action by parties, as opposed to classes or status groups, always requires the forming of an association. For it is always directed towards a goal which is pursued in accordance with a plan: the goal may be an 'objective' one, in the sense of the fulfillment of some programme for ideal or material ends, or it may be a 'personal' goal, in the sense of sinecures, power and, as a consequence, status for the leader and members, or, and indeed usually, all these things at once. Such activity is therefore only possible within a community, which, for its part, is in some way or other constituted as an association, that is, which possesses some form of rational organisation and an apparatus of personnel which is ready to bring about the goals in question. For the whole aim of parties is to influence such an apparatus and, wherever possible, to ensure that it is made up of party members. In individual cases, parties may represent interests determined by class situation or status situation and recruit their membership accordingly. But it is not necessary for a party to be purely representative of either a class or a status group: mostly, parties are such only in part, and often not at all. They may be either ephemeral or permanent structures, and their methods of achieving power can be of the most varied kinds: naked force in all its forms, soliciting votes by both crude and subtle means – money, social influence, rhetoric, insinuation, clumsy trickery – or, finally, the use of obstructive tactics, both of the cruder and the more sophisticated kind, within parliamentary bodies. Their sociological structure necessarily differs in its basis, depending on the structure of the communal action which they strive to influence: it depends, indeed, on whether or not the community is, for instance, differentiated by status groups or classes, and above all on the structure of 'domination' within it. For the aim, as far as their leader is concerned, is normally to take control of this structure. Parties, in the sense defined here, did not first emerge from specifically modern forms of domination: we wish to include under the term all ancient and medieval parties, despite the fact that they differ so much in their basic structure from modern examples. At all events, because of this difference in the structure of domination, it is wrong to say anything about the structure of the party, which is always an organisation which strives for domination and so is itself organized, often very rigidly, in terms of domination, without discussing the structural forms of social domination in general. To this central phenomenon of all social life we shall, therefore, now turn.[4]

Before doing so, however, one general point which should be made about classes, status groups and parties is that, in saying that they necessarily pre-suppose a more comprehensive association, and especially a framework of communal political action within which they function one is not saying that they themselves are confined within the boundaries of a particular political community. On the contrary, since time immemorial it has always been the case that an association, even an association which aims at the common use of military force, transcends political frontiers. Examples are the solidarity of interests amongst oligarchs and democrats in Ancient Greece, or amongst Guelphs and Ghibellines in the Middle Ages, or the Calvinist party in the time of the Wars of Religion, or more recently, the solidarity of landowners in the International Agrarian Congress, or of princes in the Holy Alliance or the Carlsbad Decrees, or of socialist workers or of conservatives (as in the longing of Prussian Conservatives for Russian intervention in 1850). The only reservation is that the goal in such cases is not necessarily to establish a new international political (that is, *territorial*) domination, but usually to influence the existing one.

4 The cross-reference most probably refers to *E&S*, pp. 941–1368, and includes the legitimate types of rulership (see Reading 7) and the non-legitimate types of city rulership.

15 Parties[1]

The term 'party' will be employed to designate associations, membership in which rests on formally free recruitment. The end to which its activity is devoted is to secure power within a group body (*Verband*) for its leaders in order to attain ideal or material advantages for its active members. These advantages may consist in the realization of certain objective policies or the attainment of personal advantages or both. Parties may have an ephemeral character or may be organized with a view to permanent activity. They may appear in all types of group bodies and may themselves be organized in any one of a large variety of forms. They may consist of the following of a charismatic leader, of traditional retainers, or of purpose- or value-rational adherents. They may be oriented primarily to personal interests or to object-ive policies. Officially or merely in fact, they may be solely concerned with the attainment of power for their leaders and with securing positions in the administrative staff for their own members. (Then they are 'patronage par-ties'.) They may, on the other hand, predominantly and consciously act in the interests of a status group or a class or of certain objective policies or of abstract principles. (In the latter case they are called 'ideological parties'.) The attainment of positions in the administrative staff for their members is, however, at the least a secondary aim and objective programs are often merely a means of persuading outsiders to participate.

By definition a party can exist only *within* a group body (*Verband*),[2] in order to influence its policy or gain control of it. Federations of party groups which cut across several bodies are, however, not uncommon.

A party may employ any one of the conceivable means of gaining power. In cases where the government is determined by a formally free ballot and legislation is enacted by vote they are primarily organizations for the attrac-tion of votes. Where voting takes a course in accord with legitimate expect-ations they are legal parties. The existence of legal parties, because of the fact that their basis is fundamentally one of voluntary adherence, always means that the business of politics is the pursuit of *interests*. (It should, however, be noted that in this context, 'interests' is by no means necessarily an economic

---

1 Taken from *E&S*, pp. 284–8.
2 Rulerships are sociologically constituted as a group body (*Verband*). See Reading 7 and p. 128 above, and pp. 350–2 below.

category. In the first instance, it is a matter of political interests which rest either on an ideological basis or on an interest in power as such.)

In this case the political enterprise is in the hands of:

1   party leaders and their staffs, whereas
2   active party members have for the most part merely the function of acclaiming their leaders. Under certain circumstances, however, they may exercise some forms of control, participate in discussion, voice complaints, or even initiate resolutions within the party;
3   the inactive masses of electors or voters (*Mitläufer*) are merely objects whose votes are sought at election time. Their attitudes are important only for the agitation of the competing parties;
4   contributors to party funds usually remain behind the scenes.

Apart from formally organized legal parties in a formal-legal group body (*Verband*), there are the following principal types:

1   Charismatic parties arising from disagreement over the charismatic quality of the leader or over the question of who, in charismatic terms, is to be recognized as the correct leader. They create a schism.
2   Traditionalistic parties arising from controversy over the way in which the chief exercises his traditional authority in the sphere of his arbitrary will and grace. They arise in the form of movements to obstruct innovations or in open revolt against them.
3   Parties organized about questions of faith (*Glaubensparteien*). These are usually, though not necessarily, identical with (1). They arise out of a disagreement over the content of doctrines or declarations of faith. They take the form of heresies, which are to be found even in rational parties such as the socialist.
4   Appropriation parties (or spoils-oriented parties) arising from conflict with the chief and his administrative staff over the filling of positions in the administrative staff. This type is very often, though by no means necessarily, identical with (2).

Organizationally, parties may conform to the same types as any other group bodies. They may thus be charismatically oriented by devotion to the leader, with the plebiscite as an expression of confidence. They may be traditional with adherence based on the social prestige of the chief or of an eminent neighbor, or they may be rational with adherence to a leader and staff set up by a 'constitutional process' of election. These differences may apply both to the basis of obedience of the members, and of the administrative staff. Further elaboration must be reserved to the Sociology of the State. [The *Staatssoziologie* was never written.]

It is of crucial importance for the economic aspect of the distribution of power and for the determination of party policy by what method the party activities are financed. Among the possibilities are small contributions from the masses of members and sympathizers; large contributions from disinterested sympathizers with its cause; direct or indirect sell-out to interested parties; or taxation either of elements under obligation to the party, including its members, or of its defeated opponents. These details, too, belong in the *Staatssoziologie*.

1   As has been pointed out, parties can exist by definition only within a group body, whether political or other, and only when there is a struggle for its control. Within a party there may be and very often are sub-parties; for example, as ephemeral associations they are typical in the nomination campaigns of presidential candidates of the American parties. On a permanent basis an example is the 'Young Liberals' in Germany. Parties which extend to a number of different polities are illustrated by the Guelphs and Ghibellines in Italy in the thirteenth century and by the modern socialists.

2   The criterion of formally voluntary solicitation and adherence in terms of the rules of the group within which the party exists is treated here as the crucial point. It involves a distinction of major sociological significance from all associations which are prescribed and controlled by the polity. Even where the order of the polity (*Verbandsordnung*) takes notice of the existence of parties, as in the United States and in the German system of proportional representation, the voluntarist component remains. It remains even if an attempt is made to regulate their constitution. But when a party becomes a closed group which is incorporated by law into the administrative staff, as was true of the Guelphs in the Florentine statutes of the thirteenth century, it ceases to be a party and becomes a part of the group body.

3   Under genuinely charismatic domination, parties are necessarily schismatic sects. Their conflict is essentially over questions of faith and, as such, is basically irreconcilable. The situation in a strictly patriarchal body may be somewhat similar. Both these types of parties, at least in the pure form, are radically different from parties in the modern sense. In the usual kind of hereditary monarchy and estate-type organization, it is common for groups of retainers, composed of pretenders to fiefs and offices, to rally around a pretender to the throne. Personal followings are also common in organizations of *honoratiores* such as the aristocratic city states. They are, however, also prominent in some democracies. The modern type of party does not arise except in the legal state with a representative constitution. It will be further analyzed in the Sociology of the State.

4   The classic example of parties in the modern state organized primarily around patronage are the two great American parties of the last generation. Parties primarily oriented to issues and ideology have been the older type of Conservatism and Liberalism, bourgeois Democracy, later

the Social Democrats and the (Catholic) Center Party. In all, except the last, there has been a very prominent element of class interest. After the Center attained the principal points of its original program, it became very largely a pure patronage party. In all these types, even those which are most purely an expression of class interests, the (ideal and material) interests of the party leaders and the staff in power, office, and remuneration always play an important part. There is a tendency for the interests of the electorate to be taken into account only so far as their neglect would endanger electoral prospects. This fact is one of the sources of public opposition to political parties as such.

5   The different forms which the internal organization of parties take will be dealt with separately in the proper place. One fact, however, is common to all these forms, namely, that there is a central group of individuals who assume the active direction of party affairs, including the formulation of programs and the selection of candidates. There is, secondly, a group of 'members' whose role is notably more passive, and finally, the great mass of citizens whose role is only that of objects of solicitation by the various parties. They merely choose between the various candidates and programs offered by the different parties. Given the voluntary character of party affiliation this structure is unavoidable. It is this which is meant by the statement that party activity is a matter of 'play of interests'. (As has already been stated, it is political interests and not economic interests which are involved.) The role of interests in this sense is the second principal point of attack for the opposition to parties as such. In this respect, there is a *formal* similarity between the party system and the system of capitalistic enterprise which rests on the recruitment of formally free labor.

6   The role in party finance of large-scale contributors is by no means confined to the 'bourgeois' parties. Thus Paul Singer was a contributor to the Social Democratic Party (and, by the way, humanitarian causes) of grand style (and purest motives so far as is known). His whole position as chairman of the party rested on this fact. Furthermore, the parties of the Russian Revolution in the Kerensky stage were partly financed by very large Moscow business interests. Other German parties on the 'Right' have been financed by heavy industry, while the Center party occasionally had large contributions from Catholic millionaires.

For reasons which are readily understandable, the subject of party finances, though one of the most important aspects of the party system, is the most difficult to secure information about. It seems probable that in certain special cases a 'machine' has actually been 'bought.' Apart from the role of individual large contributors, there are two basic alternatives: On the one hand, as in the English system, the electoral candidate may carry the burden of campaign expenses, with the result that the candidates are selected on a plutocratic basis. On the other hand, the costs may be borne by the 'machine,' in which case the candidates become dependent on the party organization. Parties as permanent organizations have always varied between these two fundamental types, in the thirteenth century in Italy just as much as today. These facts should not be covered up by fine phrases. Of course, there are limits to the power of party finance. It can only exercise an influence insofar as a 'market' exists, but as in the case of capitalistic enterprise, the power of the seller as compared with the consumer has been tremendously increased by the suggestive appeal of advertising. This is particularly true of 'radical' parties regardless of whether they are on the Right or the Left.

Further reading

A good introduction to Weber's ideas on power and politics are the essays by Wolfgang J. Mommsen in his *The Political and Social Theory of Max Weber*, Cambridge, Polity Press, 1989. David Beetham provides a more democratic oriented viewpoint to Weber in his *Max Weber and the Theory of Modern Politics*, London, Allen & Unwin, 1974. It offers a counterweight to Wolfgang Mommsen's nationalist reading of Weber (*Max Weber and German Politics 1890–1920*, Chicago, Chicago University Press, 1984 [German edn 1959]). Part 3 of Wolfgang Schluchter's *Rationalism, Religion, and Politics*, Berkeley, University of California Press, 1989, is devoted to the subject of domination.

Weber's own formulations on rulership and legitimacy went through a number of versions. For a more historical account, see *E&S*, pp. 941–1204, and in a more typological account *E&S*, pp. 212–97. *Weber. Political Writings*, edited and translated by Peter Lassman and Ronald Speirs, Cambridge, Cambridge University Press, 1994, provides a valuable set of translation of Weber's major political writings. Weber's extensive writings on Russia have been translated and edited by Gordon Wells and Peter Baehr, *The Russian Revolutions*, Cambridge, Polity Press, 1995.

The debates on class, status, and party are now somewhat dated, revolving as they did around fundamental approaches to social theory and whether Marx or Weber provided the best overall account. Karl Löwith gives an eloquent and brief account of the Marx–Weber contrast in his *Max Weber and Karl Marx*, London, Allen & Unwin, 1982. Norbert Wiley has edited a collection on the same theme: *The Marx–Weber Debate*, Beverly Hills, Sage, 1987. Frank Parkin's *Max Weber*, London, Routledge, 2002, provides an introductory guide to power and to stratification debates. Peter Saunders, in *Social Class and Stratification*, London, Routledge, 1990, illustrates how Weberian ideas on stratification can be applied to contemporary societies. Catherine Brennan, in *Max Weber on Power and Social Stratification. An Interpretation and Critique*, Aldershot, Ashgate, 1997, considers the form and significance of Weber's thinking on stratification.

Ralph Schroeder has edited a volume of essays on Weber's relevance to modernization on a comparative basis: *Max Weber, Democracy and*

Democratization, Basingstoke, Macmillan, 1998. The volume also has some important essays on Weber and democracy, in particular those by Stefan Breuer. Randall Collins' *Weberian Sociological Theory*, Cambridge, Cambridge University Press, 1986, is a fine example of Weberian theory applied to stratification, institutions and societal change. *Reading Weber*, edited by Keith Tribe, London, Routledge, 1989, examines some of Weber's contemporary analyses of German society and social structure.

Writings on the nation and ethnicity are now voluminous and it needs only to be noted that Weber's work on these subjects is axiomatic to the field, especially his scepticism that a national people or common ethnicity were 'primordial' qualities. See Ernest Gellner, *Nations and Nationalism*, Oxford, Blackwell, 1983.

Weber's writings on the ancient world can hardly be regarded to be central to contemporary classical scholarship. On the other hand, the developmental axes within the Mediterranean basin may well be due for reformulation and this work could draw profitably on Weber's agrarian sociology of the ancient world. For a recent assessment, see Mohammad Nafissi, 'On the Foundations of Athenian Democracy', *Max Weber Studies*, 1, 1, 2000, pp. 56–83.

Richard Swedberg has restored Weber's economic sociology to the prominence it deserves in *Max Weber and the Idea of Economic Sociology*, Princeton, NJ, Princeton University Press, 1998. On the modern firm, see S. Jagd, 'Weber's Last Theory of the Modern Business Enterprise', *Max Weber Studies*, 2, 2, 2002, pp. 210–38.

Weber's writings on the household and the position of women in society are somewhat limited, although his *General Economic History*, London, Allen & Unwin, 1927 should be consulted. He both advised and drew on the work of Marianne Weber, for whom the claim can be made as the first sociologist of gender. On Marianne Weber, see 'Marianne Weber. (1870–1954): A Woman Centered Sociology', by Patricia Madoo Lengermann and Jill Niebrugge-Brantley in their *The Women Founders. Sociology and Social Theory 1830–1930*, Boston, McGraw-Hill, 1998.

Part III
The dilemmas of modernity

Introduction

Reading 16 (Intermediate Reflection on the Economic Ethics of the World Religions) straddles two major areas of Weber's interest: his diagnosis of modernity and his continuing interest in the economic consequences of religious ethics. The 'Intermediate Reflection' was written primarily to conduct the reader of his 'Economic Ethics of the World Religions' from his presentations of Protestantism and Confucianism to that of Hinduism and Buddhism. Indian religiosity was, says Weber, 'the cradle of theoretically and practically the most world-denying forms of religious ethic that the world has ever known'. This provides Weber with the basis of his well-known contrast between two types of the search for salvation. At its typological extreme, Indian religiosity seeks salvation through contemplation and mysticism. Divinity is present as an immanence within the individual, the person is a vessel of divinity and religious practice is a matter of taking possession of that quality. It is a religiosity that looks inward and fears any involvement in the affairs of the world as a dangerous distraction on the path to discovering salvation. In sharp contrast, Puritanism is a religious practice of asceticism carried out in the world. The individual is an instrument of God, and salvation can be gained only by taming man's creaturely instincts through hard work and sober conduct. Puritans look outward to the world and their ascetic conduct has a potentially transforming effect upon the world. The Buddhist religious person, by contrast, seeks in his religious asceticism to efface himself from the ways of the world.

Having introduced this typology, Weber almost immediately allows variant types. Many forms of Christianity are involved in contemplation and lead to a flight from the world, and importantly Hinduism has contemplative religious practices that remain very much within the orders of the world – and for Weber this makes Hinduism one of the most successful of the world religions. It has what he calls an 'organic social ethic', where religion takes account of the social stratification of society. Clearly, in comparative historical terms, the extent to which a religious ethic turns towards the world, flees the world, or accommodates with the world is a very significant factor for the development of different societies. This is the main purpose of the economic ethics of world religions project.

Religious ethics, as we have seen (p. 69), are like switches that point human activity in certain directions according to the salvation message. In the 'Intermediate Reflection' Weber pursues a related and crucial question: what is the process behind the construction of these salvation messages? Here Weber becomes as interested in the common process of message formulation as in their different soteriological content. It was a topic that he had already considered in his 'Introduction to the Economic Ethics of the World Religions', where the problem was to explain how salvation messages ever took hold in the face of magical practices. By comparison, promises and prophecies of salvation are high-level messages. They appeal to *one* non-earthly divinity as a permanent entity. The vast array of magical practices are embedded in terms of time and space into their host societies and they therefore remain complex, particularistic rituals and material practices rather than the pure abstract idea of a transcendental god or an immanent divinity. Weber's answer in the 'Introduction' was one of hybridity. A high-level salvation message is grafted on to existing magical practices. Whether the graft 'takes' is dependent on circumstances – it is a matter of chance – and actually a very low probability, which is why there are so few salvation religions, argued Weber (see above, p. 64).

In the 'Intermediate Reflection' essay Weber identifies intellectuals as the source of salvation messages. In the shaping of a message priests are intellectually pressured to achieve some sort of consistency. While the idea of salvation is non-rational (because it depends on revelation and prophetic insight) it is, as an intellectual idea, subject to what Weber terms *ratio* – that is, reason. Weber was well aware that in his ideal-typical presentation he was forcing clarity upon religious ideas, but he also perceived that salvation messages have a clarity and consistency in real life and as such they exert power over people's behaviour. Compared to the material forces in historical life, ideas remain frail; but organized into consistent wholes they can have a determining influence.

One consequence of the demand for consistency is that salvation messages can be driven beyond any pragmatic reconciliation with normal everyday life. In their different ways, the devout Calvinist and the wholly absorbed Buddhist mystic are religious virtuosi whose lives are dedicated to religious practice as they carry out the full tenets of their respective salvation messages. This sets up a tension between religion and what Weber terms the other orders of life. These other orders of life number kinship groupings, economic life, politics and power, aesthetic and sexual life, and intellectual and scientific life. Most religions, as normally pursued, lessen and compromise the full tension contained within the complete salvation message, and we have noted how Hinduism makes explicit acknowledgement of caste stratification. But where the tension is maintained, in historical and comparative terms this has a strong effect on societal development. Religions tend to routinize, become somewhat lazy in their observance, become what Weber sometimes terms 'morally indifferent'. But equally, all religions are prone to reform movements which restore the full purity of the salvation message, and in doing this, create enormous tensions with the other orders of society. For this reason reform movements (for example, in Christianity, Islam, Judaism, or Buddhism) have the capacity to greatly affect the development of society.

Religious 'rationalism', like its modern counterpart scientific rationalism, is a significant part of Weber's understanding of the dynamics of societal development. In both cases pure reasoning is used to gain accounts of the nature of the world – the products of the mind are not simple reflections of a surrounding empirical reality. (This is irrespective of the underlying irrationality of religious belief.) Where rationalism is embedded within a society and 'carried' by an important or rising stratum, then it contributes to the processes of rationalization. To give some examples: the Calvinists rationalized their everyday conduct in the light of 'rationalist' views of predestination, the Temple priests in Judah in the fifth century BC rationalized Jewish law and its observance, at the end of the eighteenth century Abd al-Wahhab preached a return to simple faith and obedience in Islam that led to a political unification of Arabian tribes, and scientific rationalism carried into the capitalist cosmos by the universities in the nineteenth century unleashed massive rationalizing forces in technology and the organization of production and consumption.

So far, then, the 'Intermediate Reflection' is a continuation of the arguments to the 'Introduction to the Economic Ethics of the World Religions'. On the basis of the peculiar distinctiveness of salvation messages and the religious sphere, Weber then embarks on a systematic exposition of the tensions generated with each of the non-religious life orders. He allows the development of the life orders to run up to the present, so examining the contemporary predicament of those moved by soteriological sentiments and how these can be reconciled with a person's attitude to the other spheres of his or her life. Moreover, the various orders of life with their respective value spheres, to use Weber's complete terminology, exist in tension with each other and not just religious ethics. The essay develops into an acute and frequently agonized diagnosis of modernity and its existential conflicts.

What religions and the value spheres of the other life orders have in common is the intellectual drive to consistency and closure. Each of the life orders is prone to an internal dynamic. Overall this process is referred to as rationalization, despite the fact that some orders have a far more rational basis (for example, economics and science) than others such as religion, art, and sexuality. To see how this process works, we need to understand what Weber means by sublimation.

It will be remembered from Part I (p. 67) that prior to a religious attitude towards salvation, human cultures would provide release from the everyday world through ecstasy and frenzy using magic, rhythm, feasts, and intoxicants as a means to acquiring those extraordinary states. A high-level salvation message is a sublimation of these more naturally given states of ecstasy. Weber uses sublimation in its chemical sense. Impure substances are refined, or sublimated (for example, through heat treatments), into a pure element.

Religions take impure magical and ritualistic practices and refine them, sublimate them, into a higher quality element. This is a process that occurs in all the life orders. Values that are at first only simple and uncouth become sublimated and transformed into something more elevated, more civilized, and more universal than its particularistic and material origins. Chivalry is the sublimation by warriors of the treatment of women as objects of booty into a courtly code of exaggerated respect for women. Neighbourliness, and the practice of helping a neighbour who is in great need, as a practice embedded in a social community, is sublimated into a religious ethic. The norm of helping another, therefore, was originally a communal obligation. Religious ethics raised community from a taken-for-granted given into a moral idea. Eroticism is the sublimation of naturalistic sexuality into a cultural code, which can sometimes actually deny the sexual in favour of its cultural enhancement. Examples of this would be the troubadours in medieval Provence, or Japanese geishas.

Weber argues that once values within the various life orders are subject to sublimation, which is an intellectual process of refinement, it becomes practically unstoppable. In the original 'lifeworld' of people, they had a direct involvement in economic subsistence, communal obligations of help and defence, magical practices, legal adjudication, and artistic practices. All of these would in developmental terms exist at a low level of rationality. Sublimation breaks this direct link. For Simmel this constituted the 'tragedy of culture', for Freud it involved the repression of instinctual urges, and for Weber it represented the disenchantment of the modern world. The peasant, says Weber, dies sated with life. He lives close to the life cycles of nature, and can regard his own life in that way. He can die a satisfied man. Not so the modern, civilized person. Culture and civilization are subject to continuous rationalization, placing the forms of life beyond the ken of an individual, who must die knowing that he or she has sampled only a fraction of life.

The dilemma of modernity is living with this dissatisfaction; also that salvation which offers the chimera of universal brotherhood or oneness with the universe can never be attained because of the separate rationalization of the life orders and the fragmentation of any common value into values whose validity is underpinned by the particular life order. In economic activity the pursuit of profit at the expense of another person is condemned in various ways by the world religions. Under modern capitalism, the rational enterprise and the impersonal and calculable medium of money assert their advantage over the non-rational qualities of religious or moral altruism. The values of each belong to separate spheres with their own internal dynamic. Likewise with politics that, as we have seen in Part II, is comprehensively the realm of power. The 'Intermediate Reflection' has a number of biographical traces, and it was written at the time of the First World War. A nation at war raises community to the highest possible level, so that dying for one's country becomes more meaningful than any religious message of salvation. The modern state borrows religion's consecration of death for secular and political purposes. Likewise religiously inspired pacifism has to be rejected in favour of the state's *realpolitik*.

One might say that Weber is a secular realist in his recognition of the inevitability of this value fragmentation and the priority certain life orders now command. His diagnosis of modernity does not offer happiness – for him, the search for salvation and release is a constant in a world that offers only conflict and tension between the life orders. The modern, civilized individual instead seeks out surrogates of salvation in contemporary enchantments of political and lifestyle anarchism, or art and culture, or eroticism where the 'cold skeletal hand of the rational orders' can be eluded in the salon or under the duvet. But these are essentially flights from the realities of modern politics, economics, and science. Any attempt to transfer real or pseudo salvation goods into these last three orders of life can only be disastrous and cause fundamental unhappiness.

Reading 17 (Bureaucracy) represents the functional triumph of the administrative machine and the elimination of any personal, religious, or ethical traits from the running of organizations. While Reading 16 revolved around the universal need of human beings to confer an ultimate meaning on their activity, Reading 17 stands for its removal and the complete adherence to rational rules. Fixed jurisdiction, clear hierarchy, written and organized files, specialized training, full-time career jobs, and the existence of general rules have propelled modern bureaucracy to be the indispensable form of administration in modern government, the political party, the business enterprise, and every other large permanent organization, such as churches, trade unions, and so on. It is able to optimize efficiency through the dehumanization of its processes. It pursues impartiality in place of any favouritism for friends, family, religion, or party. It runs on calculable rules that make it congruent with the 'peculiarity of modern culture', which in terms of technical and economic base is a matter of 'calculability' of results.

Reading 18 (Formal and Substantive Rationalization: Theocratic and Secular Law) takes up the issue of rationalization in the field of law and justice. It was an area in which Weber could use his own considerable subject specialism, and the reader is able to see just how complex a matter the rationalization process is in empirical reality. Reading 17 ends with the observation that impersonal bureaucracy, specialist and neutral in regard to person, status, and sentiment, had also established the basis of the administration of rational law. But, Weber continued, it would be a mistake to assume that the abstract and general rules, which characterize rational bureaucracy, are the same thing as specialist expertise and objectivity when it comes to the field of justice. Legal adjudication involves conflicts or injustices of a substantive nature. Legal administration can be made more rational in terms of evidence, procedure, and accessibility. But the former – substantive issues of justice – can never be exactly reconciled with the latter.

It is perfectly true that 'objectivity' ('*Sachlichkeit*') and 'expertness' ('*Fachmäßigkeit*') are not necessarily identical with the rule of general and abstract norms. Indeed, this does not even hold in the case of the modern administration of justice. The idea of a 'law without gaps' is, of course, under vigorous attack. The conception of the modern judge as an automaton into which legal documents and fees are stuffed at the top in order that it may spill forth the verdict at the bottom along with the reasons, read mechanically from codified paragraphs – this conception is angrily rejected, perhaps because a certain approximation to this type would precisely be implied by a consistent bureaucratization of justice.

(*E&S*, pp. 978–9)

Weber is reflecting the contemporary opposition to the idea that a legal code (which covers every legal eventuality and is therefore 'gapless') in combination with an automated legal process could possibly deliver acceptable justice. Weber is not unsympathetic, but he also offers an historical account of how justice and its administration have remained apart. Reading 18, which is taken from his *Economy and Society*, gives a fuller analysis of this.

Weber effectively offers a periodization of magic, religious, and political rationalization, and secular and modern law. In all three periods Weber refers to the issues on which people seek adjudication as being substantive (*material*). Some real or perceived harm or advantage leads individuals to seek adjudication. Weber does not spell out the obviously infinite number of wrongs for which people seek redress through legal process; instead he simply refers to them as substantive or material. In tribal and kinship communities adjudication is arrived at through strictly observed magical procedures and the judgement is revealed by oracles or other magical revelation or signs. Both procedure and adjudication remain irrational, although not necessarily out of line with the community's substantive requirements. (Durkheim, in his *Division of Labour in Society*, put this point far more strongly – primitive lawmaking defines the sense and structure of the community.) With the rise of ecclesiastical and patrimonial rulership, royal and religious law offer adjudication on a more rational basis, both in court procedure, such as the process of entering pleas, and the introduction of rules of evidence. Justice is not however arrived at according to rational criteria. Instead judges will use substantive criteria such as morality, or kingly interests, or their own application of equity; also the rationalization of law is very often checked. In English common law, historically that is, adjudication remained stubbornly 'empirical', each case being taken on its 'merits', and in this sense justice was substantive. This could be 'sublimated' to a higher level through the use of analogies (precedents that suggest the rule), but the guild of English lawyers opposed any codification of law, as had occurred in the Roman Republic in Antiquity (*c.* 450 BC) and was also taken up (through the Justinian Code) in the French and German legal systems in the nineteenth century.

Weber is using 'substantive' in more than one sense. First, judges who have sufficient freedom in making their judgements can resolve cases according to their substantive notion of justice (fairness, equity, ethics, and khadi justice where the judgement is subjective). Second, the rules of adjudication and legal procedure still remain in touch with the substance of grievance. With the rationalization of legal codes that provide abstract norms for judgement distanced from the particular substantive features of a case, and the rationalization of legal procedures in favour of impersonal administration, we arrive at Weber's legal machine with the judge as automaton. This renders justice calculable, predictable, and formally free. But as such it can no longer render substantive justice in terms of various criteria such as social justice, welfare, or morality, and so on. In addition, when the administration of justice falls into the hands of experts – whether university trained or the English guild – this becomes an effective denial of justice to the common people who cannot afford the legal fees. The reverse also holds: where popular justice is installed, it is hostile to any formalism in adjudication, and reverts instead to substantive criteria of justice such as social justice and economic equity.

Reading 18 in its detail suggests far more than the above summary, and Weber's ideal types remain submerged within his historical examples – certainly compared to the very high-level ideal typification of the 'Intermediate Reflection'. One common thread is the jury. Under magical adjudication (for example, among the Anglo-Saxons prior to the eleventh century), jurors swore what was right as revealed by magical actions and not on the basis of evidence or witness. In the English royal courts of justice, juror deliberation was based on more rational rules of evidence, but in reaching a judgement jurors could be swayed both by fear of the judge (the king or his representative) as well as by sympathy for the defendant. For substantive reasons, then, jury trials can be unpredictable and are not fully rational. But as Weber notes, the complete formalization of justice ends up with only a *relatively* best option that refuses substantive criteria, still gives the judge discretion, and denies justice to the masses on grounds of expense.

As a historical footnote, we may note that Weber's younger brother Alfred lectured on these same themes in Prague, where the young Kafka was one of his students. Kafka's novel *The Trial* takes the theme of automated justice to its terrifying extreme – cruel, impersonal, and an internal logic whose rationality remains unfathomable to the defendant.

Rationalization should not be taken for perfectibility. One might choose to optimize either substantive justice or the formal rationality of legal process. There is not a one-to-one fit between the two, however nice that might be thought to be. The features of rationalization include sublimation, the distancing from the 'raw material' of social life and the experiential, the mediation through rules, the working of an autonomous intellectual dynamic, and the differentiation of tasks and values (for example, religious ethics and legal rules, or laymen and officials).

Reading 19 (The Vocation of Politics) and Reading 20 (The Vocation of Science) are not quite so studiously academic in tone as his other writings in this anthology. They were originally given as lectures to the Bavarian Union of Free Students at the University of Munich towards the end of the war when both the political and the university system were in crisis. Extreme politics, strong enthusiasms, and a deep disgust with the traditional ways were surging through the student population. Weber was an exception among his academic colleagues in publicly speaking out against the policies of the Wilhelmine government. He had also gained a reputation for debating on equal terms with any viewpoint, whether religious, cultural, anarchist, or political. As we have seen from the 'Intermediate Reflection', it would be quite reasonable to expect Weber to have a sympathy with those who thought the modern world was increasingly disenchanted and without meaning.

His two lectures on politics and on science develop a particular rhetorical style. Each lecture opens with an exposition of the sociological development of the realities of the situation in politics and science. Then, because the students had invited him as something of a sage on the course of modern civilization, Weber systematically disabuses them of each of their possible enthusiasms and solutions, hoping to lead them to a mature analysis and recognition of the demands of the day. Weber does not defend rationalization in itself but instead points out its inevitability and indispensability. The pursuit of politics and of science has to be rebuilt in the light of these realities. Any other option is an illusion, and as Weber somewhat prophetically notes in relation to Bolshevism, a dangerous illusion.

His lecture on politics continues the sociological analysis we have already covered in Part II and in the 'Intermediate reflection' (and for this reason this part of the lecture is omitted in Reading 19). The particular concern in this lecture was to spell out the specific qualities an individual requires in order to pursue the job of a politician. Despite the title of the lecture '*Politik als Beruf*' (Politics as a vocation or occupation), Weber's major sociological query is whether modern politics *is* a vocation. Historically, leaders were traditionally princes or kings or, alternatively, leaders by virtue of their charismatic qualities. Leadership, therefore, was a matter of either inherited or an achieved charisma. Likewise political officials used to belong to a status group, and in historical and comparative terms, Weber identifies five strata: religious clerics as in India, Japan, and medieval Europe, humanistically educated literati as in China, the court nobility, the gentry as in England, and the university trained jurist as in Europe. Historically then, both leader and political official belonged to a fixed status group with a prescribed education, outlook, and conduct of life, and in this sense the vocation of politics was unproblematic (*FMW*, pp. 92–4).

In the modern world, however, there is no obvious career path to becoming a politician. There is an immediate problem as to whether one is to live 'for politics' or 'from politics'. The first requires an inner commitment, the second is a source of income, says Weber. By the nineteenth century the state has monopolized as legitmate all the sources of power and force within a territorial unit, and it is supported and maintained by a bureaucratic machine. If the political aspirant is to climb to the pinnacle of this apparatus under conditions of modern democratic constitutions, he has to consider a number of options. Under democracy the leader achieves power through the organized political party, and the activists in the party canvass on his behalf seeking the support of passive voters. (Weber varies this description for the different situations of Imperial Germany, the United States, and Britain.) The aspirant politician either obtains a position in the political party and seeks patronage to propel himself into Parliament. Alternatively, he can get a job as a journalist as a kind of preliminary career. These paths in themselves do not offer an entirely convincing training for the rising politician, and Weber more or less leaves his question unanswered. Weber assumes in his analysis of modern democratic politics that the leader has to be demagogue, whose rise and influence is based on the power of words. Weber states this as a fact not as a negative value-judgement, and he refers to Pericles (to whom we are partially indebted for the *demos*) as a positive example. This was inevitable in a world of mass franchise and mass media, and the propaganda successes of Lord Northcliffe's *Daily Mail* did not escape his attention – a paper that supported the career of the democratic demagogue Lloyd George.

Reading 19 takes up the lecture with Weber's exposition of what the politician will face as a leader. Immediately it will be the sensation of power, that is its own reward, and for which a leader must have an instinct. But at the same time the politician has to be true to a cause and not indulge his own vanity. Weber then rehearses the arguments we have seen in the 'Intermediate Reflection' that the life order of politics has its own values, and the business of politics ultimately concerns the pragma of power and violence. Weber offers three qualities for the politician to perform his task: passion, the capacity to take responsibility for political action, and a sense of proportion (see below, p. 257). In his conclusion, he restates this with a prosaic emphasis: 'Politics means slow, strong drilling through hard boards, with a combination of passion and a sense of judgement.'

Weber delivered this lecture in January 1919 in Munich in the Free State of Bavaria. For a short period, Government had become the soviets of workers and soldiers. Weber's only direct comment on this was the wry observation that government was now open to amateurs – anybody who could handle a machine-gun. This context did, however, transform the academic nature of the argument in the 'Intermediate Reflection' into an actual and imminent danger. In the lecture Weber is far more extreme in his exclusion of ethics from the sphere of politics. The outbreak of soviets, revolution, and anarchism in Germany, Austria, and Russia opened up the possibility of the reformulation of the boundaries between the life orders of politics, economics, and Christian ethics and, for Weber, the misplaced search for salvation in new ideals of community and brotherliness. To displace a communal, pacifist ethics into politics was, argued Weber, to pursue absolute convictions with no heed of the consequences. It was naïve to believe that from good actions, good will result. Politics and powers have a diabolical element because their primary means is violence. Only the mature political leader is capable of acknowledging the ethical irrationality of the world and realizing that a sense of both conviction and responsibility is required of the politician and that these are irreconcilable goods.

Reading 20 parallels the arguments in the politics lecture. It starts out with the pertinent question: why make a career in science? In Weber's view a scientific career often means enduring no advancement according to merit, bad pay, and no just recognition by colleagues. Moreover, science by its very nature will render any discovery redundant and obsolete after a period of years. Weber deliberately goes out of his way to rebuff the aspirations of his student audience, who felt that both science and politics needed to be revital-ized. They demanded that politics should rediscover its soul, and that science should celebrate the experiential, life, and personality and that it should not be a dry-as-dust form of specialist knowledge. Once again, Weber argues that this is a diplacement of the search for community and salvation into the life order of intellectual knowledge. Science cannot confer ultimate meaning on life. The individual has to discover and pursue ultimate meanings outside the classroom and it is not the job of a professor to peddle such ultimate values within the lecture hall. Science provides information and explanations about how particular (policy) goals can be achieved and what the consequences of implementing those goals will be. It does not have the capability of assessing the ultimate value of any goal – for instance, its ethical, or political value. Science can never provide a *Weltanschauung* (an overall view of world), nor leadership, nor answer Tolstoy's grand question – how should we lead our lives? Science is part of the rationalization of the world and as such leads to its disenchantment. Modern science has divorced itself from the Christian metanarrative of progress, even though many professors – 'big children' – still pursue this illusion. There is no necessary unity of truth, beauty, and good-ness; indeed as Baudelaire and Nietzsche show, the opposite may be the case. The only enthusiasm Weber himself shows is for Plato's discovery of 'the concept' where the pursuit of truth can be a kind of frenzy. Weber warns his audience not to place false expectations on science, and to pursue truth and the vocation of science only if that is the demon in one's soul.

16 Intermediate reflection on the Economic Ethics of the World Religions[1]

Theory of the stages and directions of religious rejection of the world

The motives of world-rejection (*Weltablehnung*) – towards the rational construction of their meaning

Indian religiosity, which we wish to explore, was the cradle of theoretically and practically the most world-denying (*weltverneinend*) form of religious ethic that the world has ever known – in the strongest contrast to China. Equally, its corresponding 'technique' was the most highly developed. It is in India that monasticism and the typical manipulation of asceticism and contemplation occurred earliest and were most consistently built up, and it is from here that their rationalization has perhaps historically even spread through the world. Before we turn to this religiosity, it will be useful to make clear in a short schematic and theoretical construction from what motives world-denying religious ethics have originated and in what directions they have proceeded. Thus, of what their possible 'meaning' could consist.

Such a schema is obviously constructed only as a *means of orientation*, and it does not teach a philosophy all of its own. Its intellectually (*gedanklich*) constructed types of conflicts of the 'life orders' (*Lebensordnungen*) seek solely to say that in these positions only these inner conflicts are *possible* and 'adequate'. What it does *not* say is that there is no standpoint whatsoever from which they could be thought to be 'overcome' (*aufgehoben*). As one will readily see, the individual value-spheres (*Wertsphären*) are elaborated as rationally closed wholes and as they *seldom* appear in reality; but, to be sure, they could so appear and *have done* so in important historical cases. Where a historical phenomenon approximates to one such whole either in its individual traits or overall character, it is possible for the typological position of that historical phenomenon to be established by determining how close to, or far away, it is from the theoretically constructed type. The construction, therefore, is solely a technical aid for facilitating clarity and terminology.

But thereafter, under certain circumstances, it could nevertheless be something more. Also, what is rational in the sense of the logical or teleological

1 Taken from *GARS*, vol. 1, pp. 536–71.

'consistency' of an intellectual and theoretical, or practical and ethical, stance has (and always has had) power over human beings, whatever in general are, and were, its limitations and frailties in the face of the other powers of historical life. Quite simply, where religious interpretations of the world (*Weltdeutungen*) and ethics have been created by intellectuals according to rational purposes, they have been strongly exposed to the demand for consistency. But as little as they obey in individual cases the demand for the absence of contradiction and as much as they may fit their ethical postulates to a stance that is *not* rationally derivable, so nevertheless the effectivity of reason (*ratio*) – and especially the teleological derivation of practical postulates – has been in some way very remarkable amongst all religious interpretations and ethics. For these material (*sachlich*) reasons we should also hope to facilitate the presentation of the otherwise ungraspable (*unübersehbar*) manifold complexity through the purposeful construction of rational types; that is, through the elaboration of the internally most 'consistent' forms of a practical behaviour derived from fixed, given presuppositions. And finally, most of all, an essay in religious sociology of this sort at the same time has to be, and will be, a contribution in itself to the typology and sociology of rationalism. It therefore starts from the most rational forms which reality *can* assume, and seeks to establish how far certain theoretically presentable, rational consequences have followed in reality. And possibly, why they did not follow.

Typology of asceticism and mysticism

The great significance of the conception of a transcendental (*überweltlich*) creator god for the religious ethic has already been touched upon in the introductory and later remarks.[2] In particular, the actively ascetic search for salvation was contrasted to the contemplative mystical direction and its internal relatedness to the depersonalization (*Verunpersönlichung*) and immanence of divine power. This was not, however, an unlimited relation of dependency,[3] and the transcendental (*überweltlich*) god purely as such has not determined the direction of asceticism in the Occident. Consideration has to be given to the Christian Trinity with its human-yet-divine saviour (*gott-menschlicher Heiland*) and its saints (*Heiligen*) that basically presented a rather less transcendental conception of God than the god of Judaism – especially late Judaism – or that of the Islamic Allah.

Moreover, Judaism has even developed mysticism but more or less no asceticism of the occidental type. And in early Islam asceticism was directly rejected, while the distinctiveness of Dervish religiosity originated from completely different sources (mystical and ecstatic) than the relationship to a

---

2 See Reading 3.
3 [Weber] E. Troeltsch has repeatedly and correctly stressed this dependency.

transcendental creator god, and also it was distanced by its inner nature from occidental asceticism. The transcendental conception of god, important as it was, evidently therefore worked, in spite of its relatedness to emissary prophecy (*Sendungsprophetie*) and ascesis of behaviour, not alone but only in combination with other circumstances. Probably most important of all was the type of religious promises and the ways to salvation those promises thereby determined. This will be discussed further in greater detail. What is first needed here is a clarification of the terminology, the expressions 'asceticism' and 'mysticism', which have already been much used as polar opposites, but will now be somewhat further refined.

In the introductory remarks on the subject of the rejection of the world (*Weltablehnung*) the contrast was presented between, on the one side, active asceticism as *activity* willed by god as an instrument of god, and, on the other, the mystic's contemplative *possession* of salvation, which signifies not active behaviour but a 'possessing' ('*Haben*') and by which the individual is not an instrument but a 'vessel' ('*Gefäß*') where action in the world must consequently appear as endangering the thoroughly irrational and extra-worldly state of salvation (*außerweltliche Heilszuständlichkeit*). This is a radical opposition, if, on the one side, the asceticism of action realizes itself within the world as its rational moulder (*Gestalterin*) for the taming of the creaturely and the corrupt (*kreatürlich Verderbten*) through work in a worldly 'vocation' ('*Beruf*') (innerworldly asceticism); and if mysticism, from its side, assumes the full consistency of radical world-flight (contemplation that flees the world). The opposition is lessened, if, on the one side, the asceticism of action limits itself to the keeping down and the overcoming of what is creaturely and corrupt in its own nature, and it consequently concentrates more on the active accomplishment of salvation as defined and willed by God to the detriment of activity in the orders of the world (world-fleeing asceticism), and so comes close in external behaviour to world-fleeing contemplation. Or if, on the other side, the contemplative mysticism does not assume world-flight fully consistently, but remains within the orders of the world similar to the innerworldly ascetic (innerworldly mysticism). In both of these cases the opposition can actually disappear in practice and any combination of each type of search for salvation can occur.

But the opposition can also remain in place disguised by externally similar appearances. For the genuine mystic the principle asserts that the creature must be still, so that then God can speak. He 'is' in the world and 'resigns himself' ('*schickt sich*') in outward behaviour to its orders. But he does this not for the world but against it; for in order to assure his state of grace, he resists the temptations of the world and does not regard its ways as important. As we were able to see in the case of Lao-tzu, its typical attitude is a specifically humble bearing (*gebrochene Demut*), a minimization of action, a manner of religiose incognito in the world. He affirms himself *against* the world, that is, *against* his activity in the world. Whereas the innerworldly ascetic affirms himself, directly conversely, *through* activity. For the innerworldly ascetic the behaviour of the mystic is an indulgent self-absorption. For the mystic the behaviour of the innerworldly activist ascetic is a vain self-justifying and suborning entanglement in the ways of a god-forsaken world. With that 'happy bigotry' which one tends to associate with the typical Puritan, innerworldly asceticism executes the positive and godly decrees (*Ratschlüsse*) whose ultimate meaning remains hidden to the ascetic, as they exist in the rational orders of the creaturely (*Kreatürlichen*) ordained by God.

For the mystic, it is simply the grasping of that final, wholly irrational sense in mystical experience that alone is important for salvation. The world-fleeing forms of both ways of behaving are distinguishable by similar opposites, whose discussion we reserve for the separate studies.

We now turn to a detailed look at the tensions that exist between the world and religion, linking this to the observations made in the 'Introduction' but also giving them a different consideration.[4]

As has already been said, the presuppositions of magic were the starting point for those ways of behaving which developed into a methodical conduct of life (*Lebensführung*) and have formed the basis of asceticism as well as mysticism. Magic was used either for the awakening of charismatic qualities or for the protection against evil spirits. The first case was clearly of more importance in historical-developmental terms, since already at its inception it showed its Janus-face: on the one side, the rejection of the world (*Weltablehnung*) and, on the other, the mastery of the world (*Weltbeherrschung*) by the magical powers that could be attained through that rejection.

In historical-developmental terms, the magician was the forerunner of the prophet – both exemplary and emissary as well as the saviour. As a rule, the prophet and the saviour legitimized themselves through the possession of a magical charisma. But it was used only as a means to gain recognition and respect for their personality in its exemplary significance, mission, or the qualities of a saviour. What was important was the content of the prophecy or the commandment for salvation: the orienting of the conduct of life for the salvation good (*Heilsgut*). This means, at least relatively speaking, the rational systematization of the conduct of life, either in its individual aspects or as a whole. The latter was the case in those religions that were specifically 'redemption' religions; that is, all those religions that offered to their followers the prospect of deliverance from *suffering*. This was more likely to occur, the more the nature of suffering was made more sublimated, more internalized and more principled. What counted was to place the followers in a *permanent* situation that gave them an internal immunity against suffering. In place of an acute and extraordinary (*außeralltäglich*) state of holiness attained predominantly through orgy, asceticism, or contemplation, for the

4 See Reading 3.

redeemed a holy and permanent habitus that assured salvation would be attained. Put in abstract terms, this was the rational purpose of a salvation religion. Where a religious community developed among the following of a prophecy or in the propaganda of a saviour, the duty for the regimentation of life at first fell into the hands of the charismatically qualified successors, pupils, and disciples of the prophet or saviour. Then, under definite and regularly occurring conditions, which we cannot go into here, this duty fell into the hands of a priestly – hereditary or official – hierocracy. But, as a rule, the prophet or saviour himself stood in opposition to the traditional hierocratic powers, that of the magicians and the priests, against whose traditionally consecrated rank (*Würde*) he placed his own personal charisma in order to break their power or to force it into his own service.

As already stated and taken for granted as a presupposition, prophetic and saviour religions exist not only in an acute but in a continuous state of tension with the world and its orders; this is so for the large majority of cases and for the majority of the important cases that are of particular significance in historical and developmental terms (as should be obvious from the terminology being used). The more a religion was truly a religion of redemption, the greater this tension has been. This was a consequence of the meaning (*Sinn*) of redemption and the nature of prophetic salvation teaching as soon as these developed themselves into an ethic, and even more so as these became more principled as rational and so as *inward* (*innerlich*) religious salvation goods (*Heilsgüter*) oriented towards the means of redemption (*Erlösungsmitteln*). Using the normal terminology, we can say that the tension became greater the more ritualism was sublimated towards a religiosity based on convictions (*Gesinnungsreligiosität*). Indeed, the tension itself became stronger, as the rationalization and sublimation of the external and inward possession of 'worldly' goods (in its widest sense) progressed.[5] What the rationalization and the conscious sublimation of the relation of human beings to the different spheres, in which external and inner (*inner*), religious and worldly goods were possessed, then forced into the open was a consciousness of the *internal and autonomous working* (*innere Eigengesetzlichkeit*) of the individual spheres in their consistency. This brought into play those tensions between the value spheres that in the original openness (*Unbefangenheit*) of man's relation to the external world remained hidden. A very important consequence – one general to the history of religion – of the development of the possession of goods (*Güterbesitz*) (innerworldly and

---

5 Weber's terminology and argument are quite novel. In general, Weber says, human beings seek to acquire 'goods'. In the economic sphere these are goods in the normal sense. But Weber extends his usage of 'goods' to the spheres of the kinship group, politics as well as economics, culture, the erotic, and the intellectual sphere. These all come into conflict with the religious sphere and its salvation 'goods'. Depending on the historical context, a good may be an inner value – love of poetry, or belief in God, or it can be an external acquisition – such as power or wealth or ostentation.

other-worldly) was a tendency to the rational, the consciously striven for and, through knowledge, the sublimated. Analysing a series of these goods, we will elucidate the typical phenomena which recur in very different religious ethics.

Directions of world rejection

Where salvation prophecy has created communities on a purely religious basis, then the first power it came into conflict with, and with which it had most to fear from devaluation, was the naturally occurring **kinship** community (*Sippengemeinschaft*). Whoever is not able to be hostile to his household companions, or his father, and mother, then he cannot be a disciple of Jesus: 'I have not come to bring peace, but the sword' (Matthew, 10, 34), but (we should note carefully) this applies only in this context. The overwhelming majority of all religions have certainly regulated the innerworldly bonds of piety. That the saviour, prophet, priest, confessor, and brother in faith have stood ultimately closer to believers than the family relatives and marriage partners becomes more explicable in itself, the more far-reaching and inward the goal of salvation has been conceived. Where those relationships have been devalued, at least relatively, and where the bonds of magic and the exclusivity of the kinship group have been shattered, prophecy – where it has become a soteriological[6] religious community – has created a new social community. It developed within this a religious ethic of brotherliness. It did this mostly by simply taking over the original and fundamental principles of social-ethical behaviour as it occurred in the neighbourhood band: the community of the village, kin, guild, and partners in hunting, shipping, and military expeditions. These communities recognized two basic principles: (1) the dualism of in-group morality and an out-group morality (*Binnen- und Außenmoral*), (2) the principle of reciprocity – 'do to me, as I do unto you' – operated in the in-group morality. The economic consequence of these principles – that is, the obligation to provide fraternal assistance at times of emergencies – was confined to the morality of the in-group. It included on the part of the propertied and the noble the free loan of utility items, interest-free credit, free hospitality and support for those without any means, and the performance of unpaid labour at the request of a neighbour, as though it was manorial service, in return for mere sustenance. Naturally all of this occurred not for rationally *considered* principles but according to the general *sentiment* that what your need is today, so it might be mine tomorrow. It also followed that haggling (over exchange and loans) and permanent enslavement (following on, for example, from unpaid debts) was reserved to the out-group morality and those not members of the community.

Communal religiosity imposed the old economic neighbourhood ethic on the relationship of a brother in faith (*Glaubensbruder*). The obligation of the

---

6 The adjective for salvation.

noble and the wealthy to give aid in emergencies to widows and orphans and to the sick and the poor of the same faith, and above all the charity of the rich, on which the sacred singers, magicians as well as the ascetics were economically dependent, became fundamental commandments of all ethically rationalized religions of the world. In prophecies of salvation it was especially *suffering* – actual or continually threatened, external or internal – that was common to all believers and became the constitutive principle of the community. Indeed, the more rational and the more sublimated the idea of salvation became as a conviction ethic, the more it thereby intensified itself as an internal and external commandment that was derived from, but raised above, the ethic of reciprocity of the neighbourhood band. Externally, it became a commandment of the communism of brotherly love, internally a conviction of charity for, and love of, suffering as such, and so love of one's neighbour, of humanity, and finally love of one's enemy. The barriers of the band of believers and ultimately the facticity of hate, which once was a feature of a conception of the world as a place of undeserved suffering, now appeared to be the result of imperfection and corruption common to everything empirical, and thus responsible for suffering.

The curious euphoria of all sorts of sublimated religious ecstasy has notably operated in the same general direction, when considered purely psychologically. From devout emotion to the feeling of direct possession of communion with god, ecstasy has inclined to stream out into an acosmic love without object.[7] The deep and peaceful bliss of every hero of acosmistic goodness has always merged therefore, in the salvation religions, with the compassionate knowledge of the natural imperfection of one's own being and so of all others. The psychological coloration as well as the rational-ethical significance of this inner attitude obviously could take on very different forms. But its ethical demand towards a universalistic brotherhood was located somewhere well beyond the boundaries of the social group, including frequently the band of believers (*Glaubensverband*) themselves. The more this religious brotherliness was consistently established, the sharper was the conflict with the orders and values of the world. Indeed the more religion from its side has tended to be rationalized and sublimated according to its own autonomous working (*Eigengesetzlichkeit*), the more irreconcilably polarized the conflict has become. This is what now needs to be shown.

This has most obviously been the case in the **economic** sphere. Every form of influencing the original spirits and gods (be they magical or mystagogical) for the benefit of *individual* interests strove for wealth as a taken-for-granted purpose, alongside long life, health, honour, descendants, and perhaps the improvement of one's destiny in the Beyond. This has been the case for the Eleusian mysteries, as well as Phoenician and Vedic religion, the Chinese folk religion, ancient Judaism, ancient Islam, and the promises for the pious lay

---

7 On acosmos, see the discussion above, p. 67.

person in Hinduism and Buddhism. In contrast to this, the sublimated religion of salvation has come into increasing tension with the rationalized economy.

Rational economic activity (*rationale Wirtschaft*) is a matter of fact business (*sachlicher Betrieb*). It is oriented to *money* prices, which originate from the *market* where people are in conflict with one another. No form of *calculation* is possible without evaluation in money terms and its accompanying struggle. Money is the most abstract and most 'impersonal' thing in all human life. The more the cosmos of the modern rational capitalist economy followed its own autonomous working, the more it became inaccessible to every imaginable ethic of religious brotherhood. And this was ever more the case, the more rational and so more impersonal the economy became. One could regulate the personal relationship of lord and slave in a completely ethical manner, simply because it was personal. This cannot be said of – at least in the same *sense* and with the same *result* – of the relationship between the changing holders of credit-notes and to the (to them) unknown and also changing debtors of a mortgage lending institution, between whom no possible personal relationship could exist. If however one did attempt to establish personal relationships, then the result would be the *restriction* of formal rationality, as we have seen in China; for here formal and material rationality stand in conflict with one another. Although the salvation religions have a tendency towards a peculiar depersonalization of love in the sense that it obtained in acosmic views, it is quite clear that they have viewed with deep distrust the unfolding of impersonal economic powers, albeit in a different sense of the impersonal, which are thereby specifically hostile to an ethic of brotherliness. The Catholic saying 'It is not possible to please God' ('*Deo placere non potest*') was for a long time the characteristic position towards acquisitive activity, and salvation religions rationally and methodically warned against the accumulation of money and goods, so much so that this amounted to an abomination. It is the dependence of the religious communities themselves, their propaganda and self-advertising, that has compelled them to make compromises with economic expediency and an accommodation with the cultural needs and everyday interests of the masses; the history of the prohibition against charging interest is just *one* example of this.[8] For a genuine ethic of salvation, however, this tension in the last instance could scarcely be surmounted.

It is the religious ethic of virtuosi, through their rejection of the possession of economic goods, that has externally reacted most radically to this conflictual relationship. The monk in his world-fleeing asceticism is forbidden individual possessions, he keeps himself alive through his own work, and above all his needs are correspondingly limited to the absolutely indispens-

---

8 Making a living from charging for money loans (usury) was considered a sin in the Bible. The medieval church none the less permitted it.

able. This has resulted in the paradox of all rational asceticism: that the wealth which it has created is at the same time what it seeks to reject, and this is what has always tripped up monasticism. Throughout the world, temples and cloisters have from their side become places of rational economic activity (*rationale Wirtschaft*). World-fleeing contemplation could only take the view in principle that the propertyless monk ought only to enjoy in general what is freely offered to him by nature and man – berries, roots, and free charity; work was something that detracted from his concentration on the contemplation of the good of salvation (*Heilsgut*). Similarly, contemplation has made compromises by creating districts for begging (as in India).

There were only two consistent ways to escape the tension in principle and from *within*. One was the paradox of the Puritan's ethic of vocation (*Berufsethik*), which as a virtuosi religiosity renounced the universalism of love and rationally objectified all action in the world (*Wirken in der Welt*) as being in the service of God's will and the testing of his divine grace. Ultimately, God's positive will was unknowable, and one therefore accepted the objectification of one's action in the economic cosmos – which being part of the creaturely and corrupt world was devalued – as willed by God and as a way of fulfilling one's duty. This was the main reason for the renunciation of salvation as a goal that was attainable through the actions of each and every person in favour of a grace that was always particularistic yet without reason. In truth this standpoint of unbrotherliness did not represent a true 'salvation religion' anymore. The only other way [to escape the tension], presented in pure terms, was to exaggerate brotherliness into that of the acosmistic love of the mystic, which has no real interest in the person to whom and for whom it sacrifices. In the final analysis devotion is made not for a person but out of disinterested goodness: if the mystic is asked by someone he accidentally meets for his coat, he will always give his shirt – for no other reason than this accidental meeting took place. This is a distinctive flight from the world in the form of an objectless devotion to anybody. It is done not for the sake of somebody but is a form of abandonment that in Baudelaire's words is made for the sake of 'the soul's sacred prostitution'.[9]

The tension with the **political** orders of the world must have been equally acute for the ethic of brotherliness in salvation religions where this ethic was held consistently. This was not a problem for a religiosity of magic and functional gods. The ancient gods of war and the god who guaranteed the legal order were functional deities who protected what were clearly everyday goods (*Alltagsgüter*). The god of locality, tribe, and empire was concerned only with the interests of his own group. He had to struggle against other gods of a similar nature, just as did the community itself, and through this struggle he had to affirm his own godly power. The problem only first came about when universal religions were able to break those barriers with a unified conception

9 Charles Baudelaire, French lyric poet. The quotation comes from the poem, 'Les Foules'.

of god and the world that at its strongest was conceived of as a god of 'love'; for salvation religions this was based on the demand of brotherliness. As with the economic sphere, the more rational the political order became, the greater its tension with religion.

The bureaucratic state apparatus runs on impartial lines 'without respect to person', without anger and enthusiasm (*sine ira et studio*), and without hate and therefore without love. It has this in common with the rational *homo politicus*, who is incorporated into the apparatus, as well as *homo oeconomicus*. Its business, including the punishment of wrongs, is performed when it is directly based in its most ideal sense on rational rules of the state's organization of power (*staatliche Gewaltordnung*). By virtue of its depersonalization it is less amenable to a material ethicization, despite appearances to the contrary, in contrast to the patriarchal orders of the past, which because of personal obligations of piety and the concrete personal worthiness of the individual case are influenced 'by respect of person'. The whole course of the internal political functions of the state apparatus in respect to the maintenance of law (*Rechtspflege*) and administration (*Verwaltung*) is unavoidably and continuously regulated by the impartial pragmatism of reasons of state (*Staatsräson*) whatever the final goals of 'welfare policies'. This is an absolute goal in its own right for the maintenance (or transformation) of the internal and the external distribution of power (*Gewaltverteilung*), even though for every universal religion of salvation this, in the final analysis, appears as meaningless. This holds, and has held, most definitely for the state's foreign policy. The appeal to naked power as a means of coercion in both internal and foreign policy is quite simply essential for every political body (*Verband*). In our terminology this is what makes a political organization: the 'state' is the organization which claims the monopoly of the *legitimate use of violence* (*legitime Gewaltsamkeit*), and it cannot be defined in any other way.

Where the Sermon on the Mount says 'ye shall not resist evil with force',[10] against this the state says 'you *should* use *force* in order for law to triumph – or you will be responsible for injustice'. Where force is absent, then there is no state, and there would be pacifist 'anarchism' in its place. But force and the threat of force, according to the inescapable pragma of all action, unavoidably breed the ever new use of violence. Reasons of state follow their own autonomous workings, both internally and externally. And the *success* of force, or its threat, obviously is finally dependent on power relations and *not* upon what is ethically '*right*', even if one believed that objective criteria for what was ethical were in general discoverable. At any rate, in a situation which is typical of the rational state – in contrast to the unconstrained naturalness of the warrior hero – each party will sincerely claim to be in the right in a power dispute (*Gewaltkampf*) with other groups or holders of power. This

10 The New Testament, Matthew, 5, 39.

can only appear on reflection to every form of religious rationalization as a travesty of ethics. The drawing of a divinity into a political power dispute is reckoned as an especially unproductive use of his name, and the complete exclusion of everything ethical from political reasoning is regarded as purer and as the only honourable course. The whole of politics, especially as it becomes more 'impartial' and calculating – indeed the more it is free from passionate sentiments, anger and love – has to be reckoned by religion as more hostile to the ethic of brotherliness.

As each sphere, political and religious, reaches full rationalization, the alienation of one to the other becomes particularly acute. In contrast to the economic, the political sphere has the capability of acting as a direct competitor to that of the religious ethic. *War*, as the realized threat of force, is able to create in the modern political community a pathos and a feeling of community and thereby releases an unconditional community of sacrifice among the combatants. Furthermore, war releases the work of compassion and love for the needy which breaks through all the barriers of naturally given groups, and it does this as a mass phenomenon. Religion, from its side, can only in general provide a similar ethic of brotherliness in the heroic-warrior communities. And furthermore war performs something for the combatant himself that is quite distinctive in his sensibility: the perception of the meaning and consecration of death, which belongs to him alone. The community of the standing army in the field is today aware of itself as a community until death, the greatest of its kind – just as in the times of the warrior bands. And of that death, which comes to us all and beyond which is nothing, about which we cannot ask why me and why now, death in arms is distinguishable from the normal inevitability of death. While cultural goods (*Kulturgüter*) develop ever more intensively and are sublimated to an immeasurable degree, death still marks an end where only a beginning can seem to be meaningful. Death in arms, *only* here in this massiveness of death, can the individual believe he *knows* that he dies 'for' something. The why and for what he must endure death, which he shares with others who face death as part of their 'profession', becomes as a rule an irrelevance when faced with its certainty. The 'meaning' of death in this most general sense, about which salvation religions are forced to be preoccupied with, here requires no such assumptions about its causes.

Death has to be installed within a series of meaningful and consecrated occasions and this lies at the root of all attempts to provide the political body that exercises violence (*politische Gewaltsamkeitsverband*) with its own dignity. But the manner of how death can be conceived of as meaningful lies in a radically different direction to the theodicy of death in the religiosity of brotherliness. The banding together in war of groups of men as brothers can only appear as devalued to such a religiosity – as a mere reflex of the refined brutality of conflict and where the innerworldly consecration of death in arms is a glorification of fratricide. The sheer extraordinariness of brothers in arms and death in war, something it shares with holy charisma and the experience of holy communion, raises the competition to a very high level. There are only two consistent solutions to this, as in the economic sphere. First, the particularism of grace of the Puritan's asceticism of work (*Berufs-askese*) which believes in the fixed and revealed decrees of an otherwise incomprehensible god. Here the will of God is understood as decreeing that this creaturely world, subject as it is to violence and ethical barbarism, should be brought under control by the same means, namely force. And this then requires some limitations on the obligation of brotherhood in the interests of God's 'cause'.

The other solution is the radical anti-politics of the mystical search for salvation and its acosmistic goodness and brotherliness, for which all political action is intrinsically tied up with the pragma of violence. It escapes the political with the saying 'resist not evil' and the maxim 'turn the other cheek', which for the self-confident and worldly heroic ethic is common and without dignity. All other solutions are weighed down with compromises or with dishonourable and unacceptable presuppositions from the point of view of a genuine ethic of brotherliness. Some of these solutions, however, are interesting in principle as types.

Every organization of salvation as an *institution* for the dispensation of universalist grace will feel itself responsible before god for all the souls entrusted to it. To this end it will feel justified and obliged to counter any danger of straying from belief even if this involves ruthless force, and it will support the spread of its saving means of grace. Also the salvation-aristocracy bears the sign of active 'warriors of the faith' where it is commanded by its god to discipline the sinful world for the glory of God, as in Calvinism (and in a different way in Islam). At the same time, however, there is a clear distinction between a 'holy' or 'just' war – that is, undertaking war as carrying out God's decree for the sake of faith, which always in some sense is a religious war – and all other wars of a purely worldly and so deeply devalued nature. The compulsion to take part in wars of the political powers is therefore rejected by the salvation-aristocracy. These wars are not holy. They do not correspond to God's established will and are not affirmed by individual conscience. For this reason mercenaries are preferred for military service in place of compulsory service – as was the case in Cromwell's victorious army of the saints that stood out against conscription.[11] Where the will of God has been violated by men, in particular in matters of belief, the religious aristocracy will decide on the side of active revolution for their faith – on the basis that one must obey God and not man.

The stance taken, for example, by the institutional religion of Lutheranism

---

11 As a military commander in the English Civil War, Oliver Cromwell favoured and promoted 'religious men'. See Weber's discussion, *The Protestant Ethic and the Spirit of Capitalism and Other Writings*, translated and edited by Peter Baehr and Gordon Wells, London, Penguin, 2002, p. 192.

is exactly the reverse. It has rejected war over matters of faith and the active right of resistance against the secular violation of belief, regarding these as drawing salvation into the arbitrariness of power and the pragma of violence. Instead Lutheranism accepted only passive resistance, and there again it did not see obedience to the power of the state as objectionable even when the authorities ordered a secular war. This was because the state and not the individual bore the responsibility, and the secular order of power was recognized as ethically independent – in contrast to the universalistic claims in matters of inner belief of the (Catholic) institutional church. Luther's own personal Christianity with its element of mystical religiosity failed to draw the full conclusions in this matter.

The truly mystical or pneumatic, religiously charismatic search for salvation of the religious virtuoso has everywhere by its nature been completely apolitical or anti-political. It has been quite willing to accept the independence of the earthly orders, but only then to assert their radically diabolical character; or at the very least have assumed an absolute indifference to them, as expressed in the saying 'give unto Caesar, what is Caesar's due'[12] (for how can these matters be concerned with salvation?).

The involvement of religious organizations in the interests and conflicts of power, the continual and unavoidable collapse of the extremely tense relationships with the world into compromise and relativization, the appropriation and use of religious organizations for the political domestication of the masses, and the need in particular for the religiously consecrated legitimation of the existing powers conditioned the attitude taken by the religions towards political activity. History shows that the empirical stances taken by religions have greatly varied with one another. Almost all the stances were forms of the relativization of their sacred values (*Heilswerte*) and their ethically rational autonomy (*Eigengesetzlichkeit*). Their most significant type, in practice, has been the '*organic*' social ethic which has spread in various forms.[13] Its concept of calling was in principle the most important counter-image to the idea of calling held by innerworldly asceticism.

Where it has been religiously supported, an organic social ethic is founded on 'brotherliness'. But, in contrast to mystical acosmic love, the requirement of a cosmic and rational brotherliness has prevailed. The inequality of religious charisma seen in experience is the starting point. What is unbearable for the sense of brotherliness is that holiness could be accessible only to some and not to everyone. Its social ethic therefore seeks to bend this inequality of charismatic qualifications that is tied to the secular stratification of status groups towards a cosmos of tasks, willed and ordained by God, that are

---

12 The New Testament, Mark, 12, 17.
13 Weber uses this term for his analysis of Hinduism, though it could also apply to medieval Christianity. *Within* both these religions there will be those who make pragmatic compromises with the world and those who pursue salvation unconditionally.

divided by occupation. For every individual and group there falls certain tasks according to personal charisma and according to the social and economic position that has been given to them by fate. As a rule these tasks work for the realization of the world that despite its compromise character is pleasing to God. The world is interpreted as both socially utilitarian and providential. In the light of its corrupted and sinful nature, this permits at least a relative control of sin and suffering and the preservation and saving of as many endangered souls as possible for the heavenly kingdom.

The situation is directly the reverse in the far greater pathos of the Indian doctrine of karma, which in the context of the organic doctrine of society gives the pragmatic control of salvation (*Heilspragmatik*) purely to the interests of the individual, as will soon be shown.[14] Aside from this very distinctive linkage [of salvation to the individual], every organic social ethic remains from the standpoint of the radical, mystical religious ethic of brotherliness an accommodation with the interests of the privileged strata of this world. This latter ethic of brotherliness is regarded in its turn from the standpoint of innerworldly asceticism as lacking the impetus for the complete ethical rationalization of individual life. For what is missing is the premium placed on the rational and *methodical* structuring of the life of the individual himself in the interests of his own salvation. From its side the salvation pragmatism of the organic social ethic must regard the innerworldly asceticism of aristocratic salvation (*Heilsaristokratismus*) with its rational objectification of the orders of life (*Versachlichung der Lebensordnungen*) as the harshest form of lovelessness and lack of brotherliness; it also must regard the mystic's search for salvation as a sublimated and, in truth, an unbrotherly indulgence with one's own charisma where an unmethodical acosmic love seeks its own salvation by egoistical means alone. Both [mysticism and innerworldly asceticism] condemn the social world ultimately to absolute meaninglessness or to the complete unknowability of God's purposes for the world. These ideas are too much for the religious rationalism of the organic doctrine of society, which seeks instead to comprehend the world as bearing traces of a divine plan of salvation and so at least a rational cosmos, despite its sinful corruption. But for the absolute charismatism and religiosity of the virtuosi even this relativization is actually reprehensible and alien to salvation.

As rational action in the economic and the political spheres follows its own lawlike autonomy, so every other rational action in the world remains inseparably linked to worldly conditions that are alien to brotherliness. Rational action, which must treat these conditions as its means or ends, finds itself somehow in tension with the ethic of brotherliness. There is also a deep tension within rational action itself, since there appears to be no way of resolving the most basic of questions: just where in the individual case is the ethical value of an action to be decided? Should it be located in its

---

14 A reference to Weber's study on Hinduism and Buddhism. See *India*.

success (*Erfolg*) or from the action's *intrinsic* value alone (*Eigenwert*) – however this is to be ethically defined? This is a matter of whether, and how far, the responsibility of the actor for the consequences of an action sanctifies the means; or conversely, whether the value of the conviction (*Gesinnung*) which the action carries should justify refusing the responsibility for the consequences, passing them over to God or the corruption and foolishness of the world which God permits.

The ethic of conviction, as a sublimation of religious ethics, will incline to the latter alternative. 'The Christian does right and leaves success to God.' But in carrying this through with real consistency, one's own action in relation to the lawlike autonomy of the world is judged as irrational in its effects.[15] In the face of this, the consistency of a sublimated search for salvation leads towards an increase in acosmism (*Akosmismus*), and instrumental action (*zweckrationales Handeln*) purely as such is rejected as action that falls into the categories of means and ends, so as tied to the world and estranged from God. This, as we will see, has occurred with various forms of logical consistency – starting with the biblical parable of the lilies of the field[16] through to the more principled formulations, for example, in Buddhism.

The organic social ethic is generally an eminently conservative power opposed to all revolution. The religiosity of virtuosi, by contrast, can under certain circumstances pursue other *revolutionary* consequences. But this only occurs when the pragma of violence (*Gewaltsamkeit*) summons force (*Gewalt*) and leads only to a change of rulers and at best changes in the methods of violent rule (*gewaltsamen Herrschens*) which are not recognized as the permanent character of the creaturely world. According to its complexion, the religiosity of virtuosi in its revolutionary turn can in principle take one of two forms. One springs from innerworldly asceticism in the overall situation where it was able to oppose the creaturely and reprehensible empirical orders of the world with an absolute and divine 'natural law'. This was the realization of the saying, as a matter of religious obligation, that one should rather obey God than man; a maxim that can be found more or less generally in the rational religions. One such type are the genuine Puritan revolutions, and other counterparts can be found elsewhere. Its attitude is one of complete obligation to religious war (*Glaubenskrieg*).

Quite different is the case of the mystic, who fulfils the always possible psychological transformation from having the possession of God to being possessed by God (*von Gottbesitz zur Gottbesessenheit*). This is meaningful and then realizable when the eschatological expectations for the immediate arrival of the epoch of acosmistic brotherliness breaks out, and when therefore

---

15 [Weber] As we will see, this is carried through theoretically most consistently in the *Bhagavad-Gita*. (See *India*, pp. 180–91.)

16 The New Testament, Matthew, 6, 28: 'And why be anxious about clothes? Consider how the lilies grow in the fields; they do not work, they do not spin.'

the belief in the eternal tension between the world and the irrational, hidden realm of redemption disappears. The mystic then turns into the saviour and the prophet. But the commands, which he proclaims, have no rational character. As products of his charisma, they are revelations of a concrete sort, and they quickly transform the radical rejection of the world into a radical *anomism*.[17] As someone possessed by God, the commands of the secular world are no longer valid for his own assured state of security (*panta moi exestin*). All chiliasm[18] up until the revolution of the Baptists draws in some way upon this substratum. The type of behaviour of the mystic lacks significance for salvation, given the nature of his redemption through 'possessing God' ('*Gott-Haben*'). We will find something similar among the Indian *jivanmukhti*.[19]

If the religious ethic of brotherliness stands in a relationship of tension with the autonomous working of instrumental rational action in the world, this is no less the case with those innerworldly powers of life, whose nature and character are fundamentally arational or anti-rational. This tension occurs above all with the aesthetic and the erotic spheres.

Magical religiosity stands in the most intimate relationship with the **aesthetic sphere**. From time immemorial religion has been an inexhaustible source of artistic developments; on the other hand, religion through its ties to tradition has been a source of stylization. These two tendencies are demonstrated in idols, icons and other religious artefacts; magical stereotyping in its proven forms as a first stage in the overcoming of naturalism through a fixed 'style'; music as a means to ecstasy, exorcism, or apotropaic magic; the magician as a sacred singer and dancer; the magically proven and so magically stereotyped tonal relations as the earliest stages of musical tonality; dance steps as a means to ecstasy that, as magically proven, become the sources of rhythm; temples and churches as the largest building forms where the style has become stereotyped in the face of building demands, which have to meet purposes fixed once and for all and building forms that satisfy magical tests; ornaments and ecclesiastical implements of all sorts as artistic objects linked to the religious zeal for the richness of temples and churches.

Art as a bearer of magical effects has, however, been not only devalued but regarded as suspicious by the religious ethic of brotherliness as well as by aprioristic rigorism.[20] The sublimation of religious ethics and the search for salvation on the one hand, and the unfolding of the autonomous working of art on the other, have brought out a relationship of increasing tension with

---

17 A rejection of all law.
18 The doctrine which holds that after a thousand years the Kingdom of God will arrive – often referred to as 'millenarianism'.
19 A person who is in a state of being in the world but not of it. The name comes from the Sanskrit 'liberated in this life'. See *India*, pp. 178–9.
20 The idea that morality is to be derived from abstract, philosophical principles.

each other. Every sublimated religion of redemption has looked only to the meaning and not to the form of those things and actions which are relevant for salvation. Form devalues itself through its propensity to the accidental, the creaturely and its distraction from meaning. From the point of view of art, the unconstrained attitude (*das unbefangene Verhältnis*) [to the world] can remain undisturbed (*ungebrochen*), or always further reproduce itself so long as the conscious interest of the recipient is naïve in respect to the content of the formed and does not adhere to the form purely as such; also so long as the work of the creators does not regard itself as an (originally magical) charisma of 'know-how' ('*Können*'), nor as free play.

Furthermore, the development of intellectualism and the rationalization of life alters this situation. Art now constitutes itself as a cosmos of ever more consciously grasped, free-standing autonomous values (*Eigenwerte*). It takes over the function of an innerworldly *redemption* (no matter how this is conceived) in the face of the everyday and above all the increasing pressure of theoretical and practical rationalism. But in making this claim it comes into direct competition with redemptory religion. In contrast to this irrational innerworldly redemption, every rational religious ethic must turn against what it sees as a realm of irresponsible enjoyment and a concealed lovelessness (*geheime Lieblosigkeit*). In fact, in the rejection of responsibility for an ethical judgement, which is a feature of intellectualistic periods due to reasons of subjectivist demands and the fear of appearing as traditionally philistine in one's ethical rigidity, there is a tendency to reformulate an ethically intended value-judgement into a judgement of taste ('lack of taste' replaces the 'reprehensible') whose inaccessibility to appeal excludes discussion. The 'universal validity' of the ethical norm at least supports community insofar as a person is prepared to live alongside another whose action he ethically rejects, knowing as he does his own creaturely limitations and so being prepared to subordinate himself to the ethical norm. In contrast, the flight from the necessity of taking a rational ethical attitude *can* very readily present itself to the redemptory religion as the deepest form of unbrotherly mentality. The ethical norm, however, may easily appear to the artistic creator as well as the aesthetically stimulated recipient, as an imposition upon the truly creative and what is most personal.

But the most irrational type of religious behaviour, mystical experience, is in its inner being not only alien to form and without form and inexpressible but also hostile to form, since it simply believes in its feeling of the bursting of all forms to be able to enter into the all-oneness that lies the other side of every sort of determination and the formed. To the mystic the undoubted psychological affinity of art with religion in their ability to shock only indicates a symptom of the diabolical character of art. Certainly music, which is the most 'inward' of the arts, has the capacity in its purest form of instrumental music with its own internal development (*Eigengesetzlichkeit*) to feign a realm that does not reside within the soul (*eines nicht im Innern lebenden Reiches*) and to appear as an irresponsible surrogate form of the primary religious experience. The well-known position of the Council of Trent may be traced back to this sentiment.[21] Art then becomes a 'creaturely idolatry' ('*Kreaturvergötterung*'), a competing power and a deceiving illusion, turning the portrayal and allegory of purely religious things into blasphemy.

Quite clearly in the empirical reality of history this psychological affinity has always led to renewed alliances between art and religion that have been significant for the development of art itself. The great majority of all religions have entered into this alliance in one way or another. The more a religion has wanted to be a universal religion, the more systematic it has become and the more it has demonstrated its efficacy with the masses and its emotional propaganda. All truly virtuosi religions – both actively ascetic and mystical – have stayed very much aloof from art because of the nature of the inner contradictions. This is more pronounced the more religion has emphasized either the transcendality of its god or the extra-worldliness (*Außerweltlichkeit*) of redemption.

As with the aesthetic sphere, so the religious ethic of brotherliness in salvation religions has stood in a relation of high tension with the greatest irrational power of life, **sexual love**. Indeed this has been more stark, the more sexuality has been sublimated on the one hand, and the more ruthlessly consistent has been the development of the salvation ethic of brotherliness on the other hand. Again, the original relationship was very intimate. Sexual intercourse was very often a part of magical orgiastics,[22] and holy prostitution, which had nothing to do with the alleged 'original promiscuity',[23] was mostly a remnant of the situation when all ecstasy counted as 'sacred'. Profane prostitution, both heterosexual and homosexual, was very old and often quite refined (the training of tribades[24] occurs among so-called primitive peoples).

The transition from prostitution to legally formed marriage was fluid, because of the existence of all manner of intermediate forms. The conception of marriage as an economic arrangement for the security of the wife and the inheritance rights of the child – and thereby an important institution for the gaining (*Gewinnung*) of children for the purposes of improving one's fate in the hereafter from sacrifices (*Totenopfer*) made by the descendants – occurs prior to the prophets and is universal and has nothing to do with asceticism. Sexual life as such had its spirits and gods, just as every other function did. A certain tension is only revealed in the quite ancient and temporary cultic chastity of priests. This was probably conditioned by the view easily taken by

21 In 1592 the Council of Trent banned undisciplined and impure organ and choir music.
22 [Weber] Or the unwanted effect of orgiastic excitement. The Skoptsi (eunuchs) sect in Russia was founded as a way of escaping the effect of the orgiastic dance (the radjani) of the Chlysts that was considered as sinful.
23 A reference to Friedrich Engels' view that marriage was an institution created for the preservation of private property within the male line. Engels drew on the research of J.J. Bachofen on matriarchy. See *GEH*, pp. 28–30.
24 A reference to female homosexuality.

the strongly stereotyped ritual of the regulated community cult that sexuality was the dominion of something specifically demonic. But further, it was certainly not accidental that the prophecies as well as the life orders controlled by the priests have regulated, almost with no noteworthy exception, sexual intercourse in favour of *marriage*. It is here that we find the opposition of all rational regulation of life against magical orgiastics and all types of irrational frenzy.

A further increase in the tension was then conditioned by respective moments in the development of sexuality and religion. On the side of sexuality, through its sublimation of the 'erotic' – and in opposition to the plain naturalism of the peasant – there was cultivated a *conscious* sense of being *beyond the everyday* (*außeralltäglich*), and this erotic sphere did not have to be – not even necessarily – opposed to convention. It was usual for knightly convention to turn the erotic into an object of regulation, although to be sure it did this through the concealment of the natural and organic basis of sexuality. The experience of being outside the everyday lay far beyond the unconstrained naturalism of the sexual. The reasons and significance of this are interrelated with the universal context of the rationalization and the intellectualization of culture.

We now wish to outline in a few sketches the phases of this development, taking our examples from the Occident.

The stepping outside of the totality of existence (*Gesamtdaseininhalte*) of the organic cycle of peasant existence and the increasing enrichment of life, whether intellectually or in other supra-individual cultural values (*überindividuell gewertete Kulturinhalte*), was realized through the movement of the contents of life away from what was naturally given and at the same time towards the intensification of the special position of the erotic. The erotic was raised up into the conscious sphere of the enjoyable in its most sublime sense. It appeared none the less and even thereby as a portal to the most irrational, and so the most real, kernel of life in the face of the mechanisms of rationalization. The degree and manner, by which the erotic as such was given a value accent (*Wertakzent*), was historically extremely variable. In the uncouth (*ungebrochen*) sentiment of the warrior band, the ownership of women and conflict over them were the near equivalents of treasure and the seizure of power. In pre-classical Greece in the era of knightly romance, an erotic disappointment could, for Archilochos,[25] be an experience of great and permanent gravity and the theft of a woman an occasion for a heroic war without equal.[26] And the tragedians also recognized the echoes of these myths as a genuine force of destiny. But on the whole it was a woman, Sappho, whose

25 Archilochos (*c.* 650 BC) was a Greek lyric poet. Lycambes had promised his daughter in marriage to him, but then withdrew his consent. Archilochos recited a satire that ridiculed Lycambes and his daughter, who subsequently hanged herself.
26 A reference to the Trojan War.

capacity for erotic experience surpassed that of men. But the classical Hellenic age, the period of the hoplite army, regarded – as all the statements of the time show – these matters in relatively plain (*nüchtern*) terms, even more plainly than the Chinese educated class. Not that they would no longer have known about the deadly seriousness of sexual love. Instead they were *characterized* by the opposite sentiment, and one recalls here – despite Aspasia – the speech of Pericles and, especially, the well-known remark of Demosthenes.[27] In the exclusively masculine character of this epoch of 'democracy', the treatment of erotic experiences with women as 'life's destiny' – to use our modern expression – would have been regarded as almost puerile sentimentality. The 'comrade', the boy was a desired object with all the ceremonial of love at the centre of Hellenic culture. Plato's eros following on from that, despite its grandeur, was a very *restrained* feeling; the beauty of the *bacchanalian passion* purely as such was not officially accepted.

The possibility of a problematic and tragedy of a principled sort was first introduced into the erotic sphere by definite demands for responsibility whose provenance in the Occident was Christian. The accent (*Wertakzent*) placed on the purely erotic sensation as such, however, unfolded primarily under the cultural conditions of feudal concepts of honour. This was conveyed into erotically sublimated relationships by the symbolism of vassalage of the knightly courts. In the vast majority of cases eroticism was combined with some sort of value accent of crypto-erotic religiosity, or combined directly with asceticism as happened in the Middle Ages. The troubadours (*Ritterminne*) of the Christian Middle Ages were well known for an erotic vassal service *not* towards maidens (*Mädchen*) but instead exclusively to married ladies, who they did not know (*fremd*), and involving (in theory!) abstinent nights of love and a casuistic code of submission (*Pflichtenkodex*). With this there began – in sharp contrast to the masculinity of Hellenism – the 'testing' ('*Bewährung*') of the man not before his peers, but as part of the 'lady's' erotic interest in the man. It was through this process that the concept of the lady was first created.

A further intensification of eroticism's character, as sensation, developed in the transition from the essentially masculine and agonal conventions of the Renaissance around the time of Cortegiano[28] and Shakespeare to the increasingly unmilitaristic intellectualism of salon culture; Renaissance convention,

---

27 Pericles played a leading role in the Athenian state, most notably during the Peloponnesian War. Aspasia was an Athenian courtesan who built a reputation on her beauty and accomplishments. She became the mistress of Pericles in 445 BC. Demosthenes is attributed with saying: 'Mistresses we keep for the sake of pleasure, concubines for the daily care of our persons, but wives to bear us legitimate children and to be faithful guardians of our households.'

28 Courtier. Baldassare Castiglione wrote a style book for courtiers, *Libro del cortegiano*, first published Venice, 1528.

despite major differences, was related to Antiquity – but stripped of the asceticism of Christian chivalry. Salon culture was based upon the conviction in the value of the creative power of conversation between the sexes, which was fed by the open or latent erotic sensation and the cavalier's agonal proving of himself (*Bewährung*) in the face of the essential stimulant (*Anregungsmittel*) of the lady. From the time of the *Lettres Portugaises* women's love as a genuine problematic developed a market value as a specifically intellectual topic and the amatory correspondence of women became 'literature'.[29]

A final intensification of the accenting of the erotic sphere was completed on the ground of intellectualistic cultures where it collided with the unavoidable ascetic element of the world of vocational specialism (*Berufsmenschentums*). Under conditions of tension with the rational everyday world, sexual life liberated from marriage became an experience beyond the routine of the everyday and appeared as if it could be the only tie that could link man to the natural source of all life, now that humanity had stepped completely out of the cycle of the old simple organic peasant existence. What welled up here was a powerfully accentuated valuing of this specific sensation of inner-worldly salvation from the rational world. This was a joyful triumph, and it corresponded in its radicalism to the no less radical rejection held by every sort of salvation ethic, whether extra-worldly or transcendental (*außer- oder überweltlich*),[30] for which the triumph of the spirit over the body should be its specific culmination and so leaving sexual life as the only ineradicable connexion with the animalistic. But in the case of the systematic cultivation (*Herauspräperierung*) of the sexual sphere, where the animalistic relationship is transfigured into a supreme erotic sensation, the tension with religious salvation will be at its unavoidably most acute – especially where the salvation religiosity takes on the character of love, whether brotherly or neighbourly. This is because the erotic relationship with its declared state of an insurpassable pinnacle in its fulfilment of the demands of love appears to offer the direct breaking through of one soul to another. In the most radical contra-distinction to the mundane, the rational, and the general, there occurs the limitless devotion (*Hingabe*) in the unique sense here of what one being in its irrationality has for another being, and only this one other being. In this sense, and therefore the value conferred on the relationship itself, from the aspect of the erotic there exists the possibility of a communion which is felt as the merging into *one* (*Einswerdung*) and the disappearance of the intimate other (*Du*). This is so overpowering that this fusion is thought of as 'symbolic', as *sacramental*. This is an experience akin to mystical possession (*Haben*) in its ungroundedness, its inexhaustibility and incommunicability. By

---

29 *Lettres Portugaises traduites en français* was a series of five letters written by a woman – and published anonymously in 1669 – who had been abandoned by her male lover.

30 The distinction Weber is making is between supramundane belief, such as Puritanism, and the outside-the-world experience of the mystic.

virtue of not only the intensity of experience but also the directly possessed reality, the lover knows himself to be transported to the kernel – always inaccessible to rational endeavours – of what is truly alive, and to have completely escaped the cold skeletal hand of the rational orders as well as the dullness of the everyday. The lover, who knows himself to be in touch with what is most alive, stands opposite the mystic's experience of a world devoid of objects, as if facing a pale, twilight realm (*wie einem fahlen hinterweltlichen Reich*). The knowing love of the mature man in relation to the passionate enthusiasm of the young man is like the deadly seriousness of this eroticism of intellectualism in relation to the chivalry of the courts of love. In contrast to courtly love, intellectualism affirms the naturalness of the sexual sphere and more than this makes it into an embodied creative power (*leibgewordene Schöpfermacht*).

A consistent ethic of religious brotherliness is radically hostile to the whole of this. A sensation of salvation purely as such within the earthly realm (*innerirdische Erlösungssensation*), which is how it looks to salvation religion, is the most extreme competition there could be when compared to the devotion to a transcendental god or to an ethically rational divine order or to the mystical bursting apart of individuation that alone is 'genuine'. Certain psychological affinities in both spheres directly make the tension between them more acute. The most intense eroticism has a psychological and physiological equivalence (*Vertretbarkeit*) with certain sublimated forms of heroic piousness. In contrast to rational and active asceticism, which already disapproves of the sexual because of its irrationality and regards the erotic as a mortally hostile power, there exists a relation of equivalence especially with the mystical finding of God within oneself (*Gottinnigkeit*). This has in consequence an always threatening, deadly refined revenge of the animalistic, or a direct sliding from the mystic experience of God into the realm of the all-too-human. Quite simply, this psychological proximity naturally increases the hostility of the inner sense of meaning. As seen by the religious ethic of brotherliness, the more the erotic relationship is sublimated the more it is attached to brutality in a most specifically refined degree. Religion cannot but help see the erotic relationship as a relationship of conflict, not just only or predominantly because of jealousy and possessiveness to the exclusion of a third person, but rather far more because of the most inward violence (*Vergewaltigung*) upon the soul of the less brutal partner – something that is never noticed by the partners themselves. This is a refined and deceiving form of pleasure because of its most human devotion.

No complete erotic relationship will be established in its own right other than through a mysterious *destination* for the other – *fate* in the highest sense of the word – and will thereby know itself (in a wholly unethical sense) 'legitimated'. But this 'fate' for salvation religion is nothing other than a purely accidental offshoot of the flames of passion. It is this that supports a pathological state of possession, idiosyncrasy, and a disturbed sense of proportionality and of any objective justice, which to religion must appear as the total denial of all brotherly love and of submission to God. The feeling of 'goodness' and euphoria of the fortunate lovers with their friendly need to poetize the entire world with their joyful countenance, or else to enchant it with their naïve desire to spread happiness always comes up against the chilling ridicule of the genuine, religiously founded and radical ethic of brotherliness. (This is found, for example, in the psychologically most effective parts of the early work of Tolstoy.[31]) For the latter, the extreme sublimation of the erotic is a relationship, which by necessity in its complete inwardness is exclusive and, in the highest way imaginable, subjective and absolutely incommunicable, that in these regards has to be the polar opposite of any religiously oriented ethic of brotherliness. This is so quite apart from the fact that the passionate character of the erotic as such obviously appears to be an unworthy loss of self-control and of orientation to either the rational good sense (*rationale Vernunft*) of God-ordained norms or to the mystical possession of the divine. Whereas for the erotic, *genuine* 'passion' purely in itself is a type of *beauty* and any refusal of it is a blasphemy (*Lästerung*).

Erotic rapture (*Rausch*) for psychological reasons as well as in terms of meaning is in accord only with the orgiastic and beyond the everyday (*außeralltäglich*) form of religiosity, although it is in accord with inner-worldly religion in a particular sense. The recognition by the Catholic Church of the *consummation* of marriage (*Eheschluss*), the '*copula carnalis*' as a 'sacrament' is a concession to this sentiment. Mysticism that is at the same time both otherworldly and outside the everyday operates in the most acute inner tension with the erotic. On account of their psychological equivalence they are only too easily able to enter into an unconscious and labile surrogate relationship and to fuse, from which a collapse into the orgiastic easily follows. Innerworldly rational asceticism (vocational asceticism) can only accept the rational regulation of marriage, decreed by the divine orders, for the 'concupiscence' of the hopelessly fallen and creaturely state of human beings. Husband and wife should live by, and only by, this regulation whose rational purposes are the procreation of children and their upbringing and to mutually support each other in the state of grace. Any refinement in the direction of eroticism has to be rejected as the idolization of the creaturely of the worst sort. From its side the original and natural *un*sublimated sexuality of the peasant is embedded into a rational order of the creaturely: all 'passionate' elements are then reckoned as residues of the fall of man, at which according to Luther 'God peeks through his fingers' – in order to stop anything worse.[32] The extra-worldly (*außerweltlich*) rational asceticism (the

---

31 [Weber] In *War and Peace* particularly. Nietzsche's well-known analyses in *The Will to Power* perfectly reflect the situation, despite – indeed on account of – the clearly recognized inversion of values (*umgekehrte Wertvorzeichen*). The position of salvation religiosity is clearly established by Açvagoscha.

32 Luther's sermons, 'A sermon of the state of matrimony', *Luthers Werke*, vol. 2, Weimar, Hermann Böhlau, 1884, p. 215.

active asceticism of monks) also rejects these elements and with them everything sexual as a diabolical power that endangers holiness.

It is probably the Quaker ethic (as expressed in the letters of William Penn to his wife)[33] that has best succeeded in going beyond Luther's rather crude interpretation of the meaning of marriage and has attained a genuinely humane interpretation of its inward religious values. Seen from a purely innerworldly approach, it is only the linkage of marriage to the idea of ethical responsibility for one another – and so a category heterogeneous to the *purely* erotic sphere – that offers the sentiment that throughout all the nuances of the organic cycle of life there exists a consciously responsible feeling of love; in the giving of each to the other (*Einander-Gewähren*) and the indebtedness of each for the other (*Einander-schuldig-werden*) (in Goethe's sense) up until the 'pianissimo of old age' there can reside something distinctive and supreme. This is seldom in its pure form conferred upon life, and to whom it is given, so one may speak of the good fortune and favour (*Glück und Gnade*) of destiny – but not of having 'earned it' ('*Verdienst*').

The rejection of all unconstrained surrender to the most intense types of experience of existence (*Dasein*) – the artistic and the erotic – is in itself to be sure only a negative attitude. But it does, however, offer the possibility of increasing the capacity with which energies can flow in the direction of rational performance – both the ethical as well as the purely intellectual.

But it has to be accepted that the greatest and most principled tension is, finally, the conscious tension of religion in relation to the realm of **intellectual knowledge** (*denkendes Erkennen*). An unbroken unity can exist in the field of magic and the purely magical worldview, as we have seen in China.[34] A far-reaching mutual recognition is also possible for purely metaphysical speculation, although this can easily lead to scepticism. For this reason religion often considers purely empirical and also scientific research as more in line with its interests than philosophy; this is especially so for ascetic Protestantism. But where rational empirical knowledge has consistently carried through the disenchantment (*Entzauberung*) of the world and its transformation into a causal mechanism, there emerges a tension with the claims of ethical postulates – that the world, for religion, is ultimately willed and ordained by God and is therefore, in whatever way oriented, an ethically *meaningful* cosmos. For where the world is considered through the empirical and – most completely – the mathematical, there develops in principle the rejection of every form of consideration that searches out the 'meaning' of innerworldly occurrences. With each acceptance of the rationalism of empirical science, religion is thereby forced increasingly out of the realm of the

33 Marianne Weber quotes a letter from William Penn to his wife Guli on his leaving for the American colonies: *Ehefrau und Mutterrecht in der Rechtsentwicklung*, Tübingen, Mohr Siebeck, 1907, pp. 289–90.
34 See above, pp. 35–6.

rational and into the irrational, so that now it is simply *the* irrational or anti-rational transcendental force.

The degree to which this opposition is consciously, or even consistently, perceived is to be sure very varied. In the case of Athanasius, as has been suggested, it is not unimaginable to think that his simply absurd formula (from a rational viewpoint), which established a conflict with the majority of the contemporaneous Hellenic philosophers, was really an attempt to compel the explicit sacrifice of the intellect and a fixed limit on rational discussion.[35] Immediately after this, however, the Trinity was itself grounded and discussed in rational terms. Directly on account of the irreconcilability of an apparent tension, both prophetic as well as priestly religions are always in an intimate relationship with rational intellectualism.

The less religion is magic or sheer contemplative mysticism and the more it is 'doctrine', so there is a corresponding need for rational apologetics. The priesthood took over the functions of the magicians. The latter were the typical keepers of myths and heroic sagas, because they had taken part in the upbringing and education of young warriors for the purposes of awakening of heroic ecstasy and the rebirth of heroes (*Heldenwiedergeburt*). The priests alone were capable of maintaining a perennial tradition, the education of youth in the law and often also in the purely technical and administrative skills, and above all in writing and counting. The more religion became a religion of the book and doctrine, the more literary it became and was able to provoke rational thinking by lay persons, independently of priests. But from lay thinking repeatedly arose prophets who were hostile to the priests, as well as mystics and sectarians who sought their religious salvation independently of priests, and lastly the sceptics and philosophers hostile to belief. A further rationalization of priestly apologetics then reacted against all of these. Anti-religious scepticism as such was just as well represented in China, Egypt, in the Vedas, and in the post-exilic Jewish literature as it is today. There are almost no new arguments to advance against religion.

The monopolization of the upbringing of youth is therefore the central issue of power for the priesthood. This power could expand with the increasing rationalization of political administration. Initially they alone were competent scribes for the state in Egypt and Babylonia, as also was the case for the medieval princes when writing entered into administration. Of the great systems of pedagogy, only Confucianism and Mediterranean Antiquity – the first due to the power of its state bureaucracy, the second, conversely, because of the complete absence of bureaucratic administration – have deliberately escaped the power of the priesthood and thereby excluded priestly

---

35 Athanasius (293–373) was Bishop of Alexandria. He argued that God the father and Jesus his son were of one nature. To regard Jesus as a person, separate to God, living and dying on earth was, Athanasius argued, to admit a creaturely nature that did not distinguish Jesus from any other Greek deity.

religion. Otherwise, the priesthood have as a rule been the carriers of education. It was not only these particularly priestly interests, however, that conditioned the ever new linkage with intellectualism, but also the internal necessity due to the rational character of the religious ethic and the specifically intellectualist need for salvation. In effect every religiosity stood in a different relation to intellectualism in respect to its psychological and intellectual substructure (*Unterbau*) and its practical consequences. This did not lead, however, to the disappearance of the effects of that last inner tension which resided in the unavoidable disparateness of the ultimate forms of the worldviews of religion and intellectualism. There is overall *no* unbroken religion, which is effective as a life-power, that has not had to demand at *some* point the 'sacrifice of the intellect' on the basis of 'I believe not what is absurd but *because* it is absurd' ('*credo non quod, sed quia absurdum*').

To outline the stages of the tension between religion and intellectual knowledge, is hardly necessary and also would not be possible. Salvation religion defends itself against the claim of a self-sufficient intellect, and naturally claims, especially in principle, that its own knowledge takes place in another realm in a way and sense that is wholly heterogeneous and disparate to what the intellect can provide. What religion offers is not an ultimate intellectual knowledge about the existing or the normatively valid, but an ultimate stance taken towards the world (*Stellungnahme*) by virtue of the grasping of its 'meaning'. And it discloses this meaning not by means of understanding but through the charisma of illumination, to which it alone is party. The charisma of illumination frees itself through the techniques that lie to hand from the misleading and deceptive surrogates that offer, as knowledge, the erroneous impression of the sensate world and the abstractions of understanding, which are in truth vacuous and of no consequence for salvation. Religion instead knows in itself how to be ready for the reception (*Aufnahme*) of grasping the meaning of the world, which is alone of practical importance, and one's own place in the world. The efforts of philosophy to demonstrate that ultimate meaning and through that meaning to grasp the (practical) ((*praktische*))[36] attitude to the world, as well as philosophy's attempts to gain intuitive knowledge of whatever sort – and so having another kind of dignity but nevertheless a concern with the 'being' ('*Sein*') of the world – are seen by religion as nothing more than the strivings of the intellect to escape its own autonomous working (*Eigengesetzlichkeit*). These attempts are above all entirely the specific product of just that rationalism, which intellectualism would so ardently wish to elude.

But salvation religion, in terms of its own position, is itself guilty of the same inconsistent infringements, as soon as it gives up the unassailable incommunicability of mystic experiences, for which it can only be a means of bringing about an *event*. What it is not able to do is to communicate and

---

36 'Practical philosophy' may be read as ethical philosophy, as in Kant's 'practical reason'.

demonstrate adequately such an experience. When it attempts to do this and to influence the world, it runs the danger of taking on the character of propaganda. Despite this danger, every attempt at a rational interpretation of the meaning of the world (*Weltsinn*) has always been repeatedly made.

All in all, the 'world' can come into conflict with religious postulates under different viewpoints. The pertinent viewpoint is always most important substantively for the direction of the type of striving for *salvation*.

Stages in the rejection of the world

The consciously pursued need for salvation, which is the substance of religiosity, has originated always and everywhere as the result of the efforts for a systematic and practical rationalization of the realities of life. This universal need – although there has been much variation in how clearly this is established – can be alternatively expressed as the demand that the course of the world (*Weltverlauf*), as it touches upon the interest of human beings, is in some way a *meaningful* process. At this level, this demand is the specific presupposition of every religion. The demand first surfaced, naturally enough, as the common problem of undeserved suffering, as we have seen;[37] thus as a postulate of a just balancing out of the unequal distribution of individual good fortune within the world. As such, it tended to develop in stages into an ever greater devaluation (*Entwertung*) of the world. For the more intensively the problem of a just, compensatory equalization was taken up by rational thought, the less its purely innerworldly solution was credible and the more an explanation belonging to the external world appeared to be probable or meaningful.

So far as one can see, the way of the world, as it actually is, did not worry itself with the postulate of just distribution. For not only was the unequal distribution of good fortune and suffering ethically unmotivated – and its equalization imaginable – but the sheer facts of the existence of suffering as such must have remained as irrational. The universal dissemination of suffering could then only be replaced by another, more irrational problem, the origins of sin – which according to the teaching of the prophets and priests should have explained suffering as a punishment or a means of discipline. But a world created for sinfulness must have appeared as ethically more imperfect than a world condemned to suffering. At any rate the absolute imperfection of this world was firmly established for the ethical postulate of a just compensation. It was only because of this imperfection that the transitoriness of the world appeared to be meaningfully justified. But this justification could seem to make the still further devaluation of the world appropriate. It was more than the merely worthless who were included in the transitoriness of the world.

37 See above, pp. 60–4.

Death and decay overtook both the best as well as the worst of human beings and things, and as such could appear as a devaluation of the supreme innerworldly values (*Güter*) once the idea of the eternal duration of time, an eternal god, and an eternal order was conceived. This stood in contrast to the values that were the most highly prized, and transfigured as being 'timeless', and whose meaning as realized in the 'culture' was secured independently from their temporal existence in their concretely realized appearance. The idea of religious eternity could then lead to a further increase in the ethical disparagement (*Verwerfung*) of the empirical world. A new train of thought could appear on the religious horizon that was of far greater significance than the imperfection and transitoriness of the world in general, since it was able to attack directly the otherwise supremely placed 'cultural goods'. To those values there now attached the mortal sins of an unavoidable burden specifically of guilt. Charisma of artistic taste and charisma of the intellect were burdened in this way and their cultivation appeared to presuppose unavoidably forms of existence (*Daseinsformen*) which ran counter to brotherliness and could only be adapted to it through self-deception. The barriers of educated culture and the culture of artistic taste are the most innermost and most difficult to cross of all status group distinctions. Religious guilt could now appear no longer as only something occasional and accidental but as an integrating element of the total culture, of all action in the civilized world (*Kulturwelt*) and lastly all formed life in general. Quite simply, everything that this world had to offer as supreme values (*Güter*) then appeared to be burdened with the greatest of guilt.

The external order of the social community, the more it became a cultural community within the cosmos of the state, was obviously concerned only to uphold its own power with brutality with justice a nominal and occasional concern and only permitted in accordance with its own *ratio*. This in itself generated unavoidably further acts of power – both external and internal to the state – and moreover insincere pretexts for these acts. This meant, therefore, an explicit lovelessness, or what must appear worse, hypocritically (*pharisäisch*) disguised lovelessness.

The objectified (*versachlichte*) economic cosmos, thus for every innerworldly culture simply the most highly rational form of indispensable material provision, was a structure to which lovelessness was intrinsically attached. All types of action in the formed world [of society and culture] appeared to be entangled in the same guilt. Veiled and sublimated brutality, idiosyncrasy hostile to brotherliness, and the illusionary displacement of just measure (*Augenmaß*) unavoidably accompanied sexual love; and the more powerfully sexual love develops its force, the more it is pharisaically disguised – something not recognized by the participants themselves.

The rational knowing of the world (*Erkennen*) constructed, autonomously and following its own innerworldly norms, a cosmos of truths, and then had nothing more to do – certainly not with the systematic postulates of a rational religious ethic that either the world as a cosmos satisfied *its* demands or should exhibit some 'meaning'. Ethical religiosity had itself appealed to rational knowledge, but was rejected in principle. The cosmos of natural causality and the postulated cosmos of ethical compensatory causality (*Ausgleichskausalität*) stood in a mutual relation of unreconcilable contradiction. And although the science, which created the former cosmos, appeared not to be able to give a secure explanation of its own final presuppositions, it entered in the name of 'intellectual integrity' (*'intellektuellen Rechtschaffenheit'*) the claim to be the only possible form of intellectual (*denkende*) consideration of the world. Like all cultural values, the intellect created an unbrotherly aristocracy of the rational possession of culture that was independent of all the personal and ethical qualities of human beings. Alongside its ethical burden of guilt, there now attached to cultural possession – and so, for the innerworldly person, to what was supreme in the world – the loss of meaning (*Sinnlosigkeit*), which must have been a far more definitive devaluation when this was judged against the standards of cultural values themselves.

The meaninglessness of the purely innerworldly perfection of self of the cultural person (*Kulturmensch*) – that is, of the final values to which 'culture' appeared to be reducible – already followed for religious thought and its innerworldly presuppositions from the obvious meaninglessness of death. So, under conditions of 'culture' this appeared to give the meaningless of life its definitive accent. The peasant could die 'sated with life' like Abraham. Likewise the feudal lord and heroic warrior. Both fulfilled the cycle of their existence, beyond which they did not reach. They could attain in their own manner an inner completion within their earthly life, as it followed the naïve clarity of its contents. But this was not the case for the 'educated' person who strove after self-perfection in the sense of an acquisition or creation of 'cultural contents' (*'Kulturinhalte'*). He could indeed be 'tired of life' but not 'sated with life' in the sense of the completion of the course of life. For his perfectibility was as limitless in principle as that of cultural goods. And the more the aims of cultural goods and self-perfection differentiated and diversified, the more trivial became the fraction that an individual – as a passive recipient or as an active creator – could encompass in the course of a finite life. The individual was less likely to be able to absorb the range of the internal and external cultural cosmos, either in its totality or in whatever sense was 'essential' to culture, for which moreover there was no ultimate measure; also that culture and the striving for it could have any innerworldly meaning for the individual. To be sure culture existed for the individual not in the *amount* of 'cultural goods' gathered, but in the form of their *selection*. But there was no guarantee that by the end-point of an individual's life, which was 'accidental' in its term, this was a meaningful conclusion to life. And if he turned away from life in a superior manner – 'I have had enough, life has offered (or denied) to *me* everything worth having' – this proud attitude would appear to salvation religion as a blasphemous belittling of the ways of life and destiny as ordained by God. No religion of salvation positively *approves* of the taking of one's own life (*Freitod*) – which has been transfigured (*verklärt*) only by philosophies.

In this light, the whole of 'culture' is a stepping out from the organically determined natural course of life, and the cultural person with every further step is condemned to ever more annihilating loss of meaning. The more the service to cultural goods was turned into a sacred undertaking and into a 'vocation', the more it became a senseless rush into the service of worthless purposes which were, moreover, contradictory and mutually antagonistic.

The world of culture, when seen purely ethically from the religious postulate of a divine 'meaning' for its existence, appeared to be both fragmented and devalued. For it was a place of imperfection, injustice, suffering and transitoriness, and culture's ever increasing meaninglessness stemmed from its irremovable burden of guilt and its unstoppable further development and differentiation. This devaluation of the world was a consequence of the conflict between the rational claims of the world and its reality, and between the rational ethic and its in part rational, in part irrational values. With every elaboration of the specific distinctiveness of each of the world's separate spheres the conflict became ever more acute and more insoluble. As the thinking about the 'meaning' of the world becomes more systematic, the more the world is rationalized in its external organization, and the more sublimated the conscious experience of the world's irrational contents becomes, so – exactly paralleling this process – the religious began to be constituted in such a way that its specific contents were more unworldly and more hostile to all formed life. It was not perhaps only theoretical thinking which led to the disenchantment of the world, but also the direct attempt of the religious ethic to carry through practically an ethical rationalization of the world.[38]

---

38 Weber concludes the essay with three types of theodicy.

17 Bureaucracy

Characteristics of modern bureaucracy[1]

Modern officialdom functions in the following manner:

I   There is the principle of official *jurisdictional areas*, which are generally ordered by rules, that is, by laws or administrative regulations. This means:

    1   The regular activities required for the purposes of the bureaucratically governed structure are assigned as official duties.

    2   The authority to give the commands required for the discharge of these duties is distributed in a stable way and is strictly delimited by rules concerning the coercive means, physical, sacerdotal, or otherwise, which may be placed at the disposal of officials.

    3   Methodical provision is made for the regular and continuous fulfillment of these duties and for the exercise of the corresponding rights; only persons who qualify under general rules are employed.

In the sphere of the state these three elements constitute a bureaucratic *agency*, in the sphere of the private economy they constitute a bureaucratic *enterprise*. Bureaucracy, thus understood, is fully developed in political and ecclesiastical communities only in the modern state, and in the private economy only in the most advanced institutions of capitalism. Permanent agencies, with fixed jurisdiction, are not the historical rule but rather the exception. This is even true of large political structures such as those of the ancient Orient, the Germanic and Mongolian empires of conquest, and of many feudal states. In all these cases, the ruler executes the most important measures through personal trustees, table-companions, or court-servants. Their commissions and powers are not precisely delimited and are temporarily called into being for each case.

---

1 Taken from *E&S*, pp. 956–8.

II   The principles of *office hierarchy* and of channels of appeal (*Instanzenzug*) stipulate a clearly established system of super- and subordination in which there is a supervision of the lower offices by the higher ones. Such a system offers the governed the possibility of appealing, in a precisely regulated manner, the decision of a lower office to the corresponding superior authority. With the full development of the bureaucratic type, the office hierarchy is *monocratically* organized. The principle of hierarchical office authority is found in all bureaucratic structures: in state and ecclesiastical structures as well as in large party organizations and private enterprises. It does not matter for the character of bureaucracy whether its authority is called 'private' or 'public'.

When the principle of jurisdictional 'competency' is fully carried through, hierarchical subordination – at least in public office – does not mean that the 'higher' authority is authorized simply to take over the business of the 'lower'. Indeed, the opposite is the rule; once an office has been set up, a new incumbent will always be appointed if a vacancy occurs.

III The management of the modern office is based upon written documents (the 'files'), which are preserved in their original or draft form, and upon a staff of subaltern officials and scribes of all sorts. The body of officials working in an agency along with the respective apparatus of material implements and the files makes up a *bureau* (in private enterprises often called the 'counting house', *Kontor*).

In principle, the modern organization of the civil service separates the bureau from the private domicile of the official and, in general, segregates official activity from the sphere of private life. Public monies and equipment are divorced from the private property of the official. This condition is everywhere the product of a long development. Nowadays, it is found in public as well as in private enterprises; in the latter, the principle extends even to the entrepreneur at the top. In principle, the *Kontor* (office) is separated from the household, business from private correspondence, and business assets from private wealth. The more consistently the modern type of business management has been carried through, the more are these separations the case. The beginnings of this process are to be found as early as the Middle Ages.

It is the peculiarity of the modern entrepreneur that he conducts himself as the 'first official' of his enterprise, in the very same way in which the ruler of a specifically modern bureaucratic state [Frederick II of Prussia] spoke of himself as 'the first servant' of the state. The idea that the bureau activities of the state are intrinsically different in character from the management of private offices is a continental European notion and, by way of contrast, is totally foreign to the American way.

IV   Office management, at least all specialized office management – and such management is distinctly modern – usually presupposes thorough training in a field of specialization. This, too, holds increasingly for the modern executive and employee of a private enterprise, just as it does for the state officials.

V   When the office is fully developed, official activity demands the *full working capacity* of the official, irrespective of the fact that the length of his obligatory working hours in the bureau may be limited. In the normal case, this too is only the product of a long development, in the public as well as in the private office. Formerly the normal state of affairs was the reverse: Official business was discharged as a secondary activity.

VI The management of the office follows *general rules*, which are more or less stable, more or less exhaustive, and which can be learned. Knowledge of these rules represents a special technical expertise which the officials possess. It involves jurisprudence, administrative or business management.

The reduction of modern office management to rules is deeply embedded in its very nature. The theory of modern public administration, for instance, assumes that the authority to order certain matters by decree – which has been legally granted to an agency – does not entitle the agency to regulate the matter by individual commands given for each case, but only to regulate the matter abstractly. This stands in extreme contrast to the regulation of all relationships through individual privileges and bestowals of favor, which, as we shall see, is absolutely dominant in patrimonialism, at least insofar as such relationships are not fixed by sacred tradition.

The technical superiority of bureaucratic organization over administration by notables[2]

The decisive reason for the advance of bureaucratic organization has always been its purely *technical* superiority over any other form of organization. The fully developed bureaucratic apparatus compares with other organizations exactly as does the machine with the non-mechanical modes of production. Precision, speed, unambiguity, knowledge of the files, continuity, discretion, unity, strict subordination, reduction of friction and of material and personal costs – these are raised to the optimum point in the strictly bureaucratic administration, and especially in its monocratic form. As compared with all collegiate, honorific, and avocational forms of administration, trained bureaucracy is superior on all these points. And as far as complicated tasks are concerned, paid bureaucratic work is not only more precise but, in the last analysis, it is often cheaper than even formally unremunerated honorific service.

Honorific arrangements make administrative work a subsidiary activity: an

2 Taken from *E&S*, pp. 973–5.

avocation and, for this reason alone, honorific service normally functions more slowly. Being less bound to schemata and more formless, it is less precise and less unified than bureaucratic administration, also because it is less dependent upon superiors. Because the establishment and exploitation of the apparatus of subordinate officials and clerical services are almost unavoidably less economical, honorific service is less continuous than bureaucratic and frequently quite expensive. This is especially the case if one thinks not only of the money costs to the public treasury – costs which bureaucratic administration, in comparison with administration by notables, usually increases – but also of the frequent economic losses of the governed caused by delays and lack of precision. Permanent administration by notables is normally feasible only where official business can be satisfactorily transacted as an avocation. With the qualitative increase of tasks the administration has to face, administration by notables reaches its limits – today even in England. Work organized by collegiate bodies, on the other hand, causes friction and delay and requires compromises between colliding interests and views. The administration, therefore, runs less precisely and is more independent of superiors; hence, it is less unified and slower. All advances of the Prussian administrative organization, for example, have been and will in the future be advances of the bureaucratic, and especially of the monocratic, principle.

Today, it is primarily the capitalist market economy which demands that the official business of public administration be discharged precisely, unambiguously, continuously, and with as much speed as possible. Normally, the very large modern capitalist enterprises are themselves unequalled models of strict bureaucratic organization. Business management throughout rests on increasing precision, steadiness, and, above all, speed of operations. This, in turn, is determined by the peculiar nature of the modern means of communication, including, among other things, the news service of the press. The extraordinary increase in the speed by which public announcements, as well as economic and political facts, are transmitted exerts a steady and sharp pressure in the direction of speeding up the tempo of administrative reaction towards various situations. The optimum of such reaction time is normally attained only by a strictly bureaucratic organization. (The fact that the bureaucratic apparatus also can, and indeed does, create certain definite impediments for the discharge of business in a manner best adapted to the individuality of each case does not belong into the present context.)

Bureaucratization offers above all the optimum possibility for carrying through the principle of specializing administrative functions according to purely objective considerations. Individual performances are allocated to functionaries who have specialized training and who by constant practice increase their expertise. 'Objective' discharge of business primarily means a discharge of business according to *calculable rules* and 'without regard for persons'.

'Without regard for persons', however, is also the watchword of the market and, in general, of all pursuits of naked economic interests. Consistent bureaucratic domination means the leveling of 'status honor'. Hence, if the principle of the free market is not at the same time restricted, it means the universal domination of the 'class situation'. That this consequence of bureaucratic domination has not set in everywhere proportional to the extent of bureaucratization is due to the differences between possible principles by which polities may supply their requirements. However, the second element mentioned, calculable rules, is the most important one for modern bureaucracy. The peculiarity of modern culture, and specifically of its technical and economic basis, demands this very 'calculability' of results. When fully developed, bureaucracy also stands, in a specific sense, under the principle of *sine ira ac studio*. Bureaucracy develops the more perfectly, the more it is 'dehumanized', the more completely it succeeds in eliminating from official business love, hatred, and all purely personal, irrational, and emotional elements which escape calculation. This is appraised as its special virtue by capitalism.

The more complicated and specialized modern culture becomes, the more its external supporting apparatus demands the personally detached and strictly objective *expert*, in lieu of the lord of older social structures who was moved by personal sympathy and favor, by grace and gratitude. Bureaucracy offers the attitudes demanded by the external apparatus of modern culture in the most favorable combination. In particular, only bureaucracy has established the foundation for the administration of a rational law conceptually systematized on the basis of 'statutes', such as the later Roman Empire first created with a high degree of technical perfection. During the Middle Ages, the reception of this [Roman] law coincided with the bureaucratization of legal administration: the advance of the rationally trained expert displaced the old trial procedure which was bound to tradition or to irrational presuppositions.

18 Formal and substantive rationalization

Theocratic and secular law[1]

The considerations of the last section raise the important problem, already touched upon in various places, of the influence of the form of political authority on the formal aspects of the law. A definitive analysis of this problem requires an analysis of the various types of authority which we shall not undertake until later. However, a few general remarks may be made at this point. The older forms of popular justice had originated in conciliatory proceedings between kinship-groups. The primitive formalistic irrationality of these older forms of justice was everywhere cast off under the impact of the authority of princes or magistrates (*imperium*, ban) or, in certain situations, of an organized priesthood. With this impact, the substance of the law, too, was lastingly influenced, although the character of this influence varied with the various types of authority. The more rational the administrative machinery of the princes or hierarchs became, that is, the greater the extent to which administrative 'officials' were used in the exercise of the power, the greater was the likelihood that the legal procedure would also become 'rational' both in form and substance. To the extent to which the rationality of the organization of authority increased, irrational forms of procedure were eliminated and the substantive law was systematized, i.e., the law as a whole was rationalized. This process occurred, for instance, in Antiquity in the *ius honorarium* and the praetorian remedies, in the capitularies of the Frankish Kings, in the procedural innovations of the English Kings and Lords Chancellor, or in the inquisitorial procedure of the Catholic Church.[2] However, these rationalizing tendencies were not part of an articulate and unambiguous policy on the part of the wielders of power; they were rather driven in this direction by the needs of their own rational

---

1 Taken from *E&S*, pp. 809–15.
2 These are all cases where an increase in the power of the ruler(s) has led to the introduction of more rational methods of adjudication in place of irrational customary law. The Roman *praetor* (a leading public official who directed a variety of types of court actions) came to lay down directions on how cases should be tried, which then became new law. The Frankish kings in the eighth century AD overrode strong customary law with royal decrees, the English royal courts of justice were developed by the Angevins in the twelfth century and marked a move towards the rational use of evidence with the use of writs and juries, and in the late Middle Ages church law developed an inquisitorial method of adjudicating cases that provided the model for civil legal procedures.

administration, as, for instance, in the case of the administrative machinery of the Papacy, or by powerful interest-groups with whom they were allied and to whom rationality in substantive law and procedure constituted an advantage, as, for instance, to the bourgeois classes of Rome, of the late Middle Ages, or of modern times.

Where these interests were absent the secularization of the law and the growth of a strictly formal mode of juridical thought either remained in an incipient stage or was even positively counteracted. In general terms, this may be attributed to the fact that the rationality (*Rationalismus*) of ecclesiastical hierarchies as well as of patrimonial sovereigns is *substantive* in character, so that their aim is not that of achieving that highest degree of formal juridical precision which would maximize the chances for the correct prediction of legal consequences and for the rational systematization of law and procedure. The aim is rather to find a type of law which is most appropriate to the expediential (*praktisch-utilitarisch*) and ethical goals of the authorities in question. To these carriers of legal development the self-contained and specialized 'juridical' treatment of legal questions is an alien idea, and they are not at all interested in any separation of law from ethics. This is particularly true, generally speaking, of theocratically influenced legal systems, which are characterized by a combination of legal rules and ethical demands. Yet in the course of this kind of rationalization of legal thinking on the one hand and the forming of associational relationships on the other, the most diverse consequences could emerge from the nonjuridical components of a legal doctrine of priestly make. One of these possible consequences was the separation of *fas*, the religious command, from *ius*, the established law for the settlement of such human conflicts which had no religious relevance. In this situation, it was possible for *ius* to pass through an independent course of development into a rational and formal legal system, in which emphasis might be either upon logical or upon empirical elements. This actually happened both in Rome and in the Middle Ages. We shall discuss later (*E&S*, pp. 815–16, 828–31) the ways in which the relationship between the religiously fixed and the freely established components of the law were determined in these cases. As we shall see hereafter (*E&S*, pp. 823–8), it was quite possible, as thinking became increasingly secular, for the sacred law to encounter as a rival, or to be replaced by, a 'natural law' which would operate beside the positive law partly as an ideal postulate and partly as a doctrine with varying actual influence upon legislation or legal practice.

It was also possible, however, that the religious prescriptions were never differentiated from secular rules and that the characteristically theocratic combination of religious and ritualistic prescriptions with legal rules remained unchanged. In this case, there arose a featureless conglomeration of ethical and legal duties, moral exhortations and legal commandments without formalized explicitness, and the result was a specifically *non-formal* type of law. Just which of these two possibilities actually occurred depended upon the already mentioned characteristics of the religion in question and the principles that governed its relation to the legal system and the state; in part it depended upon the power position of the priesthood *vis-à-vis* the state; and finally, upon the structure of the state. It was because of their special structure of authority that in almost all the Asiatic civilizations the last mentioned of these courses of development came to emerge and persist.

But although certain features in the logical structure of different legal systems may be similar, they may nevertheless be the result of diverse types of domination. Authoritarian powers resting on personal loyalty, such as theocracy and patrimonial monarchy, have usually created a nonformal type of law. But a nonformal type of law may also be produced by certain types of democracy. The explanation lies in the fact that not only such power-wielders as hierarchs and despots, and particularly enlightened despots, but also democratic demagogues may refuse to be *bound* by formal rules, even by those they have made themselves, excepting, however, those norms which they regard as religiously sacred and hence as absolutely binding. They all are confronted by the inevitable conflict between an abstract formalism of legal certainty (*Rechtslogik*) and their desire to realize substantive goals. Juridical formalism enables the legal system to operate like a technically rational machine. Thus it guarantees to individuals and groups within the system a relative maximum of freedom, and greatly increases for them the possibility of predicting the legal consequences of their actions. Procedure becomes a specific type of pacified contest, bound to fixed and inviolable 'rules of the game'.

Primitive procedures for adjusting conflicts of interest between kinship groups are characterized by rigorously formalistic rules of evidence. The same is true of judicial procedure in *Dinggenossenschaften*.[3] As we have seen, these rules were at first influenced by magical beliefs which required that the questions of evidence should be asked in the proper way and by the proper party. Even afterwards it took a long time for the law to develop the idea that a fact, as understood today, could be 'established' by a rational procedure, particularly by the examination of witnesses, which is the most important method now, not to speak at all of circumstantial evidence. The compurgators of earlier epochs did not swear that a statement of fact was true but confirmed the rightness of their side by exposing themselves to the divine wrath. We may observe that this practice was not much less realistic than that of our days when a great many people, perhaps a majority, believe their party task as witnesses to be simply that of 'swearing' as to which party is 'in the right'. In ancient law, proof was therefore not regarded as a 'burden' (*Pflicht*) but at least in large part as a 'right' of the party to which it was attributed. The judge, however, was strictly bound by these rules and the traditional methods of proof. The modern theory of as late a period as that of 'common

---

3 A *Dinggenossenschaft* was a village community in the early Middle Ages in Germany.

law' procedure[4] is different from ancient procedure only in that it would treat proof as burden. It, too, binds the judge to the motions of, and the evidence offered by, the parties and, indeed, the same principle applies to the entire conduct of the suit: in accordance with the principle of adversary procedure the judge has to wait for the motions of the parties. Whatever is not introduced or put into a motion does not exist as far as the judge is concerned; the same is true of facts which remain undisclosed by the recognized methods of proof, be they rational or irrational. Thus, the judge aims at establishing only that relative truth which is attainable within the limits set by the procedural acts of the parties.

This exactly was the character of adjudication in its oldest known, most clear-cut form: arbitration and composition between contending kinship groups, with oracle or ordeal constituting the trial procedure. This ancient legal procedure was rigorously formal like all activities oriented towards the invocation of magical or divine powers; but, by means of the irrational supernatural character of the decisive acts of procedure, it tried to obtain the substantively 'right' decision. When, however, the authority of, and the belief in, these irrational powers came to be lost and when they were replaced by rational proof and the logical derivation of decisions, the formalistic adjudication had to become a mere contest between litigants, regulated so as to aim at the relatively optimal chance of finding the truth. The promotion of the progress of the suit is the concern of the parties rather than that of the state. They are not compelled by the judge to do anything they do not wish to do at their own initiative. It is for this very reason that the judge cannot comply with the quest for the optimal realization of substantive demands of a political, ethical or affective character by means of an adjudication which could give effect to considerations of concrete expediency or equity (*Billigkeitsgefähl*) in individual cases. Formal justice guarantees the maximum freedom for the interested parties to represent their formal legal interests. But because of the unequal distribution of economic power, which the system of formal justice legalizes, this very freedom must time and again produce consequences which are contrary to the substantive postulates of religious ethics or of political expediency. Formal justice is thus repugnant to all authoritarian powers, theocratic as well as patriarchic, because it diminishes the dependency of the individual upon the grace and power of the authorities. To democracy, however, it has been repugnant because it decreases the dependency of the legal practice and therewith of the individuals upon the decisions of their fellow citizens. Furthermore, the development of the trial into a peaceful contest of conflicting interests can contribute to the further differentiation of economic and social power. In all these cases formal justice, due to its necessarily abstract character, infringes upon the ideals of substantive justice.

4 I.e. prior to the reform and codification of the laws in nineteenth-century Europe.

It is precisely this abstract character which constitutes the decisive merit of formal justice to those who wield the economic power at any given time and who are therefore interested in its unhampered operation, but also to those who on ideological grounds attempt to break down authoritarian control or to restrain irrational mass emotions for the purpose of opening up individual opportunities and liberating capacities. To all these groups nonformal justice simply represents the likelihood of absolute arbitrariness and subjectivistic instability. Among those groups who favor formal justice we must include all those political and economic interest groups to whom the stability and predictability of legal procedure are of very great importance, i.e., particularly rational, economic, and political organizations intended to have a *permanent character*. Above all, those in possession of economic power look upon a formal rational administration of justice as a guarantee of 'freedom', a value which is repudiated not only by theocratic or patriarchal-authoritarian groups but, under certain conditions, also by democratic groups. Formal justice and the 'freedom' which it guarantees are indeed rejected by all groups ideologically interested in substantive justice. Such groups are better served by khadi-justice than by the formal type. The popular justice of the direct Attic democracy, for example, was decidedly a form of khadi-justice. Modern trial by jury, too, is frequently khadi-justice in actual practice although not according to formal law; even in this highly formalized type of a limited popular adjudication one can observe a tendency to be bound by formal legal rules only to the extent directly required by procedural technique. Quite generally, in all forms of popular justice decisions are reached on the basis of concrete, ethical, or political considerations or of feelings oriented toward social justice. Political justice prevailed particularly in Athens, but it can be found even today. In this respect, there are similar tendencies displayed by popular democracy on the one hand and the authoritarian power of theocracy or of patriarchal monarchs on the other. When, for example, French jurors, contrary to formal law, regularly acquit a husband who has killed his wife's paramour caught in the act, they are doing exactly what Frederick the Great did when he dispensed 'royal justice' for the benefit of Arnold, the miller.[5] Even more so does the distinctive characteristic of a theocratic administration of justice consist entirely in the primacy of concrete ethical considerations; its indifference or aversion to formalism is limited only in so far as the rules of the sacred law are explicitly formulated. But in so far as norms of the latter apply, the theocratic type of law results in the exact opposite, *viz.*, a law which, in order to be adaptable to changing circumstances, develops an extremely formalistic casuistry. Secular, patrimonial-authoritarian administration of justice is much freer than theocratic

---

5 Arnold was a poor miller who was ejected from his mill for the non-payment of rent. The Prussian King ordered the courts to overturn their decision to uphold the eviction.

justice, even where it has to conform with tradition, which usually allows quite a degree of flexibility.

Finally, the administration of justice by honoratiores presents two aspects depending on what legal interests there are involved, those of the honoratiores' own class or those of the class dominated by them. In England, for instance, all cases coming before the central courts were adjudicated in a strictly formalistic way. But the courts of justices of the peace, which dealt with the daily troubles and misdemeanors of the masses, were informal and representative of khadi-justice to an extent completely unknown on the Continent.[6] Furthermore, the high cost of litigation and legal services amounted for those who could not afford to purchase them to a denial of justice, which was rather similar to that which existed, for other reasons, in the judicial system of the Roman republic. This denial of justice was in close conformity with the interests of the propertied, especially the capitalistic, classes. But such a *dual* judicial policy of formal adjudication of disputes within the upper class, combined with arbitrariness or de facto denial of justice for the economically weak, is not always possible. If it cannot be had, capitalistic interests will fare best under a rigorously formal system of adjudication, which applies in all cases and operates under the adversary system of procedure. In any case adjudication by honoratiores inclines to be essentially empirical, and its procedure is complicated and expensive. It may thus well stand in the way of the interests of the bourgeois classes and it may indeed be said that England achieved capitalistic supremacy among the nations not because but rather in spite of its judicial system. For these very reasons the bourgeois strata have generally tended to be intensely interested in a rational procedural system and therefore in a systematized, unambiguous, and specialized formal law which eliminates both obsolete traditions and arbitrariness and in which rights can have their source exclusively in general objective norms. Such a *systematically codified* law was thus demanded by the English Puritans, the Roman Plebeians, and the German bourgeoisie of the nineteenth century. But in all these cases such a system was still a long way off.

In the administration of justice of theocratic type, in adjudication by secular honoratiores (as judges or private or officially patented jurisconsults), as well as in that development of law and procedure which is based upon the *imperium* and the contempt powers of magistrates, princes, or officials holding in their hands the direction of the lawsuit, the view is at first strictly adhered to that fundamentally the law has always been what it is and that no more is needed than an interpretation of its ambiguities and its application to particular cases. Nonetheless, as we have seen (*E&S*,

6 A khadi is a judge in an Islamic sharia court. Weber characterizes their adjudication as following ethical, religious, or expediential grounds rather than the strict enforcement of the law; 'it is written but I say unto you . . .' was a typical preamble to a judgement.

pp. 753–76), the emergence of rationally compacted norms is in itself possible even under rather primitive economic conditions, once the hold of magical stereotypization has been broken. The existence of irrational techniques of revelation as the sole means of innovation has often implied a high degree of flexibility in the norms; their absence, on the other hand, has resulted in a higher degree of stereotypization, because in that event the sacred tradition as such remained the sole holy element and would thus be sublimated by the priests into a system of sacred law.

19 The vocation of politics[1]

What kinds of inner joy does politics have to offer, and what kinds of personal qualifications does it presuppose in anyone turning to this career?

Well, first of all, it confers a feeling of power. The professional politician can have a sense of rising above everyday existence, even in what is formally a modest position, through knowing that he exercises influence on people, shares power over them, but above all from the knowledge that he holds in his hands some vital strand of historically important events. But the question facing such a person is which qualities will enable him to do justice to this power (however narrowly circumscribed it may actually be in any particular case), and thus to the responsibility it imposes on him. This takes us into the area of ethical questions, for to ask what kind of a human being one must be in order to have the right to seize the spokes of the wheel of history is to pose an ethical question.

One can say that three qualities are pre-eminently decisive for a politician: passion, a sense of responsibility, and a sense of proportion (*Augenmass*). Passion in the sense of *concern for the thing itself* (*Sachlichkeit*), the passionate commitment to a 'cause' ('*Sache*'), to the god or demon[2] who commands that cause. Not in the sense of that inner attitude which my late friend Georg Simmel was wont to describe as 'sterile excitement'.[3] This is characteristic of a particular type of intellectual (especially Russian intellectuals, but of course not all of them!), and also plays such a large part amongst our own intellectuals at this carnival which is being graced with the proud name of a 'revolution'; it is the 'romanticism of the intellectually interesting', directed into the void and lacking all objective (*sachlich*) sense of responsibility. Simply to feel passion, however genuinely, is not sufficient to make a politician unless, in the form of service to a 'cause', *responsibility* for that cause becomes the decisive lode-star of all action. This requires (and this is the decisive psychological quality of the politician) *a sense of proportion*, the ability to maintain one's inner composure and calm while being receptive to

1 Taken from *Weber: Political Writings*, edited by Peter Lassman and Ronald Speirs, Cambridge, Cambridge University Press, 1994, pp. 352–69.
2 [All footnotes in this Reading are by P. Lassman and R. Speirs.] In this instance Weber is using *Dämon* in the same sense as the English 'demon'; elsewhere he uses it without the sense of moral evil.
3 This use of *Aufgeregtheit* as a derogatory term for revolutionary fervour was prefigured in Goethe's fragmentary satire on the consequences of the French Revolution, *Die Aufgeregten*.

realities, in other words *distance* from things and people. A 'lack of distance', in and of itself, is one of the deadly sins for any politician and it is one of those qualities which will condemn our future intellectuals to political incompetence if they cultivate it. For the problem is precisely this: how are hot passion and cool judgement to be forced together in a single soul? Politics is an activity conducted with the head, not with other parts of the body or soul. Yet if politics is to be genuinely human action, rather than some frivolous intellectual game, dedication to it can only be generated and sustained by passion. Only if one accustoms oneself to distance, in every sense of the word, can one achieve that powerful control over the soul which distinguishes the passionate politician from the mere 'sterile excitement' of the political amateur. The 'strength' of a political 'personality' means, first and foremost, the possession of these qualities.

Every day and every hour, therefore, the politician has to overcome a quite trivial, all-too-human enemy which threatens him from within: common *vanity*, the mortal enemy of all dedication to a cause and of all distance – in this case, of distance to oneself.

Vanity is a very widespread quality, and perhaps no one is completely free of it. In academic and scholarly circles it is a kind of occupational disease. In the case of the scholar, however, unattractive though this quality may be, it is relatively harmless in the sense that it does not, as a rule, interfere with the pursuit of knowledge. Things are quite different in the case of the politician. The ambition for *power* is an inevitable means (*Mittel*) with which he works. 'The instinct for power', as it is commonly called, is thus indeed one of his normal qualities. The sin against the holy spirit of his profession begins where this striving for power becomes detached from the task in hand (*unsachlich*) and becomes a matter of purely personal self-intoxication instead of being placed entirely at the service of the 'cause'. For there are ultimately just two deadly sins in the area of politics: a lack of objectivity and – often, although not always, identical with it – a lack of responsibility. Vanity, the need to thrust one's person as far as possible into the foreground, is what leads the politician most strongly into the temptation of committing one or other (or both) of these sins, particularly as the demagogue is forced to count on making an 'impact', and for this reason is always in danger both of becoming a play-actor and of taking the responsibility for his actions too lightly and being concerned only with the 'impression' he is making. His lack of objectivity tempts him to strive for the glittering appearance of power rather than its reality, while his irresponsibility tempts him to enjoy power for its own sake, without any substantive purpose. For although, or rather precisely *because*, power is the inevitable means of all politics, and the ambition for power therefore one of its driving forces, there is no more pernicious distortion of political energy than when the parvenu boasts of his power and vainly mirrors himself in the feeling of power – or indeed any and every worship of power for its own sake. The mere 'power politician', a type whom an energetically promoted cult is seeking to glorify here in Germany as elsewhere, may give the impression of strength, but in fact his actions merely lead into emptiness and absurdity. On this point the critics of 'power politics' are quite correct. The sudden inner collapse of typical representatives of this outlook (*Gesinnung*) has shown us just how much inner weakness and ineffectuality are concealed behind this grandiose but empty pose. It stems from a most wretched and superficial lack of concern for the *meaning* of human action, a blasé attitude that knows nothing of the tragedy in which all action, but quite particularly political action, is in truth enmeshed.

It is certainly true, and it is a fundamental fact of history (for which no more detailed explanation can be offered here), that the eventual outcome of political action frequently, indeed regularly, stands in a quite inadequate, even paradoxical relation to its original, intended meaning and purpose (*Sinn*). That does not mean, however, that this meaning and purpose, service to a *cause*, can be dispensed with if action is to have any firm inner support. The *nature* of the cause the politician seeks to serve by striving for and using power is a question of faith. He can serve a national goal or the whole of humanity, or social and ethical goals, or goals which are cultural, innerworldly or religious; he may be sustained by a strong faith in 'progress' (however this is understood), or he may coolly reject this kind of faith; he can claim to be the servant of an 'idea' or, rejecting on principle any such aspirations, he may claim to serve external goals of everyday life – but some kind of belief must always be *present*. Otherwise (and there can be no denying this) even political achievements which, outwardly, are supremely successful will be cursed with the nullity of all mortal undertakings.

Having said this, we have already broached the last problem which concerns us this evening, the problem of the ethos of politics as a 'cause' ('*Sache*'). What vocation can politics *per se*, quite independently of its goals, fulfil within the overall moral economy of our conduct of life? Where is what one might call the ethical home of politics? At this point, admittedly, ultimate *Weltanschauungen* collide, and one has eventually to *choose* between them. The problem has recently been re-opened for discussion (in a quite wrong-headed fashion in my view), so let us approach it resolutely. . . .

What, then, is the real relationship between *ethics* and *politics*? Have they nothing at all to do with one another, as has sometimes been said? Or is the opposite true, namely that political action is subject to 'the same' ethic as every other form of activity? At times people have believed that these two possibilities were mutually exclusive alternatives, and that either the one or the other was correct. But is it in fact true that any ethic in the world could establish substantially *identical* commandments applicable to all relationships, whether erotic, business, family or official, to one's relations with one's wife, greengrocer, son, competitor, with a friend or an accused man? Can the fact that politics operates with a quite specific means, namely power, backed up by the use of *violence* (*Gewaltsamkeit*), really be a matter of such indifference as far as the ethical demands placed on politics are concerned? Have we not seen that the Bolshevik and Spartacist[4] ideologues, precisely because they use this political instrument, bring about exactly the *same* results as any militarist dictator? What, apart from the identity of the holders of power (and their amateurism) distinguishes the rule of the Workers' and Soldiers' Councils from the rule of any wielder of power under the old regime? What distinguishes the polemics directed by most exponents of the supposedly new ethics at the opponents they criticize from the polemics of any other demagogues? Their noble intentions, some will say. Very well. But the question under discussion here is the means, and their enemies lay just as much claim to noble ultimate aims, and do so with complete subjective sincerity. 'All they that take the sword shall perish with the sword',[5] and fighting is fighting everywhere. What about the ethics of the Sermon on the Mount then? The Sermon on the Mount, by which we mean the absolute ethics of the Gospel, is something far more serious than those who are so fond of citing its commandments today believe. It is not to be taken frivolously. What has been said about causality in science also applies to this ethic, namely that it is not a hired cab which one may stop at will and climb into or out of as one sees fit. Rather, the meaning of the sermon (if it is not to be reduced to banality) is precisely this: we must accept it in its entirety *or* leave it entirely alone. Hence the case of the rich young man: 'he went away sorrowful, for he had great possessions.'[6] The commandment of the Gospel is unconditional and unambiguous – 'give all that thou hast' – *everything*, absolutely. The politician will say that this is an excessive and socially meaningless demand if it is not made to apply to *everybody*, which means taxation, expropriation by taxation, confiscation, in other words, coercion and order applied to *all*. The ethical commandment disregards such questions *completely* – that is its essence. The same applies to the injunction to 'turn the other cheek!' – unconditionally, without asking by what right the other person has struck you. An ethic of indignity, except for a saint. This is the heart of the matter: it is necessary to be a saint in *all* things, or at least one must want to be one, one must live like Jesus, the Apostles, Saint Francis and men of that kind; *then* this type of ethic becomes meaningful and expresses a kind of dignity. *But not otherwise.* For while it is a consequence of the unworldly ethic of love to say, 'resist not evil with force',[7] the politician is governed by the contrary maxim, namely, 'You *shall* resist evil with force, for if you do not, you are *responsible*

---

4 The Spartakus League, led by Karl Liebknecht, was formed in 1916–17. A left socialist group opposed to war, it adopted the name of the Communist Party of Germany in December 1918.

5 The New Testament, Matthew, 26, 52.

6 The New Testament, Matthew, 19, 22.

7 The New Testament, Matthew, 5, 39: 'That ye resist not evil: but whosoever shall smite thee on thy right cheek, turn to him the other also.'

for the spread of evil.' Anyone seeking to act in accordance with the ethic of the Gospel should not go on strike, since strikes are a form of coercion; instead he should join an unaffiliated trade union. Above all, he should not talk of 'revolution', for that ethic surely does not teach that civil war of all things is the only legitimate form of war. The pacifist whose actions are guided by the Gospel will refuse weapons or throw them away, as we Germans were recommended to do, so that we might fulfil our ethical duty to end the war, and thus to end all war. The politician will say that the only sure means of discrediting war for the *foreseeable* future would have been peace on the basis of the status quo. Then the people of all nations would have asked what the point of the war was. It would have been reduced to absurdity, which is not now possible. For the war will have proved to be politically profitable for the victors, or at least for some of them. The responsibility for this outcome lies with the behaviour which made it quite impossible for us to resist. What will now happen – once the phase of exhaustion has passed – is, that *peace, not war, will have been discredited* – and this will be the result of absolute ethics.

Finally, there is the duty to be truthful. For the ethic of absolute principles this is an unconditional duty.[8] Hence it was concluded that all documents should be published, especially those which placed a burden of guilt on our country, and that a confession of guilt should be made on the basis of these documents – unilaterally, unconditionally, regardless of the consequences. The politician will take the view that the upshot of this will not serve the cause of truth, but rather that truth will certainly be obscured by the misuse of the documents and by the passions they unleash. He will take the view that the only productive approach would be a systematic, comprehensive investigation, conducted by disinterested parties; any other way of proceeding could have consequences for the nation which could not be repaired in decades. 'Consequences', however, are no *concern* of absolutist ethics.

That is the crucial point. We have to understand that ethically oriented activity can follow two fundamentally different, irreconcilably opposed maxims. It can follow the 'ethic of principled conviction' (*Gesinnung*) or the 'ethic of responsibility'. It is not that the ethic of conviction is identical with irresponsibility, nor that the ethic of responsibility means the absence of principled conviction – there is of course no question of that. But there is a profound opposition between acting by the maxim of the ethic of conviction (putting it in religious terms: 'The Christian does what is right and places the

---

8 Kant's attempt to found ethics on the 'categorical imperative' led him to argue that there was an absolute obligation to tell the truth, even where to do so might lead to the loss of human life. See, for example, *The Metaphysics of Morals*, edited by M. Gregor, Cambridge, 1991, pp. 225–7. Kant's was one of the most influential voices arguing for 'anti-consequentialism' in ethics in Germany.

outcome in God's hands'),[9] and acting by the maxim of the ethic of responsibility, which means that one must answer for the (foreseeable) *consequences* of one's actions. A syndicalist who is committed to the ethics of conviction might be fully aware that the likely consequences of his actions will be, say, increased chances for the forces of reaction, increased oppression of his own class, a brake on the rise of his class. But none of this will make the slightest impression on him. If evil consequences flow from an action done out of pure conviction, this type of person holds the world, not the doer, responsible, or the stupidity of others, or the will of God who made them thus. A man who subscribes to the ethic of responsibility, by contrast, will make allowances for precisely these everyday shortcomings in people. He has no right, as Fichte correctly observed,[10] to presuppose goodness and perfection in human beings. He does not feel that he can shuffle off the consequences of his own actions, as far as he could foresee them, and place the burden on the shoulders of others. He will say, 'These consequences are to be attributed to my actions.' The person who subscribes to the ethic of conviction feels 'responsible' only for ensuring that the flame of pure conviction (for example, the flame of protest against the injustice of the social order) is never extinguished. To kindle that flame again and again is the purpose of his actions, actions which, judged from the point of view of their possible success, are utterly irrational, and which can and are only intended to have exemplary value.

Yet we have still not reached the end of the problem. No ethics in the world can get round the fact that the achievement of 'good' ends is in many cases tied to the necessity of employing morally suspect or at least morally dangerous means, and that one must reckon with the possibility or even likelihood of evil side-effects. Nor can any ethic in the world determine when and to what extent the ethically good end 'sanctifies' the ethically dangerous means and side-effects.

The decisive means of politics is the use of violence. Just how great are the ramifications of the ethical tension between ends and means in politics can be seen in the case of the revolutionary socialists (the Zimmerwald faction).[11] Even during the war, as is generally known, they espoused a principle which one might characterize thus: 'If the choice lies between a few more years of war, followed by a revolution, and peace now but no revolution, we choose a

---

9 Although an exact source for these words (used on several occasions by Weber) has not been traced, the editors of the new *Gesamtausgabe* believe they allude to a passage in Luther's lectures on *Genesis*, 'Fac tuum officium, et eventum Deo permitte', *D. Martin Luthers Werke. Kritische Gesamtausgabe*, vol. XLIV, Weimar, 1915, p. 78.

10 Fichte quotes such sentiments from Machiavelli's *Discourses* in 'Über Macchiavelli als Schriftsteller', *Johann Gottlieb Fichtes nachgelassene Werke*, vol. III, Bonn, 1856, p. 420.

11 In September 1915 a group of radical socialists held a conference in Zimmerwald (near Berne) with the aim of founding a new (Third) International. Despite further conferences in 1916 and 1917, they could not achieve unity.

few more years of war.' If then asked what this revolution might achieve, any scientifically trained socialist would have replied that there could be no question of a transition to an economy deserving the name 'socialist' as *he* understood the term. Rather, a bourgeois economy would arise again which would have shed only its feudal elements and the remnants of dynasticism. For this modest result they would accept 'a few more years of war'! In this instance it could well be said that even a person of very firm socialist convictions might reject the end if these are the means it demands. But this is precisely how things stand with Bolshevism and Spartacism and indeed every type of revolutionary socialism. Hence it is of course utterly ridiculous for such people to condemn *morally* the 'politicians of violence' of the old regime for using precisely the same means as they are prepared to use (no matter how justified they may be in rejecting the *aims* of the other side).

It seems that the ethics of conviction is bound to founder hopelessly on this problem of how the end is to sanctify the means. Indeed the only position it can logically take is to *reject any action* which employs morally dangerous means. Logically. In the real world, admittedly, we repeatedly see the proponent of the 'ethics of conviction' suddenly turning into a chiliastic prophet. Those who have been preaching 'love against force' one minute, for example, issue a call to force the next; they call for one *last* act of force to create the situation in which *all* violence will have been destroyed for ever – just like our military leaders who said to the soldiers before every attack that this would be the last, that it would bring victory and then peace. The man who espouses an ethic of conviction cannot bear the ethical irrationality of the world. He is a cosmic-ethical 'rationalist'. Those of you who know their Dostoyevsky will recall the scene with the Grand Inquisitor, where the problem is dissected very acutely.[12] It is not possible to unite the ethic of conviction with the ethic of responsibility, nor can one issue an ethical decree determining which end shall sanctify *which* means, if indeed any concession at all is to be made to this principle.

My colleague, F.W. Foerster,[13] a man I hold in the highest personal esteem because of the undoubted integrity of his convictions (although I reject him unreservedly as a politician), thinks that he can get round the difficulty in his book with the simple thesis that only good can flow from good, only evil from evil. Were this so, the whole, complex problem would admittedly not exist. Yet it is astonishing that such a thesis could still see the light of day 2,500 years after the Upanishads were composed. Not just the entire course of world history, but any unbiased examination of daily experience, proclaims

12 F. Dostoyevsky, *The Brothers Karamazov*, Book 5, ch. 5.
13 F.W. Foerster (1869–1966) was a leading spokesman of the Society for Ethical Culture. His *Staatsbürgerliche Erziehung* (1910) ('Education for Citizenship', reprinted under the title *Politische Ethik und politische Pädagogik*) was a popular expression of the ideas of this movement for social reform.

the opposite. The development of all the religions in the world rests, after all, on the fact that the opposite is true. The age-old problem of theodicy is, after all, the question of how a power which is said to be both all-powerful and benevolent can possibly have created such an irrational world of undeserved suffering, unpunished injustice and incorrigible stupidity. Either that power is not all-powerful or it is not benevolent – or quite other principles of compensation and retribution govern life, principles which we may be able to interpret metaphysically or which will for ever elude our interpretation. This problem, the experience of the irrationality of the world, was, after all, the driving force behind all religious development. The Indian doctrine of *karma*, Persian dualism, original sin, predestination and the concept of the *deus absconditus*, all these notions have grown out of precisely this experience. The early Christians too knew very well that the world was governed by demons, that anyone who gets involved with politics, which is to say with the means of power and violence, is making a pact with diabolical powers, and that it does *not* hold true of his actions that only good can come of good and only evil from evil, but rather that the opposite is often the case. Anyone who fails to see this is indeed a child in political matters.

Religious ethics have adopted various strategies to come to terms with the fact that we are placed in various orders of life, each of which is subject to different laws. Hellenic polytheism sacrificed to Aphrodite and also to Hera, to Dionysius as well as to Apollo, knowing that these gods were often in conflict with one another. The Hindu order of life made each of the various occupations subject to a particular ethical law, a *dharma*, and forever divided them one from another into castes, setting them in a rigid hierarchy of rank from which there was no escape for the individual born into a particular caste, except through reincarnation in the next life; the different occupations were thereby placed at varying distances from the highest religious goods of salvation. Hinduism was therefore able to elaborate the *dharma* for each caste, from the ascetics and Brahmans down to the rogues and whores, according to the immanent and particular laws governing each occupation, including war and politics. How war is fitted into the totality of the orders of life can be found in the *Bhagavad Gita*, in the discussion between Krishna and Arduna. 'Do what is necessary', which means whatever 'work' is imposed as a duty by the *dharma* of the warrior caste and its rules, whatever is objectively necessary in relation to the purpose of war. According to this belief, acting thus is not injurious to religious salvation; indeed it serves this end. Admission to Indra's heaven had always been assured to the Indian warrior who died a hero's death just as certainly as Valhalla was to the Germanic warrior. But the former would have scorned Nirvana just as surely as the latter would have scorned the paradise of Christianity with its choirs of angels. This specialization of ethics made it possible for Indian ethics to treat the regal art of politics quite without reservation or scruple, following the peculiar laws (*Eigengesetzen*) of politics alone, indeed intensifying them radically. Truly radical 'Machiavellianism', in the popular sense of the word, finds its classic expression in Indian literature in the *Kautaliya Artha-Sastra* (composed long before Christianity, allegedly in the time of Chandragupta), in comparison with which Machiavelli's *Principe* is harmless. In Catholic ethics, to which Professor Foerster is otherwise sympathetic, the *consilia evangelica* are, as is generally known, a special ethic for those gifted with the charisma of holy life. Here, alongside the monk, who may spill no blood nor seek material gain, there stand the pious knight and the burgher, the first of whom may do the former, while the second may do the latter. The gradations in this ethic and its integration within an organic doctrine of salvation are less consistent than in India, as was bound to be the case, given the assumptions of the Christian faith. Because the world was corrupted by original sin, it was possible to build violence relatively easily into ethics as a means of chastising sin and heretics who endangered the soul. But the unworldly demands of the Sermon on the Mount, which represent a pure ethics of conviction, and the absolute demand for religious natural justice founded on the Sermon, have retained their revolutionary force and come to the fore with elemental power in almost every period of social upheaval. In particular they created the radical pacifist sects, one of which experimented in Pennsylvania with a state that abjured force in its relations with other states. The outcome of the experiment was tragic, however, inasmuch as the Quakers could not take up arms on behalf of their own ideals at the outbreak of the War of Independence, although this was fought on behalf of those very ideals. Normal Protestantism, by contrast, legitimated the state absolutely (and thus its means, violence) as a divine institution, and gave its blessing to the legitimate authoritarian state in particular. Luther relieved the individual of ethical responsibility for war and placed it on the shoulders of authority, asserting that no guilt could ever be involved in obeying authority in matters other than faith. Calvinism in its turn recognized as a matter of principle the use of force as a means to defend the faith, in other words religious war, which, in Islam, was a vital element in religion from the very beginning. Plainly, the problem of political ethics is *not* just one that has been thrown up by the modern lack of faith engendered by the cult of the hero during the Renaissance. All religions have grappled with it, and with very varying degrees of success; in view of what has been said above, things could not have been otherwise. The specific means of *legitimate violence per se* in the hands of human associations is what gives all the ethical problems of politics their particular character.

Anyone who makes a pact with the means of violence, for whatever purpose – and every politician does this – is at the mercy of its specific consequences. This applies particularly to the man fighting for a belief, whether religious or revolutionary. Let us simply take the present as an example. Anyone wishing to establish absolute justice on earth *by force* needs a following in order to do so, a human 'apparatus'. He must promise these people the necessary inner and outward prizes – rewards in heaven or on earth – because the apparatus will not function otherwise. Under the conditions of modern class-warfare the inner rewards are the satisfaction of hatred and revenge, of *ressentiment* and the need for the pseudo-ethical feeling of being in the right, the desire to slander one's opponents and make heretics of them. The outward rewards are adventure, victory, booty, power and prebends. The success of the leader is entirely dependent on the functioning of his apparatus. He is therefore dependent on *its* motives, not his own. He is dependent also on the possibility of providing those prizes *permanently* to his following, the Red Guard, the informers, the agitators he needs. Given these conditions of his activity, what he actually achieves does not, therefore, lie in his own hands but is, rather, prescribed for him by the, in ethical terms, predominantly base or common (*gemein*) motives prompting the actions of his following. He can only keep control of his following as long as a sincere belief in his person and his cause inspires at least some of the group, probably never in this life even the majority of them. Not only is this faith, even when held with subjective sincerity, in many cases merely the ethical 'legitimation' of the craving for revenge, power, booty and prebends (and let no-one try to persuade us differently, for the materialist interpretation of history is not a cab which may be boarded at will, and it makes no exceptions for the bearers of revolutions!), but the emotionalism of revolution is then followed by a return to traditional, *everyday existence*, the hero of the faith disappears, and so, above all, does the faith itself, or it becomes (even more effectively) a part of the conventional rhetoric used by political philistines and technicians. This development comes about particularly quickly in a war of faith, because these are usually conducted or inspired by genuine *leaders*, prophets of revolution. For it is one of the conditions of success in this, as in any apparatus subordinate to a leader, that things must be emptied and made into matters-of-fact (*Versachlichung*), and the following must undergo spiritual proletarianisation, in order to achieve 'discipline'. This is why the following of a man fighting for a faith, when it begins to rule, tends to decline particularly easily into a quite ordinary stratum of prebendaries.

Anyone wishing to practise politics of any kind, and especially anyone who wishes to make a profession of politics, has to be conscious of these ethical paradoxes and of his responsibility for what may become of *himself* under pressure from them. He is becoming involved, I repeat, with the diabolical powers that lurk in all violence. The great virtuosi of unworldly goodness and love for mankind, whether they came from Nazareth or Assisi or from the palaces of Indian kings, did not employ the means of politics, force. Their kingdom was 'not of this world' and yet they worked, and work still, in this world, and the figures of Platon Karatayev[14] and Dostoyevsky's saints are still the closest imitations of their lives. Anyone seeking to save his own soul and the souls of others does not take the path of politics in order to reach his

---

14 Platon Karatayev is a character in Tolstoy's *War and Peace*.

goal, for politics has quite different tasks, namely those which can only be achieved by force. The genius – or demon – of politics lives in a state of inner tension with the god of love, and even with the Christian God as manifested in the institution of the church, a tension that may erupt at any moment into irresolvable conflict. Even in the days of church rule people were aware of this. Again and again the interdict was imposed on Florence (something which represented at the time a far greater power over men and the salvation of their souls than what Fichte has called the 'cold approbation' of Kant's ethical judgement),[15] and yet the citizens of Florence fought against the Holy See. Machiavelli had such situations in mind when, in a beautiful passage in his Florentine histories (if my memory does not deceive me),[16] he has one of his heroes praise those citizens who placed the greatness of their native city above the salvation of their souls.

To see the problem in its current guise, replace the terms 'native city' or 'Fatherland' (which may not strike everyone as an unambiguous value at present) with 'the future of socialism' or even 'the achievement of international peace'. The 'salvation of the soul' is endangered by each of these, whenever men strive to attain them by *political* activity, employing the means of violence and acting on the basis of an ethic of responsibility. Yet if the soul's salvation is pursued in a war of faith fought purely out of an ethic of conviction, it may be damaged and discredited for generations to come, because responsibility for the *consequences* is lacking. In such circumstances those engaged in action remain unaware of the diabolical powers at work. They are inexorable, bringing about the consequences of their actions, including consequences for their inner being, to which they will fall helpless victims if they remain blind to them. 'The devil is old, so become old if you want to understand him'[17] – the saying does not refer to one's age measured in years. I too have never allowed myself to be outdone in debate simply because of a date on a birth certificate; equally, the mere fact that someone is twenty whereas I am over fifty does not persuade me that this in itself is an achievement before which I must expire in awe. What matters is not age but the trained ability to look at the realities of life with an unsparing gaze, to bear these realities and be a match for them inwardly.

For truly, although politics is something done with the head, it is certainly not something done with the head *alone*. On this point the conviction-moralists are entirely correct. But whether one *ought* to act on the basis of an ethics of conviction or one of responsibility, and *when* one should do the one

15 'Das System der Sittenlehre nach den Principien der Wissenschaftslehre', *Johann Gottlieb Fichtes sämmtliche Werke*, vol. IV, Berlin, 1845, p. 167.
16 The reference is to Machiavelli, *Florentine Histories*, Book 3, ch. 7, p. 114: 'so much more did those citizens esteem their fatherland than their souls' (in the translation by L.F. Banfield and H.C. Mansfield, Princeton, NJ, Princeton University Press, 1988).
17 Goethe, *Faust*, Part II, lines 6817–18.

or the other, these are not things about which one can give instructions to anybody. There is just one thing one can say in these times of excitement – *not*, you believe, a 'sterile' form of excitement (although excitement is not always the same as true passion) – if, *suddenly*, conviction-politicians spring up all around, proclaiming, 'The world is stupid and base (*gemein*), not I. Responsibility for the consequences does not fall on me but on the others, in whose service I work and whose stupidity or baseness I shall eradicate', then I say plainly that I want to know how much *inner weight* is carried by this ethic of conviction. For it is my impression that, in nine cases out of ten, I am dealing with windbags, people who are intoxicated with romantic sensations but who do not truly feel what they are taking upon themselves. Such conduct holds little human interest for me and it most certainly does not shake me to the core. On the other hand it is immensely moving when a mature person (whether old or young) who feels with his whole soul the responsibility he bears for the real consequences of his actions, and who acts on the basis of an ethics of responsibility, says at some point, 'Here I stand, I can do no other.'[18] That is something genuinely human and profoundly moving. For it must be *possible* for *each* of us to find ourselves in such a situation at some point if we are not inwardly dead. In this respect, the ethics of conviction and the ethics of responsibility are not absolute opposites. They are complementary to one another, and only in combination do they produce the true human being who is *capable* of having a 'vocation for politics'.

And now, ladies and gentlemen, let us return to these questions *ten years* from now. If by that time, as I am bound to fear will be the case, an age of reaction has set in for a whole series of reasons, and little has been realized of all those things which many of you and (as I freely admit) I too have wished and hoped for – perhaps not exactly none of them but apparently only very little (this is very likely, but it will not break my spirit, although I confess that it is an inward burden) – then I would very much like to see what has become of those of you – what has 'become' of you in the innermost sense of the word – who at present feel themselves genuinely to be 'politicians of conviction' and who share in the intoxication (*Rausch*)[19] which this revolution signifies. It would be fine indeed if Shakespeare's Sonnet 102 fitted the situation:

> Our love was new, and then but in the spring,
> When I was wont to greet it with my lays;
> As Philomel in summer's front doth sing,
> And stops her pipe in growth of riper days.

18 Luther is reported to have said this at the Diet of Worms in 1521.
19 In criticizing the *Rausch* (intoxication) of revolutionary enthusiasm, Weber is striking at the ready welcome given to the 'Dionysian' aspects of Nietzsche's thought by many German intellectuals at the time.

But that is not how things are. What lies immediately ahead of us is not the flowering of summer but a polar night of icy darkness and hardness, no matter which group wins the outward victory now. For, where there is nothing, not only has the Kaiser lost his rights but so too has the proletarian. When this night slowly begins to recede, which of those people will still be alive whose early summer seems now to have flowered so profusely? And what will have become of you all inwardly? Embitterment or philistinism, sheer, dull acceptance of the world and of your job (*Beruf*) – or the third, and not the least common possibility, a mystical flight from the world on the part of those with the gift for it or – a frequent and pernicious variant – on the part of those who force themselves into such an attitude because it is fashionable. In every such case I will draw the conclusion that they were *not* inwardly a match for their own actions, *nor* were they a match for the world as it really is, nor for their daily existence. Objectively and actually, they did not have the vocation they thought they had for politics in the innermost sense of the word. They would have done better to cultivate plain and simple brotherliness with other individuals, and, for the rest, to have worked soberly (*sachlich*) at their daily tasks.

Politics means slow, strong drilling through hard boards, with a combination of passion and a sense of judgement (*Augenmass*). It is of course entirely correct, and a fact confirmed by all historical experience, that what is possible would never have been achieved if, in this world, people had not repeatedly reached for the impossible. But the person who can do this must be a leader; not only that, he must, in a very simple sense of the word, be a hero. And even those who are neither of these things must, even now, put on the armour of that steadfastness of heart which can withstand even the defeat of all hopes, for otherwise they will not even be capable of achieving what is possible today. Only someone who is certain that he will not be broken when the world, seen from his point of view, is too stupid or too base for what he wants to offer it, and who is certain that he will be able to say 'Nevertheless' in spite of everything – only someone like this has a 'vocation' for politics.

20 The vocation of science[1]

But I believe that you really wish to hear about something else – the inner vocation for science. Nowadays, that inner vocation, as opposed to the organization of science as a career, is above all conditioned by the fact that science has reached a stage of specialization which was previously unknown, and that this will always be the case. Not merely on the surface but also in essence, the matter is such that an individual can be confident of having achieved something really perfect in the area of knowledge only through the most thoroughgoing specialization. Any work that encroaches on neighbouring fields, which we occasionally undertake and which for example sociologists in particular must necessarily always undertake, must be resigned to accepting that at best one can provide the specialist with useful questions, which would not occur to him so easily given his viewpoint. One's own work must however necessarily remain extremely imperfect. Only strict specialization can make the scholar feel confident, for once and perhaps for the only time in his life, that he has achieved something that will really last. A really definitive and worthwhile achievement is nowadays always a specialist achievement. Therefore, anyone who lacks the capacity to put on blinkers, so to speak, and to work himself up to the belief that the fate of his soul depends on whether he is correct in making this, and precisely this, conjecture at this point in this manuscript should have nothing to do with science. He will never undergo inwardly what one may call the 'experience' of science. Without this particular frenzy which is ridiculed by every outsider, without this passion, this conviction that 'thousands of years must pass before you enter life and thousands more wait in silence' according to whether you succeed in this conjecture, without all this one has no vocation for science and should do something else. For nothing is worth anything to a man, as a man, if he cannot do it with *passion*.

However, it is a fact that no amount of passion, however genuine and profound it might be, can come anywhere near to forcing out a result. Admittedly passion is a pre-condition of the crucial thing, which is 'inspiration'. Nowadays there is a widespread notion among young people that science has become an arithmetical problem, which is produced in laboratories or statistical card-indexes as 'in a factory', involving the intellect alone rather

1 Taken from *Science as a Vocation*, edited by Peter Lassman and Irving Velody and translated by Michael John, London, Unwin Hyman, 1989, pp. 8–31.

than the 'soul'. To which should be noted first of all that such notions show no knowledge about what goes on in either a factory or a laboratory. In both, something – indeed, the right thing – must *occur* to a person so that he can achieve something valuable. But this idea cannot be forced. It has nothing whatever to do with cold calculation. That is certainly an indispensable pre-requisite. No sociologist, for instance, should ever think himself too good, even in his old age, to do tens of thousands of quite trivial calculations in his head, perhaps for months on end. There are always penalties involved in completely offloading work on to assistants if one wants to get anything out of it – and what eventually does come out is often next to nothing. But if nothing definite about the purpose of his calculations and, while he is doing them, about the significance of his results has 'occurred' to him, then even this small result will not be gained. Normally, such an idea grows out of hard work alone, though this is certainly not always the case. In science, a dilet-tante may have an idea of exactly the same or greater significance than an expert. We owe many of our best ideas of approaching a problem and many of our best perceptions to dilettantes. A dilettante differs from an expert – as Helmholtz has said about Robert Mayer – only in that he lacks complete certainty in his working methods.[2] He is thus normally not in a position to control, gauge, or carry through his idea in all its significance. An idea does not replace work. On the other hand, work cannot replace or force out an idea, just as little as enthusiasm can. Both work and enthusiasm – above all, both *together* – can entice an idea out. But ideas come at their own time, not when we want. It is in fact true that the best ideas come as Ihering depicts – when smoking a cigar on a sofa – or as Helmholtz says of himself with scientific precision – when taking a walk on a slowly ascending street – or in some similar way. In any case, ideas come when one does not expect them and while one is racking one's brains at a desk. Admittedly ideas would not come to mind if one had not racked one's brains and passionately searched for answers. However that may be, the researcher must put up with the risk, which attends all scientific work. Will inspiration come or not? He may be an excellent worker and yet never have a valuable idea of his own. It is a grave error to believe that this is the case only in science and that things in an office are somewhat different from in a laboratory. A merchant or large industrialist who lacks 'commercial imagination' – that is, ideas or inspiration – is for his entire life merely a man best suited to being a clerk or a technical official. He will never be really creative in an organizational sense. Inspiration certainly does not – as the arrogance of the academic imagines – play a larger role in the field of science than in the mastery of practical problems by a modern entrepreneur. On the other hand – and this is something that is frequently forgotten – it plays no smaller role than in the field of art. It is childish to

---

2 Helmholtz established the laws of entropy (the dissipation of energy). He noted that Mayer had made the crucial insight without the means of verifying it.

think that a mathematician might come to any scientifically valuable result by sitting at his desk with a ruler, calculating machines or other mechanical devices. In terms of disposition and results the mathematical imagination of a Weierstrass is naturally quite differently oriented from that of an artist; indeed, there is a fundamental qualitative difference. But this difference does not extend to the psychological processes. Both have in common frenzy (in the sense of Plato's 'mania') and 'inspiration'.

Now whether somebody has scientific inspiration depends on fates which are hidden from us, but otherwise on the possession of a 'gift'. Not at least because of this undoubted truth a very popular idea has come to promote certain idols, especially among the young for understandable reasons. And today we find the cult of these idols on every street corner and in every magazine. Those idols are 'personality' and 'personal experience' (*Erleben*). Both are closely linked, and the idea prevails that the latter amounts to the former and belongs to it. One tortures oneself with efforts to 'experience', because this belongs to the proper style of life of a 'personality', and if it does not succeed one must at least pretend to have this gift of grace. Formerly this was called mere 'experience' (*Erlebnis*) or, in plain German, 'sensation'. And people had, I think, a more accurate understanding of what 'personality' is and means.

Ladies and gentlemen! Personality is only possessed in the realm of science by the man who serves only the *needs of his subject*, and this is true not only in science. We know of no great artist who would have ever done anything other than devoting himself to his work and only to his work. Even with a personality of Goethe's standing, it would have been disastrous, as far as his art was concerned, if he had taken the liberty of trying to make his 'life' into a work of art. And even if one doubts this, one would have at least to be Goethe to allow oneself to try it at all. At the very least, everyone would admit that even in the case of somebody like him, who appears once every thousand years, such a liberty has its price. Things are no different in politics, but I do not want to talk about that today. But in the field of science it is quite certain that the man who steps up on to the stage as an impresario of the subject to which he is devoted, seeks to justify himself through 'personal experience' and asks, 'How can I manage to say something in form or content which nobody else has said?' – such a man is no 'personality'. Such behaviour is to be seen on an enormous scale nowadays and in each case it detracts from and debases the man who asks such questions instead of letting an inner devotion to the subject and only to the subject raise him to the height and dignity of the subject which he claims to serve. That is also not different for an artist.

In contrast to these pre-conditions which scientific work has in common with art, science is in one sense destined to be profoundly different from artistic practice. Scientific work is harnessed to the course of *progress*. In art, however, there is no progress in this sense. It is not true that a work of art from a period which has worked out a new technique, or perhaps the laws of perspective, is for that reason greater in an artistic sense than a work of art which lacks all knowledge of such techniques or laws. If it merely did justice to its materials and forms – that is to say, if it selected and shaped its object in such a way that it could have been artistically rendered without the application of such techniques – then such a work is by no means greater. A work of art which involves genuine 'fulfilment' can never be surpassed; it will never be out of date. An individual may judge its importance for him personally in different ways. But nobody will ever be able to say of a work which involves genuine 'fulfilment' in an artistic sense that it has been made 'obsolete' by another work of equal 'fulfilment'.

On the other hand, each of us scientists knows that what one has worked through will be out of date in ten, twenty, or fifty years. That is the fate of science; indeed, it is the true meaning of scientific work, to which it is subjected and devoted in a sense specifically different from all the other elements of culture, where the same thing is generally true. Every scientific 'fulfilment' means new 'questions'; it asks to be 'surpassed' and made obsolete. Anyone who wishes to devote himself to science must come to terms with this fact. Scientific works can certainly remain important for a long time as 'things of pleasure', on account of their artistic quality or as means of training work. To be overtaken in science is, however – let me repeat – not only the fate of every one of us, but also our common goal. We cannot work without hoping that others will get further than we do. Such progress is in principle infinite, and here we come to the *problem of the meaning* of science. For it is simply not self-evident that something which is subject to such a law is in itself meaningful and rational. Why should one do something which in reality never comes to an end and never can? One does it above all for purely practical or, in the broader meaning of the word, technical ends, in order to be able to direct our practical activities to the expectations which scientific experience suggest to us. That is all well and good, but that means something only to the practical man. But what is the personal attitude of the man of science to his vocation, if indeed he is in search of such an attitude at all? He maintains that he is engaged in 'science for science's sake' and not merely in order that others may achieve commercial or technical successes or be able to feed, clothe, light, or govern themselves better. But what of significance does he believe himself to accomplish with these creations which are always destined for obsolescence? Why then does he allow himself to be tied to this specialized, endless enterprise? Some general remarks on this matter are in order.

Scientific progress is a fraction, indeed the most important fraction, of that process of intellectualization which we have been undergoing for millennia and which is generally judged in such an extraordinary negative fashion nowadays Let us first of all clarify what this intellectual rationalization through science and scientific technology actually means in practice. Does it perhaps mean that today we – for example, everybody who is sitting in this room – have a greater understanding of the conditions under which we live than a Red Indian or a Hottentot? Hardly. Not one of us who travels on trams has any idea of how trams come to move unless he is a physicist. He does not need to know anything about it. He is satisfied if he can 'count on' the behaviour of the tram; he bases his behaviour on that. But he knows nothing of how a tram is constructed so that it will move. The savage knows incomparably more about his tools. If we spend money today, I would bet that even if there are economists in this room almost every one of them would provide a different answer to the question: how is it that one can buy something – sometimes more, sometimes less – with money? The savage knows how he manages to come by his daily bread and which institutions help him to do so, thus increasing general knowledge of the conditions under which one lives. It means something else – the knowledge or the belief that, *if one only wanted to*, one *could* find out any time; that there are in principle no *mysterious, incalculable powers at work*, but rather that one could in principle master everything through *calculation*. But that means the disenchantment of the world. One need no longer have recourse to magic in order to control or implore the spirits, as did the savage for whom such powers existed. Technology and calculation achieve that, and this more than anything else means intellectualization as such.

Now, does this process of disenchantment which has gone on for thousands of years in Western culture, does this 'progress', to which science belongs as a part and as a motive force, have any meaning that goes beyond the purely practical and technical? You will find this question raised in the purest form in the works of Leo Tolstoy. He came to it by a peculiar route. The whole problem to which his meditations were directed revolved increasingly around the question of whether or not *death* was a meaningful occurrence.[3] And for him the answer was, for civilized man, no. And the reason was that the individual life of a civilized being, inserted into 'progress' and infinity, can in terms of its own immanent meaning have no end, for there is always a step further for him, which stands in the march of progress. Nobody who dies stands at this peak, which lies in infinity. Abraham or any other peasant of ancient times died 'old and satiated with life', because he stood in the organic cycle of life, because his life by its very nature had given him at the end of his days what it had to offer, because he had no more puzzles which he wished to solve and therefore he could have enough of life. But a civilized man, who is put in the midst of the continuing enrichment of civilization with thoughts, knowledge and problems, can become 'tired of life', but not 'satiated with life'. He snatches only the tiniest part of what the life of the spirit constantly produces, and then only something provisional, rather than final; thus death is for him a meaningless occurrence. And because death is meaningless, so too is civilized life as such, for it is that which condemns death to meaninglessness through its meaningless 'progressiveness'. This thought is to be found everywhere in the late novels as the keynote of Tolstoy's art.

---

3 This is discussed by Tolstoy in his story, 'The Death of Ivan Ilich'.

What should one think of that? Does 'progress' as such have a recognizable meaning that goes beyond technical ends, so that devotion to it can become a meaningful vocation? However, the question of the vocation *for* science – thus, the problem of the significance of science as a vocation for the person who devotes himself to it – is already another question: namely, what is the *vocation of science* within the totality of human life and what is its value?

Now, the contrast between the past and the present is enormous. If you remember the wonderful picture at the beginning of the seventh book of Plato's *Republic*: those chained cavemen, whose faces are turned towards the wall of rock before them; behind them lies the source of light, which they cannot see – they can occupy themselves only with the shadowy images that the light throws on to the rock and they seek to discover the relationship between them until one of them succeeds in breaking his fetters, turns around and sees the sun. Blinded he gropes around and stammers out what he saw. The others say that he is mad. But gradually he learns to look into the light, and then his task is to climb down to the cavemen and lead them up to the light. He is the philosopher, but the sun is the truth of science, which alone does not snatch at illusions and shadows but strives for the true being.

Well, who considers science in that way nowadays? Today youth in particular feels rather the reverse – that the thought processes of science constitute an unreal world (*hinterweltliches Reich*) of artificial abstractions, which with their lean hands seek to capture the blood and sap of real life without ever being able to grasp it. Here in life, which for Plato was the play of the shadows on the walls of the cave, genuine reality pulsates; the other things are lifeless ghosts, derived from life, and nothing else. How did this change take place? Plato's passionate enthusiasm in the *Republic* is in the end to be explained by the fact that at that time one of the greatest tools of all scientific knowledge was consciously discovered – the *concept*. Its significance was discovered by Socrates, though not by him alone. In India you can find the beginnings of a logic, which is very similar to that of Aristotle. But nowhere else was there this consciousness of its importance. In Greece, for the first time, one had a tool to hand with which one could put somebody in a logical vice so that he could not escape without admitting that he knew nothing, or that this and nothing else was the truth, the *eternal* truth, which would never disappear like the ways and actions of blind men. That was the tremendous experience of the pupils of Socrates. And from that seemed to follow that if one could only find the correct concept of the beautiful, the good, or even perhaps of courage, of the soul or whatever, one could grasp its true essence. This in turn seemed to open the way to being able to know and teach proper behaviour in life and above all as a citizen. For everything depended on this question for the Greeks, whose thought was thoroughly political. It was for this reason that one engaged in science.

The second great tool of scientific work made its appearance beside this discovery of the Hellenic mind during the Renaissance period – rational experiment as a means of reliably controlling experience, without which today's empirical science would be impossible. Experiments had been conducted early; for instance, in India physiological in connection with the ascetic techniques of the Yogi; in Hellenic antiquity mathematical experiments for military purposes, and in the Middle Ages for the purpose of mining. But it was the achievement of the Renaissance to have made the experiment the principle of research as such. In fact the pioneers were the great innovators in the field of *art* – Leonardo and men like that. Above all the musical experimenters of the sixteenth century with their experimental keyboards were characteristic. From these circles, the experiment entered science, especially through Galileo, and it entered theory through Bacon. And then the various exact disciplines took it over in the continental universities, in the first instance those in Italy and the Netherlands.

Now what did science mean to these men who stood at the threshold of modernity? To the artistic experimenters like Leonardo and to the musical innovators it meant the road to *true* art, which meant for them the road to true *nature*. Art should be raised to the rank of a science, and that meant above all that the artist should be raised to the rank of a doctor (of philosophy) both in social terms and in terms of the meaning of his life. That was the ambition, on which Leonardo's sketch-book for example was based. And today? 'Science is the way to nature' – that would sound like blasphemy to the young. No, quite the reverse, today's youth proclaims deliverance from the intellectualism of science in order to return to one's own nature and thus to nature as such. Science as the way to art finally? Here no criticism is needed. But much more was expected of science in the period when the exact natural sciences developed. If you remember Swammerdam's saying – 'I bring you proof of divine providence in the anatomy of a louse' – you will see what scientific work (indirectly influenced by Protestantism and Puritanism) saw as its task at that time, and that is, the way to God.[4] That way was no longer to be found through philosophers with their concepts and deductions.

All pietist theology of the time, especially Spener, knew that God was not to be found on the road on which the Middle Ages had sought him.[5] God is hidden; his ways are not our ways, nor are his thoughts ours. But one hoped to find clues about his intentions for the world in the exact natural sciences, where his works could be grasped physically. And today? Who – apart from certain overgrown children, who are indeed to be found in the natural sciences – still believes today that a knowledge of astronomy or biology or physics or chemistry could teach us anything at all about the *meaning* of the world? How could one find clues about such a 'meaning', if there is such a thing? If anything, the natural sciences tend to make the belief that there is something like a 'meaning' of the world die out at its very roots. And finally,

---

4 Swammerdam was an anatomizer and drawer of insects whose *Bible of Nature* was published (in German) in 1752.

5 Spener was an intellectual founder of German Pietism. See *PESC*, pp. 131ff.

science as the way 'to God'? Science, that specifically irreligious power? Nowadays nobody can doubt in his heart of hearts that science is irreligious, whether he wishes to admit it or not. Deliverance from the rationalism and intellectualism of science is a fundamental pre-condition of a life in communion with the divine. That or something like it in meaning is one of the basic watchwords which are constantly to be heard among our young people who are religiously inclined or who strive for religious experience. And they strive not only for religious experience, but for experience as such. The only thing that is odd is the path that is now followed; that is, the only thing which has hitherto not been touched by intellectualism, the sphere of the irrational, is now being put into the conscious realm and subjected to its scrutiny. For this is what the modern intellectualist romanticism of the irrational amounts to. This way of emancipating oneself from intellectualism leads to the exact opposite of what those who follow it see as their aim. After Nietzsche's devastating criticism of those 'last men' who 'have invented happiness', I may completely ignore the fact that science – that is, the techniques of mastering life based on science – has been celebrated with naïve optimism as the way to *happiness*.[6] Who believes that other than some overgrown children among the professoriat or in editorial offices?

Let us go back. With these internal presuppositions, what is the meaning of science as a vocation, now that all these earlier illusions – 'the way to the true being', 'the true way to art', 'the way to true nature', 'the way to the true God', 'the way to true happiness' – have been dispelled? Tolstoy gave the simplest answer to the only important question: 'What should we do? How should we live?'[7] The fact that science does not give us this answer is completely undeniable. The only question is in what sense does science give us 'no' answer and whether or not it could perhaps be of use to somebody who poses the question properly. Nowadays one often tends to speak of science 'without preconceptions'. Does that exist? It depends what is meant by that. In any scientific work the validity of the rules of logic and method, those general foundations of our orientation in the world, are presupposed. These presuppositions are, at least for our particular question, the least problematic aspects of science. But science further presupposes that what is produced by scientific work should be *important* in the sense of 'being worth knowing'. And it is obvious that all of our problems lie here, for this presupposition cannot be proved by scientific means. It can only be *interpreted* with reference to its ultimate meaning, which one must accept or reject according to one's ultimate attitudes towards life.

Moreover, the relationship of scientific work to these presuppositions

6 A reference to the Prologue of Nietzsche's *Thus spoke Zarathustra*. On the translation difficulties of 'last men' and Weber's use of the phrase, see S. Whimster (ed.), *Max Weber and the Culture of Anarchy*, Basingstoke, Macmillan, 1999, p. 1.
7 A reference to Tolstoy's essay, 'What then must we do?'.

varies greatly according to their structure. Natural sciences, as for example physics, chemistry and astronomy, presuppose as self-evident that it is worth knowing the ultimate laws of cosmic events, in so far as they can be construed by science. This is so, not only because technical advances can be made with such knowledge, but 'for its own sake' if the acquisition of such knowledge is supposed to be a 'vocation'. But even this presupposition cannot be absolutely proved. And still less can one prove that the world which these sciences describe is worthy of existence – and it has a 'meaning' or that it is meaningful to live in such a world. Science does not ask such questions. Or consider such a scientifically highly developed practical art as modern medicine. The general 'presupposition' of the medical enterprise is, to put it in a trivial way, the assertion that medical science has duty to sustain life as such and a duty to reduce suffering as much as possible. And that is problematic. The medical man uses all measures at his disposal to keep the terminally ill alive, even if the patient implores him for deliverance, even if his relatives, to whom his life is meaningless, who are willing to grant him deliverance from his sufferings and to whom the costs of maintaining his worthless life are unbearable – perhaps a wretched lunatic is involved – wish for and must wish for his death, whether they admit it or not. For the presuppositions of medicine and of the criminal code prevent the doctor from ceasing his efforts. Whether the life is worth living and when is not a question asked by medicine. All natural sciences give us the answer to the question: what should we do, *if* we wish to control life *technically*? *Whether* we should control it technically or indeed wish to, and whether that in the end has any meaning, are questions which science does not go into or which it prejudges for its own ends. Or take a discipline such as aesthetics. The fact that there are works of art is a given in aesthetics. The subject seeks to find out under what conditions this state of affairs exists. But it does not raise the question of whether or not the realm of art is perhaps a world of diabolical splendour, a realm living in this world and therefore in its core hostile to God and, given its intrinsically aristocratic spirit, hostile to the brotherhood of man. Thus, aesthetics does not ask whether there *should* be work of art. Or consider jurisprudence. It ascertains what is valid according to the rules of juristic thought, which is composed partly of logic and partly of frameworks established by convention. Thus it determines *if* certain legal rules and certain modes of interpretation are to be seen as binding. It does not answer the question of *whether* precisely these rules should be created. Jurisprudence can only declare that, if one wishes to succeed, then this legal rule is the suitable way of doing so according to the norms of our legal system. Or let us consider the historical and cultural sciences. They teach us how to understand political, artistic, literary and social phenomena in terms of their origins. They neither give us the answer to the question of whether these cultural phenomena were and are worthy of existence nor do they answer the further questions of whether it is worth the effort required to know them. They presuppose that there is an interest in participating, through this procedure, in the community of 'civilized men'.

But they cannot prove this to be the case to anyone 'scientifically', and the fact that they presuppose this interest certainly does not prove that it is self-evident.

Finally, let us consider the disciplines which are closest to us: sociology, history, economics, political science and those areas of philosophy which attempt to interpret those disciplines. It is said, and I agree, that politics has no place in the lecture-room. It has no place there as far as the students are concerned. I would for example deplore it just as much if, in the lecture-room of my former colleague Dietrich Schaefer in Berlin, pacifist students were to surround the desk and create an uproar of the sort which anti-pacifist students are said to have made in opposition to Professor Foerster whose views are in many ways as distant from mine as possible.[8] However, party politics also does not belong in the lecture-room as far as the lecturer is concerned and it belongs least of all when he is scientifically concerned with politics. For opinions on practical political issues and the scientific analysis of political structures and party positions are two different things. If in a public meeting one talks of democracy, then one makes no secret of one's personal attitudes; indeed, to take sides clearly is one's damned duty and obligation in this context. The words used are not means of scientific analysis but means of winning over the attitudes of others politically. They are not ploughshares for loosening the soil of contemplative thought; they are swords against opponents, instruments of struggle. On the other hand, it would be outrageous to use words in this way in a lecture or in the lecture-room. If for example 'democracy' is under discussion there, one should consider its different forms, analyse the way in which they function and establish the particular consequences for the conditions of life of each form. Then one should compare them with other non-democratic political systems and attempt to arrive at *one's* ultimate ideals. But the true teacher will guard against imposing any attitude on the student from the lectern, whether explicitly or through suggestion. 'To let the facts speak for themselves' is of course the most unfair method of all.

Now, why should we not do this? I would state as a premiss that some very respected colleagues are of the opinion that it is not possible to achieve this self-restraint and that, even if it were possible, it would be a whim to avoid it. Now one cannot demonstrate to anyone scientifically what his duty as an academic teacher is. One can only demand of him the intellectual integrity to see that the establishment of facts, the determining of logical and mathematical relations or the internal structure of cultural values (*Güter*), is one thing; while answers to the questions of the *value* of culture and its individual components of how one should act in the cultural community and in political associations are another. He must see that these are completely *heterogeneous*

---

8 Dietrich Schaefer was a professor of history at the University of Berlin and an advocate of Germany's expansionism by military means. Foerster was a radical pacifist and Christian.

problems. Should he then ask why he ought not to deal with both in the lecture-room, the answer is that the prophet and the demagogue do not belong at the lectern. To the prophet and the demagogue it is said: 'Go out into the streets and speak in public', that is, speak where criticism is possible. In the lecture-room, where one sits opposite one's audience, the audience must be silent and the teacher must speak. I consider it irresponsible for the lecturer to exploit the fact that students must attend a teacher's course for the sake of their careers and that nobody present can criticize him, in order to stamp them with his personal political opinions instead of being useful to his students with his knowledge and scientific experiences, as is his duty. It is certainly possible that an individual will not totally succeed in excluding his personal sympathies. He then exposes himself to the sharpest criticism in the forum of his own conscience. And it proves nothing for other, purely factual errors are possible and yet they prove nothing against the duty of seeking the truth. I regret this in the interest of pure science; I am willing to demonstrate from the works of our historians that, whenever a man of science brings in his own value-judgement, a full understanding of the facts *ceases*. But that goes beyond this evening's theme and would require lengthy discussion.

I ask only: how should one bring a devout Catholic (on the one hand) and a freemason (on the other) to the same *evaluations* in a course on the forms of church and state or on religious history? That is out of the question. And yet the academic teacher must wish and demand of himself that he is useful to both with his knowledge and methods. You will quite rightly say that the devout Catholic will never accept the view about the facts involved in the rise of Christianity that a teacher who is free of such dogmatic preconceptions might express. Certainly! The difference, however, lies in the following: science 'free from preconceptions', in the sense of a rejection of religious ties, does not know of the 'miracle' and the 'revelation'. If it did, science would be untrue to its own preconceptions. The religious belief knows both miracle and revelation. And a science 'free from preconceptions' expects no less of him – but also *no more* than an acknowledgement that *if* a course of events can be explained without those supernatural interventions, which an empirical explanation must exclude as causal factors, then it must be explained in the way that science attempts to do so. And the believer can do this without being untrue to his faith.

But does the achievement of science have no meaning at all for the person who is indifferent to the facts as such and to whom only the practical standpoint is important? Perhaps yes. Above all, there is one thing. Anybody who is a reasonable teacher has as his first duty to teach his students to acknowledge 'inconvenient' facts, I mean facts which are inconvenient for their party opinion. And there are extremely inconvenient facts for every party opinion – for mine as well. I believe that if the academic teacher forces his audience to get used to this, he achieves a more than merely intellectual achievement. I would even be so immodest as to use the expression 'moral achievement' if that does not sound too elevated for something that is so obvious.

Thus far I have spoken only of the *practical* reasons for avoiding the imposition of a personal point of view. But there is more to be said. The impossibility of 'scientific' advocacy of practical standpoints – except in the case of discussion of means to a *given*, presupposed end – is rooted in reasons which lie far deeper. Such advocacy is meaningless in principle because the different value systems of the world stand in conflict with one another. Mill, whose philosophy I would not otherwise wish to praise but who was right on this point, said in his old age: if one proceeds from pure experience, one arrives at polytheism.[9] That is superficially formulated and sounds paradoxical, but there is truth in it. If anything, we know once more today that something can be sacred not only in spite of its not being beautiful, but rather *because and in so far as* it is not beautiful. You will find evidence for this in the fifty-third chapter of the Book of Isaiah and in the twenty-second Psalm. And, since Nietzsche, we know that something can be beautiful not only in spite of its lack of goodness, but rather in that very aspect in which it is not good. You will find this idea formed earlier in the *Fleurs du Mal* as Baudelaire called his volume of poems. And it is a commonplace that something can be true although it is not beautiful and not holy and not good. But these are merely the most elementary examples of this battle between the gods of the different systems and values. I do not know how to decide 'scientifically' between the *value* of France and Germany, however one approaches the problem. For here, too, different gods struggle with each other and will do for all time. It is just like in the old world, which was not yet disenchanted with its gods and demons, but in another sense. Just as Hellenic man sacrificed on this occasion to Aphrodite and on another to Apollo, and above all as everybody sacrificed to the gods of his city – things are still the same today, but disenchanted and divested of the mythical but inwardly genuine flexibility of those customs. And destiny, certainly not 'science', prevails over these gods and their struggles. One can only understand what the divine is for one system or another, or in one system or another. Thus the matter has reached its limit as far as discussion in a lecture-room by a professor is concerned, although the great problem in *life* is naturally far from being solved. But this is an area in which powers other than universities have their say. What man would presume to 'refuse scientifically' the morality of the Sermon on the Mount, for example the sentence 'resist no evil' or the image of turning the other cheek?[10] And yet it is clear from the perspective of this world that here an undignified morality is being preached. The choice is between the religious dignity which this morality confers and the dignity of man, which preaches something quite different; 'Resist evil, for otherwise you will share the responsibility for its supremacy'. For each individual, according to his ultimate standpoint, one is the devil and the other God, and the

9 This view was expressed by J.S. Mill in his essay, 'Theism'.
10 The New Testament, Matthew, 5, 39.

individual must decide which *for him* is God and which the devil. And so it is in all aspects of life. The lofty rationalism of an ethical-methodical conduct of life, which flows out of every religious prophecy, has dethroned this polytheism in favour of 'the One that is necessary'.[11] Then, faced with the realities of the external and the interior life, it saw itself forced into those compromises and relativizations which we all know from the history of Christianity. But today there is the religious nature of 'everyday life'. The many gods of old, without their magic and therefore in the form of impersonal forces, rise up from their graves, strive for power over our lives and begin once more their eternal struggle among themselves. But what is difficult for modern man, and most difficult of all for the younger generation, is to meet the demands of such an *everyday life*. All hunting for 'experience' stems from this weakness, for not to be able to look the destiny of the time full in the face is a weakness. It is the destiny of our culture however that we will once more become more clearly aware of it, after our eyes have been blinded for a thousand years by the allegedly or presumably exclusive orientation towards the sublime pathos of the Christian ethic.

But enough of these questions which lead us far astray. The error of that part of our youth which would answer all that with, 'Yes, but we only come to a lecture in order to experience something other than mere analyses and factual statements', is that they seek in the professor something other than what stands before them – a *leader*, not a *teacher*. But our place at the lecture is solely that of a *teacher*. These are two different things, and it is easy to convince oneself that that is the case. Allow me to take you back to America, because one can often see such things in their most primitive form there. The American boy learns vastly less than ours. In spite of the incredible number of examinations, he has not yet become, in terms of *meaning* of his school life, the absolute examination candidate, as the German boy is. For the bureaucracy, which presupposes an examination diploma as a ticket of entry into the realm of office, is only in its infancy in America. The young American respects nothing and nobody, no tradition and no public office, with the exception of the personal achievement of the person concerned – the American calls *that* 'democracy'. However distorted the relationship between reality and those conceptions may be, the conception is as follows and that is what matters here. The American's conception of the teacher, who stands before him, is: he sells me his knowledge and methods in return for my father's money just as the woman in the greengrocer's sells my mother cabbage. That's all. To be sure, if the teacher happens to be a football coach, then he is a leader in this field. But if he is not a coach (or something similar in a different sport) then he is only a teacher and nothing more, and no American would think of letting the teacher sell him '*Weltanschauungen*' on rules of behaviour. Now, if put in this way, we would reject that. But the question is

11 The New Testament, Luke, 10, 42.

whether there isn't a kernel of truth in this feeling, which I have deliberately described in a somewhat exaggerated way.

Fellow students! With these demands on our qualities of leadership you come to our lectures and you fail to say to yourselves beforehand that out of the hundred professors at least ninety-nine not only do not and should not claim to be football coaches in the field of life; they cannot even claim to be 'leaders' in matters of conduct. Just think; the value of a person does not depend on whether he possesses qualities of leadership. In any case, those qualities which make somebody an excellent scholar and academic teacher are not *those* which make him a leader in the field of life's practicalities or, more particularly, politics. It is pure chance if somebody also possesses these latter qualities, and it is a serious situation if a teacher feels it expected of him to make use of them. It is even more serious if it is left to each academic teacher to play the role of a leader in the lecture-room. For those who think of themselves as leaders most are often the least capable of fulfilling the role. Above all, whether they are leaders or not, their position offers them simply no opportunity of *proving* themselves to be such. The professor who feels he has a vocation as an adviser of youth and enjoys their trust may prove himself a man in personal relations with them. And if he feels a vocation to interfere in struggles of *Weltanschauungen* and political opinions, then he may do that outside in the market-place of life – in the press, in meetings, in associations, or wherever he likes. But it is far too easy for him to demonstrate the courage of his convictions where those present, who perhaps think differently, are condemned to silence.

Finally you will pose the question: if that is so, what of positive use does science actually contribute to practical and personal 'life'? And with this we are back with the problem of science as a 'vocation'. First of all, of course, there is knowledge of the techniques by which life – both external things and the behaviour of people – can be controlled through calculation. But you will say, that is merely the American boy's greengrocer, and I would quite agree. Secondly, there is at any rate something that the greengrocer cannot do – that is, methods of thought and the tools and education necessary for it. You will perhaps say: well, that is not vegetables but it is nothing other than the means of procuring them. Good, let's leave it at that for today. Fortunately, that does not yet exhaust the contribution of science, for we are in a position to help you gain a third objective: *clarity*. That naturally presupposes that we possess it ourselves. As far as that is the case, we can make clear to you that one can in practice take up this or that position with regard to the problem of values – for the sake of simplicity, please take social phenomena as an example. *If* one takes up such-and-such a position, then according to scientific experience, one must apply such-and-such *means* in order to carry out one's belief in practice. These means are perhaps in themselves of a sort that you believe you must reject. In that case you have to choose between the end and the unavoidable means. Does the end 'justify' the means or not? The teacher can demonstrate to you the necessity of the choice. More than that he cannot do, as long as he wishes to remain a teacher and not become a demagogue. Of course, he can go further and tell you that if you want such-and-such an end, then you must also accept such-and-such secondary results, which experience shows to occur. Once again we are back in the same position. But these are all problems which can arise for any technician who in numerous cases must decide according to the principle of the lesser evil or the relative best. The only difference is that, for him, there tends to be only one thing – the *end*. But precisely that is *not the case* for us, as soon as we are dealing with truly 'ultimate' problems. And here, at last, we come to the last contribution which science as such can make towards clarity, and at the same time to the limits of that contribution; we can and should say to you that the *meaning* of such-and-such a practical standpoint can be derived consistently (and therefore honestly) from such-and-such an ultimate position in terms of *Weltanschauung*. It may be derived from only one such position or perhaps from several, but we can say that it cannot be derived from a different position. Figuratively speaking, you will serve this god *and you will offend every other* if you decide in favour of this standpoint. For you will necessarily arrive at such-and-such ultimate, internally meaningful *conclusions*, if you remain true to yourself. In principle at least, that can be accomplished.

Philosophy as a specialist discipline and the essentially philosophical discussions of principles in the other disciplines attempt to achieve this. Thus if we understand things correctly (which must be presupposed here) we can force the individual, or at least help him, *to give account of the ultimate meaning of his own actions*. That does not seem to be trivial to me, even for one's purely personal life. If a teacher succeeds in this, I am even tempted to say that he serves 'moral' forces by creating a sense of duty, clarity and a feeling of responsibility. And I believe that he will be the more capable of this achievement, the more conscientiously he avoids the desire to impose upon or suggest to his audience his own standpoint.

Admittedly, the assumption which I am presenting here derives from the one fundamental fact – that life, as long as it is to be understood in its own terms, knows only the unending struggle between those gods. Put literally, that means the incompatibility of the ultimate *possible* attitudes towards life and therefore the inconclusiveness of the battle between them. It is thus necessary to *decide* between them. Whether, under these circumstances, science is becoming a 'vocation' for somebody, and whether science itself has a 'vocation' which is objectively worthwhile, are once again value-judgements about which nothing can be said in the lecture-room. For a positive answer is a *pre-condition* of teaching. Personally I answer the question positively through my own work. And I do that precisely from the viewpoint which hates intellectualism as the worst evil, just as youth does nowadays or, more usually, imagines it does. But then the motto, 'Mind you, the devil is old; grow old to understand him', holds for youth. That does not mean age in terms of a birth certificate, but rather that one should not take flight from this devil, if one wishes to be rid of him. That happens often nowadays. Rather one must first examine his ways thoroughly before seeing his power and his limitations.

Science today is a 'vocation' conducted through *specialist* disciplines to serve the cause of reflection on the self and knowledge of relationships between facts, not a gift of grace from seers and prophets dispensing sacred values and revelations. Nor is it part of the reflections of wise men and philosophers on the *meaning* of the world. That is an inescapable fact of our historical situation, and we cannot avoid it, if we remain true to ourselves. If once more Tolstoy rises in you and asks, 'Who answers the question, "what should we do and how should we organize our lives" if not science?' – or in the words used here this evening, 'Which of the warring gods should we serve, or should we perhaps serve a completely different one?' – then one can only say, a prophet or a saviour. If there isn't one or if his prophecies are no longer believed, then you will quite certainly not compel him to appear by having thousands of professors seeking to take over his role in their lecture-rooms in the guise of state-salaried or privileged petty prophets. The one thing you will achieve in this way is to ensure that the full knowledge of the decisive fact will be denied to the younger generation; and the fact is that the prophet for whom so many of that generation yearn is just *not* there. I believe that the inner needs of a truly religious 'musical' person can never be served if the fundamental fact that he is destined to live in a godless, prophetless age is concealed from him and others by surrogates as all these prophets of the lecture-room are. The integrity of his religious voice must, it seems to me, reject that.

Now, you will be tempted to say, 'But how does one stand in relation to the fact of the existence of "theology" and its claim to be a science?' Let us answer that directly. 'Theology' and 'dogmas' are certainly not universal, but are also not limited to Christianity. Rather (going backwards in time) they exist in highly developed form in Islam, Manichaeism, Gnosticism, Orphism, Parsism, Buddhism, in the Hindu sects, in Taoism, in the Upanishads and of course in Judaism. Of course they are developed in terms of system to greatly differing degrees. And it is no accident that not only has Western Christianity – in contrast to Jewish theology, for example – worked out its theology more systematically, or at least has attempted to do so, but also that theological development has had by far the greatest significance here. The Hellenic mind produced that, and all Western theology goes back to Greece, just as (obviously) all Eastern theology goes back to Indian thought. All theology is the intellectual *rationalization* of the possession of what is sacred. No science is absolutely without assumptions. However, every theology adds a few specific assumptions to its work and thus to the justification of its own existence. Thus *every* theology, including Hindu theology for example, presupposes that the world must have a *meaning*, and the question is how to interpret that meaning so that it is intellectually conceivable. The same thing applies to Kant's theory of knowledge, which started with the assumption that ' "scientific" truth exists and is *valid*' and then asked: 'what is intellectually postulated in order to make that (meaningfully) possible'.[12] That applies similarly to modern aestheticians (either explicitly, as with G.V. Lukács for example, or implicitly), who start with the assumption that 'there *are* works of art' and then ask: 'how is that (meaningfully) possible?'[13]

However, as a rule, theologies are not satisfied with that assumption (which essentially pertains to the philosophy of religion). Rather, they generally proceed from the further assumption that certain 'revelations' are to be believed as facts relevant to salvation and thus as facts which enable one to lead a meaningful life. They further assume that certain conditions and actions possess a sacred quality, that is, they constitute a religiously meaningful way of life, or at least elements of one. Then your question is once again: how can these assumptions, which must simply be accepted, be interpreted within a conception of the universe? For theology, those assumptions themselves lie beyond the limits of 'science'. They are not 'knowledge', as it is usually understood, but 'possessions'. Whoever does not 'possess' faith or the other holy conditions cannot have them replaced by theology, let alone any other science. On the contrary, in every 'positive' theology the believer reaches the point at which the Augustinian saying holds: *credo non quod, sed quia absurdum est.* A capacity for this virtuoso's achievement – the 'sacrifice of the intellect' – is the decisive characteristic of the positively religious man. And this is shown by the fact that in spite of (or rather because of) theology (which uncovers this fact) the tensions between the spheres of value of 'science' and of religion cannot be overcome.

By rights, only the disciple offers the 'intellectual sacrifice' to the prophet, and only the believer does so to the church. As yet, a new prophecy has never emerged (and I deliberately use an image here which has been offensive to some) through the need of some modern intellectuals to furnish their souls, so to speak, with guaranteed genuine antiques and in so doing remembering that religion was once one such that they did not possess. As a substitute, they play at decorating a sort of private chapel with sacred images from all over the world or create a surrogate through all sorts of experiences, to which they ascribe the dignity of possessing mystical holiness and then peddle it on the book market. This is simply fraud or self-deception. On the other hand, it is absolutely no fraud but something very serious and genuine, though at times perhaps involving a misinterpretation of itself, when certain of those youth groups, which have quietly grown up in the last few years, interpret their own human communities as religious, cosmic, or mystical relationships. However true it is that every act of real brotherhood is linked to the knowledge that it contributes something which cannot be lost to a realm above the personal, it

---

12 A reference to I. Kant, 'Introduction' to *Critique of Pure Reason.*
13 Lukács discussed this with Weber while writing a dissertation in Heidelberg on aesthetics. See *György Lukács. His Life in Pictures,* complied and edited by Éva Fekete and Éva Karádi, Budapest, Corvina, 1981, p. 61.

seems doubtful to me that the worth of purely human relationships is increased by such religious interpretations. But that is to go beyond our theme.

The fate of our age, with its characteristic rationalization and intellectualization and above all the disenchantment of the world, is that the ultimate, most sublime values have withdrawn from public life, either into the transcendental realm or mystical life or into the brotherhood of immediate personal relationships between individuals. It is no accident that our greatest art is intimate rather than monumental, nor is it fortuitous that today only in the smallest groups, between individuals, something pulsates *in pianissimo* which corresponds to the prophetic *pneuma* which formerly swept through great communities like fire and welded them together. If we try to compel and to 'invent' a monumental sense of art, lamentable monstrosities will be produced as with the many pictures of the last twenty years. If one wishes to propound new religions without new, genuine prophecies, then something profoundly similar occurs with even worse consequences. And academic prophecy will create only fanatical sects, never a true community. One should tell somebody who cannot take this destiny of the age like a man that he would do better to return silently, without the usual public announcements of the renegade, but modestly and simply into the open, compassionate arms of the old churches. They will not make it difficult for him. To do so, he must give his 'sacrifice of the intellect' in some way – that is inevitable. We will not chide him, if he can really do it. For such a 'sacrifice' of the intellect in favour of unconditional religious devotion is morally quite different from the evasion of straight intellectual integrity, which occurs if one does not have the courage to be clear about one's ultimate standpoint but rather makes this duty easier by weak relativizations. And for me such devotion is worth more than that academic prophecy which does not make clear that within the lecture-room no virtue other than straight intellectual integrity counts. Integrity however forces us to state that, for the many who are waiting for new prophets and saviours today, the situation is the same as in that beautiful Edomite watchman's song from the period of exile which is included among the oracles of Isaiah: 'He calleth me out of Se'ir, Watchman, what of the night? The watchman said, The morning cometh, and also the night: if ye will inquire, inquire ye; return, come.'[14] The people to whom that was said asked and waited for far more than two millennia, and we know their shattering fate. From that we should draw the lesson that nothing is gained by yearning and waiting alone, and we should act differently. We should go to our work and do justice to the 'demands of the day' both in human and in professional terms. But that is plain and simple, if everybody finds and obeys the demon which holds the threads of *his* life.

---

14 The Old Testament, Isaiah, 21, 11–12. See also *Revised English Bible*: 'One calls to me from Seir:/"Watchman, What is left of the night?/ Watchman, what is left of it?"/The watchman answered:/ "Morning comes, and so does night./Come back again and ask if you will." '

Further reading

The 'Intermediate Reflection' has become a pivotal essay in Weber studies. It bridges between Weber's 'economic ethics' project and his analysis of modernity. The reading given for rationalism and rationalization, in Part I, needs to be recalled, for how this essay is interpreted has repercussions for the understanding of modernity. Tenbruck offers an idealist reading whose consequences are pessimistic for modernity, whereas Schluchter sees an emergent rationality in line with the realization of the Enlightenment project of a rational society. In this context Jürgen Habermas' *The Theory of Communicative Action*, vol. 1, London, Heinemann, 1984 comes into the debate. Habermas takes up a neo-evolutionary systems account of societal development, first advanced by Talcott Parsons (in *The Social System*, New York, Free Press, 1956) and S.N. Eisenstadt (in *The Protestant Ethic and Modernization*, New York, Basic Books, 1968). The concept of differentiation lies at the centre of these interpretations. The 'Intermediate Reflection' essay charts the fragmentation of the life orders that for neo-evolutionary thinking is a differentiation process. In place of conflict and fragmentation of the value spheres, Habermas and Schluchter chart the emergence of higher level integrative mechanisms with increasing reflexivity and rationality.

W.G. Runciman's *A Treatise on Social Theory*, vol. 2, Cambridge, Cambridge University Press, 1989, fashions a different evolutionary theory using in part a wide range of Weberian concepts, though Runciman is critical of Weber's rejection of evolutionary theory. See W.G. Runciman, 'Was Max Weber a Selectionist in Spite of Himself?', *Journal of Classical Sociology*, 1, 1, 2001, pp. 13–32.

Historical development but without evolutionary theorizing is represented by the tradition of Reinhard Bendix. Historical outcomes are the result of conflicts of power, interests, and ideas between different social strata. His undervalued *Nation-building and Citizenship*, Berkeley, University of California Press, 1977, provides some superb theoretical insights as well as historical case-studies. Equally worthwhile are the essays of Bendix and Guenther Roth in *Partisanship and Scholarship*, Berkeley, University of California Press, 1971. While the case studies are now somewhat dated, the approach still remains viable with new case studies of nation-building awaiting to be researched.

Related to the Bendix tradition is Ernest Gellner whose work emphasized the interrelation of culture, religion, and language with social structures. He also outlined different trajectories of historical development, in particular that of the Islamic world, noting the concatenation of factors that led to 'the conditions of liberty' as well as their historical contingency if not transience. See E. Gellner, *Plough, Sword and Book*, London, Collins Harvill, 1988; also John Hall, *Powers and Liberties. The Causes and Consequences of the Rise of the West*, London, Penguin, 1986. Michael Mann combines Weberian with Marxist ideas and has in common with the previous authors a concern with citizenship. For Weber, the issue was more one of citizenry as a middle-class (or burgher) phenomenon, whereas for Mann it was a universal entitlement but one that had to be demanded and extracted from the late nineteenth- and twentieth-century nation states. Mann's ideas are summed up most succinctly in his book of essays, *States, War and Capitalism*, Oxford, Blackwell, 1988. Anthony Giddens also incorporates Weberian ideas, most notably in *Nation State and Violence*, Cambridge, Polity Press, 1985.

These debates can all be summed up under the heading of the processes of modernity: how was it achieved, by which historical and cultural paths, and what are its dominant structures? New work on globality seeks to displace modernity as a central issue, and here the arguments turn on discovering new processes at the global level that supersede central features of modernity such as capitalism, democracy, and rationality. On this, see Martin Albrow, *The Global Age*, Cambridge, Polity Press, 1996.

As noted in the Introduction to Part III, the 'Intermediate Reflection' essay links to Readings 19 and 20 (the vocations of 'Politics' and of 'Science'). The concern here is with the meaning and significance of modernity for conduct, lifestyle, and the validity of values. The literature to an extent divides on these issues between those who discuss the significance of modernity in relation to its emergence, and those who treat modernity as a given and open to philosophical debate.

Thus, in the category of the former, the writers mentioned above may be briefly glossed. The Habermasian school discern immanent modes of integration and the possibility of a transcendent discourse on science, culture, and politics. The Gellner 'school' see values such as liberty and tolerance as delivered through the agency of ideas and the ability of social strata to implement ideas. The neo-Marxist school attach the values of modernity to struggles for citizenship at the level of social class. Giddens' approach is distinctive for the small but important addition he makes to Weber's theory of social action. Where Weber conceives of rational action as in part only half-conscious, Giddens sees a learning effect in modernity whereby individuals can reflexively monitor their actions and become more effective agents of their own destiny.

The work of Wilhelm Hennis is clearly alert to the historical categories of Weber's sociology, especially the way in which social strata inhabit a status position in society with a well-defined conduct of life (*Lebensführung*) – something that Hennis advances as the key to Weber's work. What at first sight is a historically informed enterprise, however, turns out to be a philosophical anthropology. Weber has a normative standard of what constitutes the formation of a social stratum in terms of human development, education, sense of position, and conduct of life. The mandarin, the Brahman, the feudal knight, and, nearest to Hennis' heart, the public official and public politician all possess a social formation of personality which should not be relativized through sociological reductionism. Hennis has expounded his views in a series of essays collected together in *Max Weber's Central Question*, Newbury, Threshold Press, 2000, and *Max Weber's Science of Man. New Studies for a Biography of the Work*, Newbury, Threshold Press, 2000 – both translated by Keith Tribe.

Hennis' use of Nietzsche is quite distinctive. Weber outlined the rise of the expert (*Fachmensch*) who in Nietzsche's critique is, to be blunt, a nonentity with no aspirational values other than work and contentment. Hennis takes this as a challenge to revitalize contemporary conduct, especially that of the political class. Hennis is sometimes placed in the conservative, natural law critique associated with Leo Strauss, *Natural Right and History*, Chicago, Chicago University Press, 1953. Although Strauss is equivocal in his reading of Weber, both praising and blaming him, his disciple Allan Bloom in *The Closing of the American Mind*, New York, Simon & Schuster, 1987, had no such inhibitions. According to Bloom, Weber has fallen prey to Nietzschean relativism and has negated the Western tradition of the possibility of identifying and living by universal values and truths. One interpretation of the Vocation lectures is that if the individual has to make up her own mind on ultimate values, there is no value hierarchy but only a plurality of values whose worth is evaluated by the individual. In modern thought this position is best represented by Isaiah Berlin's *Liberty*, Oxford, Oxford University Press, 2002. Another more extreme position is to close down the ever open-endedness of values, which under certain circumstances could lead to an anarchy within the social and political orders, and to argue for 'decisionism'. This option was argued for by Weimar legalist Carl Schmitt. It is controversial because it 'decides' ultimate values on what are taken to be arbitrary grounds; also his writings became implicated with the legitimation of the Hitler regime. On these debates see Wolfgang J. Mommsen, *Max Weber and German Politics, 1880–1920*, Chicago, Chicago University Press, 1984, and Sven Eliaeson, *Max Weber's Methodologies*, Cambridge, Polity Press, 2002. There are also a number of interesting essays in *The Barbarism of Reason. Max Weber and the Twilight of Enlightenment*, edited by A. Horowitz and T. Maley, Toronto, Toronto University Press, 1995. Roslyn Bologh's *Love or Greatness*, London, Unwin Hyman, 1990 has a number of penetrating insights, including Weber placed in gender terms.

A Nietzschean interpretation of these issues is pursued by David Owen, *Maturity and Modernity: Nietzsche, Weber, Foucault and the Ambivalence of Reason*, London, Routledge, 1994. An assessment of Nietzsche and Weber, and the accompanying literature is made by Ralph Schroeder, 'Nietzsche and Weber: Two "Prophets" of the Modern Age', in S. Whimster and S. Lash (eds), *Max Weber, Rationality and Modernity*, London, Allen & Unwin, 1987, pp. 207–21; this same collection also contains an important essay on the continuities of Weber's thought with Foucault's views on governmentality; see Colin Gordon, 'The Soul of the Citizen. Max Weber and Michel Foucault on Rationality and Government', pp. 293–316.

Issues of cultural rationalization, disenchantment, the polytheism of values, and the debates of which Weber was part at the turn of the century (*c.* 1900) are brilliantly laid out by Lawrence Scaff, *Fleeing the Iron Cage. Culture, Politics, and Modernity in the Thought of Max Weber*, Berkeley, University of California Press, 1989. Nicholas Gane takes up the theme of similarities and dissimilarities between Weber's and postmodernism's treatment of Nietzsche, cultural disenchantment, and re-enchantment, and the polytheism of values, in *Max Weber and Postmodernism. Rationalization versus Disenchantment*, Basingstoke, Palgrave, 2002.

On Weber's sociology of law, Weber himself wrote a book-length treatment of the subject; see *E&S*, pp. 641–900. Secondary works on law include Anthony Kronman, *Max Weber*, London, Edward Arnold, 1983, and Alan Hunt, *The Sociological Movement in Law*, Basingstoke, Macmillan, 1978.

On bureaucracy there is an enormous literature, because Weber's exposition of bureaucracy, which may be read in further detail in *E&S*, pp. 956–1003, underlies the corpus of organizational theory. For a starting point into this literature, see Larry Ray and Michael Reed (eds), *Organizing Modernity. New Weberian Perspectives on Work, Organization and Society*, London, Routledge, 1994.

Part IV
Methodology of the social sciences

Introduction

Methodology occupied no especially privileged place in Weber's writings. As we have already experienced in this volume, Weber was engaged in path-breaking studies in the historical development and analysis of different societies and cultures. For this purpose, he created new methodological tools and devices and wrote clarifications about where he stood in relation to other social scientists and historians. But unlike his contemporary Emile Durkheim, he wrote no prior methodological book that would define the territory of sociology as a discipline and its specific methods, as did Durkheim in his *Rules of Sociological Method* (1895). Instead he wrote essays, often very argumentative ones, that sought to identify his own position and its correctness in relation to the many opposed overall approaches to studying history and social science.

So far in this volume, readers will have more or less grasped how Weber uses ideal types, how he thinks about causality, how we can interpret the actions of other people and even their inner motivations, and why objectivity and value-freedom are important for the validity of social science. Leaving aside ideal types for the moment, Weber did not believe that the theories and methods of social science were distinctively different from how most people think about social interaction. The issue for him was to make this intuitive understanding of social processes and people's own part in that process methodologically explicit. When this was done, scientific issues of causality, verification, explanation, and validity could be properly addressed, so that social scientists would and should know what methodological points had to be dealt with if their work was going to claim scientific status.

Two major essays have been selected for Part IV. When Weber wrote these (in 1904 and 1920 respectively) his viewpoint was far from receiving any general assent. For a start, until Weber no one had really sat down and sorted out the problems of what we mean when we say what caused an individual to act in the way she did, what were the consequences, how individual choice was to be related to collective determination, and how these matters could be scientifically studied. There were few studies that had faced up to the methodological issues prompted by Weber's substantive studies such as *The Protestant Ethic and the Spirit of Capitalism*. This is reflected in the preamble to 'Basic Sociological Concepts' (see below) where Weber provides a very short reading list of books that were of relevance – and as Weber admits often difficult in their exposition. But today a bibliography on causality and explanation in interpretative sociology and philosophy would itself be book-length. Weber's influence, therefore, has been seminal even though he himself regarded methodological work as of no intrinsic value other than problem solving.

In reading his methodology, we need to be aware of the context within which Weber framed his position. Weber was faced with a formidable array of opposing methodological positions. He addresses and often attacks these counter-positions, sometimes naming his target explicitly, but sometimes he assumes the reader will know the implicit reference. I will briefly outline his main methodological and theoretical opponents. Sociological positivism heads the list. This was the tradition founded by Auguste Comte that developmental laws of society could be discovered, and that these laws acted as an external and causal force upon the individual. The enthusiasm for using the scientific methods, which had proved so successful in the progress of science from Galileo to Isaac Newton, Weber thought was simply misplaced. Causal agency, he argued, was not some external force, like gravity, that would be discovered to control the individual atoms of society. There would be no laws in the sense of the gravitational laws of the solar system that can predict with almost complete accuracy the position of planetary bodies in space. Weber, as we will see, was certainly in favour of discovering socio-logical regularities and rules of society, but this was not going to be achieved by importing natural scientific methods and assumptions. This form of positivism has subsequently been subject to massive critique throughout the twentieth century, but in Weber's day, the aspirations and ambitions for a positivist sociology ran very high. They were, of course, expressed with great sophistication by Weber's contemporary Emile Durkheim. Weber seems to have remained unaware of this body of work and instead he confined himself to criticizing those in the tradition of Comtean postivism.

Weber's opposition to what today is termed positivism, (i.e. the methods of natural science need to be copied in social science, individuals are determined by exterior laws, and science should concern itself only with facts and not values or inner states of mind and motivation) should not be regarded as a principled opposition to natural science. Social scientists as well as natural scientists are faced with the duality of appearance and reality. Astronomers, for instance, will be well aware that they have theories and observation statements on one side; what, however, occurs 'out there' in reality may ultimately be unknowable. All scientists are faced with the problem of construing reality, whether social or natural, that in logical terms lies beyond or outside their minds and thinking. This assumption has been well established in the philosophy of science from David Hume through to Karl Popper, and Weber's thinking lies within this tradition of dualism (even though he expresses the position in somewhat different terms). All scientists need to think hard about reality, to use devices to model the world in order to establish regularities, laws, and explanations. The capacity to discover regularities in social and physical reality Weber terms nomological knowledge (from the Greek word *nomos* or law). Sociology may not be able to construe *laws* of meaningful social behaviour, but it will certainly establish regularities or sociological rules of experience.

Weber's acceptance of nomological knowledge as part of the aims and methods of the social sciences should not, however, be extended to any blurring of the dualism of the world of science and reality itself. Where this line is crossed, or is indeed deliberately abolished, Weber becomes highly critical. Biology and zoology were disciplines that saw spectacular growth and enjoyed great scientific prestige in Weber's day. It was even more dominant than today's endeavours by evolutionary biology and psychology to explain the soul, human consciousness, the working of the brain, free will, and differences between individuals. Today, evolutionists use genetics and neuro-biology as their techniques. Around 1900 the techniques were the analysis and development of cells, what is termed embryology. The aspiration behind both of these endeavours – then and now – is a properly based materialist account of human behaviour and development.

Weber was very much against this scientizing movement, which technically in philosophy is called monism. Like positivism, the scientific monists sought to identify external laws that controlled our behaviour, but they also dispensed with the appearance/reality divide that many natural scientists take as axiomatic. Monists take the view that our thinking is determined by physical realities, and these realities can be revealed in their regularities. Science, then, not only discovers external laws but also overcomes the ontological divide of how human beings perceive the world and reality itself. These evolutionistic theories were also dominant in Marxism. Marx's own dialectic that explicitly acknowledged the appearance and reality divide was junked by Marxist philosophers contemporary with Weber. They reduced class-consciousness and the open-ended unfolding of societal development to inevitable laws of evolution.

This line of thought drove Weber to impassioned argument, which we have already witnessed in his two lectures on science and politics as a vocation (in Part III). The dilemma of modernity, as Weber sees it, is that science – while supremely successful and genuinely world-changing – cannot ever capture reality in its entirety within its explanatory nets. It follows from this insight that, unlike the monists, science cannot be used to explain all of human behaviour. In addition, it cannot be used as a basis for erecting ethical, racist, political, or cultural arguments in the public realm of politics and social policy. The danger presented by certain conceptualizations of science is that it can use and abuse its high status as knowledge as the justification of policies whose goodness, rightness, or desirability cannot be established in scientific terms alone. Weber's position, properly understood, in 'The Vocation of Science' is that social and natural scientists must engage with public debate, but they are not entitled to claim scientific infallibility over the ultimate values by which people choose their lives to be guided. Political, cultural, and ethical values, while benefiting from professorial analysis and reasoning, remain the property of citizens' debate and convictions. Weber's position here is often referred to as 'value-freedom'. A better formulation is 'freedom *for* values'.

Opposed to the positivistic and naturalizing tendencies were the disciplines of the humanities which we can label 'idealism'. These disciplines may be broadly characterized as being concerned with cultural values. The concern was normative in the sense of prizing certain 'human', aesthetic, or religious values – for example, values such as authenticity, beauty, goodness, artistic style. Education and upbringing meant cultivating these values and ensuring their transmission. In addition, there was the more technical analysis of how cultural values could be analysed and better understood. Here, the different disciplines in the humanities in the German universities had proved very successful in the hundred-year period prior to Weber. Theology, linguistics, ethnography, ethno-musicology, the historical sciences, aesthetics, and philosophy as well as epistemology had all registered progress – so much so that the German university and school system had become something of a template for educational reformers in most other leading countries.

There has been a tendency to depict Weber as belonging to the idealist tradition. Comtean positivism, evolutionism, and Marxist historical materialism, all lumped together on one side, are countered by an idealist perspective that considers values as transcendent over materialist and natural processes. At the technical level, Weber's aim was to incorporate cultural values – such as Calvinist predestination beliefs, or Indian karmic beliefs – in his societal analysis. For many decades in the mid-twentieth century Weber's Protestant ethic thesis was seen as the bourgeois retort to the Marxist account of historical development. However, to recall the points made in the Introduction to Part II, Weber was seeking an equivalence for cultural and religious values with those of material factors of geography, trade, economics, and politics. He wanted to include cultural factors as part of his explanatory methodology, but this did not mean material factors were to be excluded.

Weber developed a critique of the shortcomings within the idealist tradition, if it was to be considered as part of the social sciences. What particularly irritated Weber was the insistence of German historians in arguing that their disciplinary concern was with particular events and that this clearly demarcated them from natural science and its concern with nomological knowledge. For instance, in the field of economics Weber welcomed the developments in theoretical economics, which used a model of the rational economic actor to predict market behaviour. This was a more promising line of development for economics than the insistence that markets can be explained only in terms of their particular historical circumstances.

To give another instance, historians wished to assert that the motivation of historical personalities must remain unknowable. They made this point to buttress a different issue: that the course of history was always non-determinable because the essence of human freedom lay in acting contrary to any historical or sociological determination. Weber's interpretative sociology, however, aimed to establish rational motivation as one of the key devices for understanding social behaviour. To defend the idea of human autonomy by postulating the right of anybody to act irrationally (and unknowably), and so prove themselves free of any prior determination, was for Weber a complete misreading of the methodology of social action. His idea of autonomy was for the individual to act in his or her own interests, and therefore rationally. Individuals exist as part of a complex social world and they take account of the nature of constraints in that world and act accordingly. Individuals may of course choose to act differently from the conditions rationally predicted. They are not slaves to those conditions, or any higher law. Nevertheless there are clear regularities of social behaviour which it is the task of the social scientist to investigate.

> The error in the assumption that any freedom of the will – however it is understood – is identical with the 'irrationality' of action, or that the latter is conditioned by the former, is quite obvious. The characteristic of 'incalculability', equally great but not greater than that of 'blind forces of nature', is the privilege of the insane. On the other hand, we associate the highest measure of an empirical 'feeling of freedom' with those actions which we are conscious of performing rationally.
>
> (*MSS*, p. 124)

Weber levelled this criticism against the historian Eduard Meyer, whose studies of the Mediterranean basin in antiquity Weber both greatly admired and used. The picture therefore emerging of Weber as a methodologist is of someone who moves easily between different schools of thinking and exercises decisive intellectual judgement about which parts of each tradition are valid as well as usable (and also which are plain wrong and misguided) in his new science of interpretative sociology.

Finally, the influence of Nietzsche in Weber's thinking has to be noted. Nietzsche defies any classification within philosophy, and he is closely associated today with the developments of post-structuralist social theory – for example, in the work of Michel Foucault – as well as in contemporary pragmatist thought as represented by Richard Rorty. Published in the 1870s and 1880s, Nietzsche's work, like a sadistic dentist, probed the roots of the major traditions in European thought. His best-known aphorism declares: God is dead. European intellectuals had of course reached a similar awareness sometime before Nietzsche, and had shown that, for instance, the Christian tradition rested on revelation and magic and not on historically ascertainable facts. Nietzsche however went on to argue that Christianity and modern science both share an unfounded belief that truth is permanent and universal. God and scientific laws are identical in playing the role of an immutable and unchangeable reference point for truth and explanation, the one metaphysical, the other secular.

Reality for Nietzsche was a process of continual change. Appeals to higher laws in science were illusionary because they presupposed a reality that was essentially eternal and unchanging. The objective world of reality was composed of objects in flux, not as neutral facts to be encompassed by science, but as points of resistance to our human will. They obtrude into our human world as brute hard objects. Truth is the feeling of mastery over an object world and is obtained only by the projection of human will over objects.

This deconstruction of truth was far too wide-ranging for Weber, whose purpose was to construct a workable social science, but, having read Nietzsche, it reinforced his opposition to the strong programmes of both positivism and idealism. For Nietzsche idealism was doomed as part of a decadent tradition of European values. For Weber, while cultural values could not be substantiated by reference to any rock-solid set of assumptions, it none the less remained an option for people to choose and to stand by the values that they held to be ultimate. (This is sometimes referred to as anti-foundationalism.) So, to return to the lectures on vocation in 'Science' and 'Politics', at some point in his of her thinking a politician has to realize that the virtues of a political programme, while demonstrable and persuasive, lack any ultimate foundation. It is the same for the scientist. His or her ultimate value is truth, but this cannot be underpinned by a system idea such as positivism, monism, or Marxism (which were then contenders for validating scientific truth). Instead truth for the scientist is a passion, pursued through vocation. Likewise, for Nietzsche, the commitment to the individuality of truth was a passionate obligation in the face of a senseless object world.

So, summarizing, positivism, idealism, and the ideas of Nietzsche form the wider field of Weber's methodological writings.

Reading 21 (Basic Sociological Concepts) was one of the last pieces Weber wrote. It has been a somewhat underestimated and underused text, mainly because Weber compressed into it almost the totality of his thinking on how an interpretative sociology was possible in the light of his comparative and world-historical studies. It forms the opening chapter of one of his most important projects, *Economy and Society*. This in its turn was one volume in a multi-volume encyclopedia series – also edited by Weber – called the *Outline of Social-Economics*.

The overall function of *Economy and Society* was to outline the various sociological forms (for example, the household, the enterprise, the types of rulership, the basics of social stratification, ethnic groups, law, and religion) *not* as a general sociology but as constructs (as he calls them) in relation to economic action and its forms. Just as *The Protestant Ethic and the Spirit of Capitalism* undertook to examine the relation between a religious disposition and a capitalist mentality, so in *Economy and Society* Weber is interrelating the major sociological structures in their reciprocal determination of economic behaviour. In Part I of this volume, we have already obtained a very broad picture of the economic and historical development of different societies in relation to the predominant type of religiosity as practised in everyday behaviour and thinking. In Part II, a large range of Weber's sociological constructs was outlined. These, then, constitute the substantive content of *Economy and Society* (although not exclusively that work – and, out of necessity, in a somewhat slimmed-down presentation).

What Chapter 1 of *Economy and Society* lays down are the rules for how we should conceptualize the full range of sociological constructs. When a sociologist uses terms such as the state, the legal order, a structure of rulership, the clan, the nation, class, status group, how are these constructs to be thought of? Weber's answer is: as a social relationship and not as some reified entity. Lawyers, as well as common language use, may speak of the state as a real thing or entity, but for the sociologist it always has to be perceived as a complex set of social relationships. Put more simply, nothing can be taken for granted by the sociologist. Every sociological construct has to be broken down to its component social relationships.

What then is a social relationship? Weber says it is the manner in which one person orients his or her behaviour to another individual taking account of the *context of meaning (Sinnzusammenhang)* which forms the content of any social relationship. The ways in which a child interrelates with his mother, a courtier to his king, how two lovers treat each other, how government officials interact with each other, how a judge interacts with a plaintiff in a court of law – these are all examples of social relationships that are informed by a context of meaning. These meanings range very widely: from the personal and the emotional to the official, impersonal and authoritarian.

Thus sociological constructs are broken down to their most rudimentary bond: the social relationship. Weber's next task in 'Basic Sociological Concepts' is to characterize social relationships. He elaborates these progressively in seventeen sections. Just to list them gives the idea of how he proceeds. He starts with his definition of how sociology investigates the meaning context of social action. In §2 he lists in ideal-typical presentation the four major forms of social action to which all meaningful social behaviour can be related. These consist of two different types of rational orientation (instrumental and value-rational) and two types of non-rational action (affectual or emotional and traditional). In §3 he provides his definition of social relationship. §4 concerns how regularities should be thought of in social relationships: as customs and practice that achieve high-level chances that behaviour will be regular (but *not* the outcome of external laws, as the positivists would argue). §5 introduces a significant step in his scaling up of his sociological constructs: a great deal of social action is structured through a belief in the legitimacy of an order – social, legal, political, religious and so on. §6 elaborates the types of belief that guarantee a social order, in particular the role of convention and law. §7 relates the belief in the legitimacy of an order back to the social action types of §2. §8 diverts away from order to consider conflict and struggle, which, as we have already seen in this volume, is one of the constants in Weber's analysis of societies.

§9 can claim to be one of the most important pieces of thinking in sociology: How should we conceptualize community and its contrasting partner associational relationships? This is a 'classic' statement because throughout the length and breadth of sociological writing (and not just Weber's) the idea of community and associational forms such as organizations, markets, political parties, and so on are invoked continually without a precise understanding of what is denoted. Weber's crucial insight was to advise that they should not be thought of as pre-formed entities (even though, as we have seen in Part III and 'Intermediate Reflection' the urge to community, is an enormously strong force in all societies) but as something that is always in the process of being formed.

§10 considers the processes of closure and openness that operate in all social relationships. §11 considers the coalescing factors in social relationships: we attribute a solidarity with another person either because we treat them as part of a traditional group, or we accept their representative status that is underwritten by some form of legal statute. Closure is considered further in §12, and we enter in §§13, 14, and 15 the social world of group bodies, organizations, administrative bodies, executives, permanent institutions, and voluntary associations.

§16 explains conceptually what Weber means when he uses the terms power, rulership or domination, and discipline. §17 supplies the conceptualization to how political power is operated by a state and by religions (hierocratic power).

The chapter is a *tour de force*, not only because Weber informs his readers with great precision what he means when he uses a sociological term, but also because in the succeeding numbered parts to each section he tells us what he does not mean and how he differs from other approaches. Much of this latter material is addressed to the wider contextual field which I have already indicated above. The other dimension to be grasped is that Weber has presented the methodological basis not only of sociology as an interpretative science but how one can pursue a comparative sociology of civilizations.

It is quite easy also to overlook a crucial feature: his concepts apply to *all* societies insofar as sociology is concerned with meaningful behaviour. The chapter often reads as if Weber was referring only to modern societies. But, for Weber, all societies have to have mechanisms, rooted in social relationships, that deal with order, conflict, group and community formation, rulership and power.

In addition to this exposition of basic concepts Weber provides a major methodological subsection after §1. Subsection is a misnomer, and it should be read as a separate essay in its own right. Within it Weber calmly summarizes many of the methodological features he had developed during his career.

The 'Methodological Foundations' establishes that 'interpretative sociology' is concerned with subjectively intended meaning of a social actor's behaviour. Using methods that had been established by Dilthey, Weber argues that we can understand the motivation behind other people's behaviour. We can empathize with their behaviour and, in addition, we can, in our imagination, relive someone else's experience. Much of this empathetic reconstruction of someone else's actions, which may include the past action of a historical person, is intuitively obvious to us. Weber calls it evident (although self-evident might be a better term). Weber is not saying that all human action is meaningful or that all events are meaningful. For instance, cognitive psychologists today establish the extent to which our behaviour is shaped by factors of which we are not actually conscious. Weber refers to something similar as 'psycho-physical' phenomena. Events such as natural disasters also shape human activity and are not in themselves meaningful. Likewise climate and geography are conditions that shape human activity. So, quite clearly there can be neighbouring disciplines such as cognitive psychology and physical geography which contribute to our overall knowledge of society. Weber is quite happy to accept the existence of neighbouring disciplines whose methods are nomological in character, seeking out laws and frequency regularities. But their methods are not centred on the meanings that social actors give to their behaviour and it is here that Weber develops the distinctive procedure of an interpretative sociology.

Interpretative sociology is based on understanding meaning and this is a capacity all social beings are given. Sociologists, however, have to observe certain checks and pursue certain special methods. Weber quotes the well-known saying, 'One does not need to be Caesar to understand Caesar'. Thus a historian can reconstruct Julius Caesar's motivation in ceasing to be a mere general and reaching for the status of emperor. The historian constructs as best she may the objective conditions facing Caesar at his point of decision, and then interprets Caesar's decision as, in part, rationally motivated. Some part of his behaviour may, however, be driven by non-rational or affectual motives – for instance, vanity. Weber's advice in general is to gauge all social action in terms of rational motivation, so as to expose the non-rational motivations – emotions, or just sheer habit. We also need to check our intuition about motives and meanings against observed behaviour. If Caesar was motivated by vanity, he might be expected to have created empty titles and rituals for himself – whether he did this in historical fact requires empirical validation.

Out of this procedure we derive two parts of sociological explanation. We place a social action in its context of meaning and intuit motives for actions and decisions. This is the reason for action, which Weber terms 'adequacy of meaning'. This first part does not sound all that important, but in actuality it constitutes what we mean when we say that we understand someone's reason for acting. As such it is a high-level explanation, which we as social actors exercise all the time, even though we do not do this fully reflexively and conscious of our reasons for acting. It is the job of the sociologist to lay bare such reasons. The second component is what Weber calls 'causal adequacy'. If we attribute rational motivation to people holding on to good currency and spending bad currency (Gresham's Law), can this be corroborated through historical examples? Here, the sociologist or economic historian is empirically establishing a causal regularity. 'Correct causal interpretation for a concrete action requires its apparent course and motive to be accurately recognized and meaningfully understood in its context' (*MSS*, p. 9). These are the required two parts of an interpretative science of society.

Of course, much explanation is one-sided. Statistical frequencies are established between social phenomena to which no meaningful motivation may be attributed. Conversely, motivations are intuited that have no warrant in observed behaviour. For an interpretative sociology both of these cases would be deficient.

Weber refers to this method as a science. The philosophy of science in the twentieth century would find it hard to accept this description. Science is now more exactly concerned with efficacy of predictive laws and statements (and it has also moved on from the crude positivist assumption that *all* events are deducible from nomological laws). In the German tradition, however, science (*Wissenschaft*) also includes systematic methods for establishing regularities in social behaviour. Weber likened his approach to the processes of establishing guilt or liability in a court of law.[1] Leaving aside the procedural context of the court itself, in a great many legal systems it is crucial, first, to establish the motivation for a criminal act, and then, second, evidence that the course of action follows and is in line with such imputed motivation. This is analogous to what Weber recommends for understanding all social action. First, we can never establish correct motivation with certainty – it involves instead the reconstruction of the context of meaning and motives as we are able to understand them. Second, establishing the linkage between an effect and an imputed cause is intrinsically open to doubt and uncertainty. So, an interpretative science of social reality needs to be regarded as a pragmatic and not as an exact science, and like a legal court it will have to follow certain (methodological) rules.

Weber's pragmatic simplification of an interpretative science has subsequently triggered a very wide debate about this dual method: adequacy of meaning (motives or reasons for acting) and causal adequacy (establishing the relationship between two events in concrete, empirical reality). This is taken up in the Further reading.

In Part II of the 'Methodological Foundations', Weber expounds his preferred method, the ideal type. This is a device that Weber developed and made distinctively his own, and almost every page of Parts I, II, and III of this Reader works with ideal-typical presentation. Weber notes that we can

---

1 Stephen P. Turner and Regius A. Factor elucidate the whole lawyerly frame to Weber's thinking in their *Max Weber: The Lawyer as Social Thinker*, London, Routledge, 1994.

interpret the motivation of an individual using our existing and uncodified rules of experience. He goes on to argue for the desirability of modelling meaning and motivation, so as to clarify and simplify our sociological attribution.

Unlike everyday rules of experience through which we interpret the meaning and reasons for action in the social world, ideal types are rationalistic in inspiration. Weber explicitly says they have nothing to do with empirical reality, they are not created through a process of induction from experience. Instead they are purely mental constructs or imaginative experiments. Ideal types 'are necessarily relatively *empty* of contents as compared with the concrete reality of the historical'. We need them, Weber argues, to enhance our conceptual precision about meaningful action. Ideal types can and should be constructed for all sorts of meaningful behaviour whether rational or irrational. One can have an ideal type of the mystic as much as the rational businessman. In addition, to remove a possible confusion, ideal types are not 'ideal' as judged by beauty or ethics or some other criterion. One can construct an ideal type of a drug dealer, or a call-girl, or a saint.

Weber suggests that proceeding with fully rational ideal types is a better way of probing meaningful behaviour than constructing an irrational, say, an affectual motivation. In analysing the decisions of opposing generals in a battle, we run a thought experiment as if both generals were acting fully rationally, and for this a model of rational battle action would have to be devised. We then compare how far short the generals' strategy and tactics deviated from the rational model. As Weber notes, it is at this point that we can identify false information, errors, failures in thinking, temperamental factors in the personalities of the generals, and so on.

Models of perfect rationality, or, in Weber's terms, attributing instrumental rationality to people's decisions, is now a fairly commonly accepted part of social science. However, it should be emphasized that the ideal type extends to the modelling of cultural meanings. For instance, the legitimacy of rulership can be modelled. In a patrimonial rulership loyalty of an 'official' is owed to the ruler by virtue of piety and the lack of rights. Under feudalism, loyalty of a baron to the ruler is a mutual form of allegiance and is based on rights on each side. In historical reality (for example, Anglo-Norman rulership) historians will point to the co-existence of both patrimonial and feudal ideal types (if they have read Weber). In working out the causal explanation of historical individuals, Weber suggests that modelling their motivation according to separate ideal types will clarify a historian's work. Within an actual rulership (for example, the English king Henry II), different courtiers acted according to different understandings of legitimacy – some were patrimonial, others feudal in orientation. This is an important distinction in terms of developmental possibilities, for patrimonial legitimacy offers rulers a far greater capacity to centralize their rule in comparison with feudal structures. Weber offers his rationalist services to the historian to identify effective rulership strategies and so clarify what would otherwise be an unexplained muddle of behaviours. The individual causation of what historically actually happened is, however, the business of the historian to establish.

In his second subsection (see below, pp. 327–9), Weber introduces his conceptualization of social action. It excludes purely private behaviour, or economic activity that has no effect on a third party, or religious behaviour that remains private in its scope. It also excludes imitative behaviour, which as we know can be effectively caused and manipulated, for it is not meaningful on the part of the social actor. Action, then, is social when it takes into account the behaviour of other people. Social action can include inner conduct (for example, religious motivations whose outcome does affect other people). This last mentioned conduct is a methodological principle vital for the validity for Weber's whole project studying the world religions.

So far in this Introduction I have highlighted aspects of Reading 21. It should now be read in its entirety, especially since it is in itself a clear and systematic exposition of Weber's own thinking. Having done that, the reader then has to take stock of the 'learning outcome'. Weber has expounded a programme for an interpretative sociology and a methodology that makes clear the logic of his own historical and cultural studies. Let us work his Protestant ethic study (outlined in Part I) through the exposition of Reading 21 as a way of realizing the learning outcome.

The historical thesis of the Protestant ethic states that certain Puritan religious beliefs and practices were conducive to the emergence of a modern capitalistic mentality. Weber is arguing his thesis on the basis of meaningful conduct. In the controversy among historians that his thesis triggered, one of the opposing options was to argue that belief was not a relevant factor. For instance, an argument may be constructed that points to a growing population, the rise of technology, and the development of markets as adequate grounds for explaining the emergence of modern capitalism in North-west Europe. These are trends that affect human behaviour and attitudes, but do not place any great dependence on attitudes or religious values as a crucial factor in the rise of capitalism. Weber would allow hypothetically that this could have been the case, and, if this was established, there would be no point in advancing a factor based on meaning. Weber, however, saw no such alternative argument being established, hence his thesis still remained on the table.

By insisting on an argument based on the context of meaning, Weber was being counter-intuitive. The conventional wisdom of historians held that with the rise of capitalism there was a decrease in religious belief, so how could religion be a causal factor except negatively? Weber, in contrast, argues that it was precisely the intensity of Puritan beliefs that switched European capitalism into a higher phase of growth. Technology, population, cities, markets are all necessary components of the causal mix that determined the emergence of modern capitalism, but it was a rational and calculative mentality that animated those structural factors and gave modern capitalism its distinctive character.[2]

So, Weber feels more than justified in defending his interpretative method that explains to us the distinctive trait of a system which now has universal significance and global diffusion. Conventional economic historians would have overlooked or misidentified the causal variable of belief and would have left the explanation at the level of meaning obscured. The achievement of a culturally aware historical sociology, i.e. the interpretative method, pinpoints not only a crucial historical factor but one that haunts us – 'the idea of "duty in one's calling" prowls about in our lives like the ghost of dead religious beliefs' (above, p. 33).

In order to identify the factor of religion, Weber has had to employ his ideal-type method to isolate and clarify Puritan beliefs in their everyday practice. Religious historians and theologians, by contrast, would have entered into the sheer complexity of belief systems without any intellectual sharpening of factors that in respect of economic development (a matter of sheer unconcern to such historians) would have remained unnoticed.

In the opening paragraph to his Prefatory Remarks to his studies in the sociology of religion (above, p. 109), Weber announces that the rise of the West can be accounted for only in terms of a combination of factors. How then can Weber establish his meaningful cause (religion) as crucial in relation to the many other possible and interrelating factors? Weber's reply to this, an issue which so far we have not discussed, is that there is no objective way to do this. There is no nomological realm of science that will identify each and every cause and weight its efficacy in respect of a defined outcome. Here we need to return to the analogy of legal culpability. Historians and sociologists are, so to speak, members of a scientific court who in devising their questions restrict the number and presentation of possible causes. In an actual court of law there are numerous accidental factors that could have caused, say, a road accident. Had one of the drivers involved in a crash not woken up late because her alarm clock failed to function, she would not have been at the particular place of the accident when it occurred. But this is excluded as irrelevant to the deliberations of the court. Likewise with social and historical scientists, who allow only so many factors or causes to be debated using specific rules. In Reading 22, Weber argues at length that academic issues are selected from the infinite complexity of past and current reality on the basis of relevance and interest to the scientist.

Methodology can help with the attribution of cause. Again in his Prefatory Remarks Weber elaborates his comparative studies as a way of isolating the distinctive rationalism of the West. The research is designed to examine cases (India, China, Antiquity) where rationalism, as defined by Weber, is absent.

---

2 For this point, I am indebted to Ola Agevall's *A Science of Unique Events. Max Weber's Methodology of the Cultural Sciences*, Uppsala, Uppsala University Press, 1999, pp. 231–46.

Where there is a rough equivalence of a civilization in terms of population, cities, markets, technology, we can then gauge the efficacy of the missing factor. Weber does not claim to have proven the causal role of rationalism in the rise of the West, but rather to have established it against opposing explanations. What in reality has occurred belongs to the world of individual events, the only level where truth can be established.

Finally, what are we supposed to learn from the basic sociological concepts? In the case of the Protestant ethic thesis we have been working with a historical or genetic ideal type. Within a given historical situation these genetic types can marshal the causes and meanings and allow attribution. What is the function of the more abstract basic concepts? As a basic concept, Puritan ethics correspond to value-rationality, which as a social action type is clearly differentiated from other types. Rational action oriented to a goal whose value lies beyond question is a distinctive characteristic in a great many societies. Reform movements in any religion are a form of value-rationality whose consequences for a society (and neighbouring societies) are often far-reaching. In this way, basic concepts can operate as an aid in the orientation of research. As already noted, they also serve as a reminder to treat all institutions, structures and societies in terms of social relationships, not as pre-formed entities.

Reading 22 (The 'Objectivity' of Knowledge in Social Science and Social Policy) was written in 1904 as Weber was publishing *The Protestant Ethic and the Spirit of Capitalism*. It is one of the great essays of scientific humanism, defending the case for scientific method but attacking the pretensions of the derivation of social behaviour from laws or lawlike statements – even though it starts as a pragmatic guide for policy science and was written on the occasion of Weber, Jaffé, and Sombart's assumption of the editorship of the *Archiv für Sozialwissenschaft und Sozialpolitik*. Weber persistently attacks the confusion of the two levels of statements of law and statements of empirical fact that occurs in a great many guises: the German historical school, monism, Marxism, idealism, marginalist economics and psychology, Hegelianism, and evolutionism. In arguing for a science of reality that will elucidate the role of cultural meaning in socio-economic processes, Weber, in this essay, indicated his reliance on the 'neo-Kantian' writings of his colleagues Simmel, Windelband, and Rickert. These authors emphasized the gulf – far more than a neutral dualism – between an infinitely complex empirical reality and its knowability through laws and conceptual constructions. Indeed the gulf, for them, was unbridgeable and they often referred to it as an irrational hiatus – a kind of epistemic tear in the fabric of the world. Faced with this, the best we can do is construe reality according to our cultural interests.

The label 'neo-Kantian' is slightly misleading in that Kant's epistemology (the theory of how we obtain valid knowledge of the world) was designed specifically to overcome the scepticism that the world was ultimately unknowable to the human mind. Kant devised solutions to the problem of knowing the world, and to the validation of morals, that were in part rationalist in inspiration. Neo-Kantianism, with its insistence on the particularity of the cultural world and its denial of universal statements, opens the door to both cognitive and moral relativism. The heroic features of the 'Objectivity' essay – in 'scare' quotes because there is no final court of objectivity – is an acceptance of this condition as well as firmly shutting the door to both kinds of relativism. At the end of the essay Weber reveals his mentors: Kant for whom concepts are the cognitive means of mastering empirical reality; Nietzsche (unnamed): 'The light given off by these highest evaluative ideas falls upon an ever-changing finite part of the monstrously chaotic stream of events that flows through time.' And Goethe, the exemplar of holding a light to reveal new cultural problematics in a world knowable only in its uncertainties.

21 Basic sociological concepts[1]

Preamble. No claim of novelty is made for the method employed in these introductory conceptual definitions. It would however be imprudent to forgo them, notwithstanding their inevitably abstract character, and their disengagement from reality. They do in fact merely seek to clarify, somewhat pedantically perhaps, the actual meaning of expressions commonly found in empirical sociology when referring to the same problems, rendering these terms more appropriate and precise. This is also the case when apparently unfamiliar or new expressions are employed. The terminology has been simplified as far as possible by comparison with my *Logos* essay,[2] and has therefore been altered in many respects to make it as easy to understand as possible. None the less, the demands of unconditional popularization could not always be reconciled with the need for conceptual precision, and in such cases the former has had to give way to the latter.

On 'understanding' ('*Verstehen*') see Jaspers' *General Psychopathology*, together with some remarks by Rickert in the second edition of his *The Limits of Concept Formation in the Natural Sciences* (1913, pp. 514–23) and by Simmel in *Problems of Historical Philosophy*. With respect to the methodology I refer the reader here, as elsewhere, to that followed by Gottl in his *Dominion of the Word*, not the most well-written and easily understood of texts, and certainly in places not fully thought through; for the subject-matter see F. Tönnies' admirable book *Community and Civil Society*. See also the very misleading book by R. Stammler, *Economy and Law in the Materialist Conception of History*, together with my critique in the *Archiv für Sozialwissenschaft und Sozialpolitik*, vol. 24 (1907), which contains the foundations of much that follows here. I deviate from the method adopted by Simmel in his *Sociology* and *Philosophy of Money* in that I make as clear as possible a distinction between *intended* and objectively *valid* 'meaning' ('*Sinn*'), a distinction which Simmel not only sometimes fails to make, but often deliberately runs together.

---

1 Ch. 1 of *WuG*, pp. 1–30. Translation by Keith Tribe.
2 The *Logos* essay was published in 1913 and represents Weber's first approach in defining sociological concepts. It has been translated by Edith E. Graber: 'Some Categories of Interpretive Sociology', *The Sociological Quarterly*, 22, 1981, pp. 151–80.

§1. **Sociology**, a word often used in quite diverse ways, shall mean here: a science which seeks interpretative understanding (*deutend verstehen*) of social action, and thereby will causally explain its course and effects. By 'action' is meant human behaviour linked to a subjective *meaning (Sinn)* on the part of the actor or actors concerned; such behaviour may be overt or occur inwardly – whether by positive action, or by refraining from such action, or by acquiescence to some situation. Such behaviour is 'social' action where the meaning intended by actor or actors is related to the behaviour of *others*, and conduct so oriented.

I Methodological foundations

1. 'Meaning' is here either:

(a) an actual, subjectively *intended*, meaning

   (i) occurring in a historically given instance in respect of one actor, or
   (ii) approximating to the average among a given number of instances on the part of several actors; alternatively it is a

(b) subjective meaning conceived as a *pure*, conceptual type ascribed to the behaviour of one, or several, *hypothetical* actors.

But not, for instance, some kind of objectively 'correct' meaning, or one founded metaphysically upon some 'real' meaning. In this there lies the difference between the empirical sciences of action – of sociology and of history – and those dogmatic sciences, such as jurisprudence, logic, ethics, aesthetics, which seek 'true' and 'valid' meanings in their objects of study.

2. An extremely fluid border separates meaningful action from what is here called solely reactive behaviour, which is unrelated to subjectively intended meaning. A very significant part of all sociologically relevant behaviour, especially purely traditional action (see below), is placed directly on this border. Meaningful action, in other words action that can be understood, is often entirely absent from psycho-physical events, or is in other cases only evident to the specialist. Mystical events, by definition only incompletely communicable in words, cannot be fully understood by those untouched by such experiences. By contrast, one's capacity to replicate an action does not imply its understanding: 'One need not be Caesar to understand Caesar.' Being able to 'relive' an experience ('*Nacher-lebbarkeit*') plays an important part in forming an understanding, but is not an absolute condition of the determination of meaning. Often the under-standable and the non-understandable elements of an event are blended and related.

3. All interpretation seeks 'evidence'[3] – this is common to all the sciences. Evidence of understanding can be either

(a) of a rational character (and as such either logical or mathematical); or:
(b) founded upon an empathetic re-experiencing, or artistically appreciative in character.

In the domain of action, rational evidence primarily takes the form of a complete, unclouded *intellectual* understanding of the context of an intended meaning. Empathetic evidence consists in the empathetic realization of an emotional context. Rational understanding (defined here as meaning which is, directly and unambiguously, intellectually accessible) occurs for the most part with respect to meaningful contexts created by the relation of mathematical or logical propositions. We understand the meaning quite unambiguously when someone, in thought or in argument, employs the proposition $2 \times 2 = 4$, or makes use of Pythagoras' theorem, or 'correctly' completes a chain of reasoning – correct that is to our way of thinking. We likewise understand if, for given ends, someone uses 'facts of experience' that we 'know' to be valid in selecting those 'means' that are in our experience uniquely appropriate to his action. Any such interpretation of rationally oriented instrumental behaviour possesses – for an understanding of the *means* employed – the greatest amount of evidence. A lesser degree of evidence, but one quite sufficient for our need for explanation, is used to understand 'errors' (including here problems whose elements have become entangled one with another) to which we ourselves might be liable, or whose origins can be empathetically realized. On the other hand, our understanding of many of the ultimate 'aims' and 'values' to which, in our experience, human action can be oriented is not fully evident. We are sometimes only capable of taking account of them intellectually; and the more radical the divergence of such ultimate values from our own, the greater also our difficulty in understanding them through imaginative *re-experiencing*. We must then, as circumstance dictates, be satisfied with an intellectual interpretation; or, failing that, simply accept them as givens, making the best of such intellectual or empathetic re-experiencing as can be mustered in understanding the course which action motivated by them takes. Among these belong, for example, many acts of religious or charitable virtuosity whose motivating force is inaccessible to those not susceptible to such values, or extreme, rationalistic fanaticism (involving, for instance, 'human rights') whose standpoint eludes those who have radically repudiated its mandate. The more we ourselves are open to emotional reactions such as anxiety, anger, ambition, envy, jealousy, love, enthusiasm, pride, vengefulness, piety, dedication, desires of every sort, and their (from the standpoint of

---

3 Weber uses 'evidence' in the sense of intuitively obvious or self-evident and his use does not indicate forensic or empirical verification.

instrumentally rational action) irrational consequences, the greater the degree
to which we emotionally understand them; and even when they far exceed our
own capacities in intensity we are none the less able to empathize with them,
and take account intellectually of the orientation and chosen means of action
motivated by them.

A *typological* scientific approach in general treats all irrational, emotionally determined, meaningful behavioural contexts influencing action as
'deviations' from a pure construct of instrumentally rational action. For
example: explanation of the course taken by a stock exchange panic will first
establish what *would* have happened if action had *not* been influenced by
irrational emotions, following which these irrational elements are introduced
as 'disturbances'. Similarly, in the case of a political or military action it
would first be established how things *would* have developed if the action
taken had been informed by complete knowledge of circumstances and
participants' intentions, consequently selecting those instrumentally rational
means which in our experience appeared most appropriate. Only after this
has been done is it possible to impute causal influence to those irrationalities
which determine deviations from this construct. This construct of rigorous,
instrumentally rational action therefore furthers the evident clarity and
understandability of a sociology whose lucidity is founded upon rationality.
In this way a *type* is presented ('ideal type') from which real action, influenced
by all manner of irrationalities (emotions, errors), can be presented as a
'deviation' from processes directed by purely rational conduct.

The method of an 'interpretative' sociology is 'rationalistic' only in this
strictly *limited* sense, out of regard for methodological convenience. In no
respect does this approach reflect sociology's rationalistic disposition, it is
just a methodological procedure; it should not be thought to imply a belief
that life is really governed by rational factors. It suggests absolutely nothing
about the extent to which, in reality, *actual* action might or might not be
determined by a rational evaluation of ends. (Which is not to deny that there
is a constant danger of misplaced rationalistic interpretations. Experience,
unfortunately, shows this to be all too manifest.)

4. Events and objects which are devoid of meaning are considered by all
sciences of action with respect to the manner in which they stimulate, or
result from, foster or inhibit human action. 'Devoid of meaning' is not the
same as 'lifeless' or 'non-human'. Every artefact, for instance, a machine, can
only be interpreted and understood by reference to the meaning which
human action of quite diverse kinds lends, or sought to lend, to its production and use; in the absence of such reference the artefact remains entirely
beyond understanding. What is therefore here 'understood' is the relation of
the artefact to human *action*, as a 'means' or as an 'end' envisaged by actor or
actors, and to which their actions are oriented. Understanding of such
objects can *only* be effected through these categories. By contrast, all events
or circumstances – animate or inanimate, human or non-human – without an
intended meaning remain senseless so long as they *cannot* be related to the

'means' and 'ends' of action, but merely stimulate or foster or inhibit such action. Perhaps the flooding of the Dollart in the late thirteenth century had 'historical' significance, prompting a pattern of resettlement which had considerable historical significance.[4] Mortality and the life cycle, from the helplessness of the child to that of the elderly, naturally has pre-eminent sociological significance on account of the different ways in which human action has been, and is, oriented to this existential fact. Or again, statements devoid of meaning regarding the experience of physical or psycho-physical episodes such as fatigue, habituation, memory and so on belong to the same class of phenomena, together with, for instance, euphoric states typical of certain forms of ascetic mortification, or typical differences in speed, form and precision of modes of reaction. Ultimately, the substantive content here is the same as with any other class of factor which cannot be understood: they are treated as 'data' by both pragmatic actor and sociological understanding.

It is possible that future research might find regularities that *cannot* be understood underlying apparently *meaning*ful action, although this remains a discovery yet to be made. Hereditary biological differences (between 'races'), for example, would have to be accepted by sociology as given data if statistically persuasive proof were produced indicating their influence upon the form taken by sociologically relevant behaviour – that is, social action in its relation to *meaning*. Such acceptance would be equivalent to that granted to physiological facts such as the nature of nutritional need or the effect of ageing on action. Recognition of its causal significance would not of course alter the task of sociology, and of the sciences of action, in the slightest; this would remain, as before, the interpretative understanding of meaningfully oriented action. *Non*-interpretable facts would simply be introduced at certain points into the interpretative understanding of motivational contexts. (For instance, it may be discovered that particular goal-directed action, or the degree of its typical rationality, interrelates with a typical frequency with cephalic index, skin colour or any other kind of physiologically heritable characteristic.)

5. Understanding can mean:

(a) the *direct* and *immediate* (*aktuell*) understanding of the intended meaning of an action, including a verbal utterance. Our 'understanding' of the meaning of the proposition $2 \times 2 = 4$ is immediate in this sense, since we hear or read it (the rationally immediate understanding of thoughts). We understand in like fashion a fit of anger manifested in a facial expression, in an interjection, or an irrational movement (the irrationally immediate understanding of emotions). Similarly, we understand the behaviour of a woodcutter, or someone who reaches for the handle of a door, or who

---

4 In 1277 the dykes at the mouth of the River Ems in the Low Countries burst.

aims a gun at an animal (the rationally immediate understanding of actions). But understanding can also mean:

(b) *explanatory* understanding. We 'understand' the *motivational* meaning attached by the person expressing, or writing, the proposition $2 \times 2 = 4$ moving him *to do* just this now and in this context, if we see him to be involved in an accounting calculation, a scientific demonstration, a technical computation or some other kind of action in the context of which this proposition 'belongs' in a *sense* that we understand. In other words: it acquires a *contextual* meaning that we understand (rational understanding of motivation). We understand the chopping of wood not only directly, but motivationally, if we know that the forester is working for a wage, or is pursuing his own needs, or is simply taking some exercise (rational); or that he is possibly working off a fit of anger (irrational). Likewise we understand the aiming of a gun motivationally if we know that the rifleman is under orders as part of a firing squad, or firing at enemies (rational); or that he is acting out of revenge (emotional, and therefore in this sense irrational). Finally, we understand motivationally a fit of anger if we know that jealousy, affronted vanity, or wounded honour underlie it (emotionally determined, hence motivationally irrational). All of these are understandable *contexts of meaning* (*Sinnzusammenhänge*), understanding of which we treat as an *explanation* of the actual course taken by an action. For a science concerned with the meaning of action, 'explanation' amounts to: identification of the meaning *context* to which a directly understandable action belongs, corresponding to its subjectively intended meaning. (See the following section, no. 6, for clarification of the causal significance of this 'explanation'.) In all of these cases, including emotional events, we shall call the subjective meaning of such episodes, together with their context of meaning, their 'intended' meaning ('*gemeinten*' *Sinn*). This goes beyond common usage, where 'intention' generally refers only to rational and instrumentally intentional action.

6. In all these cases 'understanding' denotes the interpretative grasp of

(a) what was historically actually intended in an individual instance, or
(b) what a broadly based sociological assessment might conclude was a probable and likely intention, or
(c) a *pure* type constructed scientifically out of a frequently recurring phenomenon, an 'ideal type' of an intended meaning, or meaning context.

Ideal-typical constructions of this kind are, for instance, those concepts and 'laws' developed in pure economic theory. They represent the course which a particular sort of human action *would* follow *if* its instrumental rationality were rigorously formulated, its execution undisturbed by error and emotion, and *if* moreover it were quite unambiguously oriented to one (economic) objective. Only in rare cases (for example, the stock exchange) does action in reality follow this course, and then only as an approximation to that defined by the ideal type. (On the purpose of such constructions see my article 'The "Objectivity" of Knowledge in Social Science and Social Policy', *Archiv für Sozialwissenschaft und Sozialpolitik*, Bd. 19, 1904, pp. 64ff.)[5]

All interpretation seeks evidence (see (3) above). An interpretation whose meaning is evident cannot however, simply by virtue of this, claim to be a causally *valid* interpretation. It remains instead only an especially evident causal *hypothesis*.

(a) supposed 'motives', and 'repressed factors' such as unacknowledged motives, often enough conceal from the actor himself the real context forming his action, to such a degree that only limited value can be attached to sincere personal expression of an actor's motivation. Sociology has here the task of identifying this context and establishing its appropriate interpretation, *although* this context has not, or usually has only incompletely, been fixed in *consciousness* as something which was definitely 'intended'. This is a borderline instance of the interpretation of meaning.

(b) External properties of action which appear to us as 'the same' or 'similar' can have quite different contextual meanings for an actor or actors, and we 'understand' varied, and sometimes quite contrasting, actions on the basis of situations which we regard as in themselves to be alike. (See the examples given by Simmel in his *Probleme der Geschichtsphilosophie*.)

(c) Acting human beings very often find themselves, in given situations, driven by contradictory imperatives that we 'understand'. All experience tells us that very often we cannot be certain – in many cases we cannot even begin to form a judgement – of the relative *strength* with which meanings underlying this motivational conflict are expressed in action, meanings which are nevertheless to us *equally* intelligible. Only the actual outcome of this motivational struggle clarifies this. As with every hypothesis, it is vital that the evaluation and reappraisal of our understanding of interpretative meaning is made on the basis of the eventual real outcome. This can be done more or less precisely only in those (unfortunately very few) special cases suited to psychological experiments. Variable degrees of approximation can be achieved in a similarly limited number of cases of mass phenomena susceptible to numerical representation and exact statistical calculation. For the remainder, the only option is a comparison of as many historical or everyday events as possible. Although these might be otherwise very similar, they can be differentiated by *one* significant factor: according to the practical significance of the 'motive' or 'impulse' that closer investigation discloses. This

5 Translated in this volume; see below, pp. 387–8.

is an important task for a comparative sociology. Unfortunately, we are often compelled to employ the uncertain means of 'thought experiments' in imputing a cause, simplifying *in thought* by eliminating some elements of a motivational chain and constructing out of this its probable course.

What is known as Gresham's Law,[6] for example, is a rationally evident interpretation of human action under given conditions and assuming ideal-typical instrumentally rational action. How far action does *in fact* correspond to this law is a matter for experience, ultimately for statistical estimation: the actual disappearance of undervalued coinage from circulation. In this case experience shows the general validity of this principle. Cognition here took the following path: *firstly* observations based upon experience existed, subsequent to which an interpretation was formulated. In the absence of an adequate interpretation our need to identify a causal mechanism would remain unsatisfied. On the other hand, without proof that a theoretically predicted course of events does in fact occur to some sort of degree, even such an apparently substantive law would be a worthless construct for knowledge of real actions. In this case the coincidence of meaningfulness and empirical test is quite persuasive, and instances are numerous enough to treat the test as having been met satisfactorily. To take a different example, Eduard Meyer has put forward an inspired hypothesis concerning the causal significance of the battles of Marathon, Salamis, and Platea for the specific developmental character of Greek, and therefore occidental, culture. His hypothesis proceeds from symptomatic events – the behaviour of Greek oracles and prophets towards the Persians – that are open to meaningful elucidation, and can be verified only by reference to the behaviour of Persians in cases where they were victorious (Jerusalem, Egypt, Asia Minor), and in many respects it must remain incomplete.[7] Resort therefore has to be made to the general plausibility and rationality of the hypothesis itself. But in many cases, even such seemingly plausible (*evident*) historical imputations cannot be tested in the limited manner possible here. Consequently, imputation necessarily there remains a matter of 'hypothesis'.

7. A 'motive' is the meaningful context (*Sinnzusammenhang*) which appears, to the actor himself or to an observer, as the significant 'reason' for a

---

6 Generally known as 'bad money drives out good', the 'law' suggests that where coins of differing base metal content circulate at equal face values, the more 'valuable' coins will tend to be withdrawn from circulation.

7 Meyer's argument is that the Greek oracles made a decisive contribution to stiffening Greek resistance to the Persian invasion. Weber's point is that its crucial significance can only be estimated by comparison with cases where the oracles played no such role. See Volume 4, Book 2 of Eduard Meyer's *Geschichte des Altertums*, Stuttgart, Cott'sche Buchhandlung, 1944, pp. 340ff. (1st edn, 1900). Weber makes the same point at greater length in his essay on Eduard Meyer, 'The Logic of the Cultural Sciences', in *MSS*, p. 138.

mode of behaviour. We consider contextual conduct of this kind to be 'mean-ingfully adequate', according to our usual ways of thinking and feeling, to the extent that we consider the relationship between its elements form a typically meaningful context – or, as we usually say, the 'correct' context. 'Causal adequacy' by contrast refers to a sequence of events where it is known from *experience* that in all likelihood (*Chance*) the sequence will recur in exactly the same manner. (In these terms we understand by *meaning*fully adequate for instance our usual *norms* for calculating or conceiving *correct* solutions to an arithmetical problem. Causal adequacy on the other hand concerns the statistical probability that there exists – or rather, that by applying the usual rules we know from experience that the probability exists – a 'correct' and a 'false' solution, in the form of a typical 'calculation mistake' or 'procedural confusion.') Causal explanation therefore involves the idea that some degree of probability exists – ideally (although rarely) exactly quantifiable – that one particular observed (internal or external) event will be succeeded by another particular event (or will occur at the same time).

Correct causal *interpretation* of a concrete action requires its apparent course and motive to be *accurately* recognized and meaningfully *understood* in context. A correct causal interpretation of a *typical* action (those actions open to understanding) requires that the origin typically claimed for such action appears to a degree both meaningfully adequate, and that this origin can to some extent also be described as causally adequate. In the absence of such meaningful adequacy we have only an *incomprehensible* (or incompletely understandable) *statistical* probability, even where there is a very significant, precisely quantifiable probability of a regular event occurring (whether overt or psychic). By contrast, even the most unambiguous meaningful adequacy has significance for sociological knowledge only to the extent that a correct causal statement, as proof of the existence of a (somehow specifiable) *likelihood* that the action *in fact tends* to take an apparently meaningful course with specifiable frequency, or something close to it (either on average, or in a 'pure' case), can be instanced. Only those statistical regularities which correspond to the *understandably* intended meaning of a social action are in the sense used here understandable types of action, i.e. 'sociological rules'. Only such rational constructions of meaningfully intelligible action are sociological types of real events observable in reality to some degree. It is certainly not the case that in parallel with the degree of inferred meaningful adequacy the actual likelihood of frequency of the corresponding events *always* increases. Whether or not this occurs must be demonstrated for each instance through external experience. There are *statistics* for events lacking *meaning* (mortality statistics, statistics on fatigue, machine performance statistics, rainfall statistics) in exactly the same way that there are meaningful statistics. *Sociological* statistics on the other hand (crime statistics, occupational statistics, price statistics, tillage statistics) are composed of only the latter sort (with cases that include *both* being of course frequent: crop statistics, for instance).

8. Processes and regularities not amenable to understanding are not 'sociological events' or rules in the sense used here, but are of course no less *important* on this account. This also goes for sociology as defined here, a definition which limits it to a 'sociology of *understanding*' which cannot be, ought not be, forced upon anyone. They move instead – methodologically quite unavoidably – into a category distinct from that of intelligible action: the 'conditions', 'causes', 'inhibitions' and 'promoters' of such action.

9. Action, in the sense of meaningfully understandable orientation of one's own behaviour, is for us always understood as the behaviour of one or more *individual* persons.

It may be useful or necessary for other cognitive ends to conceive of this individual as, for example, a consociation of 'cells' or as a complex of bio-chemical reactions, or consider his 'psychic' life as one composed of individual elements, however these might be qualified. Important things are learned in this way about, for example, causal rules. But we do not *understand* the behaviour of these elements and the rules which express it. This is also true of psychic elements, and in fact the more scientifically exact their expression, the *less* we understand them; this never opens a path to the interpretation of an intended meaning. For sociology in the sense used here, as for history, the object under consideration is the *meaning* with which behaviour is endowed. We can (at least in principle) observe the behaviour of physiological units, of cells, for example, or some form of psychic elements; or seek to derive rules ('laws') based upon such observation with the aid of which we can arrive at causal 'explanations' of discrete processes, which means: subsume them under a rule. However, the interpretation of action pays as much regard to these facts and rules as it does to any other meaningless psychopathological events, or the scientific conditions of technical events – whether physical, astronomical, geological, meteorological, geographic, botanic, zoological, physiological, or anatomical.

For other cognitive purposes such as in law, or for purely practical ends, it might be useful (and indeed unavoidable) to treat social constructs (*Gebilde*) (the 'state', 'association', 'companies', 'charitable foundations') as if they were individual persons with rights and duties, or as the performers of legally relevant action. For the interpretative understanding of action by means of sociology these constructs remain merely processes and specific behavioural relationships on the part of *individual* people, since for us these are the sole understandable agents (*Träger*) of meaningfully oriented action. But of course even for its own ends sociology cannot simply *ignore* the collective thought constructs of other intellectual perspectives. For the interpretation of action has a threefold relationship to these collective concepts:

(a) It is itself often compelled to operate with very similar collective concepts, frequently characterized in exactly the same way in order that some kind of intelligible *terminology* can be established. Thus, for instance, in both legal and everyday language the term 'state' is used both as a legal *concept* and in referring to the circumstances of social action which should be governed by legal rules. As far as sociology is concerned the object 'state' is by no means necessarily constructed from *legal* components. And in any case sociology does not recognize the existence of 'acting' collective personalities. If it talks about the 'state', or the 'nation', or a 'commercial company', or a 'family', or an 'army corps' or any other similar kind of construct, then this *solely* refers to a specifically conditional sequence of actual, or conceivable, social actions on the part of individuals, imputing a completely different meaning to a legal concept which is employed for the sake of its precision and familiarity.

(b) The interpretation of action has to acknowledge a fundamental and important fact: that the *conceptions* associated with a collective construct – whether drawn from everyday thought or derived from some specialized discipline, such as the law – are related to things which real people (not just judges and officials, but also the wider 'public') think of as both positively and normatively existent. Their action is *oriented* in accordance with such conceptions, and they have a powerful, indeed often overwhelming, causal significance for the type and course of action on the part of real people. This is especially true of conceptions relating to what should or should not exist. (A modern 'state' is to a great extent of this sort – as a complex arising out of the mutual action of men – *because* specific men and women orient their action in regard to their *conception* that the state exists in this form, or *should* exist in this form; that in other words legally oriented regulations of this kind *have validity*. More about this later.) While it would be possible, if extremely pedantic and long-winded, for sociology to completely eliminate from its language such legal and commonly used terminology and replace them with neologisms, this could not be done in this important instance.

(c) The methodology of so-called 'organic' sociology (classically represented by Schäffle's stimulating book, *The Structure and Life of the Social Body*) seeks to explain mutual social action by starting with the 'whole' (for example, an 'economy'), and proceeding to interpret the individual and his behaviour in much the same way that physiology relates the location of an anatomical 'organ' within the 'household economy' of the organism, considering it, for instance, as an element contributing to the maintenance of the whole. (As when a physiologist states in a lecture: 'Section Ten: The Spleen. We know nothing about the spleen, gentlemen. That deals with the spleen.' In fact he knew rather a lot about the spleen: its position, size, shape, and so on. But he could not say what its 'function' was, and this incapacity he called 'knowing nothing'.) How far this kind of *functional* consideration of the relation between '*parts*' and a '*whole*' is definitive for other disciplines cannot be discussed here; we know that the biochemical and the biomechanical perspective are quite unwilling to stop at this. For an interpretative sociology this much can be said:

1   This functional frame of reference serves for practical illustration and provisional orientation (and is as such extremely useful and necessary, although it must be said that an overestimation of its cognitive value and a faulty conceptual realism (*Begriffsrealismus*) can have very detrimental effects). And

2   In some circumstances this is the sole way of identifying social action whose interpretative understanding is *important* for the explanation of context. But the task of sociology (as understood here) simply *begins* at this point. In the case of 'social forms' (and in contrast to 'organisms') we can rise above the mere registration of functional relationships and rules ('laws') typical of all 'natural science' (where causal laws are established for events and patterns, and individual events then 'explained' on this basis) and achieve something quite inaccessible to natural science: namely, an '*understanding*' of the behaviour of participating *individuals*, whereas we do *not* for example 'understand' the behaviour of cells, but merely register them functionally, and then determine their activity by reference to *rules*. The superiority of interpretative over observational explanation is of course bought at the cost of the substantially more hypothetical and fragmentary character of its results. None the less: *this* is what is specific to sociological knowledge.

The extent to which we find the behaviour of animals meaningfully 'understandable', and vice versa (both of these of a very uncertain nature and of problematic scope) must here remain unexamined. Hence likewise the extent to which there can be a sociology of the relation of humans to animals (whether pets or hunting animals) – many animals 'understand' commands, anger, love, hostility, and quite obviously often do not react to these in an exclusively mechanical and instinctive way, but with respect to some consciousness of meaning and experience. The extent of our empathy for the behaviour of 'primitive men' ('*Naturmenschen*') is certainly no greater. But we either lack any *certain* means of establishing subjective content for an animal, or can assess it only in a very incomplete way – the problems of animal psychology are known to be both interesting and riddled with pitfalls. Animals associate of course in the most varied manner: monogamous and polygamous 'families', herds, packs, even functionally structured 'states'. (The degree of functional differentiation of these animal associations is unrelated to the degree of physical or morphological development of the species concerned. The functional differentiation displayed by termites and consequently that of their artefacts is more highly differentiated than is the case for ants and bees.) In these cases the purely functional perspective establishes what, for the time being, is the most definitive knowledge attainable by research: ascertaining the conditions for the preservation of animal societies (their sustenance, defence, reproduction, and social reconstitution) together with the functions of specific types of individuals – 'kings', queens', 'workers', 'soldiers', 'drones', 'propagators', 'surrogate queens', and so on. Anything beyond this was for a long time mere speculation, or studies of the degree to which heredity or environment contributed to the development of these 'social' proclivities. (This marked the controversy between Weismann and Götte: Weismann claimed an 'omnipotence of natural selection' underpinned in fact by deductions made with little empirical foundation.) Genuine scientific research assumes that this necessary restriction to functional knowledge is merely provisional. (See, for instance, the state of termite research in Escherich 1909.[8]) One would wish to go beyond the relatively simple registration of a functional importance of individually differentiated types and its relation to preservation of the whole; together with attempts to explain – without resort to an assumption that acquired characteristics are inherited, or, if making such an assumption, the manner it might be interpreted – how such differentiation might be explained. We need also to know

(a) what *determines* the specific form assumed by the differentiation of an originally neutral, undifferentiated individual;
(b) what *moves* the differentiated individual to behave on the average in such a way as to actually further the interest in survival of the differentiated group.

Wherever research has made any progress then it was through experiments with *solitary* individuals, demonstrating, or hypothesizing, the presence of chemical stimulation, or physiological circumstances such as nutritional procedures or parasitic castration. Today only an expert could judge the degree to which there might be hope of substantiating experimentally 'psychological' or 'meaningful' orientation. The idea that we could have a verifiable image of the psyche of these individual social animals founded upon meaningful 'understanding' seems scarcely attainable even as an ideal objective. We cannot expect an 'understanding' of human social action from this direction, rather the reverse: human analogies are used in such research, and must continue so. But we might perhaps expect that these analogies will become of use to us in posing the question: how in the early stages of human social differentiation we might judge the relation between *instinctive* mechanical differentiation and the domain of individual meaningful understanding and hence *conscious* rationally formed differentiation. An interpretative sociology has to be quite clear on this point: that in the early stages of human development the first of these factors is entirely dominant, and in later stages a sociology of this kind must continue to register their constant and decisive influence. 'Traditional' action (see §2) and large areas of 'charisma'[9] (wherein lie the seeds of psychic 'contagion' and hence sociological

8 Karl Escherich, *Die Termiten oder weissen Ameisen.*
9 See above, pp. 138–45.

spurs to developmental processes) are in fact very close to those phenomena conceivable only in biological terms and which are either inaccessible to interpretative understanding and motivational explanation, or if in some way accessible, then only in a very fragmentary fashion. But none of this absolves a sociology of *Verstehen* from its obligation to do what it alone *can* do, conscious as it is of the narrow limits to which it is confined.

The various works of Othmar Spann – often full of suggestive ideas alongside occasional misunderstandings and, above all, arguments based upon value-judgements not accessible to empirical investigation – have quite rightly laid emphasis upon the importance for any sociology of a *preliminary* functional orientation, a 'universalistic method' (his terms) disputed by no one. We certainly need to know first of all what kind of action is functionally *important* for 'survival' (and more, the maintenance of a specific 'cultural type'!), together with its importance for a deliberate development of a type of social action. Then we can pose the question: How does this action come about? What motives define it? One first has to know what a 'king', or an 'official', or a 'businessman', 'pimp' or 'magician' *does*. It is important to know for any analysis with what typical 'action' we are dealing that stamps the action as one of the preceding categories, and this has to be decided before analysis can be initiated in H. Rickert's sense of 'value-relation'. It is only this sort of analysis that accomplishes what sociology should and can perform – the sociological understanding of action of typically differentiated individual human beings (and *only* human beings). We should discount the monstrous misapprehension that an 'individualistic' *method* involves an individualistic *evaluation* of *any* kind, just as we preclude the view that the inevitably rational character of *concept* formation involves a belief in the *primacy* of rational motives, or even a positive *evaluation* of 'rationalism'. Even a socialist economy has to be interpretatively *understood* 'individualistically', on the basis of the *actions* of *individuals*, the types of functionaries that emerge in it; just as exchange transactions are understood by marginal utility theory (or a yet-to-be-found 'better' alternative method which in *this* respect has a similar method). For even there the most significant empirical sociological work always begins with the question: Which motives *determined* and *do determine* the individual functionaries and members of this 'association' to behave in such a way that the association was *created*, and *continues to exist*? All functional concept formation which begins at the level of the 'whole' is only a *preliminary* for such an investigation, a preparation whose utility and indispensability – if done properly – no one can dispute.

10. It is usual to call some principles of interpretative sociology 'laws', Gresham's 'Law', for example. These represent the typical *likelihood* (substantiated from observation) that under given circumstances we might *expect* a certain pattern of social action which can in turn be *understood* in terms of the typical motives and typical intentions of the actor. Where instrumentally rational motives underlie the typically observed pattern – or underlie the

methodologically constructed type employed for heuristic ends – such action is both exceptionally intelligible and unambiguous. In such cases experience will clearly identify the relation between means and ends (where, for instance, the choice of means was 'inevitable'). In this case we might say: *if* action is strictly instrumentally rational, *then* action *has to take this course and no other* (for the participants, in pursuing their explicit ends, can for 'technical' reasons avail themselves of these and no other means). This goes to show how wrong it is to regard some form of 'psychology' as the ultimate foundation of an interpretative sociology. Each has his own understanding of 'psychology' today. The quite specific methodological aims of a natural scientific study of particular processes justifies the separation of the 'physical' from the 'psychic', a separation which is *in this* sense quite alien to the specialist study of action. The results of a 'psychic' science working *solely* in terms of natural scientific method (whatever form this took), and hence *not* along the same lines as a psychology of human behaviour and its intended *meaning*, could of course have quite specific consequences for sociological investigation, and has done so to an important extent. But in this it is just the same as any other science. But sociology's relation to psychology is *not* generally any closer than to any other discipline. The mistake lies in the concept of the 'psychic': what is not 'physical' is supposed to be 'psychic'. But the *meaning* of an arithmetical calculation which someone makes is of course not 'psychic'. When a person makes a rational assessment of whether the anticipated outcomes a particular course of action advance or injure specific given interests, and according to the result of this assessment makes a particular decision, no 'psychological' considerations will make this process a jot more intelligible. Sociology, and economics, construct most of their 'laws' on just such rational assumptions. By contrast an *interpretative* psychology can do a great deal to explain the *irrationalities* of action. But that does not alter the fundamental methodological position in any respect.

11. Sociology constructs concepts of *types* and seeks *general* rules in events – this much has been repeatedly assumed in the foregoing. This contrasts with the manner in which history is oriented to the causal analysis and imputation of *individual* and *cultural* significance to actions, constructs, and personalities. Conceptual formation in sociology takes its *material* largely, but not wholly, from realities of action also encountered in the historical perspective. In forming its constructs and seeking their rules it *also* considers whether, in so doing, it can be of any service to causal historical imputation in respect of important cultural phenomena. As with any generalizing science abstractions are necessarily relatively *empty* of content as compared with the concrete reality of the historical. On the other hand, it does provide an enhanced conceptual *precision*. This enhancement in precision is achieved through the optimization of *meaningful* adequacy for which sociology strives. As has been recognized, such optimization has been quite completely achieved in respect of *rational* concepts, whether they be value-rational or

instrumentally rational. But sociology also seeks to develop theoretical, meaningfully adequate concepts in respect of irrational phenomena (mystic, prophetic, pneumatic, and affectual). In each case, whether rational or irrational, sociology distances itself from immediate reality and contributes to our knowledge by registering the degree to which a historical phenomenon can be assigned to one or more of these concepts. Components of the same historical occurrence can be characterized as 'feudal', as 'patrimonial', as 'bureaucratic', or as 'charismatic'. If these words are to mean anything *precise*, sociology has for its part to form 'pure' ('*ideal*') types of such constructs, each of which exhibits the rigorous uniformity associated with the maximization of *meaningful* adequacy, but which because of this degree of conceptual consistency probably never assume this absolutely *ideal* form in reality, in the same way that a physical reaction occurring in absolutely empty space might be calculated. Sociological casuistry is only possible in terms of *pure* ('ideal') types. Of course, sociology also on occasion employs the idea of a statistically *average* type, a construct which does not require any special methodological elaboration. But when '*typical*' cases are referred to here, it should ordinarily be assumed that the reference is to *ideal* types, whether rational or irrational, and which are for the most part constructed rationally (in respect of economic theory, always), and are always meaningfully adequate.

One should recognize that in the sociological domain 'averages' and 'average types' can be constructed with some degree of precision only where there are clear differences of *degree* in action whose meaning is determined by qualitatively uniform factors. This does occur. But in the majority of cases historically or sociologically relevant action is influenced by qualitatively *heterogeneous* motives from which a genuine 'average' cannot be struck. Those ideal-typical constructions of social action which can be found, for example, in economic theory are 'unrealistic' in this respect since they ask: Given ideal, and hence purely economically oriented, instrumental rationality, how *would* an actor behave? The question is posed in this way either to assist understanding of action not purely economically determined, but which is in actuality influenced by traditional constraints, emotions, mistakes; or to seek an understanding: (1) of a concrete action which does have an *element* of instrumental-rational motivation, or tends on average to have such a disposition – but also (2) precisely because of the *distance* separating the actual course of events from their ideal-typical course, it aids in the understanding of *real* motivation. An ideal-typical construction of a consistent, mystically determined, acosmic way of life (in, for example, politics, or the economy) would necessarily proceed in this way. The sharper and more precise ideal types are (in other words, the more *unreal* that they are in this sense) the better they serve – terminologically, classificatorily, heuristically. Substantive causal imputation with respect to individual events in historical studies here proceeds no differently. If, for example, one seeks to explain the course of the 1866 campaign, we must first determine, for both Moltke and

Benedek,[10] how, assuming ideal instrumental rationality, they would have manoeuvred had they possessed complete knowledge of their own position and that of their opponent. Then we can compare this with how they did in fact dispose their forces, and hence causally *explain* the observed difference, attributable as it may be to false information, genuine error, intellectual failure, personal temperament, or extra-strategic considerations. Even here an ideal-typical instrumentally rational construction is employed, if implicitly.

The structuring concepts of sociology are ideal typical not merely overtly, but also inwardly. Agents engage in *real* action for the most part in a dulled half-aware condition, perhaps entirely unaware of its 'intended meaning'. The actor 'senses' the meaning more indefinitely than consciously or positively, and generally acts by instinct or habit. Only occasionally, involving very frequent repetition of the same action, does anyone become conscious of a rational or an irrational meaning, and even then this could involve a very small number of individuals. Effective, fully conscious and explicitly meaningful action is always in reality quite a marginal case. Analysis of *reality* through historical or sociological study has to keep this circumstance constantly in mind. But this should not prevent sociology from employing *concepts* in the classification of possible 'intended meanings', as if action were actually conducted with conscious orientation to its meaning. The remoteness of this conception from reality must be constantly kept in mind when dealing with actual events, taking account both of distance and of quality.

Methodologically, one very often has only a choice between imprecise terminology on the one hand, and on the other terminology which though precise, is unreal and 'ideal typical'. In such a case the latter are scientifically preferable.[11]

II The concept of social action

1. Social action (including refraining from action, or acquiescence to some situation) can be oriented to the past, present or future anticipated behaviour of others (revenge for earlier assaults, resistance to present assault, defence measures in respect of future assaults). The 'others' can be individual and familiar, or an indefinite number of unfamiliar people ('money', for example, signifies an exchange good which the actor accepts in exchange because his action is oriented to the expectation that numerous others, be they unknown and of indeterminate number, will for their part be prepared in future to accept it in exchange).

2. Not every form of action – even overt action – is 'social' action in the sense defined here. Overt action is not social action when it is solely oriented to the anticipated behaviour of material objects. Inner conduct is only social

10 Two opposing generals in the war between Prussia and Austro-Hungary.
11 See the 'Objectivity' essay below, pp. 388–91.

action when oriented to the action of others. Religious behaviour, for example, is not social action when it assumes the form of contemplation, or solitary prayer. Or again, economic activity (by an individual) only when it takes account of the behaviour of third parties. To put it quite generally and formally: insofar as it reflects acknowledgement by a third party of one's own effective power of disposal over economic goods. Materially: insofar as in consumption the future desires of others are taken into account and one's own form of 'saving' is oriented accordingly. Or insofar as in production the future desire of a third party directs his orientation, and so forth.

3. Not every form of human contact is social in character, only when one's own behaviour is sensibly oriented to that of others. The collision of two cyclists is, for instance, a mere event, just like any natural occurrence. On the other hand their prior efforts to avoid each other, and the succeeding dispute, fisticuffs or amicable discussion are all 'social action'.

4. Social action is identical with neither

(a) *similar* action on the part of many, or
(b) every action *influenced* by the behaviour of others.

(a) If on the street at the beginning of a shower of rain a number of people put up their umbrellas simultaneously, normally the action of any one is not oriented to that of the others, but instead the action of all is a common response to the need for protection against the rain.

(b) It is well known that the action of the individual is strongly influenced by the mere fact of being part of a crowd in a confined space (the object of research in 'mass psychology', for example, in the work of Le Bon). This is action *determined* by the mass. Even within a dispersed mass it is possible for the individual to be subject to simultaneous or successive influence, for example, through the press, where the sensed behaviour of the many influences that of the individual. Particular forms of reaction are facilitated, or hindered, by the mere fact that the individual feels himself part of the 'mass'. Consequently a specific event, or human behaviour, can evoke quite varied responses: laughter, anger, enthusiasm, despair, passions of every form that would not be so prompted in a solitary individual, or at least not so easily. In the majority of cases none of this requires that a *meaningful* relationship exist between the behaviour of the individual and the fact of his being part of a mass. Behaviour prompted by a reaction to the mere presence of a mass, or to which such presence contributed, without there being a meaningful *relation*, is not 'social action' in the sense used here. Naturally the distinction is a highly fluid one. Differences – both of degree and of intelligible extent – in meaningfulness can be attributed to the 'mass condition' not simply in the case of demagogues, but also with a mass public itself. Simple 'imitation' of another's action (the importance of this is rightly emphasized by G. Tarde) should not be conceptualized as *specifically* 'social action' where it is purely reactive, lacking the orientation of one's own action to that of the other. The boundary is so fluid that often a clear distinction seems impossible. The simple fact that a person adopts from someone else an apparently useful procedure is not social action in our sense. The action is not oriented to the behaviour of the other, but the actor has, *through* observation of this behaviour, become aware of certain objective possibilities and it is to *these* possibilities that his action is oriented. His action is *causally*, but not meaningfully, determined by the behaviour of others. If by contrast the action of another is imitated because it is 'fashionable', is considered to be traditional, exemplary, 'proper', or for any similar reason, then meaning is oriented either to the behaviour of the source of imitation, or to that of third parties, or to both. Naturally these shade into each other. Both instances, that of mass determination and of imitation, are unstable and are borderline cases of social action, as we shall see below in dealing with traditional action, for instance. The reason for this instability is to do with the fact that orientation to the behaviour of others and the meaning of one's own action cannot be established unambiguously, or is *unconscious*, and rarely completely conscious. Mere 'influence' and meaningful 'orientation' are for this reason not always easily distinguishable. Conceptually, of course, they can be distinguished, although it goes without saying that simple 'reactive' imitation has at least the same sociological *consequence* as that which represents 'social action' in a genuine sense. Sociology is *not only* concerned with 'social action'; for the sociology pursued here this is simply its central referent, what could be said to be *constitutive* for it as a science. But this is to say nothing about the importance of this referent as compared with that of others.

§2. As with any form of action, social action can be determined by:

(a) **instrumental rationality**:[12] through expectations of the behaviour of external objects and other people, together with the employment of this expectation as a 'condition' or 'means' for the realization of one's own intended, premeditated *aims and purposes*;
(b) **value rationality**: through conscious belief in the unconditional and *intrinsic value* – whether this be understood as ethical, aesthetic, religious or anything else – of a specific form of personal behaviour for itself, unrelated to its success;
(c) **affect**, especially *emotion*: through actual emotions and feelings;
(d) **tradition**: through ingrained habituation.

1. Rigorously traditional action, just like purely reactive imitative behaviour (see the preceding section), lies at the very extreme of what one could dub

---

12 *Zweckrational* is the German term and has the literal meaning of rationality in terms of an *end*, and so offers a clear contrast to the *means* of achieving an end. The use of the less precise 'purpose' is unavoidable if the term is to be translated at all.

'meaningfully' oriented action; often quite beyond it. For it is very frequently merely an empty reaction to familiar stimuli following an ingrained pattern. The greater part of ingrained everyday actions approach this type, and not only represents a marginal case for any systematic taxonomy, but also because contact with the familiar can be sustained with various degrees of self-consciousness (more about this later) and in different senses; in this case the type approaches (b) above.

2. Rigorously affectual behaviour likewise lies at the boundary, and often beyond, what is consciously 'meaningfully' oriented; it can be uninhibited reaction to some exceptional stimulus. It is *sublimated* when affectually determined action involves the *consciously* controlled release of feeling; in which case it usually, but not always, finds itself on its way to 'value-rationalization', or to instrumental action.

3. Affectual and value-rational action differ in their conscious elaboration of the ultimate point of direction of action and *consistent* planned orientation with respect to these details. Otherwise they share in common the idea that the meaning of action lies not in its success, but in the particular form taken by the action itself. He who acts according to emotion seeks instant revenge, instant enjoyment, instant dedication, instant contemplative bliss, or seeks to satisfy through abreaction current emotions (no matter how great or sublime they might be).[13]

Value-rational action pays no regard to the expected consequences of action; the person acts out of a conviction that duty, honour, beauty, religious pronouncement, piety, or the importance of a 'cause' of whatever kind so demand. Value-rational action is in our sense always an action governed by 'decree' and according to 'demands' which the actor believes are imposed upon him. We will talk here of value-rationality only where human action is oriented to such demands – something which occurs in greatly varying degrees, and mostly only in a very small number of cases. As we shall see, this form is important enough to be distinguished as a special type, although there is no intention here of establishing an exhaustive typology of action.

4. Instrumentally rational action is oriented to the purpose, means and associated consequences of an act, rationally *estimating* the relation of means to ends, that of the ends to the associated consequences, as well as that of the various ends; hence an action which is *neither* affective (especially not emotional) *nor* traditional. A *value*-rational orientation can be employed in any decision concerning competing and conflicting aims and consequences; in this case only the means are selected by instrumentally rational criteria. Alternatively, the individual can deal with competing and conflicting aims without resort to value-rationality, taking 'decrees' and 'demands' as given subjective feelings of need arranged in a scale consciously *balanced* according

---

13 Abreaction is the immediate release of emotional energy. Sublimation involves its working out through controlled and conscious direction.

to their urgency and so orienting his action that they will be satisfied in the relevant sequence (the principle of 'marginal utility'). Hence there are many ways in which the value-rational orientation of action can relate to the instrumental rationality. From the perspective of instrumental rationality, however, value-rationality must always be *irrational*, the more so when action is governed by absolute values. For the more that action elevates such absolute values, the less it reflects upon the consequence of such action, and the more unconditional do considerations of inner disposition, beauty, the absolute good, absolute duty become. However, *absolutely* instrumental rational action is for the most part a marginal case.

5. Action is very rarely oriented *solely* to the one *or* the other type. Similarly, these types of orientation are in no way exhaustive in respect of types of action, but are instead created for sociological ends, conceptually pure types to which real action more or less conforms, or, more often, are compounded in reality. Their utility for *us* is judged by results.

§3. **Social 'relationship'** shall refer in its meaningful content (*Sinngehalt*) to the mutual *attitude* of several persons to one another and behaviour arising from such an orientation. A social relationship therefore *consists* entirely and quite exclusively in the *likelihood* that action will be social in a (meaningfully) manifest sense, leaving to one side for the moment the basis of this likelihood.

1. A leading characteristic of the concept shall therefore be the existence in the relationship of a minimum of *mutual* orientation *one to another*. The content can be quite various: conflict; enmity; sexual love; friendship; piety; market exchange; 'fulfilment', 'evasion' or breach of an agreement; economic, erotic, or other forms of 'competition'; or communal relations based upon status, nation, or class (in the event that these last circumstances create 'social action' that goes beyond the mere sharing of this circumstance). Hence the concept implies *nothing* about 'solidarity' between the actors, or its direct negation.

2. It is always a matter of the *intended*, empirical meaning of participants for each actual or average case, or in a constructed 'pure' type – never of a normatively 'correct' or metaphysically 'true' meaning. A social relationship – even where it is a matter of 'social constructs' such as 'state', 'church', or 'co-operative association' – *consists* exclusively and solely in the *likelihood* that action occurred, occurs, or will occur whose meaningful content manifestly arises from its mutual orientation. This must be constantly born in mind if one is to avoid an 'essentialist' interpretation ('*substanzielle*' *Auffassung*) of these concepts. A 'state', for example, ceases to 'exist' sociologically with the disappearance of the *likelihood* that particular forms of meaningfully oriented social action might occur. This likelihood might be very great or infinitely small. Together with the meaning and *degree* of this likelihood existing or having existed the relevant social relationship likewise exists or did exist. There is no alternative and clearer meaning for the statement that a 'state', for instance, 'exists', or 'no longer exists'.

3. This in no respect means that those involved in mutually oriented action attribute in each case the *same* meaning to a social relationship, or that each inwardly reciprocates the orientation of the other, so that 'mutuality' arises in *this* sense. 'Friendship', 'love', 'piety', 'contractual fidelity', 'national spirit' – everywhere the sentiments of one side can encounter quite different attitudes on the other. In this case participants attribute a different meaning to their action – here the social relationship is regarded by both sides to be objectively 'one-sided'. But such action is nevertheless mutually related to the degree that the actor *assumes* (perhaps entirely, or in part, mistakenly), that the partner has a particular disposition towards him and orients his own action to such expectations, this can have, and usually will have, consequences for the ensuing action and the construction of a relationship. The relationship is naturally also only objectively 'mutual' to the degree that the meaningful content for each – according to their average *expectations* – 'corresponds', such that, for example, the child's attitude relates to the father's in a manner which at least approximates to that which the father expects, whether for each instance, or on average, or typically. A social relationship based upon a perfectly *symmetrical* correspondence of such attitudes is in reality a rarity. Absence of mutuality should in our terminology only rule out the existence of a 'social relationship' if there is an actual lack of *reciprocity* in mutual action. As elsewhere, in reality all kinds of transitional cases are the rule.

4. A social relationship can be quite transitional, or long-lasting – such that there is a likelihood that behaviour corresponding to its meaning will *recur*, i.e. anticipated behaviour conforming to its meaning. To avoid any misunderstanding we must always remember that it is *only* the existence of this likelihood – the greater or lesser *probability* that action corresponding to this meaning takes place, and *nothing* more than this – which signifies the '*continuance*' ('*Bestand*') of the social relationship. That a 'friendship' or a 'state' exists, or did exist, means exclusively and uniquely that: *we* (the *observers*) think that a *likelihood* exists or, did exist, that on the basis of a specifically formed orientation particular persons will *act* according to a meaning understood by each to be the *generally intended* meaning – no more and no less (see (2) above). From a legal perspective the reverse seems to be true – that a *legal* statute with a certain meaning is either legally valid or not, that a *legal* relationship either exists or not – but this is not applicable to a sociological perspective.

5. The substantive meaning of a social relationship can alter – for instance, a political relationship can out of solidarity change into a conflict of interest. In such cases, whether one says that a 'new' relationship has been created, or that the existing relationship has gained a new 'substantive' meaning is only a matter of terminological utility and the degree of *continuity* in the transformation. Substantive meaning can be partly constant, partly subject to variation.

6. The *constant* substantive meaning constituting a social relationship can be formulated in 'maxims', general adherence to which participants *expect*

from their partner(s), and according to which they in return generally orient their action. This is more frequently the case the more (instrumental or value) rationally oriented the general character of the action is. With an erotic relationship, or emotional relationships in general (for instance, a relationship of 'piety'), the prospect of a rational formulation of the intended substantive meaning is quite naturally much less than that in a contractual business relationship.

7. The substantive meaning of a social relationship can be *agreed* by mutual consent. Those involved make *promises* regarding their future behaviour, whether towards each other, or otherwise. Each participant – insofar as each calculates rationally – initially assumes (with a varying degree of certainty) that the *other* will orient his action to that meaning of the agreement held by the first actor. He orients his own action to this expectation partly in an instrumentally rational manner (expressing some degree of 'loyalty'), partly value-rationally as his 'duty' to 'adhere' for his part to the concluded agreement as understood by him. All this is by way of preliminaries (see also below §§9 and 13).

§4. **Actual regularities** can be observed within social action, i.e. regularities whose *intended meaning* is typically similar in actions repeated by the same actor, in actions replicated by many actors, or in both of these at the same time. Sociology is concerned with *typologies* of such modes of action, unlike history, which concerns itself with causal imputation in respect of important, fateful singular events. An actually existing likelihood of *regularity* in the orientation of social action will be called **practice** (*Brauch*) if the likelihood of its existing among a group of people depends *solely* on its actual performance. A practice which has become *familiar* through lengthy exercise shall be called a **custom**. A custom is regarded as having been *conditioned by interests* insofar as its likelihood of empirical existence is determined *solely* by the instrumentally rational orientation of individual action to similar *expectations*.

1. 'Fashion' is also a practice. By contrast with the definition of 'custom', fashion is a 'practice' if the source of an action's orientation becomes the *novelty* of the relevant behaviour. It is close to the meaning of 'convention', for these both arise from the prestige accruing to *status differences* and the interests formed around them. This will not be considered any further here.

2. By contrast with 'convention' and 'law', 'custom' does *not* involve an externally guaranteed rule to which the actor voluntarily adheres (whether such adherence be 'unthinking', for 'convenience', or for any other reason) and whose probable observance he can for these reasons expect on the part of other members of this group of people. Custom does not have the 'validity' of an established law: no one can 'require' its observance, that one conform to it. There is a fluid convergence here with established *convention* and *law*. Established actual practices have always the source of that which is later enforced. Today it is 'customary' that we breakfast every morning in a more

or less predetermined way; but there is nothing 'obligatory' about this (except for hotel guests) and it was not always a custom. By contrast, the form of dress, even where it is derived from 'custom', is today for the most part not only custom, but convention. The relevant passages on practice and custom from Ihering's *Purpose in Law*, vol. II can still be read with benefit today. . . .

3. Many very obvious regularities in the course of social action, especially (but not exclusively) in the case of economic action, are in fact quite independent of some 'valid' prescribed norm, or of custom. They arise instead from the circumstance that the form of social action adopted generally corresponds most closely to the normal, subjective evaluation by participants of their *interests*, hence orienting their action according to this subjective opinion and understanding; an example of this can be found in the process of price formation in a 'free' market. Market agents orient their behaviour instrumentally, employ it as a *means* in the realization of their 'end' – their subjective, *typified*, economic interests – and treat the prospective behaviour of others as so many 'conditions' for the realization of this end. The more *rigorously* instrumentally rational their behaviour – the greater the degree to which means are matched to a desired end – the more that they react in similar ways to any given situation. From this there arise similarities, regularities, and continuities in outlook and action; and these are often a great deal stronger than action oriented by norms and duties thought of as 'binding' for a particular group of people. Orientation to the naked self-interest of oneself and to that of others creates effects entirely similar in character to those sought (often vainly) in the forcible imposition of uniform conditions; this phenomenon is well known in the economic domain, and was a principal source for the development of political economy as a science. But this holds for all domains of action in a quite similar manner. The self-awareness and lack of scruple associated with self-interest is the polar opposite of any kind of inner commitment arising from conformity with the familiar, with 'custom'; it also contrasts with a dedication to norms, belief in which is value-rational in character. An important component in the 'rationalization' of action is the replacement of this inner conformity to habitual custom by planned adaptation to given interests. This process does not however exhaust the concept of the 'rationalization' of action. The process can be positive where there is a conscious rationalization of values; negative where it is not only at the expense of custom, but also of emotional action; and ultimately can also work in favour of nihilistic, instrumentally rational action at the expense of action linked rationally to absolute values. This *ambiguity* in the concept of the 'rationalization' of action will be returned to again. (Some conceptual remarks on this can be found in the conclusion.)

4. The strength of (mere) *custom* derives for the most part from the fact that he who fails to orient his action to it acts 'inappropriately', has to put up with greater or lesser humiliations and mortification so long as the action of the majority observes the relevant custom and is so oriented.

Likewise, the strength of *given interests* derives from the fact that he who fails to orient his actions to the interests of others – does not 'reckon' with them – provokes their opposition, or succeeds in a manner he had neither wanted nor foreseen and, consequently, risks damaging his own interests.

§5. Action, especially social action, and even more specifically, a social relationship, can be oriented on the part of the actor in the *idea* (*Vorstellung*) of the existence of a **legitimate order**. The likelihood that this actually occurs will be called the 'validity' of the relevant order.

1. The 'validity' of an *order* means more here than a regularity in the course of social action brought about by custom or by given interests. If removal firms routinely advertise their services when new lettings are made then this regularity is dictated by their given interests. If a door-to-door salesman seeks out a specific group of customers on particular days of the month or of the week, then that is either a familiar custom, or alternatively a product of his particular interests (it is his turn to work a given patch). But if an official routinely appears in his office at the same time each day, then that is not *only* the result of a familiar custom, nor *only* determined by given interests to which he can conform or not as he pleases. He is generally subject to a 'prevailing' order (an office rule) infringement of which would not only bring disadvantage, but which would normally be abhorrent to his 'sense of duty', a sentiment linked to value-rationality but which can manifest itself in numerous ways.

2. We will call the meaningful content (*Sinngehalt*) of a social relationship an 'order' only when action is generally oriented to definite 'principles'. Secondly, we shall only speak of the 'validity' of this order if this actual orientation to given principles is *also* in practice followed because these principles are in some way or another recognized as binding or exemplary *for* the action. In fact the orientation of an action to an order occurs for a wide variety of motives. For at least a proportion of actors the order seems exemplary, or obligatory, and hence is something that *should* have validity, and this circumstance, *besides* other motives, frequently increases the likelihood that action will be oriented to this order. An order which is internalized *only* for purely instrumental motives is generally a great deal more volatile than an orientation based upon custom, from the sheer familiarity of a mode of behaviour; this is the most frequently encountered internalized (*innegehaltene*) attitude. But the former is even more unstable than an order which is considered exemplary or obligatory, or as we might say, which enjoys '*legitimacy*'. The transition from an orientation to an order motivated simply by traditional or instrumental factors to an orientation based on a belief in its legitimacy is of course in reality an extremely fluid one.

3. 'Orientation' of action to the validity of an order does not only imply 'adherence' to its (averagely understood) meaning. Even where this averagely understood meaning is 'evaded' or 'infringed', it is likely that this validity will still to some extent remain *effective* as a binding norm, especially when seen

instrumentally. The thief orients his action with respect to the 'validity' of criminal law even as he infringes it. The prevalence of an order in a human group is expressed in the fact that the thief must conceal his violation of the order. Besides this extreme case, violation of an order is mostly limited to numerous more or less partial infringements, or such violations might be represented, with varying degrees of good faith, as legitimate infringements. Or it might happen that several conceptions of the meaning of an order co-exist, which (for sociology) can in turn have 'validity' in that they actually determine behaviour. Sociology has no difficulty with the idea of a variety of co-existing, *contradictory* orders within a given human group. For even the individual can orient his action to mutually inconsistent orders. And this can occur not only successively, as happens daily, but in the selfsame action. Anyone involved in a duel and who seeks to hide this fact orients his action to the code of honour; or, conversely, orients his action to the criminal code if he gives himself up to the police. Of course, if evasion or violation of the generally accepted meaning of an order becomes the *rule* then the order retains only a limited 'validity', or loses it altogether. For sociology (unlike jurisprudence with its inflexibility of purpose) there exists no absolute alternative between the validity and the invalidity of a particular order. There is instead a gradual shift from one case to the other, and as noted above mutually inconsistent orders can be simultaneously 'valid' – each to the extent that there is a *chance* that action will *actually* be oriented to it.

Those familiar with the literature will recall the role played by the concept of 'order' in the work by R. Stammler cited above, which is no doubt quite brilliantly written but is nevertheless fundamentally misconceived and fatally confused in its appreciation of the problems (see my critique, which became rather sharp in its form because of my irritation with the confusion engendered).[14] Stammler not only fails to distinguish empirical and normative validity, he also fails to recognize that social action is not *only* oriented to 'orders'; above all, he develops a quite mistaken logical argument in which order becomes the 'form' of social action, which is related to a 'content' in a manner analogous to the contrast of 'form' and 'content' in epistemology (this quite apart from his other mistakes). For instance, action which is predominantly economic in character (see the following chapter)[15] is oriented to the scarcity of means available to satisfy demand compared with the assumed demand, and to the present and expected action of third parties who have in view these same means. But this *also involves* an orientation in the *choice* of 'economic' measures to those orders which the agent recognizes as having 'valid' laws and conventions, that is, this recognition implies an expectation that a third party will react in a specific manner if these laws and conventions

---

14 English translation: *Critique of Stammler*, introduced and translated by Guy Oakes, New York, Free Press, 1977.
15 Weber refers to ch. 2 of *E&S*.

are flouted. Stammler has quite hopelessly muddled these quite simple empirical principles and in particular declared the conceptual impossibility of a
causal relationship between an 'order' and actual action. There is of course
no causal relationship between the normative validity of an order in the
strictly legal sense and an empirical event; there is only the question: Does the
order *properly* interpreted in the legal sense 'apply' to the empirical event?
Should the order have a normative force over the empirical? If so, what does
this normative *prescription* imply for it? By contrast, there is of course a
causal relationship in its quite usual sense between the *chance* that action will
be oriented by the *belief* (of whatever kind) in the validity of an order and
economic action. But for sociology, as opposed to the law, it is the chances of
orientation by this *belief* (*Vorstellung*) that alone is 'constitutive' of 'the'
validity of an order.

§6. The **legitimacy of an order** can be *guaranteed*:

I   purely through inner impulse (*innerlich*), either

    1   through pure affect: by emotional dedication (*Hingabe*); or
    2   through value rationality: by a belief in its absolute validity as the
       embodiment of ultimate, obligatory values (ethical, aesthetic or of
       whatever kind); or
    3   through religion: by the belief that salvation depends upon inner
       adherence to the order; and (also: or merely)

II by an expectation linked to specific external consequences, and so, by the
    interest situation; but also expectations of a quite particular *kind*.

An order will be called a

(a) **convention**, where its validity is externally underwritten by a likelihood
    that deviation from its observance will, in a given human group, result in
    relatively general and tangible *disapproval*.
(b) **law**, where its validity is externally underwritten by the likelihood that
    physical or mental coercion will be applied by a specialized *staff* whose
    task is to enforce conformity or punish contravention.

On 'convention', see besides Ihering, Weigelin, also F. Tönnies, *Die Sitte*
(1909).

    1. The term 'convention' denotes a 'custom' adhered to *by a human group*,
which endorses its validity, and where disapproval acts as a guarantee against
infringement. By contrast with the law (as here defined), there is no specialized staff charged with its enforcement. Stammler distinguishes convention
from law in terms of the absolutely 'voluntary' nature of subordination to it,
but this does not coincide with common usage, nor is it appropriate for his
own examples. Following a 'convention' (in the usual sense) – for instance:

ordinary greetings, what counts as decent clothing, and the rules governing the form and content of social intercourse – have an obligatory or exemplary force for the individual, upon whom such conventions are most definitely imposed, without option, and have nothing in common with the merely 'customary' manner in which an individual elects to prepare his meals. Violation of a convention, of a mark of status, for example, is often more effectively and painfully penalized through social boycott than any legal compulsion could effect. All that is missing is the specialized staff charged with enforcing conformity to a specific mode of action (in our case: judges, state prosecutors, officials, executioners, and so on). There is however no hard and fast distinction. The conventional guarantee of an order that comes closest to a legal guarantee is the formal institution of a threatened and *organized* boycott. In our terms this would be a legal means of compulsion. We are not concerned here with the fact that a convention can be effected by means other than simple *disapproval* – for example, the invocation of house rules where behaviour flouts convention. For what is again decisive here is the fact that it is the *individual*, and not a dedicated and specialized *staff*, who, by virtue of conventional disapproval, applies these often quite drastic coercive means.

2. For the concept of 'law' as employed here the existence of a *staff* dedicated to its enforcement is its most decisive feature, although for other purposes it might be defined quite differently. This agency does not of course have to resemble, in any respect, that with which we are today familiar. There is no necessary requirement, for instance, that a 'judicial' body exists. A clan fulfils the requirements of this staff in reprisals and feuds, if the form of its reaction validates orders of some kind. Of course this is an extreme case of what we otherwise refer to as 'legal compulsion'. The 'legal' character of international law has often been disputed because of the absence of transnational coercive force. For the sake of convenience, the terminology employed here for an order guaranteed externally solely through anticipation of disapproval and retaliation on the part of injured parties, hence guaranteed conventionally and according to given interests, but lacking a staff whose action is *exclusively* directed to enforcing adherence to this order, cannot be treated as a *legal* order. None the less, in legal terminology the opposite could well be the case. The *means* of coercion are not relevant. Even the 'brotherly admonishment' that was commonly used by many sects as the first step of gentle pressure on sinners – if conforming to a rule and applied by a staff – belongs here. Likewise the use of the censorious reprimand as a means of guaranteeing 'moral' behavioural norms. And also of course the psychic coercion exercised by church disciplinary methods. There is of course law enforced ecclesiastically, politically, through the statutes of an association, through domestic authority as well as through co-operatives and other unions. The rules of a 'student fraternity' ('*Komment*') are in these terms 'law'. The case of Para. 888 Section 2 of the German Code of Civil Procedure, dealing with unenforceable rights, belong quite naturally here too. 'Leges imperfectae' and 'natural obligations' are likewise forms of legal

language which express *indirect* restrictions or conditions on the use of coercion. A coercively imposed 'rule of moral conduct' is in this respect *law* (BGB Paras 157, 242).[16]

3. Not every valid order necessarily has an abstract and general character. A valid 'legal principle' and a 'legal decision' arrived at in a given case, for instance, would not be as distinct in every circumstance as we are today accustomed to think. An 'order' *can* be simply the order governing a single situation. Everything else is a matter for legal sociology. To begin with, where not stated otherwise, we shall take for granted the modern appreciation of the relationship of legal principle and legal decision.

4. Orders which are guaranteed 'externally' can also be guaranteed 'internally'. Sociology has no problem with the relation between law, convention, and 'ethics'. An 'ethical' standard is for sociology simply one to which a specific type of value is attributed, and, because of this *belief*, it is treated as a norm for human action which can be labelled 'ethically good' – in the same way that an action labelled 'beautiful' is evaluated in terms of aesthetic standards. Conceptions of ethical norms of this kind can have a very profound influence while doing entirely without any kind of external guarantee. This tends to occur if the interests of others are barely affected by the violation of such norms. They are frequently religious guarantees. But, in the sense used here, they can also be conventional: guaranteed through disapproval of their violation together with the imposition of a boycott; or also legal, guaranteed by the criminal law, the response of the police, or the consequences of civil law. Every actually 'valid' ethic (in the sociological sense) tends to be guaranteed by the chance that disapproval will follow from its violation – that is, by convention. By contrast, not every conventionally and legally guaranteed order (necessarily) lays claim to *ethical* norms. Legal orders, often formulated in a purely instrumental manner, make far fewer ethical claims than conventional orders. *Whether* or not a prevailing conception of validity is to be ascribed to the domain of 'ethics' – and not to 'mere' convention or 'mere' legal norm – is a problem to which an empirical sociology can only respond by examining the concept of 'the ethical' *actually* current among that human group. For this reason nothing can be said *about this* in general.

§7. **Legitimacy** can be ascribed to an order by virtue of:

(a) **tradition**: the validity of the ever-existing;
(b) **affectual**, especially emotional, belief: the validity of the newly revealed, or the exemplary;

---

16 [Weber] For an account of 'good customs' (i.e. customs which might be approved of and which thus enjoy the sanction of the law), see Max Rümelin in *Schwäbische Heimatgabe für Theodor Häring* (1918).

(c) **value-rational** belief: the validity of that which has been revealed to be absolutely certain;
(d) **positive** statute: the *legality* of which is believed.

The legality of this last instance can be treated as *legitimate* by participants by virtue of:

(i)   an agreement among those interested parties; or
(ii) imposition (on the basis of the legitimacy ascribed to the rule of man by man) and compliance (see §13).

Further details (apart from some concepts which will be elaborated below) will be dealt with in the sociology of rulership (*Herrschaft*) and of law. Here it can be observed that:

1. The original and most universal validity ascribed to orders lies in the sanctity of tradition. Fear of magical penalties reinforces the psychic inhibition with respect to any sort of change to habitual action, together with the many interests that tend to underwrite compliance to an existing order, support its maintenance. This will be discussed further in ch. III [of *E&S*].[17]

2. *Conscious* formation of new orders was originally almost exclusively the outcome of prophetic oracles, or at least sanctioned by prophecy and as such thought of as holy proclamation, right down to the statutes of the Greek aisymnetai.[18] Conformity depended on belief in the legitimacy of the prophet. When a rigorous traditionalism prevailed, the formation of new orders – those that would be *perceived* to be new – was only possible without revelation unless it was claimed that they had always been valid though not hitherto *properly* recognized for such, or that they had been obscured for a long time and were now for the first time *restored* to their rightful place.

3. The purest type of value-rational validity is that of 'natural law'. However limited it may be in comparison with its ideal claims, it cannot be disputed that no little part of its real influence derives from its logically constructed principles, and this can be distinguished both from revealed, statute, or traditional law.

4. Today, the most common form of legitimacy is a belief in *legality*: conformity with *formally* correct statutes which have been established in the usual manner. The contrast between an order based upon assent and one that is simply imposed is relative, not absolute. For as soon as the assenting type of order ceases to depend on *unanimous* agreement – often thought in the past to be a requisite of genuine legitimacy – but depends for its existence on the acquiescence of a dissenting minority to the will of the majority (as frequently happens), then an order agreed among a majority is in fact

---

17 For this volume see Reading 7.
18 Greek monarchs.

imposed upon this minority. But the reverse of this is also common: where a minority imposes an order by force, or by virtue of a certain ruthlessness and clarity of purpose, which order is then subsequently accepted as legitimate by those who had previously resisted it. Where 'voting' is a legal means for the creation or alteration of orders it is very common for the minority will to gain a formal majority, and that the majority acquiesces in this, such that the principle of majority is mere facade. There is a fairly lengthy tradition of belief in the legality of freely agreed orders and examples can be found among so-called primitive peoples, although this is nearly always reinforced by the use of oracles.

5. Apart from cases where fear or instrumentalism is the motivating factor, acquiescence in the face of an imposed order on the part of one or more persons is founded upon conceptions of legality, a belief in some form of legitimate power of *rulership* enjoyed by hegemonic agent or agents (this is dealt with separately below).[19]

6. As a rule, and besides circumstantial interests of all kinds, acquiescence to order is secured through a mixture of an allegiance to tradition and conceptions of legality, except in the case of entirely new statutes. In many instances an acquiescent actor is quite unconscious of the role of custom, convention, or law in such action. Here it is the task of sociology to determine the *typical* form of validity.

§8. A social relationship will be called a **struggle** where the actor is oriented to the imposition of his own will upon an unwilling partner or partners. 'Peaceful' means of struggle are those which do not actually involve physical force. 'Peaceful' struggle will be called 'competition' where there is a formally peaceful attempt to gain control of opportunities which are also desired by others. 'Regulated competition' is where the ends and means of competition are oriented to an order. 'Selection' refers to the (latent) struggle for existence or for survival among humans or types, although such struggle is not a conscious intention: 'social selection' refers to opportunities arising in the lifetime of an actor, and 'biological selection' where it is a matter of the chances of the survival of inherited characteristics.

1. There is an entirely seamless transition between the two extremes of struggle: from a struggle aimed at the destruction of an opponent's life, refusing any binding rules of engagement, to the conventionally regulated encounters of medieval chivalry. Typical for the latter was the cry of a herald before the battle of Fontenoy: 'Messieurs les Anglais, tirez les premiers.'[20] Other instances are regulated games (sport), unregulated erotic competition among admirers for the attention of a woman, the regulated, competitive struggle for exchange opportunities constrained by market order, regulated artistic 'competitions',

---

19 See §13, §16, and pp. 133–45 above.
20 'Englishmen, please fire your opening shots.'

and finally 'electoral struggle'. The conceptual distinction of violent from non-violent struggle can be justified by the special nature of the normal means employed and the particular characteristics of the sociological consequences following from their use (see ch. II of *E&S* and elsewhere).

2. Typical, repeated struggle and competition eventually leads, despite all manner of decisive chances and twists of fate, to the 'selection' of that actor who has the greater endowment of those personal qualities essential for success. These qualities might be quite various: greater physical strength or unscrupulous cunning; a greater intensity of intellectual capacity; or greater stamina; or a superior demagogic technique; a greater devotion to superiors, or to the flattering of masses; greater originality or greater social adaptability; more extraordinary qualities, or on the other hand, a greater than average degree of ordinariness. Whatever traits possessed by adversaries, the conditions of conflict and competition work in favour of those who, besides all conceivable forms of such qualities, belong to the *orders* to which behaviour in the course of conflict is oriented – whether it be traditional, value-rational or instrumentally rational. *Each* of these influences the prospect of social selection. Not *every* form of social selection is 'struggle' in the sense used here. 'Social selection' means rather that particular forms of behaviour, and probably also personal qualities, are favoured in the possibility of achieving a certain social *relationship* (as a 'lover', 'husband', 'Member of Parliament', 'official', 'site foreman', 'company director', 'successful businessman', and so on). There is no implication here that this social advantage will be necessarily realized in 'struggle', or indeed whether the biological *prospect for survival* of the type is thereby improved, or damaged.

We shall only talk of 'struggle' where there is genuine *competition*. All experience has shown that it is only in this sense of 'selection' that conflict is actually inescapable, only in the sense of *biological* selection is it inevitable in *principle*. Selection is 'eternal' since no means have been conceived which might bring it to a halt. A rigorously pacifist order is only able to deal with conflict by systematically controlling the specific means, objects and aims of conflict. But this would mean only that *other* forms of conflict would emerge through open competition; or even on the utopian assumption that all competition were eliminated, conditions would still lead to a latent process of selection in opportunities for existence and survival, favouring those who were best adapted, whether by dint of biology or of education. The abolition of conflict is empirically limited by social selection, and limited in principle by biological selection.

3. 'Struggle' and 'selection' which involve social *relationships* must naturally be distinguished from struggle on the part of an *individual* for existence and survival. In this case one can only use these concepts in a metaphorical sense. For 'relationships' *exist* only as substantive meanings arising out of human *action*. 'Selection' or 'conflict' between them means that a particular form of action is *displaced* over time by another, involving the same people,

or a different group of people. This can happen in different ways. Human action can be:

(a) *consciously* oriented to the disturbance of specific, existing social relationships, or to more generally conceived social relationships whose substantive meaning corresponds to particular *actions*; or seek to prevent their foundation, or persistence. Examples would be to seek the destruction of a 'state' by war or revolution, or of a conspiracy put down by bloody suppression, the control of prostitution by police measures, and of usurious commercial dealings by denial of legal protection and punishment. Human action can involve preference for one type of social relationship and the influencing of other types. Individuals, or a number of conjoined individuals, might pursue such ends. It can also be:
(b) the unanticipated consequence of a course of social action and the many circumstances conditioning it, so that specific concrete relationships, or specific forms of relationship (i.e. whatever is the relevant *action*) have a reduced chance of persistence, or of being created anew.

Changes to natural and cultural conditions of all kinds work in some way or another to alter the differential probabilities of survival of different social relationships. Anyone can in such circumstances talk of the 'selection' of social relationships – for example, that among states the 'strongest' (in the sense of the 'fittest', the best adapted) prevails. It needs to be remembered that this alleged 'selection' has nothing to do with the selection of human *types* in either the sociological or the biological sense; that in every single case one must examine *reasons* for the displacement of chances for this or that form of social action and social relationship; or what shatters a social relationship; or what has permitted its persistence as compared with others, and that these reasons are so many and various that no single expression seems inappropriate. There is always a danger here of importing *evaluations* unchecked into empirical research, and above all justifying the *success* of a single case where quite individual and 'coincidental' reasons played the major part. There have been more than enough examples of this in the past few years. The fact that an actually or qualitatively specific social relationship has been eliminated for reasons particular to a given situation proves nothing about its 'adaptability' in *general* terms.

§9. **The formation of community** ('*Vergemeinschaftung*') shall refer to a social relationship if and to the extent that the orientation of social action – whether in the individual case, or average case, or as a pure type – rests upon subjectively *felt* (affectual or traditional) *mutual* belonging (*Zusammengehörigkeit*) of the participants.

The formation of association ('*Vergesellschaftung*') shall refer to a social relationship if and to the extent that the orientation of social action rests upon the rationally motivated (either value-rational or instrumentally rational) *balancing* out of interests or upon similarly motivated linking of interests. Such associative action is rationally oriented either in value-rational terms in the belief in one's *own* sense of obligation, or in instrumentally rational terms in the expectation of the loyalty of one's *partner*.

1. This terminology echoes that distinction used by F. Tönnies in his pioneering volume *Gemeinschaft und Gesellschaft*. However, Tönnies used the distinction in a much more specific way than would be useful here. The purest types of association are:

(a) the rigorously instrumental, freely agreed *exchange* in a market, where opposed but complementary interests reach a comprise;
(b) the pure voluntary *instrumental association*, established on a continuous basis and where both intentions and means reflect pursuit of the material (economic or other) interests of members;
(c) the voluntary association of individuals sharing a common value-rational *disposition* (*Gesinnung*): a rational sect to the extent that it disregards emotive and affectual relationships, seeking only to dedicate itself to a 'cause' (this only arises as an entirely pure type in very special cases).

2. Community formation can have any kind of affective, emotional or traditional basis. Examples are a religious brotherhood, an erotic relationship, a relation based upon reverence, a 'national' community, and a military unit bound together by comradeship. The easiest example is that of the family. The great majority of social relationships are made up of *both* communal and associative elements. The most soberly conceived instrumentally rational association (for example, of retailer and customers) can evoke an emotional allegiance that transcends its instrumental purpose. Any social relationship between the same members of such an instrumental association which is not from the very first strictly limited to specific individual procedures but lasts for a long time – for example, the association provided by a military unit, by the same classroom, by the same office or workshop – tends in this direction, albeit to very different degrees. By contrast, a social relationship normally thought of as communally based can be shifted towards instrumentalism if some or all of its members determine upon instrumental ends. The degree to which a 'family' is felt by its members to be communal, or might be exploited for instrumental ends is of course quite unpredictable. The concept of 'community formation' employed here is quite deliberately general and hence covers a wide range of circumstances.

3. The intended meaning of the 'community formation' is here radically contrasted with '*struggle*'. But this should not divert our attention from the fact that violations of all kinds routinely occur in the most intimate communal associations with respect to those who are spiritually more pliant, and that 'selection' by type leading to differences of existence and survival occurs within these associations in just the same way as anywhere else. Associative

relationships are by contrast frequently based *exclusively* upon a compromise between antagonistic interests, a compromise which eliminates (or seeks to eliminate) just one element of this antagonism while leaving unaltered the existing conflict and *competition* for pre-eminence arising from it. 'Struggle' and community are relative concepts; struggle can assume many forms, the means used being violent or 'peaceful', and the degree of ruthlessness with which such means are applied is likewise quite variable. And as has already been stated, every order of social relations, however constituted, permits the existence of an actual process of *selection* to occur as the product of competition between different human types over life-chances.

4. Not every quality, situation or behaviour shared *in common* engenders the formation of communality. For example, the possession of a common biological stock thought to be a racial characteristic naturally implies nothing further about those bearing this characteristic. It cannot of itself imply communality. External restrictions upon marriage and commercial relations might well impose similarities arising from their common orientation to this external environment. But even if they react similarly to this common situation, this does not constitute communality, nor of itself does 'fellow-feeling' arising out the common situation and its consequences. It is only when their behaviour is in some way mutually *oriented* because of this feeling that a social relation is formed among them, a relation between each of them and the external world is insufficient; and it is only when this social relationship is registered as such that a 'community' can be said to have formed. For example, besides Zionist circles and the activities of a few other associations concerned with Jewish interests, Jews have relatively weak social relationships of this sort, and indeed Jews often repudiate the notion of a Jewish 'community'. A common *language*, created by a similarity of tradition reinforced by family and neighbourhood, greatly facilitates mutual understanding, and hence the formation of social relationships. But of itself it implies no sort of communal relationship, it only fosters intercourse among the relevant group, i.e. the formation of associations. Hence it is *not* the existence of a common language which promotes communality, but rather a relationship between *individuals* based upon interests of a particular kind; an orientation to the rules of a common language is primarily a means of mutual understanding, and does not provide a substantive basis for social relationships of itself. It is only the emergence of conscious differences with respect to third parties that place those in a linguistic community in a common situation, prompting fellow feeling and associations whose conscious foundation rests on their common language. Participation in a 'market' (see ch. II of *Economy and Society*) is structured differently. A market creates associational relationships between individual exchanging parties and a social relationship (principally one of 'competition') between prospective exchanging parties, for in each case these agents have to orient their behaviour towards each other. But associational activity only develops from this if some of the participants seek to improve their competitive situation, or reach agreement on ways to

regulate and stabilize transactions. (The market and the commercial economy (*Verkehrswirtschaft*) based upon it is incidentally the most important type of mutual influence of action through the sheer *self-interest*, characteristic of modern economic organization.)

§10. A social relationship, whether communal or associational, will be called '**open**' to outsiders to the degree that participation in mutually oriented social action linked to the substantive meaning constitutive of the relationship is, according to the prevailing order, not systematically denied to anyone so inclined and able to participate. By contrast, a social relationship is '**closed**' to outsiders to the extent that its substantive meaning or its prevailing order exclude such participation, or restrict it, or permit it only according to specific conditions. Openness and closedness can be defined traditionally or affectually, by value-rationality or by instrumental rationality. *Rational* closure can in particular arise for the following reasons: admission to a social relationship lends participants the prospect that inward or external interests can be satisfied, whether this be on account of the purpose of the relationship itself or because of its successful prosecution, whether it arises from solidaristic action or from a balance of interests. If the participants anticipate that wider dissemination of the relationship will improve the degree, nature, certainty, or value of their own chances, then they are interested in the openness of the relationship; if on the other hand they anticipate that their own chances are improved by monopolizing it, then they will be interested in closure against *outsiders*.

A closed social relationship can guarantee its monopolized prospects (*Chance*) to participants in a number of ways. Such allocation might be (a) *freely* arrived at, (b) *regulated* or rationed by degree and form, or (c) *appropriated* on a more or less permanent basis by specific individuals or groups. This represents *internal* closure. Appropriated prospects can be called 'rights'. Such appropriation can result from rules established (1) by those participating in particular communities and associations (for example, households); or (2) by individuals, and here a distinction can be made between (a) purely personal appropriation, and (b) appropriation through inheritance, where a succession to the enjoyment of prospects is established either through birth, or by nomination on the part of the previous holder. It can also result from (3) the holder (a) more or less freely alienating such prospects to specific persons, or (b) by agreement to any other party. This is 'alienable' appropriation. A party to a closed relationship will be called a *member* (*Genosse*), and where participation is regulated in such a way as to secure prospects to that party, a *privileged member* (*Rechtsgenosse*). Prospects which are appropriated through inheritance on the part of individuals, communities, or associations will be termed *property* (of the relevant individuals, communities, or associations); prospects which are appropriated through alienation will be termed *free* property.

The seemingly useless and 'wearisome' definition of these circumstances is illustrative of the fact that what is 'taken for granted', because it is intuitively obvious, tends to be 'thought' about least.

1. Relationships which are:

(a) traditionally closed social relationships tend to be communities whose membership is based on kinship;
(b) affectually closed tend to be based on personal relations (of an erotic or reverential nature);
(c) relatively closed by virtue of rational adherence to values tend to the strict observance of communal beliefs;
(d) closed by virtue of instrumental rationality are economic associations of a monopolistic or plutocratic character.

A few examples can be cited here:

The extent to which a conversational group is open or closed depends upon content (light conversation as opposed to intimate or business communication). Market relations tend mostly to be open. It can be observed that many communities and associations *alternate* between expansion and exclusiveness. This is true of guilds, and also of the democratic city-states of ancient and medieval times, whose members alternately expanded and contracted their number, sometimes seeking as great a number as possible as a means of securing their power, while at other times they sought to restrict such growth in the interest of their monopoly. A similar process can be observed in monastic orders and sects, shifting from expansion in the interests of religious propaganda to restriction as a way of maintaining ethical standards, or for material reasons. There is a similar relationship between the extension of the market in the interest of greater turnover, and its monopolization. The promotion of linguistic uniformity is today in the interests of writers and publishers, whereas in earlier times language differed according to estate and also included secret languages.

2. The means and extent of regulation and external closure can be quite various, the change from openness, to regulation, to closure being a seamless one. Various conditions for participation can be set: qualifying tests, probationary periods, the purchase of a share in the membership, election of new members by ballot, membership or eligibility by birth, or by virtue of accomplishments open to anyone, or (where there is closure and the appropriation of rights) through the attainment of an appropriate right – membership conditions are graduated in a wide variety of ways. 'Regulation' and 'closure' are therefore relative concepts. An exclusive club, a theatre performance for which entry is by ticket, a widely advertised party rally, a church service open to all, the act of worship of a sect and a secret society (*Mysterium*) – these different examples all shade into one another.

3. *Inner* closure – among the members themselves and in their relationship to each other – can also assume the most various forms. For example, a caste, a guild, or stock exchange association can be closed with respect to external

members while at the same time the allocation of opportunities so monopolized are left to free competition among members. Or it might strictly allocate to each member specific opportunities for life with respect to clients or business prospects, or on a heritable basis, as in India. Or a closed group of settlers may allow its members either free use of its resources, or allocate them strictly to households; while a closed community might permit use of land in common, or assign specific holdings on a permanent basis. In all these cases a wide variety of intermediate conditions can be found. Historically, closure of eligibility to fief, benefices and offices within the group, and their assignment to those with right of enjoyment, has assumed a wide variety of forms. The development of rights to particular positions in the workplace, and succession to them, runs from the [English] closed shop on the one hand to a right to a particular position on the other; a preliminary stage for this is prohibition of dismissal without the agreement of a workers' representative. 'Workers' Councils' *could* form the first phase in this process, but not necessarily so. Details of this must be reserved for substantive individual studies. The greatest extent of permanent appropriation occurs where particular rights are guaranteed to an individual, or particular groups of individuals such as households, clans (*Sippen*), families in such a way that:

(1) in case of death their transfer to specified persons is regulated and guaranteed by orders, or
(2) the possessor of such rights is free to transfer the rights on any third party, who *hence* become participants in a social relationship.

Where complete *internal* appropriation occurs in this last fashion the group becomes in this respect relatively *open* to *outsiders*, so long as the inheritance of membership is not subject to agreement on the part of the existing members.

4. The *motivation* for closure can be:

(a) the maintenance of quality and also probably of prestige, with the associated prospect of honour and profit. Examples here are: groups of ascetics, monks (especially the Indian case of mendicant orders), religious sects like the Puritans, groups of warriors, ministerial and other officials, and of political citizenry (e.g. in Antiquity), craft guilds;
(b) the shortage of opportunity in relation to the needs of consumption (the balance of the food supply). An example is the monopoly of consumption (the most developed form the autarchic village community);
(c) the restriction of opportunities for acquisition. Examples are trade monopolies such as the guilds, or the ancient monopolies of fishing rights.

The first motivation is usually found in combination with the second or third.

§11. A social relationship governed by a traditional or statutory order can have the following consequences for its members:

(a) certain kinds of action can be *attributed* by *each* to *all* ('**solidary fellow members**') or

(b) certain kinds of action can be *attributed* by particular members ('**representatives**') to others ('the represented')

such that they either enjoy the opportunities or bear the consequences. Power of representation (authority) can be conferred as the prevailing order dictates:

(1) completely, in all its forms (independent authority) or

(2) in accordance with particular criteria, whether permanently or for a specified time or

(3) by specific acts on the part of members or third parties, temporarily or permanently (statutory authority).

Whether social relationships, communal or associative, are treated as solidary or as representative is determined by a number of factors, and it can be said quite generally that the degree to which action is directed towards (a) violent conflict or (b) peaceful exchange is here decisive, while recognizing that individual studies would identify particular circumstances critical to this issue. Where purely *ideal* goods are pursued with peaceful means this tends naturally enough to be the least common occurrence. Solidary or representative authority appears to be generally linked to the degree of closedness, but not always.

   1. 'Attribution' ('*Zurechnung*') can imply in practice:

(a) Both passive and active solidarity: everyone is answerable for the action of one person in the same way that that person is answerable; likewise all can legitimately enjoy the opportunities secured by the action of one member. Or responsibility is oriented to human beings and in the case of convention operates for and against privileged members (as in blood feuds with members of a clan, or reprisals against the inhabitants of a city or fellow nationals). Alternatively, responsibility is based on law (the punishment of relatives, members of household and members of the commune, and the personal liability of each member of a household or a commercial partnership for another member's debts). Solidaristic responsibility in relation to gods has also had important consequences for ancient Israelite, Christian, and Puritan communities.

(b) But, on the other hand (at the very least), attribution of responsibility can also merely mean that those involved in a closed relationship governed by tradition or legal statute consider themselves *legally* entitled to the enjoyment of various benefits (especially economic opportunities) procured by a representative. Examples are the 'validity' of powers of disposal exercised by the 'executive committee' of an 'association', or on the part of the representative of a political or economic association, with respect to material goods which are intended for use by the association.

2. Solidarity is typically found in the following cases:

(a) in traditional communities based on birth or the sharing of a common way of life (typically, the household and the clan);
(b) in closed relationships where opportunities are monopolized through the exercise of their own force (this is typical of political groups, especially in the past, but most extensively during wartime, including the present);
(c) in profit-making organizations whose activity is directed by the participants in person (typically, an open trading company);
(d) in some cases, in societies based upon labour (typically, the artel).[21]

Representation is most frequently encountered in associations formed for a specific purpose, or statutory bodies, especially where funds have been collected for a specific purpose and require administration (more on this in my treatment of legal sociology).

3. Representative authority is conferred according to 'criteria' when, for example, this occurs by seniority or some other rule.

4. The details of these circumstances cannot be dealt with here, and must be investigated in individual sociological studies. The most ancient and universal phenomenon here is that of *reprisal*, whether for purposes of revenge or of hostage-taking.

§12. A social relationship which is either closed to outsiders, or restricts their admission according to set rules, will be called a **group body** (*Verband* [literally, a banded-together group of people]) when the maintenance of order is guaranteed by the action of specifically designated persons: an *executive* (*Leiter*) and probably also an *administrative staff* which usually has representative powers. Exercise of executive powers or participation in the work of the staff – the '*powers of government*' – can be:

(a) appropriated, or
(b) permanently, temporarily, or for particular cases, exercised by persons selected by prevailing rules, by the possession of certain characteristics, or according to specific procedures.

21 A co-operative organization of Russian peasant workers of the nineteenth century that aimed to restrict the division of labour within home industries.

Action by the 'group body' is either:

(a) the legitimate action of the administrative staff itself in executing its powers of government or of representation, or
(b) action on the part of members under the direction of the administrative staff.

1. The communal or associational nature of a group has no consequences for conceptual definition here. The presence of an 'executive' is entirely sufficient: that the action of a head of a household, chairman of an association, chief executive, prince, state president, or head of a church is directed to the implementation of a group order. This form of *action* is oriented not simply to the order itself, but rather to its *enforcement*, and adds sociologically an entirely new feature to the existence of a closed 'social relationship'. For not every closed community or association is a 'group body' – not, for instance, an erotic relationship, or a clan without a leader.

2. The 'existence' of a 'group body' depends entirely on the presence of a leader, and possibly of an administrative staff. To put it more exactly: on the existence of the *likelihood* that the *action* of certain persons occurs and is directed to the execution of order of the group: that there are people '*disposed*' to act accordingly in every sense. It is a matter of *conceptual* indifference whether this disposition arises from traditional, affective or value-rational dedication (feudal fealty, loyalty to an office, or to a service), or from instrumental *interests* (the salary paid). For our purposes, the 'group body' exists sociologically only insofar as action conforms to that outlined here. In the absence of a staff or an individual performing action in the manner defined there is in our terminology no 'group body', although a 'social relationship' does exist. For as long as the prospect of such action being performed exists, the 'group body' exists, sociologically speaking; *despite the change of personnel* who orient their action to the order in this way. (The purpose of this form of definition is to include exactly this circumstance.)

3. (a) In addition to the action of the administrative staff itself, or under its leadership, there may be other cases where action of the participants is intended to uphold the authority of the order (contributions or personal services of all kinds serving the common good, such as jury or military service).

(b) The prevailing order can also include norms to which the action of members should be oriented in circumstances *other* than those directly concerned with the group: for example, the regulation by the state of 'private' economic interests beyond those which are directly the concern of the group body; and in 'civil' law. In case of (a) we can refer to 'action related to the group body', while in (b) we might refer to 'action *regulated* by the group body'. Only the action of the administrative staff itself and all planned activity under its direction should be called 'group action'. 'Group action' for all participants would be, for example, a 'war' which a state 'waged', or a contribution decided upon by an association's managing committee, a 'contract' concluded by the executive and whose 'validity' is compulsorily imposed upon members of the group, and to which it is assumed that all will conform (§11), and also 'legal proceedings' and 'administration'. (See also §14.)

A group body can be:

(a) autonomous or heteronomous;
(b) autocephalous or heterocephalous.

Autonomy means that the order cannot (as in heteronomy) be subordinated to the statutory action of outsiders, but only by group members on their own authority, and regardless of how this is done. Autocephaly means that the executive and the group staff act according to the directives of their own group order, and are not subject to directives (of whatever kind) from outsiders, as with heterocephaly.

An instance of heterocephaly occurs where Canadian provincial governors are appointed by the central government. A heterocephalous group body can also be autonomous, and an autocephalous heteronomous. A group body can be *partly* the one, and partly the other, in both respects. Autocephalous federal German states (*Bundesstaaten*) were, despite their autocephalous status, heteronomous within the sphere of competence of the Reich, while autonomous in matters relating to church and school. Alsace Lorraine enjoyed a degree of autonomy within the German Reich before 1918, but also heterocephalous since the governor was appointed by the Kaiser. All of these circumstances can co-exist to an extent. A group body which is entirely heteronomous *as well as* heterocephalous (like a 'regiment' within an army) can usually be said to be a 'part' of a larger whole. Whether this is in fact the case or not depends on the actual *extent* of independence in the orientation of action in each individual case and is terminologically a pure matter of convenience.

§13. The **statutory order** of an associative relationship may originate:

(a) by voluntary agreement; or
(b) through imposition and acquiescence.

The governing power of the group may claim a legitimate power to impose new orders. The *constitution* of the group denotes the *actual* likelihood – varying in degree, form and preconditions – of acquiescence to the power of *imposition* enjoyed by the existing governing bodies. Prevailing rules might specify that among these preconditions particular groups or sections of the group membership be heard, or express their agreement, in addition to which there is a wide variety of other possible preconditions.

A group body can impose its rules upon members, but also upon non-members in specific *circumstances*. Territorial circumstances are here especially relevant (presence, place of birth, performance of certain actions within a territory). This is 'territorial authority'. A group body whose order is imposed primarily by virtue of territorial authority will be called a territorial group, regardless of the extent of its authority internal to the group. *Only* territorial authority is claimed in relation to the members of the group body (*Verband*), and it is confined to what is possible or what occurs in a limited degree.

1. An imposed order in the sense used here is *any* order not established on the basis of a free personal agreement by all participants. This includes therefore a 'majority decision' in which a minority acquiesce. The legitimacy of a majority decision therefore often goes unrecognized for a long time or gives rise to problems (see, for example, the position of medieval estates, or the Russian *obschina* right up to the present day).[22]

2. It is generally acknowledged that formally 'free' agreements are often in fact imposed (as in the *obschina*). As far as sociology is concerned it is the *actual* nature of the relationship that is important.

3. The concept of 'constitution' used here is the same as that used by Lassalle.[23] It is not the same as a 'written' constitution, and is certainly quite distinct from the legal sense. The sociological question is simply: When, involving which objects, *within which boundaries*, and (probably) under which special conditions (e.g. approval on the part of gods or priests, or the assent of elected bodies) do the members of a group body accept the leadership of the executive, and under what conditions is the administrative staff and group action at his disposal when the executive 'makes decisions' or in particular, when the executive imposes orders?

4. The principal types of imposed 'territorial authority' within political bodies are the norms of criminal law and many other 'legal statutes' where residence, birthplace, location of action or place of realization, etc. in the territories of the group body are preconditions for the application of the order.

§14. An order that regulates the action of a corporate body will be called an **administrative order**. An order that regulates other kinds of social action and thereby protects the opportunity of actors that are made available by such rules will be called a **regulatory order**. A group oriented only to the first kind of order will be called an administrative group, one oriented exclusively to the second, a regulatory group.

1. Of course, the majority of group bodies (*Verbände*) include both characteristics. A *solely* regulatory order would for instance be the theoretically possible pure form of a state based on the rule of law allowing a regime of

---

22 Weber refers the reader to his sociologies of rulership and law at this point. The *obschina* was a Russian peasant commune responsible for dividing up communal land.

23 Ferdinand Lassalle was a founder of the German social democratic movement. He criticized the Prussian constitution for providing unequal voting rights.

absolute *laissez-faire*, which would naturally also involve the transfer of monetary regulation to the private sector.

2. On the concept of 'group action' see §12, No. 3. The concept of 'administrative order' embraces all rules which govern not only the behaviour of the administrative staff but also the behaviour of members in their relation to the group body. This includes those goals whose attainment the administrative order endeavours to secure through the deliberately (*positiv*) prescribed and planned activity of the administrative staff and its members. In a pure communist economic system practically *all* social action would fall under this category, while in a state strictly based on the rule of law only the actions of judges, police authorities, jurors, soldiers, and the activity of legislators and voters would do so. In general – although not in every case – the boundary between administrative and regulatory orders coincides with the distinction of 'public' and 'private' law in the corporate group. (More detail on this is given in ch. 1 in *The Sociology of Law*.)

§15. An **enterprise** (*Betrieb*) will refer to continuous goal-directed activity of a particular sort, and its organizational group (*Betriebsverband*) will refer to an associational administrative staff whose activities are continuous and goal-directed.

A **voluntary association** (*Verein*) will refer to a group formed through agreement, whose statutes have valid authority only for members who have joined out of personal choice.

An **institution** (*Anstalt*) will refer to a group whose statutes can be imposed with relative success within a given domain on all behaviour that conforms to specific characteristics.

1. The concept of 'enterprise' naturally includes the prosecution of political and ecclesiastical affairs as well as that of voluntary associations so long as these are characterized by purposeful continuity.

2. 'Voluntary association' and 'institution' are both group bodies (*Verbände*) with *rational* (planned) statutes. Or more exactly: a group body should be called a 'voluntary association' or an 'institution' *insofar* as it has rational statutes. The prime instance of an 'institution' is the state, along with all its auxiliary heterocephalous groups – and the Church, so long as its statutes are rational. The orders of an 'institution' claim validity for all who *meet* particular characteristics (place of birth, residence, use of certain facilities), regardless of whether or not they have joined in person (as with a voluntary association), or contributed to the formation of the group's rules. They are therefore *imposed* orders in a quite specific sense. The institution in particular can be a *territorial* group.

3. The contrast between a voluntary association and an institution is only *relative*. The rules of a voluntary association can affect the interests of third parties, and recognition of their authority can then be imposed on such third parties by usurpation by the simple power of the association, or by legal statute (for example, the law regulating share dealing).

4. It hardly needs emphasizing that 'voluntary association' and 'institution' do not exhaust *all* conceivable group bodies. They are indeed 'polar' contrasts (as, for instance, are 'sect' and 'church' in the religious domain).

§16. **Power** (*Macht*) can be defined as the chance, within a social relationship, of enforcing one's own will against resistance, whatever this chance might be based on.

Rulership (*Herrschaft*) will be termed the chance that a command of a certain kind will be obeyed by a given group of people. **Discipline** will be termed the chance that by virtue of habituation a command will promote automatic, stereotypical responses among a definite number of persons.

1. The concept of 'power' is sociologically quite amorphous. Any conceivable quality of a person, and all conceivable constellations can place someone in a position of being able to enforce one's own will in a given situation. The sociological concept of 'rulership' must therefore be more precise and can be used only in the sense of a chance that a *command* will meet with acquiescence.

2. The concept of 'discipline' includes the 'habituation' characteristic of uncritical and unresisting *mass* obedience.

The existence of rulership turns only on the presence *of one* person successfully issuing commands to *others*, independently of the existence of an administrative staff or of a group body; although in all normal cases *one* of these is true. A group body will be called a *rulership group body* (*Herrschaftsverband*) to the extent that its members are subordinated within a relationship of power on account of the validity of an order.[24]

1. The head of a household rules without an administrative staff. The Bedouin chief, who raises tribute from caravans, persons, and goods passing his stronghold, exercises power over a changing and indefinite number of people who while not associated with each other find themselves in a common situation. In order to do this, his following act as the occasion demands as his administrative staff in enforcing his will. (This kind of rule would also be theoretically conceivable where one person acted without any administrative staff.)

2. Thanks to the existence of an administrative staff a group body is always to some extent a rulership group body. The concept is a relative one. The normal rulership group is also as such an administrative group body. The character of the group body is determined by a number of factors: the manner as well as the character of the administrative personnel, the objects of administration, and the extent of its effective power. The first two of these are especially dependent upon the *legitimate* basis of rulership. (On this see ch. III in *E&S*.)

---

24 A 'rulership group body' (*Herrschaftsverband*) is a topic taken up at greater length by Weber in 'The Three Pure Types of Legitimate Rule'; see Reading 7.

§17. A rulership group body (*Herrschaftsverband*) will be called **political** to the extent that its existence and authority can be continually guaranteed within a given geographical *area* by the application and threat of *physical* coercion by an administrative staff. A political *institutional organization* will be called a **state** to the extent that an administrative staff can successfully exercise a *monopoly of legitimate* physical force in the execution of its orders. Social action is 'politically oriented', especially in relation to the action of the group, when it is directed to influence over the leadership of a political group; in particular, the appropriation, expropriation, redistribution, or allocation of powers of government where this does not involve violent means (see No. 2 below).

A rulership group body will be called **hierocratic** where it guarantees its order through the employment of psychic coercion through the distribution or denial of religious benefits (hierocratic coercion). A **church** is a hierocratic *institutional organization* where its administrative staff *monopolize* legitimate hierocratic coercion.

1. Violence is of course neither the sole, nor the usual administrative means employed by political group bodies. Their leaders have instead made use of all possible means for the realization of their ends. But the threat of violent means, and possibly their use is *specific* to political groups and always the last resort when other means fail. The use of violence as a legitimate means has *not been*, and *is not unique* to political groups: clans, households, guilds, and in the Middle Ages sometimes all those entitled to bear arms. Besides the use of violence as a means of securing 'order', the political group is characterized by the manner in which its administrative staff claim rulership over a definite *territory* and secure it by force. Where groups make use of force – whether it is a village community, single households, or groups of guilds or workers ('councils') – they are *to this extent* political group bodies.

2. A political group, or a 'state' cannot be defined in terms of the *purpose* of the action of its group body (*Verband*). All the way from the provision of food to the patronage of art, there is *no* conceivable purpose which at one time or another has not been pursued. And from the protection of personal security to the administration of justice there is none which all have recognized. The 'political' character of a group body can therefore be defined only in terms of the *means* (which sometimes becomes an end in itself) not necessarily unique to it, but all the same *indispensable* for its nature: violence. Normal linguistic usage does not entirely conform to this, but without being made more precise it is quite unusable. One talks of the 'foreign exchange policy' of the Reichsbank, of the 'financial policy' of an association, of the 'educational policy' of a local council (*Gemeinde*). We mean by this the planned treatment and *control* of a particular substantive matter. We approach the present meaning more closely when we distinguish the 'political' aspect or implication of a question. Thus there is the 'political' official, the 'political' newspaper, the 'political' revolution, the 'political' club, the 'political' party, and the 'political' consequences of an action, as distinct

from others such as the economic, cultural, religious aspect of the persons, affairs or processes in question. Here we generally mean by 'political' that which is linked to relations of authority within (in our terms) a political organization, the state. We refer in this way to factors likely to maintain, to alter, overthrow, hinder, or promote the interests of the state, as distinct from persons, things, and processes which have nothing to do with it. This usage therefore seeks to bring out the features shared by the various *means* of exercising 'domination' used within the state to enforce its order, abstracting them from the ends they serve. Hence it is legitimate to claim that the definition made here is only a more precise form of common usage in that it sharply emphasizes the most characteristic of those means: the actual or threatened use of violence. Of course, everyday language applies the term 'political' not only to groups which are the agents of the legitimate use of violence, but also to parties and clubs which seek to influence the action of a political group quite peaceably. We will distinguish this kind of social action, which will be called 'politically oriented', to distinguish it from genuine 'political' action (the action of group bodies as political as defined in §12, No. 3).

3. Since the complete development of the concept of the *state* is quite modern, it is best to define it in terms of the modern type, while at the same time abstracting from those changing substantive purposes with which we are familiar today. Formally characteristic of the modern state is an administrative and a legal order subject to change by statute, to which the organized group activity of the administrative staff, likewise governed by statute, is oriented. This order claims authority not only over its members, the majority of whom have acquired membership by birth, but also to a great extent over all action taking place under its jurisdiction. Today the use of force is considered 'legitimate' only to the degree that it is permitted or prescribed by the state (e.g. reserving the 'right of chastisement' to the head of the household, a survival of the former independent authority of the head which right to violence extended to a power of life or death over children and slaves). This manner in which the state lays claim to the monopoly of rule by force is as essential a current feature as is its character as rational 'institution' and continuous 'organization'.

4. In formulating the concept of a hierocratic group body (*Verband*) we cannot use the *nature* of its prospective religious salvation benefits – worldly, other-worldly, external, inner – as decisive characteristics, rather their ministration can form the basis for spiritual *dominion* (*Herrschaft*) over human beings. What is most characteristic of the concept of the Church, even in common (and practical) usage, is that the forms of its orders and administrative staff are expressive of a rational, compulsory organization and that it claims monopolistic dominion. It is normal for a church institution to *strive* for its own hierocratic territorial rulership and to establish this through parochial or territorial organization, although the means through which this monopolistic claim is realized varies from case to case. But, unlike the

political group, actual monopolistic rulership of a given *territory* was not essential, and is not at all so today. This 'institutional' character, especially the circumstance that one is 'born into' a church, distinguishes a 'church' from a 'sect', whose characteristic feature is that of an 'association', and admits on a personal basis only those who are religiously qualified.

22 The 'objectivity' of knowledge in social science and social policy[1]

The first question posed to a new social science journal (especially one directed to social policy), or a new editorial board, concerns its 'tendency'. We too find this question unavoidable, and following on from the remarks already made in the 'Geleitwort' we present here a more systematic treatment of the issues. This gives us an opportunity to shed light on the specific character of what we understand as 'social scientific' work in a variety of domains, if not of use to the expert, then of interest to the reader detached from practical scientific activity; even though, or perhaps directly because, we are here dealing with 'self-evident' matters.

The express aim of the *Archiv* has been since its foundation, alongside the enlargement of our knowledge of 'social circumstances of all countries' – i.e. the *facts* of social life, the training of *judgement* in respect of *practical problems* arising from these social circumstances; and hence, given the very modest degree to which such an aim can be pursued by private scholars, the

---

1 'Die "Objektivität" sozialwissenschaftlicher und sozialpolitischer Erkenntnis', *WL*, pp. 146–214. Translation by Keith Tribe. [Weber] Where in Section I of the following reference is made explicitly to the views of the editors, or tasks proposed for the *Archiv*, the statements in question have been expressly endorsed by the joint editors, and are not of course the private views of the author. In Section II the author bears *sole* responsibility for both form and content.

The *Archiv* will never be swayed by any one particular school of thought, and the fact that contributors and editors alike lack a common standpoint or methodological view ensures this. Of course, agreement on certain basic views was a presupposition for the joint assumption of editorial control. This agreement concerns in particular a common estimation of the value of *theoretical* knowledge among 'one-sided' viewpoints, as well as in furthering the *formation of clear concepts* and the strict *distinction between empirical knowledge (Erfahrungswissen) and value-judgements*, as represented here, without any claim being made as to the 'novelty' of such an enterprise.

The wide-ranging argument and frequent repetition of the same idea in Section II is aimed exclusively at achieving the greatest possible *common understanding* in such discussion. Often, although not I hope too frequently, this interest is sacrificed to precision of expression, and it is this interest which has dictated that no effort has been made to replace a review of some methodological viewpoints with a *systematic* investigation. This would have made necessary the introduction of a number of epistemological problems that to some extent lie much deeper. This is not an exercise in logic, rather the established results of modern logic should be set to work for us; problems will not be solved, but their significance made plain to the lay person. Anyone familiar with the writings of modern logicians – here I cite only Windelband, Simmel, and especially for our concerns Heinrich Rickert – will notice immediately that in most important respects this essay takes its starting point from them.

elaboration of a critique of practical socio-political work reaching as far as legislative factors. Nevertheless, from the very first the *Archiv* aspired to be an exclusively scholarly journal, employing only the means of *scientific* research – and so the problem arose of how such an aim might in principle be reconciled with these means. If the legislative and administrative measures together with related practical suggestions found in its columns were open to *judgement* – what does that mean? What are the *norms* for such judgements? What sort of *validity* inheres in the value-judgements expressed by an individual, or those which a writer employs to support practical proposals? In what sense does he, in so doing, enter into the terrain of *scientific* discussion, for of course the leading characteristic of scientific knowledge must be the 'objective' validity of its results as *truth*. First of all we shall elaborate our own position on *this* question, so that we might later raise another: in what *general* sense *are* there 'objectively valid truths' in the domain of the sciences of cultural life? This is an inescapable question, given the constant state of change and bitter conflict over what appear to be the most elementary problems of our discipline, its method of working, the manner in which it constructs concepts, and their validity. We offer no solutions here, but seek rather to indicate problems – those problems to which our journal, if it is to be true to its past and future purpose, will have to direct its attention.

I

We all know that our science, as every science concerned with human cultural institutions and cultural processes (excepting perhaps political history), arose historically from *practical* perspectives. Its immediate, and initially sole, purpose lay in the production of value-judgements in respect of specific instances of state economic policy. It was a 'technique' in the sense, for instance, that the clinical disciplines of medical sciences are 'techniques'. It is now known how this situation was gradually modified. This modification was not, however, accompanied by a formulation of a *principled* distinction between 'existential knowledge', knowledge of what 'is', and 'normative knowledge', i.e. knowledge of what 'should be'. Such a distinction was blocked first of all by the view that immutably invariant natural laws determined economic processes, a view then succeeded by the idea that such processes were determined by a specific developmental principle; hence *that which should exist* coincided either, in the first instance, with the immutably *extant*, and in the second, with the inevitably *emergent*. With the growth of historical awareness, a combination of ethical evolutionism and historical relativism became the predominant attitude in our science, seeking to strip ethical norms of their formal character and hence, through incorporation of the entirety of cultural values, lend *substantive* definition to the domain of 'morals'. Economics would thus be raised to the dignified status of an empirically founded 'ethical science'. By 'morally' endorsing all possible cultural ideals one did away with the specific virtue of the ethical imperative without gaining anything with respect to the 'objective' validity of such ideals. We can and must leave debate over principles to one side here; and we hold fast solely to the fact that, even today, the mistaken opinion that economics does and should produce *value-judgements* formed on the basis of a specifically 'economic worldview' not only persists, but is (understandably) especially widespread among practical men of affairs.

As a representative of a specialized empirical discipline (as will be demonstrated below) our journal has to *reject fundamentally* this view; for we are of the opinion that the task of an experiential science can never be the determination of binding norms and ideals, from which in turn guidelines for practical application might be derived.

But what follows from this statement? In no respect is it here implied that value-judgements should be kept entirely out of scientific discussion because of their ultimate dependence upon particular ideals, that they are thus 'subjective' in origin. Both in practice and purpose our journal would always rebut such a statement. Critical argument does not stop short at value-judgements. The question is rather: What is the *meaning* and *purpose* of scientific criticism of ideals and value-judgements? This demands rather more detailed consideration.

Any thoughtful reflection on the ultimate elements of meaningful human action turns first of all on the categories 'means' and 'ends'. Specifically, we want something either 'for its own sake', or as a means of acquiring something ultimately desired. The suitability of means to given ends is the prime question accessible to scientific consideration. Taking into account the prevailing bounds of our knowledge, we can determine *which* means are either suitable or not for a given end. We can also estimate the chances of achieving a particular end with the given available means, and so in this way indirectly determine whether the ends themselves, given the prevailing historical situation, are practically meaningful, or criticize them as meaningless in the given circumstances. Furthermore, *if* the conditions for attaining a given end seem to be present (always of course within the limits of current knowledge), we can determine the *consequences* that the application of the requisite means within the total context of events will have *besides* the attainment of the intended end. In this way we offer to the actor the possibility of weighing these intended consequences against the unintended, and hence an answer to the question: What does the attainment of the desired end *'cost'* in the context of foreseeable injury to *other* values? Since in the great majority of cases every sought-for end does or can 'cost' something in this sense, no person behaving reflectively and responsibly can avoid this balancing of the ends of an action against its consequences; and one of the most important functions of the *technical* criticism considered so far is to provide for this. Turning an assessment of this kind into a decision is certainly *not* the business of science, but of the desiring person: he weighs and chooses between the values concerned according to conscience and personal viewpoint. Science can help him to a *consciousness* that *all* action – naturally likewise in some circumstances a *lack of action* – has as its consequence *endorsement* of particular values; but today that this also involves the consistent *rejection of other values* is too often readily overlooked. Making a choice is his own affair.

In the making of such a decision we can further offer: *knowledge* of the *significance* of that which is wished for. We can elucidate the desired ends between which he chooses according to context and significance, first of all by indicating and developing in a logically consistent manner the 'ideas' that do, or can, underlie the concrete end. For it is obvious that one of the most important tasks of a science of human cultural life is to open up to intellectual understanding these 'ideas' over which men have actually or supposedly struggled, and still do. This does not transgress the bounds of a science seeking the 'conceptual (*denkend*) order of empirical reality', nor the means serving this interpretation of intellectual values – 'inductions' in the usual sense. Such a task certainly falls at least in part beyond the bounds of the discipline of economics as defined by customary divisions of specialization; it belongs among the tasks of *social philosophy*. But the historical power of ideas has become, and remains, so powerful in the development of social life that our journal will never exclude this task from its pages, but include its treatment among its most important duties.

None the less, the scientific treatment of value-judgements seeks not only to facilitate understanding and evocation of desired ends and their underlying ideals, but also to teach how they might be critically 'judged'. Of course, *this* criticism can only be of dialectical character, i.e. it can only be a formal and logical judgement of the material content of historically given value-judgements and ideas, testing ideals against a postulated *lack of contradiction* inhering in the desired end. Hence the desiring actor can in this way be prompted to reflect upon those ultimate axioms governing the content of his desires, upon the ultimate standards of value upon which he unconsciously acts, or, to be consistent, upon which he must act. Rendering *conscious* these ultimate standards, as manifested in substantive value-judgements, is the most that such scientific treatment can achieve without entering the realm of speculation. Whether these ultimate standards *should* be acknowledged by the judging subject is his own affair, a question of his desire and conscience, and not of experiential knowledge.

An empirical science cannot teach anyone what he *should* do, only what he *can* do and, in some circumstances, what he *wants*. It is true that personal views constantly enter into scientific argument and blunt it, arbitrarily varying the weight of scientific arguments even when investigating simple causal relationships between facts, so that the result might diminish or enhance the prospect of realizing personal ideals, the possibility of desiring something definite. Even the editors and contributors to our journal will regard 'nothing human as alien' in this respect. But it is a long way from this confession of human weakness to belief in an 'ethical' science of economics which is supposed to produce ideals from its material, or which through the application of general ethical imperatives is supposed to produce concrete norms. It is true that we feel those innermost elements of 'personality' to be 'objectively' valuable, those highest and ultimate value-judgements that govern our action and lend meaning and significance to our life. We are only able to adopt them so long as they appear to us as having validity, flowing from our highest values and formed in the struggles of daily life. And it is certain that the integrity of 'personality' flows from the existence of values to which its own life is related. And if on occasion these values were located exclusively *within* the sphere of its own individuality, then 'self-realization' with respect to *just those* interests for which it claims *validity as values* is the idea to which personality relates itself. The open espousal of value-judgements in any case presupposes a belief in values. *None the less: judgement* of the *validity* of such values is a matter of *belief; perhaps* also a task for speculative observation and interpretation of the meaning of life and the world; but is certainly not the object of an experiential science in the sense to be practised here. In making this distinction the empirically demonstrable fact that ultimate ends are historically mutable and subject to dispute is not decisive, despite widespread belief to the contrary. For even knowledge of the most certain statement of the theoretical sciences (for example, the natural or mathematical sciences) is above all a cultural product, just like the clarification and refinement of the conscience.

We only need to consider the practical problems of social and economic policy (in its usual sense) to find numerous, even countless practical *individual questions* discussion of which by general agreement treats specific ends as *self-evident* – examples are, for instance, emergency credit, concrete problems of public health, poor relief, measures such as factory inspection, industrial tribunals, employment exchanges, and a large part of protective labour legislation – where it seems at least that only the *means* for the achievement of ends are an issue. But even if here we take the seemingly obvious for reality – something that science would never do without cost – and proceed to regard as purely technical questions of expedience inconsistencies arising out of any attempt at practical execution (which is a mistake recurring quite regularly), then we would have to note that this apparent obviousness of governing value standards disappears as soon as we move from the domain of concrete problems (of charitable welfare work and welfare and economic services) to questions of economic and social policy. The social and *political* character of a problem is distinguished by the fact that it *cannot* be resolved by the application of mere technical considerations to fixed ends, that *argument* can and *must* arise over the regulating standards of value, and because the problem reaches into the region of general *cultural* questions. And there is dispute not only between 'class interests', as we too readily think today, *but also between worldviews* – which however leaves quite unaffected the truth that *whatever* the worldview to which the individual adheres, among many other influences one feature tends to be increasingly decisive: the degree of elective affinity that unites it with 'class interest' – if we can here use a concept whose lack of ambiguity is quite superficial. In all circumstances one thing is completely certain: the more 'general' a problem, that is, the greater the scope of its *cultural significance*, the less accessible is it to an unambiguous response based upon experiential knowledge, the greater the role played by the ulti- mate and highest axioms of belief and ideas of value. It is simply naïve to believe – notwithstanding occasional evidence of continuing faith on the part of specialists – that it is sufficient for practical social science merely to put forward and scientifically corroborate 'a principle' from which the norms for the solution of individual practical problems can be unambiguously deduced. However important discussion of the principles underlying indi- vidual practical problems is to social science, i.e. reconnecting unreflecting value-judgements to their conceptual content, and however much our journal intends to devote itself especially to them – the creation of a practical lowest common denominator for our problems in the shape of generally valid ulti- mate ideals can quite certainly be neither the task of this journal, nor indeed of any experiential science (*Erfahrungswissenschaft*): as such it would be not only practically insoluble, but also an absurdity. And however the basis and nature of commitment to ethical imperatives might be interpreted, it is certain that normative *cultural contents* cannot be unambiguously *deduced* from these norms for the concretely determined action of the *individual*; and the more comprehensive the contents concerned, the weaker such a proposition becomes. Only positive religions – more precisely, dogmatically ordered *sects* – are capable of lending the content of *cultural values* the dignity of unconditionally valid ethical imperatives. Outside such sects the cultural ideals that an individual *wishes* to realize, and the ethical duties that he *should* fulfil, are of quite differing degrees of dignity. The fate of a cultural epoch that has eaten from the tree of knowledge is that it must know that we cannot read the *meaning* of world events out of the results of any analysis, no matter how complete that might be; but that it has to be prepared to create such a meaning itself, that 'worldviews' can never be the product of enhanced experiential knowledge, and that therefore the highest ideals that move us most strongly are forever formed in struggle with other ideals, ideals which are as dear to others as ours are to us.

Only the kind of optimistic syncretism that results from a historico- developmental relativism can deceive itself with respect to the immense seriousness of this situation, or practically evade its consequences. Naturally in individual cases the practical politician can subjectively find himself duty- bound to mediate between antagonistic opinions, or alternatively take sides with one of them. But this has nothing at all to do with *scientific* 'objectivity'. The 'middle way' is *not one jot closer to scientific truth* than the most extreme party ideals of left or right. Nowhere is the interest of science worse off in the long term than when one refuses to acknowledge uncomfortable facts and the stark reality of life. The *Archiv* will struggle unconditionally against the ser- ious delusion that one can, through synthesis of several party lines, or by drawing a line mediating between them, derive practical norms having *scien- tific validity*; for this belief, fond of relativizing and hence disguising its own standards of value, is far more dangerous for the freedom of research than the older naïve party political belief in the scientific 'verifiability' of their dogmas. The capacity of *distinction* between perception and judgement, together with discharge of the scientific duty to see factual truth, as well as in practice defending one's own ideals – these represent the programme to which we wish to adhere.

There is and remains an eternal, unbridgeable difference – and *this* is what is of importance for us – separating the manner in which argument is directed to our feelings, and our capacity to be enthused in respect of concrete practical aims, cultural forms, and cultural contents; or by contrast, where once the validity of ethical norms is questioned, to our conscience; *or* finally, directed to our ability and need *for conceptually ordering* empirical reality in such a manner as to lay claim to *validity* as experiential truth. As we shall see, the truth of this proposition is not diminished even where those highest 'values' of *practical* interest are and will remain of decisive importance for the *path* taken up by the ordering activity of thought within the domain of the cultural sciences. It has been and continues to be true that a methodologically correct form of proof in the social sciences, if thought to be complete, has to be recognized as correct even by a Chinaman, or – more precisely – that it must at any rate *strive* to reach a goal perhaps not completely attainable for lack of material. Moreover, even *logical* analysis of an ideal with respect to its content and its ultimate axioms, together with demonstration of the logical and practical consequences arising from pursuit of such an ideal should, if they are to be deemed successful, likewise have to be valid for this Chinaman. Although he might be 'deaf' to our ethical imperatives, can and certainly often will reject this ideal and the concrete *evaluations* flowing from it, this in no respect detracts from the scientific value of such conceptual *analysis*. Our journal will certainly not ignore the constant and unavoidable recurrence of efforts to arrive at unambiguous definitions of the *meaning* of cultural life. On the contrary, they are part of the most important creation of this cultural life itself, at times becoming its most powerful motive forces. We will therefore at all times follow carefully the course taken by 'social philosophical' debates in *this* sense. Besides, there is here no trace of the prejudice according to which those observations of cultural life that seek a metaphysical interpretation of the world going beyond the conceptual ordering of the empirically given *could*, because of this character, serve no useful purpose for knowledge. What this purpose might be is primarily a problem for epistemology, response to which cannot, and need not, trouble us here. For there is one thing to which *our* work holds fast: a social scientific periodical as we understand it should, inasmuch as it is *scientific*, be a space where truth is sought, truth which can claim to be a valid conceptual ordering of empirical reality, a validity which – keeping to our example – even holds true for our Chinaman.

Of course, the editors cannot once and for all proscribe any expression of their own, or of their contributors', innermost ideals in value-judgements.

But two important obligations arise out of this. First of all, both readers and editors should be at all times entirely aware *which* standards are here applied for the measurement of reality, and from which a value-judgement is derived; contrasting with the all too frequent practice of an imprecise mingling of the most diverse values, confounding the conflict between ideals in an effort to 'offer something to everyone'. If this obligation becomes sufficiently rigorous then the expression of practical judgement in a purely scientific interest is not only inoffensive, but directly useful, even requisite. In the scientific criticism of legislation and other practical matters the full implication of the legislator's motivation, and the ideals of a criticized writer, can very often only be made entirely clear through *confrontation* of their value-standards with others, and ideally: with one's own. Any meaningful *evaluation* of alien *aspirations* can only be a critique formed from one's own 'worldview', a struggle against *alien* ideals on the basis of one's *own* ideals. *If* in individual cases the ultimate value-axiom underlying a practical aspiration is not only identified and subjected to scientific analysis, but its relationships with *other* value-axioms made clear, then 'positive' criticism of the latter through systematic exposition is unavoidable.

Thus the columns of the journal – especially where reviewing laws – will inevitably include discussion of *social science* (the conceptual ordering of facts) alongside *social policy* (the exposition of ideals). But we would not think of presenting such discussions as '*science*', and we will strive with our best efforts to prevent such muddle and confusion. It is no longer *science* which is speaking, and the second fundamental rule of scientific impartiality is therefore: in such cases to make at all times clear to the reader (and, we repeat, above all to oneself!) *when* and *where* the thoughtful researcher stops speaking and the needing human being begins, *where* arguments are addressed to understanding and *where* they are directed to feelings. The continual fusion of scientific discussion of facts with evaluative rationalization is one of the most widespread, but also most damaging, features of work in our discipline. The following remarks are directed against this *fusion*, and *not* against advocacy of one's own ideals. *Lack of inner conviction* and *scientific* 'objectivity' have no essential connection. The *Archiv* never has been, at least intentionally, a place where polemic against particular political or socio-political parties was to be found, nor must it become one; and it was never a place where political or socio-political ideals were either promoted or denounced – there are other publications for that sort of thing. The special character of the journal from the very first was that bitter political opponents came together in its pages to make scientific contributions – a character which the editors have to continue. Hitherto it has not been a 'socialist' periodical; henceforth neither shall it be 'bourgeois'. No one who is prepared to work within the framework of scientific discussion is excluded from its circle of contributors. It is not an arena for 'objections', replies and rebuttals; but it protects no one – not its contributors, and certainly not its editors – from exposure in its columns to the sharpest conceivable material and scientific criticism. Whoever finds that too difficult, or refuses to work with people serving ideals different to their own, even in the context of scientific knowledge – such people can remain uninvolved.

However, we cannot deceive ourselves that today this last sentence says rather more than is apparent at first glance. First, and as already indicated, experience shows that everywhere, and especially in the German context, there are psychological barriers limiting opportunities for open co-operation, be it social or intellectual, between political opponents on neutral ground. While these must be opposed as signs of narrow party fanaticism and a poorly developed political culture, this becomes all the more important for a journal such as ours, since in the domain of the social sciences the impulse to debate scientific questions regularly comes (in our experience) from *practical* 'questions', such that mere recognition that a scientific problem exists is united personally with a human being having specific wants and desires. In the columns of a periodical originally brought into existence under the influence of general interest in a concrete problem will regularly be found contributors with a personal interest in this problem, for particular concrete circumstances conflict with their ideal values, and appear to threaten those values. The elective affinity of similar ideals will therefore cement this group of contributors and recruit new members to the circle; and at least in the treatment of practical social-*political* problems, this will lend a specific 'character' to the journal. This results inevitably from any collaborative endeavour among lively and sensitive people who, even when engaged in theoretical work, cannot entirely suppress their evaluative positions, which find, under the conditions discussed above, quite legitimate expression in criticism of *practical* proposals and measures. . . .[2]

With this comment we arrive at an issue so far undiscussed: the *material demarcation* of our field of work. However, no answer to this can be given until we have dealt with the goal of social scientific knowledge in general. Up to now we have, in making a principled distinction between 'value-judgements' and 'experiential knowledge', assumed that there really is a definite and valid form of knowledge, i.e. the conceptual order of empirical reality, for the domain of the social sciences. This assumption will now become a problem as we discuss what the objectively 'valid' truth to which we aspire *can* mean in our field. No one can evade the fact that the problem exists, and is not simply created by our ruminations; this is clear to anyone who observes the struggle over method, 'basic concepts' and presuppositions, the constant change of 'viewpoints' and the continual redefinition of 'concepts' – it is evident that theoretical and historical deliberations still seem to be separated by an unbridgeable chasm: '*two* sciences of economics!' as a bewildered Viennese examinee once peevishly complained. What does

---

2 Weber enters into a brief discussion of the character of the journal under its previous editor.

objectivity means in this context? The following discussion is devoted solely to this question.

II

The *Archiv für Sozialwissenschaft und Sozialpolitik* has from the first treated its subject matter as socio-*economic* in nature.[3] While there is here little purpose in embarking upon the definition of concepts and the demarcation of sciences, we none the less need to clarify briefly what that means.

Our physical existence, just like the satisfaction of our most ideal needs, constantly encounters the actual quantitative limit and qualitative inadequacy of the appropriate external means. Their satisfaction requires careful forethought, effort, a struggle with nature, and the need to work in association with people. Expressed most imprecisely, these are the fundamental factors to which all those phenomena that we call 'social-economic' in the broadest sense are related. That a process (*Vorgang*)[4] is a 'social-economic' phenomenon is not something that is objectively inherent. Rather, it is determined by the direction of our cognitive *interest*, arising out of the specific cultural meaning that we attribute to the individual process in question. Wherever the specific character of an event in cultural life has for us particular *meaning*, and is either directly or very indirectly rooted in that circumstance, there we do, or at least can, find a social-scientific *problem* – a task for a discipline that takes the clarification of the significance of that underlying circumstance for its object of study.

Among these social and economic problems we can distinguish: processes, complexes of the same, norms, institutions, etc., all of whose cultural significance to us rests upon their economic aspect, and which initially – for example, in the operation of banks and bourses – really only interest us from *this* perspective. This becomes usually, but not exclusively, the case when it concerns institutions *deliberately* created (or used) for economic aims. Such objects of our knowledge can be more exactly called 'economic' processes or institutions. Other processes – for instance, those associated with *religious* life – do not strike us primarily in terms of their economic significance and do not interest us as such. But all the same they can from this perspective gain significance because their *effects* are of interest from the economic perspective and so are 'economically relevant' phenomena. Finally, there are phenomena that we would *not* classify as 'economic' and whose economic effects are of little or no interest to us: for instance, the nature of artistic taste in any

---

3 The journal was co-edited by Edgar Jaffé, an expert in financial economics, and Werner Sombart, an economic historian. Weber's own professorship was in economics (*Nationalökonomie*).

4 In a literal sense a *Vorgang* is an antecendent event, or series of events (when used in the plural).

particular era, the character of which is however sometimes greatly influenced by economic motives; in this case the way in which the social structure of the public taking an interest in artistic matters is more or less strongly *influenced* and so are economically *conditioned* phenomena. That complex of human relationships, norms and relations determined by norms we refer to as the 'state' is, for example, an 'economic' phenomenon with respect to state finances: to the extent that it has an impact on economic life through legislation and so on (and indeed in those aspects where its behaviour is governed by factors far removed from economic perspectives) it is 'economically relevant'; finally, where its behaviour and its attributes are determined by motives other than those of its 'economic' relationships, then it is 'economically conditioned'. It is obvious from the above that on the one hand, the sphere of 'economic phenomena' is fluid and not capable of sharp delineation; and on the other, that in no respect are the 'economic' aspects of a phenomenon *only* 'economically conditioned' or *only* 'economically effective'. Also, a phenomenon has an 'economic' quality only to the degree that – and only *so long* as – our *interest* is exclusively directed to the *significance* it has for the material struggle for existence.

Our journal concerns itself therefore, like social and economic science itself since Marx and Roscher,[5] not only with 'economic' phenomena, but also with 'economically relevant' and 'economically conditioned' phenomena. Quite plainly, the domain of such objects reaches – following whatever path our interest takes – throughout the entirety of cultural processes. Specific economic motives – that is, motives whose individual significance to us is rooted in the fundamental circumstance outlined above – operate everywhere that the satisfaction of even quite immaterial needs is related to the use of *limited* external means. Everywhere the impact of economic motives can be traced not only in the form of their satisfaction, but at the same time in defining and transforming cultural needs, reaching even to their innermost core. The indirect influence of social relationships, institutions and human groupings pressurized by 'material' interests extends, sometimes unconsciously, across all cultural domains without exception, into the finest nuances of aesthetic and religious sensibility. The processes of everyday life, no less than the 'historical' events of high politics, collective and mass phenomena, the 'singular' actions of statesmen, or individual literary or artistic achievements are 'economically conditioned' in this way. In return, the totality of lived phenomena and conditions within a historically given culture influences the formation of material needs, the manner in which they are satisfied, the formation of material interest groups and the nature of their coercive means – hence on the course of 'economic development' – all these are 'economically conditioned'. To the extent that our science attributes *economic* cultural phenomena in a causal regression to their individual origins,

5 Wilhelm Roscher (1817–94) was a leader of the historical school of economics.

whether they be economic or non-economic in character, it can be said that it seeks 'historical' knowledge. To the degree that it traces the cultural significance of *one* specific element of cultural phenomena – the economic element – through the most diverse cultural relations (*Zusammenhänge*) it seeks historical *interpretation* from one particular point of view. In doing this, it provides part of the picture that is the *preliminary work* for complete historical knowledge.

A socio-economic *problem* does not exist everywhere that economic factors, either as consequence or as cause, are in play – for such a problem arises only when it is certain that the significance of those factors is *problematic* and can only be determined by the application of the methods of social-economic science – and hence the field of research for the socio-economic perspective appears to be quite without limit.

Hitherto our journal has generally excluded many highly important specialist areas of our science – such as descriptive economics, economic history in the strict sense, and also statistics. Similarly it has left to other publications debate over technical financial issues and the techno-economic problems of market and price formation in the modern exchange economy. It concerned itself instead with constellations of interests and conflicts of interest arising out of the leading role played by capital in search of investment opportunities in modern developed economies (*moderne Kulturländer*), their present significance, and their historical formation. In so doing it has not limited itself to those practical and developmental problems associated with the 'social question' in its narrowest sense – the relationship between the modern classes of wage labourers and the existing social order. Of course, greater scientific understanding of an interest, which became widespread in Germany during the 1880s, dictates that this special question will initially be one of its most important tasks. But as practical treatment of labour relations becomes a constant object of legislative activity and public debate, scientific work should concern itself increasingly with identification of the universal context within which these problems belong. In turn this shift of emphasis should open out into the task of analysing *all* those problems formed by the particular nature of the economic foundations of our culture, and hence specifically modern cultural problems. Very early on the journal had begun to deal historically, statistically, and theoretically with the most varied, in part 'economically relevant', in part 'economically conditioned' living conditions of the other large classes of the modern cultural nation – together with their mutual relationships. We merely draw the consequences of this stance when we characterize the prime work of our journal to be the scientific investigation of *the general cultural significance of the social-economic structure of human communal life* and its historical forms of organization. In calling our journal the *Archiv für Sozialwissenschaft* we mean just this, and nothing else. This title is intended to cover the historical and theoretical pursuit of those same problems whose practical solution is the task of 'social *policy*' in its widest sense. We thus make use of the term 'social' in the significance given to it by material problems of the present. If we call 'cultural sciences' those disciplines that view the events of human life from the viewpoint of their *cultural significance*, then social science in our sense belongs to this category. We will shortly see what principles follow from this.

There is no doubt that the accent on the *social-economic* side of cultural life introduces a very tangible restriction to our topic. It will be said that the economic perspective upon cultural life, or as has been said imprecisely, the 'materialistic' perspective, is one-sided. It certainly is, and this one-sidedness is intentional. Belief that progress in scientific work will cure the 'one-sidedness' of this economic point of view by extending it into a *general* social science labours first of all under the illusion that the 'social' perspective, concerning the relation between humans, possesses clarity sufficient for some kind of delimitation of scientific problems only if attached to a predicate indicating a specific content. Otherwise, considered as the object of a science, it naturally includes philology as well as church history, and in fact all those disciplines concerned with the most important constitutive elements of cultural life: the state, and with it the most important form of its normative regulation: the law. The fact that social economics deals with 'social' relations is no reason to think it to be a necessary harbinger of a 'general social science'; nor that it should be part of biology because it deals with life-forms, or think of it, because of its preoccupation with life on a planet, as belonging to an augmented and improved astronomy of the future. Scientific domains are constituted not by the '*objective*' (*sachlich*) relation of 'things', but by the relationship of *problems* in *thought*: a new 'science' emerges wherever new methods are applied to a new problem and, in this way, truths discovered which disclose significant and new perspectives.

It is no accident that the concept of the 'social', which seems to have a very general meaning, turns out to have a particular and esoteric (if indefinite) meaning when its use is examined more carefully. The 'generality' of its meaning actually depends upon this lack of specificity. The concept in this 'general' sense offers no specific *viewpoints* from which one might shed light upon the *significance* of particular cultural elements.

Liberated as we are from the obsolete belief that the totality of cultural phenomena can be *deduced* from 'material' constellations of interests, whether as product or function, we do however believe that the *analysis of social phenomena and cultural events* from the particular perspective of their *economic* determination and importance was a creative and fruitful scientific principle. Used carefully and without dogmatic bias it will remain so for the foreseeable future. The so-called 'materialist conception of history', whether as a '*Weltanschauung*' or as the lowest common denominator in the causal explanation of historical reality, is to be most decidedly rejected – one of the most important aims of our journal is the advancement of historical *interpretation* from an economic perspective. This needs further elaboration.

The so-called 'materialist conception of history' in the *older* primitive, yet inspired, sense to be found in the *Communist Manifesto* turns today only the

heads of laymen and dilettantes. Here we can still find the distinctive circumstance that their need for a causal explanation of a historical event is never
satisfied until somehow or somewhere economic causes are shown (or seem)
to be operative. If this is the case then they content themselves with the most
threadbare hypothesis and the most general maxims, for their dogmatic
need to locate economic 'motives', the 'genuine', sole 'truth' of 'universal
determination in the last instance' is satisfied. This phenomenon is by no
means unique. Almost all the sciences, from philology to biology, have at one
time or other claimed to be the source not only of specialized economic
knowledge but of '*Weltanschauungen*' as well. Under the impression of the
profound cultural significance of *modern* economic transformations and the
special importance of the 'labour question' the ineradicably monistic tendency of all knowledge uncritical of itself naturally drives it along this path.
With the increasing intensity of political and commercial struggles among
nations for world dominance the same tendency is now appearing in anthropology. There is a widespread belief that 'in the final analysis' all historical
events are the outcome of the interplay of innate 'racial qualities'. In place of
uncritical descriptions of 'national characters' there emerge the even more
uncritical concoction of 'social theories' based on the 'natural sciences'. We
shall carefully follow the development of anthropological research in our
journal insofar as it has significance for our perspective. It is to be hoped that
this causal reduction of cultural events to 'race' testifies to our complete *lack*
of knowledge – in much the same way that reference is made to a 'milieu', or
before that to the 'prevailing circumstances' – and can be gradually overcome
by work guided in a methodical manner. If there is anything that has hitherto
hindered this kind of research, it is the notions of eager dilettantes who have
thought they could contribute something different and more weighty in place
of the enlargement of the possibility of certain imputation of individual *concrete* cultural events occurring in historical reality to *concrete, historically*
given causes through the acquisition of *exact* observational material fur-
nished by specific perspectives. Only to the extent that they are able to do this
are their results of interest to us, and only then does 'racial biology' become
something more than a product of the modern rage for founding new sciences.

It is no different with the significance of the economic interpretation of the
historical process. If today, following a period of unrestrained overestimation, there is almost a danger that its scientific applicability will be
*under*valued, this is only because of its quite unprecedented and uncritical use
as a 'universal' method for the interpretation of reality. This construes all
cultural phenomena – that is, all such phenomena that are important to us –
as determined in the last instance by the economic. Today the logical form in
which this appears is not entirely uniform. Wherever the pure economic
explanation gets into difficulties various means are available to sustain its
general validity as the decisive causal moment. One can treat everything that
in historical reality can*not* be linked to economic motives as *on this account*
scientifically *insignificant* 'flukes'. Or alternatively, one can stretch the

concept of the economic beyond all recognition, so that it subsumes all human interests in some way connected to external means. If it can be historically ascertained that in two situations *identical* in economic respects differing reactions occur – resulting from differences in political, religious, climatological, and countless other *non*-economic determinants – then to maintain the supremacy of the economic all these moments are reduced to historically unintended 'conditions' within which economic motives continue their 'causal' work. It is obvious, however, that all those aspects which from the economic viewpoint are 'coincidental' (*zufällig*) follow their own regularities in exactly the same way as the economic; but these same given *economic* 'conditions' appear equally 'historically coincidental' when considered from the point of view of these other regularities. A favourite final ploy, seeking to rescue the overwhelming significance of the economic, is to interpret the constant mutual interaction among the individual elements of cultural life in terms of a causal or functional *dependency* of one or more, or more exactly, of them all, upon the economic instance. Where a specific, individual non-economic institution acquired a 'function' serving an economic class interest, where, for example, a particular religious institution allowed itself to be used as 'black police', then the institution in question is represented as being created for this purpose, or (quite metaphysically) influenced by an economically founded 'developmental tendency'.

Today, specialists do not need convincing that *this* version of the purpose of the economic analysis of cultural life followed partly from a particular historical constellation attracting scientific interest to cultural problems of a specifically economic kind, and partly from a rabid scientific parochialism and aggrandizement (*Ressortpatriotismus*) which is today at best obsolete. Reduction to *exclusively* economic causes is in no sense sufficient in *any* sphere of cultural phenomena, not even in that of 'economic' processes. In principle, a history of banking in a particular country that adduced only economic motives as explanations is just as unworkable as an 'explanation' of the Sistine Madonna in terms of the contemporary socio-economic foundations of cultural life; and it is in no respects any more exhaustive than, for instance, the derivation of capitalism from certain transformations of religious consciousness that played a part in the genesis of the capitalist spirit, nor the derivation of a political structure from geographical conditions. Decisive in *all* these cases for the degree of significance given to economic conditions is the class of causes to which are imputed *those* specific elements of the phenomenon at issue that have a *meaning* of interest to us. The *one-sided* analysis of cultural reality from specific 'perspectives' – here, in respect of their economic determination – finds its purely methodological justification in the circumstance that considerable advantages arise from a division of labour based upon practised observation of the effect of qualitatively similar causal categories and the consistent use of the same conceptual and methodological apparatus. This is not 'arbitrary' so long as it meets with *success*; that is, it provides knowledge of relationships (*Zusammenhänge*) that prove to be *valuable* in the causal imputation of concrete historical events. *None the less*: the *'one-sidedness'* and lack of reality inhering in the pure economic interpretation of the historical is only a special case of a general principle valid for the whole of scientific knowledge of cultural reality. The paramount aim of what follows is to make clear the logical foundations and general methodological consequences of this principle.

There is *no* absolutely 'objective' scientific analysis of cultural life – or to put it perhaps more precisely, without however materially altering our meaning – there is no 'objective' analysis of 'social phenomena' *independent* of special and 'one-sided' perspectives, on the basis of which such phenomena can be (explicitly or implicitly, consciously or unconsciously) selected as an object of research, analysed and systematically represented. The reason for this arises from the specificity of the cognitive aim of social scientific work which seeks to move beyond a purely *formal* consideration of legal or conventional *norms* governing social association.

The social science that we wish to pursue is a *science of reality* (*Wirklichkeitswissenschaft*). Our aim is an understanding of the *uniqueness* (*Eigenart*) of the lived reality within which we are placed. We wish to understand on the one hand the context and cultural *significance* of individual phenomena in this lived reality; and on the other, the reasons for their being historically so and not otherwise. As soon as we seek to reflect upon life as it presents itself we encounter a simply endless variety of events, which are both 'internal' and 'external' to us, and appear and fade away both successively and concurrently. The sheer infinity of this variety is entirely undiminished if we isolate an individual 'object' for examination – for example, a given act of exchange – and remains so if we merely seek in all seriousness an *exhaustive* description of this 'individual' in all its parts, let alone comprehend its causal determination. All cognitive knowledge of infinite reality by the finite human mind thus rests upon the implicit presupposition that at any one time only a finite part of this reality can be subjected to scientific scrutiny, that only this part is 'material' in the sense of 'worth knowing'. But according to what principles has this part been isolated? It has always been thought, in the cultural sciences as well, that the decisive feature could ultimately be found in the 'lawlike' recurrence of particular causal associations. Hence, in this view, the 'laws' that we thought to find among the manifold succession of events must themselves represent what alone is 'essentially' scientific about such events. Once we could demonstrate the 'regularity' of a causal connection to be universally valid by applying the methods of historical induction, or made it directly plausible for our subjective experience, then all subsequent similar cases, however numerous, can be ordered to this formula. Having extracted this 'regularity' from a given individual reality, those elements not included within it are treated as a residue awaiting scientific investigation, to be eventually incorporated within a more elaborated system of 'laws'; or they remain 'coincidental', *hence* scientifically inconsequential *just because* they resist 'law-based comprehension' – they are not considered 'typical' of the event

and so can only be the object of 'idle curiosity'. The idea constantly recurs –
even among representatives of the historical school – that the ideal to which
all cultural knowledge strives, or could strive into the distant future, would be
a system of doctrinal propositions from which reality might be 'deduced'. It
is well known that a leading natural scientist believed that the ideal (if factually unattainable) aim of such an assimilation of cultural reality could be
taken to be the creation of an *'astronomical'* knowledge of life's events.[6] Let
us not begrudge the effort required to look at this rather more closely, no
matter how often these things have been discussed before. It strikes us first of
all that the 'astronomical' knowledge in question is in *no* respect a knowledge
of *laws*; instead, the 'laws' with which this science works draw their *presuppositions* from other disciplines, such as mechanics. Astronomy concerns
itself with the question: What *individual* result is created by the effect of these
laws on an *individual constellation*, for it is these individually formed constellations that are of *significance* to us. Each individual constellation that it
explains or predicts is of course causally explicable only as a consequence of
another individual constellation that preceded it; and no matter how far we
reach back into the gloom of the distant past, the reality *to* which the laws
apply remains individual and *irreducible to* these laws. A cosmic 'primeval
state' either lacking in individual character, or with less individual character
that that of the present cosmic reality, would of course be a ridiculous idea.
But can we not detect a remnant of this way of thinking in our domain when
propositions are derived from natural law, or from observation of 'primitive
peoples', concerning a socio-economic 'original state' without historical
'accidents' – characterized as 'primitive agrarian communism', 'sexual
promiscuity', etc. – from which individual historical development emerges as
a kind of fall from grace into the material world?

The point of departure of social scientific interest is doubtless the *real*
individually constituted social and cultural life that surrounds us in its *universal*, but not in any respect less *individually* formed, relationships; and its
emergence from other social and cultural circumstances that are in turn individually formed. Obviously the issue that we sought to illustrate as a limiting
case (*Grenzfall*) in astronomy (often used by logicians to the same end) is to
be found here in an especially heightened form. While in astronomy we are
interested in the heavenly bodies only with respect to *quantitative* relationships susceptible to exact measurement, it is the *qualitative* aspect of events
that interests us in social science. In addition to this there is the fact that the
social sciences deal with events influenced by *intellectual* factors whose
'understanding' through re-experiencing (*nacherlebend*) is naturally a task
quite different to the formulae that exact natural knowledge could or would
wish to solve. But these differences are not a matter of principle, as it might at
first sight appear. Apart from pure mechanics, the exact natural sciences

6 Probably a reference to Wilhelm Ostwald (1853–1932), a chemist and Nobel prize winner.

cannot do without qualities; furthermore, we encounter in our domain the quite erroneous idea that the fundamental part that money plays as a means of economic exchange, at least in our culture, is quantifiable and can *hence therefore* be expressed in terms of 'laws'. And finally it depends upon the wider or narrower definition of the concept of 'law' whether one includes regularities that, since they are not susceptible to quantification, cannot be registered numerically. Where the influence of 'intellectual' motives is concerned, this does not preclude the formation of *rules* of rational conduct. Above all, the point of view persists which claims that the task of *psychology* is to play a role for the human sciences comparable to that of mathematics, in the sense that it analyses the complicated phenomena of social life into their psychic conditions and effects, reduces them to the most elementary possible psychic factor, classifies these factors by type (*gattungsmäßig*), and then analyses their functional interdependencies. Thereby, a sort of 'chemistry' if not 'mechanics' of the psychic foundations of social life would be created.

Whether such investigations can produce valuable and – what is something else – useful results for the *cultural* sciences, we cannot seek to decide here. But this would be irrelevant to the question as to whether the *aim* of social-economic knowledge, in our sense: knowledge of *reality* with respect to its cultural *significance* and its causal relationships can be attained through the quest for regularly recurrent sequences. Let us assume that we have succeeded by means of psychology or otherwise in analysing all the observed and imaginable relationships of the phenomena of human social life into some ultimate elementary 'factors', that we have exhaustively analysed and classified them, and then formulated rigorously exact laws covering their behaviour – what would be the significance of these results for our knowledge of the *historically* given cultural world or any individual phase thereof, such as capitalism, in its development and cultural significance? As an analytical *means*, it would be as useful, or useless, as, for instance, a textbook of organic chemical combinations would be for our *biogenetic* knowledge of the animal and plant world. Each case would certainly represent useful and important preliminary work. But neither permits the reality of life to be *deduced* from these 'laws' and 'factors' – and not because there are some higher and more clandestine 'powers' ('dominants', 'entelechies' or whatever) concealed within the life's phenomena. This is a problem in its own right – the real reason that such a deduction cannot be made is that for our knowledge of reality it is the *constellation* formed by the grouping of those (hypothetical!) 'factors' into a cultural phenomenon that is of historical *significance* to us. *If* we then wished to 'explain causally' this individual grouping we would of necessity have to refer back to other equally individual groupings from which we would seek an 'explanation' for the first grouping, employing of course those (hypothetical!) concepts of 'law'. The determination of these (hypothetical) 'laws' and 'factors' would be only the *first* of several pieces of work that would lead us to the knowledge that we sought. The next task would be analysis and ordered representation of each historically given, individual grouping of those 'factors', their *significant* consequent material interaction, and above all *rendering intelligible* the basis and nature of this significance; this would be worked through with the aid of the preliminary studies, but in comparison to them a completely new and *independent* task. The third task would be to trace back the formation of a grouping's individual character- istics retaining significance for the *present* as far into the past as possible, deriving their historical explanation from earlier, likewise individual constel- lations. A fourth task would finally be the estimation of possible future constellations.

For all such purposes the availability of clear concepts and knowledge of these (hypothetical) 'laws' would obviously be of great value as a *means* of knowledge, but *only* as such, and for this purpose they would certainly be indispensable. But even in this function their substantive limits are immedi- ately revealed at *one* decisive point, and in establishing this we arrive at the most decisive quality of the cultural scientific approach. We have defined as 'cultural sciences' those disciplines that seek to identify the cultural *signifi- cance* of life's phenomena. The *significance* inherent in the formation of a cultural phenomenon and the *basis* for this significance cannot be taken, founded and rendered intelligible from a system of law-like concepts, no matter how complete, for the significance of cultural phenomena implies a relationship to *evaluative ideas* (*Wertideen*). The concept of culture is an *evaluative concept*. Empirical reality is for us 'cultural' in the sense, and to the extent that, it is related to evaluative ideas; it comprises those elements of reality rendered *meaningful* by this relationship, no more. A tiny part of the given observed individual reality is coloured by the interests arising out of these evaluative ideas, and this part alone has significance for us; it has sig- nificance because it highlights a relationship *important* to us by virtue of its connection to evaluative ideas. It is only for this reason, and to this extent, that we believe its individual character to be worth knowing. But what has significance for us cannot be ascertained by some 'presuppositionless' study of the empirically given; determination of such a significance is rather the presupposition that something becomes the *object* of our investigation.

What is significant naturally fails to coincide with any law as such, and the more general the law is, the less the coincidence. For the specific *significance* that a component of reality has for us is *not* to be found in the relationships that it has with numerous other such components. The relation of reality to those evaluative ideas lending it significance, and the selection and ordering of those elements of reality so coloured from the perspective of their cultural *meaning*, represent a quite heterogeneous and disparate viewpoint when set against the analysis of reality in terms of *laws* and its ordering with respect to general concepts. These two modes of ordering the real in thought have no necessary logical relationship. They may coincide in isolated cases, but it would be fatal if we were to conclude from this chance correspondence that they were not distinct *in principle*. The cultural significance of a phenomenon such as exchange in a money economy lies in the fact that it appears in the form of a mass phenomenon, which is a fundamental component in modern cultural life. But if we are to understand the cultural *significance* of the *historical* fact that it plays this role, then its historical emergence has to be causally explained.

Investigation of the *general* nature of exchange and the *technique* of market transactions is extremely important and indispensable *preliminary* work. But this not only fails to answer the question of how exchange historically came to have the fundamental *significance* that it has today; above all, our ultimate interest in the *cultural significance* of money economy, the only reason we might have an interest in transaction techniques, and for which purpose alone there exists today a science that concerns itself with that technique – none of this follows from any such 'laws'. The generic features of exchange, purchase, etc. is of interest to lawyers – but we are concerned with the task of analysing the *cultural significance* of precisely the *historical* fact that today exchange is a mass phenomenon. In the case of Antiquity, where exchange has exactly the same generic qualities as it does today, what should be explained and what we need to understand is what separates our socio-economic culture from theirs – what therefore is the *meaning* of the 'money economy' and here logical principles of entirely heterogeneous origin push their way into the investigation. We shall use as *means* of representation the concepts produced by investigation of the generic elements in economic mass phenomena inasmuch as they contain meaningful components of our culture. But even the most exact delineation of such concepts and laws does not realize the *goal* of our work; for the question of what should be the object of such generic concept formation is not posed 'without presupposition'; a response is required with respect to the *significance* that particular components of the infinite diversity of what we call 'trade' (*Verkehr*) have for culture. We are seeking knowledge of a historical phenomenon, i.e. a phenomenon whose *individuality* is *significant*. What is decisive here is that only through the presupposition that a finite part of the infinite array of phenomena is alone significant does the idea of a knowledge of *individual* appearances become logically meaningful.

Armed even with the most comprehensive knowledge of *all* 'laws' of events conceivable, we would still be helpless faced with the question: how is the *causal explanation* of an *individual* fact at all *possible*? – for even a *description* of the smallest extract from reality can never be thought exhaustive. The number and type of causes that have determined an individual event is always *infinite*, and there is nothing in the material itself warranting the selection of one part for our consideration. Any serious attempt at creating cognition of reality 'without presupposition' would simply produce a chaos of 'existential judgements' with respect to innumerable individual observations. And even this result only appears to be a possibility, for the reality of every single observation always, on closer examination, reveals an infinity of component parts that can never be expressed exhaustively in observational judgements. Order is brought to this chaos *only* through the circumstance that in each case only a *part* of individual reality is of interest to us, has *significance* for us, since only this part relates to the *cultural evaluative ideas* that we bring to reality. Only particular aspects of infinitely diverse individual phenomena are therefore worth knowing; those to which we attribute a general *cultural significance* – these alone are the object of causal explanation. This causal explanation in turn discloses the same phenomenon: an exhaustive causal regress from the *full* reality of any particular concrete phenomenon is not only impossible in practice, it also makes no sense. We select only those causes that can, in each individual case, be *attributed* to the '*material*' ('*wesentlich*') components of an event. Where the *individuality* of a phenomenon is concerned the question of causality does not concern *laws*, but rather concrete causal *relationships*; not a question in which the event simply becomes an exemplar of something else, but instead a question of to which individual constellation it should be attributed as a result: it is a question of attribution, of *imputation*. Wherever causal explanation of a 'cultural phenomenon' is considered – of a '*historical individual*',[7] to use a term occasionally used in the methodology of our discipline, and now, more precisely formulated, increasingly common in logic – knowledge of the *laws* of causation can never be the *objective* of investigation, but only a *means*. It facilitates and makes possible causal imputation of individual, culturally significant elements of phenomena to their concrete causes. To the extent, and only to the extent that it does this, then it is valuable for the knowledge of individual contexts. The more general, that is the more abstract, that the laws are, the less work they do for the requirements of causal imputation of *individual* phenomena, and hence indirectly for understanding of the significance of cultural processes.

What follows from the above?

Not, of course, that in the domain of the cultural sciences knowledge of the *general*, the formation of abstract generic concepts, knowledge of regularities and the attempt to formulate 'law-like' relationships is without scientific justification. On the contrary: if the causal knowledge of the historian consists of the *imputation* of concrete effects to concrete causes, then a *valid* imputation of any one effect is entirely *impossible* without the use of 'nomological' knowledge – knowledge of the regularities of causal relationships. Whether a single individual component of a relationship is, in reality, to be assigned causal responsibility for an effect, the causal explanation of which is at issue, can in doubtful cases *only* be determined by estimating the effects that we *generally* expect from it and *other* components of the same constellation: which includes consideration of '*adequate*' results (*Wirkungen*) of the original elements concerned. The extent to which the historian (in the broadest sense), his imagination sharpened by life's experience and methodological training, can effect this imputation with certainty, and insofar as he avails

---

7 '*Historisches Individuum*' is a term taken from the epistemology of Heinrich Rickert. It refers to any specific historical entity, both person or event.

himself of assistance from special disciplines which make this possible – this all depends on the individual case. But everywhere, and so also in the sphere of complex economic processes, the more certain and comprehensive our general knowledge, the greater the *certainty* of imputation. This proposition is not in the least diminished by the fact that even in the case of so-called 'economic laws', we are without exception concerned with 'laws' not in the narrow natural scientific sense, but rather with *adequate* causal relationships expressed in rules, with 'objective possibility' (a category whose use will not be further elaborated here).[8] The establishment of such regularities is not the *end*, but a *means* of knowledge; whether there is any point in formulating a regularly recurring causal relationship in every experience as a 'law' is a matter of expediency in every individual case. For the exact natural sciences 'laws' are the more useful and important, the greater their *general validity*; while for knowledge of the concrete presuppositions of historical phenomena the *most general* laws are, because of their lack of content, commonly the least valuable. For the more comprehensive a generic concept is – its *reach* – the more it leads us *away* from the richness of reality; for if it is to include the common factor shared by as many phenomena as possible, it has to be as abstract as possible, and hence *poor* in content. In the cultural sciences knowledge of the general is in itself never of any value to us.

From the above it follows that an 'objective' treatment of cultural processes – in the sense that the ideal aim of scientific labour is the reduction of the empirical to 'laws' – is nonsense. But this is *not* because (as is often claimed) the unfolding of cultural or intellectual processes is 'objectively' any less law-governed. It is because (1) knowledge of social laws is not knowledge of social reality, but instead just one of the means which we might use to attain such knowledge; and (2) no knowledge of *cultural* processes can be conceived separately from the *meaning* which the consistently individual shaping of life's reality has for us in respect of *specific* individual relationships. No law will tell us in *what* sense and in *which* relationship this is the case, since this is determined by those *evaluative ideas* through which we perceive 'culture' in any one instance. 'Culture' is a finite, meaningful selection from the meaningless infinity of world events endowed with its meaning and significance by a *human* perspective. This is even true when the humans perceive the culture *in question* to be their mortal enemy and seek to 'return to nature'. For a human being can only come to this conclusion by *relating* such a culture to his evaluative ideas and finding it 'too soft'. It is this *purely formal logical* circumstance that is meant when we talk here of the logically necessary rootedness of all historical individuals in 'evaluative ideas'. The transcendental presupposition of any *cultural science* is *not* that we find one or any 'culture' to be *of value*, but that we are cultural *beings* endowed with the

---

8 'Objective possibility' refers to the options that can be *thought of* as possible. See above, p. 329.

capacity and the desire to adopt a position with respect to the world, and lend it *meaning*. Whatever this meaning might be, it will lead to our *judging* those phenomena arising from human association, from this perspective ascribing to them a positive or a negative *significance*. Whatever the significant content might be, these phenomena possess cultural *significance* for us, and upon this significance alone rests their scientific interest. If we make use here of the terminology of modern logicians when talking of the determination of cultural knowledge by *evaluative* ideas (*Wertideen*), we do so in the hope that we will not be subjected to such crude misunderstandings of the type that cultural meaning is only ascribed to *highly valued* phenomena. Prostitution is a cultural phenomenon, just like religion or money. All three are cultural phenomena *only* because and *only* insofar as their existence and the form which they *historically* assume touch directly or indirectly on our cultural *interests*, prompting our desire for knowledge in terms of perspectives originating in evaluative ideas that render the piece of reality comprehended by those concepts *significant* for us.

As can be seen, all knowledge of cultural reality is always a knowledge from a *specific point of view*. If we ask of the historian or social investigator that, as an elementary prerequisite, they be able to distinguish between the important and the unimportant, and that they possess the 'perspective' necessary for such a distinction – then all this means is that the events of reality have, consciously or unconsciously, to be related to universal 'cultural values' and hence *those* relationships that are of importance to us made plain. If the view does constantly recur that such perspectives can be 'taken from the facts themselves' this is due to naïve self-deception on the part of the academic specialist, who fails to take account of the fact he has already selected a tiny part from an absolute infinity thanks to the evaluative ideas with which he unconsciously set about his work, and that observation of this tiny part is his *sole concern*. In this perpetual and everywhere conscious or unconscious selection of *individual* special 'aspects' of events there also prevails that feature of cultural scientific endeavour underlying the oft-heard claim that the 'personal' element in a scientific work is what is really valuable, and that if there is any further justification for such work then it has to be as an expression of 'a personality'. To be sure, without the investigator's evaluative ideas, there would be no principle of selection of subject matter and no meaningful knowledge of individual reality; and just as in the absence of the *belief* on the part of an investigator in the *significance* of a particular cultural content all work regarding knowledge of *individual* reality is quite meaningless, so the direction of his personal belief, the refraction of his values in the prism of his mind, gives direction to his work. And the values to which the scientific genius relates the object of his inquiry may determine, i.e. decide the 'conception' of a whole epoch, not only concerning what is regarded as 'valuable' but also concerning what is regarded as significant or insignificant, 'important' or 'unimportant' in the phenomena.

Cultural scientific knowledge in our sense is thus *tied* to 'subjective' pre-suppositions to the extent that it is concerned only with those components of reality that connect in some way to events to which we attribute cultural *significance*. It is none the less pure *causal* knowledge in the same sense as the knowledge of significant individual natural events of a qualitative nature. To the many confusions that formal juridical thinking has already introduced into the cultural sciences a new one has recently been added: the attempt to 'refute' in principle the 'materialistic conception of history' by introducing a number of brilliant fallacies, arguing that, since all economic life must be conducted according to conventionally or legally *regulated forms*, all economic 'development' must therefore take the shape of efforts to create new *legal forms*. Therefore, the argument goes, it can only be understood in terms of *moral* principles; and *for this reason* it differs from every form of 'natural' development. Knowledge of economic development is therefore held to be teleological in character.[9] Without here wishing to go into the ambiguities of 'development' for social science, or into those of the logically no-less ambiguous concept of the 'teleological', it can be stated that such knowledge does not have to be 'teleological' in *that* sense presumed by the criticism. Prevailing legal norms can remain formally identical while the cultural *significance* of norm-governed legal *relationships*, and hence the norms themselves, are fundamentally overturned. If we might fantasize about the future for a moment, we could visualize the 'socialization of the means of production' as in theory complete, without any 'endeavour' aimed at such a result being made, or that any paragraph of our legislation disappeared, or that new paragraphs were added. The statistical frequency of individual norm-governed legal relationships would of course be fundamentally changed, in some cases disappearing entirely; and a great number of legal norms would *in practice* become meaningless, their entire culture meaning altered beyond recognition. Discussion of prospective law (*de lege ferenda*) could therefore be justifiably disregarded by the 'materialist' theory of history, for its central proposition was of course the inevitable change in the *significance* of legal institutions. Whoever thinks unpretentious work on the causal understanding of historical reality to be of minor importance can disregard it – but it is impossible to supplant it with a 'teleology'. In *our* view, a 'purpose' ('*Zweck*') is the conception of a *consequence* whose *cause* is an action; and as with *every* cause that does or can contribute to a *significant* consequence, we take account of it. Its *specific* meaning rests entirely upon our wish and ability not only to *register* human action, but to *understand* it.

---

9 Rudolf Stammler (1856–1938) was a legal philosopher who in his *Economy and Law According to the Materialist Principle* (German edn 1896) argued that material life had to be contained within legal forms which in their turn operated according to moral principles and purpose (telos).

Without doubt all such evaluative ideas are 'subjective'. Between a 'historical' interest in a family's history and interest in the greatest conceivable cultural phenomena common to a nation or to mankind over epochs there is an infinite scale of 'significances', whose degrees will have a different sequence for every one of us. These are also historically variable according to the character of culture, and to prevailing human ideas. But it does *not* of course follow from this that cultural scientific *research* itself can only have *results* that are 'subjective', in the sense of being valid for *one* person and not for another. What changes is rather the degree to which such results *interest* one person, but not another. In other words: it is the investigator and the prevailing ideas of the time that determine *what* becomes the object of investigation, and how far this investigation extends back into the infinity of causal relationships. In the method of investigation the guiding 'viewpoint' determines, as we shall see, the composition of the conceptual resources that it employs. But the investigator is of course here, as everywhere, bound to the norms of our thought in the way in which they are used. For scientific truth is only valid for those who *seek* truth.

From this one thing follows: the meaninglessness of an idea, sometimes prevalent even among the historians of our discipline, according to which the goal of the cultural sciences could be the creation of a closed conceptual system, in which reality might in some sense be *finally* and *permanently* configured so that reality could in turn be deduced from it. The stream of infinite events flows constantly towards eternity. The cultural problems that sway humankind are constantly renewed and reformulated; that which assumes individual meaning and significance for us in that constantly unending stream becomes a 'historical individual'. The conceptual context in which it is considered and scientifically comprehended alters. The points of departure for the cultural sciences remain mutable throughout an endless future, so long as a Chinese ossification of intellectual life does not render mankind incapable of posing new questions to eternal, inexhaustible life. A system of the cultural sciences – even if only in the sense of a definitive, objectively valid, systematic final determination of questions and spheres with which it would henceforth deal – would be an absurdity. All that can emerge from such a project is the listing of several, particularized, mutually heterogeneous and disparate viewpoints through which reality is for us a given 'culture', that is, whose specific character was or is significant.

Following on from this wearisome discussion we can now turn finally to the question that interests us *methodologically* in considering the 'objectivity' of cultural knowledge: what is the logical function and structure of the *concepts* with which our science, as every science, operates; or with special reference to the decisive problem: what is the significance of *theory* and the theoretical conceptualization for knowledge of cultural reality?

Economics was originally – as we have already seen – a 'technique' insofar as the central focus of its attention went; it viewed the phenomena of reality from an apparently unambiguous and stable practical evaluative standpoint:

namely, the increase of the 'wealth' of a state's population. But it was from the very beginning more than mere 'technique', for it was integrated into the powerful eighteenth-century *Weltanschauung* uniting natural law and rationalism. The optimistic faith in the theoretical and practical rationalizability characteristic of this *Weltanschauung* of the real had the effect of *hindering* the discovery of the *problematic* character of a standpoint assumed to be self-evident. Just as the rational consideration of modern society arose in close connection with the modern development of natural science, so its entire approach remained connected to natural science. In natural scientific disciplines the practical evaluative orientation towards what was directly technically useful was closely associated from the very first with the hope, inherited from Antiquity and further elaborated, of attaining, by means of generalizing abstraction and analysis of the empirical, law-like relationships that would constitute a purely 'objective' (that is, freed of all values and individual 'fortuitousness', hence rational) monistic knowledge of reality in its totality. Those natural science disciplines linked to evaluative standpoints, such as clinical medicine, and even more so, what is usually referred to as 'technology' became purely practical 'industrial arts' ('*Kunstlehre*'). The values that they served – the health of the patient, the technical perfection of a concrete process of production – these were fixed for each of them. The means that they employed consisted and could only consist in the use of the law established by the theoretical disciplines. Every theoretical advance in the construction of these laws was, or could also be, an advance for the practical disciplines. With a given end, the progressive reduction of concrete practical questions (e.g. a case of illness, a technical problem, etc.) to the status of special cases of generally valid laws meant that extension of theoretical knowledge was associated and identical with the extension of technical-practical possibilities. When modern biology then subsumed under a universally valid evolutionary principle those aspects of reality which interest us *historically*, i.e. why something happened thus and not otherwise – a principle which at least seemed (none the less speciously) to permit the inclusion of everything essential in this reality within the schemata of universally valid laws, this appeared to herald a final twilight of the gods (*Götterdammerung*)[10] for all evaluative standpoints in all the sciences. Since the so-called historical event was a segment of the total reality, and since the principle of causality, the presupposition of all scientific work, seemed to require that all events be dispersed into generally valid 'laws'; and in view of the overwhelming success of the natural sciences which in all seriousness had taken up this idea, it seemed that there was in general no conceivable meaning for scientific work other than the discovery of the *laws* of events. It was only 'law-governed' aspects of phenomena that could be scientifically material; 'individual' processes could only be considered as 'types', as illustrative representatives of

---

10 A disparaging term Weber takes from Nietzsche meaning effectively 'game over'.

laws. An interest in such events for their own sake did not appear to be a 'scientific' interest.

It is not possible to trace here the formidable repercussions of the certainties of natural scientific monism on economic disciplines. As socialist criticism and the work of historians began to transform the original evaluative points of view into problems, the vigorous development of biological research on the one hand and the influence of Hegelian panlogism on the other prevented economics from attaining a clear and full understanding of the relationship between concept and reality. The result, to the extent that it interests us here, is that in spite of the massive bulwarks erected against naturalistic dogma – by German idealistic philosophy since Fichte, the achievements of the German historical school of law, and the work of the historical school of German economics – nevertheless, and in part *as a result* of all this work, the naturalistic perspective remained unvanquished.[11] To this in particular there belongs the still problematic relationship within our discipline between 'theoretical' and 'historical' work.

There remains today a direct and apparently unbridgeable gulf in our discipline between 'abstract'-theoretical method and empirical-historical research. Proponents of the first approach quite properly recognize the methodological impossibility of replacing historical knowledge of reality through the formulation of 'laws', or alternatively creating 'laws' by the simple juxtaposition of historical observations. To derive such laws – from this point of view it is evident that this is the ultimate aim of science – they take for granted as a fact that we have a constant and direct appreciation of the real structure of human action, and hence – so they think – it is possible to render the course of such action axiomatically intelligible, and as a consequence reveal its 'laws'. The sole exact form of cognition – the formulation of directly perceptible *evident* laws – is also at once the only one that permits conclusions to be drawn concerning processes that are not directly observable; hence, at least for the fundamental phenomena of economic life, the creation of a system of abstract and consequently purely formal propositions analogous to that of the natural sciences is the sole means of intellectually mastering social diversity. Despite the fundamental methodological distinction between historical knowledge and knowledge of laws, which the creator of the theory had made the *prime* and *sole* such distinction, empirical *validity* is now claimed for the principles of abstract theory in the sense of the *deducibility* of reality from 'laws'. True, that is not meant as a claim that abstract empirical laws themselves are empirically valid, but rather that when equally 'exact' theories have been constructed for all other factors, taken *together* these abstract theories

11 See Keith Tribe, 'Historical Schools of Economics: German and English', in J.E. Biddle, J.B. Davis and W.J. Samuels (eds), *The Blackwell Companion to the History of Economic Thought*, Oxford, Blackwell, 2003.

must contain the true reality of things – i.e. what is worth knowing in reality.

Exact economic theory is said to presuppose one psychic motive, while the task of others is thought to be the formation of similar hypothetically valid principles covering all other motives. Quite fantastic claims are made on occasion for the consequence of theoretical work, such as abstract theories of price formation, rent, and interest: that they might be employed, supposedly quite analogously with the principles of physical science, to *deduce* from given real premises *quantitatively determined* results having validity for lived reality, for human economic activity is with respect to a given end unambiguously 'determined' in relation to means. This claim overlooks the fact that, to arrive at such a result in even a very simple case, the *totality* of a given historical reality together with all its causal relationships would have to be taken as 'given' and *known* in advance. But if *this* knowledge were accessible to the finite mind it would not be possible to conceive the cognitive value of abstract theory. The naturalistic prejudice that such concepts should create something analogous to the natural sciences has led to a mistaken appreciation of the purpose of theory construction. It was thought to be a matter of psychological isolation of a specific human 'impulse', the acquisitive instinct, or the isolated study of a specific maxim of human conduct – the so-called economic principle. Abstract theory considered it possible to support itself upon psychological axioms, and the outcome was that historians called for an *empirical* psychology so that the invalidity of those axioms could be demonstrated and also that the course of economic events could be derived psychologically.

We do not wish to enter here into a thoroughgoing critique of belief in the significance of a (prospective) systematic science of social psychology as a future foundation of the cultural sciences, and especially of social economics. Those psychological interpretations of economic phenomena that we have, some of which are quite brilliant, do however demonstrate that the logical movement is not from analysis of the psychological qualities of human beings to the analysis of social institutions, but the exact reverse: that the illumination of the psychological presuppositions and effects of institutions *requires* exact knowledge of the latter and their relationships. In individual cases psychological analysis can offer an extremely valuable deepening in our knowledge of the historical *cultural determination* and cultural *significance* of such institutions. What interests us in the social relationships of human psychic behaviour is in each case differentiated by the specific cultural meaning of the relationship in question. This involves quite heterogeneous and concretely combined psychic motives and influences. Social psychological research sorts out a variety of *individual* and mutually quite disparate kinds of cultural elements according to their interpretative susceptibility for our empathetic (*nacherlebend*) understanding. Starting from knowledge of individual institutions, we increasingly learn to intellectually *understand* their cultural specificity and cultural significance; we do not wish to deduce such institutions from psychological laws, or seek to *explain* them in terms of elementary psychological phenomena.

The elaborate polemic that has grown up around the question of the psychological justification of abstract theoretical propositions, of the scope of the 'acquisitive instinct', of the 'economic principle' and so on is thus of little consequence.

That the construction of abstract theory requires 'deductions' from basic psychological motives is an illusion; such deductions are in truth merely a special case of conceptual formation characteristic of the sciences of human culture, however indispensable. It is worthwhile here outlining this process of concept formation in greater detail, for this will bring us closer to the main question concerning the significance of theory for social scientific knowledge. In so doing we will leave entirely unexamined the question of whether the theoretical constructions upon which we draw for examples, or to which we allude, do themselves serve the end that they seek; that is, whether they are materially *fitting* to this end. How much further present-day 'abstract theory' should be elaborated is ultimately a question of the economy of scientific labour, and such labour has other problems to pursue. The 'theory of marginal utility' is after all subject to the 'law of marginal utility'.

Abstract economic theory offers us an example of synthetic constructs that have been dubbed 'ideas' of historical phenomena. It gives us an *ideal* impression of processes in the commodity market of a social organization based upon an exchange economy, free competition, and consistently rational action. This construction brings together certain relationships and events of historical life into an internally coherent *conceptual* cosmos. This construction has the substantive character of a *utopia* arrived at by the conceptual accentuation of particular elements of reality. Its sole relation to the empirically given facts of life is where relationships there represented abstractly, i.e. events related to the 'market', can be *identified* or *supposed* as existing in reality; and we are therefore able to make the characteristic features of this relationship pragmatically *lucid* and understandable in terms of an *ideal type*. This procedure can be of value, even indispensable, heuristically as well as in exposition. The concept of the ideal type can direct judgement in matters of imputation; it is not a 'hypothesis', but seeks to guide the formation of hypotheses. It is not a *representation* of the real, but seeks to provide representation with unambiguous means of expression. It is therefore the 'idea' of the *historically* given modern commercial organization of society developed with the same logical principles as used in, for instance, the idea of the medieval 'town economy' as a 'genetic' concept.[12] In so doing, one does not construct the concept 'town economy' as an *average* of the economic principles observable in all towns, but rather as an *ideal type*. It is formed by a one-sided *accentuation* of one or *several* perspectives, and through the

12 Genetic here means specific or individual and the sense of its historical effect.

synthesis of a variety of diffuse, discrete, *individual* phenomena, present sometimes more, sometimes less, sometimes not at all; subsumed by such one-sided, emphatic viewpoints so that they form a uniform construction *in thought*. In its conceptual purity this construction can never be found in reality, it is a *utopia*. *Historical* research has the task of determining in each *individual case* how close to, or far from, reality such an ideal type is; how far, therefore, the economic character of relations in a particular town can be thought of as a 'town economy' in the conceptual sense. If employed with care, this concept has specific uses in research and exposition.

To take another example, one can in a similar manner outline the 'idea' of 'craft industry' in a utopia, one-sidedly accentuating particular features that can be found scattered among craft workers of the most various times and countries, bringing them together as a coherent ideal image, linking this to a *conceptual* expression that one finds there manifest. One can then further attempt to outline a society in which all branches of economic, even of intellectual activity, are dominated by what appears to us to be an application of the same ideal-typical principle of a 'craft' system. To this craft ideal type there could then be juxtaposed a corresponding ideal type of capitalist indus-try (*Gewerbeverfassung*), abstracting from particular features of modern large-scale industry, seeking finally to sketch out a 'capitalist' utopia, a cul-ture where the realization (*Verwertung*) of the interests of private capitals predominates. The character of diffuse, existing individual features of mod-ern material and intellectual life would be enhanced and then brought together as a coherent ideal image lacking all internal contradiction. This would amount to an outline of *an 'idea' of capitalist culture* – but quite whether, and how, such an idea might be formed we shall here have to leave to one side. It is possible – or rather, it must be seen as a certainty – that several utopias of this kind could be constructed, of which *no* two would be the same, *none* of which could be observed in empirical reality as an actually existing order of social conditions, but where *each* of them claims to be a representation of the 'idea' of capitalist culture, and where *each* of them *can* make this claim on the grounds that the features so characterized are taken from *significant* parts of our lived culture and rendered into a unified ideal image. For those phenomena that interest us as cultural phenomena routinely derive their '*cultural significance*' from a diversity of evaluative ideas that we can in turn relate to them. Just as there are quite different 'points of view' from which these will appear significant to us, so entirely different principles can be used for the selection of those traits that are to be applied to the construction of an ideal type of a particular culture.

What then is the significance of such ideal-typical concepts for the *experiential* science (*Erfahrungswissenschaft*) that we wish to pursue? First of all it must be said that we wish carefully to distance an idea of what *ought* to be, the 'ideal', from these thought constructs which are 'ideal' only in a purely *logical* sense. We are concerned with the construction of relation-ships which seem to our *imagination* sufficiently motivated and 'objectively possible', hence appearing *adequate* from the standpoint of our nomological knowledge.

Whoever takes the position that knowledge of historical reality should or could assume the form of a 'disinterested' representation of 'objective' facts will deny the value of the ideal type. Even those who recognize that there is in reality no such thing as 'disinterestedness' in its logical sense; that even the most simple extract from statute or document can only have some kind of scientific sense by reference to 'significations', and hence ultimately to evaluative ideas – these will view the construction of some kind of scientific 'utopia' as a form of representation that endangers the impartiality of historical work, or perhaps more often as little more than a travesty. And it is a fact: the question of *whether* this is a matter of a pure thought experiment, or scientifically fertile conceptual construction is not something that can be determined a priori. There is only one standard here: that of success in developing knowledge of concrete cultural phenomena and their context, their causal determination and their *significance*. The construction of abstract ideal types is not an aim, but a *means*. All careful observation of the conceptual elements of historical representation shows that as soon as the historian seeks to go beyond the mere registration of material relationships and 'characterize' the *cultural significance* of even a very simple process, he is forced to work with concepts that can only be defined sharply and unambiguously in ideal types.

Or is it the case that concepts – such as 'individualism', 'imperialism', 'feudalism', 'mercantilism', 'the conventional', and countless similar conceptual constructs that we use to master reality in thought and understanding – can be won through 'disinterested' *description* of a concrete phenomenon, or by the abstract analysis of that which is *common* to *several* material phenomena? The language of the historian contains hundreds of words that are ambiguous constructs created by the unreflecting need for the expression of thought constructs, words whose meaning is only sensed, but not clearly conceived. In the vast majority of cases, especially in the domain of descriptive political history, the lack of substantive clarity does no harm to the clarity of the account. It is here sufficient in individual cases that one *senses* what the historian has in mind, or one can assume that a *specific* definition of conceptual content had *relative* significance for the individual case in hand. But the greater the clarity with which the significance of a cultural phenomenon has to be defined, so the need becomes ever more inescapable for working with clear concepts, defined not merely particularly, but universally. A 'definition' of this synthesis of historical thinking according to the schema, *genus proximum, differentia specifica*[13] is of course nonsense; but let us examine it. This mode of defining the meaning of words

---

13 Similar genus (as in plants) and different species – for example, the Linnean system of classification.

exists only in those axiomatic disciplines that work with syllogisms.[14] There is no simple 'descriptive reduction' of the concepts to their elements, or only apparently, for here it is a question of *which* of these components is to count as essential. All that remains, if a genetic definition of conceptual substance is to be attempted, is the form of the ideal type in the sense elaborated above. It is a thought construct; not historical reality, and most certainly not 'genuine' reality. Even less is it for employment in the service of a method for which reality is reduced to an *exemplary* instance, but rather functions instead as a purely ideal *limiting* concept (*Grenzbegriff*), against which reality is *compared*, so that particular significant component parts of its empirical content can for the sake of clarification be *measured*. Concepts of this sort are constructs in whose terms we formulate relationships through the employment of the category of objective possibility; and these constructs are *judged* with respect to their adequacy by an *imagination* oriented to, and guided by, reality.

The ideal type is in this function an attempt to comprehend historical individuals or individual components through *genetic* concepts. Take the concepts 'church' and 'sect'. They can be dissolved through pure classification into complexes of characteristics; in this not only the boundaries separating the two concepts, but also their substantive conceptual content, has to remain fluid. If however I wish to grasp the concept 'sect' *genetically*, that is, in relation to particular important cultural meanings that the 'sect spirit' has for modern culture, then particular characteristics of both concepts become *essential*, because they stand in an adequate causal relationship to those influences. The concepts then become *ideal typical*, since they do not appear in complete conceptual *purity*, or only in individual instances. Here as everywhere else a concept that is not *purely* classificatory leads away from reality. But the discursive nature of our knowledge – the circumstance that we grasp reality only through a chain of modifications in our apprehension of it – presumes such a conceptual shorthand. Our imagination can often do without explicit conceptual formulation as a means of *research* – but for *exposition*, so far as it seeks to be unambiguous, its use in the domain of cultural analysis is in numerous cases quite indispensable. Whoever takes a principled decision to do without it has to restrict himself to the formal aspect of cultural phenomena, for example, that of legal history. The universe of *legal* norms is naturally clearly definable and is *valid* (in the legal sense!) for historical reality. But the work of social science in our sense is concerned with its practical *significance*. However, this significance can very frequently only be brought unambiguously to mind by relating the empirically given to an ideal limiting case. If the historian (in the widest sense) refuses to attempt formulation of such an ideal type on the grounds that it is a 'theoretical construction', i.e. either of no use, or inessential to his given cognitive purpose, the regular outcome is that he either, consciously or unconsciously,

14 For example, logic.

uses other similar constructs *without* linguistic formulation and logical elaboration, or that he remains trapped in the realm of the ill-defined 'felt experience'.

There is certainly nothing more dangerous than the *assimilation* of theory to history engendered by naturalistic prejudices. Whether it is in the form of a belief that one has fixed the 'real' content, the 'nature' of historical reality, within those theoretical constructs; or in their use of such constructs as a procrustean bed into which history is to be forced; or perhaps that one sees 'ideas' as the 'genuine' reality underlying the flow of phenomena, hypostasized as the real 'forces' that work their way out in history.

The danger in the last case is greater if we tend to think of the 'ideas' of an epoch as thoughts or ideals that have *dominated* the masses, or a historically important section of the people during an epoch, and are therefore significant components of their cultural attributes. And two things can be added to this: first, that specific relationships exist between the 'idea' in the practical or theoretical sense, and the 'idea' in the sense of an ideal *type* of an epoch constructed as a conceptual support. An ideal type of particular social circumstances that can be abstracted from certain characteristic social phenomena of an epoch – and this happens quite frequently – appears to contemporaries themselves as an ideal to be striven for in practice, or as a principle that can be used in the regulation of certain social relationships. This is the case with the 'idea' of 'the preservation of subsistence' and many other Canonist doctrines, especially those of Thomas Aquinas, in contrast to the ideal-typical concept of the 'town economy' that we discussed above and use today. This is certainly the case with the infamous 'basic concept' of economics: that of 'economic *value*'. From Scholasticism to Marxist theory the idea that there was something 'objectively' valuable became intertwined as a *normative* ideal with an abstraction based upon the empirical process of price formation. And that thought, that the 'value' of a commodity *should* be regulated according to certain principles of natural right did have and still has immeasurable significance for cultural development, and not only of the Middle Ages. Moreover, this has had a lasting and substantial impact on empirical price formation itself. But what is and can be thought within this *theoretical* concept can *only* be made unambiguously clear with the assistance of precise conceptual constructs, which means ideal types. Those scornful of the 'Robinsonades' of abstract theory should give this matter some thought, so long as they have nothing better – which here means something *clearer* – to put in their place.

The causal relationship between a historically existing *idea* that rules men, and the components of historical reality from which its corresponding ideal *type* can be abstracted, can be formed in quite various ways. In principle we need only to remember that the two elements are fundamentally different. Now however there is another factor: the 'ideas' that govern the people of a given epoch, however diffusely, can (where a degree of complexity of thought construct is involved) only be grasped with any kind of conceptual clarity *in the form of an ideal type*, since this idea empirically inhabits the heads of an

392 Methodology of social sciences

indeterminate and constantly changing number of individuals, and as such assumes the form of extreme variation with respect to form and content, clarity and meaning. Those elements of the spiritual life of individuals living in a definite epoch of the Middle Ages that, for example, we might designate as 'Christian' in those particular individuals would be, *if* completely represented, a chaos of infinitely differentiated and entirely contradictory complexes of ideas and feelings of all kinds; but despite all this, the medieval church was able to establish a high degree of unity in faith and morality. If we ask what in this chaos might be 'Christian' about the Middle Ages, for one after all continues to use this as a stable concept – what is 'Christian' about medieval institutions, it turns out that here, in every instance, we introduce a pure thought construct that we have created. It is a combination of articles of faith, canon law and moral norms, maxims of human conduct and numerous concrete interrelationships that we unite as an 'idea': a synthesis which, in the absence of ideal-typical concepts, we could not achieve without contradiction.

There is a very great difference between the logical structure of conceptual systems in which we represent such 'ideas' and their relation to that which is given to us directly by empirical reality. The matter is relatively straightforward with respect to cases where one (or a few) theoretical principles can easily be converted into a formula – as, for example, Calvin's doctrine of predestination – or for cases where moral principles can be clearly formulated; these have dominated people and generated historical effects, so that we are able to arrange the 'idea' in a hierarchy of thoughts developed logically from these principles. It is of course easily overlooked that however compelling the significance of pure *logical* thought has been in history – Marxism is an excellent example of this – the empirico-historical process in the heads of human beings has to be understood as a *psycho*logical process, and not one determined by logical principles. The ideal-typical character of such syntheses of historically effective ideas is revealed still more clearly when those fundamental leading principles and postulates no longer survive in the heads of individuals who are, none the less, still dominated by thoughts logically or associatively derived from them, because the historically and causally fundamental 'idea' has either died out, or has been widely diffused *only* in respect of its consequences.

The character of the synthesis as an 'idea' that *we* create emerges even more strongly if those underlying principles are from the beginning incomplete, or never fully realized in consciousness, or never at least take the form of conscious connections in thought. If we adopt this procedure, as always and must always happen, this 'idea' – for instance, the 'liberalism' of a specific period, or 'Methodism', or some kind of conceptually undeveloped variation of 'socialism' – concerns a *pure* ideal type of exactly the same character as the synthesis of 'principles' of an economic epoch from which we started. The more comprehensive the relationships that are to be represented, and the more varied their cultural *significance*, the *more* their comprehensive and systematic representation as a conceptual system approaches the character of an ideal type; and the *less* it is possible to make do with *one* such concept – hence the more natural and inevitable the repeated attempts to bring into consciousness ever new aspects of meaning through the construction of new ideal-typical concepts. All representations of the 'nature' of Christianity, for instance, are ideal types, of necessarily limited and problematic validity if they are to be viewed as historical representations of the empirically given; but they have on the other hand a high heuristic value for research, and a high systematizing value for exposition, if they are taken to be solely conceptual means for the *comparison* and *calibration* of reality. In this function they are indispensable.

But there is another, far more complicated significance implicit in such ideal-typical representations. They regularly seek to be, or are unconsciously, ideal types not only in a *practical*, but also in a *logical* sense: *model* types which – to keep with our example – include that which Christianity *should* contain from the point of view of the expositor, what is *for him* 'essential' in it *because it is of lasting value*. If this is so consciously – or more frequently, unconsciously – then they contain ideals that are related evaluatively to Christianity: tasks and goals to which his 'idea' of Christianity is directed, and which can of course diverge quite markedly from the values that, for example, early Christians related to Christianity – and this divergence will doubtless continue. In this sense however the 'ideas' no longer provide purely *logical* assistance, they are no longer concepts with and against which reality can be compared and *measured*, but ideals with which it is evaluatively *judged*. This is *no longer* a matter of a purely theoretical procedure *relating* the empirical to values, but concerns instead *value-judgements* that are included within the 'concept' of Christianity. Because the ideal type here claims empirical validity it breaks into the region of evaluative *interpretation* of Christianity: the basis of an experiential science is left behind; and we are dealing with a personal confession of faith, and *not* ideal-typical *concept* formation.

Although this distinction is quite plain, these two fundamentally distinct meanings of the 'idea' are amalgamated in the course of historical work with extraordinary frequency. It is always foreshadowed as soon as a historian begins to develop his 'conception' of a personality or of an epoch. Contrasting with the constant ethical standards that Schlosser employed in a rationalist spirit, the modern historian, schooled in relativism, seeks to understand the epoch of which he speaks 'in its own terms' – but also wants to judge it; he feels the need to draw his judgement 'from the material', i.e. to allow the 'idea' in the sense of the *ideal* to emerge from the '*idea*' in the sense of the 'ideal type'. The aesthetic allure of this procedure constantly tempts him to blur the line separating them – a half-measure that on the one hand does not permit of evaluative judgement, while on the other it tends to deny responsibility for its judgements. By contrast, it is an *elementary duty of scientific self-control*, and the sole means of defence against deception, to make a sharp distinction between the logically *comparative* relation of reality to ideal *types* in their logical sense, and the evaluative *judgement* of reality directly in terms of *ideals*. An 'ideal type' in our terms, as can be stated once more, is entirely indifferent to *evaluative* judgement, it has nothing to do with any sense of 'perfection' other than in a purely *logical* sense. There are ideal types of brothels as well as of religions, and there are ideal types of brothels which are technically 'functional' from the point of view of contemporary mores, as well as those for which the absolute opposite is true.

Detailed discussion of the most complex and interesting case – the question of the logical structure of the *concept of the state* – must be here left to one side. Here the following brief observations can be made: if we ask to what in empirical reality the thought 'state' corresponds, we encounter an infinity of diffuse and discrete active and passive human actions, relations regulated factually and legally, sometimes unique, sometimes recurrent in character, all held together by an idea, a belief in actually or normatively prevailing norms and relations of rule of man by man. This belief is partly consciously held as a developed idea, partly dimly perceived, partly passively accepted and reflected in the most varied forms in the heads of individuals who, if they really did clearly *think* this idea through, would have no need of the 'general theory of the state' that they sought to elaborate. The scientific concept of the state, however formulated, is naturally only a synthesis that *we* employ for specific cognitive ends. But it is on the other hand also abstracted from the imprecise syntheses that could be found in the heads of historical humans. The concrete form assumed by the historical 'state' in such contemporary syntheses can however be rendered explicit only through orientation to ideal typical concepts. And there is not the slightest doubt that the manner in which these syntheses were made by contemporaries, however logically incomplete, the 'ideas' that they formed of the state – the German 'organic' state metaphysic contrasted to the American 'business' view, for example – were of eminent practical significance; that in other words the *practical* idea that should, or was believed to, prevail, and the theoretical ideal *type* constructed for heuristic ends ran in parallel and tended constantly to run into each other.

In the above we mostly, if not exclusively, deliberately treated the 'ideal type' as a thought construct for the charting and systematic characterization of *individuals* – i.e. the uniquely significant relationships such as Christianity and capitalism. This was done so that we might eliminate the widespread belief that in the domain of cultural phenomena the abstract *type* can be identified with the abstractly *generic*. This is not true. Without going into analysis of the much discussed, and through misuse discredited, concept of the 'typical', we can establish on the basis of our previous discussion that the formation of concepts of type through the exclusion of 'accidentals' has its place with *historical individuals*. *Generic* concepts, constantly encountered as elements of historical representations and concrete historical concepts, can be formed into ideal types through the abstraction and intensification of those conceptually important elements. In practice, this is indeed an especially frequent and important instance of the application of ideal types, and each *individual* ideal type is composed of conceptual *elements* that are generic and have themselves been formed as ideal types. Here also the specifically logical function of ideal-typical concepts is apparent. An example of a simple generic concept (that is, a concept that is a complex of many features shared in common with other phenomena) is that of the concept 'exchange', so long as I ignore the *meaning* of conceptual elements, and analyse everyday usage. If I relate this concept to that of the 'law of marginal utility' and create the concept of 'economic exchange' as an economically *rational* process, then this involves a *judgement* of the 'typical' *conditions* of exchange, as with *every* logically fully developed concept. It assumes a *genetic* character and hence also becomes ideal typical in the logical sense; it distances itself from empirical reality, which can henceforth only be a standard of *comparison*, that can be related to the ideal type. It is much the same with the so-called 'basic concepts' of economics: in their *genetic* form they can only be developed as ideal types.[15] The contrast between simple generic concepts capable only of summarizing that which is common to *empirical* phenomena, and generic *ideal* types – as, for instance, an ideal-typical concept of the 'nature' of craft production – is one which alters from case to case. But *no* generic concept as such has a 'typical' character, and there is no such thing as a purely generic 'average' *type*. Whenever we refer to 'typical' magnitudes, for instance, in statistics, then this involves *more* than a mere average. The more that we are concerned with the simple *classification* of processes that appear in reality as mass phenomena, the more that we are involved with *generic* concepts. By contrast, the more that complicated historical relationships are conceptually formed with respect to those elements relating to their specific *cultural significance*, then the concept, or the conceptual system, will assume an increasingly *ideal*-typical form. For the objective of ideal-typical conceptual construction is *not* the conscious clarification of generic factors, but rather the clarification of that which renders cultural phenomena unique.

The fact that ideal types, including generic ideal types can be used, and are used, is of *methodological* interest only when related to another circumstance.

So far we have encountered ideal types in the main as abstract relational concepts, conceived by us as stable historical individuals in the flow of events, *in* which developments take place. Now a complication crops up, seamlessly reintroducing with the assistance of the concept of 'type' the naturalistic prejudice that the goal of social sciences is the reduction of reality to '*laws*'. Even *developments* can be construed as ideal types, and such constructions

---

15 Generic concepts as ideal types are the construction of types of phenomena found in a large variety of societal settings – for example, feudalism. Genetic concepts as ideal types isolate an aspect of meaningful behaviour such as rational profit maximization. Outside Weber's ideal-type usage, generic refers to a large group or class of phenomena, e.g. crustaceans, or hunter-gatherers, whereas genetic concerns the specific origins or causes of phenomena.

can be of very great heuristic value. But there is in this a very great danger that ideal type and reality will be driven together. One could, for instance, reach the theoretical conclusion that in a *thoroughly* 'craft-based' society land rent formed the sole source of capital accumulation. From this one could perhaps – we are not concerned here with the rectitude of the construction – form an ideal image of the transformation of craft industry into a capitalist economy, determined by simple factors such as the finitude of land, increasing population, inflow of precious metals, and the rationalization of life conduct. Whether the historical course of development is actually the one that has been constructed could only be determined with the assistance of this construction as a heuristic means through comparison of ideal type and 'facts'. If the ideal type were 'properly' constructed while the actual course of events did *not* correspond to the ideal type, this would prove that medieval society was *not* in certain respects totally 'craft-based'. And if the ideal type had been constructed in a heuristically '*ideal*' manner – whether this applies to our example is not important here – research would *then* seek a clearer understanding of the character and historical significance of these non-craft elements of medieval society. *If* it arrives at this conclusion it has fulfilled its logical aim *in that* it makes plain its own lack of reality. In this case, it was a test of a hypothesis. This procedure is unobjectionable so long as one constantly recalls that ideal-typical *constructs* of development and *history* are two elements that require sharp demarcation, and that the act of construction was in this case solely a means of *deliberately* and *validly* imputing a historical process to its real causes, selecting from the sphere of the *possible* given the prevailing state of our knowledge.

Strict maintenance of this distinction is in our experience rendered much more difficult by one factor. For the sake of the evident demonstration of the ideal type, or ideal-typical development, efforts will be made to *clarify* it by adducing illustrative material from empirico-historical reality. The danger of this procedure, in itself quite legitimate, is that historical knowledge appears here in the *service* of theory, rather than the reverse. The theoretician is strongly tempted to view this relationship as normal, or worse, push theory and history into each other and as a result take the one for the other. This situation arises more sharply if the ideal construction of a developmental sequence and conceptual classification of ideal types of particular cultural entities (e.g. commercial enterprise forms developed on the basis of 'closed domestic economy', or religious concepts developed out of 'gods of the moment') are integrated into a *genetic* classification. The series of types that results from the conceptual criteria selected then appears to be a lawfully necessary historical sequence. The logical ordering of concepts on the one hand, and the empirical ordering of the conceptualized in space, time, and causal relationship on the other, becomes so entangled that there is an almost unavoidable temptation of doing violence to reality so that the real validity of the construction might be verified in reality.

We have deliberately avoided demonstrating this with respect to what is for us by far the most important case of ideal-typical construction: that of *Marx*. This was done so that our exposition might not be further complicated through the introduction of Marx interpretations, and also so that we might not anticipate contributions to our journal that will regularly present critical analyses of that great thinker. We will limit ourselves here to the observation that all specifically Marxian 'laws' and developmental constructs – to the extent that they are free of fault *theoretically* – are of ideal-typical character. The eminent, even unique *heuristic* meaning of these ideal types, if they are used in *comparison* with reality – and likewise their danger, the moment that they are conceived as empirically realized, or even as *real* (i.e. in truth: metaphysical) 'driving forces', 'tendencies', etc. – this is familiar to all who have ever worked with Marxist concepts.

Generic concepts – ideal types – ideal-typical generic concepts – ideas in the sense of actual thought connections made by historical human beings – ideal types of such ideas – ideals that govern historical human beings – ideal types of such ideals – ideals to which the historian relates history – *theoretical* constructions combined with the *illustrative* employment of the empirical – *historical* investigations using theoretical concepts as ideal limiting cases – plus the varied possible combinations that can here only be indicated: all thought constructions whose relation to the empirical reality of the directly given are problematic in every single instance: this sample alone shows the endless ramifications of conceptual and methodological problems which remain active in the sphere of the cultural sciences. And we must simply abandon any ambition of seriously examining in any greater depth practical methodological questions that are here only briefly *exposed*, or the relation of ideal-typical to 'statutory' knowledge, and that of ideal-typical concepts to collective concepts.

After all this discussion the historian will still insist that the rule of the ideal-typical form of conceptual formation is a specific symptom of the immaturity of a discipline. And in a certain sense this is correct, although linked to consequences other than those that he would draw. Let us take a few examples from other disciplines. It is certainly true that a harassed third-former, just like the primitive philologist, first thinks of a language *'organic-ally'*, that is, as a meta-empirical *totality* ruled by norms; but assumes the business of science to be the determination of what *should* prevail as a language rule. The first task normally assumed by a 'philology' is to reduce the content of a 'written language' to *rules*, as was done by the *Accademia della Crusca*.[16] If today by contrast a leading philologist declares the 'speech of

---

16 Academy founded in Florence in 1582, itself modelled on an earlier society in Perugia (*Accademia degli Scossi*). Both names indicate the function of separating the linguistic wheat from the chaff (*crusca*) and led to the purification of the Italian language on a fourteenth-century Tuscan model.

every single person' to be the object of philology, then the creation of such a programme is only possible once a relatively stable ideal type exists in written language, with the aid of which the endless variety of speech can (tacitly) be systematically studied, and without which aid such research would lack all orientation and limit. The construction of theories of the state on the basis of natural law or an organic metaphor is no different; nor is – to introduce an ideal type in our sense – Benjamin Constant's theory of the ancient state which served as a safe haven until such time as one had found one's way about the vast sea of empirical facts. A science entering into maturity always involves *supersession* of the ideal type, insofar as it is thought to be empirically *valid*, or a *generic concept*. Use today of Constant's learned construction to demonstrate particular aspects and historical peculiarities of ancient political life is still quite legitimate, so long as one carefully remains in touch with its ideal-typical character.[17] But there are sciences destined to eternal youthfulness, and that includes all *historical* disciplines, all those disciplines to which the eternally advancing flow of culture poses new problems. Here the transience of *all* ideal-typical constructions, *but* at the same time the inevitability of constantly forming *new* constructions, is central to their task.

Attempts to determine the 'genuine', 'true' meaning of historical concepts recur incessantly, but are always incomplete. As a consequence the syntheses with which history continues to work either remain imperfectly defined, or, as soon as unambiguous conceptual content is sought, the concept becomes an abstract ideal type and stands revealed as a theoretical, therefore 'one-sided' perspective capable of illuminating the reality to which it is related. But this concept also of course proves itself to be unsuitable for use as a schema within which reality can be completely *integrated*. For no systems of thought, whose support is vital if we are to grasp given significant elements of reality, are capable of exhausting reality's infinite wealth. None of them are anything more than an attempt, on the basis of prevailing knowledge and using the conceptual constructs available to us, to bring order into the prevailing chaos of facts that we have drawn into a field circumscribed by our *interest*. The thought apparatus developed by the past through the cognitive processing of immediately given reality – which in truth means cognitive *reconstruction* – and by ordering reality in terms of those concepts corresponding to the apparatus's state of knowledge and the tendency of its interest, is constantly challenged by new knowledge that we can and *wish* to draw from reality. In the course of this struggle cultural scientific work makes progress. The outcome is a constant process of reconstruction of those concepts within which we seek to grasp reality. The history of the sciences of social life is, and thus remains, a constant shift from the attempt to order facts in thought through

---

17 Benjamin Constant (1767–1830) drew a striking contrast between the liberty of the ancients and the liberty of the moderns. Ancient liberty consisted of privileges and liberties along with devotion to the city state.

conceptual construction – the dissolution of cognitive constructs so realized by the extension and displacement of the scientific horizon – to the reformation of concepts on this changed foundation. It is not the error of seeking to construct conceptual systems *in general* that is expressed by this – every science, including simple descriptive history, operates with the conceptual stock-in-trade of its time – it expresses instead the circumstance that in the sciences of human culture the construction of concepts depends on the posing of problems, and the latter change with the content of the culture itself. The relation within the cultural sciences of the concept to the conceived implies the transience of all syntheses. Large-scale attempts at conceptual construction have in the domain of our science often been of value in revealing the *limits* of the significance of the perspectives that founded them. The greatest advances in the domain of the social sciences are *substantively* connected to the shift of practical cultural problems and disguise themselves as critiques of conceptual construction. Among the most important tasks of our journal will be to serve this critical endeavour and hence the investigation of *synthetic principles* within the domain of social science.

In the conclusions that can be drawn from the above we now come to a point at which, here and there, our views differ from many (even eminent) representatives of the historical school, among whose pupils we certainly belong. In many respects the latter still hold, explicitly or implicitly, to the opinion that the purpose and aim of every science is to organize its material as a system of concepts, the content of which is to be acquired and slowly perfected through the observation of empirical regularities, the construction of hypotheses and verification of the same; until at some time or other a 'complete' and *therefore* deductive science has been formed. Given this objective, the historico-inductive work of the present is preliminary work governed by the incompletion of our discipline: and naturally nothing is more questionable from this perspective than the formation and use of clear concepts which seems to over-anticipate an objective to be realized in the distant future. This view would be unobjectionable in principle within the context of ancient and scholastic epistemology, an epistemology that was still a reflex for the bulk of specialists of the historical school: it was assumed that the purpose of concepts lay in the *direct* representation in imagination of 'objective' reality; and so the persistent claim was made that all clear concepts were *unreal*. Whoever follows through the basic principles of modern epistemology – principles that go back to Kant – according to which concepts instead are, and can only be, cognitive means for the purpose of intellectually mastering the empirically given, would have no objection to the idea that clear genetic concepts are necessarily ideal types. From this latter viewpoint, the relationship between concept and historical work is reversed: the objective of historical work appears quite impossible, concepts are not the *objective*, but the *means* to the end, knowledge of relationships that are significant from individual viewpoints. *Because* the contents of historical concepts are mutable, they need in any given context to be as clearly formulated as possible.

One would only ask that in *use* their character as ideal constructs be carefully emphasized, that ideal type and history not be confused with each other. Since really definitive historical concepts are not in general to be thought of as an ultimate end, given the inevitable shift in leading evaluative ideas, the construction of sharp and unambiguous concepts relevant to the concrete *individual* viewpoint directing our attention at any given time affords the prospect of maintaining a clear appreciation of the *limits* of their validity.

It will be said, and we have already admitted, that in the individual case the course of a concrete historical relationship can be made quite intelligible (*anschaulich*) without the constant introduction of defined concepts. And it will be claimed for the historians of our discipline that they may speak the 'language of life', as has been said of political historians. Certainly! But it can only be said that in this procedure there is often a *very* high degree of coincidence in the conscious registration of the viewpoint from which the process gains significance. We are generally not in the favourable position of the political historian for whom the cultural contents to which his account is related are naturally unambiguous, or at least seem to be. Any intelligible description entails *artistic* representation: 'each sees what is in his own heart' – valid *judgement* everywhere presupposes the *logical* working through of what is immediately perceived, which means the use of *concepts*. It is indeed possible, and often aesthetically appealing, to keep these *in petto*, but it always endangers the security of the reader's orientation, and often that of the writer, with respect to the content and scope of his judgements.

The neglect of clear concept formation in the context of the discussion of practical, economic and social policy is especially dangerous. An outsider would find incredible the degree of confusion generated by, for instance, use of the term '*value*' – that problem child of our discipline which gains unambiguous meaning *only* ideal-typically – or words such as 'productive', 'from the economic standpoint', and so forth, terms that withstand no clear conceptual analysis. It is here chiefly *collective* concepts taken from everyday life that have had an especially unhappy impact. One can take a textbook example most transparent to the layperson, the concept of 'agriculture', as it appears in the phrase 'interests of agriculture'. If we begin by taking the 'interests of agriculture' as the empirically verifiable more or less clear *subjective* perception of their interest on the part of economically active individuals; and if we for the time being ignore the countless conflicts between cattle-keeping, animal-feeding, corn-growing, corn-feeding, schnapps-distilling, etc. agriculturalists, not every layperson is aware of what is familiar to the expert: that there is an enormous entanglement of value-relations running into each other and against each other grasped only hazily by that heading.

We shall list only a few of them here: the interests of farmers wishing to sell their property and hence solely interested in the rapid rise in land values; the exact opposite interest of those wishing to buy, rent or lease; the interest of those who wish, for the sake of social advantage, that their descendants retain the property, and are therefore interested in the stability of landed property; the opposite interest of those who, in their own and their children's interests wish to see land move into the hands of the best farmers or, not necessarily the same thing, to the buyer with the most capital; the purely economic interest in the economic freedom of the 'most efficient farmer' in the business sense; the conflict between the interests of established ruling strata in the maintenance of the prevailing social and political position of their own 'status' and that of their descendants; the social interest of the *non*-dominant farmers in the decline of those strata that oppress them; occasionally, their contradictory interest in the political leadership of those strata for the protection of their commercial interests.

The list could so easily be extended without end, despite the fact that we have been as brief and imprecise as is possible. We ignore the fact that the more 'selfish' interests of this kind are mixed and amalgamated with, constrained and diverted by, the most varied pure ideal values, in order to remark that, if we speak of the 'interests of agriculture', we generally think *not only* of those material and ideal values to which individual farmer relate their own 'interests', but also of those sometimes quite heterogeneous evaluative ideas to which *we* can relate agriculture: for example,

- the interests of production, deriving from the interest in cheaper, if not necessarily high-quality, food for the population, and in which the interests of town and country clash along many dimensions, and in which the interest of the present generation does in no respect have to coincide with the probable interest of future generations;
- the populationist interest, the especial interest in a *numerous* rural population derived from 'state' interests driven either by conceptions of national power, or domestic policy, or various other ideal interests such as an expectation that a plentiful rural population will influence the cultural character of a country. This populationist interest can clash with the diverse commercial interests of all sections of the rural population, conceivably with all contemporary interests of the mass of the rural population;
- or, for example, an interest in a particular form of social *organization* of the rural population on account of the nature of political or cultural influences resulting from that; this interest, depending on its focus, can clash with all conceivable interests held by individual farmers, even the most pressing present and future interests, as well as those of the 'state'. And – this complicates the matter even further – this 'state' to whose 'interests' we freely relate these and numerous other similar individual interests is often only a convenient covering term for utterly entangled evaluative ideas, to which it is in turn related in individual cases: – purely military external security; the securing in dominance of a dynasty or particular class internally; interest in the maintenance and extension of the formal state unity of the nation, for its own sake or in the interest

of particular objective, if varied, cultural values, to which we adhere as members of a people united by a state; transformation of the social character of the state with respect to quite varied cultural ideals. It would simply take too long even to sketch out everything that might be included under those 'state interests' to which we could relate 'agriculture'.

The example chosen here is crude and simple; more so our summary analysis. The layperson could analyse, for instance, the concept 'class interest of the worker' in a similar and more thorough fashion and see just how entangled and contradictory this term is in respect of the interests and ideals of the worker, and also in respect of the ideals in whose terms *we* regard the worker. It is impossible to do away with slogans relating to the struggle of interests by laying a purely empirical emphasis on their 'relativity': clear, precise, conceptual definition of the various *possible* viewpoints is the only path that leads us beyond the ambiguity of the phrase. As a worldview or a prevailing norm the 'argument for free trade' is simply laughable, but it has inflicted heavy damage on our discussions of trade policy – quite independently of the trading ideals to which the individual adheres – such that we have underestimated the heuristic value of maxims formulated in ideal-typical form by the greatest merchants of the earth. It is only ideal-typical conceptual formations that clarify specificity of viewpoints that become relevant in individual cases through the *confrontation* of the empirical with the ideal type. The use of undifferentiated collective concepts with which everyday language works is always a cover for a lack of clarity of thought or aspiration, often enough the tool of serious deception; but always a means of obstructing the proper formulation of a problem.

We have come to the end of this discussion, the only purpose of which has been to trace the fine line that separates science and belief, and makes clear the meaning of the search for socio-economic knowledge. The objective validity of experiential knowledge rests, solely rests, upon the fact that given reality is ordered by categories which are in a specific sense *subjective*: they represent the *presupposition* of our knowledge and are based on the presupposition of the *value* of those truths which experiential knowledge alone is able to give us. For those whom this truth has no value – and belief in the value of scientific truth is the product of particular cultures, and is not given naturally – then the means of our science has nothing to offer them. He will certainly search in vain for another truth to take the place of science with respect to those aspects that *it* alone can provide: concepts and judgements that are not empirical reality, nor represent such reality, but which allow it to be *ordered in thought* in a valid manner. As we saw, in the domain of the empirical socio-cultural sciences the possibility of meaningful knowledge of what is essential for us in the infinity of events is linked to the consistent use of viewpoints of a specifically particular character, all of which in the last instance are directed by evaluative ideas, which ideas in turn can be registered and experienced as elements of all meaningful human action, but which are *not* derived from or validated by the empirical material. The 'objectivity' of social scientific knowledge depends rather on the fact that the empirical given is always related to those evaluative ideas which alone give it cognitive *value*, and the significance of the empirically given is in turn derived from these evaluative ideas. But this empirical given can never become the pedestal upon which is based an empirically impossible proof of its validity. The *belief* that we all possess in some form or other – in the meta-empirical validity of the ultimate and highest evaluative ideas, with which we anchor the meaning of our being – does not exclude the constant change in concrete viewpoints from which empirical reality gains significance, but rather includes it: life, in its irrational reality and its store of *possible* significances is inexhaustible, the *concrete* formation of value relations remains therefore fluid, subject to change in the distant future of human culture. The light given off by these highest evaluative ideas falls upon an ever-changing finite part of the monstrously chaotic stream of events that flows through time.

None of that should lead to the misunderstanding that the real task of social science lies in the constant pursuit of new viewpoints and conceptual constructions. *On the contrary*: nothing should be here more strongly emphasized than the proposition that the knowledge of the *cultural significance of concrete historical relationships* is exclusively and alone the final end that, along with other means, the work of conceptual formation and criticism seeks to serve. There are in our sphere, to use the words of F. Th. Vischer, 'material specialists' and 'interpretative specialists'. The hunger of the first can be satisfied only with legal documents, statistical tables and surveys; he is insensitive to the quality of a new idea. The latter on the other hand dulls his taste for facts by ever newer conceptual distillations. The genuine artistry that, for example, among the historians Ranke possessed in such great measure shows itself by its capacity to link *known* facts to *known* viewpoints but none the less create something new.

All work in the cultural sciences in an age of specialization, once oriented towards particular material by a particular way of posing a problem and having created its methodological principles, will treat the analysis of this material as an end in itself. It will cease consciously assessing the value of the individual facts in terms of their ultimate evaluative values, and will lose its awareness of being ultimately rooted in these evaluative ideas altogether. And that is a good thing. But at some point the atmosphere alters: the significance of viewpoints used unreflectively becomes uncertain, the path becomes lost in the twilight. The light cast by the great cultural problems has moved onward. Then even science prepares to shift its ground and change its conceptual apparatus so that it might regard the stream of events from the heights of reflective thought. It follows those stars which alone are able to give meaning and direction to its labour:

A new impulse awakes,
I hurry forth to drink its eternal light,
Before me the day, behind me the night,
Heaven above, beneath me the waves.
>   (Goethe, *Faust*, Part One, Scene II)

Further reading

In the German language Weber's methodology is referred to as *Wissenschaftslehre*. This has a larger compass than the Anglo-American understanding of technical methods. *Wissenschaftslehre* includes ontology, epistemology, methods, and the praxis of knowledge. In this wider circle of reference, we come back to some of the issues already mentioned in the Further reading to Part III. Rather than repeat these debates I will confine my remarks to strictly expositional references, of which there are surprisingly few in English. And by implication there are a great number of works dealing with Weber's methodology in the light of twentieth-century developments in the philosophy of science and of social science. Weber is mostly treated in terms of what he *should* have said according to the post-Weberian paradigms of neo-positivism, phenomenology, interpretivism, and critical theory. On this range of interpretations, see Sven Eliaeson, *Max Weber's Methodologies*, Cambridge, Polity Press, 2002. An additional complication in the literature is that Weber, in liberating himself from German collectivist and organicist thinking, overlaps with an Anglo-American analytic tradition initiated by J.L. Austin and extended by major figures such as Quentin Skinner and John R. Searle. Martin Hollis, in *Models of Man. Philosophical Thought on Social Action*, Cambridge, Cambridge University Press, 1977, operates in the confluence of these two traditions.

Chapter 1 of L.M. Lachmann's *The Legacy of Max Weber*, London, Heinemann, 1970, presents an extremely clear account of Weber's theory of social action. Chapter 11 of Martin Albrow's *Max Weber's Construction of Social Theory*, Basingstoke, Macmillan, 1990, demonstrates how his methodology ties into the analysis of social structure – a link clearly intended by Weber but more often than not overlooked or contested by commentators. Ola Agevall provides an overall exposition of Weber's methodological essays in *A Science of Unique Events. Max Weber's Methodology of the Social Sciences*, Uppsala, Uppsala University Press, 1999. Hans Henrik Bruun expounds with scholarly conviction the principal topics of Weber's *Wissenschaftslehre* – value-freedom, the scientific study of values, the ideal type, politics, science and ethics – in *Science, Values and Politics in Max Weber's Methodology*, Copenhagen, Munksgaard, 1972. Stephen Turner and

Regis Factor, in *Max Weber. The Lawyer as Social Thinker*, London, Routledge, 1994, significantly clarify Weber's model of causality. Fritz Ringer's *Max Weber's Methodology: The Unification of the Cultural and Social Sciences*, Cambridge, MA, Harvard University Press, 1997, provides an overview, and Rogers Brubaker in his *The Limits of Rationality*, London, Allen & Unwin, 1984, provides an informative summary of the interrelation of rationality and morality in Weber's thought.

There is no English equivalent of Weber's collected methodological works (published as *Gesammelte Aufsätze zur Wissenschaftslehre* in Germany). Edward Shils and Henry Finch have published three central essays in *Methodology of the Social Sciences*, New York, Free Press, 1949, though there are some oddities in the translation of such key conceptual terms as 'value' and 'judgement'. Guy Oakes has published Weber's early methodological essays on Roscher and Knies, which are the most Rickert influenced of Weber's thinking, *Roscher and Knies. The Logical Problems of Historical Economics*, New York and London, Free Press and Macmillan, 1975. Guy Oakes has also translated Weber's caustic critique of Rudolf Stammler, *Critique of Stammler*, New York and London, Free Press and Macmillan, 1977. See also his *Weber and Rickert. Concept Formation in the Cultural Sciences*, Cambridge, MA, MIT Press, 1988.

Glossary

Abreaction   See *sublimation*.

Adequacy of meaning   The understanding by an observer of the reasons behind the motive for social behaviour. See also *causal adequacy* and *context of meaning*.

Asceticism   The technique and discipline of bodily and sensory deprivation used by religions to achieve an extraordinary psychological state.

Autonomous working (*Eigengesetzlichkeit*)   Where *rationalization* operates within its own sphere of values or specialist area as a recurring empirical regularity, independently of its original impulse. It is sometimes also translated as lawlike autonomy but any regularity should not be taken as the result of a law.

Bureaucracy   An administrative organization or apparatus based on rules, written files, hierarchy, expertise, and the impersonal treatment of individuals. In modernity, Weber's ideal type specifies these characteristics are based on rationality. Throughout history, however, bureaucracies have also operated on non-rational criteria.

Calling   The Christian or gospel idea that people are called to Christ's mission to spread the message of salvation. Derived from calling is the term *vocation* that is used to describe a dedication to an occupation, profession, trade, or labour; similarly in German *Berufung* is the notion of Christian calling, while *Beruf* is an, occupational vocation. Weber's *PESC* is an explanation of how the specific religious idea of calling in Protestantism is transmuted into the economic practice of vocation.

Capitalism   Where property or wealth is an object of trade and used by individuals for making profit in a market economy. Capitalism for Weber was a universal phenomenon. Modern capitalism is distinguished by its pre-eminence of rationality criteria such as calculability, planning, budgeting, use of free labour, and a legal–rational framework.

Capitalist spirit   *Asceticism* based on the idea of a religious *calling* infuses work, labour, and the acquisitive impulse and forms the basis of rational conduct in the economic sphere.

Carriers   A prominent social group or status group whose members bear or carry a significant and distinctive attitude towards the world.

Causal adequacy   A sequence of events that is known from experience to recur on a regular basis.

Charisma   In its religious sense a divine talent possessed by only a few. A charismatic leader is credited by followers with having superhuman and extraordinary personal powers often of a magical nature.

Church   An institution-like community with officials for the organized administration of grace to the masses. Its ideal typical opposite is the *sect*.

Class   The basis of power in the economic order. Class is stratified by the positive or negative possession of (a) property, (b) earning chances. Social class refers to the ranges of social links, like marriage, within a class.

Conduct of life or **life conduct (*Lebensführung*)**   How a life, or *style of life*, is conducted, usually rigorously, according to religious principles and status group expectations.

Confucianism   Set of beliefs and lifestyle derived from the Chinese philosopher Confucius (551–479 BC) and held by the ruling official stratum in the Chinese Empire. The world was seen as a magic garden inhabited by spirits and the lifestyle aimed at education and self-perfection.

Context of meaning (*Sinnzusammenhang*)   The ensemble of meanings in a social situation to which all attribution of motives for actions has to be referred. See *adequacy of meaning*.

Conventicles   A voluntary group of the religiously saintly within a *church* who meet together to intensify their faith. The communities formed by German Pietists were known as conventicles.

Disenchantment (*Entzauberung*)   This should be understood literally, as de-magicalization. It is a product of religious and scientific *rationalization* that removes the original, naïve and direct attitude of humans to the world and to community.

Domination   See *power* and *rulership*.

Estatist   'Estatist' is the political representation of the various estates (nobility, clergy, and townspeople or burghers) in parliamentary-type assemblies where the right to speak stems from a liberty or privilege conferred by the monarch on an estate.

Ethic of conviction (*Gesinnungsethik*)   Ethical behaviour guided by adherence to a strongly held conviction or principle.

Ethic of responsibility (*Verantwortlichkeitsethik*)   Ethical behaviour guided by the foreseeable consequences of one's actions.

Ethical irrationality   The reversal of the assumption that out of good actions comes good and from evil ones evil. Because of the irrational nature of the world, a good intention can result in harm.

Extraordinary   A concept that is frequently used by Weber and should be understood literally, i.e. out of or beyond the ordinary and the everyday.

Habitus   A disposition to behave and view the world in a particular and distinctive manner.

Hidden god (*Deus absconditus*) The idea that God's will cannot be known by mortals. Its principal application concerns *predestination*.

Historical economics Mostly associated with the work of Gustav Schmoller (1838–1917) who was a leading professor at Berlin when Weber was a postgraduate student there. Schmoller held that economic laws could be induced through building up detailed historical pictures of economic institutions. Other components in this economic tradition include the protectionist state policies of Fichte and Friedrich List, Roscher's aristotelian understanding of economic behaviour, and the political economy of Hegel and Marx. The category of historical economics overlaps with national-economy, but under the influence of price theory and *marginalism* from the beginning of the twentieth century the latter moves towards the modern conception of neo-classical economics.

Honoratiores Latin word for notables who perform administrative and governing roles from status honour rather than paid employment. Under modernity they are replaced by the salaried professional.

Ideal type A methodological instrument created by Weber to analyse cultural meanings into their logically pure components. It is essential for clarity of *understanding* and the operations of causality.

Iron cage A striking example of the effectiveness of mixing imagery. Weber's imagery at the end of *PESC* speaks of a Puritan saint who wears his worldly goods 'like a light cloak' easily cast aside. In the modern economic world this cloak has become a confining, steel-hard housing. Talcott Parsons translated the image of a housing as 'iron cage', and the phrase has become an important signifier in contemporary discourse.

Lawlike autonomy See *autonomous working*.

Legal enactment Social action oriented to the following of rules that have been written down and legislated. See also *rulership*.

Legitimacy The belief of the ruled in the validity of rulership. Legitimacy is based on tradition, charisma, or legal enactment. See also *rulership*.

Life orders and value spheres Refers to the development of society out of an original simple unity of kinship groups, magic, and a naïve attitude to the world. The family becomes differentiated from economic activity and from politics (whereas under patriarchalism these spheres overlapped). In addition religion and its sphere of values comes into opposition with the values of the developing life orders of economics and politics. This differentiation process reaches its greatest fragmentation in modernity. Weber speaks of the incommensurability of values in each of the life orders so, for example there is no way of reconciling economic rationality with religious brotherhood.

Literati Latin word for people who write literature. Weber frequently objected to writers who thought they could solve the problems of the world and especially of politics. His use of the word implies that these people are naïve dilettantes who have no idea of the seriousness of politics. His condemnation was not, however, absolute.

Marginalism   A mathematical theory that showed that frequency data should not be considered solely in terms of averages but that the last unit added to a quantum had far greater significance than the changed average. It was taken up by the Austrian economist Carl Menger (1840–1921), who used it as a new criterion for the rationality of consumer behaviour. Later in the twentieth century marginalism enabled the development of price theory and neo-classical economics. Weber was exceptional among German national-economists in including marginalism in his teaching.

Occidental   A cultural and religious designation of 'the West'. The word derives from the setting of the sun, just as 'oriental' derives from the rising of the sun, and many European and Asian religions laid/lay great significance on this horizontal occurrence.

Oikos   A unit of production and consumption based on an extended household and usually involving the use of slave labour. Widespread in the classical world of Greece, Rome, and the Near East.

Pathos   The pain that results from the tension between the imperfection of the everyday world and the perfection of a religiously transcendental world. Apathy is the state experienced when the tension is removed.

Politics   Competition for, or influence over, the distribution of power in the state and social groups.

Power   Possibility of imposing one's will over the behaviour of others in spite of their resistance. See also *rulership*.

Predestination   A religious doctrine, especially pronounced among Calvinists, that God has predetermined before the birth of a human being whether he or she is destined for heaven or hell. Those who were destined for heaven were known as the 'elect'. Calvinists sought to 'affirm' their election through hard work and success even though the ways of God were unknown to them. See also *hidden God*.

Protestant   Literally, someone who protests their freedom of conscience against the authority of church or state. Protestants, collectively, sought to reform the Christian Church, and the Reformation was a movement started in Germany by Martin Luther in 1517. Weber's *PESC* pays little attention to the large Protestant churches (Lutheranism in Germany or Anglicanism in England) and instead focuses on the *Puritan sects*.

Puritan   Someone who is pure in terms of their religious practice and conscience. Weber uses the term as a shorthand for Protestant groups (Calvinists, Pietists, Methodists, and Baptists) who are rigorous in their *asceticism*.

Rationalism   An intellectual imposition of a coherent and ordered set of ideas upon the world. Rationalism is instanced in a wide variety of forms: ascetic rationalism, Confucian rationalism, legal rationalism, scientific rationalism, technological rationalism, economic rationalism, etc. The underlying assumptions on which a rationalism is based are often irrational and even in the case of scientific rationalism it is not possible to validate its foundations as rational. Rationalism is a strong determinant of people's behaviour and is a principal component in the process of *rationalization.*

Rationality Within Weber's typology of *social action* there are two types of rational action: instrumental rationality, the rational assessment of ends and the means for their attainment, and value rationality, the rational attainment of a goal held for its own sake or from conviction. More generally, Weber speaks of formal and substantive rationality and this corresponds to the opposition between instrumental and value rationality. The tempered western musical scale is an example of formal rationality but it is unable to meet completely the substantively rational needs of musical acoustics; similarly in law there exists the substantive rationality of justice and the formal rationality of the administration of law. There is an unbridgeable gap between the two categories of rationality.

Rationalization One of Weber's most indispensable concepts for analysing the processes of change and their direction. It is a compound concept consisting of several elements. All rationalization processes originate from some form of *rationalism.* In imposing an intellectual idea upon the world in whatever sphere (politics, economics, religion, magic, sport, marketing, etc.) the rationalist kernel becomes 'objectivated' in the materiality of the structures of society. The rationalist idea takes on an independent life within the respective social process. For example, ascetic rationalism resulted in the rationalization of a methodical way of life among Puritans and legal rationalism led to a specific rationalization of the administration of law. As the example of religious rationalization demonstrates, there is no assumption that rationalization rests on rational foundations and assumptions. Rationalization processes often have irrational and sub-optimal consequences. Rationalization also involves the concept of *autonomous working.*

Routinization Ways of institutionalizing religious or political power after the death of a charismatic ruler. The House of Windsor, for example, demonstrates the success of routinization where the charismatic lineage has long been moribund.

Rulership (*Herrschaft*) Often translated as domination and sometimes as authority. The immediate requirement of any rulership is an administrative apparatus or group body through which power is exercised. Those who are ruled accept their subordination usually through a belief in the *legitimacy* of power. Legitimacy is either traditional, charismatic, or legally enacted.

Salvation benefits/goods (*Heilsgüter*) Salvation is the religious idea that a human being will be saved, i.e. on their death they will enter a state of transcendental bliss and will escape the pain of earthly life as well as divine punishment. The benefits or goods are the content of the promises given in the salvation message of a religion.

Sect   A group of the faithful that only accepts into the congregation the religiously qualified and pure. It contrasts with *church* which offers open access to the masses.

Sib   Kinship group based on extended family and equivalent to clan.

Social action   The subject matter of sociology as an interpretative science. In ideal typical terms Weber distinguished four types of social action: instrumentally rational action, value-rational action, affectual/emotional action, and traditional action.

Soteriological   The adjectival form of salvation.

State   Supreme and legitimate controller of physical force within given territorial boundaries.

Status group   The German term for status group is a *Stand* which in historical terms means an 'estate'. In feudal times the three estates of a realm consisted of those who prayed (the clergy), those who fought (the knights), and those who worked (the peasants). Modern societies are less rigidly stratified into status groups, but the term, especially in historical usage, implies that stratification is well developed. See also *estatist*.

Style of life or **lifestyle**   This is a no less ordered concept than the *conduct of life*, but is as likely to be determined by status group expectations as ethical principles. It is not as frivolous a concept as it is in Simmel and Veblen. Parsons refused to translate the term in *PESC* preferring 'life' or 'way of life' in its stead.

Sublimation   As a psychological phenomenon, the controlled and conscious direction of emotional energy; its opposite is abreaction: the immediate release of emotional energy. As a cultural phenomenon, sublimation is the refinement of natural human events such as love and death into a higher cultural form or of lower level magical practices into religious beliefs such as salvation. It is frequently a component in *rationalization*.

Theocracy   Government by a priestly order or church; for example, the Papal state or Iran under Ayotollah Khoemini. A secular state is one where the influence of religion is excluded from government.

Theodicy   The attempt to explain how an all-powerful and benevolent god could create an irrational world full of suffering, injustice, and stupidity.

Tradition   The sanctity of an order that can successfully claim to have existed since time immemorial.

Understanding   Often known by its German name *Verstehen*. Very simply, it means to understand the actions and meanings of another person or cultural artefact, and it is enabled by our capacity to empathize with the motives, thinking, and expressions of another human being.

Value freedom   The methodological demand that the values of a religion, a political party or a philosophy of life have no place in the lecture hall and in scientific research. Unlike positivism, this does not mean that the subject matter of values and meanings is excluded in the social and cultural sciences as an object of study.

Virtuoso   Someone who is exemplary or heroic in their religiosity. The word is normally used to describe supreme musical skill as is indicated by Weber when he refers to the masses as religiously unmusical.

Vocation See *calling*.

Work ethic A current term to describe the inner compulsion to work. Weber showed how this compulsion has descended from Protestant asceticism.

Worldview A perceptual lens determined by beliefs through which the world is seen and understood. Magic and the various religions produce entirely different properties of cognizing the world. One of the simplest and most important of Weber's concepts. It should not be confused with *Weltanschauung* which is an overall philosophy of life and is not a scientific concept.

Index

* Indicates glossary entry.

Abd al-Wahhab 207
abreaction 95, 330
'abstract'-theoretical method 385, 387
acosmistic 95, 99, 229
acquisitive drive 49, 96–7
adequacy of meaning 303, 319, 407*;
    see also causal adequacy; meaning,
    context of
adjudication 210, 253, 255
adjustment to the world 41, 81, 91, 97
administrative orders 353, 354
administrative staff 141–2, 350, 351
aesthetics 230–2, 278
affectual action 301, 329, 330, 339
agriculture 28, 166, 167, 400–2
all-oneness 67, 71
Anglicanism 30–1
animal behaviour 322
animism 36, 38, 41–2
anthropology 111, 372
Antiquity 5, 37, 48, 53, 58, 72, 73, 83, 84,
    85, 86, 97, 105, 161–70, 172, 174, 178,
    186, 192, 194, 201, 235, 239, 250, 276,
    378
appearance/reality divide 296–7
Aquinas, Thomas 42
arbitrary rulership 122
architecture 102
Archilochos 233
Archiv für Sozialwissenschaft und
    Sozialpolitik 308, 359–72
Aristotle 51, 101
art 26, 102, 230–1, 272, 276, 287
artisans 68
asceticism 15, 20, 37, 40, 44, 50, 53, 57,
    65, 67, 71, 73, 74, 77–8, 81, 67, 94, 205,
    215, 223, 232, 234–6, 238, 407*;
    Confucian 37; and eroticism 236, 237;
    innerworldly 22, 29, 89, 93–4, 227–9,
    237; Islam 92, 94; Judaism 88; magical
60, 68; mysticism 216–20; Protestant
15, 25–34, 35, 226; sects 78; typology
216–20
Asiatic political thought 101
Asiatic popular religiosity 97
Aspasia 234
associated relationships 302, 343–4,
    351
astronomy 375
Athanasius 239
Attica 168
Austria 146, 148, 213
authoritarian powers 252
autocephaly 352
autonomous working 47, 54, 219, 222,
    224, 230, 240, 407*
autonomy 352
average types 326

Babylonia 53, 101, 105, 168, 239
balances 104
banks 106, 163
Baptists 14, 31, 44, 45, 86
Barclay, Robert 27
Baudelaire, Charles 214, 223, 281
Baumgarten, Fritz 5
Bavaria 213
Baxter, Richard 28, 33
bearers see carriers
begging 31, 223
belief in values 363, 381, 402, 403
Benedek, Ludwig 327
Bhagavad Gita 264
biological heredity 111
biology 297, 384
Bismarck, Otto von 3, 4
Book of Sports 25
book-keeping 106, 126
bourgeois strata 72–3, 107–8, 177, 178
Brahmans 21, 57
Britain 213
brotherhoods 80

brotherliness: ethic 99–100; tension with political orders 221, 223–8
Bücher, Karl 161–2
Buddhism 19, 20, 21, 23, 55, 57, 66, 94–6, 190, 207, 222, 229, 285
Bunyan, John 30
bureaucracy 120, 122, 134–5, 209, 245–7, 291, 407*
business enterprise 48, 106, 125, 126, 167, 168, 201, 354; and book-keeping 48, 106
business forms 83–4
Butler, Samuel 26

cabala 88
Caesar, Julius 303, 312
calculability 108, 171, 209, 248, 271, 274
calculation 104, 107, 108
Calderon, Pedro 191
calling 15, 25, 31, 32, 33, 100, 407*
Calvin, John 31; Calvinism 15, 28, 31, 76, 206, 226, 265; Calvinists 45
capital accounting 171–5
capital accumulation 28, 30, 104, 105, 167
capital investment 168
capitalism 33, 407*; in Antiquity 125, 161–70; booty 51; and calculation 48; China 47–9; modern 14, 24, 83–4, 97, 126, 208; politically oriented 48, 175; and Puritanism 25–34; and world religions 96–7, 103–7
capitalist spirit 13, 407*
carriers 20, 58, 59, 407*
Carlyle, Thomas 45
castes 128, 188–9, 192
Catholicism 21, 85–7, 222, 265
causal adequacy 304, 319, 379, 380, 408*
causality 295, 296, 373, 374, 375, 376, 378, 379, 382, 391
Cavaliers 26
charisma 76, 98, 120, 227, 242, 408*
charismatic parties 196
charismatic qualification 129, 143–4
charismatic rulership 120, 121, 138–45
Charles I, king of England 25
chiliasm 230, 263
China 15–16, 17, 18, 20, 24, 39–40, 43, 44, 47–9, 53, 63, 74, 96, 101, 102, 105, 107, 109, 148, 215, 222, 238
chivalry 208
Chlysts 66
chosen people 152
Christianity 18, 19, 20, 22, 23, 58, 64, 97–100, 392, 393; early 21, 80, 81, 97–100

Christian Tertiaries 57
Church 76, 140, 356, 390, 408*
Cicero 5
citizenship 107, 122, 253, 289
city economies 162, 165
class action 184–5
class conflict 177, 178
class interest 65, 128, 363
class situation 176, 183, 184, 185, 186, 187, 193
class struggle 186
class types 176
class-consciousness 128
classes 127, 183–7, 192, 193, 200, 408*; *see also* commercial classes; social classes
Cleon 141
closure 302, 346–8
collective action 184–5
collegiate bodies 248
commenda 83, 104
commercial classes 178–9
Communist Manifesto 371
community cults 60, 233
community relationships 302, 343, 344, 345, 351
competition 342
Comte, Auguste 296
concepts 367, 377, 383, 387, 388, 389, 389–90, 394–5, 399, 400
conceptual constructs 389, 391, 398, 399
conditioning 333
conduct of life 16–17, 56, 109, 151, 218, 408*; social strata 57–8, 75
Confucianism 15–17, 408*; basis in magic 19, 23; contradictions 39–40; social strata 57; vs Puritanism 15–16, 35–54
consistency 216
consumption 26–8, 50–1
Constant, Benjamin 398
contemplation 37, 73, 205, 219, 223
context of meaning (*Sinnzusammenhang*) 408*; *see also* meaning
conventicles 33, 111, 408*
convention 33, 301, 333, 337–8, 338, 339
conviction *see* ethics
Cortegiano, Baldassare 234
Court, Pieter de la 30
craft industry 388
criminal gangs 119
cults 61, 153–4
cultural life 365, 371, 374
cultural sciences 377
cultural significance 364, 370, 371, 379, 381, 382, 388
cultural values 149, 298, 300, 364

culture 242, 244, 377, 380
custom 333, 334

da Vinci, Leonardo 276
death 225, 274
Defoe, Daniel 32
dehumanization 209
demagogues 213, 258
democracies 121, 200
democracy 213, 253, 279; leadership 145
democratic legitimacy 121–2
Demosthenes 234
depersonalization 224
Dervish orders 66, 93; religiosity 216
d'Este, Renata 47
developmental historians 122
developmental laws 296
developments 395, 396
diasporas 189
dilettantes 271
Dilthey, Wilhelm 303
disciples 139
discipline 302, 355
disenchantment 214, 238, 274, 291, 408*
distance, lack of 257–8
domination 132, 133, 302, 408*
Dostoyevsky, Fyodor 263, 266
Dowden, Edward 29
Doyle, John Andrew 28
dualism 296, 297
Durkheim, Emile 208, 295

ecology parties 129
economic capacities 127
economic conditioning 369
economic ethics *see* ethics
economic geography 16, 56
economic laws 380
economic life: Catholicism 85–7;
    Judaism 82–3, 84–5, 88; Puritanism
    85–7; and world rejection 221–30
economic phenomena 369, 372–3
economic policy 363
economic production (forms) 125
economic sociology 201
economic sphere 221–3
economic theory 386, 387
economics 298, 360–1, 367, 383–4
economy 123
Economy and Society 9, 115, 123, 300,
    301
ecstasy 40–1, 76–8, 207
ecstatic cults 40
Educational Alliance 91
Egypt 101, 105, 107, 168, 169
elective affinity 20–1, 73, 363, 367
empathy 313

empirical-historical research 385
England 28, 173, 212, 255
English law 210, 255
Enlightenment 33
entrepreneurs 127, 178, 246
ergasteria 48, 106, 162–3
eroticism 208, 233, 236; *see also* sexual
    love
Essenes 23
estate structures 136–7, 138, 408*
estatist 408*; rulership 122, 138
ethic of conviction (*Gesinnungsethik*)
    229, 261–2, 267–8, 408*
ethic of responsibility
    (*Verantwortlichkeitsethik*) 257, 260–3,
    267, 268, 408*
ethical evolutionism 360
ethical irrationality 408*
'ethical' science 360, 362
ethics 16, 22, 33, 37, 93, 207, 213–14, 225,
    259–68, 339, 364, 365, 393, 405;
    capitalistic 32; Confucian 36;
    economic 16, 20, 22, 55–80, 91,
    215–44; Jewish 84–5; medieval 31;
    Puritan 13, 16, 27, 52, 85–6; religious
    42, 43, 46, 47, 55, 56, 59, 71, 92, 94–5,
    99–100, 205–6, 208, 211, 215, 216, 220,
    229; vocational 30; work 1, 2, 15
ethnic groups 150, 154–5; disutility of
    notion 154–5
ethnic honor 152
ethnic identity 151
ethnicity 123, 124, 150–5, 201
ethnography 111
Europocentrism 114
evaluative concepts 377, 379, 381
everyday action 77, 79
everyday life 103
evidence 313, 317
evolutionary theory 288
exchange 103–4, 378, 395
executive powers 350
exemplary prophecies 73, 74
existential knowledge 360
experiential knowledge 367, 402
extraordinary 408*
extraordinary states 60, 66–8, 75, 77

factories 125
factory organization 163
factory system 125, 162, 163
faith parties 196
Fallenstein, Georg Friedrich 4
family 157; piety 42, 43
fas 251
fashion 333
Faust 32, 38, 404

feudal lords 243
feudalism 28, 53, 92, 93, 103, 120, 243
Fichte, J.G. 267, 385
files 246
finance 48, 106, 107, 175
flight from the world 37
Foerster, F.W. 263, 265
force 131, 132, 214, 224, 226, 260, 262, 263, 265, 266, 267, 356, 357
formal justice 252, 253, 254
Foucault, Michel 119, 299
fragmentation 208, 288
France 281
Franklin, Benjamin 14–15, 32, 49
Frederick the Great 254
Frederick II, Holy Roman Emperor 122
Frederick II, King of Prussia 246
free labour 107–8, 164, 172, 173
freedom 254
Freud, Sigmund 7, 18–19, 208
funding 30

Galileo 276, 296
Gellner 'school' 289
general rules 325
generic concepts 395, 397
Germany 3–4, 28, 148, 188, 197, 213, 258, 281; German society 201
Ghibellines 194, 197
Giddens' approach 289
globality 289
Gnosticism 20, 285; Gnostic communities 58, 67
Goethe, Wolfgang 32, 238, 267, 309
good fortune 60
goods 219, 243
Gothic vaults 102
Gottl-Ottlilienfeld, Friedrich von 311
government 213
governmentality 291
Greece 150–1
Gresham's Law 304, 318, 324
group bodies (*Verbände*) 120, 195–6, 302, 350–2; and rulership 133–4
Gross, Otto 8
Guelfs 194, 197
guild 192
guilt 242, 244, 261
Gummerus 164

Habermas, Jürgen 88, 289; Habermasian school 289
Hadrian 89
habitus 66, 67–8, 74, 408*
happiness 209, 277
Helmholtz, H. 271
Hennis, Wilhelm 290

heuristic 325, 326, 396
heterocephaly 352
hidden god (*Deus absconditus*) 409*
hierocracies 71, 76, 356, 357; hierocratic groups 356, 357
Hinduism 17, 19, 21, 23, 64, 81, 205, 264; *dharma* 264; social strata 57; social stratification 57, 205; vs Buddhism 96
historical development 16, 17, 121, 288
historical economics 409*
historical factors 16, 17, 56
historical individual 379, 394
historical interpretation 371, 399
historical materialism 59
historical relativism 360
history 396
Holland 28, 31
honoratiores 197, 255; *see also* notables
honorific service 247–8
household communism 159
household community 156–60
household economy 125, 201
household organization 125, 137
Hume, David 296
human nature 36
humanities 298
Hungary 128
hypotheses 317–18

ideal types 2, 211, 295, 405, 409*; medieval cities 165–6; modern capitalist enterprise 126; *oikos* 161; Protestant ethic thesis 308; Weber's preferred method 304–5, 307, 326–7, 387–99
idealism 298, 300
ideas 271, 388, 391, 392, 393
ideology 58
Ihering, Rudolf 271, 337
imitation 328–9
impartiality 209
India 16, 41, 53, 74, 93, 96, 101, 105, 109, 212, 215, 223, 307, 348
Indian Buddhism 96
Indian religiosity 205, 215
individual interests 221
industrial organization 106
inheritance 159
Innocent III 122
institutions 201, 354–5, 368, 386–7
instrumental rationality 305, 329, 330–1
instrumentally rational action 314, 330–1
intellectualism 68–71, 86–7, 238–41
intellectuals 68, 124, 206
interests 70, 128, 195, 221, 334, 335, 363, 400, 402
intermarriage 125

international houses 159
interpretative sociology 299, 302–3, 307, 314, 324, 371
Iran 74
iron cage 2, 33, 409*
Islam 18, 19, 20, 22, 23, 115–16, 199, 207, 226, 265, 285; 'adjustment' to the world 91–4; social strata 57
islamic warriors 57
Israel 150
Italy 197, 199
ius 251

Jaffé, Else, *née* von Richthofen 8
Jaffé, Edgar 308
James I, king of England 25
Japan 40, 96, 143, 212
Jaspers, Karl 311
Jesus Christ 22–3, 90, 97–9, 141, 260
Jewish business ethic 84–5
Jewish Law 22, 81, 82, 85, 87, 100
Jewish Messiah 23
Jews 91, 147, 189
joint liability 158–9
'journeyman' 165
Judaism 18, 19, 21, 22, 23, 64, 207, 285; asceticism 88; economic life 82–3, 85–7, 88; self-control 87–9; social strata 57–8; vs Puritanism 89–91; Talmudic 21, 22; as world religion 81–5
juries 211, 254
jurisdictional areas 245
jurisprudence 278
justice 209–10, 250; formal 252, 253, 254; khadi-justice 254, 255; substantive 210, 252, 253, 254

Kafka, Franz 211
Kant, Immanuel 240, 261, 267, 285, 308–9, 399
karma 64, 75, 94, 95, 228; causality 94, 95
khadi-justice 254, 255
kinship groupings 47, 220–1
knights 68; and fate 72
knowledge, objectivity 359–404

labour 31, 106, 107, 108, 370, 372; free labour 164, 172, 173; organization 106, 107, 108, 373
labourers 178
Lao-tzu 50, 217
land cultivation 173
land ownership 173
language 146, 147; groups 151
Laud, Bishop William 32

law 109, 291, 337, 338, 371, 376; English 210, 255; Jewish 22, 81, 82, 85, 87, 100; natural 340; secular 254–5; sociology of 291; substantive 208, 250, 251; theocratic 254; theocratic and secular 250–6
lawlike autonomy 56, 75, 228, 409*
Lawrence, D.H. 8
laws in science 296, 318, 324, 374, 375, 377, 379, 380, 385, 395
leaders 139, 144, 212, 213, 214, 266, 269, 282, 283
Le Bon, Gustave 328
legal authority 119, 120
legal culpability 307
legal enactment 409*
legal institutions 382
legal orders 338, 339
legal rulership 129, 133
legal system 108, 115
legality 340
legitimacy 409*
legitimacy of an order 301, 335, 337–40
legitimate rule (types) 119–20, 133–45, 200
life conduct *see* conduct of life
life orders 206, 207, 209, 213, 215, 288, 409*
lifestyles 17, 191, 192, 412
literati 110, 138, 409*
Lloyd George, D. 213
lovelessness 242
loyalty 158
Lukács, György 128, 286
Luther, Martin 141, 237, 238, 265; Lutheranism 42, 226–7, 265

Machiavelli, Niccolò 101, 120; Machiavellianism 264–5, 267
magic 16, 20, 35, 38, 41, 46, 61, 65, 96, 97, 206, 218; magicians 61
majority principle 144
mandarins 120
Manichaenism 285
manorialism 166
marginalism 331, 387, 409–10*
markets 345, 347
marriage 157, 232, 237
Marx, Karl 2, 17, 18, 123, 126, 179, 297, 369; Marxism 17, 64, 297, 392, 397
Maryology 67
mass behaviour 328
mass religiosity 77
materialist conception of history 17, 371, 382
maternal groupings 157, 158
Mayer, Robert 271

meaning 303, 312, 377; adequacy of 303, 319, 407*; context of 301, 316, 408*; cultural life 368; devoid of 314; and philosophy 284; of the world 276, 285, 364, 381
meaningfulness 241, 244, 306, 328
meaninglessness 244, 274, 383
means and ends 361–3
medical science 278
medieval cities 165–6
medieval Europe 120
medieval trading companies 115
Meister Eckhardt 75
Mencius 43
Mennonites 44
men's houses 157
merchants 68, 105
Methodism 29, 58; Methodists 14, 44
methodology 2, 24, 296, 308, 312–27, 385, 405–6
Meyer, Eduard 5, 162, 299, 318
middle classes 72–3, 107, 177, 178
middle way 364
Mill, J.S. 281
missionary prophecies 73–4
modelling techniques 298
modern capitalism 14, 24, 83–4, 97, 126, 208
modern state 120, 121, 122, 131
modernity 5, 116, 205, 208, 209, 288, 289, 297
modernization 200
Mohammed 91–2
Moltke, Helmuth von 326
Mommsen, Theodor 5, 6
monasticism 29, 38, 222–3
money 130, 222
money economy 48, 378
money-lenders 105
monism 297, 385
monks 80; Buddhist 57
morality 220, 360
mortification of flesh 27, 37, 63
motive 318
multiple modernities 116
music 70, 102, 115, 231–2
mysteries 61, 62
mystics 229–30; mysticism 74–8, 205, 216–20, 231, 237

Napoleon Bonaparte 4, 141
nation building 289
nation states 124
national solidarity 147
nation(s) 123, 124, 146–9, 201
natural relationships 46–7
natural scientific methods 296

neighbourliness 99, 208
neo-Marxist school 289
neo-Pythagoreans 20, 74
Netherlands 31
Nietzsche, Friedrich 5, 214, 277, 281, 290–1; influence on Weber 299–300, 309; religion and social class 17–19; *ressentiment* 59, 190
Nirvana 66, 67, 95, 97
nomological knowledge 298, 304, 389
Nonconformists 32
normative knowledge 360
norms 382
North American Colonies 29
Northcliffe, Viscount Harmsworth 213
notables 247–8

objectification 143
'objectivity' of knowledge 359–404
objects 300
occidental 101–9, 410*; rationalism 109
office hierarchy 246
office management 246–7
officialdom 71, 102–3
oikos economy 125, 161, 163–4, 410*
openness 302, 346
opium 40–1
organic social ethic 205, 227, 229
organic sociology 321
organization 141
organizational sociology 291
orgy 67, 68, 218, 233
Orphism 285

painting 102
Palestine 22
Papacy 251
pariahs 84, 189, 190; pariah people 57–8
Parker, Robert (?) 32
Parsism 285
parties 129, 130, 182, 193, 195–9, 200
party finance 196–9
pathos 410*
patriarchal rulership 136, 137, 138
patrimonial rulership 53, 96, 305–6
peasants 72, 243; and magic 72
Penn, William 238
Pericles 141, 234
personal relationships 222, 287
personality 42, 95, 363, 381
Petty, Sir William 31
Pharisees 22, 98
philosophy 284
Pietists 14, 44, 45, 49, 51; Pietism 58
Plato 214, 234, 272, 275

plebiscite 144
point of view 280–1, 284, 381
polis 150, 154
political communities 154–5
political enterprise 196
political groups 356–7
political interests 195
political orders 223–5
political parties 129, 130
politically oriented capitalism 175
politics 405, 410*; in the lecture room
    279; and power 119, 200; and the state
    131–2; as vocation 212, 257–69
Popper, Karl 296
positivism 296, 300, 340
possessions 27, 72
power 1, 2, 3, 302, 355, 410*; distribution
    127, 182–94, 224; political leaders 213,
    257, 258–9; and stratification 119, 126,
    129, 132, 200; structures 119, 122
practice 333
precious metals 168–9
predestination 15, 45, 46, 47, 82, 94, 207,
    392, 410*
prestige 124, 132, 149
priesthood 239–40
priests 61–2
print 102
processes 368
profit 24, 103, 173–5
progress 272–3, 274, 275
proletariat 107
proof 252–3, 365
property 106, 183–4, 186; classes 127,
    176–8; revolutions 177
propertylessness 183–4
prophecy 41, 73–4; ethical 38, 65
prophets/prophecies 62–3, 65, 73–4, 218
prostitution 232
Protestant 410*; ascetic *see* Puritan
Protestant ethic thesis 7, 9, 13–15, 25–34,
    109–10, 113–14, 298, 301–2, 306–8
Protestantism 265
Prynne, William 32
psychology 376, 386, 392
psycho-physical phemomena 303
public administration *see* bureaucracy
Puritanism 205; culture 25–26; economic
    life 85–7; self-control 87–9; and the
    spirit of capitalism 25–34; compared
    with Confucianism 15–16, 35–54;
    compared with Judaism 89–91
Puritans 22, 44–5, 410*
Pythagorean comma 70

Quakers 14, 25, 27, 44, 45, 80, 86, 238,
    265

race 124–5, 372
Ranke, Leopold von 403
rational conduct 32
rational methods 24
rational orientation 301
rationalism 116; Confucian 35, 52;
    intellectuals 68–71; Judaic 93; meaning
    24, 410*; practical 73, 231; Puritanism
    52; religious 67–70, 207, 216; scientific
    207; Western culture 24, 109, 307
rationality 1, 2, 121, 221, 411*; capital
    accounting 171–5
rationalization 59, 109, 208, 211–12, 214,
    219, 233, 244, 250–6, 273, 287, 334,
    411*; ethical 49, 75; religious 19, 20,
    24, 69, 70, 207, 216
realist approach 119
reality 296–7, 300, 327, 367, 396; science
    of 374
rebirth 68
reciprocity 220, 221
redemption 36, 69, 219, 229, 232;
    religions 218, 231
reform movements 207
Reformed Jews 91
regularities 301, 333–5, 374, 379, 380
regulatory orders 353–4
religion 29; psychological character 66,
    67, 68, 74, 79; sociology of 101–16
religions 2, 13, 66–7,
religiosity 76, 77–9, 97, 205, 215;
    animistic 39
religious ethics 208, 264
religious qualifications 75
Rembrandt 26
Renaissance 26, 43, 51, 101, 276
rentiers 177
representation 350
repression 19
responsibility *see* ethics
ressentiment 59, 64, 65, 87; *see also*
    Nietzsche
revolution 266
revolutionary conflict 177
revolutionary socialism 263
Rickert, Heinrich 308, 311, 324
rights 133
Robinson Crusoe 30
Rodbertus, Karl 107, 161
Rorty, Richard 299
Roscher, Wilhelm 369
routinization 142, 411*
rulership 200, 355, 411*; arbitrary 122;
    charismatic 120, 121, 138–45; estatist
    122, 138; groups 355–6;
    interdependence with economy 123;
    legal 129, 133–5; patrimonial 122,

305–6; structure 122; traditional 135–8; typology 1–2
Russia 146, 147, 200

St Francis of Assisi 260
St Paul 22, 81, 90, 100
salon culture 234–5
salvation 2, 68, 223, 226, 241; anxiety 13, 14; benefits (goods) 21, 67, 75, 76, 77, 411*; cults 60–2; doctrines 95; messages 206, 207; religions 60–2, 65, 219, 240
Sappho 233
saving 28, 52, 168
saviours 61–2, 218
Schaefer, Dietrich 279
Schäffle, Albert 321
Schi king 39
Schlosser, F.L. 393
Scholasticism 26, 51, 391
science 101, 108, 300, 402, 405; as vocation 270–87
scientific method 308
scientific rationalism 207
scientific validity 364–5
sects 78, 114, 358, 364, 390, 411*
secular law 254–5
selection 342–3, 345
self-perfection 37, 46, 49, 50, 243
Sermon on the Mount 260, 265, 281
servants 136, 157
sex, conjugal 22, 233, 237
sexual love 8, 82, 232–8, 242
sexuality 88
Shakespeare, William 191, 234, 268
shopkeeper mentality 47, 97
sib 125, 412*
significance 377, 378–9, 388
Simmel, George 208, 257, 308, 311, 317
Singer, Paul 198
sin(s) 37, 62, 93, 98, 241
slave labour 164, 169–70, 172
social action 304, 306, 320, 321, 327–58, 405, 412*
social circles 151
social classes 2, 17, 128, 179
social conditions 65
social constructs 301, 320
Social Democratic Party, German 18
social ethic 229
social order 182
social philosophy 362
social policy 363, 366, 370
social relationships 301, 302, 331–3, 346
social sciences 3, 359, 366, 367, 374
social strata: brotherhoods 80; conduct of life 57–8, 75, 290; contrasts within

68; hierocracy 71–3; interest situations 70; salvation religions 65; saviour myth 63
social stratification 24, 126, 200, 201
social-economic phenomena 368–71
socialism 17, 107
societal change 201
sociology 312, 321
Sohm, Rudolph 139, 140
solidarity 147, 148, 350
Sombart, Werner 22, 82, 84, 85, 104, 308
soteriological 412*
Socrates 275
Spann, Othmar 324
Spartans 158
specialism 33, 51, 52, 102, 285
specialization 271
Spener, Philip Jacob 51, 276
Ssu-ma Ch'ien 44
Stammler, R. 311, 336–7, 382
state 356–7, 371, 394, 412*; force, use of 224; modern 120, 121, 122, 131; Occidental phenomenon 103; periodization 122; politics and 131–2; traditional 121; validity 321
statistics 319
status 179–81, 200
status differentiation 190–2, 333
status groups 126, 179–81, 412*; distribution of power 182, 184, 187–8, 190, 192; political officials 212; social order 127, 128–9
statutory orders 352–3
strangers 84–5, 86, 87
structural transformations 4
struggle 341–3, 344; of interests 400, 402
style of life 412*
subjectivity 382–3
sublimation 18–19, 207–8, 219, 330, 412*; erotic 88, 236
substantive justice 210, 252, 253, 254
substantive law 250, 251
suffering 59–60, 62, 64, 218, 221
Sufism 20, 57
sultanism 120, 136
Swammerdam 276

Talmud *see* Jewish Law
Tao 43, 96; Taoism 20, 35, 37, 38, 43, 49, 50, 285
Tarde, Gabriel 328
teachers 280, 282, 283, 284
technical factors 108
technology 48, 167–8, 171
teleology 382

tensions: marriage vs priesthood 232–3; mysticism vs eroticism 237; non-religious life orders 207; rational action vs brotherliness 228; religion vs intellectual knowledge 238, 240; religions in relation to the world 36, 218, 219–20, 222, 229
terminology 320
territory 132
theatre 26
theocratic law 254
theodicy 2, 18, 60–5, 264, 412*
theology 276, 285, 286
theory 383
Thucydides 101
Tobler, Mina 8
Tolstoy, Leo 214, 237, 274, 277
Tönnies, Friedrich 311, 337, 344
Torah 79
trade 48
tradition 46, 140, 301, 329, 339, 340, 412*
traditional rule 135–8
traditional rulers 120
traditional state 121
traditionalistic parties 196
tribes 154–5
Trotsky, Leon 131
troubadours 234
trust 43, 50
truth 261, 277, 300, 383
types 325
typology(-ies) 216–20, 333

Umar-al-Khattab 94
understanding 311, 312, 315–16, 320, 322, 324, 375, 412*
United States 33, 147, 152, 154, 172, 188, 197, 282
universal history 121
Upanishads 263
urban economy 165–6
utilitarianism 30, 31

validity 317, 333, 335–6, 363, 364–5, 367, 385, 402
Vallabhacharyas 67
value freedom 298, 405, 412*
value judgements 231, 284, 360, 361, 362–3, 364, 366, 367, 393

value rationality 308, 329, 330, 340
value spheres 409*
values 363, 400, 405; hierarchy 290; ultimate 75, 290
vanity 258
Vedas 57, 239
violence 119, 131, 132, 224, 225, 229, 260, 265, 266, 356
virtuosi 21, 76–9, 222, 227, 229, 412*
virtuoso religiosity 76, 77–9
Vischer, F. Th. 403
vocation 15, 53, 79, 217, 223, 257, 269, 270, 273, 275, 283
vocationalism, *see* specialism
voluntary associations 354, 355
votes 198

war 119, 208, 225, 226, 261
warriors 57, 72, 93, 94
wealth: acquisition 104, 105; Confucianism 47, 50–1; early Christianity 99; Judaism 81; Puritanism 27, 28, 29, 33, 50
Weber, Marianne 7, 201
Weber, Max: bibliography 9; comparative sociology 23–4, 114–15; historical sociology 114–15; intellectual biography 3–9; major contributions 1–3; methodology 2
Weigelin, E. 337
Wesley, John 29–30, 50, 82
White Russians 146, 147
Whitfield Methodists 45
Wilamowitz-Moellendorff, U. von 5
Windelband, Wilhelm 308
work ethic 1, 2, 15, 412*
working-class movement 17
world flight 44, 95, 217
world religions: and capitalism 96–7, 103–7; economic ethics 55–80
world-rejection: directions 220–41; motives 215–16; stages 241–4
worldviews 20, 69, 70, 71, 363, 366, 413*
written documents 246

Zinzendorf 31
zoology 297
Zoroastrianism 20, 62, 64